1992

Chaucer and the Subject of History

Chaucer and the Subject of History

Lee Patterson

THE UNIVERSITY OF WISCONSIN PRESS

The University of Wisconsin Press
114 North Murray Street
Madison, Wisconsin 53715

5   4   3   2   1

Printed in the United States of America

Publication of this book was assisted by a grant from the Publications
Program of the National Endowment for the Humanities, an independent
federal agency.

Library of Congress Cataloging-in-Publication Data
Patterson, Lee.
    Chaucer and the subject of history / Lee Patterson.
    504 pp.   cm.
    Includes bibliographical references and index.
    1. Chaucer, Geoffrey, d. 1400—Knowledge—History. 2. Chaucer,
Geoffrey, d. 1400—Political and social views. 3. Historical
poetry, English—History and criticism. 4. History, Ancient, in
literature. 5. Social problems in literature. 6. Middle Ages in
literature.   I. Title.
PR1933.H57P38   1991
821'.1—dc20
ISBN 0-299-12830-X   90-50651
ISBN 0-299-12834-2 (pbk.)   CIP

To my mother
and in memory of my father.

Contents

Acknowledgments

Since the acknowledgments page is the one part of a book that is sure to be read, the author must be concerned that his potential audience not meet with immediate disappointment, whether of nonappearance or inclusion. But having received so much support of so many different kinds for so long, I know that acknowledgment is indispensable albeit always inadequate.

Fellowships from the National Endowment of the Humanities and the Guggenheim Foundation provided time free from other commitments; and a stay at the Rockefeller Foundation's Villa Serbelloni provided the ideal conditions for transforming a manuscript into a book. I owe a great deal to these splendid institutions and to their solicitous administrators. I have also been fortunate to have been employed by Johns Hopkins and Duke Universities and to have had as chairmen and colleagues Larry Holland, Ronald Paulson, and Stanley Fish. They had confidence in my work when at times I had little and supported me in ways small and large.

Like the ancient mariner, I have for many years been stopping one in three and pouring out my Chaucerian obsessions. A number have listened without visible discomfort, and several have even turned a monologue into a conversation. David Aers, John Baldwin, Harry Berger, Leo Braudy, Theresa Coletti, Marshall Leicester, Frank Lentricchia, Del Kolve, Jerome McGann, Anne Middleton, Michael Ondaatjee, Andy Silber, James Simpson, and David Wallace have each helped me to understand my topic a little better and on occasion to realize that I had a topic at all. Anne Middleton and Glending Olson read this book at an early stage and provided detailed and immensely helpful commentaries; Peter Travis did the same very near the end and showed me how to get over several barriers I had thought were impassable. Their collective wisdom and hard work have been a great resource to me. And once again Barbara Hanrahan has proven herself to be an ideal editor.

The manuscript of this book was mailed to the publisher from Addenbrooks Hospital, Cambridge, where I was recuperating from a bicycle accident, and its completion is inextricably linked for me to that experience. Of the friends who so generously helped me through that difficult time, I can mention here only three: Lisa Jardine presided with indefatigable kindness over the material construction of the manuscript and the bodily reconstruction of its author; and Tony and Pat Wilson gave unstintingly of their hospitality and their affection when I was sorely in need of both. I want also to record here my warm gratitude to the nursing staff of Ward 5C, whose competence and compassion I shall not forget.

No one is more happy that this book is completed than my children, if only because they are now released from having to proffer increasingly formulaic expressions of interest. But I've appreciated them nonetheless, kids, and if you keep them coming, and keep your father informed of your own vivid and admirable lives, I won't keep asking you if you've read it. As for my wife, this book is—in all the ways that matter—hers.

The epigraphs to all of the chapters are taken from Don DeLillo's *Libra* (New York: Viking, 1988). Those who are interested may find them on the following pages of that book: 181, 20, 260, 127, 248, 165, 384, 166, 45, and 65.

Early versions of portions of this book have been previously published as the following articles: "Chaucerian Confession: Penitential Literature and the Pardoner," *M&H* 7 (1976): 153–73; " 'For the Wyves Love of Bathe': Feminine Rhetoric and Poetic Resolution in the *Roman de la Rose* and the *Canterbury Tales*," *Speculum* 58 (1983): 656–95; " 'No Man His Reson Herde': Peasant Consciousness, Chaucer's Miller, and the Structure of the *Canterbury Tales*," *South Atlantic Quarterly* 86 (1987): 457–95; and " 'Thirled with the poynt of remembraunce': Memory and Modernity in Chaucer," in *Modernité au moyen âge: le défi du passé*, ed. Brigitte Cazelles and Charles Méla (Geneva: Droz, 1990): 113–51. I have also cannibalized sentences and a couple of paragraphs from two other articles: " 'What Man Artow?': Authorial Self-Definition in the *Tale of Sir Thopas* and the *Tale of Melibee*," *SAC* 11 (1989): 117–76, and "On the Margin: Postmodernism, Ironic History, and Medieval Studies," *Speculum* 65 (1990): 87–108.

A Note on Citations

Unless otherwise noted, citations from classical texts, and from Augustine's *Confessions* and Boethius's *Consolation of Philosophy*, are from the Loeb Classical Library editions. I have not included in the footnotes the titles of works cited from Migne's *Patrologia Latina*, although full bibliographical information is provided in the Bibliography.

All citations from Chaucer's works are from Larry D. Benson, gen. ed., *The Riverside Chaucer*, 3rd ed. (Boston: Houghton Mifflin, 1987). I have very occasionally altered the editors' punctuation.

Classical and medieval works that are divided into sections and/or lines are cited by numbers separated by commas (e.g., *Confessions* 10, 2; *Troilus and Criseyde* 5, 233–37). Occasionally page numbers have been added in parentheses. In other cases, volume and page numbers follow standard usage.

Except where noted, translations are my own.

List of Abbreviations

AHDLMA	Archives d'histoire doctrinale et littéraire au Moyen Age
AN&Q	American Notes and Queries
AnM	Annuale Medievale
BIHR	Bulletin of the Institute of Historical Research
BJRL	Bulletin of the John Rylands Library
C&M	Classica et Mediaevalia
CCR	Calendar of Close Rolls
CCSL	Corpus Christianorum, Series Latina
CE	College English
CFMA	Classiques français du Moyen Age
CPR	Calendar of Patent Rolls
ChR	Chaucer Review
CL	Comparative Literature
EETS, ES	Early English Text Society, Extra Series
EETS, OS	Early English Text Society, Original Series
EHR	English Historical Review
EIC	Essays in Criticism
ELH	English Literary History
ES	English Studies
JEGP	Journal of English and Germanic Philology
JMH	Journal of Medieval History
JMRS	Journal of Medieval and Renaissance Studies
JNT	Journal of Narrative Techniques
JWCI	Journal of the Warburg and Courtauld Institute
L&H	Literature and History
LCL	Loeb Classical Library
LeedsSE	Leeds Studies in English
M&H	Medievalia et Humanistica
MAE	Medium Aevum
MED	Middle English Dictionary
MLN	Modern Language Notes
MLQ	Modern Language Quarterly
MLR	Modern Language Review
MP	Modern Philology
MS	Mediaeval Studies

N&Q	*Notes and Queries*
NLH	*New Literary History*
PL	*Patrologia Latina*
PMLA	*Publications of the Modern Language Association*
PQ	*Philological Quarterly*
PRO	*Public Record Office*
REL	*Review of English Literature*
RES	*Review of English Studies*
Rot. Parl.	*Rotuli Parliamentorum*
SAC	*Studies in the Age of Chaucer*
SATF	*Société des anciens textes français*
SB	*Studies in Bibliography*
SI	*Studies in Iconography*
SN	*Studia Neophilologica*
SP	*Studies in Philology*
SSF	*Studies in Short Fiction*
TRHS	*Transactions of the Royal Historical Society*
UTQ	*University of Toronto Quarterly*
YES	*Yearbook of English Studies*

Chaucer and the Subject of History

Introduction

"He has abandoned his life to understanding that moment in Dallas, the seven seconds that broke the back of the American century."

I

In late-twentieth-century America, perhaps in the West as a whole, human life is conceived in terms of a basic unit, the autonomous, free, self-determining individual. This is a being understood as possessing a whole and undivided selfhood, an inner entity known through a sense of immediacy and plenitude and constituted above all by a self-aware consciousness and an executive will. The behavior of these individuals is in turn typically understood as freely chosen rather than socially or historically determined: people are what they choose to be. Attitudes, habits, and deportment—all those qualities that constitute "character" or "personality"—are assumed to be self-consciously adopted, a style of being that each person fashions in order to be himself or herself. In the words of Robert Bellah and his colleagues, contemporary Americans "insist, perhaps more than ever before, on finding [their] true selves independent of any cultural or social influence, being responsible to that self alone, and making its fulfillment the very meaning of [their] lives."[1]

The social effects of these assumptions are well known. In the contemporary world the realities we routinely designate by the terms "society" and "history" are at best dimly perceived, at worst subject to explicit attack. As modern life comes to focus ever more insistently upon the private world of the self, the public world becomes ever less conceivable as an arena of action. Instead of communities organized according to "an objective pattern of roles and social institutions," in the words of the Bellah group, we have instead "lifestyle enclaves" held together by

1. Robert N. Bellah et al., *Habits of the Heart: Individualism and Commitment in American Life* (New York: Harper & Row, 1986), 150. See also Alasdair MacIntyre, *After Virtue*, 2d ed. (Notre Dame: University of Notre Dame Press, 1984 [1981]), 31–35; and for an earlier, excellent version of this argument, Richard Sennett, *The Fall of Public Man: On the Social Psychology of Capitalism* (New York: Knopf, 1977).

common income levels and shared recreational interests.[2] Similarly, work has largely ceased to provide a satisfying arena for personal fulfillment: the idea of the calling, of a vocation undertaken for reasons other than self-interest, has been replaced either by a numbing bureaucratic routine endured out of economic necessity or by a "career," a life choice typically legitimized in terms of private gratifications. Most strikingly, modern men and women are less and less able to conceive of themselves in terms of a collective identity, as members of a class, an ethnic group, or even a political party—a collective identity that is the prerequisite for effective political engagement.[3] In the United States, over half the eligible population no longer bothers to vote; coalition building is typically subverted by a fragmentizing identity politics. Since Americans typically think of their true being as residing in a self that stands apart from society, they are less and less able to assess political leaders in terms of their own economic and political interests. Hence Ronald Reagan was widely judged as "amiable," a characterological analysis that ignored a vigorously prosecuted political program that ran counter to the interests of the vast majority of his supporters. Nor is this condition confined to the United States. Margaret Thatcher has perhaps best succeeded in translating the ideology of individualism into a successful political strategy based, in her words, on the belief that "there is no such thing as society; only individuals exist." Nor is it surprising that we now gaze upon a landscape in which an individualist economy of private affluence and public squalor has reached what may prove to be, if the prognoses of ecological disaster are even moderately accurate, its terminal condition.

If the category of the social has faded from view, so too has the category of the historical. Instead of understanding themselves as products of determinative historical processes, modern individuals tend to see themselves as autonomous and self-made. Insofar as it exists at all, the past is either a burden to be cast off—within our therapeutic culture, a common goal is to "take responsibility for yourself" by dispensing with outgrown cultural and parental precepts—or an array of items and practices available for nostalgic reminiscence. Miss World 1985 summed it up: "I think destiny is what you make of it." Far from being shaped much less produced by the past, the individual sees it as a by no means intractable set of facts that can, if taken in the right way, be transformed into an occasion for self-fulfillment and self-gratification.

2. Bellah et al., *Habits of the Heart*, 85, 72–75.
3. See Richard M. Merelman, *Making Something of Ourselves: On Culture and Politics in the United States* (Berkeley: University of California Press, 1984), 204–43.

Not coincidentally, at the very time that the ideology of individualism has come to dominate our culture as a whole it has been subject to a withering attack within the academy. The confident pieties of democratic liberalism, with its assertion of the centrality of the individual's rights and duties, has given way to far darker analyses that stress the dominance of economic, political, and linguistic structures. The Marxist definition of individualism as a form of false consciousness, a bourgeois illusion required by a capitalism insatiable for both workers eager to sell their labor and acquisitive consumers wanting to spend their wages, has largely demolished the once secure faith in the idea of the individual as a natural category. So too, the linguistic analyses of Saussure and Benveniste have argued that the concept of the self is the reification of a grammatical category: language allows for a subject position that speakers fill in with a reified subjectivity, naively believing that they exist because they can say they exist. Far from speaking language, we are spoken—and constituted—by it. And the sovereignty of consciousness so central to individualism has been almost wholly undone by the revival of Freudianism and its linguistic reinterpretation at the hands of Jacques Lacan.

Also not coincidentally, for recent sociologists the dark secret at the heart of modern individualism is its failure as a mode of life. The "improvisational self" of the modern American is revealed as "radically empty," an emptiness that allows for its appropriation by a range of powerful social determinants. Individuals isolated from the social whole replicate within the enclave of their personal existence the bureaucratic practices that dominate modern capitalism: the therapeutic culture preempts resistance by projecting social dissonance into the psychological realm of the self, while "the purely contractual structure of the economic and bureaucratic world . . . becom[es] an ideological model for personal life."[4] According to the anthropologist Michael Moffatt, modern college students are so absorbed within the ideology of individualism that they are unable to conceive of their cultural practices as anything other than a purely natural mode of behavior, one that flows instinctively from an autonomous, unconstrained selfhood. Consequently, friendship, understood as a relationship in which one socially undetermined entity chooses another, has become

the only culturally unproblematical tie with another human being that still exist[s] in the late twentieth century. . . . All other social connections—the relationships of work, family, class, race, and

---

4. Bellah et al., *Habits of the Heart*, 79–80, 127.

ethnicity—[are] imposed on your true self from without. . . . Your
friends, on the other hand, [are] freely chosen, mutually chosen,
egalitarian others whom you trust with the secrets of your self. . . .
Friendship [is], in fact, simply the social side of the late-twentieth-
century American individualistic self, which "naturally" desire[s] to
"relate" to freely chosen others.

And yet what is this self? To the anthropologist it is a "cultural
myster[y]—no more objectively verifiable than the odd deities believed
in by many 'primitive' peoples."[5]

Both the widespread commitment to an individualist ethic and the
academic attack upon individualism agree on a central point: the ineffi-
cacy of agency. Proclaiming their autonomy from oppressive social
structures, college students follow almost ritualistic patterns of behavior prescribed by their peer group; locating the center of their existence
within the therapeutic self, the bureaucratically equivalent workers required by the service economy submit to progressively less meaningful
working lives; and many Americans seem to agree that any effort to
change the world is doomed before it begins: politics is a corrupt and
corrupting activity in which everybody is out for personal gain. Similarly, academic analysts insist that structures of domination do not
merely control but in effect constitute the individual: to be a subject is to
be subjected.[6]

The conclusion toward which these various critiques direct us is the
paradoxical notion that the very freedom that individualism takes as its
central premise, the ability of individuals to separate themselves from
the social totality in order to choose or to change the conditions of their
lives, is being subverted by the ideology of individualism itself. The
extreme to which the contemporary world has carried individualism
threatens to annul its most precious value, its affirmation of the power
of human beings to make their own history, its insistence that the social
world is within our control and subject to our powers of reformation.
Nor is it easy to know how best to remedy this situation. A conceptual
solution, one that would both acknowledge the inescapability of social
determination and yet protect individual agency, is by no means self-

5. Michael Moffatt, *Coming of Age in New Jersey: College and American Culture* (New
Brunswick, N.J.: Rutgers University Press, 1989), 42, 67 n.19.

6. See Paul Smith, *Discerning the Subject* (Minneapolis: University of Minnesota
Press, 1988); for a powerful critique of this strain of contemporary thought, see Luc Ferry
and Alain Renaut, *French Philosophy of the Sixties: An Essay on Antihumanism*, trans. Mary
H. S. Cattani (Amherst: University of Massachusetts Press, 1990).

evident.[7] And a praxis of social engagement able to
tices of separation that characterize modern life is
as it is to achieve.

Surely it is at least in part because of our current dileⁿ
literary critics and historians have devoted so much attentioₙ
problems of individualism and subjectivity as they are staged in texts
from a wide variety of historical periods. Not surprisingly, much of this
attention has been focused upon texts deriving from the Renaissance: it
is usually assumed that the idea of the individual, and the psychological and social dilemmas that such an idea entails, arose in Western culture only at that time. Only then did people became aware of themselves as freestanding individuals, defined not by social relations but
by an inner sense of self-presence, a sense of their own subjectivity.
Previously, in the well-known words of the great nineteenth-century
cultural historian Jacob Burckhardt, "Man was conscious of himself
only as a member of a race, people, party, family, or corporation—only
through some general category."[8]

Many contemporary literary critics have accepted and developed
Burckhardt's assertion. Terry Eagleton draws a distinction between
"the old feudalist subject" of the Middle Ages, "constituted by social
bonds and fidelities," and the modern "individualist conception of the
self" as a being crushed by the "crippling burden" of subjectivity.[9] Stephen Greenblatt asserts that "there is in the early modern period a
change in the intellectual, social, psychological, and aesthetic structures that govern the generation of identities," a change away from an
(apparently) unproblematic world of identity formation and toward
the fraught arena of struggle and subjection within which Renaissance
self-fashioning takes place.[10] Jonathan Dollimore sets the "Christian/

7. The thinker who perhaps confronted this problem most directly is Theodor
Adorno. Insisting that to construe subjectivity as either wholly autonomous or wholly a
product of social forces is a mistake, Adorno argued that while nineteenth-century individualism may have been a function of bourgeois complacency, it nonetheless provided a
crucial defense against the homogenizations of both totalitarianism and mass culture. As
Adorno says in *Minima Moralia*, "In the face of totalitarian unity, which cries out for the
elimination of differences directly as meaning, something of the liberating social forces
may even have converged in the sphere of the individual. Critical Theory lingers there
without a bad conscience" (cited by Martin Jay, *The Dialectical Imagination: A History of the
Frankfurt School and the Institute of Social Research 1923–1950* [Boston: Little, Brown, 1973],
277).

8. Jacob Burckhardt, *The Civilization of the Renaissance in Italy*, trans. S. G. O. Middlemore (London: Phaidon Books, 1965 [1860]), 81.

9. Terry Eagleton, *William Shakespeare* (Oxford: Blackwell, 1986), 75.

10. Stephen Greenblatt, *Renaissance Self-Fashioning: From More to Shakespeare* (Chicago: University of Chicago Press, 1980), 1.

metaphysical" essentialism of medieval selfhood—"the medieval conception of identity as hierarchical location"—against the fractured subjectivity of the Renaissance.[11] Joel Fineman contrasts Shakespeare's sonnets to the medieval lyrics of Dante to show how it is only in the former that we can discover "the poetic invention of subjectivity."[12] And Francis Barker argues that the "coherence" of the medieval self was destroyed by "the deadly subjectivity of the modern" in the sixteenth and seventeenth centuries.[13]

Since at least the time of Petrarch in the mid-fourteenth century the Middle Ages has functioned as an all-purpose alternative to whatever quality the present has wished to ascribe to itself. The claim that selfhood becomes problematic only in the Renaissance is a prime instance of this impulse. In fact, the antagonism between the desires of the individual and the demands of society provided one of the great topics for literary exploration throughout the Middle Ages; it is hard, for example, to think of a medieval romance, and especially one derived from the great mass of Arthurian legend, that does not deal with just this topic. More to the point, the dialectic between an inward subjectivity and an external world that alienates it from both itself and its divine source provides the fundamental economy of the medieval idea of selfhood. Medieval anthropology defined the subject as desire: as the Augustinian will, with its opposed movements of *caritas* and *cupiditas;* as the Boethian *intentio naturalis* that tends ineluctably toward the *summum bonum;* as the scholastic powers of appetition, in which the intellectual appetite seeks to govern its concupiscible and irascible partners; or as *amor,* an inward sense of insufficiency that drives the Christian self forward on its journey through the historical world. Among the impediments placed in the way of the Christian is the social identity—the Stoic *persona* or *karaktera*—derived from the historical communities of the medieval world. The medieval conception of selfhood is typically understood as a dialectic between the Christian subject and this objectified historical identity.

This dialectic, in which the historically particularized self serves as the oppositional term against which a subjective interiority defines itself, is visible in a wide variety of medieval texts and contexts. We see it at work in the confessional Augustinianism in force throughout the period and

11. Jonathan Dollimore, *Radical Tragedy: Religion, Ideology and Power in the Drama of Shakespeare and His Contemporaries* (Chicago: University of Chicago Press, 1984), 155–58.

12. Joel Fineman, *Shakespeare's Perjured Eye: The Invention of Poetic Subjectivity in the Sonnets* (Berkeley: University of California Press, 1986).

13. Francis Barker, *The Tremulous Private Body: Essays on Subjection* (London: Methuen, 1984), 25.

especially remarkable in Petrarch's *Secretum;* in that great document of the struggle to form a masculine identity from the confrontation between monasticism and an emergent scholasticism, a struggle refracted through the lens of feminine desire, the *Letters of Abelard and Heloise;* in the huge body of hagiographical writing that records the intense spirituality of the later Middle Ages, ranging from Thomas of Celano's *Life of St. Francis* to *The Book of Margery Kempe;* in the many chivalric biographies, whether historical (Machaut's *La Prise d'Alexandrie,* the Chandos Herald's *Vie du Prince Noir*) or fictive (Malory's *Tale of Sir Gareth*), that record the making and unmaking of chivalric identity; in the autobiographical poetry of Hoccleve; and in the confessions of Lollards like William Thorpe and Sir John Oldcastle.

It may well be, in fact, that this interest takes on a new force in the later Middle Ages. Such a development is suggested, for example, in the transformation of the early courtly lyric into the *dit* of the later Middle Ages, as Michel Zink has recently shown.[14] If the *chanson* serves as the means by which, as Guilhem Molinier says in his *Leys d'amors,* the poet is able to "declarar e expressar son desirier e sa voluntat," it does so in a way that is highly idealized and generalized: indeed, its very mode of existence—as a song to be sung—marks it as a discourse designed to be expressive of the inner world of all of its performers, and hence one necessarily denied the inflection of a historically particularized individuality.[15] But in the thirteenth and fourteenth centuries this *poésie pure* yields to a historically situated, essentially dramatic conception of literary discourse. Hence, for instance, the early troubadour lyrics were provided with biographical prefaces and commentaries—the *vidas* and *razos*—almost entirely derived from the poems themselves, resulting in a composite form that served Dante as one model for the *Vita nuova.*[16] Hence too, as Zink has shown, the widespread presence in late medieval French writing of autobiographical and pseudoautobiographical forms of discourse—practitioners of what Zink calls the *roman du moi* are Rutebeuf, the Arrageois poets, Jean

14. Michel Zink, *La subjectivité littéraire autour de siècle de saint Louis* (Paris: Presses universitaires de France, 1985); Zink's "Time and the Representation of the Self in Thirteenth-Century French Poetry," *Poetics Today* 5 (1984): 611–27, provides a summary of the argument of the book.

15. Cited by Zink, *Subjectivité,* 71.

16. Nor is such biographical situating confined to the troubadour lyric; one of the manuscripts of Richard of Fournival's *Bestiaire d'amour* includes a prologue that provides a biographical sketch confected from material found in the text itself; see David Hult, *Self-Fulfilling Prophecies: Readership and Authority in the First* Roman de la Rose (Cambridge: Cambridge University Press, 1986), 71–72.

Bodel, Baude Fastoul, Gautier d'Arras and (especially) Adam de la
Halle, Machaut, Charles d'Orleans, and Villon. The literary history of
allegory follows a parallel course, with the radically depersonalized
and transcendentalizing forms of early allegory—which include the
bellum intestinum of Prudentius, the visionary texts of the Chartrians,
and the first part of the *Roman de la Rose*—being set aside (as I shall
argue in chapter 6) in favor of a temporally inflected autobiographical
discourse that is given its definitive articulation in Jean de Meun's La
Vieille.[17] In sum, the characteristic topic of late French medieval
writing—perhaps even of late medieval writing *tout court*—is not the
subject per se but (in Zink's words) "the confrontation of the subject
with the determinations of the exterior, present world."[18]

The medieval text that most thoroughly documents this dialectical
relationship between the subject and history—between the inner self
of desire and its external mode of self-articulation as a singular individual who traces a specific worldly career—is Dante's *Commedia*. As commentators from the poem's first appearance until the present have demonstrated, the *Commedia* represents "the state of the soul after death"
(in the words of the Letter to Can Grande) in fully historicized terms:
the translation from time into eternity does not extinguish but fulfills
each soul's earthly being.[19] But if the *Commedia* is the *locus classicus* of
the medieval "novel of the self" (in John Freccero's phrase), it is in no
sense unique.[20] For English literature of the last quarter of the fourteenth century was similarly dominated—and its extraordinary development in part provoked—by just this topic.[21] The medieval poem

17.   A somewhat different but analogous account of this process is given by Hans
Robert Jauss, "La transformation de la forme allégorique entre 1180 et 1240," in
L'Humanisme médiévale dans les littératures romanes du XIIe au XIVe siècle, ed. Anthime
Fourrier (Paris: Klincksieck, 1964), 107–46.

18.   Zink, "Time and Representation of the Self," 627.

19.   This point is powerfully argued by Erich Auerbach in *Dante: Poet of the Secular
World*, trans. Ralph Manheim (Chicago: University of Chicago Press, 1961 [1929]):
There is something quite miraculous in what the reader of the poem feels to be
self-evident (and in the last analysis, it actually is self-evident), namely, that the
situation and attitude of the souls in the other world is in every way individual and
in keeping with their former acts and sufferings on earth; that their situation in the
hereafter is merely a continuation, intensification, and definitive fixation of their
situation on earth, and that what is most particular and personal in their character
and fate is fully preserved. (88)

20.   John Freccero, "Dante's Novel of the Self," *The Christian Century* (1965): 1216–18.

21.   Not that this theme does not appear in English literature before the fourteenth
century; in *The Solitary Self: Individuality in the* Ancrene Wisse (Cambridge: Harvard University Press, 1981), Linda Georgianna shows how that early thirteenth-century text defines the solitary's task as being "to come to understand herself—her desires and memo-

most like the *Commedia* is Langland's *Piers Plowman*, because it too—as Anne Middleton has shown—is grounded in the drama of a historicized subject. To be sure, where Dante, empowered by a tradition of the *dolce stil nuovo* that "made possible a poetic celebration of the discrete mortal historical self," could confidently center his poem on "the subject's understanding as a being in historical time," for Langland "the value, autonomy, and cultural authority of personal history as a genre, and the status of a serious fictive work centered upon it" was "always at issue."[22] But that such a question *is* the poem's issue shows how profoundly central for Langland was the question of the subject and its historical relations. Another major Middle English text committed to the same project is *Sir Gawain and the Green Knight*, in which the dialectic of inner and outer is comprehensively thematized. Just as the action of the poem is enclosed within the historical frame of *translatio imperii*, and just as the exchange-of-winnings game is enclosed within the larger beheading game, so is the inner testing of Gawain set against the account of Bertilak's hunting in the wintry landscape—a dialectic that enacts the drama of identity at the center of the poem: "Þou art not Gawayn," accuses the Green Knight at the moment of narrative climax, echoing doubts that have become progressively more urgent as the poem has proceeded. How, the poem asks, does the subjectivity so delicately anatomized by the temptation scenes, and then further foregrounded by Gawain's own confession, accord with the identity established by Arthurian history?

It is within this historical context that Chaucer's explorations of the dialectic between an inward sense of selfhood—subjectivity—and the claims of the historical world should be placed. As generations of readers know, Chaucer was fascinated with what literary criticism has traditionally called "character," and he defined it as one term in an oppositional dialectic constituted on the other side by history—by which I mean both the persistent presence of the past and the pressure of social realities. Such a definition is by no means unmedieval. What is striking and important, however, is the fact that this interest in the constitution of the self feels—to us, probably also to his contemporary readers, and perhaps even to the poet himself—quintessentially modern. The

---

ries, her motives and habits of mind—as a unique individual, whose relationship with God is defined not in terms of the otherworld, which is always stable, but in terms of the everyday, which is always in flux" (6).

22. Anne Middleton, "Narration and the Invention of Experience: Episodic Form in *Piers Plowman*," in *The Wisdom of Poetry: Essays in Early English Literature in Honor of Morton W. Bloomfield*, ed. Larry D. Benson and Siegfried Wenzel (Kalamazoo: Medieval Institute Publications, 1982), 103–4.

shape we have given to cultural history teaches us that selfhood ought to be, if not a modern phenomenon, at least a modern problem. Insofar as we find it difficult to conceptualize the self, to that extent we think of it as unknown to earlier, simpler times. That this is not in fact the case is self-evident, but so is our need to think so. There is, in short, something about subjectivity that persuades people that in dealing with it they have entered into a new time, that they have cut themselves off from the past, that they have become moderns. What is striking about Chaucer's explorations into subjectivity is that he seems to have entertained the same idea—although he also seems never to have fully credited it.

As for our present cultural situation, it should be some consolation to realize that the dilemmas we now face are not a function of a wholly new phenomenon. To assume that subjectivity comes into existence only as an effect of specifically modern systems of subjection not only ignores a great deal of historical evidence to the contrary but, more important, posits selfhood as by definition beleaguered and ineffectual. But if we can understand that subjectivity is a human characteristic that has always been part of our history, albeit in different configurations and with different powers and values, we can also recognize that it has often been experienced as being set in some form of opposition to both the past from which it emerges and the social world within which its destiny is shaped. It is of course true that human self-consciousness has been reified into the concept of a wholly autonomous individual, a concept that has in turn been transformed into a fully fledged ideology of individualism. But this impeaches neither the fact of subjectivity itself nor its capacity to act within the world. A study of Chaucerian subjectivity thus seems worth undertaking not only for its own intrinsic interest, and not only in order to recover a past too easily misrepresented (the falsification of history being something always to be fought, however imperfectly), but because it can perhaps contribute to understanding the issues involved in the dialectical process of self-construction per se. And while historical knowledge may be a frail instrument with which to confront the vast economic and social forces that are shaping and misshaping our world, it is not finally to be scorned. "Our culture's form of intellectual cognition is that of critical scholarship": this assertion by a great medievalist of the past—Johan Huizinga—may seem quixotic now, sixty-five years later.[23] Yet before

23. Johan Huizinga, "The Task of Cultural History" (1926), in *Men and Ideas,* trans. James S. Holmes and Hans van Marle (New York: Meridian Books, 1959), 61.

we brush it aside, contemporary academics, and especially medievalists, would do well to consider what else we possess to put in its place.

II

When in 1700 Dryden designated Chaucer "the father of English poetry," he not only confirmed the poet's place in literary history but established lasting conceptions of both Chaucer's special achievement and of literary history itself.[24] For Dryden, Chaucer's foundational status derived from what later critics would call his realism: "Chaucer followed nature everywhere, but was never so bold to go beyond her" (280), a fidelity particularly in evidence in his representation of character. Chaucer, Dryden famously said,

> has taken into the compass of his *Canterbury Tales* the various manners and humours (as we now call them) of the whole English nation in his age. Not a single character has escaped him. . . . 'Tis sufficient to say, according to the proverb, that here is God's plenty. We have our forefathers and great-grand-dames all before us, as they were in Chaucer's days: their general characters are still remaining in mankind, and even in England, though they are called by other names than those of Monks, and Friars, and Canons, and Lady Abbesses, and Nuns; for mankind is ever the same, and nothing lost out of nature, though every thing is altered. (284–85)

The reader's ability to recognize the English nation, despite the roughness of the "old language" in which Chaucer represented it, is a guarantee that literary value can be transmitted from past to present. Literary history is underwritten by a universal human nature.

Running parallel to this continuity is another, deeper one that links the poet to his latter-day imitators. Just as our forefathers and great-grand-dames are still recognizable to the modern reader, so is Chaucer's genius available to his poetic heirs. "Milton was the poetical son of Spenser, and," says Dryden, "Spenser more than once insinuates that the soul of Chaucer was transfused into his body" (270).[25] Of course the

24. John Dryden, "Preface to Fables Ancient and Modern," in *Of Dramatic Poesy and Other Critical Essays*, ed. George Watson (London: J. M. Dent, 1962), 2:280.

25. Dryden's claim probably derived from Spenser's references to Chaucer in terms that assumed paternal originality: in the *Shepheardes Calendar* Spenser invoked "some little drops" from "the spring [that] was in [Chaucer's] learned hedde" ("June," 93–94), and in the *Faerie Queene* he called him first the "well of English vndefiled" (4, 2, 32) and then claimed that "in [his] gentle spright / The pure well head of Poesie did dwell" (7, 7,

infusion continues, both in Dryden's filial relation to Milton and, more crucially, in his direct recourse to Father Chaucer: in the course of translating the *Canterbury Tales*, he found, he tells us, that "I had a soul congenial to his" (287). This is not a casual claim. For if Chaucer is the ultimate *fons et origo* of the "lineal descents and clans" of English literary history, he is also an original who stands apart from the entire process and makes his genius available directly. He is both the great ancestor upon whom all lines are founded and the always available presence who provides direct and unmediated inspiration. Like Chaucer's readerly accessibility, this poetic paternity is enabled by a universal human nature—the spiritual congeniality Dryden shares with Chaucer—whose form time can alter but whose essence remains always the same.

Dryden's particular brand of humanism—his installation of an essential and unchanging (and male) human nature at the center of culture—both supports and entails a specific model of history. Although Chaucer "lived in the infancy of our poetry" (281) and so composed in imperfect meter, Dryden compared him not to his fellow Englishmen Gower and Lydgate (with whom commentators had linked him since the mid-fifteenth century) but to the great originators of antiquity: "I hold him in the same degree of veneration as the Grecians held Homer or the Romans Virgil" (280).[26] In linking Chaucer to the great classical poets, Dryden rescued him from the Gothic darkness of the Middle Ages by reaffirming the historical self-understanding of his own time. For Dryden, as for humanism as a whole, cultural history fell into three stages: first an antiquity whose greatness derived from its fidelity to nature, then a period of exile and errancy, when natural fitness was distorted by barbarous habits and oversubtle speculations,

---

9). These metaphors represent Chaucer as a *fons et origo* whose poetic inspiration is attained less through self-conscious imitation than through an infusion made possible by an intimate, filial relationship.

26. Dryden's most powerful precedent for this claim was Sidney, who reinterpreted the traditional designation of Chaucer and Gower as the English equivalents to Dante, Petrarch, and Boccaccio by setting both of these moderns against the ancient founders of Latin poetry; see Geoffrey Shepherd, ed., *An Apology for Poetry* (London: Nelson, 1965), 96. For the traditional linking of Gower, Lydgate, and Chaucer as three equals, see, for example, George Ashby and John Skelton in Derek Brewer, ed., *Chaucer: The Critical Heritage* (London: Routledge and Kegan Paul, 1978), 1:68 and 85, although Skelton insists on Chaucer's superiority. Ascham provides an earlier designation of Chaucer as "our Englishe Homer" (ibid., 1:100). In *The Fall of Princes* (1431–39), Lydgate had already compared Chaucer with Virgil, Dante, and Petrarch, and earlier, in the *Troy Book* (1412–20), he had provided an extensive comparison to Petrarch as Laureate (ibid., 1:57, 48). But Lydgate never located the comparison in the context of the quarrel of the ancients and moderns, as did Sidney and Dryden.

and finally a period of recovery, a rebirth or Renaissance of antique virtue. This scheme assumed a double moment of originality: the moment *then*, the antiquity that provides the model upon which the present is to be constructed, and the moment *now*, which establishes the break from the immediate past. These moments are linked—indeed, rendered virtually identical—by their mutual possession of a universal humanness, the pure being of "man" as he truly is. In between falls a time of loss, when this essence was distorted by the mediations of the historical moment: the Renaissance called this time, inevitably and ineradicably, the Middle Ages. By returning poetry to the universality of human nature, Chaucer escaped this time. And he was not merely a Renaissance rather than a medieval poet: more to the point, he was the first poet who lived in our own, postmedieval time—the first modern poet and hence the father of English poetry.

To all intents and purposes, the terms in which Dryden explained Chaucer's greatness largely continue to govern our own understanding of his poetry. Since the nineteenth century Chaucer criticism has focused almost exclusively on the question of character; just as the dominant liberal ideology has privileged the individual, so has the largely liberal tradition of academic criticism valued Chaucer for his depiction of a selfhood that is understood as at once historically particular and transhistorically recognizable.[27] It has also assumed that the key to his meaning resides in the proper understanding of his characters: how we interpret *Troilus and Criseyde* will be determined by how we understand the three protagonists; and the *Canterbury Tales* are habitually read as indexed to the ethical register of their tellers. In fact, the controversies that have traditionally preoccupied Chaucer criticism have focused not on the legitimacy of this procedure but rather on the terms of its practice. On the one hand is a self-proclaimed "historicism" that insists on the priority of stylistic and iconographic traditions, rhetorical programs, and a required exemplary meaning; on the other a "criticism" that privileges mimetic accuracy and commonsense psychology. In both cases Chaucerian character is seen as a conjunction of the specific (whether derived from stylistic imitation, rhetorical precept, or empirical observation) and the general (whether taken to be authoritative truths or universal human nature). Thus both assume that Chaucerian character is simply an object of representation, whether located in books or in the world

27. For an account of these issues in the Chaucer criticism of the last one hundred years, see Lee Patterson, *Negotiating the Past: The Historical Understanding of Medieval Literature* (Madison: University of Wisconsin Press, 1987), 3–39.

at large. But what is not considered is the possibility that it is in fact always in the process of being constructed, that it is an open site for negotiating the problematic relationship between outer and inner, historical particularity and transhistorical generality.

In this context we should realize that the humanist understanding of which Dryden was so authoritative a spokesman was by no means widely shared among Chaucer's immediate successors. Of course his fifteenth-century inheritors recognized (and were intimidated by) his achievement, but they neither endowed him with patriarchal status nor particularly admired his representation of character. When Lydgate said that Chaucer was the first to "fonde the floures . . . of Retoryke" with which to "enlumyne" "Our Rude speche," he was thinking not of origination but enhancement: finding an English that was "rude and boistous," Chaucer "Gan oure tonge first to *magnifie* / And *adourne* . . . with his elloquence."[28] Chaucer represents not a clean break from a rejected past but instead a transformation of that which was given: "Wyth al hys rethorykes swete" he *"amendede* our langage."[29] He is not source but model, the master who can teach his pupils a technical lesson rather than the father from whom derives an intangible and so all the more indispensable aptitude. With the exception only of Hoccleve, who is exceptional in other respects as well, the epithet applied to Chaucer by fifteenth-century poets is "master" not "father."[30]

Interestingly enough, this very question of paternity versus mastery is at the center of one of the earliest fifteenth-century responses to Chaucer's poetry. Henry Scogan addresses his *Moral Balade* to the children of Henry IV to whom he was tutor: he calls them "my sones" and designates himself "your fader called."[31] But we soon discover that this rather awkward invocation of patriarchy is complexly motivated, that the poem directly challenges at least the genealogical if not the sexual

28. John Lydgate, *The Life of Our Lady,* 1635–36; *Troy Book,* 3,4538–43 (Brewer, ed., *Chaucer,* 1:46, 48).

29. John Lydgate, *The Pilgrimage of the Life of Man,* 19774–76 (ibid., 1:51).

30. This is true of Lydgate, Scogan, James I, John Metham, George Ashby, John Rastell, and Skelton (ibid., 1:46, 48, 49, 51, 52, 53, 54, 59 [Lydgate], 60 [Scogan], 64 [Metham], 68 [Ashby]); for James I, Rastell, and Skelton, see Caroline Spurgeon, ed., *Five Hundred Years of Chaucer Criticism and Allusion, 1357–1900* (Cambridge: Cambridge University Press, 1925), 1:34, 73, 74. The designation "master" is also commonly used in manuscript colophons (ibid., 1:51, 54). Hoccleve alone claims personal acquaintance and is also virtually alone in addressing Chaucer as "maister deere and fadir reuerent" and "vniuersal fadir in science" (Brewer, *Chaucer,* 1:62–63); for the rare, late fifteenth-century exceptions, see ibid., 1:72, 75.

31. Walter W. Skeat, ed., *Chaucerian and Other Pieces,* Supplement to the *Complete Works of Geoffrey Chaucer,* vol. 7 (Oxford: Oxford University Press, 1897), 237–44.

assumptions of patriarchy itself. "My mayster Chaucer," says Scogan, has taught us that "the fader whiche is deed and grave, / Biquath nothing his vertue with his hous / Unto his sone" (65–69). On the contrary, virtue must be earned through virtuous deeds—an entirely conventional point: true nobility rests in virtue, not blood. But Scogan enforces the point in an unconventional way: first he cites the Wife of Bath on this point and then reproduces, verbatim and in its entirety, Chaucer's lyric "Gentilesse." The frankness of his citations confirms the model of discipleship the poem promotes: far from imitating Chaucer and so claiming a Chaucerian inspiration, Scogan relies instead upon the specific lessons the master has taught him, a wisdom that must be learned and reproduced rather than instinctively absorbed. "Therfore laborious / Ought ye to be" (69–70), he concludes; "thinke on this word, and werke it every day" (47). Both Henry's sons and Chaucer's successors are not heirs who will naturally inherit but disciples—"prentises" is the term a later royal tutor, George Ashby, applies to those who would learn from Chaucer—who must acquire for themselves the wisdom he purveys.[32]

Dryden's Chaucer provides English literature with a new and definitive origin, a father at one with the transcendent source (the "God's plenty" of character) who provides his heirs with a similarly immediate access. But Scogan's Chaucer provides instances of verbal mastery and moral perspicuity whose values can be learned only through diligent application and careful imitation. Instead of breaking with the past, Chaucer renewed it; instead of endowing the future with his genius, Chaucer offered it his example. As both the Wife of Bath and "Gentilesse" argue, all acts of invocation must be referred beyond earthly fathers to a transcendent *fons et origo*. History is a realm of mediation that can never in itself yield a definitive origin, and the lessons it teaches must be laboriously relearned. It is thus not a coincidence that the fifteenth century, unlike Dryden, declined to privilege Chaucer's depiction of character. His successors thought his most important achievement was rhetorical rather than realistic, and they had little interest in his most dramatic work, the Canterbury frame tale and the fabliaux. On the contrary, it was the elaborate courtly lyrics, like Anelida's complaint in *Anelida and Arcite*, and the exotic allegorical landscapes of the dream poems, especially the *House of Fame*, that attracted their admiration. And when they did imitate his representation of character, they often got it wrong: when Lydgate

---

32. For Ashby's phrase, see Brewer, *Chaucer*, 1:72.

provided an account of the Canterbury pilgrims in the *Siege of Thebes*, he made errors of detail that strike the modern reader as obvious.[33]

One is tempted to choose between these opposed conceptions of Chaucer's achievement.[34] But I want instead to suggest that Dryden and Scogan, and the attitudes toward history and character they represent, together declare a paradox at the center of Chaucerian writing itself. As is famously known, the Middle Ages is a time in which all forms of human activity were understood in relation to an original perfection. There is hardly an area of life—whether it be political, institutional, intellectual, spiritual, or artistic—in which medieval people did not legitimize their activity by reference to transcendent values and first principles. Medieval culture understood its own activity as the effort to ground itself upon a divinely authored originality. At the same time, medieval people also knew that this effort could only partially succeed. For them history was by definition the realm of the imperfect, and all efforts to reproduce in earthly form the absolutes in which they so firmly believed were necessarily incomplete. As Augustine had learned through his own life and taught to his medieval heirs, history is a place of temptation and loss, a geography of estrangement, a *regio dissimilitudinis* or land of unlikeness (to cite an influential Augustinian phrase) in which *homo viator* finds nothing that is like either the heavenly home toward which he journeys or the ideal self he seeks to become.[35] And yet what legitimizes the entire enterprise is a belief in a transcendental origin that can be only imperfectly known and inadequately represented.

For the humanism of the Renaissance, on the other hand, history does indeed allow for recuperation. The legitimizing origin is historically instantiated in the models of natural perfection provided by antiquity. By returning to this past the present can construct itself upon a

33. As A. C. Spearing says, "It is as though Chaucer for Lydgate was essentially a world of words, rather than, as for most modern readers, a world of people" (*Medieval to Renaissance in English Poetry* [Cambridge: Cambridge University Press, 1985], 75).

34. For another version of this choice, see below, chapter 1.

35. For *regio dissimilitudinis*, see Augustine, *Confessions*, 7, 10, 16: "I found myself to be far from you in a region of unlikeness" (trans. John K. Ryan [Garden City: Image Books, 1960), 171. For a history of the phrase, and its importance to medieval thinking about history, see Pierre Courcelle, *Les "Confessions" de Saint Augustine dans la tradition littéraire: Antécédents et postérité* (Paris: Etudes Augustiniennes, 1963), 623–40; F. Chatillon, "Regio Dissimilitudinis," in *Mélanges E. Podechard* (Lyon: Facultés Catholiques, 1903), 85–102; Robert Javelet, *Image et ressemblance au douzième siècle* (Paris: Letouzey et Ané, 1967), 1:266–85; Giuseppe Mazzotta, *Dante, Poet of the Desert* (Princeton: Princeton University Press, 1979), 151–52; and John Freccero, *Dante: Poetics of Conversion*, ed. Rachel Jacoff (Cambridge: Harvard University Press, 1986), 1–28.

secure foundation of absolute value, absolutes that allow it to escape entirely from the merely local determinations of its specific historical moment. For Dryden, as for so many other postmedieval writers, these absolutes are visible above all in human character, in what William Blake was later to call—in describing what Chaucer had represented in the *General Prologue*—"the Physiognomies or Lineaments of Universal Human Life."[36] By representing people as they truly and always are, Chaucer's poetry escapes from the limitations of its own historical moment into the timeless present of great art: it becomes a classic. In these terms, Chaucer's achievement was to be able, in Ezra Pound's phrase, "to make it new": to present a picture of human life that is felt to be always authentic and therefore always contemporary. It is in this sense, then, that Chaucer is the first modern English poet and can be appropriately designated the father of English poetry.

It is part of the argument of this book that both of these accounts are relevant to Chaucer's own conception of the historical process and his place within it. Dryden assumes the modernist model of Renaissance humanism: the Renaissance present posits a definitive break with the past (the Middle Ages) in order to ally itself with a transhistorical realm of self-presence (antiquity). Scogan assumes instead a model of continuity, in which both improvement and decline are possible but a transhistorical step out of the process as a whole is not. In trying to understand Chaucer's relation to the subject of history—to history as a topic for poetry, as a material and social world for representation, and (to shift the meaning of the word "subject") as the individual person forged in the dialectic between the subjective and the social—we must realize that he entertained both of these possibilities.

We can recognize this double allegiance in Chaucer's habit of simultaneously positing and undoing a foundational moment. He typically establishes for his poems a legitimizing genesis, an originary absoluteness whose contingency and insufficiency are then relentlessly exposed. In *Troilus and Criseyde*, for instance, the foundational status of Troy within medieval historiography is paralleled by the text's self-grounding upon its *auctor* Lollius, and then by the lovers' grounding of their actions upon an *entente* of wholly unadulterated idealism—a set of origins that the narrative as a whole undoes. In the *House of Fame* the foundational assumption is the originality of authority itself, both its location at the beginning of the line of literary imitation and its closeness to the *res* that

36. William Blake, "Prospectus of the Engraving of Chaucer's Canterbury Pilgrims," in *Poetry and Prose of William Blake*, ed. Geoffrey Keynes (London: Nonesuch Press, 1943), 637.

authorizes the disposition of all poetic *verba*. In the *Canterbury Tales* it is the initiating project of pilgrimage, a linear movement that promises to return the pilgrims to an original *patria* that stands outside the world of fallen history through which they are journeying. But the linear purposiveness of pilgrimage is undone by a persistent retracing of previous patterns, and by the rich thematic intertextuality that forces upon the reader an analogous interpretive recursiveness. As recent criticism has persuasively argued, the *Tales* articulate a shape that resembles not the straight line of pilgrimage but the circularity of a web or labyrinth.[37] And hence they issue not in a resolution but in the cancellation of the *Parson's Tale*. In his translation of Boethius's *Consolation*, Lady Philosophy says that

> ye men, that ben erthliche beestes, dremen alwey your bygynnynge, althoughe it be with a thynne ymaginacioun; and by a manner thought, al be it nat clerly ne parfitely, ye loken from afer to thilke verray fyn of blisfulnesse. (3, 3, 1–6)[38]

The Chaucerian imagination is at once caught within the middling world of history and haunted by the dream of origins.

It would be possible to understand this Chaucerian dynamic as endemic to the act of writing itself. According to Derrida, "to write is to have the passion of the origin," a passion that must remain always unfulfilled.[39] The promise of a self-present meaning offered by writing is constantly deferred: rather than providing access to an unambiguous, self-identical meaning invulnerable to historical change, writing offers instead only mediation, a set of signifiers whose internal articulation prevents us from ever arriving at, in Neil Hertz's phrase, "the end of the line."[40] But Chaucer's interest in this dilemma derives, I believe, from the complexity of his own specific cultural moment.

37. For the labyrinth, see Donald R. Howard, *The Idea of the* Canterbury Tales (Berkeley: University of California Press, 1976), 316–32; the web metaphor is proposed by Helen Cooper, *The Structure of the* Canterbury Tales (Athens: University of Georgia Press, 1983), 69–71. Howard argues that the *Canterbury Tales* deploys "a series of interlaced, interrelated themes among which everything leads to everything else; it has no beginning, no end, and no center, but is all the same coherent" (222).

38. I have cited Chaucer's *Boece* according to the convention used for the Latin text: the *prosae* are cited by arabic numerals, the *metra* by roman. Thus 3, 3, 1–6 refers to Book 3, prose 3, lines 1–6; 3, iii, 1–6 would refer to Book 3, metrum 3, lines 1–6.

39. Jacques Derrida, *Writing and Difference*, trans. Alan Bass (Chicago: University of Chicago Press, 1978), 295.

40. Neil Hertz, *The End of the Line* (New York: Columbia University Press, 1985), 217–39.

For Chaucer's poetic procedures express a typically "modernist" dilemma—a dilemma that becomes pressing when, for whatever reasons, the idea of the modern becomes an urgent possibility. According to Paul de Man's exemplary account, modernity consists in the paradoxical discovery of the impossibility of being modern. On the one hand, "modernity exists in the form of a desire to wipe out whatever came earlier, in the hope of reaching at last a point that could be called a true present, a point of origin that marks a new departure." But when writers begin to "assert their own modernity, they are bound to discover their dependence on similar assertions made by their literary predecessors; their claim to being a new beginning thus turns out to be the repetition of a claim that has always been made." Hence the paradox: "If history is not to become sheer regression or paralysis, it depends on modernity for its duration and renewal; but modernity cannot assert itself without being at once swallowed up and reintegrated into a regressive historical process."[41]

Dryden and Scogan represent the two sides of this paradox, the first responding according to the modernist model of Renaissance humanism, the second following the historicist model of medieval transcendentalism. As for Chaucer, his poetry everywhere records the attraction of modernity but is finally unwilling to annul its own historicity. And in the early poetry, the arena in which this struggle is worked out is, as we would expect, the representation of antiquity. Like his *trecento* colleagues in Italy and his sixteenth-century successors in England, Chaucer invoked the world of antiquity in order to distance himself from the immediate past. But unlike many of them, his classicism never pretends to recover antiquity as a self-coherent and autonomous cultural period.[42] Not that he naively appropriates classical *topoi* to medieval meanings: Chaucer's is no "clergial" classicism that uses the materials of antique legend simply for illustrative and ornamental purposes.

41. Paul de Man, "Literary History and Literary Modernity," in *Blindness and Insight*, 2d ed. (Minneapolis: University of Minnesota Press, 1983 [1970]), 148, 161, 151. See also Jürgen Habermas, "Modernity—An Incomplete Project," *New German Critique* 22 (1981), reprinted in Paul Rabinow and William M. Sullivan, eds., *Interpretive Social Sciences: A Second Look* (Berkeley: University of California Press, 1987), 141–56; and Gordon Teskey, "Milton and Modernity," *Diacritics* 18 (Spring, 1988): 42–53.

42. On this as the hallmark of humanism, see Erwin Panofsky, *Renaissance and Renascences in Western Art* (Stockholm: Almqvist and Wiksell, 1960), and Thomas M. Greene, *The Light in Troy: Imitation and Discovery in Renaissance Poetry* (New Haven: Yale University Press, 1982). For accounts of Chaucer's classicism that seek to align it with the humanist model, see Alastair Minnis, *Chaucer and Pagan Antiquity* (Cambridge: Brewer, 1982), Winthrop Wetherbee, *Chaucer and the Poets* (Ithaca: Cornell University Press, 1984), and Spearing, *Medieval to Renaissance*, 15–58.

But because it developed as a solution to a specific cultural problem—
the need to liberate writing, and the writer, from the constricting social
environment of the court—and because it was enacted without the
benefit of a widespread sense of cultural renewal, Chaucer's classicism
articulated the complex negotiations of past and present with special
complexity. If we must have a label for this kind of historical consciousness, perhaps we should call it postmodern.

III

That which Chaucer sought to modify in constituting a new way of
writing—that which represented the status quo against which his modernity was to enact itself—will be found not in the relentlessly didactic sententiousness that is often thought to represent medieval culture
at its most conservative. Rather, it was both within and against the
fashionable discourse of court versifying that his poetry developed. All
of Chaucer's pre-*Canterbury Tales* poetry was almost certainly written
within the environment of noble and royal courts and was directed to a
court audience.[43] Not that those who retained Chaucer—the Countess
of Ulster, Edward III, John of Gaunt, and Richard II—rewarded him
because he produced writing they admired: J. R. Hulbert showed many
years ago that Chaucer's financial support was in no way different from
that received by similar men who were not poets, and the more than six
hundred pages of the *Life-Records* contain not a single reference to literary activity.[44] Whatever other satisfactions Chaucer's writing might
have brought him, neither financial reward nor social advancement
seems to have been among them. Yet it remains true that virtually all

43.   Even the *Boece*, although we hardly need to posit a court audience to account for
its production, translates a text that was widely popular among the late medieval nobility. For the aristocratic ownership of French translations of Boethius, see A[ntoine]
T[homas] and M[ario] R[oques], "Les traductions françaises de la *Consolatio Philosophiae*
de Boèce," *Histoire littéraire de la France* 37 (1938), 437, 441, 471 n. 6; Nigel F. Palmer, "Latin
and Vernacular in the Northern European Tradition of the *De Consolatione Philosophiae*," in
Boethius: His Life, Thought and Influence, ed. Margaret Gibson (Oxford: Blackwell, 1981),
371. Glynnis M. Cropp, "*Le Livre de Boece de Consolation:* From Translation to Glossed
Text," in *The Medieval Boethius: Studies in the Vernacular Translations of* De Consolatione
Philosophiae, ed. Alastair Minnis (Cambridge: Brewer, 1987), discusses an anonymous
fourteenth-century translation, designed specifically for a noble audience, that glosses
the text with accounts of the deaths of contemporary rulers and noblemen (63–85). For
chivalry and Boethianism, see below, chapter 3, 215–16.

44.   James Root Hulbert, *Chaucer's Official Life* (Menasha: Collegiate Press, 1912); Martin Crow and Clair C. Olson, eds., *Chaucer Life-Records* (Oxford: Oxford University Press,
1966).

the writing produced prior to the *Canterbury Tales* is constructed from, as it enlarges upon, the materials and procedures of court writing. Moreover, that this poetry should concern itself above all with the subject of history—with the relation of agency to action, and with the legitimacy of historical engagement per se—is fully consistent with its address to a nobility whose class definition stressed an active role in the bringing of order to a disordinate world. The growth in the later Middle Ages of what Richard Kaeuper has called the "secular reform movement," the sense within the governing class that its task was to engage in the "constantly evolving reform" of a world in need of guidance, naturally promoted the nature and meaning of history to topics of central interest.[45]

The first two chapters of this book seek to describe the ways in which Chaucer initially explored the subject of history. Chapter 1 offers a reading of the neglected but symptomatic poem *Anelida and Arcite*. My purpose here is twofold. One is to show that the imbrications of romance and epic, love and war, the self and history here articulate an economy of historical recursiveness: the doubled self of erotic pathology—the disloyal Arcite is described as "double in love and nothing pleyn"—finds its counterpart in the historical circularity defined by the mythology of Thebes that provides the poem's narrative materials. And this economy is relevant as well to the poet's own practice: as Arcite and Anelida are afflicted with a disordered and obsessive memory, so the poet's oblique recourse to literary history reveals a similarly unsettled attitude toward his poetic past—including mighty precursors such as Statius, Ovid, Corinna, Dante, and Boccaccio. Secondly, the circularity of Theban history (expressed both here and, in greater detail, in the very similar "Complaint of Mars") stands in a complex and potentially subversive relation to the transcendental circularity of Boethianism. Invoked in both these poems as a saving alternative to the erotic absorptions they record, the Platonic circularity of Boethianism (in which being proceeds from and returns to the *summum bonum*) becomes ironically implicated in the aporia it means to foreclose.

Chapter 2 carries these concerns over into *Troilus and Criseyde*, which is here located in the context established by medieval historiography generally and specifically by the tradition of Trojan writing. In taking up the project of a Trojan poem, Chaucer raised questions about historical origin and the legitimacy of the historical life itself, questions central to aristocratic self-definition. Yet Trojan history here reveals itself to be

45. Richard W. Kaeuper, *War, Justice and Public Order* (Oxford: Clarendon Press, 1988), 271–72.

underwritten by a dark Theban subtext that argues that beginnings are always rebeginnings: the form of the historical life undoes the very possibility of the purposive movement—the *translatio imperii*—upon which the historical legitimacy of medieval Europe was often thought to rest. The poem is also in quest of psychological origins, the *entente* to love (what Boethius called *intentio naturalis*) that motivates and presumably explains the actions of the protagonists. But here too singularity evades the poet's interrogations: the actions of the lovers reveal subjectivity to be not a self-identical essence but rather a site where different selves form and reform, thwarting any effort to apprehend the *fons et origo* of the action. What the narrator calls "the cause whi" is thus hopelessly lost amid the shiftings entailed by a world of constant mediation. The final section of this chapter argues that the interpretive impasse at which the *Troilus* arrives is a function not simply of Chaucer's sceptical imagination but of the historical conditions of the 1380s in which it was written, and that it may even stage (in a necessarily displaced way) political dramas in which Chaucer was himself engaged.

But having said this, it must be acknowledged that Chaucer's meditations on history remain, throughout the pre–*Canterbury Tales* two-thirds of his career, for the most part divorced from the specificity of local events. By endowing his courtly writing with both a densely developed classical context and philosophical depth Chaucer distinguished it from the *makyng* of his contemporaries. But his poetry declined to engage the real world of late medieval England explicitly. In a recent discussion of the Modernist movement of the early twentieth century, Perry Anderson has argued that one of its necessary preconditions was "the imaginative proximity of social revolution. The extent of hope or apprehension that the prospect of such a revolution arouses varies widely, but over most of Europe it was 'in the air' during the Belle Époque itself."[46] Yet while the twentieth-century Modernists may have been empowered by the possibility of revolution, their responses were for the most part conservative, both in the explicitly reactionary political programs to which they subscribed and in the formalist aesthetic that largely governed their own cultural production. History may have enabled their innovations, but it was a history from which they more often than not sought to flee.

Something of the same could be said of Chaucer's own early meditations on history and modernity. Revolution was in the air in late

46. Perry Anderson, "Modernity and Revolution," in *Marxism and the Interpretation of Culture*, ed. Cary Nelson and Lawrence Grossberg (Urbana: University of Illinois Press, 1988), 325.

fourteenth-century Europe too, not least of all in England: the Rising of 1381 was the most visible expression of an upsurge of new forces that were felt to pervade the social, political, and economic life of post-plague England. Chaucer's relations to these dynamic forces are by no means straightforward. But in seeing modernity as an essentially literary question, by allowing his writing to remain within the highly stylized aesthetic of court culture (however modified), and in staging the problematic of historical action in terms of antiquity, Chaucer ruled out much of his contemporary historical world as an object of poetic attention. Moreover, the ostentatious formalism of his writing (a quality that has helped to preserve its canonicity in the academy) located it within the *hortus conclusus* of aristocratic aestheticism, a world where the acts of dominance and victimization, possession and privation, so common to the historical world of late medieval England were displaced into a fantasy world of amorous play. Indeed, given the seigneurial crisis of the later Middle Ages, one of the attractions of courtly *makyng* must have been just the sense of control with which it endowed the *maker* himself, a control that Chaucer deploys with effortless authority.[47] And when he does consider the problem of change directly, as what he calls in the *Anelida* "newefangelnesse," he locates it in the realm not of social and political action but of moral psychology, where it is stigmatized as an erotic instability to be diagnosed as "falsnes" and "doublenesse."

Yet this cannot, finally, be the whole story. For if Chaucer is no revolutionary (and who ever thought otherwise?), he does remain a writer committed not just to innovation but to the understanding of innovation. Certainly such self-reflection may lead to a deconstructive paralysis, and both *Anelida and Arcite* and *Troilus and Criseyde* are deeply self-cancelling texts that call into question the very possibility of historical action per se. Yet they are also bravely exploratory, at the levels of both literary construction and conceptual penetration. No one else in England, perhaps even in Europe, could have written them: in the imprecise way we usually use the word, they are *originals*. Finally, if we must measure the degree to which they stand apart from history—and de Man has reminded us that the proper antithesis to the modern is not the past but historicity itself—we should also see them as the necessary preliminary for rapprochement. For only in this way can we under-

47. As Robert Guiette has said of the courtly poet, "L'artifex, dans son monde à part, clos, limité, absolu, met sa force d'homme au service d'une chose qu'il fait" ("D'une poésie formelle en France en Moyen Age," *Romanica Gandensia* 8 [1960], 21). For this writing as an escape from history, see Daniel Poirion, *Le poéte et le prince* (Paris: Presses universitaires de France, 1965), 20–25.

stand how it could be that Chaucer concluded his career by writing the text that provides us with the shrewdest and most capacious analysis of late medieval society we possess. History impelled Chaucer toward the modern and he accepted the challenge by investigating not just the idea of history, as in *Anelida and Arcite* and the *Troilus*, but, in the *Canterbury Tales*, the historical world itself.

IV

The turn to the social world of contemporary England represents, I believe, a significant reorientation of Chaucer's way of thinking: we should take seriously the discontinuity of his career and try to understand the conditions that made the writing of the *Canterbury Tales* possible. The presence of the *Tales* is for the modern reader so unavoidable, their achievement so undeniable, that we approach them with a sense of inevitability that assumes their permanent existence. But there was a time when they had not been written, and their coming into existence was not preordained. If something rather than nothing, then why this thing rather than another?

Anelida and Arcite and the *Troilus* define the problematic of history in terms of the relation of the individual to an unfolding historical totality, a totality that both stands over against the self and is nonetheless an effect of it. And both, and especially the *Troilus*, explore with often astonishing perspicuity the complex subjectivity that constitutes the inner dimension of selfhood. It is this same dialectic—between the subject and history—that is at the heart of the *Canterbury Tales*. But there is a difference. Throughout his early poetry Chaucer had insisted upon subjectivity as the unavoidable condition of all discourse, that all writing, both that endowed with cultural authority and that which purports to render experience directly, is mediated by a historically specific human consciousness. The early complaints and the dream visions constantly call attention to the narratorial voice, while *Troilus and Criseyde* is both presided over by the go-between Pandarus and delivered by an unavoidable narrator, in effect defining itself as a study in mediation. But in the *Canterbury Tales* Chaucer goes further, for each *Tale* is not only grounded within a speaking subject but in effect serves to constitute that subjectivity. This quality has been best described by Marshall Leicester:

> The *Canterbury Tales* is not written to be spoken as if it were a play. It is written to be read, but read *as if* it were spoken. The poem is a literary imitation of oral performance. . . . While any text can be read in a

way that elicits its voice, some texts actively engage the phenomenon of voice, exploit it, make it the center of their discourse—make it their content. A text of this sort can be said to be *about* its speaker, and this is the sort of text I contend that the *Canterbury Tales* is and especially the sort that the individual tales are. The tales . . . concentrate not on the way preexisting people create language but on the way language creates people.[48]

While in practice some *Tales* may efface their speakers, Leicester is certainly right in recognizing that the very form of the *Tales* always raises the possibility of a radically subjectivized discourse.

The *General Prologue* proclaims this possibility in no uncertain terms and provides a model for the kind of selfhood the *Tales* are going to explore in detail. In *Chaucer and Medieval Estates Satire*, Jill Mann showed that although the conceptual framework of the *Prologue* was derived from an estates literature that defined selfhood in terms of social function—"the estate itself, rather than the individual, is the root idea" (14)—the *Prologue* in fact pays scant attention to "social ends" (191) and instead manages "to create the ambiguity and complexity of response which persuades us that the characters are complex individuals" (193).[49] To an extraordinary degree, Chaucer allows the members of the various estates to define themselves, a procedure that in effect undermines their definition as estates. Rather than being representatives of social functions, in other words, the pilgrims become individuals who have been assigned those functions, men and women enacting externally imposed roles toward which each has his or her own kind of relationship. They become, in short, subjects.

This definition from the inside is accomplished by several means. For one thing, Chaucer persistently filters into the narratorial description of each pilgrim an individualizing voice. Virtually every pilgrim is presented not only as a physical appearance and set of typical practices but also as a speaker, and the *Prologue* is full of references to their linguistic habits: the Prioress's fastidious oath "by Seinte Loy," her nasal "entuning" of the divine service, and her Stratford French; the Friar's "fair langage"—a pleasant absolution, solicitous *in principio*, and sweetly lisped English; the Merchant's solemn "resons" and self-promoting "sowynynge"; the Clerk's verbal economy—"short and

48. H. Marshall Leicester, Jr., "The Art of Impersonation: A General Prologue to the *Canterbury Tales*," *PMLA* 95 (1980), 221, 217.

49. Jill Mann, *Chaucer and Medieval Estates Satire* (Cambridge: Cambridge University Press, 1973).

quyk and ful of hy sentence"—that "souns" only moral virtue; the Sergeant's "wordes [that] weren so wise"; the Doctor's ponderous account
"of physik and of surgerye"; the Wife of Bath's banter—"wel koude
she laughe and carpe"; the Parson's "discreet and benygne" teaching—
"he was to synful men nat despitous, / Ne of his speche daungerous ne
digne"; the Miller's performance as a "janglere and goliardeys"; the
Summoner's drunken Latin; and the Pardoner's voice "as smal as . . . a
goot."

Even more important, throughout the *Prologue* Chaucer reminds us
that the language of his pilgrims is not just a characterizing detail but
the very material from which they are (self-)constructed. Within the
narratorial voice we hear as well the voice of the pilgrim: narratorial
objectivity is replaced by pilgrim subjectivity. Take, for example, the
case of the Parson:

> This noble ensample to his sheep he yaf,
> That first he wroghte, and afterward he taughte.
> Out of the gospel he tho wordes caughte,
> And this figure he added eek therto,
> That if gold ruste, what shal iren do?
> For if a preest be foul, on whom we truste,
> No wonder is a lewed man to ruste;
> And shame it is, if a prest take keep,
> A shiten shepherde and a clene sheep.
> Wel oghte a preest ensample for to yive,
> By his clennesse, how that his sheep sholde lyve. (496–506)

As Mann says, "It is the *character himself* who is speaking. It is not the
moralist commentator who quotes from the gospel and adds the 'figure' about rusting gold; it is the Parson himself." And she adds: "This is
no abstract, timeless figure; Chaucer envisages [the Parson] in a realistic spatial and temporal existence, and as not merely acting out a role,
but expressing his consciousness of doing so" (66).[50] Chaucer shows us that
the Parson's estate is not the sum total of his selfhood but a social identity that he deliberately adopts, a self-definition he labors to achieve.
He shows us, in other words, that character is not an object to be described but the product of a dialectical movement between a socially

---

50.   The first italicization is in Mann's text; I have added the second. That several of
the pilgrims appropriate the narratorial voice was already noted by E. Talbot Donaldson
in *Chaucer's Poetry: An Anthology for the Modern Reader*, 2d ed. (New York: The Ronald
Press, 1975 [1958]), 1040.

undefined subjectivity (content, for the moment, unspecified) and a historically determined role. Character is what emerges from the transactions between the given world outside (history) and the unspecified world within (the subject).

This essentially rhetorical conception of selfhood is at work throughout the *General Prologue*. The pilgrims' verbal energy is not just a characteristic to be described by the narrator but is itself continually demonstrated by the pilgrims themselves: usurping the narratorial voice, the pilgrims in effect represent themselves. We hear the Monk articulate his own objections to the monastic rule:

> What sholde he studie and make hymselven wood,
> Upon a book in cloystre alwey to poure,
> Or swynken with his handes, and laboure,
> As Austyn bit? How shal the world be served?
> Lat Austyn have his swynk to hym reserved! (184–88)

And we hear the Friar defend his power of confession—"As seyde hymself" (219)—and express his distaste for "sike lazars": "It is nat honest, it may nat avaunce, / For to deelen with no swich poraille" (246–47). The *Prologue* is also saturated with the pilgrims' professional jargon. The Merchant's "bargaynes" and "chevyssaunce"; the Sergeant of Law's "patente," "pleyn commissioun," "termes," and "caas and doomes alle"; the Cook's "mortreux" and "blankmanger"; the Shipman's "herberwe, and his moone, [and] lodemenage"; the Doctor of Physik's medical authorities—"olde Esculapius, / And Deyscorides, and eek Rufus," and a dozen more; the Pardoner's "reliks"—Our Lady's veil, Saint Peter's sail, the "croys of latoun" and the pig's bones: as Mann says, "the narrator assumes that each pilgrim is an expert, and presents him in his own terms, according to his own values, *in his own language*" (194).[51]

This procedure entails a specific idea of selfhood. For if the vocational objects with which the *Prologue* is packed are displayed before us not just as the habitual materials of the pilgrims' working lives but as the means by which they constitute their social identities, we are also made aware of the conscious effort required by these acts of self-fabrication. A telling case in point is the Prioress, the first portrait after the rigorously conventional and objectified opening trio of Knight, Squire, and Yeoman. John Livingston Lowes memorably described the Prioress's dilemma as "the engagingly imperfect submergence of the

51. My italics.

feminine in the ecclesiastical."[52] Telling as this description is, however, it in fact misrepresents the Prioress's situation. For her dilemma is not that of a womanly nature coerced into a constraining social role but rather of a subjectivity caught between the demands of two conflicting social definitions of femininity, those of nun and courtly lady. Represented by her ambiguous brooch, this social conflict is not an end in itself but the means by which a hidden inwardness struggles to make itself known. And this inwardness is symptomatically revealed by the activities that seem most to engage her, her eating and her petting. Quite apart from whatever social judgment we might wish to pass on these particular habits for a nun, they more profoundly witness to the pressure of an appetitive self that seeks for a satisfaction that continues to elude it. Food and animals become the signs of the Prioress's desire, the objects of a yearning to gratify the self both by incorporating the world ("she was nat undergrowe") and by entertaining feelings whose fleeting intensity—sharp but not deep—perhaps masks more permanent aches.

In sum, the pilgrims are usually conceived less as objects whose particularity is to be detailed than as subjects caught in the very process of self-construction. Usually but not always, and the exceptions are instructive. The three opening portraits—of the Knight, Squire, and Yeoman—can be unproblematically accounted for by the prescriptions of rhetorical *descriptio*.[53] The Knight's portrait, for instance, is carefully divided into two parts: the opening thirty lines describe his moral qualities, first the military experience that marks him as "a worthy man," then the virtues that comprise the *sapientia* that is the counterpart to this fortitude—"And though that he were worthy, he was wys." And the second part is an *effictio*, introduced by a marking line ("But for to tellen yow of his array") and followed by a brief but telling physical description. The carefully delineated structure matches the fully conventional quality of the portrait, a conventionality that is itself a sign of chivalric

52. John Livingston Lowes, *Convention and Revolt in Poetry* (Boston: Houghton Mifflin, 1919), 60–61; cited by Florence H. Ridley in *The Riverside Chaucer*, ed. Larry Benson, (Boston: Houghton Mifflin, 1987), 803. The phrase was even more telling in F. N. Robinson's miscitation; see *The Works of Geoffrey Chaucer*, 2d ed. (Boston: Houghton Mifflin, 1957 [1933]), 653.

53. The *locus classicus* is Cicero, *De inventione*, 1, 24, 34–36. For medieval rewritings of these prescriptions, see Geoffrey of Vinsauf, *Documentum de modo et arte dictandi et versificandi*, trans. Roger P. Parr (Milwaukee: Marquette University Press, 1968), 138–39 (who also cites Horace's *Ars poetica*, 120–74); Matthew of Vendôme, *Ars versificatoria*, 1, 38–118 (both in Edmond Faral, ed., *Les arts poétiques du XIIᵉ et du XIIIᵉ siècle* [Paris: Champion, 1924]); and the anonymous *Tractatus de attributis personae et negotio*, in K. F. Halm, ed., *Rhetores latini minori* (Leipzig: Teubner, 1863), 305–10.

virtue: the Knight has no identity other than that with which his social function endows him, and to ascribe self-consciousness to him, even were it a self-conscious submission to his role, would be to assume a subjectivity that would be itself subversive of the social order from which he derives his identity. So too for the Squire and Yeoman, whose absorption by the collective values of the social order is most dramatically marked by a single line in the Yeoman's portrait: "Wel koude he dresse his takel *yemanly*," as if the Yeoman's mode of acting in the world were fully determined by his social identity. How comforting a representative of the third estate he is!—especially at a time when many of his peers were far from being so instinctively docile. And this gratification is extended to the psychologically opaque and socially quiescent Plowman, whose portrait assiduously effaces the very real economic struggles of Chaucer's contemporary world, struggles that were in other texts expressed precisely by means of the figure of the plowman.[54]

Deriving their historical legitimacy from the very social conception that motivates estates literature, the unit of the Knight, Squire, and Yeoman is naturally represented in the purely social terms prescribed by the genre. But this is not the case for the majority of pilgrims, that broad group who are technically members of the third estate but are in fact drawn from the middle ranks that the ternary social theory accommodated only with difficulty. Men and women playing socially defined roles and largely aware of their performance, character is for them not a given fact but a construction; and it is constructed upon the ground of a socially undetermined subjectivity that resists representation and makes itself known only symptomatically. The Prioress's food, the Monk's sweat, the Friar's wintry gaze—these signs of an inward self find counterparts in other portraits: the Merchant's namelessness, the leanness of the Clerk's mount, the Sergeant of Law's "hoomly" array, the "wo" of the Franklin's cook if his sauces fall below standard and the "mormal" of the Guildsmen's Cook (two displaced expressions of social strain), the name—"Maudelayne"—of the Shipman's barge, the Physician's protectively "mesurable" diet, the Wife's "shoes ful moyste and newe," the Miller's white coat with its blue hood, the Reeve's "yshadwed" dwelling in Norfolk, the Summoner's sexual generosity, the Pardoner's "smal" voice straining to sing its "loude" song of love-longing—each of these details (and every reader can easily construct his or her own list) creates a discordance that forces us to acknowledge

54. See Rodney Hilton, *The English Peasantry in the Later Middle Ages* (Oxford: Clarendon Press, 1975), 22–23, and Hilton, "Ideology and Social Order in Later Medieval England," in *Class Conflict and the Crisis of Feudalism* (London: Hambledon, 1985), 248–50.

the distance between social function and psychological inwardness. And the process of self-constitution through discourse that is initiated in the *General Prologue* is fulfilled, in different ways and to different degrees, in the *Canterbury Tales* that follow.

The setting up of a socially undetermined subjectivity in opposition to the social definition entailed by the estates theory carries large implications. For the model of selfhood that underwrites the *Canterbury Tales*, with its emphasis upon an identity that exists prior to and even in opposition to the social order, is the foundational assumption of what will come to be humanist individualism. There is an essential human nature that exists apart from society—Dryden's "general character," Blake's "Universal Human Life"—a selfhood that constitutes our most essential being. But is not this idea itself a function of historical conditioning? As Raymond Williams reminds us, it is a characteristic of bourgeois ideology to establish "an abstract separation and distinction between the 'individual' and the 'social' . . . as 'natural' starting-points."[55] Does this mean that Chaucer should be understood as a bourgeois writer, or that he understood himself in this way? He was, after all, a son of the merchant patriciate and spent much of his life, as controller of customs in London, immersed in the commercial world of the city and surrounded by its merchants. Can we understand Chaucer's fascination with the subject of history in biographical terms?

V

While we can hardly account for Chaucer's attitudes and interests simply by reference to his position within the social world of late medieval England, it is nonetheless true that his social location was intriguingly anomalous. While Chaucer was a member of the *gentil* estate—as a squire he was entitled to bear arms—his position was somewhat unusual, in terms of wealth, of social status, and, especially, of the tasks he was called upon to perform.[56] "Royal service ennobles" was a common medieval maxim, and it was through his service to the king, rather than through lineage or the acquisition of landed wealth, that this vintner's son achieved *gentil* status.[57] The royal household in which Chau-

---

55. Raymond Williams, *Marxism and Literature* (Oxford: Oxford University Press, 1977), 28.

56. Noel Denholm-Young, *The Country Gentry in the Fourteenth Century* (Oxford: Clarendon Press, 1969), offers a description of Chaucer's arms, but without specifying his source (23–24).

57. For service and ennoblement, see Christopher Given-Wilson, *The English Nobility in the Late Middle Ages* (London: Routledge and Kegan Paul, 1987), 17–18.

cer served was hierarchically arranged, with the chamber knights—a group that included Chaucer's friends Lewis Clifford, John Clanvowe, and Philip de la Vache—near the top, and the king's squires, which included Chaucer, near the bottom. The office of chamber knight (*miles camere regis*) was first introduced by Edward III in 1348 to replace the more exclusively military household knights (*milites de familia regis*).[58] Edward originally had twelve chamber knights, but in the later years of his reign the number dwindled as low as three; under Richard II and Henry IV, the number rose again to between eight and thirteen. Attached to the personal service of the king, these men performed a wide variety of functions, as councillors, special commissioners, and diplomats. They were, in Given-Wilson's words, "an inner group of high-ranking and trusted royal servants, valued by the king for their counsel, their administrative ability and their domestic service."[59] Below them in scale were the *armigeri camere regis*, the twenty or so squires of the chamber who attended personally on the king, and the *armigeri familia regis*, squires of the household who "almost certainly came to the court on rotation."[60] It is within this latter group that Chaucer was to be found.[61]

The gap in status and power between the chamber knights at the top of the scale of royal service and Chaucer, near the bottom, was substantial. In certain documents this difference is explicit to the point of quantification. Like Chaucer, the chamber knight Richard Stury was captured in the campaign of 1359–60; he was ransomed for £50, while it cost Edward III only £16 to retrieve Chaucer. In the 1385 writ of allowance for liveries of mourning for Joan, the Dowager Princess of Wales, the recipients are

58. This account depends upon Chris Given-Wilson, "The King and the Gentry in Fourteenth-Century England," *TRHS*, 5th ser. 37 (1987): 87–102, and Given-Wilson, *The Royal Household and the King's Affinity: Service, Politics, and Finance in England 1360–1413* (New Haven: Yale University Press, 1986).

59. Given-Wilson, "King and Gentry," 92.

60. Given-Wilson, *Royal Household*, 66.

61. Chaucer is listed in three documents as a squire of the king's chamber, but Richard Firth Green's consideration of the full evidence leads him to the conclusion that Chaucer was in fact simply a squire of the household or *familia* (*Poets and Princepleasers: Literature and the English Court in the Late Middle Ages* [Toronto: University of Toronto Press, 1980], 68). As well as these knights and squires of the household, the king retained men who constituted his affinity: king's knights were paid an annuity of between £20 to £100, most payments being between £40 and £60, and king's squires received annuities of between 20 and 40 marks (approximately £13 to £26). These last two groups were comprised of men who would promote the king's interests in local affairs and whom he could call upon for service on commissions, as sheriffs and justices of the peace, and for support in Parliament. It may well be that after his move to the customs in 1374, Chaucer would have been thought to fit into this category.

divided into six categories according to the amount granted: Clanvowe, Clifford, and de la Vache are in number three, Chaucer in number five.[62] These administrative records reduce to numbers a significant economic and social divide. Take the matter of wealth. With the possible exception of Clanvowe, all the chamber knights of Chaucer's acquaintance married well, not only becoming joined by ties of kinship with the higher nobility but, in the cases of Stury and Clifford, remedying their previously landless condition. Their positions as chamber knights were also lucrative: they all flourished economically.[63] Chaucer, on the other hand, married Philippa, a *domicella reginae* who was probably the daughter of the herald Sir Payn de Roet, the Guienne King of Arms, and sister of the woman who would become John of Gaunt's mistress and third wife. While well connected, as a foreigner Philippa had neither standing among the English nobility nor a landed inheritance, and she apparently brought her husband only her modest annuity. Chaucer was never poor—his fees and annuities probably brought him around £20 per year at a time when an annual income of £10 was substantial—but neither did he flourish financially.[64] The records strongly suggest that he was financially embarrassed in the late 1380s when he lost his job as controller, and when he died he left his heir Thomas Chaucer a very modest inheritance indeed.[65]

Each of the chamber knights also had a lengthy military career—they were all "career soldiers who had seen much campaigning," says McFarlane, and "belonged to the international chivalrous class and spoke its lingua franca."[66] Clanvowe and Nevill died in 1391 near Constantinople, probably on pilgrimage but perhaps on crusade; in 1390 they had apparently asked Richard's permission to join the Duke of

62. Crow and Olson, *Chaucer Life-Records*, 24, 103–4.

63. K. B. McFarlane, *Lancastrian Kings and Lollard Knights* (Oxford: Clarendon Press, 1973), 176. It is not known whether Clanvowe married. Stury was a particularly spectacular example of a man of very humble origins who advanced both financially and socially through his service in the royal household: he was one of Edward III's chamber knights and stayed on with Richard, remaining a powerful member of the court until his death in 1395 (Given-Wilson, *Royal Household*, 57, 148–49, 186).

64. According to Christopher Dyer (*Standards of Living in the Later Middle Ages* [Cambridge: Cambridge University Press, 1989]), "For most people £10 represented a great fortune, and we are justified in regarding anyone receiving such a sum regularly as being wealthy" (18).

65. The inheritance consisted of "a property in Golding Lane in the city of London (worth £8 a year) and the recent lease of a house in the garden of the Lady Chapel of Westminster Abbey" (J. S. Roskell, *Parliament and Politics in Late Medieval England* [London: Hambledon, 1983], 154–55).

66. McFarlane, *Lancastrian Kings*, 160, 179.

Bourbon's crusade against Tunis. Clifford, who fought in the French wars from 1351 through 1378, accompanied Richard on his Scottish campaign of 1385 and joined Philippe de Mézières' crusading Order of the Passion, probably in the early 1390s. He also sat on the Court of Chivalry that gave final judgment in the famous dispute over a coat of arms between Sir Richard Scrope and Sir Robert Grosvenor—a court before which Chaucer gave testimony that referred to his single military campaign, Edward's expedition of 1359–60 when Chaucer was captured. And this was a campaign in which Chaucer was enrolled not because of his military prowess or ambition but simply because he was a member of the household.[67]

As we should expect of such prominent men, the chamber knights entered Chaucer's official life only briefly and only in circumstances when their weighty social authority was needed. Clifford and de la Vache seem in fact to have had no official dealings with Chaucer at all. On the other hand, Nevill and Clanvowe witnessed the release signed by Cecily Champaigne in 1380; the other witnesses were William Beauchamp, the heir of the earl of Warwick, John Philpot, the mayor of London and collector of customs, and Richard Morrell, a prominent London merchant.[68] Whatever the reality behind the records, Chaucer drew on the most highly placed friends he could find for support in what was certainly an unsavory and perhaps also a potentially dangerous affair. The only other appearances of these chamber knights in the *Life-Records* concern two official duties that Chaucer undertook under the direction of the prominent Stury: he went with him to Montreuil in 1377, and in 1390 he was a member of a commission on walls and ditches, which Stury headed.[69]

The chamber knights were thus both intimate royal servants with free access to the king and fully fledged members of the "international chivalrous class."[70] Chaucer, as the brevity of his military service, his modest financial means, his undistinguished position as an *armiger regis*, and his political obscurity all testify, was not.[71] Indeed, when he did

67. "The list of *vadia guerre* for the 1359–60 campaign includes the name of almost every person who received robes in the wardrobe that year" (Given-Wilson, *Royal Household*, 63).

68. Crow and Olson, *Chaucer Life-Records*, 343.

69. Ibid., 50, 490–91.

70. It should be pointed out, however, that since the chamber knights of Chaucer's acquaintance were exempted from attack by the Merciless Parliament of 1388 they were probably not among the inner circle of Richard's favorites.

71. A. J. Tuck, "Richard II's System of Patronage," in *The Reign of Richard II: Essays in Honour of May McKisack*, ed. F. R. H. DuBoulay and Caroline Barron (London: Athlone

enter the political arena, first as knight of the shire from Kent in the Parliament of 1386 and then as a member of the Peace Commission for Kent in 1385–89, it was almost certainly not because he was one of the leading members of the county gentry, who were the kind of men who habitually filled such posts.[72] On the contrary, he was there as the agent of the king. Indeed, his appointment to these positions may even have been an instance of that meddling in local affairs of which men complained a decade later when they described Richard's tyranny.[73] And if it is right to draw the obvious inference that Chaucer's dismissal from the controllership of the customs was an act of retaliation by the Appellants, then he was one of the first to pay a price for this particular form of Ricardian misgovernment.

Chaucer was thus very much on the margins of the chivalric community of honor, the small group of rich and powerful men who comprised the ruling class of fourteenth-century England and who were bound together by a shared set of values and a common life-style. Nor is it easy to find an alternative place within the social structure where he naturally fits. On the one hand, his status as *armiger regis,* his military service, and his diplomatic and political responsibilities were consistent, as Hulbert has demonstrated, with the career patterns of others of his rank. On the other hand, he was set apart from men of similar background and rank by his predominantly urban residence, his lack of significant landed wealth, and, above all, by his role—first as controller of the customs from 1374 to 1387, and then, after his return to the king's

Press, 1971), does suggest that the fact that the king may have dealt personally with Chaucer's 1385 request for a deputy implies a special interest in what would otherwise have been a routine petition (7).

72. For an account of the other members of the Commission of Peace for Kent from 1385–89, see Crow and Olson, *Chaucer Life-Records,* 359–63, and especially Hulbert, *Chaucer's Official Life,* 37–41. With the possible exception of William Topcliffe, the other commissioners were all far more substantial men, and far more deeply associated with Kentish society, than was Chaucer. It is also probably significant that when Richard, under parliamentary pressure, reorganized the commissions in order to make them more effective in controlling aristocratic violence, Chaucer was not reappointed, despite the fact that the commission for Kent retained a uniquely high proportion of its former members; see R. L. Storey, "Liveries and Commissions of the Peace, 1388–90," in *Reign of Richard II,* ed. DuBoulay and Barron, 136–41. For a description of the powerful and wealthy men who typically sat in parliament in the late fourteenth century, see K. B. McFarlane, *The Nobility of Later Medieval England* (Oxford: Clarendon Press, 1973), 293–96.

73. For the 1399 complaint that Richard had manipulated the membership of Parliament to include "certain persons" who would support his interests, see *Rot. Parl.,* 3:420, and Given-Wilson, *Royal Household,* 246–47; Anthony Tuck, *Richard II and the English Nobility* (New York: St. Martin's, 1974), 112; for the packing of local offices with the king's men, see Nigel Saul, "The Despensers and the Downfall of Edward II," *EHR* 99 (1984), 32.

service in 1389, as clerk of the king's works until 1391—in the civil service.

That we can speak of a "civil service" at all suggests the institutional changes that were redefining the roles and status of men like Chaucer. For the term witnesses to the gradual drawing of a distinction between personal service to the king and administrative service to the crown. There was developing in the latter decades of the century a sense of what Tout has called "the solidarity of the administrative profession," "a single disciplined service of the state, which, notwithstanding the increasing diversity in its sections, was becoming, more and more clearly, a unity."[74] To a degree not always fully appreciated, Chaucer entered into this unity. His role as controller of the customs was to represent, as best he could, the crown's interests against the rapacious and no doubt overbearing merchant oligarchs who were the collectors; and as clerk of the king's works he was fully integrated into the crown's administrative machinery. The extent to which his offices entailed that integration is suggested by the fact that Chaucer was, in both cases, the first layman in positions that had previously been filled by clerks.[75] He thus represented a new and somewhat anomalous phenomenon, the "gentleman-bureaucrat" who was gradually taking over the administra-

74. T. F. Tout, *Chapters in the Administrative History of Mediaeval England* (Manchester: Manchester University Press, 1926), 4:336 n. 6; 4:65.

75. For the five previous controllers, all clerks, see Crow and Olson, *Chaucer Life-Records*, 152. Chaucer's immediate successor was Adam Yerdele, a grocer (see *CPR*, 1389–92, 461); but he was in turn replaced almost immediately by John Hermesthorpe, an experienced clerical administrator (see Tout, *Chapters*, 3:451, 4:461–62). The office then alternated between lay and clerical control while the collectorship was taken away from merchant princes like Brembre and Philpot and given either to clerks or to less powerful merchants who could be properly supervised; see Anthony Steel, "The Collectors of Customs in the Reign of Richard II," in *British Government and Administration: Studies Presented to S. B. Chrimes*, ed. H. Hearder and H. R. Loyn (Cardiff: University of Wales Press, 1974), 27–39, and Olive Coleman, "The Collectors of Customs in London under Richard II," in *Studies in London History Presented to Philip Edmund Jones*, ed. A. E. J. Hollaender and William Kellaway (London: Hodder and Stoughton, 1969), 181–94. For the inadequate organization of the customs earlier in the century, with evidence drawn almost entirely from outside London and therefore of only limited relevance to Chaucer, see Robert L. Baker, "The English Customs Service, 1307–1343: A Study of Medieval Administration," in *Transactions of the American Philosophical Society*, n.s. 51, part 6 (1961): 1–76. As for the clerkship of the king's works, R. A. Brown and H. M. Colvin ("The King's Works 1272–1485," in *The History of the King's Works*, ed. R. A. Brown, H. M. Colvin, and A. J. Taylor [London: HMSO, 1963]), state that Chaucer's immediate predecessor as clerk, Roger Elmham, was the first layman (1:194). In fact Elmham was a king's clerk (see *CPR*, 1377–81, 367; *CPR*, 1381–85, 468; *CPR*, 1385–89, 259), which makes Chaucer the first lay holder of the office. After Chaucer's tenure the office reverted to clerical control until 1417.

tion of government from the clerics who had traditionally filled these positions.[76] This process, as R. L. Storey has shown, took place largely in the first decades of the fifteenth century, which indicates the extent to which Chaucer was in the vanguard of a social movement that would not become widespread until after his death.[77] The distinction at issue here, it should be stressed, is less between clerical and lay status than between professional administrator and royal servant. Chaucer's diplomatic and political duties show that he could be called upon for the kind of tasks appropriate to a king's squire. But his assumption of the highly technical duties of controller and clerk, and his entrance into the professional class of civil servants that this entailed, must inevitably have created a visible divide between himself and the courtly world within which he had come to maturity and to which he had directed, until the time of the *Canterbury Tales,* his poetry. And that he was seen by the king and his advisors as an appropriate man for these jobs must also bespeak his possession of "clerkly" attitudes and attributes that were by no means usual in a king's squire.

Chaucer's career as a servant of the crown was thus both modest in itself and entailed a social identity that distanced him from the aristocratic world into which his vintner father had inserted him. J. S. Roskell concludes his survey of Chaucer's public career with a dismissive phrase—"all of this was nothing very outstanding"—and Olive Coleman rather woundingly refers to the controllership as a "modest office for modest men."[78] Yet it remains true that Chaucer counted among his friends some of those very chamber knights from whom he was—by birth, by marriage, by wealth, by vocation—so different. William Nevill, Lewis Clifford, John Clanvowe, and Philip de la Vache were all his friends, and the latter three seem to have been particularly prominent in his literary environment. Clifford was the bearer of Deschamps's admiring "Balade" to Chaucer; his son-in-law de la Vache was the recipient of Chaucer's own "Balade de Bon Conseyl," one of his most deeply felt affirmations of the preeminence of troth; and Clanvowe wrote both *The Boke of Cupid,* a love poem that begins by quoting the *Knight's Tale,* and *The Two Ways,* a penitential treatise that

76. According to Michael Bennett, "From the late fourteenth century, . . . a dramatic rise in the number of lay officials in both government and private service can be observed" (*Community, Class and Careerism: Cheshire and Lancashire Society in the Age of* Sir Gawain and the Green Knight [Cambridge: Cambridge University Press, 1983], 194–95).

77. R. L. Storey, "Gentlemen-bureaucrats," in *Profession, Vocation, and Culture in Later Medieval England,* ed. Cecil H. Clough (Liverpool: Liverpool University Press, 1982), 90–129.

78. Roskell, *Parliament and Politics,* 152; Coleman, "Collectors of Customs," 192.

provided a precedent although not a model for Chaucer's own *Parson's Tale*. Scholars have seen this group, along with intellectuals such as John Gower and Ralph Strode, as comprising Chaucer's most immediate and supportive circle of friends, the community within which he can be most specifically and comfortably located.[79]

In fact, that these men were friends with Chaucer says far more about their alienation from the world of power and honor in which they habitually operated than it does about Chaucer's affiliations with that world. McFarlane has demonstrated their unorthodox religious beliefs, and at least one of these "Lollard knights"—Sir John Clanvowe—made explicit his critique of the honor world of chivalry.[80] For our purposes, what is important is the way in which Chaucer's friendships with these clearly unusual men witness to his own anomalous situation. When we try to define his social identity, to specify the community within which he can be securely located and from which he derived his sense of social self-definition, we find that every assertion requires a qualification. He is the son of a rich merchant, but one educated in noble households; a king's squire, but one who fulfilled the duties of a clerical administrator; a modest servant of the Crown, but one who numbered among his friends some of the king's closest associates. To specify his social identity with precision and confidence seems impossible. For what the evidence reveals is a Chaucer on the boundary between distinctive social formations. Not bourgeois, not noble, not clerical, he nonetheless participates in all three of these communities. Surely this sense of marginality, of participating in various groupings but being fully absorbed by none, is related to the sense of subjectivity, the sense of a selfhood that stands apart from *all* community, that we recognize throughout his writing and especially in the *Canterbury Tales*.

VI

Given the complexity of Chaucer's social location, and his friendship with men who seem to have stood somewhat to the side of the chivalric ideology, it is hardly surprising that he should have begun the *Canterbury Tales* with a critical account of the aristocratic world from which he was emerging. But this is criticism from the inside, an account not of

79. See Paul Strohm, "Chaucer's Audience," *L&H* 5 (1977): 26–41; Derek Pearsall, "The *Troilus* Frontispiece and Chaucer's Audience," *YES* 7 (1977), 68–74; and V. J. Scattergood, "Literary Culture at the Court of Richard II," in *English Court Culture in the Later Middle Ages*, ed. V. J. Scattergood and J. W. Sherborne (London: Duckworth, 1983), 29–43.

80. V. J. Scattergood, ed., *The Works of Sir John Clanvowe* (Cambridge: Brewer, 1975), 69–70.

the moral transgressions of medieval chivalry but of the crisis of chivalric identity that contemporary political and economic conditions were
generating. The *Knight's Tale* represents a paradox: an act of self-
conscious narration by a man whose social ideology precludes self-
consciousness. The reading of the *Tale* that I offer in the third chapter
argues that it enacts a narrativity corresponding to the Knight's chivalric identity, and that it serves Chaucer as a way of summarizing and
finally alienating (in the sense of handing over to another) the concerns
that preoccupied the first half of his career. The final section of this
chapter argues, then, that these questions, like the topic of history as it
was defined in the *Troilus,* were essentially class specific, and that such
a recognition on the poet's part lies behind his ability to escape from his
preoccupations by not only ascribing them to the Knight but by initiating an ostentatiously nonaristocratic poetic project—the tale-telling
game of the *Canterbury Tales.*

That this game is indeed opposed to the Knight's aristocratic ideology is made clear by the Miller's boisterous interruption. In displacing
the Monk whom the Host had chosen to follow the Knight, the Miller
transforms a hierarchically organized order into a *quiting* game very
like the fabliau that he himself then tells. In an important sense, the
Canterbury Tales really begin with the *Miller's Tale*—although even this
is something of a false start. Chapter 5 describes this Chaucerian hesi-
tancy in detail by focusing on the class-specific nature of the *Miller's
Tale:* the Miller's interruption is not merely a challenge to aristocratic
aesthetics but an act of political resistance directed against seigneurial
exploitation as a whole—a gesture that finds explicit analogues in the
unsettled world of fourteenth-century England. Given the radical nature of this challenge, then, it is hardly surprising that the succeeding
tales of Fragment I, the *Reeve's* and *Cook's Tales,* represent a Chaucerian
withdrawal from direct political statement. Moreover, the next two
tales—of the Man of Law and Wife of Bath—replay the contestation of
the Knight and Miller in far less highly charged and topical terms. Far
from being the wholly unmotivated act of self-disclosure it is often
taken to be, the Wife's autobiographical discourse, I argue in chapter 6,
is on the contrary a theatrical self-display that at once assumes and
legitimizes the priority of a socially undetermined subjectivity, that dialectical conception of selfhood that underwrites both the *General Prologue* and the *Canterbury Tales* as a whole. The *Wife of Bath's Prologue and
Tale* represent the instauration of the subject at the center of the *Canterbury Tales;* and by being set against the Man of Law's performance,
which itself replays an earlier and now discredited mode of Chaucerian
poeticizing, it stages Chaucer's own assumption of a new poetic author-

ity. This is an authority, however, that allows for (even if it does not prescribe) the effacement of the historical. It is, in short, Chaucer's representation of the "God's plenty" of a human nature that transcends historical specificity that serves not only for Dryden but, I shall argue, for Chaucer himself as a modernist strategy for breaking out of history altogether. And yet the break with social conditioning that the Wife's performance allows is not unconditionally embraced: as the *Summoner's Tale* shows, Chaucer may mute political challenges but nonetheless allows them a displaced presence.

The final two chapters explore the Chaucerian vacillation between history and the subject in two representative instances. On the one hand, the *Merchant's* and *Shipman's Tales* explore the dilemma of the fourteenth-century English bourgeoisie as a class without an ideology. Moreover, these *Tales* serve Chaucer as a way of coming to terms both with his own bourgeois origins and with the social location that he has gradually defined for the *Canterbury Tales*. In a way he seems almost ready to acknowledge, the *Tales* are finally defined as something like a bourgeois enterprise, if by that term we mean a class that denies its own class definition. Finally, chapter 8 examines the *Pardoner's Prologue and Tale* as a counterpart to the *Wife of Bath's Prologue and Tale*. If the Wife's performance shows Chaucer using the traditional language of misogyny to construct a feminine selfhood, the Pardoner relies on the language of penance, as it was deployed throughout a wide range of medieval texts, for a similar act of self-fabrication. And at the center of this enterprise resides, not entirely unexpectedly, the same conception of the self as we discovered in *Anelida and Arcite,* and one articulated in terms of the same Theban mythology that seems to have served Chaucer throughout his career as a locus for dark meditations on human nature.

VII

Chaucer criticism has its ancient topics of dispute, disagreements that have gathered over the decades long and for the most part honorable pedigrees of controversy. On the whole these are matters of fundamental importance, and scholars argue about them for very good reason. But while to ignore them would be irresponsible, even a book as extensive as this must begin from certain hypotheses that cannot be exhaustively reargued. Perhaps the most controversial of these is the use in chapters 5 and 6 of the Ellesmere order of the *Canterbury Tales* as an aid to understanding the *Miller's Tale* and the *Wife of Bath's Prologue and Tale;* I have also accepted both the authenticity and relevance of the *Man of Law's Epilogue*, which is missing from Ellesmere. In recent years the usefulness of the Ellesmere manuscript as a guide to Chaucer's intentions has been severely criticized, especially in relation to another, very early manuscript, Hengwrt. In asserting that Hengwrt is closer to Chaucer's original than Ellesmere, scholars have deployed a number of arguments: that the text of the *Tales* as found in Hengwrt, although incomplete, is better than that found in Ellesmere; that although both manuscripts were written in the first decade of the fifteenth century, Hengwrt is demonstrably earlier; that the very fact that Hengwrt presents the *Tales* in a jumble—that Ellesmere is a "more sophisticated interpretation of the text than that found in Hengwrt," in the words of two authorities—is itself evidence that Hengwrt more accurately reflects the chaotic state of Chaucer's papers at the time of his death; that the same scribe wrote both manuscripts, and since he was unlikely to undo an established sequence, the coherent arrangement of Ellesmere must be an effect of editorial intervention; and that Ellesmere is organized according to a sophisticated scheme derived from the academic concept of *compilatio*, a common medieval way of organizing texts that contain disparate materials.[81]

In fact, not all of these assertions can be unequivocally accepted, and even those that can serve as much to support as to undermine the authority of Ellesmere's presentation of the *Tales*. The chronological priority of Hengwrt, for example, is by no means certain: expert paleographers such as A. I. Doyle and M. B. Parkes find themselves unable to pronounce on the question.[82] And even if Hengwrt is earlier, this proves little: unless we are prepared to accept discredited genealogical assumptions about the transmission of originality in manuscripts, chronological priority cannot be translated into textual authority.[83] Nor is it

81.   N. F. Blake, *The Textual Tradition of the Canterbury Tales* (London: Edward Arnold, 1985), 59, 62, 66–67, 79, 187, and passim; Charles A. Owen, Jr., "The Alternative Reading of *The Canterbury Tales:* Chaucer's Text and the Early Manuscripts," *PMLA* 97 (1982): 237–50; A. I. Doyle and M. B. Parkes, "The Production of Copies of the *Canterbury Tales* and the *Confessio Amantis* in the Early Fifteenth Century," in *Medieval Scribes, Manuscripts and Libraries: Essays Presented to N. R. Ker,* ed. M. B. Parkes and Andrew G. Watson (London: Scolar Press, 1978), 170, 186, 190–94; the citation is from 191.

82.   A. I. Doyle and M. B. Parkes, "Paleographical Introduction," in Geoffrey Chaucer, *The Canterbury Tales: A Facsimile and Transcription of the Hengwrt Manuscript, with Variants from the Ellesmere Manuscript,* ed. Paul Ruggiers (Norman: University of Oklahoma Press, 1979): "The arguments over whether Hengwrt or Ellesmere was copied first are so complex that the present writers are not in complete agreement on this particular issue" (xx, n. 4).

83.   For a full explanation of the inadequacy of genealogical stemmatics, see Giorgio Pasquali, *Storia della tradizione e critica del testo,* 2d ed. (Florence: Le Monnier, 1962 [1934]).

certain that Hengwrt and Ellesmere were written by the same scribe: detailed examination of the spelling of accidentals has presented strong evidence to the contrary.[84] Moreover, while Ellesmere certainly provides a more sophisticated and complete representation of the *Canterbury Tales* than does Hengwrt, this hardly proves that the jumbled ordering of Hengwrt is by definition closer either to what was available after Chaucer's death or to his intention.[85] Every manuscript copy, like every edition, is a hypothesis about authorial intention; the more complete the information available, and the more fully and intelligently it is incorporated, the more likely is the hypothesis to be correct.[86] A great deal of evidence does indeed suggest that the Ellesmere order represents Chaucer's intention, as detailed studies by Talbot Donaldson and Larry Benson have argued.[87] Moreover, if the Ellesmere manuscript is organized according to the norms of the *compilatio*, this is no doubt because Chaucer himself, as an authorial presence within the *Tales*, assumed, as Alastair Minnis has shown, "the role of compiler and . . . exploit[ed] the literary form of *compilatio*."[88] Because Ellesmere accords with the authorial stance Chaucer adopted in the *Tales*, and because its order makes excellent sense, means not that we should impeach its authority but just the opposite, that it represents a plausible and intelligent hypothesis about Chaucer's intention. Ellesmere provides an excellent, near contemporary hypothesis about the order of the *Tales*, and in exploring its implications we may well be able to uncover evidence that will further bolster its authority. Chapters 5 and 6 seek to offer some of that evidence.[89]

The authenticity of the *Man of Law's Epilogue* is beyond dispute, and

84. R. Vance Ramsey, "The Hengwrt and Ellesmere Manuscripts of the *Canterbury Tales*," *SB* 35 (1982): 133–55; Ramsey, "Paleography and Scribes of Shared Training," *SAC* 8 (1986): 107–44.

85. Doyle and Parkes, "Paleographical Introduction," xix.

86. See George Kane and E. Talbot Donaldson, eds., *Piers Plowman: The B-Text* (London: Athlone Press, 1975), 212.

87. E. Talbot Donaldson, "The Ordering of the *Canterbury Tales*," in *Medieval Literature and Folklore Studies: Essays in Honor of Francis Lee Utley*, ed. Jerome Mandel and Bruce A. Rosenberg (New Brunswick: Rutgers University Press, 1970), 193–204; Larry D. Benson, "The Order of *The Canterbury Tales*," *SAC* 3 (1981): 77–120.

88. A. J. Minnis, *Medieval Theory of Authorship: Scholastic Literary Attitudes in the Later Middle Ages*, 2d ed. (London: Scolar Press, 1988), 210.

89. For other arguments supporting Ellesmere in relation to Hengwrt, see Ralph Hanna III, "Problems of 'Best Text' Editing and the Hengwrt Manuscript of *The Canterbury Tales*," in *Manuscripts and Texts: Editorial Problems in Later Middle English Literature*, ed. Derek Pearsall (Cambridge: Brewer, 1987), 87–94; M. C. Seymour, "Hypothesis, Hyperbole, and the Hengwrt Manuscript of the *Canterbury Tales*," *ES* 68 (1987): 214–19.

its exclusion from Ellesmere is usually explained as a function of Chaucer's change of mind about order and the assignment of tales to tellers.[90] But we should also remember that it is in the *Man of Law's Epilogue* that the Host accuses the Parson of Lollardy: "I smelle a Lollere in the wynd," he says, warning the pilgrims that "this Lollere wil prechen us somwhat" (II, 1173, 1177). This accusation accords with other elements of the Parson's representation that would have led a contemporary audience to identify him as one of the Wycliffite "Bible men," as Margaret Aston and Anne Hudson have shown.[91] This is not to say that the Parson is a Lollard in any strict sense: he is not only on pilgrimage, but his *Tale* is a thoroughly orthodox treatise on confession. But his portrait and his attack on the Host's swearing in the *Epilogue* would have led contemporary readers to associate him with the general reform movement in which Lollards were the most explicit and programmatic participants. And one can consequently well imagine why, in the first decade of the fifteenth century, when the alarmed Archbishop Arundel was mobilizing the ecclesiastical and governmental forces of repression against the Lollards, that a scribe or editor putting together a deluxe copy of the *Tales* would skip over a passage that explicitly identified this otherwise ideal figure as a Lollard.

As well as assuming the Ellesmere order, my discussion of the *Canterbury Tales* in chapters 3 and 5 through 8 also exploits another of this manuscript's assertions about the literary form of the text. In order to study an argument from beginning to end, academic compilers typically arranged their material according to a *summa* structure.[92] The structure or *ordinatio* by which Ellesmere organizes the compilation that is the *Canterbury Tales* is different: as Parkes says and as Minnis has shown, "the *Canterbury Tales* is divided according to pilgrims rather than into books and chapters."[93] Ellesmere accomplished this *ordinatio* both by its careful rubrics, which identify each element of the text according to its speaker, and by its illuminations: in the margin next to

90. See Ralph Hanna III in *Riverside Chaucer*, 1126.

91. In "Lollardy and Sedition," first published in 1960, Margaret Aston pointed out that "the Lollard inclinations of the parson [of the *General Prologue*] must strike anyone with an acquaintance of Lollard literature" (*Lollards and Reformers: Images and Literacy in Late Medieval Religion* [London: Hambledon, 1984], 16 n.61; Anne Hudson, *The Premature Reformation: Wycliffite Texts and Lollard History* (Oxford: Clarendon Press, 1988), 390–92.

92. M. B. Parkes, "The Influence of the Concepts of *Ordinatio* and *Compilatio* on the Development of the Book," in *Medieval Learning and Literature: Essays Presented to Richard William Hunt*, ed. J. J. G. Alexander and M. T. Gibson (Oxford: Clarendon Press, 1976), 121.

93. Ibid., 130; Minnis, *Medieval Theory*, 201.

each *Tale* is a portrait of the pilgrim as described in the *General Prologue*. At the beginning of each *Tale*, then, the reader is not only reminded that it is to be told by someone other than the poet—who thus functions as the compiler of the words of his authors, the pilgrims—but is referred back to that pilgrim's description in the *General Prologue*. A "dramatic reading" of the *Canterbury Tales*, which understands each *Tale* primarily in terms of its teller, can certainly permit extravagances, as recent critics have complained.[94] But it is not by definition anachronistic, and its legitimacy should be assessed in each individual case. To read the *Tales* as the Ellesmere manuscript recommends, then, seems a thoroughly appropriate enterprise.[95]

Finally, my understanding of Chaucer's writing, both in the *Tales* and before, has been guided throughout by a principle well enunciated by Anthony Giddens:

> To study the production of the text is at the same time in a definite sense to study the production of its author. The author is not simply "subject" and the text "object": the "author" helps constitute him- or herself through the text, via the process of production of that text.[96]

This may seem a perverse assumption to apply to a writer who typically conceals himself within a mask, whether of a narratorial persona or a pilgrim. But it is not Chaucer's personality that is the object of scrutiny: it is Chaucer's self-constitution as a poet. Dryden saw Chaucer as the father of English poetry because he recognized in Chaucer the first English writer who possessed the ideas of both the poet and poetic history.[97] But we have seen that there is another conception of Chaucer's role in history—as an enhancer rather than an originator—that does indeed locate him *within* history. The humanist model of poetic original-

94. David Lawton, *Chaucer's Narrators* (Cambridge: Brewer, 1985); C. David Benson, *Chaucer's Drama of Style: Poetic Variety and Contrast in the* Canterbury Tales (Chapel Hill: University of North Carolina Press, 1986).

95. For a discussion of the way in which Ellesmere directs us to a "Chaucerian" reading of the *Tales*, see Martin Stevens, "The Ellesmere Miniatures as Illustrations of Chaucer's *Canterbury Tales*," *SI* 7–8 (1981–82): 113–34.

96. Anthony Giddens, *Central Problems in Social Theory* (Berkeley: University of California Press, 1979), 43–44.

97. As Spearing says, Chaucer "*was* the father of English poetry in the sense that before him there was no such thing as an *idea* of English poetry; and this is to say that he was the father of English literary history—the first English poet to conceive of his work as an addition, however humble, to the great monuments of the classical past and as continuing to exist in a future over which he would have no control" (*Medieval to Renaissance*, 34).

ity has always located itself in a space above and beyond the impurity of historical action: Dante's "bella scola" of poets live in a timeless elysium, Petrarch's self-constituted Academy of intellectuals avoids (or occludes) political engagement while it contemplates the timeless value embodied in its cultural monuments.[98] That Chaucer was attracted to this alternative is undeniable; that his privileging of a socially undetermined subjectivity was his way of achieving it is also true. But that he was finally too much in and of the world—too fully a historical creature and too fully aware of it—to find either of these solutions fully satisfying is also true. This making of himself as a man at once in and out of history—a making enacted in and through writing—is the ultimate subject this book seeks to understand.

98. Dante, *Inferno*, 4, 94; on Petrarch, see David Wallace, "'Whan She Translated Was': A Chaucerian Critique of the Petrarchan Academy"," in *Literary Practice and Social Change in Britain, 1380–1530*, ed. Lee Patterson (Berkeley: University of California Press, 1990), 156–215.

Chapter 1
"Thirled with the Poynt of Remembraunce": The Theban Writing of Anelida and Arcite

"I don't like the kind of double-minded feeling I have about this thing."

The social meaning of Chaucer's poetry—the institutional context from which it derived, the audience to which it was addressed, above all the class values it expresses—has been and remains an open question.[1] For the most part fifteenth-century poets valued Chaucer as a source of the kind of writing admired in aristocratic circles: as the learned expositor of "fructuous sentence" and the eloquent celebrant of *fine amor*, Chaucer provided the texts they imitated, rewrote, and sometimes simply rehearsed.[2] At the same time, however, the wide-ranging provenance and often modest format of the sixty or so fifteenth-century manuscripts of the *Canterbury Tales* argue for an appeal to less highly placed readers.[3]

1. The question has been most recently and usefully discussed by Paul Strohm, *Social Chaucer* (Cambridge: Harvard University Press, 1989).
2. The Chaucerian roots of fifteenth-century didacticism are visible in Lydgate's *Fall of Princes*, which although based on a French translation of Boccaccio's *De casibus virorum illustrium* finds its precedent, its characteristic rhyme scheme, and its generic definition (as Lydgate makes clear in Book 5, lines 3118–22) in the *Monk's Tale;* and in Hoccleve's *Regement of Princes*, a *miroir de prince* analogous to the *Tale of Melibee*. For Chaucer as the source of fifteenth-century amorous verse, see Rossell Hope Robbins, "The Vintner's Son: French Wine in English Bottles," in *Eleanor of Aquitaine: Patron and Politician*, ed. William W. Kibler (Austin: University of Texas Press, 1976), 147–72, and his chapter "The Lyrics," in *A Companion to Chaucer Studies*, ed. Beryl Rowland, rev. ed. (New York: Oxford University Press, 1979), 380–402.
3. It should be noted, however, that the tales chosen for anthologizing in the fifteenth century suggest a conservative attention to moralizing and courtly writing; see Daniel Silvia, "Some Fifteenth-Century Manuscripts of the *Canterbury Tales*," in *Chaucer and Middle English Studies in Honor of Rossell Hope Robbins*, ed. Beryl Rowland (London: Allen and Unwin, 1974), 153–61, and Paul Strohm, "Chaucer's Fifteenth-Century Audience and the Narrowing of the 'Chaucer Tradition'," *SAC* 4 (1982): 3–32.

These two versions of Chaucer—the courtly versus the popular—have similarly dominated modern scholarship from its nineteenth-century beginnings. One strain of criticism has seen Chaucer as a royal favorite who promoted noble values: according to one Victorian commentator, Chaucer was a celebrant of "chivalrous love" who was "careful to remember that he was writing for a courtly audience, studious to guard against giving offense to the chivalrous mind."[4] On the other hand was the more romantic view that "it was in Chaucer that the literary spirit of the English people, vigorous, simple, and truthful, found its voice. . . . The sympathies of Chaucer are not those of coteries and courts, they are with common and universal feelings."[5]

Twentieth-century critical opinion has on the whole been organized by a similar dichotomy. One position, vigorously prosecuted throughout the century although still a distinct minority, holds that Chaucer's poetry is essentially and often explicitly confirmatory of established medieval values and institutions, including those of the court within which he came to maturity and whose patronage provided him with his livelihood.[6] The other, majority position is that Chaucer is not a spokesman for any opinions at all, much less those of the court. On the contrary, to the liberalism that has held sway in the university for most of this century, Chaucer's poetry richly expresses the "common and universal" values with which literature has always concerned itself. To immure him within the court and to understand his poetry as in consequence ideologically constrained is not merely to subject subtle and searching poetry to crassly reductive readings; it is also, since literature

4.   Derek Brewer, ed., *Chaucer: The Critical Heritage* (London: Routledge and Kegan Paul, 1978), 2:186–87; the passage is from an article by William Minto, professor of logic and English at Aberdeen University, published in the ninth edition of the *Encyclopedia Britannica* (1876).

5.   Ibid., 1:315; from an anonymous article published in the *Edinburgh Review* in 1837.

6.   The latest version of this argument can be found in Paul Olson's *The* Canterbury Tales *and the Good Society* (Princeton: Princeton University Press, 1985). For Olson the *Tales* deal directly with matters under debate in the Ricardian court of the 1380s and 1390s: peace versus war, the nature of kingship, the relation of the monastic orders to secular government, the abuses of the contemporary church, and so on. In effect, Olson's Chaucer is a court apologist, expressing through the *Tales*, as through the earlier poems, opinions that Olson takes to be those of the court. Olson's work is a natural extension of D. W. Robertson, Jr.'s, *A Preface to Chaucer* (Princeton: Princeton University Press, 1962). For Robertson's own account of Chaucer as a court poet, see his "The Historical Setting of Chaucer's *Book of the Duchess*," in *Medieval Studies in Honor of Urban Tigner Holmes*, ed. John Mahoney and John Esten Keller (Chapel Hill: University of North Carolina Press, 1965), 169–95; "The Probable Date and Purpose of Chaucer's *Troilus*," *M&H* 13 (1985): 143–71; and "The Probable Date and Purpose of Chaucer's *Knight's Tale*," *SP* 84 (1987): 418–39.

is by definition a disinterested discourse, to deny to the father of English poetry his legitimate title.

The view promoted in this book is that these opposed positions are at once right and wrong. That Chaucer was at least until the initiation of the *Canterbury Tales* a court poet can hardly be disputed; that he found this condition uncomfortable and constraining is also clear, especially in light of poems like the *House of Fame* and the *Legend of Good Women*. But even given a desire to break away from the confining conditions of court production, what were the alternative discourses available to him and how were they to be exploited? *Anelida and Arcite* and *Troilus and Criseyde* bespeak Chaucer's efforts to expand the cultic language of the court beyond its prescribed limits, thus examining and implicitly challenging the largest presuppositions of aristocratic culture. The *Canterbury Tales*, on the other hand, register the process by which he forged a way of writing that was at once oppositional and nonpolitical. In effect, the course of his career shows a writer of coterie verse expressing values that now seem quintessentially literary, and it traces the route by which a court poet came to be the father of English poetry.

I

The development of a court poetry—a poetry, that is, specifically of the court and not merely a "courtly" poetry expressive of aristocratic values in general—is a relatively late phenomenon in England.[7] To be sure, the twelfth-century court of Henry II supported a highly developed literary culture that included vernacular writers such as Benoît de Sainte-Maure, the author of the *Roman d'Eneas*, Wace, probably Marie de France, and perhaps even the young Chrétien de Troyes—not to speak of a large number of Latin writers.[8] But not only was this an exclusively French-speaking court but also one that stands in lonely eminence in relation to the next century and a half. While there are of course numerous examples of aristocratic and royal patronage throughout this period, they are isolated instances rather than parts of a coordinated program of cultural development and ideological promotion.

7.   The distinction between poetry of the court and courtly poetry is drawn, in somewhat different terms, by Derek Pearsall, *Old English and Middle English Poetry* (London: Routledge and Kegan Paul, 1977), 212.

8.   For the literary culture at the court of Henry II, see Walter F. Schirmer and Ulrich Broich, *Studien zum literarischen Patronat im England des 12. Jahrhunderts* (Cologne: Westdeutscher Verlag, 1962); for Chrétien and the author of the *Roman d'Eneas*, see my *Negotiating the Past: The Historical Understanding of Medieval Literature* (Madison: University of Wisconsin Press, 1987), 157–95, and the references cited there (158 n. 4).

Only in the second half of the reign of Edward III—beginning, that is, about the 1360s—does there develop an extensive and sophisticated literary culture centered on and fostered by the court and serving to articulate a court ideology.[9] And in part—perhaps in large part—this is a function of certain structural changes in the role of the royal household. In the latter years of the reign of Edward III and throughout that of Richard II there was not only a gradual concentration of the business of government in the *camera regis,* but the royal household came to function less as the focus of the aristocratic community as a whole than as the king's *privata familia.*[10] And under Richard, this concentration of power in the court, and the parallel development of a specifically court-ier nobility, became a matter of royal policy.[11]

The first sign of a *literary* court culture in England is the presence of Jean Froissart at the court of Edward III: a Hainaulter, he entered the service of Queen Philippa in 1361 and remained in England until about 1369.[12] In the first book of the *Chroniques* Froissart describes himself as one of the queen's "clers et familiers," and he later memorialized Phil-ippa as one "à laquelle en ma jeunesse je fus clerc et la servoie de beaulx dittier et traités amoureux."[13] The next sign is the emergence of Geof-frey Chaucer, whose *Book of the Duchess,* written to commemorate the death of Blanche of Lancaster in 1368, drew upon Froissart's poetry, as

9.   See Gervase Mathew, *The Court of Richard II* (London: John Murray, 1968).

10.   For these developments, see Christopher Given-Wilson, *The Royal Household and the King's Affinity* (New Haven: Yale University Press, 1986).

11.   This process is described by Anthony Tuck, *Richard II and the English Nobility* (London: St. Martin's, 1974). For the political meaning of the cultural attitudes of the Ricardian court, see Patricia J. Eberle, "The Politics of Courtly Style in the Court of Rich-ard II," in *The Spirit of the Court: Selected Proceedings of the Fourth Congress of the International Courtly Literature Society,* ed. Glyn S. Burgess and Robert A. Taylor (Cambridge: Brewer, 1985), 168–78.

12.   In a later poem, Froissart says that while in England he wrote poetry not only for the queen but for her daughter, Isabelle de Coucy, and daughter-in-law, Blanche of Lan-caster; for Humphrey of Bohun, the Earl of Hereford; for John Hastings, the Earl of Pembroke; for Lord Edward Despenser; and for a number of French knights then in England: Anthime Fourrier, ed., *Le Joli buisson de jonece* (Geneva: Droz, 1975), lines 230–373. We also know that he sent a balade to Philippa, the eldest daughter of Henry of Lancaster: see Elizabeth Salter, *Fourteenth-Century English Poetry: Contexts and Readings* (Oxford: Clarendon Press, 1983), 62–63.

13.   These passages are cited by Peter F. Dembowski, *Jean Froissart and his* Meliador: *Context, Craft, and Sense* (Lexington: French Forum, 1983), 43, 163 n. 43. Dembowski calls these years at the English court "without doubt the period of [Froissart's] most intense poetic activity. It was then that he composed the greater number of his lyric poems and much of his other poetic output. There is no doubt that Froissart flourished in those years as a court poet and, at the same time, underwent a period of preparation and apprentice-ship for his future profession as a chronicler" (42–43).

well as that of his more prominent French colleague Guillaume de Machaut, and was in turn imitated by Froissart himself.[14]

That Chaucer, a king's esquire in the households of both Edward III and Richard II, was very much a court poet—at least until he began writing the *Canterbury Tales* in the late 1380s—is clear from the poetry itself. The *Book of the Duchess* was written for John of Gaunt, in the absence of the Black Prince the most powerful member of the royal family in England and a man deeply involved in royal and metropolitan affairs in the period around 1370. The *Parliament of Fowls* also reflects royal interests in its reference to the negotiations for the marriage of Richard and Anne of Bohemia in 1380.[15] So too *Troilus and Criseyde*, the preeminent courtly poem of the English Middle Ages, is also a specifically *court* poem: it not only includes a royalist commentary on the Wonderful Parliament of 1386 but speaks in other, subtler ways to the dilemma of the Ricardian monarchy in the 1380s.[16] There are as well the short poems—two balades, four complaints, eight epistles, and the delicate "ABC"—that presuppose for their audience "a circle of gentlemen and clerks" derived from if not always located within the royal household.[17] Hence Chaucerians have reasonably assumed that the "many a song and many a leccherous lay" (X, 1087) to which Chaucer refers in the Retractions appended to the *Parson's Tale* designate the kind of occasional lyrics that were routinely produced at court, poems written to provide "intellectual and social diversion and amorous dalliance among a miniscule élite group," in the words of Rossell Hope Robbins.[18] In Gower's *Confessio amantis* Venus describes Chaucer as "mi disciple and mi poete" and says that "in the floure of his youthe" he wrote so many "ditees and . . . songes glade, / . . . for mi sake" that

14. For Chaucer's borrowings from Froissart's *Paradys d'Amour,* see Barry A. Windeatt, ed. and trans., *Chaucer's Dream Poetry: Sources and Analogues* (Cambridge: Brewer, 1982), 41–57; for the reverse process, see James I. Wimsatt, "The *Dit dou Bleu Chevalier:* Froissart's Imitation of Chaucer," *MS* 34 (1972): 388–400.

15. See Larry D. Benson, "The Occasion of the *Parliament of Fowls,*" in *The Wisdom of Poetry: Essays in Early English Literature in Honor of Morton W. Bloomfield,* ed. Larry D. Benson and Siegfried Wenzel (Kalamazoo: Institute for Medieval Studies, 1982), 123–44.

16. See below, chapter 2, 155–62.

17. See R. T. Lenaghan, "Chaucer's Circle of Gentlemen and Clerks," *ChR* 18 (1983–84): 155–60; Paul Strohm, "Chaucer's Audience," *L&H* 5 (1977): 26–41; Derek Pearsall, "The *Troilus* Frontispiece and Chaucer's Audience," *YES* 7 (1977): 68–74.

18. Rossell Hope Robbins, "The Structure of Longer Middle English Court Poems," in *Chaucerian Problems and Perspectives: Essays Presented to Paul E. Beichner,* ed. Edward Vasta and Zacharias P. Thundy (Notre Dame: University of Notre Dame Press, 1979), 245. See also Robbins's "The Middle English Court Love Lyric," in *The Interpretation of Medieval Lyric,* ed. W. T. H. Jackson (New York: Columbia University Press, 1980), 205–32.

"the land fulfild [was] overal": that we now have only a few of these poems indicates not the size of Chaucer's production but only the fragility of so ephemeral a product.[19]

If Chaucer wrote poetry both about and for the court, it derived not from a native tradition of courtly lyricism—there was virtually none— but instead from contemporary French writing, the writing that Froissart no doubt first introduced into the royal court.[20] As Robbins has said, "What separated Chaucer . . . from other comparable poets living in regional courts of the great nobles (the Warwicks, the Mortimers, the Bohuns, the Beauchamps, the Percys) is that Chaucer went to the currently fashionable *dits amoureux* [of Machaut and Froissart] for his models, and not to the old-fashioned French romances (as did the author of *Sir Gawain and the Green Knight*)."[21] Certainly we could overestimate this division—Elizabeth Salter has well shown how cosmopolitan tastes were throughout England—but it is real nonetheless and suggests that the late Edwardian and Ricardian courts were developing a distinctively royal literary style.[22]

Chaucer's court poetry, both the largely vanished "ditees and songes glade" and the extant longer poems, are examples of what he and his contemporaries called *makyng*.[23] That is, they were poems designed above all to serve the recreative needs of the court. The *maker* provided the materials of courtly diversion, the texts that were not merely the occasion for courtly conversation (as is clearly envisaged, for instance, by the *demande d'amour*) but both provided paradigms for and constituted that conversation.[24] It is from the world of what the

19. John Gower, *Confessio amantis* 8:*2942–47, in G. C. Macauley, *The Complete Works of John Gower* (London: Clarendon Press, 1900), 2:466.

20. The absence of a native tradition is well illustrated by the courtly lyrics of Harley 2253, which represent virtually the only pre-Chaucerian body of love lyric in English: these are courtly poems written without a court to sustain them, a situation reflected in a series of odd incongruities, as Derek Pearsall has shown (*Old English and Middle English Poetry*, 128).

21. Rossell Hope Robbins, "Geoffroi Chaucier, Poète Français, Father of English Poetry," *ChR* 13 (1978–79), 106; see also Robbins's "Chaucer and the Lyric Tradition," *Poetica* 15/16 (1983): 107–27, and "The Vintner's Son."

22. Salter, *Fourteenth-Century English Poetry*, 52–85.

23. See the seminal article by Glending Olson, "Making and Poetry in the Age of Chaucer," *CL* 31 (1979): 272–90.

24. See John Stevens, *Music and Poetry in the Early Tudor Court* (London: Methuen, 1961), 147–232, Daniel Poirion, *Le poète et le prince* (Paris: Presses universitaires de France, 1965), 59–139, Richard Firth Green, *Poets and Princepleasers: Literature and the English Court in the Later Middle Ages* (Toronto: University of Toronto Press, 1980), and Glending Olson, "Toward a Poetics of the Late Medieval Court Lyric," in *Vernacular Poetics in the Middle Ages*, ed. Lois Ebin (Kalamazoo: Medieval Institute Publications, 1984), 227–48.

Gawain-poet called "luf-talkyng" that these texts arise and to which they refer: they are surviving fragments of an ephemeral social activity. In this sense, *makyng* was defined as a purely aesthetic practice. Constantly drawing attention to its technical intricacy, basing its generic distinctions on prosody rather than content, and deploying a polysemous discourse of riddles, *doubles entendres,* allegory, and allusion, *makyng* explored the potentialities inherent in language as both a signifying and a phonetic system. As Robert Guiette has said, it is a "jeu des formes," a practice that aspires to pure aestheticism.[25] And the total effect is to create what Paul Zumthor has suggestively called a cultural *hortus conclusus,* a site where an aristocratic "culte égocentrique" can find an unconstrained fulfillment denied it in the threatening world of late fourteenth-century history.[26]

Yet of course the aesthetic is in no sense outside ideology, nor can history be so willfully set aside. The aristocratic privileging of play served itself as an important marker of social identity, declaring the nobility to be, as a class, released from the penance of both labor and prayer. And the aestheticization of life, of which the formalism of *makyng* was simply one aspect, was central to the ideological project of class self-definition and self-legitimization in which late medieval aristocratic culture was ceaselessly engaged. Just as its cuisine transformed food into art, just as its fashion transformed the body into a visual display, so the *makyng* of the court transformed words into elegant discursive artifice.[27] What the courtly *maker* taught was, again in the words of the *Gawain*-poet, "the teccheles termes of talkyng *noble.*" The obsessive focus upon love that characterizes this verse supports this project as well, not just by demonstrating over and over again that "pitee renneth soone in *gentil* herte," but by fashioning the turbulence of erotic feeling into the elegant artifice of lyric. As Derek Pearsall has said of the complaint, perhaps the most quintessentially courtly of lyric forms, "There is no movement, no action, only the lover and his mistress for ever frozen into ritual gestures of beseeching and disdain."[28] Like the other kinds of fetishized objects with which the aristocratic world adorned

25. Robert Guiette, "D'une poésie formelle en France en Moyen Age," *Romanica Gandensia* 8 (1960), 17; see also Roger Dragonetti, *La technique poétique des trouvères dans la chanson courtoise* (Bruges: De Tempel, 1960).

26. Paul Zumthor, *Essai de poétique médiévale* (Paris: Seuil, 1972), 243, 267. The social and economic constraints to which the late medieval English nobility were subjected are described in relation to the *Knight's Tale* in chapter 3.

27. For the importance of cuisine and fashion in the late medieval court, see Mathew, *Court of Richard II,* 23–31.

28. Derek Pearsall, *John Lydgate* (London: Routledge and Kegan Paul, 1970), 92–93.

itself (tapestries, jewelry, books), the complaint beautifully stages, over and over again, a reified extravagance, a petrified excess. In Anne Middleton's words, it serves a "socially or cultically reaffirmative function," and Zumthor has shown how the "register" of the *grand chant courtois* articulates the shared assumptions that bind together poet and audience.[29] It constructs, objectifies, and beautifies—but declines to analyze or understand—courtly subjectivity, just as the books in which these texts were inscribed were themselves objects placed in the service of ostentatious self-display.[30] Correspondingly, the task of the *maker* was to provide the aristocracy with languages, pastimes, modes of feeling, and objects that confirmed their nobility. Social historians have shown that in the late fourteenth century the English aristocracy was seeking, under the pressure of far-reaching economic changes, to transform itself from a loosely organized and permeable class into a hereditary caste defined by a highly distinctive life-style.[31] The *aesthetic* transformations accomplished by courtly *makyng* served a crucial ideological function in fulfilling this purpose.

29. Anne Middleton, "Chaucer's 'New Men' and the Good of Poetry," in *Literature and Society,* ed. Edward W. Said (Baltimore: Johns Hopkins University Press, 1980), 32; Zumthor, *Essai de poétique,* 239–40. As Zumthor says, the *grand chant courtois* "tend à la fois à convaincre l'auditeur d'une manière 'nouvelle,' inattendue, de quelque chose que, en un certain sens, il ignorait; et à manifester les conclusions inéluctables de quelque chose qu'en un autre sense il savait déjà. D'où une oscillation incessante entre information et redondance" (239).

30. When Froissart presented a copy of his poems to Richard II, he tells us that the king "opened it and looked inside and it pleased him greatly. Well it might, for it was illuminated, nicely written and illustrated, with a cover of crimson velvet with ten studs of silver gilt and golden roses in the middle and two large gilded clasps richly worked at their centres with rose-trees" (cited by Green, *Poets and Princepleasers,* 64). What Richard valued was the book as an object of beauty rather than as a source of understanding. As Green says, "Books were regarded as an important part of the prince's assets, able to take their place alongside the more predictable items in the aristocratic showcase" (60). And Mathew argues that "a court fashion in *objets de luxe* may best explain some of the new developments in book production and illustration" in the later fourteenth century (*Court of Richard II,* 39).

31. For a summary of these transformations, see Chris Given-Wilson, *The English Nobility in the Late Middle Ages* (London: Routledge and Kegan Paul, 1987). The difference between class and caste is succinctly described by Edmund Leach, "Caste, Class and Slavery: The Taxonomic Problem," in *Caste and Race: Comparative Approaches,* ed. Anthony de Reuck and Julie Knight (Boston: Little, Brown, 1966): "A 'ruling class' may be defined as a *caste* when the fact of class endogamy is strikingly obvious and when the inheritance of privilege has become narrowly restricted to members of that 'caste' in perpetuity. This kind of situation is likely to arise when the ruling group is distinguished from the inferior group or groups by *wide* differences of standard of living or by other easily recognizable labels" (9).

This writing served other ideological functions as well. For if it entertained court servants, it also trained them: it provided what *la belle dame sans merci* called a "school" of "fayr langage," teaching its students to "parler mignon" (Christine de Pisan's wonderful phrase).[32] From the time of its medieval beginnings in the eleventh century, courtliness made verbal facility a central value: *facetus* is virtually a synonym for *curialis*, and it means both "elegant" and "clever," both "refined" and "witty."[33] According to another medieval definition, a man who is *facetus* is one who can get what he wants out of words, whether it be a subtle meaning or a desired effect.[34] And if to be courtly is to be adroit with words, the riddles, acrostics, *jeux partis*, and *demandes d'amour* that are preserved, either intact or in allusion, are evidence of the assiduity with which this talent was practiced and displayed.[35]

A correlative talent is the capacity to interpret, to be able to read the elegantly metaphoric and topically allusive language of the court poem. According to Thomas Usk, an ill-fated sergeant-of-arms in Richard's court, Love teaches her servants "to endyten letters of rethorike in queynt understondinges," and in the *Prison amoureuse*, Froissart explains that a courtly poem is "a gloss of something which cannot or must not be openly stated."[36] In the *Livre messire Ode*, written by Oton de Grandson while at the Ricardian court in the 1370s and 1380s, the narra-

32. For the first two phrases, see Walter W. Skeat, ed., "La Belle Dame Sans Merci," *Chaucerian and Other Pieces*, Supplement to the *Complete Works of Geoffrey Chaucer*, vol. 7 (Oxford: Oxford University Press, 1897), lines 328–29 (309); for "parler mignon," see Christine de Pisan, *Cent ballades d'amant et de dame*, ed. Jacqueline Cerquiglini (Paris: Union Générale d'Editions, 1982), poem 8, line 11 (39).

33. See C. Stephen Jaeger, *The Origins of Courtliness: Civilizing Trends and the Formation of Courtly Ideals 939–1210* (Philadelphia: University of Pennsylvania Press, 1985), 162–68; on the meaning of *facetus*, see Alison Goddard Elliott's introduction to her translation of "The *Facetus*: or, The Art of Courtly Living," *Allegorica* 2 (1977): 27–57.

34. This definition is given by Donatus in his commentary on Terence's *Eunuchus*, cited by Laura Kendrick, *The Game of Love: Troubadour Wordplay* (Berkeley: University of California Press, 1988), 53.

35. Stevens, *Music and Poetry*, 163; Part I of the *Knight's Tale* itself provides the occasion for a *demande d'amour*, as do the *Franklin's Tale* and the debate among the noble suitors in the *Parliament of Fowls*. Apparently *demandes* were not always as highminded as these instances: for a collection of *demandes* that turn on racy *doubles entendres* and so require fast-paced verbal banter rather than lofty eloquence, see Eustache Deschamps, *Oeuvres complètes*, ed. Gaston Raynaud, SATF (Paris: Firmin-Didot, 1893), 8:112–25. For examples of linguistically playful poems in English, see Rossell Hope Robbins, ed., *Secular Lyrics of the XIVth and XVth Centuries*, 2d ed. (Oxford: Clarendon Press, 1955), poems numbers 172, 173, and 177.

36. Thomas Usk, "Testament of Love," in Skeat, ed., *Chaucerian and Other Pieces*, 12; for Froissart, see William W. Kibler, "Poet and Patron: Froissart's *Prison amoureuse*," *L'Esprit Créateur* 18 (1972), 38.

tor overhears a lover grieving for the loss of his sparrowhawk but fails to understand that he is speaking "par poetrie" and really means his lady.[37] In the *Book of the Duchess* Chaucer had already used the same device but had laid bare the social meaning it contains: his narrator's inability to understand the Black Knight's metaphor of the chess game is a sign of his social inferiority. It is this interpretive alertness, even suspicion, that led Puttenham in the sixteenth century to call the trope of allegory—"which is when we speake one thing and thinke another"—"the Courtly figure," one known not only to "euery common Courtier, but also [to] the grauest Counsellour."[38] Court poetry, in other words, is not simply a form of entertainment but a social practice, the means by which courtiers both learned and displayed the talents needed for success.

As literary historians have shown, court writing was in no sense the preserve of a special group of professional poets.[39] In fact, the demise of the minstrel in the late fourteenth century represents not merely the shift from one kind of taste to another but the deprofessionalization of writing per se. No longer was literary activity confined to a particular group of specially trained men but became instead the preserve of the court as a whole. Hence the fact that not only do none of the large number of documents that record Chaucer's career refer to him as a writer, but that his career was probably not advanced by his literary activity.[40] To have acknowledged that Chaucer could do something special that other members of the court could not would have been to undermine the socially legitimizing function of courtly *makyng*. According to Deschamps' *Art de dictier*, there are two kinds of music: a "musique artificiele" played on instruments by "le plus rude homme du monde," and a "musique naturelle," the harmony of verse ("une musique de bouche en proferant paroules metrifiées") inspired by the "amorous desire to praise ladies" that inhabits gentle hearts.[41] In fact, a great many courtiers did write poetry: we have the names and some of the poems of over a dozen noble *makers* from late medieval England, as well as the rather bizarre fact that Richard II wanted his epitaph to compare him to Homer.[42] Indeed, one of the tasks of the professional

37. *Le livre messire Ode*, in Arthur Piaget, *Oton de Grandson, sa vie et ses poésies* (Lausanne: Librairie Payot, 1941), line 1478 (439).
38. George Puttenham, *The Arte of English Poesie* (London: Richard Field, 1589 [printed in facsimile: London: Scolar Press, 1968]), 155.
39. See especially Green, *Poets and Princepleasers*, 101–34.
40. See J. R. Hulbert, *Chaucer's Official Life* (Menasha: Collegiate Publishing, 1912).
41. Green, *Poets and Princepleasers*, 107; Glending Olson, "Deschamps' *Art de dictier* and Chaucer's Literary Environment," *Speculum* 48 (1973): 714–23.
42. A list of English aristocratic poets of the late fourteenth and fifteeenth centuries

poet (if the title be admitted at all) was to colloborate with the patron in the production of the courtly text. Froissart's *Prison amoureuse,* for instance, records the way in which the poet instructed his patron, Wenceslas of Brabant, in the art of *makyng,* and both this text and the later *Meliador* contain poems by both authors.[43] The same is true of Machaut's *Fonteinne amoureuse,* which describes the departure of Jean, duc de Berri, into exile and incorporates several of his laments. Indeed, it is possible that the rather inept lyrics ascribed to the grieving Black Knight in the *Book of the Duchess* really were written by John of Gaunt.

This expansion of literariness to include the court as a whole also helps to account for a pronounced generic shift in the literary system of fourteenth-century England. Romances and histories, almost entirely in prose, continued to be copied and read, as library lists and manuscript survivals demonstrate. But the literature of fashion produced within the court—excluding, that is, works of instruction—was almost exclusively lyric. This category includes not only lyrics per se, the many "compleyntis, baladis, roundelis, virelais" that Lydgate ascribed to Chaucer and that must have been written by other courtly versifiers in the hundreds, but also the new genre of the *dits amoureux* produced by Machaut and Froissart.[44] For all their apparently narrative form, these works are in fact sets of lyric performances enclosed within a narrative frame: they provide lyrics with a context that is, in their usual, freestanding state, only implied. The *Book of the Duchess,* largely derived from the *dits amoureux,* is the first poem to transfer this form into English; and while there are no Chaucerian poems that fully replicate French models, we can recognize in the roundel of the *Parliament of Fowls,* in the complaint of *Anelida and Arcite,* in the balade of the *Prologue* to the *Legend of Good Women,* and above all in the many lyric mo-

---

(compiled largely from Green's discussion) includes John Montagu, earl of Salisbury; Edward Plantagenet, second duke of York; Richard Beauchamp, earl of Warwick; William de la Pole, duke of Suffolk; John Tiptoft, earl of Worcester; Anthony Woodville, Earl Rivers; Sir Richard Roos; and of course Sir John Clanvowe. As K. B. McFarlane has said, "In what other century has the peerage been so active in literature?" (*The Nobility of Later Medieval England* [Oxford: Clarendon Press, 1973], 242). Non-English noble *littérateurs* include Marshall Boucicaut and his friends, like the Duc de Berri, who composed the *Livre de cents ballades;* James I of Scotland; René of Anjou and his son, Jean, Duc de Calabre; Wenceslas de Brabant; Charles d'Orléans; and Jean II, Duc de Bourbon.

43. See Kibler, "Poet and Patron," 32–46, and Dembowski, *Jean Froissart.*

44. According to Robbins, "The Middle English Court Love Lyric," there survive perhaps three hundred love lyrics and thirty "love aunters," by which he means poems such as Lydgate's *Temple of Glass, The Flour and the Leaf,* and *The Court of Love* (207).

ments, both celebratory and lamenting, of *Troilus and Criseyde*, the overwhelming pressure of the lyric impulse.[45]

While Chaucer is the first English court poet, if not the first in England, his own relation to this kind of writing was deeply problematic. On the one hand, as the fifteenth-century rewriting of his poetry shows, he provided the materials for courtly writing for several generations of successors. As John Stevens has said, "Chaucer was, above all, the Articulate Lover, the 'well of eloquence,' the master of the language of the heart. To read *The Knight's Tale* or *Anelida and Arcite* was a sentimental education," and the courtier wrote his poems "out of *Troilus and Criseyde*, the great poem in which he could study and find how 'most felyngly' to speak of love."[46] Nor was it only lovers who recognized in *Troilus and Criseyde* the authentic language of the court: in the fifteenth century a courtier poet included Pandarus's warnings to Criseyde about the dangers of unbridled speech (3, 302–22) in a poem on the dangers of truth-telling and the burdens of service at court.[47] Yet the *Prologue* to the *Legend of Good Women* shows that Chaucer found the court to be deeply unsatisfactory as a place both to write and to be read. Here an irascible God of Love (with unmistakable affinities to *Richard II*) reads the complex contextualization of eroticism accomplished by the *Troilus* as a simplistic attack on love per se. Insisting upon turning all cultural products to the task of self-legitimization, the patron seeks to govern both the production and the reception of the text, insisting that it signify a monolithic, self-identical meaning, that it rehearse and celebrate but never analyze much less criticize court values.[48] This is an absolutism that the poem resists through its own incomplete submis-

45. The influence of the *dits amoureux* on Chaucer has been most vigorously argued by Robbins, "Chaucer and the Lyric Tradition," and "The Vintner's Son;" and by James I. Wimsatt, *Chaucer and the French Love Poets* (Chapel Hill: University of North Carolina Press, 1968). For the lyric presence in the *Troilus*, see James I. Wimsatt, "The French Lyric Element in *Troilus and Criseyde*," *YES* 15 (1985): 18–32. For an argument that Chaucer's poetry develops out of these lyric moments, see W. A. Davenport, *Chaucer: Complaint and Narrative* (Cambridge: Brewer, 1988).

46. Stevens, *Music and Poetry*, 213.

47. The poem is printed by Frederick J. Furnivall, ed., *Odd Texts of Chaucer's Minor Poems*, Chaucer Society, 1st series, nos. 23, 60 (London: Trübner, 1868–80), xi–xii. As Gervase Mathew argues, Pandarus should not be "misconceived as a comic character; he is an experienced English courtier of the late fourteenth century, . . . a man of cultivated sensibility, facilely expressed emotions and quick strategems—all qualities then prized" (*Court of Richard II*, 68).

48. For a well-documented account of Richard's "high-handed notions of regality," see George B. Stow, "Chronicles versus Records: The Character of Richard II," in *Documenting the Past: Essays in Medieval History Presented to George Peddy Cuttino*, ed. J. S. Hamilton and Patricia J. Bradley (Woodbridge: Boydell, 1989), 155–76.

sion both to the patron's commission and to its source texts, and then ironically restages in the tyranny to which its saintly heroines are subjected. In short, for all the linguistic playfulness and apparent recreative freedom claimed by courtly *makyng*, it is represented in the *Legend of Good Women* as ideologically and discursively imprisoning.

Moreover, the *House of Fame* presents a trenchant commentary on both the vagaries of service in the prince's court and its effect on literary ambition.[49] In Fame's court writers become mere agents of the powerful: whether they are "mynstralles / And gestiours that tellen tales" (1197–98) or the great *auctores* of antiquity, their mutual task is simply to bear up the fame of the mighty. In this world, even the greatest of poets are simply propagandists. After listing the classical poets from Homer to Claudian, Chaucer sadly and dismissively comments that Fame's court is as full "of hem that writen olde gestes / As ben on treës rokes nestes" (1515–16): they are little better than the "pursevauntes and heraudes / That crien ryche folkes laudes" (1321–22). Set against this dismissive recognition, however, is the poem's invocation, in its structure and patterns of allusion, of the vast cultural ambitions and achievement of Dante. These are ambitions Chaucer comes to share: recent critics have well shown how both the *House of Fame* and, especially, *Troilus and Criseyde*, bespeak the poet's heroic desire to forge a vernacular literary tradition equivalent to those of classical Rome and *trecento* Italy.[50] If, as A. C. Spearing has said, Chaucer was "the father of English poetry in the sense that before him there was no such thing as an *idea* of English poetry," this was an idea derived in large part from the example of the antique poets and Dante.[51]

It was, in sum, by means of what he called *poetrye*—the writings of the ancients and of their *trecento* inheritors, Dante, Petrarch, and the unacknowledged but all the more ubiquitous Boccaccio—that Chaucer prised himself loose from an imprisoning court ideology. According to

49. See Laura Kendrick, "Fame's Fabrication," in *Studies in the Age of Chaucer Proceedings, 1, 1984: Reconstructing Chaucer,* ed. Paul Strohm and Thomas Heffernan (Knoxville: New Chaucer Society, 1985), 135–48. See also below, 197.

50. See Winthrop Wetherbee, *Chaucer and the Poets: An Essay on* Troilus and Criseyde (Ithaca: Cornell University Press, 1984); on the *House of Fame*, see Karla Taylor, *Chaucer Reads the* Divine Comedy (Stanford: Stanford University Press, 1989), 20–49.

51. A. C. Spearing, *Medieval to Renaissance in English Poetry* (Cambridge: Cambridge University Press, 1985), 34. For the importance of Dante, see Piero Boitani, "What Dante Meant to Chaucer," in *Chaucer and the Italian Trecento,* ed. Piero Boitani (Cambridge: Cambridge University Press, 1983), 115–39, David Wallace, "Chaucer's Continental Inheritance: The Early Poems and *Troilus and Criseyde,*" in *The Cambridge Chaucer Companion,* ed. Piero Boitani and Jill Mann (Cambridge: Cambridge University Press, 1986), 19–39, and Salter, *Fourteenth-Century English Poetry,* 123.

a familiar ratio, Chaucer sought to be modern through a return to antiquity; by establishing a relation to a recuperated past he projected himself into a new future. The distinction between courtly *makyng* and the *poetrye* of the ancients and of their imitators was, as Glending Olson has shown, ubiquitous within Chaucer's literary world, and one that he himself maintains rigorously throughout his work.[52] Yet as he makes explicit at the conclusion of the *Troilus,* and as is implicit throughout, he cannot quite conceive of himself as a poet:

> Go, litel bok, go, litel myn tragedye,
> Ther God thi makere yet, er that he dye,
> So sende myght to make in som comedye!
> But litel book, no makyng thow n'envie,
> But subgit be to alle poesye;
> And kis the steppes where as thow seest pace
> Virgile, Ovide, Omer, Lucan, and Stace. (5, 1786–92)

In the final line Chaucer reconstitutes Dante's "bella scola" of *Inferno* 4, with the significant substitution of the epic Statius for Horace the satirist—a Statius who plays a crucial role in Chaucer's attempt to write a more than courtly poetry in both the *Troilus* and in *Anelida and Arcite.* But far from allowing himself to be incorporated within this group as an equal, as had Dante, Chaucer remains "subject," a petitioner whose humble posture reinvokes the courtly configuration of dominance and submission that Dante's vision of humanistic fellowship—"each shares with me the name [of poet]," says Dante's Virgil—had supplanted. Even the form in which the *maker* imagines his relation to *poetrye* figures his distance from it.[53]

Moreover, although Chaucer's initial impulse toward classicism clearly derived from the Italian humanists—there is hardly an ancient text that he does not approach through their mediation—the relation he establishes to antiquity is in fact far different. Rather than seeking to recuperate antiquity in its otherness, an otherness that can then provide the terms by which a modern or Renaissance self can define itself, Chau-

---

52. See note 23.

53. In the *Vita nuova* Dante had already asserted that vernacular versifiers were equal in status to the classical poets: "It is only recently that the first poets appeared who wrote in the vernacular; I call them 'poets' for to compose rhymed verse in the vernacular is more or less the same as to compose poetry in Latin using classical meters" (trans. Mark Musa [Bloomington: Indiana University Press, 1973], 54. For the role of the *trecento* poets in mediating Chaucer's access to the classics, see Charles Muscatine, *Poetry and Crisis in The Age of Chaucer* (Notre Dame: University of Notre Dame Press, 1972), 118–28.

cer is persistently, even painfully aware of the affiliations that bind together past and present into a seamless and finally inescapable web.
Similarly, while the humanist conception of the poet offers the court
maker an opportunity to establish a secure professional identity within a
posture of cultural superiority, its grandiose claims seem to have struck
Chaucer as both intimidating and foolish. In the *House of Fame* he both
attacks the tradition of visionary poetry and questions his own fitness as
a *vates;* presents the classical poets as points of stability within a chaotic
literary tradition who are nonetheless victimized by demeaning acts of
appropriation; and dismisses the very idea of fame while unmistakably
asserting his own superior virtue. But the classics do provide Chaucer
with two things: first, a form of writing that allows for meaningfulness—
for interpretability—while resisting the preemptive hermeneutics of allegorical exegesis; and second, a prospect upon life that is capacious and
synoptic but not dismissively transcendental—in other words, a historiography. For Chaucer, as for many other medieval readers, the classical
poets, and especially Virgil and Statius, were essentially historians; and
they provided him with a historical vision that allowed him to step outside the suffocating narcissism of court *makyng* and to recognize the mutual interdependence of subjectivity and history.[54] And yet this effort at
escape was incomplete: the failure of classical history, and of the poets
who are its historians, to provide an escape from history is, as we shall
see, a large part of the topic of both the *Troilus* and the *Knight's Tale.*

It is also the topic of *Anelida and Arcite.* Here a series of terms derived
from the lexicon of court poetry—especially "doublenesse," "newefangelnesse," and "trouthe"—are stretched beyond their usual meaning in order to encompass a far larger reference. And the court form of
complaint is here rewritten so as to function not just as an aesthetic
object but as an occasion to explore the relation of language to the speaking subject. In this apparently modest and little read poem, in other
words, we can begin to see the way in which Chaucer began to use the
idea of history, and specifically classical history, to transform himself
from a court maker into a European poet.

II

The poem is entitled in the manuscripts "The Compleynt of Feire
Anelida and Fals Arcite"—a title that misleadingly attempts to fit into a

54. As Wetherbee well says, "It is clear that one of the things [Chaucer] valued most
highly in the *poetae* was their ability to link the enactment of historical change with the
most complex kinds of human experience" (*Chaucer and the Poets,* 27).

familiar courtly category a poem that in fact asserts an almost *sui generis* idiosyncracy.[55] For a number of reasons the poem is no critical favorite.[56] It is radically, almost self-destructively segmented, being composed of what appear to be two distinct fragments: first are ten rhyme royal stanzas that invoke Mars, introduce Theseus, and recapitulate the story of the Seven against Thebes; then follows a wholly amorous account of a love affair between the two protagonists, an account that itself falls into two parts, a 140-line narrative of love won and then betrayed, and Anelida's 140-line complaint in an elaborate French rhyme scheme. This second, two-part romantic fragment bears apparently no relation to the epic opening, a discontinuity that critics have usually explained by pleading incompletion. But while four of the thirteen witnesses to the text do append a stanza that promises more to come, this addition is almost certainly scribal, while the explanation of incompletion is in any case a desperate remedy that begs the questions the poem poses.[57] Indeed, the reduplicative structure of the poem as we have it—an opening 70 lines that are then doubled into a 140-line segment that is then itself in turn replicated by another 140 lines—is itself thematically expressive; and despite its peculiarity the poem is in fact a recognizable kind of Chaucerian writing. It is a miniaturized conjunction of epic and romance as they are articulated, in more fully amplified forms, in *Troilus and Criseyde* and the *Knight's Tale;* and its closest analogue in the Chaucerian canon is the so-called "Broche of Thebes," a diminutive poem with similarly divided loyalties that literally fell apart in the fifteenth century, becoming the poems we now know as the

55. For the title, and other textual information, see Eleanor Prescott Hammond, *Chaucer: A Bibliographical Manual* (New York: Macmillan, 1908), 355–58. A. S. G. Edwards, "The Unity and Authenticity of *Anelida and Arcite:* The Evidence of the Manuscripts," *SB* 41 (1988): 177–88, has questioned Chaucer's authorship of the entire poem, and especially lines 1–120 and 351–57 (the final stanza). But Lydgate's attribution of the "compleynt" of "Anneleyda and of fals Arcite" to Chaucer in the Prologue to the *Fall of Princes* (lines 320–21), and his allusion to the poem in the *Siege of Thebes* (see below, note 86), provides at least some external attribution other than that ambiguously inscribed on the manuscripts. Furthermore, the present discussion means to demonstrate the unity of the poem (less the final stanza), its poetic sophistication, and above all its profoundly Chaucerian character.

56. The almost entirely dismissive criticism to which the poem has been subjected is surveyed by Russell A. Peck, *Chaucer's Lyrics and* Anelida and Arcite: *An Annotated Bibliography (1900–1980)* (Toronto: University of Toronto Press, 1983).

57. John Norton-Smith persuasively argued the scribal nature of this final stanza in "Chaucer's *Anelida and Arcite*," in Peter Heyworth, ed., *Medieval Studies for J. A. W. Bennett* (Oxford: Clarendon Press, 1981), 81–99; see also Edwards, "Unity and Authenticity," 181.

"Complaint of Mars" and the "Complaint of Venus."[58] These four poems are structured, in typically Chaucerian fashion, according to a series of oppositions: love is juxtaposed with war as both astrologized mythography (Venus and Mars) and genre (romance and epic); a transcendental rationality conceived in Boethian terms is set against the irreducible specificity of individual experience; and above all, the discourse of contemporary courtly *makyng* is set within a classical context derived primarily from Virgil, Ovid, and Statius, with Dante, Petrarch, and Boccaccio as mediatory figures. The result are poems that explore the relation of past to present as both cultural and psychological events: the cultural project of classicism is inflected into the psychology of a lover's memory, and the recovery of antiquity is enacted in terms of the drama of loss and reparation staged by the amorous complaint.

As I have suggested, *Anelida and Arcite* is double in both inspiration and structure. Establishing at the outset a literary context that is martial in tone, narrative in form, and male in ideology, it then modulates into a venerean world of amorousness that culminates in a highly aestheticized female lyricism. Chaucer ascribes these two elements of his poem to two different sources: "First folowe I Stace, and after him Corynne" (21). The *Thebaid* is a powerful if significantly obscured presence throughout the first ten stanzas, but we cannot be sure even whom Chaucer means by Corinna: he may be thinking of the Theban poetess of that name, or a feminine Ovidian voice with links to the *puella* of the *Amores*, or both.[59] But whoever she is, she functions as both

58. That these two poems are probably one has been argued by Rodney Merrill, "Chaucer's *Broche of Thebes:* The Unity of *The Complaint of Mars* and *The Complaint of Venus,*" *Literary Monographs* 5 (1973): 3–61.

59. Edgar F. Shannon, *Chaucer and the Roman Poets* (Cambridge: Harvard University Press, 1929), claims that "Corinna" was a name commonly applied to Ovid's *Amores* (15–47); but Douglas Bush, "Chaucer's 'Corinne,' " *Speculum* 4 (1929): 106–8, refutes this claim and argues that the Theban poetess is not only an appropriate but a likely referent. In support Bush cites Lydgate's inclusion of Statius and "Corrynne" in a list of poets in the *Troy Book* and suggests that Chaucer "met the name of Corinna in some such list" (107). But what list? Lydgate's authority for the name is doubtless Chaucer himself, and lists of the seven or nine great poets of the classical world seem not to include Corinna; see Servius's commentary on *Aeneid* 1, 12, and *Eclogues* 7, 21; and Quintilian, *Institutio oratoria* 10, 1. Greek sources do list her (see Vincent DiMarco's headnote in the *Riverside Chaucer*, 991), but Chaucer could not have known these. Not even Vincent of Beauvais seems to have heard of her, and while Statius mentions her in Eclogue 3 of the fifth *Silvae* (line 158), there is no evidence that the *Silvae* were read in the Middle Ages between the ninth century and 1416, when the text was rediscovered at St. Gallen. She is also mentioned in Propertius, *Elegies* 2, 3, 21, a text Chaucer might possibly have read; but Propertius's reference is glancing and makes no reference to Thebes. For Chaucer to know the very obscure fact that Corinna was a Theban poetess—and the context of the reference

an alternative and a counterpart to Statius, enforcing the differences between the poem's two parts but suggesting as well a complementary relationship. We are thus encouraged to read this female romanticism as both a modern graft onto an antique epic and as a coherent part of the poem as a whole, a gloss that constitutes as well as interprets the text. It is at once superior to the epic history it explicates and yet absorbed by and made one with it. And the ambiguous relationship between these two literary elements typifies the ambivalence that inhabits Chaucer's thought about the relationship of both the classical past to the medieval present and of the epic world of history to the romantic world of love. On the one hand, the erotic is an organon to explain the historical: just as the failed love of Troilus and Criseyde can presumably teach us about the failure of Troy, so can Theban compulsions be explicated by reference to Anelida and Arcite. But conversely, the historical is a determinant of the erotic and the past of the present: historical precedents impose dark coercions upon young lovers seeking to escape a similar fate, and the local enclave of love is subsumed by the tangled world of history it seeks to explicate. Hence we are forced to acknowledge that a linear model of cause and effect (love engenders war, war dooms love) must be replaced by a model of equivalence, in which love equals war. And the ultimate cause—the origin—must either lie somewhere else or, more likely, be itself subsumed within the pattern of replication.

The terms in which Thebanness is represented in *Anelida and Arcite* are suggested by the Muse to whom the poet calls for inspiration. Ignoring epic Calliope and lyric Erato, Chaucer here invokes Polyhymnia (15). Literally the muse of many songs, Polyhymnia was in the classical period given responsibility for the mimic arts, while medieval mythographers ascribed to her the *magna memoria* necessary for all poetry; in this poem she sings with "vois memorial in the shade, / Under the laurer which that may not fade" (18–19).[60] *Anelida and Arcite* is an expli-

---

here makes it almost certain that he did—argues for an intense and persistent interest in the Theban story.

60. For the medieval Polyhymnia, see, for example, Fulgentius, *Mythologicon,* ed. August van Staveren, *Auctores Mythographi Latini* (Amsterdam: Wetstenium and Smith, 1742), 1, 14: "Πολύμνια, . . . id est multam memoriam faciens dicimus; quasi per capacitatem est memoria necessaria" (643). Thomas Walsingham's *De archana deorum,* ed. Robert A. van Kluyve (Durham: Duke University Press, 1968), written about 1400, cites the same definition, and adds that Polyhymnia is Saturn's Muse (16–17). Norton-Smith, "Chaucer's *Anelida and Arcite,*" also makes this identification, and cites (unconvincingly, to my mind) Boccaccio's commentary on Dante and the *Genealogie* as Chaucer's probable sources for the information (92–93).

citly memorial poem, seeking to preserve an "olde storie" (10) that "elde . . . Hath nygh devoured out of oure memorie" (12–14). Moreover, when Anelida turns to "write" *her* "compleynynge" (208–9), she is impelled by what she calls "the poynt of remembraunce"—a phrase that is in the first instance a recollection of Dante, and then of itself, serving the complaint as both its opening and closing lines (211, 350). Indeed, the poem witnesses to and represents the workings of a memory that is at once compulsive and incomplete. Both Anelida's complaint and the poem in which it is embedded are ostentatiously and deliberately incomplete; each represents a consciousness *in medias res*, burdened with a multiplicitous past but incapable of being subordinated to a controlling understanding that would allow for a satisfactory closure. *Anelida and Arcite* articulates a form of consciousness that remembers everything yet understands nothing, that recapitulates an unforgettable past by unwittingly reliving it in the present, that finds no ending because it is unable to grasp its beginning.

Most tellingly, this disturbed mnemonics is represented in the poem in terms not only of the abandoned lady and her false lover but also of the recording poet: in effect, it is allowed to define Chaucerian literary modernity itself. While Chaucer engages in a continuous and respectful recourse to his predecessors, he is simultaneously aware that such recourse is typical of all literary production, including theirs; and his scepticism about his own achievements, implicit in the diminutive and even dismissive self-representations that pervade his work, extends to a larger scepticism about the availability of a legitimizing originality. On the one hand, the modern poet is in danger of becoming nothing more than an impersonator standing at an alienating distance from the sources of Western writing; on the other hand, those very sources are of uncertain reliability.

III

The poem establishes the thematic opposition between Anelida and Arcite in the apparently straightforward and unqualified terms of her singleness of purpose set against his duplicity. She is "pleyn" (116) while he is "double in love and no thing pleyn" (87); her "entent" is set wholly "upon trouthe" (132) while he is "fals" and "feyned" (97 and passim).[61]

---

61. In *his* Theban poem, the *Siege of Thebes*, Lydgate understands doubleness neither amorously nor metaphysically but as moral and hence political instability: the cause of the Theban war is the "doublenesse of Ethiocles" (1778), which is elaborately contrasted to truth (1747–59); ed. Axel Erdmann, EETS, ES 108 (London: Kegan Paul, 1911).

Butwhile thenarrativeispositeduponAnelida'smoralintegrity,itsimul-
taneously reveals her love to be almost literally self-divisive. Compulsively thinking of Arcite, Anelida barely attends to her food (134–35);
lying in bed, "on him she thoghte alwey" (137); "when that he was absent any throwe, / Anon her thoghte her herte brast *a-two*" (93–94). And
having thus warred against herself in a futile effort to become wholly at
one with her lover, Anelida reacts to her abandonment with a violence
that brings her to the edge of self-extinction:

> She wepith, waileth, swowneth pitously;
> To grounde ded she falleth as a ston;
> Craumpyssheth her lymes crokedly;
> She speketh as her wit were al agon;
> Other colour then asshen hath she noon;
> Non other word speketh she, moche or lyte,
> But "Merci, cruel herte myn, Arcite!" (169–75)

This is a scene that mixes pathos with horror and invites sympathy
while insisting upon judgment. If Anelida is betrayed by Arcite, she is
also self-betrayed; and when Arcite unjustly accuses her of duplicity—
he swears that "he coude her doublenesse espie, / And al was falsnes
that she to him mente" (159–60)—we recognize that beneath the literal
falsehood lies a metaphoric truth. Divided against herself first in her
love and then in her grief, Anelida surrenders herself to a necessarily
interminable process of self-destruction. As she herself says in her subsequent complaint, "For thus ferforth have I my deth [y]-soght? / Myself I mordre with my privy thoght" (290–91).[62]

The extent of Anelida's self-division is made vivid by the way in
which the complaint aspires to the self-possession of understanding—
to recollection as self-collection, in the Augustinian sense—and yet

62. If we accept the suggestion of Boyd Ashby Wise, *The Influence of Statius upon
Chaucer* (Baltimore: J. H. Furst, 1911), 70 n. 1, that Anelida's designation as "the quene of
Ermony" (71–72) is meant to recall Harmonia, the daughter of Mars and Venus, rather
than Armenia, then we can see that her career in the poem traces a movement from an
original if unstable unity to a characteristically Theban discord. In this connection, it is
relevant to recall that it was for Harmonia that Vulcan made the fatal Brooch of Thebes as
a wedding gift for her marriage to Cadmus, as Chaucer points out in the "Complaint of
Mars." Anelida is in this case the outsider who is undone by Theban divisiveness: Creon
forces "the gentils of that regioun / To ben his frendes and dwellen in the toun," one of
whom is "Anelida, the quene / Of Ermony" (68–72). Given the implied geography of the
poem, Harmonia would seem to fit better than Armenia and is certainly a *durior lectio*. In
the copy of Clanvowe's *Boke of Cupide* preserved in Bodleian MS Fairfax 16, "harmony" is
spelled "ermonye" (ed. V. J. Scattergood [Cambridge: Brewer, 1975], line 83).

falls far short.[63] Anelida begins in the confident voice of the moralist: the *sententia* she seeks to demonstrate is the sad lesson that "whoso trewest is, hit shal hir rewe" (217), and the illustrative *exemplum* is the speaker herself. "I wot myself as wel as any wight" (220), she says, meaning three things: she knows the lesson herself, she knows herself as well as anyone else knows her, and she knows herself as well as anyone else knows herself or himself. But these ambitious claims are undone by the rest of the complaint, which shows Anelida as still possessed by the very experience she seeks to understand. Far from standing outside her experience and looking back upon it, she remains wholly absorbed within it. "That I have seid, be seid for evermore!" (246), she bravely asserts, yet she is referring not to the moralizing *sententia* that would seek to categorize and so dismiss the past as a grievous if instructive mistake but to her earlier and foolish commitment to a faithless lover. The complaint is baffled at every turn, and by composing it as a letter for Arcite she acknowledges her self-chosen imprisonment. "I wil ben ay ther I was ones bounde" (245), she says, using an amorous metaphor that also has powerful, if here unacknowledged, Boethian implications.[64] While the mood of the complaint is largely interrogative, only once do the questions rise to the level of philosophical inquiry: "Almyghty God, of trouthe sovereyn, / Wher is the trouthe of man? Who hath hit slayn?" (311–12). But no answer is forthcoming, and Anelida's questioning remains merely rhetorical: "Who may avaunte her beter of hevynesse / Then I?" (296–97); "Shall I preye or elles pleyne?" (282); "Allas! Wher is become your gentilesse?" (247); "My swete foo, why do ye so, for shame?" (272). The very possibility of enlightenment is preempted by the anxiety of the fearful lover: "Now merci, swete, yf I mysseye! / Have I seyd oght amys, I preye?" (317–18).[65]

The final stanza of the complaint opens with a brave effort at conclusiveness: "Then ende I thus, sith I may do no more, / I yeve it up for

63. Augustine presents the recollection of autobiography as a re-collecting of a self dispersed among earthly pleasures by sin; see, for example, *Confessions* 2, 1, with its punning on *recolo* and *colligo*; and 10, 11, which connects *cogo* and *cogito*.

64. For the Boethianism of the term, see Stephen Barney, "Troilus Bound," *Speculum* 47 (1972): 445–58.

65. The strikingly interrogative mood of Anelida's complaint is created by the fact that a fifth of its lines are questions: 238–40, 247–52, 253–54, 272, 273–74, 275–77, 281–82, 283, 296–97, 299, 301, 311–12, 315–16, 318. Yet none of these questions actually anticipates an answer, and they serve merely to express the bafflement and emotional turmoil of the amorous complaint. For a discussion of questioning as a stylistic element of the French complaint, see Charles Muscatine, *Chaucer and the French Tradition* (Berkeley: University of California Press, 1957), 24–25, and the earlier studies cited there.

now and evermore" (342–43). But what is being abandoned is not her love for the faithless and unworthy Arcite but her attempt to understand that love: "But me to rede out of this drede, or guye, / Ne may my wit, so weyk is hit, not streche" (340–41). Anelida will never "lerne of love the lore" (345), neither an *ars amatoria* nor the wisdom that unhappy love might teach. Hence she misunderstands the genre of the *Chauntepleure*, taking it to be not a moralizing poem that instructs one in the falseness of a passing world but rather as a vehicle for expressing, and reenacting, the turmoil of uninstructed emotion.[66] In attempting to understand her past, Anelida has revealed how powerfully present it is; trying to append a dismissive *explicit*, she finds herself hopelessly implicated. The conclusion to the complaint is thus appropriately inconclusive. The last line—"thirled with the poynt of remembraunce" (350)—exactly replicates the first (211): memory encapsulates the complaint as it engrosses the speaker, and her ending returns her to her beginning in an endless cycle of repetition. This is surely why the complaint is, as Skeat long ago noted, formally circular: the first six stanzas are exactly matched, in content as well as form, by the last six.[67] Lacking a fixed perspective outside her experience from which to understand it, Anelida is condemned to repeat it.

The final stanza of the complaint also contains an allusion to another famous complaint that serves to raise larger questions about the shape of literary history as a whole, and about the position of the medieval poet within this history:

> But as the swan, I have herd seyd ful yore,
> Ayeins his deth shal singen his penaunce,
> So singe I here my destinee or chaunce. (346–48)

This is a citation of Dido's epistle in the *Heroides*, and by alluding to it here Chaucer invokes both the specific text that ultimately underwrites the amorous elements of *Anelida and Arcite* and the classical genre upon which he modeled the epistolary complaints that appear throughout

66. Anelida says, "I fare as doth the song of *Chaunte-pleure*, / For now I pleyne and now I pleye" (320–21). But as Skeat, *The Works of Geoffrey Chaucer* (Oxford: Clarendon Press, 1894), points out in his note to these lines, according to Godefroy the *Chauntepleure* "was addressed to those who sing in this world and will weep in the next. Hence also the word was particularly used to signify any complaint or lament, or a chant at the burial service" (1:537).

67. Ibid., 536 (note to line 220).

his work.[68] Both Anelida's complaint and the poem as a whole are pervaded with echoes of Dido's epistle, and there is a deep affinity of purpose between the two texts: both are largely interrogative efforts to
achieve a self-understanding that will emancipate the speaker from the
corrosive ambivalence of her feelings, and both come ultimately to
naught.[69] There are as well obvious affinities between "quene Anelida"
(47) and *Dido regina*.[70] Both are royal, both exiles, both in love with a

68. For the swan image, see *Heroides* 7, 1–2; Chaucer also cites the lines at the end of
the Legend of Dido in the *Legend of Good Women:*

"Ryght so," quod she, "as that the white swan
Ayens his deth begynnyth for to synge,
Right so to you make I my compleynynge." (1355–57)

Both Shannon (*Chaucer and the Roman Poets*) and Nancy Dean ("Chaucer's *Complaint*, A
Genre Descended from the *Heroides*," *CL* 19 [1967]: 1–27) argue that Chaucer's insistence
upon the specificity of the narrative setting, and his incorporation of details of that setting into the lyric complaint, mark his complaints as Ovidian. In "Guillaume de Machaut
and Chaucer's Love Lyrics," *MAE* 47 (1978): 66–87, James I. Wimsatt argues on the contrary that Anelida's complaint is derived from Machaut's *chant royal*, "Amis, je t'ay tant
amé et cheri" (no. 254 in *Poésies Lyriques*, ed. V. Chichmaref, SATF [Paris: H. Champion,
1909], 1:223–24). But a comparison of the two texts does not, in my view, support his
claims. In an earlier article, *"Anelida and Arcite:* A Narrative of Complaint and Comfort,"
ChR 5 (1970–71): 1–8, Wimsatt assimilates the poem to the pattern of the French *dits
amoureux* and suggests that it would have fulfilled this pattern more fully had it been
completed. But it is exactly the variation from the pattern that is important.

69. As well as the swan image, for specific Ovidian allusions, compare *Anelida*, 134–
37 and 256–58 to *Heroides* 7, 25–26 and 64, 76, 195, respectively; for more general analogies between the emotional condition described by Anelida and Dido, see, for example,
Heroides 7, 6, and 168. The interrogative nature of *Heroides* 7 is suggested by the eighteen
questions that Dido poses in the course of the poem, fifteen of them in the first half (see
lines 7–8, 9–10, 11–12, 15, 16, 19–20, 21–22, 41, 45, 53–54, 66, 71–72, 77, 78, and 83; the
other three are lines 125, 141–42, and 164). Aware of her responsibility for her own condition (see lines 23–24, 33, 85–86, 97–98 and 104), of her own self-delusions (35), and of the
complexity of her feelings (29–30), Dido struggles toward self-understanding in the
course of her complaint but finally remains baffled. It is that struggle, however, that
distinguishes the classical complaint, both in the *Heroides* and in *Aeneid* 4, from its French
descendent, which seeks above all to encase a static emotional posture in the beautifully
wrought reliquary of its ritualistic language. The point is that *Anelida and Arcite* represents Chaucer's attempt to explicate the continuities between the antique past and the
modern present.

70. Ovid's Dido never, it is true, refers to herself as a queen; but *Aeneid* 4 is structured by the repeated invocation of her title: see lines 1, 296, and 504. Interestingly
enough, one of the manuscripts of the *Anelida and Arcite* (Longleat 258, a Shirley manuscript) gives as the title *Balade of Anelyda Quene of Cartage* (see DiMarco's textual notes in
the *Riverside Chaucer*, 1144). It may even be that Anelida's name is a compilation of elements of the three female names of *Heroides* 7—*An*na, *Eli*ssa, and *Di*do.

man who represents a great political hegemony (Thebes, Rome) and
yet proves to be "fals" (*perfidus*), and false in ways that are, as we shall
see, oddly similar.

By invoking Dido here Chaucer establishes a curious but telling chronological disjunction. In terms of the fictive time of her complaint,
Anelida speaks now as Dido will come to speak later, a priority that is
stressed by having Anelida *close* with the image of the swan song with
which Dido will "later" *begin*. But in terms of the time of literary history,
priority goes to Dido: the image of the swan song is originally hers. The
effect of this temporal amalgamation is thus not to adjudicate originality but to challenge the very concept of an origin. Complaint is a form of
speech that transgresses the usual temporal categories, both in the individual sense that it elides temporal divisions—before and after, then
and now, past and present are distinctions the plaintive voice refuses to
observe—and in the general sense that it is always with us: Anelida
speaks in Thebes as Dido speaks in Carthage and, as the elaborately
contemporary rhyme scheme of her complaint reminds us, as women
still speak in the courts of Chaucer's England.[71] The swan song of complaint is thus both always original and already belated: a first utterance
that breaks a lifelong silence, it issues forth at the point of extinction
and bespeaks a helplessness before the temporality that has inflicted a
mortal wound. This is what it means, then, to speak while "thirled with
the poynt of remembrance." Apparently "pleyn," Anelida's "compleynynge" is an echoic doubling that turns back upon itself not only
formally and psychologically but also temporally.

As with Anelida's self-division, Arcite's duplicity—"he was double

71. In "*Anelida and Arcite:* A Narrative of Complaint and Comfort," Wimsatt points
out that a generic "feature [of the complaint] which Machaut evidently tried to establish
is the use of different rhyme-endings for each stanza; in the *Remède de Fortune* the poet
states explicitly that a complaint is a poem with 'sad matter and many different
rhymes'. . . . In the complaint of the later *Fonteinne amoureuse,* as the lover boasts, there
are a hundred different rhymes without one repetition" (5–6). In contemporary French
poetry there are stanzas very like Chaucer's elaborate *aabaabbab,* such as Deschamps's
Complainte pour la religieuse Marguerite (*aabaabbabaa*) and the Sénéchal d'Eu's *Complainte
pour sa femme* (*aabaabbabba*). Indeed, subsequent literary history suggests that Chaucer's
example in the *Anelida* did in fact succeed in establishing the complex metrics and rhyme
scheme of Anelida's complaint as a generic norm for his fifteenth-century Scots disciples.
The *Anelida* stanza was used by Gavin Douglas for Parts 1 and 2 of *The Palice of Honour* and
for the Prologue to Book 3 of the *Aeneid,* and by Dunbar in *The Golden Targe.* It was used as
well in three poems found in MS Arch. Selden B.24: "The Quare of Jelusy," "The Lay of
Sorrow," and "The Lufaris Complaynt." But its most brilliant use was by Henryson for
Cresseid's complaint in *The Testament of Cresseid,* a poem that both anatomizes the workings of retrospection as erotic yearning, penitential regret, and literary indebtedness and
stresses the inadequacy of complaint as a vehicle for self-understanding.

in love and no thing pleyn" (87)—is an erotic disorder with an Ovidian aetiology. His "falsnes" mimics the Ovidian Aeneas's perfidiousness, and his restless questing after "another lady" (144) parallels Aeneas's attraction to an always beckoning *alter amor* (17).[72] "Put by your wanderings," Dido urges Aeneas, and her phrase—*ambage remissa* (149)—points as well to the evasive circumlocutions with which he first won her love and has now rejected it. Whether the goal be empire or love, the questing impulse remains the same, and both Aeneas and Arcite are insatiable, satisfied only with dissatisfaction. *Facta fugis, facienda petis* (13), Dido accuses Aeneas: "You flee what has been done; what is to be done, you seek." If for Ovid the characteristically feminine erotic disorder is endless pining, the masculine counterpart is endless discontent.[73] As the *Amores* explore in detail, the elaborate system of impediments and frustrations that typifies Ovidian eroticism, and that Chaucer here and elsewhere calls "daunger" (186, 195), is established for no other reason than to forestall the disappointment of full possession. As Ovid says to an inattentive rival, "If you feel no need of guarding your love for yourself, you fool, see that you guard her for me, that I may desire her the more! What is permitted is unwanted, but what is forbidden burns all the more sharply."[74]

Chaucer's term for this discontent, in this poem and elsewhere, is "newefangelnesse" (141), a condition that "naturally" afflicts men:

> The kynde of mannes herte is to delyte
> In thing that straunge is, also God me save!
> For what he may not gete, that wolde he have. (201–3)

72. Ovid stresses the compulsive and impersonal nature of Aeneas's desire by having Dido use the word *alter* five times in order to designate the object to which that desire is directed—as if the precise goal did not matter as long as it were other than that which he now has: see lines 14 (twice), 17 (twice), and 18.

73. Chaucer explores male dissatisfaction at length in the *Legend of Good Women*, and nowhere more extensively than in the account of another questing deceiver, Jason. In the "Legend of Medea" he describes Jason as "of love devourer and dragoun" (1581; and see 1369):

> As mater apetiteth forme alwey,
> And from forme into forme it passen may,
> Or as a welle that were botomles,
> Ryght so can false Jason have no pes. (1582–85)

Derived from Guido delle Colonne's *Historia destructionis Troiae*, these lines represent male desire not as surplus or excess but as lack or inadequacy, as loss rather than endowment. It is perhaps appropriate, then, that Jason's third wife (after Hypsiplye and Medea) is Creusa, the daughter of Creon of Thebes—a name that locates Jason within the economy of Theban recursion and that also links him with that other adventurer, Aeneas.

74. *Amores* 2, 19, 1–3; for instances of similar statements, see 1,5, 2,5, 2,19, 3,4, 3,14.

Although this condition, like Anelida's "languisshing" (178), can be adequately glossed by reference to Ovidian texts, Chaucer in fact thinks of it in larger, philosophical terms. This is suggested in part by the anachronistic reference to Lamech, "the firste fader that began / To loven two, and was in bigamye" (152–53); the biblical Lamech is not only a bigamist but a homicide, a self-confessed member of the fratricidal race of Cain—a scriptural analogue, as it were, to the Thebans of classical mythology.[75] Evidently more is at issue than Ovidian wit would suggest, and this allusion begins to invoke the darker passions that lie behind Arcite's eroticism.

We can locate the center of Chaucer's concern by collating the new-fangledness of *Anelida and Arcite* with cognate texts from elsewhere in Chaucer's poetry. Most directly relevant is the complaint of the falcon in the *Squire's Tale*, a complaint that echoes *Anelida and Arcite* in a number of other instances as well.[76] In explaining the tercelet's infidelity, the falcon has recourse to a Boethian allusion:

I trowe he hadde thilke text in mynde,
That 'alle thynge, repeirynge to his kynde,
Gladeth hymself;' thus seyn men, as I gesse.
Men loven of propre kynde newefangelnesse,
As briddes doon that men in cages fede. (607–11)

Even if a bird is fed on delicacies, continues the falcon, it will prefer worms, "So newefangel been they of hire mete, / And loven novelries of proper kynde" (618–19). In the *Manciple's Tale* the same *exemplum* reappears, again designed to show that "flessh is . . . newefangel" and that men "konne in nothyng han plesaunce / That sowneth into vertu any while" (193–95).[77]

Both of these cognate texts are in the first instance comic and even frivolous: the falcon's objection to her avian lover is that he has, unsurprisingly, behaved just like a bird, while the Manciple's allusion is part of a complex set of evasive insults. But in both instances a serious question is at issue: by what means can the natural man be redeemed?

75. See Genesis 4:19–24.
76. See the note to line 105 in the *Riverside Chaucer*, citing earlier suggestions by Skeat and Tupper. These analogies suggest that if the *Knight's Tale* is a mature rewriting of *Anelida and Arcite*, then the *Squire's Tale* is a satiric version.
77. This image of the bird-in-the-cage, derived from Boethius, reappears in a submerged form and with a sharply different valence in the *Miller's Tale*: Alisoun, who sings "as loude and yerne / As any swalwe sittynge on a berne" (3256–57), is kept by her jealous husband "narwe in cage" (3224) but of course manages to escape.

In the *Squire's Tale* it is the redemptive powers of culture—what the Squire calls "gentilesse"—that are tested and found wanting, while the vividness with which the Manciple's classical fable represents the corruptions of the flesh preempts any possibility of social redemption and thus provides a fitting preparation for the Parson's terminal Christian prescriptions. Moreover, the seriousness of all three of these Chaucerian meditations on the newfangledness of sexual infidelity becomes clear when we invoke the Boethian subtext that lies behind them. This is meter ii of Book 3, which describes how Nature "restreyneth alle thynges by a boond that may nat be unbownde" (3, ii, 6–7). Boethius gives several examples of this binding: tamed lions that become wild again upon tasting blood, the caged bird that scorns the luxurious food of its captivity and sings always of the shadowed wood, the bent bough that springs upright when released, the westering sun that returns to its orient source. These natural bindings are small instances of the cosmic binding that orders the universe as a whole. "Alle thynges seken ayen to hir propre cours [*recursus*]," says Boethius in the same meter, "and alle thynges rejoysen hem of hir retornyng ayen to hir nature" (39–42). Just as it is right for the bird to return to the wood, so the proper course for man is to return to his heavenly origins. This is a homecoming that is to be accomplished through a philosophical pedagogy that will enable man to gaze once again upon that "clere welle of good" (3, xii, 1–2) that is itself both "the begynnynge of alle thinges" (3, 10, 100) and the "oon ende of blisfulnesse" (3, 2, 8). To possess this knowledge is to enjoy "the ferme stablenesse of perdurable duellynge" (3, 11, 185–86), what Boethius elsewhere calls "the ende of alle thinges that ben to desire, beyonde the whiche ende ther nys no thing to desire" (4, 2, 165–67).

Man is impelled on this quest for stability by a force that Boethius metaphorically designates "ayen-ledynge fyer" or *ignis revertus* (3, ix, 38) and, in more philosophical language, *intentio naturalis* or "naturel entencioun" (3, 11, 154–55). This intention is a kind of love: Boethius calls it *caritas*, a word Chaucer translates with the doublet "this charite and this love" (3, 11, 175–76). It represents at the level of subjectivity the force that governs the recursive action that characterizes being as a whole: all things are "constreynede . . . into roundnesses" and "comen . . . eftsones ayein, by love retorned [*converso . . . amore*], to the cause that hath yeven hem beinge" (4, iv, 56–59). And at the level of ethics it is the love that "halt togidres peples joyned with an holy boond, and knytteth sacrement of mariages of chaste loves" (2, viii, 21–23). Its opposite is what Boethius calls the "willeful moevynges of the soule" (3, 11, 153–54) that deflect men into "myswandrynge errour [and] mysledeth hem into false goodes" (3, 2, 24–25). It is above all else that regressive Ovidian love that possesses Orpheus, in Boethius's most famous meter, and that persuades him to turn his eyes backward, in an infernal parody of the authentic recursive gaze, upon the doomed Eurydice.

Chaucer's depiction of the "newefangelnesse" of Arcite's erotic restlessness invokes this kind of Boethian critique. Willfully rejecting Anelida's chaste love, Arcite rejects as well a fully human nature that ineluctably tends toward the true end of things, aligning himself instead with a less than human self that "delyte[th] / In thing that straunge is" (201–2). Hence he is throughout the poem subjected to metaphors drawn from the animal world. He behaves "ryght as an hors, that can both bite and pleyne" (157); "His newe lady holdeth him so narowe / Up by the bridil, at the staves ende" (183–84); and in following her "he is caught up in another les" (233). Anelida herself completes this pattern of judgment with a final, plaintive question that returns us to the Boethian passage from which we began: "Is that a tame best that is ay feyn / To fleen away when he is lest agast?" (315–16). It is this self-division, between a truly human nature and a less than human hankering after the unavailable and the forbidden, that most profoundly defines Arcite as "double in love" (87) and that links him to the ironically self-divided lady whom he seeks to abandon. What also links him to Anelida is his disordered memory, for his negligence of his lady is a sign of a larger forgetfulness. Arcite is one of those who has, in Lady Philosophy's words, "foryeten hymselve" (1, 2, 22): he no longer "remembre[s] of what cuntre" he is born (1, 5, 16–17) nor "remembres . . . what is the ende of thynges, and whider that the entencion of alle kynde tendeth" (1, 6, 37–39). "Drerynesse hath dulled my memorie" (1, 6, 41), says the prisoner in the *Consolation*, and the philosophical understanding to which the dialogue with Philosophy is devoted is defined as a process of remembering or anamnesis.[78] Man, says Lady Philosophy, "alwey reherceth and seketh the sovereyne good, al be it so with a dyrkyd memorie; but he not by whiche path, ryght as a dronke man not nat by whiche path he may retourne hom to his hous" (3, 2, 83–88)—a passage that is later cited by the Arcite of the *Knight's Tale* (1260–67). Just as Anelida's obsessive memory forecloses her future, so does Arcite's darkened memory keep him wandering in quest of a "suffisaunce" that was once his but that he has now aban-

78. "And if so be that the Muse and the doctrine of Plato syngeth soth, al that every wyght leerneth, he ne doth no thing elles thanne but recordeth, as men recorden thinges that ben foryeten" (3, xi, 43–47).

doned. And as Arcite is alienated from his true origin so is Anelida denied access to a transcendent end: together they are condemned to an endless repetitiveness that stands as a sad parody of the authentic recursions of Boethianism.

In soliciting a Boethian reading of its lovers, *Anelida and Arcite* prefigures the more extensive Boethianism of "The Complaint of Mars," *Troilus and Criseyde* and the *Knight's Tale*. What is important for interpretive purposes, however, is that such a reading opens a prospect upon the complex affiliations that Chaucer establishes throughout his work among Boethian philosophy, Ovidian love, and Thebanness. In exploring these affiliations we shall come to understand how insecurely grounded is the interpretive authority we are encouraged to cede to Boethianism. For if Thebanness stands as the other that Boethianism suppresses, this is because its configurations provide a dark mirroring of Boethian idealism that raise disquieting and finally unanswerable questions. The Theban story is itself about disordered memory and fatal repetition, about the tyranny of a past that is both forgotten and obsessively remembered, and about the recursive patterns into which history falls.

In its fullest form, the story begins with acts of sexual violence—the abduction of Europa by Jove—and paternal tyranny: Agenor unfairly commands Cadmus either to recover his sister Europa or go into permanent exile, a command that in the *Metamorphoses* Ovid designates as *pius et sceleratus eodem* (3, 5). Necessarily failing in his quest, Cadmus wanders in exile until Apollo leads him to Boeotia where he is to found Thebes. But this originary act, despite its divine superintendence, is both flawed in itself and proleptic of the disasters to follow: slaying a serpent sacred to Mars, Cadmus is told that he will himself end his days as a serpent, and when he sows the serpent's teeth there spring up warriors who engage in fratricidal slaughter. Born from the earth, these first Thebans now return to it; in Ovid's phrase (which Chaucer remembered when writing the *Pardoner's Tale*), they beat on the warm breast of their mother for reentry: *tepido plangebant pectora matrem* (3, 126). Here is the central, recursive act of Theban history, the first instance of a chthonic return that is then endlessly repeated.

The details of this recursion are articulated in the history of "the broche of Thebes" to which Chaucer alludes in the "Complaint of Mars." The brooch is itself a sign of illicit sexuality: it is made by Vulcan as a bitter wedding gift for Harmonia, the daughter of Mars and Venus, when she marries Cadmus—a marriage that causes their exile from their city and transformation into the originary serpents. The next owner is Semele, struck by Jove's lightning; then Agave, driven mad by the Furies; then Jocasta; then Argia, wife of Polynices, who gives it to Euripyle if she will reveal the hiding place of her husband Amphiauraus so that he may become one of the seven against Thebes, an act of betrayal that issues in his all-too-Theban engulfment in the earth. When Euripyle is then murdered by her vengeful son Alcmaeon, Ovid tellingly designates the crime as *pius et sceleratus eodem* (9, 408), the same phrase he had earlier applied to Agenor's exile of Cadmus at the beginning of Theban history. The final owner of the brooch is Orestes, whom it incites to repeat an identical act of filial vengeance against *his* mother, Clytaemnestra.[79] Like the boar that becomes the heraldic device of the Theban family of Tydeus in the *Troilus*, the brooch is an object of desire whose possession is inevitably fatal; as Chaucer's Mars says in his complaint, its owner has "al his desir and therwith al myschaunce" (241).[80] It arouses emotions that are in the first instance erotic (Harmonia, Semele, Agave, Jocasta) but that entail deadly consequences, and it functions in a context in which the venerean and the martial are in a continual process of mutual subversion, in which amorousness and violence are metamorphosed and finally fused, whether as internecine vengeance or romantic betrayal. Descending down through the Theban line—*longa est series*, says Statius (2, 267; cf. 1, 7)—the brooch metonymically represents the primal polymorphousness of Theban emotions and the self-destructive regressiveness that results from submitting to a self unknown.

At the center of Theban history is Oedipus, the tragic figure who encapsulates the Theban fate with terrifying economy. The profound circularity of Thebanness, its inability ever to diverge from the reversionary shape ordained in and by its beginning, is reflected in the details of Oedipus's life as the Middle Ages reconstructed them. At once malevolent and pitiable, Oedipus becomes both agent and victim of the self-imposed genocide that decimates Thebes. As a son he kills his father Laius—one medieval text has him say that he "struck iron through my father's loins"—and as a father he reenacts his primal crime by cursing his sons with what the same text has him describe as "the

79. The fullest medieval survey of the genealogy of the Brooch is provided by the Second Vatican Mythographer; see Georg Bode, ed., *Scriptores rerum mythicarum latini tres romae* (Celle: Schulze, 1834), 1:101. A modern account is offered by Neil C. Hultin, "Anti-Courtly Elements in Chaucer's *Complaint of Mars*," *AnM* 9 (1968): 58–75.

80. The device of the boar signifies the Calydonian boar killed by Meleager and then given by him to Atalanta as a love gift, an act that enraged his uncles and led to the family feud in which the nephew slaughtered his uncles and was, in revenge, consigned to death by his own mother. The story is told in a compressed form by Cassandra as an explication of Troilus's dream (5, 1471–84).

sword of my tongue."[81] Similarly, he reenacts the return of the dragon-warriors to their mother earth in his incest with Jocasta: his union with his mother is described by both Statius and Seneca as a *revolutus in ortus*.[82] Even the smallest details of his life express the compulsions of repetition and circularity: exiled as an infant to Mount Cithaeron by his father, he is in his old age exiled there once again by Creon, and the riddle that marks him as extraordinary presents his life, and all life, as inescapably replicating. In the *Roman de Thèbes* and its prose adjuncts the riddle is itself given a duplicative form: "I have heard tell of a beast," says the Sphinx, "that when it first wishes to walk on the ground it goes on four feet like a bear; and then comes a time when it has no need of the fourth foot and it moves with great speed on three; and when it has greater strength it stands and goes on two feet; and then it has need of three, and then four. Friend, tell me if you have ever seen such a beast?"[83] Man is the beast, and whether he is figured as a bear or, as in the *Troilus*, as a boar, it is his irredeemable animality that lies at the heart of Theban history, just as it lies at the center of Arcite's Theban consciousness in *Anelida and Arcite*.

Thebanness is a fatal doubling of the self that issues in a replicating history that preempts a linear or developmental progress. Theban history in its pure form has neither origin nor end but only a single, infinitely repeatable moment of illicit eroticism and fratricidal rivalry—love and war locked together in a perverse fatality. In its circular recursions moreover, it stands as a dark echo of the idealistic *recursus* of Boethianism, a specular impersonation that destabilizes the interpretive authority with which the *Consolation* is usually invested. Like the Theban

---

81. These are two lines from the so-called *Planctus Oedipi*, an eighty-four-line poem that survives in at least twelve manuscripts, both by itself and with the *Thebaid*. I have here translated lines 30 ["vibrans ferrum per patris ilia"] and 79 ["ut gladium linguam exacui"] from the transcription of Berlin lat. 34, fol. 113, printed by Edélestand du Méril, *Poésies inédites du moyen âge* (Paris: Franck, 1854), 310–13.

82. Seneca, *Oedipus*, line 238, and see also lines 638–39; Statius, *Thebaid* 1, 235.

83. Leopold Constans, ed., *Roman de Thèbes*, SATF (Paris: H. Champion, 1890), lines 281–91. The same circularity is stressed by the Second Vatican Mythographer: "quod primo quatuor, deinde tribus, deinde duobus, deinde tribus, deinde quatuor graditur pedibus?" (Bode, ed., 1:150–51). It is also prominent in Lydgate's version in the *Siege of Thebes*, who sums up the Oedipal condition as one of return to mother earth: "And fynaly this the trouthe pleyn, / he retourneth kyndely ageyn / To the matere which that he kam fro"; "And for he may no whyle here soiourne, / To erthe ageyn he most in hast retourne, / Which he kam fro, he may it not remewe" (Erdmann, lines 673–75, 723–25). This Oedipal return to mother earth is also figured by Chaucer in the Old Man of the *Pardoner's Tale*: see below, chapter 8. In "Oedipus in the Middle Ages," *Antike und Abendland* 22 (1976): 140–55, Lowell Edmunds points out that "in the ancient sources the riddle is always simpler: first four, then three, then two feet" (144 n. 15).

dragon-warriors and their Oedipal descendants, the Boethian philosopher is also engaged in a *revolutus in ortus*, a return to the *fons et origo* from
which all being descends. For Boethius this origin is celestial: as Chaucer's most securely Boethian poem advises its readers, "Know thy
contree, look up, thank God of al; / Hold the heye wey and lat thy gost
thee lede."[84] But the lesson about origins that the Theban legend teaches
is epitomized in a phrase from the *Thebaid: crudelis pater vincit*. Whether
personified as father Oedipus or the dragon-warriors' mother earth, the
parent ineluctably calls the Theban back, either temporally by enacting
the past or spatially by reentering the earth, the chthonic source of life.
According to Boethius's Platonic rationalism, moral failure is a function
of intellectual error: an undiverted *intentio naturalis* directs us to the
"good [that] is the fyn of alle thinges" (3, 2, 230), and it is only
"myswandrynge errour [that] mysledeth [men] into false goodes" (3, 2,
23–25; cf. 3, 3, 6–8). Boethian *caritas* is an *amor conversus* that irresistibly
returns us to the divine origin. But the *amor* that motivates the Theban,
however well intentioned, has a twofold character (*pius et sceleratus
eodem*) that leads him inevitably to disaster. The Theban legend harshly
argues that the natural self is by definition ill-behaved and self-
defeating, an unconstrained appetitiveness that bespeaks not a transcendent origin but one that is primordial and earthbound.

IV

This Theban economy has a powerful relevance as well to a poet like
Chaucer, whose own habits of literary recall witness to a dynamic strikingly similar to that articulated by Theban history. If we return now to
Anelida and Arcite in order to examine the intertextual relations that
inform it, we can begin to understand the way in which Chaucer's poetics of memory stand as a compositional version of Thebanness. An
important instance is Anelida's echoed phrase, "the poynt of remembraunce" (211, 350)—a phrase that derives from *Purgatorio* 12, where
Dante and Virgil tread upon the figured pavement of the cornice of
pride. This is the terrace where the "gran tumor" (*Purg.* 11, 119) of
Dante's own artistic pride is put down by a discussion of the fruitless
rivalry between artistic generations. The divine images with which the
cornice is adorned are compared with the sculptured paving stones
that cover the tombs set into the floor of the church nave: "In order that
there be memory of them, the stones in the church floor over the buried
dead bear figured what they were before: wherefore many a time men

84. "Truth," 19–20; in the *Riverside Chaucer*, 653.

weep for them there at the prick of the memory [*la punctura de la rimembranza*] that spurs only the faithful."[85] Bearing an artistic refiguring of the original that lies within, the sculptured stones are memorial images that spur the pious with the *punctura de la rimembranza*. Chaucer's own poem is a similar act of piety toward his dead poetic precursors: Corinna, Ovid, Statius, Dante himself, even the stubbornly unacknowledged Boccaccio. As with Anelida's lament over the departed Arcite, the poem testifies to the presence of those who are absent, and Chaucer presents himself, here as elsewhere, as a merely curatorial figure. He is the scribe who will *"endyte /* This olde storie" (9–10) and will loyally "folowe" (21) in the footsteps of Statius and Corinna. But the poem itself refuses to endorse even the possibility of such an unmediated access to the past. For it argues throughout, and especially in the first ten stanzas, that the foundations of the poet's literary heritage are only fitfully available in their original and authentic form, and that he must instead make do with artful refigurings, modern rewritings that stand always at some distance from the original.[86]

Such an understanding of the poetic past is implicit in the enigma of Corinna, whether she be the Theban *tenuis Corinna* (artful Corinna) of Statius's *Silvae*, who could have been at most only a name to Chaucer, or the Roman *versuta Corinna* (well-versed Corinna), who is implied throughout Ovid's *Amores* but, represented only as the figure of the poet's desire, has herself no voice.[87] Whoever she is, the name signifies a presence that devouring time has taken away, leaving behind only a verbal image. Time has likewise but differently distanced the poem's other announced source: Statius's *Thebaid* is everywhere present in the first ten stanzas, but present in a way that insists upon distance. For what a close comparison of these ten stanzas with the *Thebaid* reveals is that Statius appears in the poem only accompanied by his belated imita-

85. Come, perché di lor memoria sia,
   sovra i sepolti le tombe terragne
   portan segnato quel ch'elli eran pria,
      onde lì molte volte si ripiagne
   per la punctura de la rimembranza,
      che solo a' pii dà de la calcagne. (*Purg.* 12, 16–21)

86. Lydgate cited this Chaucerian phrase in the *Siege of Thebes:* Cupid's arrow strikes the lovers (Polymyte and Argyve, and Tideus and Deyfyle) with "the poynt of remembraunce, / which may not lightly raced ben away" (Erdmann, lines 1487–89).

87. In *Silvae* 5, Eclogue 3, Statius refers to "the hidden thought of subtle Corinna" (*tenuisque arcana Corinnae* [158]); the girl to whom Ovid addresses most of the *Amores* is referred to in 21, 19 as "Corinna the artful" or, more literally, "well-versed Corinna" (*versuta Corinna*). On the problems of assigning a Statian source to Chaucer's use of the name, see above, note 59.

tor Boccaccio, whose own version of the master's poem—the *Teseida*—permeates these lines. If we start with the three opening stanzas, we find them to be a rewriting of the comparable opening stanzas of the *Teseida*, itself a rewriting of the *Thebaid*. They are, moreover, a rewriting with a difference, for they both reverse the order of Boccaccio's stanzas—1, 2 and 3 here become 3, 2 and 1—and in one crucial point flatly contradict them. Whereas Boccaccio says that the *storia antiqua* he will tell has never been told by a Latin author, Chaucer assures us that he found the "olde storie" precisely "in Latin" (10).[88] Contravening his authority in order to invoke an authority, Chaucer uses the same gesture both to demonstrate and to deny his own originality; and he implies that it is not pious accuracy that characterizes the relation of follower to precursor but deformation and even reversal.

The next three stanzas of *Anelida and Arcite*, however, do return us directly to a Theban master source in Statius's *Thebaid*: describing the return of Theseus from the conquest of Hippolyta, they begin by closely translating sixteen lines from Statius's last book (12, 519–35).[89] But before they finish they again veer off into the *Teseida* by invoking the non-Statian Emily and establishing the terms of Boccaccio's story (38–42). When Statius does appear, then, and even here in what are close to his own words, it is in service to Boccaccio, the imitator from whom he

---

88. This is Boccaccio's account of the genesis of the *Teseida*, ed. Mario Marti, *Opere Minori in Volgare* (Milan: Rizzoli, 1970), 2:257:

E' m'é venuto in voglia con pietosa
rima di scrivere una istoria antica,
tanto negli anni riposta e nascosa
che latino autor non par ne dica,
per quel ch'io senta, in libro alcuna cosa. (1, 2)

"The desire has come to me to set down in plaintive verse an ancient tale, set aside and left long undisclosed over the years, so that no Latin author appears to have recounted it in any book, as far as I know" (*The Book of Theseus*, trans. Bernadette Marie McCoy [New York: Medieval Text Association, 1974], 20). In his gloss to this passage, Boccaccio makes it clear that he is claiming not originality for the *Teseida* but a more profound form of authenticity than would be the case if his source were Latin: "Non è stata di greco translata in latino" (662)—"It has not been translated from Greek into Latin" (47). By returning to an original Greek account, Boccaccio is claiming an authenticity comparable to Dares's or Dictys's accounts of the Trojan War (both of which were originally written in Greek although known to the Middle Ages in Latin translations).

89. Chaucer's rewriting of Statius's lines is preceded in the manuscripts of the *Anelida* by a citation of *Thebaid* 12, 519–21, the same lines as several of the manuscripts of the *Canterbury Tales* include at the start of the *Knight's Tale*. In terms of the chronology of the events, the *Anelida* takes place before the *Knight's Tale*, and few scholars have doubted that it also stands earlier in Chaucer's career; but the precise nature of the relationship remains obscure.

seems never to be quite free. Then in the seventh stanza Chaucer begins a final effort to return to the original version of the Theban story: leaving Theseus "in his weye rydynge" (46) toward Athens, the poet doubles back to the chronologically prior Theban War of which Statius is the chronicler, describing both his rhetorical turn and the Theban matter itself with the provocative phrase, "the slye wey."[90] But this return to the origin is also predictably thwarted: when in stanzas 8–10 the story of the Theban War is summarized, it appears in a précis drawn not from the *Thebaid* but from the unavoidable *Teseida*. The Theban matter cannot, it seems, be represented in its original Statian form; just as classical texts are encrusted with medieval glosses, so does Statius come to Chaucer embedded within a Boccaccian context.

Nor should we assume that the difference between original and imitation is so radical as to guarantee their distinction. However unlike the *Thebaid* the *Teseida* may appear to us, it is clear that Boccaccio intended his poem to be a vernacular recreation of the classical epic. Divided into twelve books and containing, in some manuscripts at least, the identical number of lines as the *Aeneid*, the *Teseida* deploys elaborate mythographical and even archaeological allusions, articulates sentiments and values appropriate to the pre-Christian past, and appends to its classicized text a medieval gloss. Even as it draws heavily upon the vernacular *romanzi* of contemporary Italy, it locates medieval forms in the service of a classicizing project. Unlike *Anelida and Arcite* and the *Knight's Tale*, the *Teseida* declines to acknowledge that its historicist piety may be itself a form of Thebanness. Arcita may be a victim of the Theban curse, but he is the last victim, and his finally selfless love for Emilia makes possible a healing reconciliation with Palemone that lays the past to rest. For Boccaccio, modern love can appease ancient hatreds, and his romantic grafts onto the epic stock are not infected by the original malignity but claim to redeem the whole.[91] But if for Boccaccio

90. Chaucer leaves Theseus riding towards Athens:

And founde I wol in shortly for to bringe
The slye wey of that I gan to write,
Of quene Anelida and fals Arcite. (47–49)

The striking phrase is elliptical, referring both to the means by which the subject matter of the poem will be introduced and that subject matter itself, "the slye wey" with which Arcite dealt with Anelida. The ambiguity thus serves to correlate Arcite's Theban action with Chaucer's Theban writing, not only suggesting that doubleness pervades both but demonstrating its workings through the lexical instability of a double meaning.

91. That this redemptiveness is to be understood as working in both individual and collective ways is clear from the poem's concluding movements. As Arcita lies dying, he

the *Teseida* bespeaks a medieval mastery over the classical past, for Chaucer, here as in the *Troilus* and the *Knight's Tale*, antiquity bears a dark, almost atavistic power.

Finally, if it is true that for Chaucer the original Theban voice is confusingly doubled by later echoes—and he seems to have heard not only Statius, Ovid, and Seneca but also the so-called *Histoire ancienne jusqu'à César*, the anonymous authors of the *Roman de Thèbes* and the *Planctus Oedipi*, and Dante—is it any longer possible to speak of an original or authentic story at all?[92] Indeed, what effect does the mysterious Corinna have upon Statius's authority? Can we any longer assume that the poet whom Chaucer in the *House of Fame* identified as a native of Toulouse is himself the original Theban poet?[93] Just as *Anelida and Arcite* is hardly the last word on Thebes, neither surely is the *Thebaid* the first. Statius himself implies as much at the beginning of his own poem: *longa retro series*, he says (1, 7), and whatever starting point is chosen must be arbitrary.[94] Every beginning is *in medias res*, every account a selection,

---

prays that he not be consigned to a place among the other Theban damned since he has always sought, even if unsuccessfully, to evade the Theban fate (10, 96–99); the subsequent account of his ascent through the spheres (the source for Troilus's ascent at the end of *Troilus and Criseyde*), and of his enlightenment about "la vanitate / . . . dell'umane genti" (11, 3), shows that his prayer has been answered. Then when the question of marrying Emilia is suggested to Palemone, he demurs on the grounds that he is "the sole heir of the great infamies of my ancestors" (12, 24 [trans. McCoy, 317]), but is dissuaded by Teseo. The elaborate account of the wedding with which the poem then concludes affirms the rightness of the reconciliations that consolidates: modern love redeems ancient wickedness.

92. For the *Roman de Thèbes*, see Wise, *Influence of Statius*, 116–37. For the *Histoire ancienne*, see Paul Meyer, "Les premières compilations françaises d'histoire ancienne," *Romania* 14 (1885): 36–76; this text included prose versions of the *romans d'antiquité*: see Guy Raynaud de Lage, "Les romans antiques dans l'*Histoire ancienne jusqu'à César*," *Moyen Age* 63 (1957): 267–309. In the Middle Ages the *Histoire* was known as, among other things, the *Livre des histoires*, the *Trésor des ystoires*, and the *Livre d'Orose* (since it adopted Orosius's chronology). For an edition, see the version ascribed to C. de Seissel and entitled *Le premier volume de Oroze*, 3 vols. (Paris: A. Verard, 1509). There is no evidence that Chaucer actually read Seneca's *Oedipus* (although see Skeat's note to the *Parliament of Fowls*, line 176); but it was known throughout the Middle Ages, and Nicholas Trevet, whose *Chronique* and whose commentary on Boethius's *Consolation* Chaucer did read, wrote a commentary on it and other Senecan plays. Several manuscripts of the *Thebaid* include the *Planctus Oedipi*, so it was certainly available to Chaucer; see Edmunds, "Oedipus in the Middle Ages," and Paul M. Clogan, "The *Planctus* of Oedipus: Text and Comment," *M&H* 1 (1970): 233–39.

93. *House of Fame*, 1460. Statius identified himself as a native of Naples, but the Middle Ages assigned him to Toulouse: see Charles Singleton's note to *Purgatorio* 21, 89.

94. Statius, for example, begins the story with the struggle between Eteocles and Polynices, while the *Roman de Thèbes* goes back to Oedipus's killing of Laius (see *Troilus and Criseyde*, 2, 100–103).

every telling a retelling. Far from being a straightforward linear development, the history of Theban writing is what Chaucer in the *Boece* calls a "replicacioun of wordes" (3, 12, 160–61), and to enter upon it is to broach a labyrinthine way, "so entrelaced that it is unable to ben unlaced" (3, 12, 157). Haunted by a past that is at once sustaining (like a pavement) and galling (like a spur), Theban writing simultaneously salves and reopens the wound caused by "the poynt of remembraunce;" and Chaucer, by invoking Thebes as an early and recurrent locus of his own work, and as a metaphor for his own poetics of memory, sets himself in a relationship with origins so sceptical that it will never receive a final resolution until (which will never happen) the pilgrims arrive at Canterbury.

Chapter Two

Troilus and Criseyde
and the Subject of History

"He believed that nothing can be finally known that involves human motive and need. There is always another level, another secret, a way in which the heart breeds a deception so mysterious and complex it can only be taken for a deeper kind of truth."

In the late fourteenth as in the late twentieth century, Chaucer's *Troilus and Criseyde* attracts attention for reasons that go far beyond its famous tale of love betrayed, however engrossing at the level of psychological realism. In rewriting Boccaccio's romance, Chaucer was, to be sure, engaging the erotic literature of contemporary aristocratic society. But his poem went far beyond the *Filostrato* in exploring the idea of antiquity—not in its own right precisely (whatever that might mean) but rather for what it could tell him about his own place in historical time. For Chaucer, the story of Troilus and Criseyde was a definitive moment in the founding myth of Western history in the Middle Ages, the myth of Trojan origins. And as a poem of origins, the *Troilus* was by definition available to a meditation upon the nature of history per se.

The context of that meditation was, initially, the contest between Augustinianism, with its supervening transcendentalism, and the late-medieval counterimpulse to preserve and create a secular historiography. The linked genres by which this secular tradition could be carried were legendary history and romance, narrative forms that allowed for a more ambitious program than "literature" is sometimes thought capable of sustaining. But when Chaucer embarked on his own essay into the philosophy of history, he soon discovered that the project was fraught with internal contradictions. Nor was it only history-as-event whose unanticipated difficulties Chaucer staged in the poem; it was also history-as-story. For the *translatio verborum* by which the text of history was rewritten proved to be as errant as the line of descent posited by the translation of empire itself.

The second context of Chaucer's project, both enabling and disabling, was Christian spiritualism's opposite—the resistance to human praxis of the material conditions of medieval life. The sheer inertia of medieval society, its difficulty in imagining and fulfilling specific historical programs, encouraged the Middle Ages to conceptualize progress not as the directed advancement toward a future goal but as the recovery of a golden past. Change was experienced as loss, development understood as reformation.[1] It is in "the former age," as Chaucer calls it, when men's "hertes were al oon," that value is to be found; "cursed was the tyme" when men embarked upon the civilizing ventures that have brought them only "doublenesse, and tresoun, and envye, / Poyson, manslawhtre, and mordre in sondry wyse."[2] This yearning for an original, unitary state, uninfected by "doublenesse," is a profoundly and pervasively Chaucerian theme and nowhere more extensively than in the *Troilus*. It must have been given special urgency for Chaucer by the disasters of the 1380s. For this was a decade that saw alarming threats to the kingdom from both within (the Rising of 1381) and without (the anticipated French invasion of 1386, the victory of the Scots at Otterburn in 1388); that witnessed an unnerving increase in both the military incompetence of the ruling class (the Despenser crusade of 1383, Richard II's impressively prepared but miserably anticlimactic campaign against Scotland in 1385, Gloucester's dismal *chevauchée* of 1387) and its political fragmentation (the "loyal conspiracy" of the Lords Appellant and their Merciless Parliament of 1388). Even Chaucer's own financial and personal security came under threat.

It is remarkable (and often remarked) how little of the pressure of historical events is directly recorded in the poem itself. While Gower placed the analogy between Troy and London at the center of his diatribe on the Rising of 1381, Chaucer provides only oblique glances at current events in his explicitly Trojan poem. Instead we have a progressively more inward focus on the subjectivity of the protagonists, a self-reflexive attention to the problematics of writing, and above all, a conceptualization of history not as a series of temporally contingent and humanly tractable events but instead as a total form of being, history as

1. Gerhart B. Ladner, *The Idea of Reform: Its Impact on Christian Thought and Action in the Age of the Fathers* (Cambridge: Harvard University Press, 1959).

2. *Riverside Chaucer*, 650–51. See James Dean, "Time Past and Time Present in Chaucer's Clerk's Tale and Gower's *Confessio Amantis*," *ELH* 44 (1977): 401–18, and "The World Grown Old and Genesis in Middle English Historical Writing," *Speculum* 57 (1982): 548–68.

a transhistorical idea rather than as a material reality. *Troilus and Criseyde* is (or tries to be) a meditation on history that effaces the historical. And what replaces the historical, as we should know from similar strategies in our own time, is the meditating mind itself, a consciousness that rises above and incorporates the conflicting interests of the medieval historical imagination.

This is precisely the moment of modernism, the moment that absorbs the past into a fully present selfhood from which an equivalently self-present significance can issue. Reality is founded in, and controlled by, the self: the disappointments of history are redeemed by an act of understanding that empowers consciousness and projects it forward into the future.[3] But as I have already argued, Chaucer was not in fact able to rest with the modernist moment, to proclaim the dominion of the transcendent mind. On the contrary, *Troilus and Criseyde* everywhere proclaims the fragmentation of subjectivity, both that of its protagonists and of its author. In so doing, it admits that there is no immunity from historicity, that the attempt to find it in thought is as great or greater a betrayal as that of faithless love.

I: The Medieval Writing of History

It is a truism that the development of a secular, causal historiography is impeded in the Middle Ages by the radical devaluation of both historiography and the historical life entailed by the spiritual imperatives of Christianity. History is the realm of the mundane and the unstable, a welter of events whose meaning remains resolutely hidden to the human observer. We are living in the Sixth Age, in the time of the Fourth Empire; the world is growing old (*mundus senescens*), traversing a vacant and meaningless period of time about which nothing useful can be said.[4] History may be, as Augustine put it, God's poem, but only God can read it; and those who are living it should concern themselves not with the means by which He works His mysterious purposes but with

3. See above, Introduction, 3–7, 11–13, 20–21; David Kolb, *The Critique of Pure Modernity: Hegel, Heidegger, and After* (Chicago: University of Chicago Press, 1986); and Gordon Teskey, "Milton and Modernity," *Diacritics* 18 (Spring, 1988): 42–53.

4. As Amos Funkenstein points out, for an Augustinian historiography, "all that could be said about [the present] was that the world grows older" ("Periodization and Self-Understanding (the Middle Ages and Early Modern Times," *M&H* in 5 [1974], 8); and see R. A. Markus, *Saeculum: History and Society in the Theology of St. Augustine* (Cambridge: Cambridge University Press, 1970): "There is no sacred history *of* the last age: there is only a gap for it *in* the sacred history" (23).

the pressing needs of their own salvation.[5] History is significant only as the stage on which to enact individual choices between the City of God and the City of Man; it is a *via peregrinationis*, a place of exile, a land of unlikeness.[6] Since the usefulness of post-Incarnation history resides solely in its ability to teach us to disdain history, its value is wholly personal. It is a locus not of accomplishment but purification, not of fulfillment but healthful loss. Whether conceived as a desert place of exile, a chaos of random events, or, as in Boethius's view, a repetitive cycle of meaningless acts of rise and fall, history is significant only in terms of its impact upon the inner spiritual lives of those caught in its web.[7]

Much of the history that was actually written in the Middle Ages reflects these assumptions. Monastic historians, who have provided so much of the material with which we now reconstruct the medieval past, were in fact deeply divided about the legitimacy of the very scholarly activity in which they were engaged. For Peter Damian, history amounted to nothing more than "ludicrously useless annals, frivolous telling of frivolous old wives' tales"; while Ernald, Abbot of Rievaulx, commissioned William of Newburgh to write his history of England because he did not want any of his own monks engaged in so dubious an activity.[8] Monks displayed an admirable concern with factual inclusiveness and, especially, chronological accuracy; but rarely is the monastic historian concerned with structural coherence or linear development.[9] For Henry of Huntingdon, writing in the early twelfth century, the succession of foreign dominations that God has imposed upon Britain—the Romans, Picts and Scots, Angles, Danes, and now

5. On history as God's poem, see Augustine, *PL* 33:527, *PL* 34:410, and *De civitate Dei*, 11, 18; 4, 17; Bonaventure, *Breviloquium*, in *Works*, trans. José de Vinck (Paterson: St. Anthony Guild Press, 1960), 2:11–12; on the dangers of an overcurious interest in the interpretation of history, see Augustine, *PL* 33:420 and *De doctrina christiana*, 2,44.

6. Augustine, *De civitate*, 1, preface; 18, 51.

7. According to F. P. Pickering, *Literature and Art in the Middle Ages* (Coral Gables: University of Miami Press, 1970), all medieval Christian literature "falls into one of the two categories, according to Augustine *or* according to Boethius" (179). But as far as the problem of the legitimization of the historical life is concerned, there is little difference between the two: for both Augustine and Boethius, history is exile.

8. For Peter Damian, see Marie-Dominique Chenu, *Nature, Man, and Society in the Twelfth Century*, trans. Jerome Taylor and Lester Little (Chicago: University of Chicago Press, 1968), 164 n. 4; for Ernald of Rievaulx, see Bernard Guenée, *Histoire et culture historique dans l'occident médiéval* (Paris: Aubier, 1980), 47–48. In his important review article in *History and Theory* 12 (1973), Robert Hanning discusses the "tensions between the historian's craft and the world-rejecting monastic profession" (423).

9. See Guenée, *Histoire*, 110–11.

Normans—are punishments for wickedness. They have no legitimacy
in and of themselves but stand as part of a scenario whose meaning is to
be read entirely in the spiritual terminology of human sinfulness and
divine wrath.[10] R. W. Southern's comments on monastic annals can be
extended to include more ambitious monastic historical projects as
well: "They are a resolute, undeviating record of human disorder in the
midst of cosmic order. . . . This ambiguity in history, which made it at
once wholly irrational and [from a divine perspective] wholly rational,
at once wholly coherent and wholly incoherent, was one of the most
carefully cultivated experiences of the early Middle Ages."[11]

The sense of coherence, of history as divinely superintended, did of
course find historiographical expression, although rarely in a form that
encouraged the development either of causal modes of historical explanation or explorations of the relation of the individual to the course of
historical events. The genre of history writing that best expressed the
medieval sense of providential order without violating its equally powerful sense of the worthlessness of the historical (i.e., secular) life was
the ecclesiastical history. Perhaps the most familiar instance is Bede's
Ecclesiastical History of the English People; its origins were in Eusebius's
Ecclesiastical History, and its assumptions continued in force in Orderic
Vitalis's twelfth-century history, also entitled *Ecclesiastical History.*[12]
The purpose of these histories—enacted in a pure form only by Bede
but providing the legitimizing assumptions for the others—is to show
how God's chosen people come together in the Church in preparation
for history's apocalyptic fulfillment. Secular events are of interest only
insofar as they are relevant to the workings of this process, and they
enter into the historical record only when appropriated by the totalizing force of the Church.[13] Yet despite its severity, this model historiography is compromised by the intrusion of secularity in two forms.
One is the simple interest in historical events of all kinds, regardless of
their ecclesiastical relevance, that is a growing characteristic of histori-

10.   For Henry of Huntingdon, see Nancy F. Partner, *Serious Entertainments: The Writing of History in Twelfth-Century England* (Chicago: University of Chicago Press, 1977), 11–
48. As she says about the form of the monastic chronicle, "The essential point is simply
the universality of episodic, nondevelopmental, serial organization" (202).

11.   R. W. Southern, "Aspects of the European Tradition of Historical Writing: 1. The
Classical Tradition from Einhard to Geoffrey of Monmouth," *TRHS,* 5th ser., 20 (1970),
180–81.

12.   See Arnaldo Momigliano, *Essays in Ancient and Modern Historiography* (Middletown: Wesleyan University Press, 1975), 107–26.

13.   Walter Ullmann speaks of a "'totalitarian' ecclesiastical history" underwritten by
"the ecclesiologically conceived theme of totality—the Church embracing the totality of
life" (*Medieval Foundations of Renaissance Humanism* [London: Elek, 1977], 64).

cal writing from the twelfth century on. The other is the development, also most marked in the twelfth century but derived from earlier models, of a full-fledged *Heilsgeschichte*, in which not just ecclesiastical but also secular foundations are endowed with a role in God's providential design.

This latter historiographical conception, which is often (and wrongly) taken to be not only the characterizing form of medieval historiography as a whole but a straightforward and unproblematical expression of medieval religious values, in fact runs counter to Augustinian principles. For Augustine denied not only the so-called Augustus-theology that would make of the Roman Empire an earthly *imperium* underwritten by God for special historical purposes but also the claim that *any* moment of secular history, no matter how momentous, can be understood in terms of a providential purpose.[14] As Theodor Mommsen has said, "To him history was the *operatio Dei* in time, it was 'a one-directional, teleological process, directed towards one goal—salvation,' *the salvation of individual men, not of any collective groups or organizations.*"[15] And R. A. Markus points out that "Augustine's excision of Roman history from sacred history has left not only Rome, but all historical achievement, problematic."[16]

But this Augustinian severity could withstand neither the late classical devotion to the idea of Rome nor the more general commitment to the belief that the historical life is per se significant. Augustine denied special value to either the rise or fall of Rome, but his own rigorous dismissals were being softened at the very moment they were being put in place: Orosius's *Seven Books of History Against the Pagans* was supposed to be an expression of Augustinian historical conceptions but proved in the event to foster attitudes diametrically opposed to an authentic Augustinianism. For while Orosius devalues the Roman empire by analogizing it to Babylon and by almost entirely suppressing the myth of Trojan origins in favor of the fratricidal violence of the founders Romulus and

14. For the phrase "Augustus-Theologie," see Theodor Mommsen, "Aponius and Orosius on the Significance of the Epiphany," in *Medieval and Renaissance Studies*, ed. Eugene Rice (Ithaca: Cornell University Press, 1959), 319. There was, it is true, one very brief moment, around 399–400, when Augustine entertained the possibility of an *imperium Romanum* in which divine providence and secular dominion would come together so that God's purposes might be enacted historically through the agency of an earthly foundation; see Markus, *Saeculum*, 33–37.

15. Theodor Mommsen, "St. Augustine and the Christian Idea of Progress: The Background of *The City of God*," *Medieval and Renaissance Studies*, 293; my italics. The cited phrase in Mommsen's statement is from Karl Löwith, *Meaning in History*.

16. Markus, *Saeculum*, 63.

Remus, he simultaneously accords to Rome the special status of being the bearer of God's final earthly purpose and so invests a sense of development and progress in the *translatio imperii* from Troy to Babylon, to Persia, and then to the fourth of Daniel's four empires, Rome. It is this "Christian progressivism," as Mommsen calls it, that in the last analysis drives Orosian historiography and that served to legitimize the topos of translation for medieval historians.[17] Hence it was almost to be expected that in the secularizing twelfth century, with its interest in historicizing values that had previously been regarded as atemporal absolutes, a writer like Otto of Freising would subvert Augustine's insistence on the internal and private nature of the two cities. Asserting the primacy of an institutional unity denominated "Christendom," whose existence was marked by its political formation into the significantly named Holy Roman Empire, Otto declared that historical actuality should be endowed with providential legitimacy.[18] Otto's *Geschichtstheologie* was widely shared throughout the later Middle Ages, and not only by historians: it also underwrites, perhaps by way of Joachim of Flora's prophetic history, the political vision of Dante's *Commedia*.

Troilus and Criseyde is, of course, located within the *other* tradition, the body of foundational narratives inspired precisely by what Augustine rejected—Virgil's Roman mythography and what followed from it. Throughout the Middle Ages historians constructed Trojan genealogies for the later European *imperia:* in his authoritative *Historia destructionis Troiae*, Guido delle Colonne designates first Britain (Brutus), then France (Francus), Venice (Antenor), Sicily and Tuscany (Sicanus), Naples (Aeneas), and Calabria (Diomedes) as Trojan foundations; and other claimants included the Danes and the Normans (Antenor again), Turkey (Turcus), Fiesole (Dardanus), Belgium (Bavon), the Saxons, the

17. Mommsen, "St. Augustine," and "Orosius and Augustine," in *Medieval and Renaissance Studies*, 325–48. Robert W. Hanning, *The Vision of History in Early Britain* (New York: Columbia University Press, 1966), provides a valuable account of these issues (1–43).

18. Markus, *Saeculum:* "Augustine's conception of history as the careers of two [historically] interwoven [if] eschatologically opposed cities has here become the very thing which it was designed to undermine: the theological prop of a sacral society, of a Christian political establishment in which the divine purpose in history lay enshrined" (164). For discussions of the development of an imperial ideology, with suggestions as to its relation to the topos of *translatio*, see Walter Ullmann's "Reflections on the Medieval Empire," *TRHS*, 5th ser., 14 (1964): 89–108, and "Dante's 'Monarchia' as an Illustration of a Politico-Religious 'Renovatio,' " in *Traditio-Krisis-Renovatio aus theologischer Sicht: Festschrift Winfried Zeller*, ed. Berndt Jaspert and Rudolf Mohr (Marburg: Elwert, 1976), 101–13; and Geoffrey Barraclough, *The Mediaeval Empire: Idea and Reality*, Historical Association Pamphlets, G17 (London: Historical Association, 1950).

German Emperors, and the Capetians.[19] Even at the very end of the Middle Ages the famous historian Johannes Trithemius proved the Trojan origins of the German emperor Maximilian by inventing two nonexistent scholarly sources, and it cost Polydore Virgil much labor, and obloquy, to disprove the Trojan foundation of Britain.[20] For virtually all medieval historians, Troy represented an originary moment analogous to the biblical moment of Genesis. According to Isidore of Seville, Moses is the first sacred historian and Dares the first pagan, and in most universal chronicles it is with the Troy story that pagan history enters into the controlling context of scriptural history.[21] Jean Malkaraume, for instance, goes so far as to insert the thirty thousand lines of Benoît de Sainte-Maure's *Roman de Troie* into his versification of the Bible, appropriately introducing it after Moses's Pentateuch.[22] Other writers use

19. Nathaniel Edward Griffin, ed. (Cambridge: Mediaeval Academy of America, 1936), 11–12. The claim for the Britains was originally made in the ninth century by Nennius and for the Franks in the seventh or eighth by "Fredegar." For Denmark (and the Normans), see Benoît de Sainte-Maure, *Chroniques des Ducs de Normandie*, ed. Carin Fahlin (Uppsala: Almqvist and Wiksells, 1951), 1:19–20 (lines 645–60); for Turcus, see pseudo–Vincent of Beauvais, *Speculum Historiale* 2, 66 (Douai: Bellerus, 1624), 68; for Fiesole, see the *Chronica de origine civitatis* (before 1231), discussed by Nicolai Rubinstein, "The Beginnings of Political Thought in Florence: A Study in Medieval Historiography," *JWCI* 5 (1942): 198–227. The Trojan origin of the Saxons was first promulgated by Widukind, for the Normans by Dudo of St. Quentin, for the German emperors by Ekkehard, and for the Capetians by Suger and the Monks of St. Denis: see Southern, "Aspects, I," 173–96. Lovato Lovati, a judge at Padua (1241–1309) who devoted much of his energy to the recovery of ancient texts, "also tried his hand at archaeology, and identified a skeleton which some workmen had turned up as the remains of the legendary founder of Padua, the Trojan Antenor, a gorgeous error" (L. D. Reynolds and N. G. Wilson, *Scribes and Scholars* [Oxford: Clarendon Press, 1968], 104). The *Chronicon Briocense*, a chronicle of Brittany begun in 1394, claims that the Breton language is the purest surviving form of Trojan; see Michael Jones, " 'Mon Pais et ma Nation': Breton Identity in the Fourteenth Century," in *War, Literature and Politics in the Late Middle Ages*, ed. C. T. Allmand (Liverpool: University of Liverpool Press, 1976), 145.

20. For Trithemius and the Emperor Maximilian, see Guenée, *Histoire*, 144; on Polydore Vergil, see F. J. Levy, *Tudor Historical Thought* (San Marino: Huntington Library, 1967), 63–68.

21. For Isidore, see *Etymologiae* 1, 42, 1: "Historiam autem primus apud nos Moyses de initio mundi conscripsit. Apud gentiles vero primus Dares Phrygius de Graecis et Trojanis historiam edidit" (*PL* 82:122–23). Isidore doubtless promotes Dares above Dictys because Dares was a Trojan. For the chronicles, see Karl Heinrich Krüger, *Die Universalenchroniken*, Typologie des sources du Moyen Age, fasc. 16 (Turnhout: Brepols, 1976). For a fourteenth-century English instance, see Ranulf Higden's *Polychronicon*, ed. Churchill Babington, Rolls Series (London: Longmans, 1885), 2:402–18.

22. J. R. Smeets, ed., *La Bible de Jehan Malkaraume*, 2 vols. (Assen: Gorcum, 1978). Benoît had already posited this chronology by asserting that Calchas's tent had previously belonged to the Pharaoh who was drowned in the Red Sea (Leopold Constans, ed., *Le Roman de Troie*, SATF, 6 vols. [Paris: Firmin Didot, 1904–12], lines 13819–21).

less drastic strategies of incorporation: in the *Story of England*, a translation of Langtoft's *Chronicle*, Robert Mannyng of Brunne traces the genealogy of the Trojan kings back to Noah and describes Troy as the first city built after the flood;[23] and several Troy stories prefaced their account with the Judgment of Paris in order to assimilate Eve's apple to the golden apple of Discord.[24]

As we should expect, Trojan origins provided a powerfully legitimizing tool for medieval rulers. The location of historical authority in a single source naturally appealed to a medieval monarchy interested in promoting its own role as an exclusive source of political power, and the linearity of *translatio imperii* was convenient support for hereditary dynasties and genealogical claims.[25] This was especially the case in England, where the stability of the monarchy and even the continuity of national identity (from Celts to Anglo-Saxons to Danes to Normans) was so much in question. While Geoffrey of Monmouth's political sympathies remain obscure, his narrative was quickly appropriated by the initially insecure and then imperialistic Henry II, who almost certainly sponsored Wace's translation; and it was again at Henry's court that Benoît wrote *Le Roman de Troie*, the central document of Trojan historiography for the Middle Ages and a crucial model for *Troilus and Criseyde*. Moreover, at the end of Henry's reign Joseph of Exeter composed his *Bellum Troianum*, a text that perhaps provided Chaucer with one of the most powerful and enigmatic moments of his own poem.[26] But the

23.   Robert Mannyng of Brunne, *The Story of England*, ed. F. J. Furnivall, Rolls Series (London: Longmans, 1887), 1:15–16. The same genealogy is given in one of the manuscripts of the so-called *Histoire ancienne jusqu'à César;* see Paul Meyer, "Les premières compilations françaises d'histoire ancienne," *Romania* 14 (1885), 68.

24.   Two instances are the *Libro de Alexandre* and the *Ovide moralisé;* see E. Bagby Atwood, "The *Excidium Troiae* and Medieval Troy Literature," *MP* 35 (1937–38), 125. See in general, Margaret J. Ehrhart, *The Judgment of the Trojan Prince Paris in Medieval Literature* (Philadelphia: University of Pennsylvania Press, 1987).

25.   For the centrality of lineage in medieval thought, see R. Howard Bloch, *Etymologies and Genealogies: A Literary Anthropology of the French Middle Ages* (Chicago: University of Chicago Press, 1983); Gabrielle M. Spiegel, "Genealogy: Form and Function in Medieval Historical Narrative," *History and Theory* 22 (1983): 43–53; and for a literary-philosophical insight, Patricia Drechsel Tobin, *Time and the Novel* (Princeton: Princeton University Press, 1978): "By an analogy of function, events in time come to be perceived as begetting other events within a line of causality similar to the line of generations, with the prior event earning a special prestige as it is seen to originate, control, and predict future events. When in some such manner ontological priority is conferred upon mere temporal anteriority, the historical consciousness is born, and time is understood as a linear manifestation of the genealogical destiny of events" (7–8).

26.   On Henry II as a patron, see Walter F. Schirmer and Ulrich Broich, *Studien zum literarischen Patronat im England des 12. Jahrhunderts* (Cologne: Westdeutscher Verlag,

invocation of Trojan origins was not confined to England: in 1204 Pierre de Bracheux tried to justify the unjustifiable Latin conquest of Byzantium by claiming that since the Franks were descendants of the Trojans they were now reconquering territory the Greeks had wrongfully seized some two thousand years before.[27]

The power of Trojan precedents was still in force in late medieval England. Not only did Trojan historiography continue to interest royal and noble families—Edward II's Queen Isabelle owned a volume called *De bello troiano*, and Humphrey of Bohun, Earl of Hereford (d. 1322), named his youngest son Eneas—but it appears in some unexpected contexts.[28] One of the charges laid against Nicholas Brembre by his opponents in 1386 was that he wanted to change the name of London to *Parva Troia* and have himself styled duke of Troy—in effect, an accusation of harboring royalist ambitions.[29] On the other side, during Richard II's elaborate tournament at Smithfield in October 1390—for which Chaucer as clerk of the king's works supervised the building of the scaffolds—London was referred to as "la neufe troy."[30] Not surprisingly, the usurping Lancastrians appropriated Trojanness: Bolingbroke's son, the future Henry V, commissioned Lydgate's *Troy Book* as well as a personal manuscript of *Troilus and Criseyde*.[31] And on the other side of the channel, the aspiring dukes of Burgundy were avid collec-

---

1962), 27–203; Diana B. Tyson, "Patronage of French Vernacular History Writers in the Twelfth and Thirteenth Centuries," *Romania* 100 (1979): 180–222, 584; and Reto R. Bezzola, *Les Origines et la formation de la littérature courtoise en Occident, 500–1200*, vol. 3, pt. 1 (Paris: Champion, 1963). I have provided a more detailed account of both the specific question of Henry's historiographical interests, Arthurian and Norman as well as Trojan, and of the ideological function of the *Gründungsagen* in general, in *Negotiating the Past: The Historical Understanding of Medieval Literature* (Madison: University of Wisconsin Press, 1987), 199–210.

27. Robert de Clari, *La conquête de Constantinople*, ed. Philippe Lauer (Paris: Champion, 1924), 102.

28. For Isabelle's book, see Juliet Vale, *Edward III and Chivalry: Chivalric Society and Its Context, 1270–1350* (Woodbridge: Boydell Press, 1982), 50; for Eneas de Bohun, see John Barnie, *War in Medieval English Society: Social Values and the Hundred Years War* (London: Weidenfeld and Nicolson, 1974), 101.

29. John P. McCall and George Rudisill, Jr., "The Parliament of 1386 and Chaucer's Trojan Parliament," *JEGP* 58 (1959), 284 n. 25.

30. The proclamation or Crie des Joustes for the tournament is printed in F. H. Cripps-Day, *The History of the Tournament in England* (London: Quaritch, 1918), xli–xlii; see Sheila Lindenbaum, "The Smithfield Tournament of 1390," *JMRS* 20 (1990): 1–20. See also Juliet R. V. Barker, *The Tournament in England, 1100–1400* (Woodbridge: Boydell, 1986), 100.

31. The Campsell manuscript, described by R. K. Root, *The Textual Tradition of Chaucer's Troilus*, Chaucer Society, 1st ser., 99 (London: Kegan Paul, Trench, Trübner, 1916), 5.

tors of Trojan materials. Philippe le Bon owned seventeen manuscripts dealing with Troy, two of which may even have been copies of the *Troilus*, and he also commissioned Raoul Lefèvre's *Recueil* and founded the Order of the Golden Fleece, which took as its exemplary chivalric event the voyage of the Argonaut that stood, in many Trojan histories, as the initiating event of the war.[32] So too, in Italy the library of the ambitious Visconti contained no less than four manuscripts of Guido delle Colonne's *Historia destructionis Troiae* and six other "Troy books."[33] Substantial and specific political value was thus invested in the idea of Trojan origins—a fact that gives the literary initiative undertaken by Chaucer, who remained loyal to his beleaguered monarch throughout the factional 1380s, an inevitably political dimension.

The invocation of Troy assumes that a legitimizing power is located within the processes of secular history itself, that earthly foundations can find authorization within the scope of their own historical existence, with no necessary recourse to a transcendental realm of value. That these powerful interests ran counter to medieval spiritualism was occasionally made explicit. In 1153 Hugh of Fouilloy attacked bishops who adorned the walls of their palaces with pictures of Trojans rather than giving their riches to the poor: his concern was with not only episcopal charity but the intrusion of secular historiography into the ecclesiastical world.[34] And in his *Scalacronica*, written in the 1350s and 1360s, Sir Thomas Gray began with a vision of the ladder of history resting upon two books, the Bible and "la gest de Troy." But once having established this familiar equivalence, Sir Thomas hastily revised it: according to the Sibyl who is his guide, "veiez cy sen et foly, le primer livre la

---

32. Alphonse Bayot, "La légende de Troie à la cour de Bourgogne," *Société d'Emulation de Bruges, Mélanges* 1 (Bruges: de Plancke, 1908); Muriel J. Hughes, "The Library of Philip the Bold and Margaret of Flanders, First Valois Duke and Duchess of Burgundy," *JMH* 4 (1978): 145–88; for the Burgundian ownership of a manuscript of the *Troilus*, see Eleanor Hammond, "A Burgundian Copy of Chaucer's *Troilus*," *MLN* 26 (1911): 32. See also André Bossuat, "Les origines troyennes: leur rôle dans la littérature historique au xve siècle," *Annales de Normandie* 45 (1963): 91–118.

33. R. A. Pratt, "Chaucer and the Visconti Libraries," *ELH* 6 (1939), 195. For the Trojan story in other aristocratic libraries in the later Middle Ages, see Pierre Champion, *La Librairie de Charles d'Orléans* (Paris: Champion, 1910), 40–41; S. Edmunds, "The Library of Savoy: Documents," *Scriptorium* 24 (1970): 318–27; 25 (1971): 253–84; 26 (1972): 269–93 (especially items number 106 and 148); and Margaret Kekewich, "Edward IV, William Caxton, and Literary Patronage in Yorkist England," *MLR* 66 (1971): 481–87.

34. Antoine Thomas, "Le *De claustro anime* et le *Roman de Troie*," *Romania* 42 (1913): 83–85. I am indebted to Prof. David Jacoby for this reference, who accepts the ascription of this work to Hugh of Fouilloy (Thomas, following Migne, ascribes it to Hugh of St. Victor).

bible, le secounde la gest de Troy."[35] Similarly, in the *Miroir de mariage*, Eustache Deschamps says that he will rest his argument

> En saincte Escripture esprouvée,
> Non pas en histoire trouvée
> D'Erculès ou des Troïens.[36]

More centrally, the founding text of English legendary history— Geoffrey of Monmouth's *Historia regum Britanniae* (c. 1136)—was by implication and design antiecclesiastical. In about 1200 the monastic historian William of Newburgh unfavorably compared Geoffrey's work with its theologically orthodox predecessor, Bede's *Historia ecclesiastica gentis Anglorum*. The point for William was not simply that "our Bede, . . . of whose wisdom and integrity none can doubt," was truthful whereas Geoffrey told lies, but that Geoffrey's narrative substituted for ecclesiastical history (in which the crucial event was the conversion of the *gens Anglorum*) a purely secular history centered on the rise and fall of the *reges Britanniae* and both climaxed and encapsulated by the career of Arthur.[37] Hence, William pointed out, Geoffrey allowed Arthur's exploits to preempt the central event of Bede's *Historia*, the conversionary moment of the arrival of St. Augustine in England. In Geoffrey's account the conversion of the British passes virtually unnoticed, and Bede's Ethelberht, who "embraced the easy yoke of Christ at the preaching of Augustine," is displaced by the fraudulent hero Arthur. In sum, the history that Geoffrey traces is governed not by a Christian providence but by a *translatio imperii* whose shape was first sketched not in Eusebius's *Historia ecclesiastica* (Bede's mastertext) but in Virgil's *Aeneid;* and the fatality that brings down the Arthurian empire locates causality at the level not of divine superintendance but human action.

35. Ed. Joseph Stevenson (Edinburgh: Maitland Club, 1836), 2. For this text, see Beryl Smalley, *English Friars and Antiquity in the Early Fourteenth Century* (Oxford: Basil Blackwell, 1960), 13–14; Derek Pearsall, *John Lydgate* (London: Routledge and Kegan Paul, 1970), 122; M. D. Legge, *Anglo-Norman Literature and Its Background* (Oxford: Clarendon Press, 1963), 283–87; and especially Antonia Gransden, *Historical Writing in England II: c. 1307 to the Early Sixteenth Century* (London: Routledge and Kegan Paul, 1982), 92–96.

36. Eustache Deschamps, *Le Miroir de mariage*, lines 9101–4, in Le Marquis de Queux de Saint-Hilaire, ed., *Oeuvres complètes d'Eustache Deschamps*, SATF, vol. 9 (Paris: Firmin Didot, 1880).

37. Joseph Stevenson, trans., *The Church Historians of England*, vol. 4, part 2 (Glasgow: Seeleys, 1856), 399, 401. William's *Historia rerum Anglicarum* is edited in the Rolls Series by Richard Howlett, *Chronicles of the Reigns of Stephen, Henry II, and Richard I*, vols. 1–2 (London: Longmans, 1884–85). For this citation, see the Proemium, in which William characterizes Bede as "de cujus sapientia et sinceritate dubitare fas non est" (1:18).

The secular and causal historiography articulated by Geoffrey's *Historia* began to flourish in the twelfth century and continued to develop in many forms.[38] To be sure, only in *quattrocento* Italy did there emerge a fully and confidently humanist historiography that sought to explain "the inner workings of historical phenomena and particularly of political institutions" by reference to "psychological elements."[39] But it was the legendary histories and the romances of the Middle Ages that served in the interim to protect this humanist interest against the effacement of historically specific secondary causes entailed by religious imperatives. With their focus upon the nature of the self and its relation to its society, and their freedom from the necessarily limiting plot ordained by Christian history, these ubiquitous narratives provided the environment in which events could begin to be understood in human terms. At the center of the narrated action is a human agent who does not merely react to events but also creates them: in the world of romance, history is less given than made. And the linearity of romance narrative, as distinct from that of ecclesiastical history, implies a causality that is, however obscured by enigma or thwarted by chance, finally grounded in the human will. As we shall see, Trojan historiography provided a particularly focused opportunity for this kind of historiographical interest, and the efflorescence of Trojan writings, first in the twelfth and then in the fourteenth centuries, corresponds to the analogous flourishing of various forms of secular and causal historiography.[40]

There was, however, a philosophical problem inherent in this new secular history, a problem raised by precisely that principle of continuity expressed in the idea of *translatio imperii*. This was the problem of repetition. In the *City of God* Augustine cited the Psalmist's phrase, "the ungodly will walk in a circle," in order to attack pagan theorists of history who believe in the idea of temporal recurrence. The phrase is relevant, he says, "not because their life is going to come round again in the

38.   The secularization of twelfth-century historiography is a commonly observed phenomenon; see, for example, Ullmann, *Medieval Foundations*, 61–67. On the "historicization" of culture generally in the twelfth century, see Chenu, *Nature, Man, and Society*, 162–201.

39.   Donald J. Wilcox, *The Development of Florentine Humanist Historiography in the Fifteenth Century* (Cambridge: Harvard University Press, 1969), 45.

40.   The dominance of secular modes of understanding in later medieval historiography is shown by the virtual disappearance of the monastic chronicle, with its insistence upon the random nature of historical events relieved only by an occasional invocation of providential intervention, and its replacement by the aristocratic history, with its location of the motive force of history in the human will and its concern to provide causal explanations for events; see Bernard Guenée, "Histoires, annales, chroniques: essai sur les genres historiques au moyen âge," *Annales* 28 (1973), 1007.

course of those revolutions which they believe in, but because the way of their error, the way of false doctrine, goes round in circles." These pagan philosophers are wandering in "a circuitous maze, finding neither entrance nor exit, for they do not know how the human race, and this mortal condition of ours, first started, nor with what end it will be brought to a close."[41] Contrasting the unidirectional linearity of Christian history, firmly anchored by the biblical paradigm of an initiatory Genesis and a conclusive Revelation, with the Platonic circularities of eternal return, Augustine's faith in a God who transcends and encompasses history offered itself as an antidote to the pagan entrapment within the historical cycle itself. Yet he also articulated the condition of all men living in the Sixth Age, whose historical life bears a meaning that remains resolutely unavailable to them and for whom the translations of secular history articulate a meaningless pattern of ceaseless rise and fall. The only significant history is that lived within the church (i.e, ecclesiastical history) since it is Fortune's turning wheel that controls the dynastic world. And as Origen's history implied, each successive empire articulates the same pattern: as Troy, so Babylon, so Persia, so Rome—and so on until the empty recursions of history have been finally brought to a definitive end.

This specter haunts the romances and the legendary histories, for which heredity is both the basis of legitimacy and the cause of failure. Troy is the original city, the *Parva Troia* or Troynovaunt of London heir to its glory.[42] Yet as Gower hysterically insists in the first book of the *Vox clamantis*, just as Troy was brought down by internal dissension so will London collapse into the chaos of the Rising of 1381.[43] A purposive

41. Henry Bettenson, trans. (Harmondsworth: Penguin Books, 1972), 488–89. "*In circuitu impii ambulabunt* [Psalm 11:9]; non quia per circulos, quos opinantur, eorum vita est recursura, sed quia modo talis est erroris eorum via, id est falsa doctrina. Quid autem mirum est, si in his circuitibus errantes nec aditum nec exitum inveniunt? quia genus humanum atque ista nostra mortalitas nec quo initio coepta sit sciunt, nec quo fine claudatur" (Bernhard Dombart, ed. [Leipzig: Teubner, 1909], 12, 14–15). Momigliano shows that the idea that pagan historians posited a circular pattern for historical time is derived not from classical histories themselves but from polemical Christian misrepresentations (Momigliano, *Essays in Ancient and Modern Historiography*, 179–204).

42. See John Clark, "Trinovantum—The Evolution of a Legend," *JMH* 7 (1981): 135–51. A text written in the same place and at the same time as the *Troilus* (London in the second half of the 1380s) that also stresses the continuity between the contemporary city and its Trojan origins is *St. Erkenwald*. For a suggestive discussion, see Gordon Whately, "Heathens and Saints: *St. Erkenwald* in its Legendary Context," *Speculum* 61 (1986): 330–63.

43. The following passage from 1, 13 is not untypical: "The Trojan victory was lost in defeat, and Troy became a prey to the wild beast, just like a lamb to the wolf. The peasant

linearity cannot maintain itself, and the historical process gives way to reveal an underlying recursiveness, a circularity that calls into question all merely historical beginnings and endings. *Troilus and Criseyde* represents, I believe, Chaucer's investigation of this central dilemma of the medieval historical consciousness. And he makes his point by extending the line of descent backwards, by showing the specular resemblance that exists between the events of Trojan history and those that took place earlier, at Thebes. If this resemblance is deeply troubling, it followed that the later connections forged by medieval historians between Troy and their own societies must be ridden by the same disastrous determinism.

In choosing Thebes as his starting point, Chaucer was somewhat eccentric. That Theban history preceded Trojan was of course known to the Middle Ages, but Thebes never attained the same historiographical status.[44] For one thing, it lacked the Virgilian mythography that served to define Troy as the originary moment; and for another it was known to the Middle Ages primarily through a variety of literary sources that lacked the historical authority that Dares' and Dictys' "eyewitness" accounts could claim. Indeed, the Thebes story functioned in medieval historiography primarily as a prefiguration of Troy: it is significant, for instance, that the *Roman de Thèbes*, in both its original, versified forms and in its prose *remainiements*, always appears in the manuscripts only within the context of ancient history and almost always as linked specifically to Troy, while the Troy story often stands on its own or as the initiatory movement from Troy to Rome and so to the modern world.[45]

---

attacked and the knight in the city did not resist; Troy was without a Hector, Argos without its Achilles. No boldness of a Hector or Troilus defeated anything then, but instead those who were defeated suffered the whole affair without courage. Priam did not shine then with his usual honor; instead, the master put up with whatever the servant did to him. Even Hecuba's chambers could scarcely remain undisturbed, without suffering agitating [sic] the faint hearts within them. Nor indeed could Ilion then defend from the madmen the man enclosed within its lofty towers" (Eric W. Stockton, trans., *The Major Latin Works of John Gower* [Seattle: University of Washington Press, 1962], 71–72).

44.   For example, the early thirteenth-century compilation called by scholars the *Histoire ancienne jusqu'à César* is divided into seven parts: Genesis; the founding of the kingdoms of Assyria, Egypt, and Greece; the early days of Assyria and Greece; Theban history; the stories of the Minotaur, Amazons, and Hercules; Trojan history; and the founding of Rome (Meyer, "Les premières compilations," 1–81).

45.   On the manuscripts of the *Roman de Thèbes*, see Giovanna Angeli, *L' "Eneas" e i primi romanzi volgari* (Milan: Ricciardi, 1971), 60 n. 1; on the prose *remaniements*, see Brian Woledge, *Bibliographie des romans et nouvelles en prose française antérieurs à 1500* (Geneva: Droz, 1975), 120–21. Of the twenty-eight (more or less) complete manuscripts of the *Roman de Troie*, sixteen present the *Roman* alone, while only two precede it with the *Roman*

But Chaucer seems to have intuited what it was about Theban history that might well have caused its strategic marginalization: he shows that the Trojan origin, and all historical origins, are undone by a subtext that repudiates the very idea of originality.

II: *The Wicker Cage of History in* The House of Fame

Before turning to his reading of the Troy story in terms of the Theban legends, more needs to be said about Chaucer's early explorations in history writing. In this respect, the *House of Fame* is a pertinent introduction, not least because its concern is historiographical in the strict sense, focusing on both history as a subject and historical writing as a procedure.[46] It may well have been written with the *Troilus* in mind. Both its concern with the grounds of historical writing (the Dido-Aeneas story in Book 1, the primarily historical poets in the House of Fame in Book 3) and its specific reference to Lollius as a Trojan author (1468) point forward to the *Troilus*. The two poems match in another way as well: the *House of Fame* concludes with the promised but unfulfilled appearance of "a man of gret auctorite" (2158), while the *Troilus* begins by invoking but then setting aside "a lord of gret auctorite" (1, 65), Calkas.

In *Histoire et la culture historique*, Bernard Guenée describes how in the Middle Ages historical texts become authoritative by being approved by an authority: "To be truly worthy of belief, an historical work had to be authenticated and approved by a public authority."[47] In other words, historical authenticity derives from "a man of gret auctorite" whose authority is itself supported by historically authentic texts. The *House of Fame* stages just this circularity. In his *Historia adversum paganos*, Orosius argued that pre-Christian history reveals only a circulation of calamity, a process that Orosius represents by the telling metaphor of basket weaving:

---

de Thèbes; in five manuscripts it is followed by the *Roman d'Eneas.* The manuscripts are described by Constans, *Le Roman de Troie,* 6:1–105. See also the *Excidium Troiae,* which provides a version of the Troy story, then a prose *Aeneid,* and finally a history of Rome to Augustus (E. Bagby Atwood and Virgil K. Whitaker, eds. [Cambridge: Mediaeval Academy of America, 1944]). A similar text is the *Compendium historiae Troianae-Romanae,* H. Simonsfeld, ed., *Neues Archiv der Gesellschaft für ältere deutsche Geschichtskunde* 11 (1886): 241–51.

46. See John M. Fyler, *Chaucer and Ovid* (New Haven: Yale University Press, 1979), 23–64.

47. Guenée, *Histoire:* "Pour être vraiment digne de foi, une oeuvre historique doit être authentique et approuvée par une autorité publique" (137).

I have woven together strands of unrelated events into a historical wickerwork that cannot be unraveled [*inextricabilem cratem*], and following the evidence closely, I have worked in a description of the uncertain cycles of wars waged here and there with uncontrolled fury. I could do this because, as I see it, the more I retained the order of events, the more was my account without order. Who can arrange either by number, chronology, or logic the disturbances springing from every kind of hatred?[48]

Further, Orosius describes Greek legendary history, and specifically the Theban stories, as "inextricable recursions of alternating evils" (*inextricabiles alternantium malorum recursus* [1, 21]) equivalent to the "inextricable wars of the East, which rarely ever begin or end without crimes."[49] And the Orosian metaphor is repeated in Ranulf Higden's statement in his *Polychronicon* that the historian's materials are a "Daedalini labyrinthus, inextricabilis intricationis," which in Trevisa's fourteenth-century translation reads "laborintus, Dedalus hous."[50]

It is striking, then, to observe that Chaucer's procedure in the *House of Fame* is to stage the fruitless waiting for the "man of gret auctorite" in a House of Tydynges that is compared to "Domus Dedaly, / That Laboryntus cleped ys" (1920–21) and subsequently described as a "cage" (1938, 1985) "mad of twigges" (1936). Whether or not Chaucer's House of Tydyngs finds its textual source in Orosius's *Historiae*—and certainly Orosius's *inextricabilem cratem* intriguingly prefigures Chaucer's wickerwork—the metaphor of labyrinthine interweaving does invoke a recursive secular history. The wicker cage in which the eagle deposits Geoffrey is this insubstantial but inescapable historical world, a world that from the inside is stable and promises authoritative knowledge but that from the outside is seen to whirl about precariously and to be founded upon nothing but Aventure

48. Irving Woodworth Raymond, trans. (New York: Columbia University Press, 1936), 114. "Contexui indigestae historiae *inextricabilem cratem* atque incertos bellorum orbes huc et illuc lymphatico furore gestorum verbis et vestigio secutus inplicui, quoniam tanto, ut video, inordinatius scripsi, quanto magis ordinem custodivi" (Karl Zangemeister, ed., *Historiarum adversum paganos libri septem*, 3,2 [Leipzig: Teubner, 1889], 68).

49. ". . . Orientis illa inextricabilia bella . . . , quae raro umquam nisi sceleribus aut incipiunt aut terminantur" (ibid., 5,–4; 148).

50. "Cujus negotii, velut Daedalini labyrinthi, inextricabilem attendens intricationem, rogata sum veritus attemptare" (Babington, ed., *Polychronicon*, 1, 1, 7 [1:8]). In Trevisa's fourteenth-century English translation the passage reads: "Þoo toke I hede þat þis matir, as laborintus, Dedalus hous, haþ many halkes and hurnes, wonderful weies, wyndynges and wrynkelynges, þat wil nouȝt be vnwarled, me schamed and dradde to fynde so grete and so gostliche a bone to graunte" (ibid., 1:9).

(1982). The history represented by the House of Tydyngs is, moreover, history verbalized, the history of the historian, for whom events necessarily exist only as language. In the House of Tydyngs Geoffrey witnesses the creation of the historical record through vocalization: the inhabitants "rouned everych in others ere" (2044) until they produced a tiding that then escaped into the world to become a reality. The referential model on which historiography is traditionally founded (*historia est narratio rerum gestae*, to cite Isidore's authoritative definition) is subverted by this genesis: words do not refer to but constitute the events they purport to describe.[51] The House of Tydyngs is thus the labyrinth not only of history but of the writing of history, and in it the Chaucerian quester after historical truth discovers that the *res gestae* he seeks to recover are not merely hidden or distorted by the process by which they are mediated in their *translatio* from past to present (the truth offered in the House of Fame proper) but that they are actually *constructed* by that process. The labyrinth of historical writing is an unfounded and ceaseless process of mediation, a *translatio* of nothing but itself.

In focusing on the Derridean question of "arche-writing," the *House of Fame* articulates a problem central to medieval literary culture as a whole. The governing assumption of the verbal training of the Middle Ages was that the same thing can be said in different words: the *res*— the referent that underwrites all verbal expression—can be expressed in an infinite number of different *verba* and yet remain always the same. The task of the medieval writer was not to invent new matter—hence the withering away of *inventio* in both late classical and medieval rhetorical theory—but to rewrite the original, the authoritative text bequeathed to the present by the past.[52] This rewriting is an amplification (or, less commonly, abbreviation) to be accomplished by recourse to the tropes catalogued by the rhetorical handbooks. These tropes are, as Geoffrey of Vinsauf put it, "of one general class, distinguished by the figurative [*improprius*] status of the words and the uncommon meaning [*peregrina sumptio*] assigned them."[53] In sum, it is through the applica-

51. For Isidore's definition, see *Etymologiae*, 1, 41, 1 (*PL* 82:122).

52. The medieval disappearance of *inventio* can be illustrated both by its absence from rhetorical and poetic handbooks and by the fate of the classical *topoi*, which were degraded from devices by which arguments could be discovered into clichéd set pieces to be inserted into a discourse at the proper moment (Richard McKeon, "Rhetoric in the Middle Ages," in *Critics and Criticism*, ed. R. S. Crane [Chicago: University of Chicago Press, 1952], 291–92).

53. *Poetria nova*, trans. Margaret F. Nims (Toronto: Pontifical Institute of Medieval Studies, 1967), 50. For the original, see Edmond Faral, *Les arts poétiques du XIIᵉ et du XIIIᵉ*

tion of figures—*translationes*—that the *auctoritas* of the past can be translated into the present.[54]

The success of this process of historical transmission depends on the transparency of the mediating agency: the *res* of the original must remain unchanged by the new *verba* into which it is rewritten. But as modern criticism has insisted, and as the Middle Ages well knew, figuration is never innocent.[55] Figuration is the transfer of a word from its proper use to an improper one (hence *translatio*): says Curtius, "an old school example is *pratum ridet*, 'the meadow laughs.' Human laughter is 'transferred' to nature."[56] According to Geoffrey, the translated word should "avoid its natural location, travel about elsewhere [*loca propria vitet / et peregrinetur alibi*], and take up a pleasant abode on the estate of another."[57] But such wandering away from the proper always runs the risk of an illicit, even promiscuous vagrancy, and hence rhetoricians insist on the restraint that must be applied to figuration. "In using figurative lan-

siècle (Paris: Champion, 1924), 227: "Genus omnibus unum: / Scilicet improprius vocum status et peregrina / Sumptio verborum" (962–64). In his *De schematibus et tropis*, Bede defines a trope as "a figure in which a word, either from need or for the purpose of embellishment, is shifted from its proper meaning to one similar but not proper to it." Metaphor is therefore defined as "a transference of qualities and words,"—as, that is, not simply one kind of trope or *figura sententiarum* but rather as, in effect, tropism itself. Bede's text is translated by Gussie Hecht Tannenbaum in *Quarterly Journal of Speech* 48 (1962): 237–53; reprinted in Joseph M. Miller, Michael H. Prosser, and Thomas W. Benson, eds., *Readings in Medieval Rhetoric* (Bloomington: Indiana University Press, 1973), 96–122; for these citations, see 106. For the original, see *Opera*, Pars I: *Opera Didascalica*, ed. C. W. Jones (Turnhout: Brepols, 1975), 151–52. This use of *translatio* (or, in Greek, *metaphora*) as a term for figurative language per se goes back to Aristotle's *Rhetoric*: "two classes of terms, the proper or the regular and the metaphorical—these and no others— are used by everybody in conversation" (1404ᵇ; trans. W. Rhys Roberts [New York: Random House, 1954], 168).

54. Douglas Kelly, "*Translatio Studii*: Translation, Adaptation, and Allegory in Medieval French Literature," *PQ* 57 (1978): 287–310.

55. For a more benign reading of medieval metaphor than that which I shall offer here, see Judson Boyce Allen, *The Ethical Poetic of the Middle Ages* (Toronto: University of Toronto Press, 1982), 198–206. Allen argues that medieval metaphorizing was underwritten by a belief in the *convenientia* of a divinely ordained universe.

56. E. R. Curtius, *European Literature and the Latin Middle Ages*, trans. Willard R. Trask (New York: Harper & Row, 1963), 128.

57. De Vinsauf, *Poetria nova*, tr. Nims, 43.
Noli semper concedere verbo
In proprio residere loco: residentia talis
Dedecus est ipsi verbo; loca propria vitet
Et peregrinetur alibi sedemque placentem
Fundet in alterius fundo: sit ibi novus hospes
Et placeat novitate sua.
Faral, *Les arts poétiques*, 220–21, lines 758–63.

guage," says Cicero, "comparisons should seek out strangeness modestly [*verecunde*]," and the *Ad Herennium* cautions that "figurative language ought to be shamefast [*pudentum*], so as to transfer reasonably to a similar thing and not seem to rush indiscriminately, boldly and eagerly [*sine dilectu temere et cupide*] across to a dissimilar thing."[58] For Geoffrey, the transfer must also be to likeness [*similis*] and accomplished decorously [*decenter*], and he sums up his discussion by simultaneously assuring and cautioning his reader that "if you heed the directives carefully and suit words to content [*rebus verba*], you will speak with precise appropriateness [*proprie*]."[59] And according to Alberic of Monte Cassino, in his influential *Flores rhetorici,*

> *translatio* turns one's attention from the particular qualities of the object; somehow, by this distraction of attention, it makes the object seem something different. . . . If a meal were served up in this way, it would disgust us, would nauseate us, would be thrown out. . . . [Hence], build up your vigilance with great care, so that you may watch over, protect, defend your own property, both in thought and deed.[60]

The threat to the proper is a threat to those very truths that the process of rewriting seeks to transmit. The continuity of literary transferral is undone by the wandering of the mediatory figures by which the transferral is to be accomplished. Just as within the economy of the individual text figuration serves to frustrate the unfolding of the narrative line, so in the larger economy of literary history does it invert the linearity that connects the writer to his original into a periphrastic circumlocution. And insofar as *translatio* is not merely the central but the only form of literary activity, the act of interpretation is similarly ceaseless. When Eustache Deschamps described Chaucer as a "grant translateur" he was thinking of him as a poet of Troy and hence as an agent of the *translatio studii* that is the literary corollary to the translation of empire: that is why his ballade designates England as "le regne d'Eneas" and "l'isle aux Geans—ceuls de Bruth."[61] Moreover, he understood that Chaucer's task in fulfilling this role was to instruct those

58. Cicero, *De optimo genere oratorum,* 2, 4; *Ad Herennium,* 4, 34, 45.

59. De Vinsauf, *Poetria nova,* tr. Nims, 82; and see Nims's note, 108, on the importance of *proprietas* to Geoffrey both here and in the *Documentum.*

60. Translated by Joseph M. Miller in Miller, Prosser, and Benson, *Readings in Medieval Rhetoric,* 146–48. For the original, see D. Mauro Inguanez and H. M. Willard, eds., *Alberici Casinensis Flores Rhetorici* (Monte Cassino: Miscellanea Cassinese, 1938), 31–59.

61. For the text of the ballade, see Deschamps, *Oeuvres complètes,* 2:138–39.

who were "ignorans de la langue Pandras" (ignorant of the language of Pandarus).[62] This is the language of mediation—the language of the go-between or, to give him his Latin title, the *interpres*—that Chaucer must negotiate in rewriting the story of Troilus and Criseyde. At once defined by difference and itself differing from the originary moment it seeks to represent, the medium of representation—"la langue de Pandras"—is thus inscribed with both the reason for its aspiration and the inevitability of its failure.

III: History versus Romance

There is, it must be acknowledged at the outset, something inherently paradoxical about either a historiographical or a historical reading of *Troilus and Criseyde*. For the action of the poem seems conspicuously, even aggressively, to resist the attention to either its Trojan or its contemporary context that would encourage us to regard history as its ultimate reference. The poet defines his project at the outset in entirely amorous terms: he addresses his bidding prayer to "ye loveres, that bathen in gladnesse" (1, 22), defines his subject as "swich peyne and wo as Loves folk endure" (1, 34), and calls himself "the sorwful instrument, / That helpeth loveres, *as I kan*, to pleyne" (1, 10–11). And he shortly issues a polemical statement explicitly disclaiming any historical interest:

> But how this town com to destruccion
> Ne falleth naught to purpos me to telle;
> For it were a long digression
> Fro my matere, and yow to long to dwelle.
> But the Troian gestes, as they felle,
> In Omer, or in Dares, or in Dite,
> *Whoso that kan* may rede hem as they write. (1, 141–47)[63]

---

62. That Deschamps is referring here to Pandarus is ably argued by Gretchen Mieszkowski, "'Pandras' in Deschamps' Ballade for Chaucer," *ChR* 9 (1974–75): 327–36.

63. "Whoso that kan:" while this gently qualifying phrase seems in the first instance directed to those without Latin, since Homer was unavailable to virtually *every* medieval reader Chaucer begins by invoking one of the original accounts of the Trojan War only to remind us of its absence. The phrase, and the preceding "as I kan" of 1, 11, also echos the opening "if I kan" of the *House of Fame* ("I wol now synge, if I kan, / The armes and also the man" [143–44]), a phrase that simultaneously marks the difference between the medieval minstrel and the classical poet and registers, in John Fyler's words, "the uncertain ability of art to be true to the facts," especially when—as in the case of the Dido-Aeneas episode—those facts are notoriously in dispute (Fyler, *Chaucer and Ovid*, 33; see A. C.

This disclaimer is then matched at the end of the poem by an analogous stanza that justifies the poet's lack of interest in the martial deeds that comprise the public record:

> And if I hadde ytaken for to write
> The armes of this ilke worthi man,
> Than wolde ich of his batailles endite;
> But for that I to writen first bigan
> Of his love, I have seyd *as I kan,*—
> His worthi dedes, whoso list hem heere,
> Rede Dares, he kan telle hem alle ifeere. (5, 1765–71)

Having initially defined his project in wholly amorous terms, the narrator feels justified in referring us elsewhere for historical details that are, for him, simply distractions from the matter at hand.

But before assuming that the narrator's dehistoricizing of the Troy story represents a straightforward Chaucerian initiative, we should take note of two other textual facts. One is that in subordinating the historical world of events to the inner world of erotic action the narrator's behavior imitates that of his protagonists, thus following a program that we know better than to regard as exemplary. When Troilus first falls in love, "Alle other dredes weren from him fledde, / Both of th'assege and his savacioun" (1, 463–64). This does not mean, however, that he abandons his martial duties. As soon as Pandarus leaves Troilus at the end of Book 1, Chaucer adds a passage to the *Filostrato* to tell us that

> Troilus lay tho no lenger down,
> But up anon upon his stede bay,
> And in the feld he pleyde tho leoun;
> Wo was that Grek that with hym meete a-day! (1, 1072–75)

And this martial prowess continues even during the height of the love affair:

> In alle nedes for the townes werre,
> He was, and ay, the first in armes dyght

Spearing, *Medieval to Renaissance in English Poetry* [Cambridge: Cambridge University Press, 1985], 22 n. 18). Moreover, the phrases prefigure the nervous "I have seyd as I kan" with which the poem concludes; see the next citation in the text.

And certeynly, but if that bokes erre,
Save Ector most ydred of any wight;
And this encrees of hardynesse and myght
Com hym of love, his ladies thank to wynne,
That altered his spirit so withinne. (3, 1772–78)

"Bokes"—the "Troian gestes" of Homer, Dares, and Dictys are doubt-less meant—testify to Troilus's bravery, and the narrator here explains its inner meaning. A matching phrase later locates in the *records* of hero-ism ("As men may in thise olde bokes rede" [5, 1753]) the fact that Troilus continues his martial ferocity after Criseyde's departure, though now motivated by rage and jealousy. Inspired first by love and then by hate, Troilus enacts throughout the narrative a heroism that is admirable (historically worthy of record) because it both testifies to the intensity of his amorous feelings and shows him fulfilling his role as an *alter Hector*—"and next his brother, holder up of Troye" (2, 644).

In effect, then, the narrator manages to provide for the "Troian gestes" a rich texture of private motivation and psychological depth without ignoring their significance as history. He thereby protects his story from the simplistic moralization that characterizes so much medi-eval historiography—and too much modern criticism.[64] The problem with moralizing Trojan history, whether Chaucer's or those of Benoît and Guido, is not that it is wrong, in the sense that it ignores another, more obviously correct understanding, but that categorical moral judg-

64. In "The Trojan Scene in Chaucer's *Troilus*," *ELH* 29 (1962), John P. McCall as-cribes the fall of the city to "the criminal lust of Troy" (263 n. 3), claiming that this interpre-tation is common in "the medieval encyclopedic tradition" (264 n. 4). This may well be so, but it is almost entirely absent from historiographical accounts, including those of Benoît de Sainte-Maure, Joseph of Exeter, Guido delle Colonne, and the various prose histories (e.g., *L'Histoire ancienne jusqu'à César*), the primary means by which classical history was transmitted to the medieval aristocratic world within which Chaucer wrote. Modern readings of the poem in these terms are offered by such diverse critics as D. W. Robert-son, Jr., *A Preface to Chaucer* (Princeton: Princeton University Press, 1962), 472–502, and "The Probable Date and Purpose of Chaucer's *Troilus*," *M&H* 13 (1985): 143–71; Chauncey Wood, *The Elements of Chaucer's* Troilus (Durham: Duke University Press, 1984), especially 32–33 and 63–98; Winthrop Wetherbee, *Chaucer and the Poets*, for whom "an excessive preoccupation with love is the folly at the heart of the *Troilus*, . . . and the ultimate downfall of Troy is foreshadowed by the intensity of this preoccupation, the importance assumed by the 'siege of Criseyde' in the midst of the larger war" ([Ithaca: Cornell University Press, 1984], 118); and Eugene Vance, "Mervelous Signals: Poetics, Sign Theory, and Politics in Chaucer's *Troilus*," *NLH* 10 (1979): 293–337, who argues that "the heroic young prince is not only reenacting Adam's loss of primal innocence, but Mars's erotic downfall in a coma of heroic inactivity as well" (324). But Chaucer takes pains to show us that Troilus is far from inactive.

ments reduce complex patterns of motivation to simple ideas of choice, or, more seriously, make all stories alike. For, while this narrative foregrounds private amorousness, it also resists the structure of blame. It not only refuses to draw any straightforward causal connections between Troilus's failed love and the fall of Troy, but seems to imply that there is no connection between these two events at all. As I shall argue, in this poem the private stands wholly apart from and seeks to efface the public, just as, at the level of genre, romance, a story focused on the fate of a single individual, seeks to preempt tragedy, a story about (in the definition of Isidore of Seville) *res publicas et regum historias.*[65] And at a still further level of complexity, the reader is so entangled in the inward world of eroticism and delicate feeling that, if he or she has learned anything from modern discussions of reading, the experience should be one not of moral superiority but rather complicity. For the characters, their narrator go-between, and the poem's audience all come to share the desire to suppress the historical consciousness.[66]

At certain points this inwardness is dramatized within the poem itself and thematized in particularly intricate ways. One telling instance is the scene at Deiphoebus's house, where Pandarus's manipulations have succeeded in momentarily creating a space within which the lovers can, in a necessarily constrained and tentative way, begin to express their love. Pandarus's busy weavings create a bustle of activity, both physical and interpretive, that allows for the brief appearance of a local enclave of pure privacy, and one which not even the reader is fully

65. In medieval literary discussions private and public concerns are generically distinguished in terms of comedy and tragedy, as in the authoritative definition by Isidore cited in the text: "Sed comici privatorum hominum praedicant acta, Tragici vero res publicas, et regum historias; item tragicorum argumenta ex rebus luctuosis sunt, comicorum ex rebus laetis" (*Etymologiae,* 8, 7, 6 [*PL* 82:308]; see below, chapter 4, 242–43). Paul Strohm has shown that the term *romaunce* is most often used to designate a narrative about an individual rather than a society: "the majority of the works designated in this way recount the chivalric (martial and occasionally amatory) deeds of a single notable hero" ("The Origin and Meaning of Middle English *Romaunce,*" *Genre* 10 [1977], 13); see also Strohm's important *"Storie, Spelle, Geste, Romaunce, Tragedie:* Generic Distinctions in the Middle English Troy Narratives," *Speculum* 46 (1971): 348–59. In terms of medieval genre theory, the *Troilus* wants to be a romantic comedy but is reluctantly constrained to the form of a historical tragedy; and when Chaucer at the conclusion designates his poem "litel myn tragedye" (5, 1786) he has implicitly acknowledged the triumph of history.

66. A fifteenth-century example is described in Patterson, *Negotiating the Past,* 115–53; for twentieth-century instances, see E. Talbot Donaldson, ed., *Chaucer's Poetry,* 2d ed. (New York: Ronald Press, 1975), 1129–44, and his "Criseide and Her Narrator," *Speaking of Chaucer* (London: Athlone Press, 1970), 65–83; Evan Carton, "Complicity and Responsibility in Pandarus' Bed and Chaucer's Art," *PMLA* 94 (1979): 47–61; and Richard Waswo, "The Narrator of *Troilus and Criseyde,*" *ELH* 50 (1983): 1–25.

able to penetrate.[67] The same process is at work in an even more elaborately articulated form in the consummation scene, where we are simultaneously made complicit in the eroticism enacted before us and yet
denied full access precisely by the ostentatious mediations of both
Pandarus and the narrator, a series of multiform goings-between designed to persuade us that at their center is a moment of utterly
unmediated confrontation. In part our conviction derives from the
sense of progressive inwardness that the very topography of the setting communicates. Situated within a room that is itself surrounded by
another room, itself surrounded by the house and its walls, by the city
and *its* walls, then by the beseiging Greeks, and with the whole encased within a rainstorm, the lovers retreat first to a bed, then to a
mental space that only they share, and finally to a wordless union that
leads them (and perhaps us) to believe that they have passed beyond
the world of history to a transcendent "Love, that of erthe and se hath
governaunce" (3, 1744).

We are likewise made aware throughout the first three books of the
poem that the historical is both unavoidably present and nonetheless
placed at the service of the erotic action. Although the poem opens
with Calkas's defection to the Greeks because of his understanding of
the shape that events will assume, this dark premonition is quickly
preempted by the theatrical scene of Criseyde pleading before Hector.
And Calkas is reduced in these opening lines from "a lord of gret
auctorite" (1, 65) and "a gret devyn" (1, 66) to a "traitour" who has
committed a "false and wikked dede" (1, 87, 93)—a reduction in which
the narrator himself participates with his trivializing pun, "whan this
Calkas knew by calkulynge" (1, 71). As I have already suggested, by
describing Calkas as a "lord of gret auctorite," Chaucer recalls the final
line of the *House of Fame*—"A man of gret auctorite" (2158)—and invokes in this new context the questions of literary authority with which
that earlier poem deals. These questions, moreover, become insistent a
few lines later when Chaucer states, both gratuitously and disingenuously, that his sources do not tell him whether or not Criseyde had
children; in fact, of course, Boccaccio explicitly describes her as child-
less (*Filostrato* 1, 15). In dispensing with Calkas's authority, therefore,
the poet opens the way for other forms of deviation from authority,

67. The phrase "local enclave" is taken from Norbert Wiener, *The Human Use of Human Beings: Cybernetics and Society* (Garden City: Doubleday, 1954): "While the universe as
a whole, if indeed there is a whole universe, tends to run down, there are local enclaves
whose direction seems opposed to that of the universe at large and in which there is a
limited and temporary tendency for organization to increase. Life finds its home in some
of these enclaves" (12).

implying that the story as a whole can be told only if both the Trojan history that is its context (presided over by Calkas) and the literary history that provides its materials (here represented by Boccaccio) can be set aside.

Yet—and this is our second textual fact—if the events of the war seem to enter the narrative only as occasions for erotic action, the historical consequence that is excluded nonetheless reenters by the textual back door. Criseyde's first sight of Troilus is as he returns from battle, and her romantic admiration fastens on, but hardly effaces, the signs of his heroic achievement. Pandarus uses as a pretext to visit Criseyde the arrival of a Greek spy with news (2, 1111–13), and while he never tells her, or us, what the news might be, it remains a disturbing possibility. More tellingly, the gathering at Deiphoebus's palace is called to solve a problem whose triviality seems to efface the larger historical crisis it displaces: Pandarus imagines some kind of legal action against Criseyde managed by "false Poliphete," an obscure figure whom Criseyde fears only because of "Antenor and Eneas, / That ben his frendes" (2, 1467, 1474–75)– although even then she regards the threat as insignificant: "No fors of that; lat hym han al yfeere" (2, 1477). Yet in fact this confected conspiracy is derived from a real conflict. Antenor and Aeneas will shortly join together in a plot against Troy itself, and there is evidence that Chaucer thought of Poliphete as a co-conspirator. For the name derives not from medieval versions of the Troy story but from Virgil's "Polyphoetes [or Polyboetes] sacred to Ceres" in *Aeneid* 6, one of the fallen Trojans whom Aeneas sees in the underworld.[68] There Polyphoetes is linked with the group Virgil calls "tris Antenoridas," Glaucus, Medon and Thersilochus, and Servius's gloss says that "multi supra dictos accipiunt quod fals[os] esse Homerus docet, qui eos commemorat."[69] However Chaucer may have understood this gloss, he seems to have believed that "false Poliphete" was an associate of Antenor, and that the conspiracy Pandarus imagines against Criseyde, and which she here dismisses as trivial, was later to be enacted in a darker, less fictive form. Similarly, just as a crucial moment in Trojan history is here prefigured in a trivialized form so does the "tretys and . . . lettre" with which Troilus distracts

68. "Cererique sacrum Polyphoeten [Polyboeten]" (6, 484); for an earlier version of this suggestion, see G. L. Hamilton, *The Indebtedness of Chaucer's* Troilus and Criseyde *to Guido delle Colonne's* Historia Trojana (New York: Columbia University Press, 1903), 97 n. 3. As I discovered after completing this chapter, the reference to Virgil's Polyphoetes is also proposed by John Fyler, *"Auctoritee* and Allusion in *Troilus and Criseyde," Res Publica Litterarum* 7 (1984): 73–92.

69. G. Thilo and H. Hagen, eds. (Leipzig: Teubner, 1884), 2:72–73.

Helen and Deiphoebus involve a public matter of grave importance—"If swych a man was worthi to ben ded, / Woot I nought who" (2, 1699–1700)—that serves as a pretext to occupy two of the leaders of Trojan society who have themselves, we suspect, an amorous agenda that will also figure in the final catastrophe.[70]

This dynamic of simultaneously invoking and suppressing the crucial issues of Trojan history also shapes the exchange between Troilus and Criseyde in the temple that initiates the erotic action in the first place. The event takes place on the feast of the Palladion, here represented as a moment of natural impulses, as

> the tyme
> Of Aperil, whan clothed is the mede
> With newe grene, of lusty Veer the pryme,
> And swote smellen floures white and rede. (1, 155–58)

Because the Greeks "hem of Troie shetten, / And hir cite biseged al aboute" (1, 148–49), the Trojans are denied access to the extramural world of nature where springtime celebrations traditionally take place; and yet they nonetheless continue to perform their "observaunces olde" (1, 160). To those familiar with Trojan history, however, the feast of the Palladion signifies more than springtime release. For at its center is the "relik" (1, 153) whose theft, according to Trojan historians, is one of the conditions of the fall of Troy.[71] The Trojans' turn away from the war into a sanctuary where they can celebrate the reappearance of a springtime from which they are excluded—a turn then reenacted by Troilus in his retreat into first his chamber and then the "mirour of his mynde" (I, 365)—is thus shadowed by a linear temporality that will finally overcome them. However brave or persistent, their attempts to evade the demands of the historical world are evidently bound to fail.[72]

70. These suspicions are discussed by McKay Sundwall, "Deiphobus and Helen: A Tantalizing Hint," *MP* 73 (1975): 151–56, and by John V. Fleming, "Deiphoebus Betrayed: Virgilian Decorum, Chaucerian Feminism," *ChR* 21 (1986–87): 182–99. On Helen's thematic function in the poem, see Christopher C. Baswell and Paul Beekman Taylor, "The *Faire Queene Eleyne* in Chaucer's *Troilus*," *Speculum* 63 (1988): 293–311.

71. In his commentary to *Aeneid* 2, 13, Servius says that the survival of Troy was dependent upon the preservation of three things: the Palladion, the tomb of Laomedon, and the life of Troilus; see E. K. Rand et al., eds., *Servianorum in Vergilii Carmina Commentariorum* (Lancaster: American Philosophical Society, 1946), 2:316–17. In the *Filostrato* Boccaccio refers to this relic as "il Palladio fatale" (1, 18); and in his gloss to *Aeneid* 2, 166, Servius has a long discussion of the theft of the Palladion by Ulysses and, significantly, Diomedes; see Rand et. al., 2:367–69.

72. Another echo of an excluded but visible Trojan history are the ominous suggestions of a connection among Criseyde, "Eleyne [and] Polixene" (1, 455), all of whom

If Books 1 through 3 show us lovers, and a society, determined to avoid their implication within a tragic history, Books 4 and 5 show instead that the local enclave of love can neither withstand nor transcend the pressures of history. "It shal be founde at preve" (4, 1659), says Troilus as Criseyde leaves Troy, and the proving of the affair is devastating in its results. For what is revealed is a fatal weakness not just in Criseyde but in the constitution of the affair as whole: whatever it is that makes her unwilling either to stay or to return has been an element of her character that has, from the beginning of the story, been both manipulated and overlooked by a devious Pandarus and an enamoured Troilus. Is the weakness of the private world of love then morally identical with (if not responsible for) the weakness that brings down Troy? Not only the narrative symmetry between the fate of the city and the fate of the lovers solicits such a question. For the exchange of Antenor for Criseyde fulfills another of the dark prophecies about Trojan history, that Troy would not fall as long as Troilus lived: in removing from Troilus his reason for living, the exchange removes as well a necessary condition for the survival of the city.[73] Are we then to think that Troilus, falling in love in such a way and with such a woman, rendered

---

brought their lovers to disaster. Helen appears at Deiphoebus's house, and in circumstances that disturbingly prefigure her later liaison with (and betrayal of) her host; and Polyxena is then referred to explicitly by Troilus when, in Book 3, he offers to be a go-between for Pandarus with "my faire suster Polixene" (409). Perhaps it is also Polyxena who is the composer of the song Antigone sings in Book 2. The song is written, we are tantalizingly told, by "the goodlieste *mayde* / Of gret estat in al the town of Troye, / And let hire lif in moste honour and joye" (2, 881–82) and is addressed to an absent lover ("Now good thrift have he, whereso that he be!" [2, 847]). These are conditions that would seem to fit particularly aptly a Polyxena who was pining for Achilles.

    73.   Chaucer could have found this prophecy implicit in the ecphrasis in the temple of Juno in *Aeneid* 1, 474–78, where not only does the *infelix puer* Troilus stand for all the victims of the Trojan War, and of the Italian Wars to come, but his death fits into a larger pattern of prophecy that Aeneas reads but fails to understand. An example of a medieval history that promotes the military role of Troilus in order to link his death to the city's destruction is the *Chronique Martinienne*, a translation of the *Cronica* of Martin of Poland made in 1458 by Sébastien Mamerot (Pierre Champion, ed., *Cronique Martiniane* [Paris: Champion, 1907], xlvi). The connection between the eponymous Troilus and his city is exploited by a number of Trojan texts: for instance, Albert of Stade's *Troilus* establishes in its proem an analogy between the fact that Troilus was named after the city and that the poem is also called *Troilus* because it is named after the Trojan War, which is its subject: "Troilus est Troilus Troiano principe natus / Et liber est Troilus ob Troia bella vocatus" (Albertus Stadensis, *Troilus*, ed. T. Merzdorf [Leipzig: Teubner, 1875], 9: these lines may be an interpolation into Albert's original). According to the *Compendium historiae Troianae-Romanae*, Troy was named after Troilus: first it was called Neptunia, but "que post modo, a Troiulo eius nepote, Troia apellata fuit" (ed. Simonsfeld, 242).

himself vulnerable to a loss that served to undermine the city to which
he owed his largest allegiance?

The poem forces us to ask this question, but it declines to provide a
clear answer. Chaucer's narrative persistently resists the equation of the
erotic and the martial, even at the level of analogy or synecdoche—as
Troilus, so Troy. Rather, the fate of the city is seen to be overdetermined
by a multitude of causes, and Troilus's behavior, if anything, to be *less*
culpable, more genuinely heroic, than Trojan society in general. We
have already seen how even after the loss of Criseyde Troilus maintains
his heroic defense of the city (5, 1751–57); more to the point, the events
surrounding the exchange of Criseyde for Antenor are themselves embedded in a set of explanations that preclude Troilus's culpability. In
describing the capture of Antenor at the beginning of Book 4, Chaucer
returns to the "authentic" accounts of Benoît and Guido that show that
Antenor was captured not *with* the other listed Trojans but *despite*—
"maugre"—their presence.[74] His purpose is evidently to present this
event as a military misadventure caused by an overly aggressive Trojan
militarism: the Trojans themselves initiate the battle—"Ector, with ful
many a bold baroun, / Caste on a day with Grekis for to fighte" (4, 33–
34)—and yet (in a passage original with Chaucer) "The folk of Troie
hemselven so *mysledden* / That with the worse at nyght homward they
fledden" (48–49). Yet another explanation for the fall of the city, and one
that also posits a general Trojan culpability, is provided by Calkas immediately prior to the scene of exchange: he explains to the Greeks (in a
passage also added by Chaucer) that because Laomedon failed to recompense Apollo and Neptune for building the walls of the city the gods will
now bring down vengeance on the "folk of Troie" (4, 122). And yet a third
explanation is then provided by the account of the Trojan parliament
(another of Chaucer's additions), in which the expediency of the "folk"
(4, 198, 202) overrides the moral force of Hector's blunt objection: "We
usen here no wommen for to selle" (182). In sum, the event that Chaucer
presents as decisive for the fall of Troy—the ironically designated "de-
liveraunce" (202) of Antenor—is *also* represented as a function of Trojan
folly in a wide variety of forms.

Moreover, while we are certainly entitled to see Troilus's love for
Criseyde as self-deluded, the poem is careful to exculpate its protagonist from simple selfishness. For just as Hector seeks by his intervention to protect Criseyde (as he had promised), so does Troilus by his
silence. "With mannes herte he gan his sorwes drye" (154), and his

74. On the revision of 4, 50–54, see Stephen Barney's notes in the *Riverside Chaucer*,
1044–45.

thought is "*First,* how to save hir honour" (159). At the very moment Criseyde is being sold by his fellow citizens, Troilus is seen as preferring "resoun" to "love" by choosing silence over speech (162–68), an act that defines his devotion to Criseyde—his "trouthe"—as very different from the narrow self-interest that motivates the "peple" (183) of Troy. Far from being complicit in the process that is to bring about their downfall, the lovers are here represented as victims, set apart at the levels of both practice and morality from the world of military, religious, and political action that will serve to drive them apart.

In sum, Chaucer forces upon his historiographically informed reader an interpretive dilemma that allows no easy solution, perhaps even no solution at all. Ostentatiously setting aside the historical context, he then persistently if surreptitiously reinvokes it; and yet having done so, he not only fails to impart any clear sense of its relevance but offers explanations that insist upon its irrelevance. In allowing the collapse of the local enclave of love and the civic world in which it is nested to be occasioned by the same event, Chaucer establishes a connection at the level of event that is then denied at the level of causality. This denial is all the more unsettling because he implies that both events are motivated by a self-destructive blindness: "O nyce world, lo, thy discrecioun" (4, 206) he apostrophizes the Trojan parliament, echoing his earlier apostrophe to the love-struck Troilus—"O blynde world, O blynde entencioun!" (1, 211). But then by here setting Troilus's "reasonable" silence (further legitimized by Hector's high-minded defense) against the clamorous "noyse of peple" (183), the poet insists upon the moral difference between two similar acts of self-destruction.

The effect of this juxtaposition is to bring the reader to an interpretive impasse. We have been encouraged to see the complex erotic relationship that constitutes the subject matter of the poem as providing an interpretive purchase upon the large historical event in which it is embedded; but then at this moment of crisis we are denied the means to do so. Troilus's love fails, Troy fails: these symmetrical events come finally to provide a statement not about the meaning of history but instead about its profound meaninglessness. We can of course find reasons for each individual failure, but it is the lack of connection that is distressing, especially since the narrative seems to assert it so insistently. At best, we are allowed only a metaphoric relation: both Troilus and the Trojans behave foolishly. Not only is this conclusion banal, but it leads to the monkish conclusion that history is by definition simply a record of human folly. Denied a stance within the historical world itself, then, the only critical purchase we can gain upon the action is one that stands outside history altogether—a position that necessarily denies the significance that the poem, by its very definition as a Troy book, seeks to express. How far this impasse can be attributed to a structural weakness in medieval historiography (as distinct from looking beyond Chaucer's poem to its own historical environment) must be our next question; and the first route to its answer is an investigation of previous Trojan history writing, especially that of Benoît de Sainte-Maure in the *Roman de Troie*.

IV: Trojan Historiography

The foundational texts of Trojan historiography were the purportedly eyewitness accounts of Dares and Dictys, bare-bones records that claimed to be *ephemeroi* or diaries, day-to-day records of the actual events. But the Middle Ages also had access to other, far richer accounts of the war: the *Ilias Latina*, a first-century epitome of Homer ascribed to Silius Italicus, the late classical *Excidium Troiae*, "historical" poems like the *Aeneid*, and, especially, the numerous mythographical handbooks and commentaries by writers such as Fulgentius, Hyginus, Servius (on Virgil), and Lactantius Placidus (on Statius).[75] Given this archive, the task of the medieval historian was to fill out Dares (and, to a lesser extent, Dictys) with a careful selection of this material plus whatever else might make the meaning of the events clear. This is the process that Joseph of Exeter designated with the word *explicare*, by which he meant both an unfolding and a clarification: "I have explicated the complaints and laments about the fall of Troy from the confused abridgements of the ancient truth, even when they come from my author, however special he may be."[76] Explication was required not only because of the strategic plainness of Dares and Dictys, their status as eyewitnesses being enforced by their lack of interpretive commentary, but because of the enigmatic character of the Trojan story itself. That the fall of Troy was a tragic event was agreed upon by all: Horace

75. There is no up-to-date account of this tradition. Older studies are Hermann Dunger, *Die Sage von trojanischen Kriege in den Bearbeitungen des Mittelalters und ihre antiken Quellen* (Leipzig: Vogel, 1869); Wilhelm Greif, *Die mittelalterlichen Bearbeitungen Trojanersage* (Marburg: Friedrich, 1885); Egidio Gorra, *Testi inediti di Storia Trojana* (Turin: C. Triverio, 1887); and Hans Matter, *Englische Gründungssagen von Geoffrey of Monmouth bis zur Renaissance* (Heidelberg: Winter, 1922).

76. *Frigii Daretis Yliados* in *Werke und Briefe*, ed. Ludwig Gompf (Leiden: E. J. Brill, 1970):

Hactenus Yliace questus lamenta ruine
Confusa *explicui* veteris compendia veri,
Etsi quando auctor, rarus tamen. (Book 6, lines 959–61)
See also Guido delle Colonne, *Historia*, ed. Griffin, 86.

called it the "lacrimosa Troiae funera" and when Joseph referred to "the complaints and laments about the fall of Troy" he was accurately characterizing the tone of Trojan historiography.[77] But as Joseph and his colleagues knew, complaint was not enough. What did the story mean?

For the Middle Ages, the authoritative version of Trojan history was Benoît's *Roman de Troie*, in large part because Benoît did not evade the challenge of historical explanation. His expansive narrative—it is almost thirty thousand lines long—defined the problem of Trojan history in terms of two, interrelated questions: how could a society destroy itself in the process of enacting its most deeply held values? and why was it unable to withdraw from the course of disaster even when the outcome had become terrifyingly clear? In confronting these questions, his poem finally settled on the logically incoherent but all too familiar proposition that human enterprises are at once radically adventitious in their development and yet, in retrospect, entirely inevitable. Benoît gives voice to this paradox through a language of beginnings and endings that reappears later in Guido's historicization of Benoît's poem and then becomes central to Chaucer's contribution to the genre. And in Chaucer's version this discourse of origins is set, as we shall see, in awkward opposition to a semantically similar but philosophically antithetical Boethianism. For whereas Boethius's Stoic vision anchors the course of the individual life in a *summum bonum* that provides both alpha and omega, Chaucer's poem explores a world of such historical density and particularity that it precludes both the discovery of a clearly demarcated beginning—in the sense both of chronological initiation and of "the cause whi" (5, 1028)—and a stable conclusion.

In Benoît's telling, the war begins almost by inadvertence, by a combination of miscalculation and happenstance in which no individual act is decisive but each contributes to an inescapable, overwhelming conclusion. The poem opens with Jason's mission to capture the golden fleece, a project that is itself motivated by a dark familial history. When Jason and his companions harbor in Trojan territory on their way to Colchis, King Laomedon—misinformed and wrongly apprehensive— refuses them hospitality. This is a rebuff for which Hercules, one of Jason's companions, later exacts a brutally excessive revenge, razing Troy on the return trip and slaughtering or enslaving her inhabitants. The next stage of this gradually escalating tragedy occurs when Laomedon's son Priam, having rebuilt the city, seeks to redeem Trojan honor by recovering from the Greeks Hesione, Laomedon's sister, whom Hercules had abducted and whom Telamon is now using as a

77. Horace, *Carmina* 1, 8, 14–15.

concubine. When the Greeks not only refuse but scorn this request, Priam unwisely consents to Paris's plan to carry off Helen in retaliation, an act that calls forth the inevitable retaliatory campaign: the war is now begun. Yet its origins are hopelessly entangled both practically and ethically: while it may be possible to mark points at which events could have been foreclosed or redirected, the process itself resists any large-scale categories of explanation. The agents who bring catastrophe about are the human beings who are themselves its victims, and it is by no means easy to make moral distinctions among either the individuals involved or their actions. Like so much human behavior, the acts that lead up to the war are as individually understandable as they are incomprehensible in their totality, and they finally resist any interpretive epithet other than the tautological "all too human."

When Antenor returns from his fruitless mission he offers advice to his fellow Trojans that is at once apt and irrelevant: "For this is what authorities tell us: whoever wishes to begin a great thing, if he is wise, will pay attention to the conclusion at which he ought to arrive so he does not bring about shame and disaster."[78] If at this stage in the narrative Antenor's words seem to constitute only a simple plea for prudence, in the course of the poem this topos is reinvoked in contexts that make it clear that its prescriptions are at once indispensible and impossible. Hector warns the Trojans that for a project to arrive at its wished-for conclusion it must have an appropriate beginning (3796–808); Agamemnon in his turn tells the Greeks that a work begun "par orgueil" can never come to a happy ending (6085–88). Yet despite their best efforts the work goes awry for both, and when, much later on, Agamemnon says that the work must be finished as it was begun he speaks now with resignation and bitter irony.[79] This is an irony that becomes yet more intense in Achilles' lament when he discovers that the woman with whom he has fallen in love is Polyxena, and in Helen's summary of her career, which shows a full awareness of how beginning and ending fit together to fulfill a curve of action that is tragically inescapable: "I

78. Quar ço nos diënt li autor:
   Qui grant chose vueut envaîr,
   La fin a qu'il en deit venir
   Deit esguarder, se il est sages,
   Que n'en vienge honte e damages. (3646–50)
All citations are from Constans, *Le Roman de Troie*.

79. In lines 18378–81, where Agamemnon is trying to preempt the position of unconditional struggle just assumed by the intransigent Thoas, and is in fact rephrasing, ironically, some of Thoas's very words; see 18299–304, and compare 18335–37 and 18364–65, with their shared allusions to Rolandian heroism.

began in a cursed hour and I will finish in a much worse one."[80] Beginnings open onto a field of uncertainty, but as the action rounds toward its conclusion it reveals a gradually coalescing inevitability that now appears to have been present all along. And while the actors acknowledge throughout the inescapability of this process, the knowledge does them no good.

Whence comes this inevitability? To be sure, Benoît invokes the almost obligatory figures of Destiny and Fortune throughout his narrative: "The thing was to happen, and nothing could change it."[81] According to Calchas, Fortune hates Troy and wants to bring her down (13091–98), and when Priam sees that the end is near he turns his lament to an attack upon "Fortune dolorose, / . . . pesme e tenebrose" (25215–16); correspondingly, the death of virtually every hero elicits the phrase that Achilles first uses about Patroclus: "Ha! las, com dure destinee!" (10337).[82] But despite their ubiquity, these terms provide little more than rhetorical coloring. Far from establishing a philosophical context within which the narrative can be interpreted—even of so simplistic a kind as the wheel of Fortune—these statements assure us only that what happened had to happen: they ratify the facts without explaining them. The prophets who repeatedly appear throughout the narrative—Panthus, Helenus, Cassandra, and Calchas—have a similarly restricted relevance: they proffer their dark prophecies as truthful advice, and yet were they believed they would immediately become false prophets, belied by the very history over which they claim authority. It is this paradox that motivates the curse by which Cassandra is condemned to speak a truth that is never believed.[83] Like Fortune and Destiny, prophecy asserts inevitability without explaining it, and its effect upon the narrative is not clarification but mystification. As with the language of beginnings and endings, the irrelevance of prophecy suggests not that men foolishly ignore good advice but rather that they are able to understand their history only retrospectively, when it is too

80. "En maudite hore començaí, / En plus male definerai" (22955–56).

81. "Si ert la chose a avenir / Que rien nel poëit destolir" (10185–86). Benoît also refers, here and occasionally elsewhere, to Aventure (10180).

82. See also 16416, 16233 (Hector), 18815–18, 18844–45 (Sarpedon), 22132–35 (Achilles), 22641–42 (Paris), 29973–74 (Ulysses), 3134, 4159–66, 12754–58, 26060 (Troy). When Briseïda is sent to the Greek camp, "'Lasse,' fet el, 'quel destinee'" (13277), a response that Chaucer's Criseyde echoes in her "'Allas, that swich a cas me sholde falle!'" (5, 1064).

83. Indeed, she herself seems to recognize the meaning of this paradox: see lines 4912, 10431, 10444–46.

late. Or to reverse the chronology, ignorance of the consequences is a prerequisite for action.

If retrospective understanding is all that is possible, then Benoît's own project, and those of the other Trojan historians, is an exercise in futility: historiography, including the *Roman de Troie* and its descendants, teaches us that we cannot learn from history. This is not, finally, a conclusion that Benoît wholly avoids, and hence he too assumes the Trojan historian's traditional role of passive mourner: rather than provide the reader with interpretive guidance, he enters the narrative only to lament the disaster that is overtaking the world he has depicted with such proprietary care. But if this is the conclusion to which the logic of his own narrative ineluctably directs him, he defers his reluctant arrival there with a series of elaborately staged romantic counterplots. Running, albeit in vain, against the grain of the main narrative line, these counterplots are not merely amorous distractions from the grim self-destructions of the war. On the contrary, they are interpretive purchases upon the narrative line pursued by characters who themselves struggle toward understanding *in medias res.* Jason and Medea, Paris and Helen, Troilus and Briseïda, Achilles and Polyxena: each pair provides, in its own way, both an exemplary instance of disaster and, especially in the case of the latter two pairs, an awareness of human complicity in and victimization by the larger historical calamity within which their fates are enacted.

As Benoît moves through his narrative these explanatory glosses provide a progressively more acute analysis of the paradoxical relation of the individual to a history of which he or she is at once cause, instance, and effect. The lesson taught at the outset by the complementary manipulations and betrayals of the story of Jason and Medea is consolingly simple: the calamities of history are caused by bad people who themselves come to a bad end. But this simplistic interpretation will not hold even for the case of Paris and Helen. Their love may be an effect of the Trojan desire for revenge for the abduction of Hesione and may be in itself illicit. But Benoît nonetheless represents it in terms that invoke a different, brighter world, in which *Amors* is not a device of statecraft and where the gifts of Venus entail only happy consequences. Adulterous love is the efficient cause of the Trojan War, but the straightforward link between personal immorality and historical disaster established by the narrative is then undone by Benoît's empathy for lovers yearning for a realm in which private but by no means solely carnal desire can be fully legitimized.

In his account of Troilus and Briseïda, Benoît fully severs the causal link between private and public, for the poem never suggests that the failure of the love affair bears anything more than a metaphoric relation to the fall of the city. Moreover, even the analogy largely ignores Troilus and focuses almost exclusively on Briseïda: as unreliable as the whirligig world she manipulates, her feminine treachery is the ethical equivalent to the instability that afflicts the historical world, and her betrayal of Troilus expresses in amorous terms not only the individual betrayals of the Trojan story but the topsy-turvey reversals that characterize all historical action. Yet not even here does Benoît unproblematically align the private and the public. For the attack on Briseïda derives not from a philosophically informed meditation on history but instead from the bitter disappointments of an abandoned lover, and it is conducted in the terms of a virulent misogyny generated by injured male pride. Moreover, Briseïda's behavior, as both motive and effect, has a complexity and texture that resists reduction to *any* simple explanatory formula, whether antifeminist or more disinterestedly philosophical. When, for example, she scornfully accepts from Diomede a horse he has captured from Troilus, and then all the more scornfully offers it back to him when he in turn loses his own, her action comments with bitter self-awareness on the arbitrariness of the fortunes of war. She has learned sooner than anyone else that merit will not decide the fate of those caught up in this historical disaster; and ought we really to condemn her for choosing survival over heedless self-destruction?

In the fully self-aware interior monologue with which she concludes her appearance in the poem, she alone is able to articulate the complex mixture of complicity and victimization that constrains all of the protagonists; and she recognizes that this inextricably confounded situation will not yield a straightforwardly moral significance. Misogynist clichés stand ready to categorize and finally to discard her, as she knows (20257–58); but they offer no greater interpretive force at the level of biography than do, at the level of history, the clichés about Fortune. Briseïda lives within herself the moral complexity that the other characters enact, but far from asserting the power of consciousness to transcend history her career displays the inevitable implications by which history subsumes the individual life. For the most that she can wish for from *her* history is that she might forget it (20321–24), and her counterplot comes finally to function less as a gloss upon the historical text than a recapitulation, less an access to understanding than an expression of bafflement.

The subsumption of the individual by history is most intensely expressed in the story of the last of these pairs, Achilles and Polyxena. Here love and war are most fully set in opposition, but that very opposition is finally and tragically revealed to be itself an illusion of which the lovers must be painfully divested. As soon as Achilles falls in love with Polyxena, he knows that he is irrevocably alienated from the war, and while he retires from battle ostensibly in order to win Priam's support in his suit, he is now in fact permanently opposed to the very idea of battle. Hence when Ulysses appeals to Achilles by warning him that he is losing his *pris* and will be called *recreant*, Achilles pours scorn upon both Ulysses' concept of honor—"You will die of it, this honor, just as many already have"—and the war by which it is purportedly to be won: "You are set amidst a savage work, without honor and without reason, and for such a wretched reward you mince up all these men."[84] Achilles' love for Polyxena brings to the end, for him, the historical imperative of the war—"Quar c'est la fin, jol vos di bien" (19715)—and turns him toward the enclave of a romantic counterplot in which *fine amor* can find its home.

Inevitably, of course, love is swept aside by war: Priam sees in Achilles' infatuation a political opportunity and soon entangles him in a net of complicity from which death is the only release. But Benoît's larger point is that love is itself a war, a *bellum cordis* that provides not a purchase upon the turmoil that engulfs Achilles but a turmoil of its own, not an interpretation but a replication. When he first sees Polyxena Achilles defines his condition in a long *complainte d'amour* (17638–746) in which the politically illicit nature of his affection—he is in love with the sister of the man he has just slain—gives special point to the oxymora of the amorous lexicon. The metaphors of courtship—the lady as mortal enemy, love as self-betrayal, as a mighty conqueror, as a mortal wound—are in his case literalized by the larger context of the war as a whole. "Jo aim ma mort e mon encombre" (17696), he says, a phrase that he uses as part of an explicit comparison to Narcissus but that also invokes the death-directed heroism of the warriors among whom he is set and the intransigent fatalism of Troy.[85] Achilles says that Polyxena "has so entrapped and captured me that I cannot escape," but the imprisonment is more general, the interlacement more universally bind-

---

84.   Vos en morreiz, ço iert honor,
      Si come en sont ja fait plusor. (19609–10)
      En fiere uevre vos estes mis,
      Qui senz honor e senz reison
      E por si mauvaise acheison
      Vos faites ci toz detrenchier. (19616–619)

85.   When the Trojans celebrate the entrance of the wooden horse into their city, the narrator mordantly comments, "Om ne set pas conter la joie / Que de lor mort fout cil de Troie" (25943–44): "One does not know how to describe the joy that the people of Troy made over their deaths."

ing.[86] Not just his love but the war as a whole is a "mortel dolor" (17641) and both Greeks and Trojans are afflicted with the "deseperance" that Achilles explicitly acknowledges (17743). Achilles' love begins and ends at the tomb of Hector: it is there that he reenacts with Polyxena the amorous gaze that initially entangled Paris and Helen, and it is there that he falls prey to Paris's ambush.[87] In his beginning Achilles finds his end, a tragic circularity that he glimpsed at the outset but that he was unable either to understand or evade: "I will be dead at the end, I know and feel it. I have had a very dark beginning; I would very much like to be a prophet in order to know what will be the ending."[88] Like his life, Achilles' death shows how thoroughly amorous desire has become indistinguishable from the darker urgings of war. Blinded by *amors* (22132–35) and betrayed by Polyxena's beauty—"The beauty of her face draws him into . . . error"—he is killed by and for his love. "Now I grant you," mocks Paris, as he strikes home, "that you have paid for [or earned] these love gifts."[89]

Achilles' fate demonstrates that there is no escape from history into romance. This amorous episode so thoroughly encapsulates the themes of the *Roman* as a whole that its absorption into the larger narrative is imperceptible: counterplot becomes plot. Far from explaining the course of events, the experience enacted by Achilles and Polyxena, like that of Troilus and Briseïda, repeats it in a minor key. And if this repetition dooms the protagonists, it bespeaks as well the narrator's analogous failure to achieve a critical purchase upon his own history. Benoît's story is finally a dark tale of internecine self-destruction. The narrative begins with Jason and the golden fleece, itself a story of families turned against themselves: Peleus against his nephew Jason, Medea against her father Aeëtes, and (in preview only) Jason and Medea against each other and themselves.[90] And it concludes with the death

86. "M'a si lacié e pris / Que jo ne li puis eschaper" (17650–51).

87. The eye-play of Achilles and Polyxena in Hector's huge mausoleum, during ceremonies to honor the fallen warrior, provided Boccaccio and then Chaucer with their model for Troilus's first sight of Criseyde.

88. Morz sui en fin, jol sai e sent.
    Mout en ai grief comencement:
    Mout en voudreie estre devin
    Saveir quel en sera la fin. (17731–34)

89. "La resplendor de sa semblance / Le fait ester en . . . errance" (22139–40); "Or vos otrei . . . / Que compareiz ces druëries" (22289–90).

90. A further, submerged expression of this self-destructiveness is the fact that Peleus, who as a way to dispose of Jason devises the quest for the fleece (the event which, with the rude reception granted to the voyagers by Laomedon, initiates the hostilities between Greeks and Trojans), is the father of Achilles: his malevolence eventually costs him the life of his son.

of Ulysses at the hands of his son Telegonus, the final disaster that caps and completes the general disaster of the homecoming.[91]

It is within this dark frame that Benoît's story of the seige of Troy plays out its irrational logic. In the war itself, all efforts at peace are overwhelmed by the sheer weight of past calamity. The principles for which it is being fought soon become submerged in a mire of blood and vengeance: national purpose, the heroic self-transcendence of the warrior, even the thrill and beauty of war—all disappear before the grinding attrition of implacable slaughter. What comes finally to dominate the combatants is a sense of nihilistic doom, of efforts that must be made in order to be true to a past that itself renders any future hopeless: the warrior rides into battle both to avenge his fallen comrades and to find his own, inevitable death.[92] Even the rhetoric of heroism, upon which the chivalric life depends for its self-justification, undergoes a process of devaluation. After Achilles has fallen in love with Polyxena he proposes abandoning the war—"I would rather be a knight at home than abroad," he says[93]— but Thoas answers him with a traditional, and unanswerable, assertion of what constitutes true *chevalerie*. "Whether it's foolish or wise," the Greeks have begun this war and so must finish it, and he alludes, anachronistically but decisively, to the most potent exemplar of heroism available to an Anglo-Norman, Roland himself: "He is greatly shamed who sounds his horn in battle while he can still strike with naked sword."[94] The final appearance in the poem of this heroic rhetoric is at Priam's last council. All of Priam's sons are now dead, and the peace party, led by Antenor and Aeneas, is urging the Trojans to return Helen and make peace. Now it is Amphimachus, the youngest of the *bastarz*, who resists: "Whether they should all die or we should all die—let's not talk of any other kind of peace," and he eagerly awaits the time when the final destruction that has been so long delayed will at last be upon them: "This

91.   Benoît does include a brief gesture toward reconciliation: Andromache has two sons, Laudamanta by Hector and Achillidès by Pyrrhus, who are brought up together and become fast friends. But he omits the most obvious consolatory argument, that the fall of Troy issued in the rise of Rome and the other Western nations; for the use of this argument by Guido and others, see below, 124.

92.   A characteristic statement of this attitude is Paris's powerful lament for the death of Deiphoebus (18711–743). On the importance of vengeance as a motive for fighting, see Menelaus's speech during the second battle (8747–52).

93.   "Mieuz vueil jo estre chevaliers / En ma terre que en estrange" (18224–25).

94.   O seit folie, o seit saveir. (18283)
Mout est honiz qui recreüe
Corne, tant com d'espee nue
Puisse ferir en grant bataille. (18335–37).
For Roland as an Anglo-Norman hero, see David Douglas, "The 'Song of Roland' and the Norman Conquest of England," *French Studies* 14 (1960): 99–116.

business has not reached such a pass that peace or an end should be discussed except as it could be brought about with naked swords—so that either we or they should be dead and conquered: that's the way I think it will be. And so it should be immediately—it's a great shame that it delays so long—let it not last much longer."[95] Heroic rhetoric is here reduced to an incoherence that expresses little more than uncontrollable violence, a discourse the poet designates as "orgoillose, laide e *vilaine*" (24605): the *chevalerie* that the Trojan War was meant to confirm has been undone by its means of confirmation.[96]

Benoît's poem matters for an understanding of *Troilus and Criseyde* because it establishes the terms in which later Trojan historiography attempts to understand its subject. That the originary moment of secular history should be an overwhelming catastrophe is itself an unsettling fact, but that it should also be a catastrophe whose causes are obscure, whose events stand in a painfully enigmatic relation to the individual, and whose ultimate meaning resists decipherment—these are qualities that made the Trojan story a continual anxiety for the medieval historical consciousness, and run counter to, or subterraneously undermine, the uses of Trojan descent and *translatio imperii* in the service of secular interests. A salient instance is provided by Guido delle Colonne's thirteenth-century *Historia destructionis Troiae*. Even though it tried to absorb and domesticate Benoît's poem by rewriting it according to the familiar norms of medieval historical writing, the narrative maintained its capacity to disturb.[97] Guido defines the purpose of his *Historia* as being to

95.   O tuit morront, or tuit morrons:
      Ja d'autre pais ne parlerons.
      N'est pas l'uevre en tel sen alee
      Que pais en deie estre parlee
      Ne fin s'o les branz non toz nuz.
      Que morz en seient e vencuz
      O nos de ça o il de la:
      Ensi cuit jo que il sera.
      E ensi seit d'ore en avant:
      Ço est granz maus qu'il targe tant;
      Ja n'ait il mais longe duree! (24593–603)
This speech, delivered at Priam's last council by the only remaining *bastarz*, echoes the reproach delivered to the cautious Helenus at the first council by the now dead Troilus (4006–12).

96.   If we locate Benoît's poem within the context of Plantagenet ambitions, we can see that it offers with its legitimization a powerfully cautionary message. For a discussion of the same strategy in Chrétien's *Erec et Enide*, see Patterson, *Negotiating the Past*, 183–95.

97.   On Guido, see C. David Benson, " 'O Nyce World': What Chaucer Really Found in Guido delle Colonne's History of Troy," *ChR* 13 (1978–79): 308–15 and his *The History of Troy in Middle English Literature* (Woodbridge: Brewer, 1980), 3–31.

examine the "primordialis causa" of the war in order to understand its "causa finalis" or ultimate effect.[98] He is distressed above all by the disparity between the apparent triviality of the initiating events and their cataclysmic effects: "Even if these many woes were pleasing to the gods, still, the original cause of these things, as trifling as unimportant, rightly troubles human hearts."[99] And so too for the final results: was the fall of Troy a *felix culpa?* Unlike Benoît, Guido produces the inevitable answer—it gave rise to the European empires. But he has finally too comprehensive a sense of the story's range of meanings to settle for so narrow an answer: "The human mind is uncertain whether the cause of such a great betrayal was finally the cause of subsequent good."[100] Hence he follows Benoît in allowing Fortune and the Fates to function more as metaphors than explanatory devices, supernatural agencies to whom the story can be referred but who are not allowed to reduce its complexity. By paying painstaking attention to the web of often petty and always misguided human motivations, he securely locates responsibility on the human plane, yet his invocation of these higher agencies simultaneously suggests that the meaning of these events transcends easy moralization.

This is not to say that Guido does not himself obligingly provide many of the events with appropriate exemplary readings: in using Hesione as a concubine rather than legitimizing her as a wife, Telamon violates universally recognized ethical norms; Priam's desire for revenge teaches us not to undertake missions whose end is unforeseen— a lesson that Hector enforces with a speech whose prominence suggests authorial sanction; the meeting of Helen and Paris in the temple elicits an outburst against not only pagan temples but the assignations and flirtations that, from Ovid through Boccaccio, seem to have been so much a part of temple going; and Medea, Helen, and Briseïda call forth the antifeminist diatribes that are always available to medieval searchers after the cause of human ills.[101] Yet finally Guido's history admits that the "origo inimicitiarum et scandali" that it seeks to understand is capable of being explicated only by the course of events itself. "Far-seeing men should diligently consider that in this world the effects of things are blind;" if the quality of an action is known only in the effect,

98. Guido, *Historia*, 4, 11, 12.

99. Trans. Mary Elizabeth Meek (Bloomington: Indiana University Press, 1974), 9; see also 43, 114, 146–47.

100. Ibid., 10.

101. For these passages, see ibid., 180, 185, 190; for similar invocations of antifeminist clichés as historical explanation, see Joseph of Exeter, *The Iliad of Dares Phrygius*, trans. Gildas Roberts (Capetown: A. A. Balkema, 1970), 62–63.

then historical action is always unseeing.[102] As Deiphoebus says in response to Hector's warning, "If in every affair which is to be undertaken one would wish to examine carefully with particular deliberation
the individual events which could take place in the future, there would
never be anyone who would boldly submit himself to the burden of any
undertaking."[103] Although in the interest of historical seriousness
Guido substitutes exemplary moralization for Benoît's romantic counterplots, he too arrives at the same interpretive impasse: history
teaches us that history teaches us nothing.

The legacy of Benoît and Guido tends to be split into two reactions,
each intelligible as self-protective. On the one hand, a historian like
Lydgate laved his *Troy Book* in confident moralisms, and in *L'Epistre
d'Othea* Christine de Pisan treated the Trojan story as a storehouse of
exemplary instances.[104] This is also the tradition of the moral ency-
clopedists, whose influence has weighed disproportionately in the criticism of *Troilus and Criseyde*. But on the other hand, many courtly writers
detached the Trojan protagonists entirely from history by treating them
as wholly amorous figures: in Machaut's *La Fonteinne amoreuse*, for example, the fountain is engraved with stories of the lovers of Troy, and
Venus asserts her authority by telling the story of the Judgment of
Paris, while in Froissart's *Paradys d'Amours* Achilles, Polyxena, Troilus,
and Paris appear simply as individual lovers among many others.[105] Of

102. "Viri providi diligenter advertant quales sunt in hoc mundo ceci rerum
eventus" (Guido, *Historia*, 43; my translation).

103. Meek, 61.

104. See Benson, *History of Troy*, 116–29. But even Lydgate has problems with the
meaning of Trojan history. When Paris leaves Troy on his journey of abduction, the poet
confidently asserts that the war can be explained as the triumph of lust (Venus) over
wisdom (Minerva) and wealth (Juno); but then at the conclusion of the episode he complains that Fortune is against the Trojans "causeles" (2, 3283), and he later declares (with
telling indecisiveness), "Almost for nou3t was þis strif be-gonne" (2, 7855). Derek Pearsall acutely notes that Lydgate consistently seeks to avoid the very history he is engaged
in recounting: "Endless digression, description, astronomical periphrasis, apostrophe,
exclamation, prophecy, lament, philosophical reflection, moral exhortation—these are
what Lydgate adds to the translation, but they are in a sense the body of the work, for it is
through them that Lydgate makes sense in his own terms of a historical narrative which
for the Middle Ages could make sense in no others" (*Lydgate*, 129). Pearsall argues that
"the significance in the story" for Lydgate was "its profound meaninglessness" (143).

105. In her *Epistre d'Othea*, Christine de Pisan uses the commonplace that chivalry
began at Troy to promote Hector as the ideal knight, quite apart from his role within the
narrative itself; see Stephen Scrope, trans., *The Epistle of Othea to Hector*, ed. George F.
Warner (London: Roxburghe Club, 1904). For another poem that uses the Trojan material
to provide simply exemplary instances of chivalric achievement in love and war, see Jean
de Condé's *Li Recors d'armes et d'amours*, ed. Auguste Scheler, *Dits et contes de Baudouin de*

all the dehistoricizations of the Troy story, however, the most extensive is Boccaccio's *Filostrato:* abandoned by his lady, the poet surveys ancient histories to find a means of representing his secret grief, and with Troiolo and Criseida he finds the "forma alla mia intenzione."[106] Amorous lyricism governs his poem throughout, and the historical questions that so troubled Benoît and Guido disappear from his narrative. In reinserting the story of Troilus and Criseyde into history, then, Chaucer was returning to the authentic, or at least authentically medieval, tradition of Trojan historiography as defined by Benoît.[107] And in being true to that tradition he encourages us to read his poem both as an attempt to clarify the enigma of the Trojan experience through the experience of his two lovers and as an ironic and knowing tribute to the failures of earlier historical exegesis.

V: The "Lavor Doppio" of Troilus and Criseyde

The Italian phrase of my subtitle appears in Petrarch's *Rime* 40, where he describes the "double work" upon which he is currently engaged—probably the *Africa*—as caught "between the style of the moderns and ancient speech."[108] *Troilus and Criseyde* is also ambivalent between an-

---

Condé et de son fils Jean de Condé (Brussels: Devaux, 1866–67), 2:98–105. A number of similar instances are cited by Constans in volume 6 of his edition of *Le Roman de Troie.* This dehistoricization of the Trojan past is not always undertaken uncritically: Machaut's *Fonteinne amoureuse* uses the Trojan materials as part of a critique of the aristocratic trivilization of history implicit within the cult of *fine amor,* an irresponsibility that the poet himself simultaneously challenges and abets; see Margaret J. Ehrhart, "Machaut's *Dit de la fonteinne amoureuse,* the Choice of Paris, and the Duties of Rulers," *PQ* 59 (1980): 119–39.

106.   *Opere Minori in Volgare,* ed. Mario Marti (Milan: Rizzoli, 1970), 15–16.

107.   Wetherbee argues, on the other hand, that Chaucer uses the classical poets, especially Virgil, Ovid, and Statius, "as a standard of authenticity" by which to free himself from the medieval historiographical tradition "with its more limited historical validity" (*Chaucer and the Poets,* 25). For him, Chaucer is interested not in the historical problem of Troy but in the possibilities for personal transcendence over the historical world, a transcendence for which the classical poets provided exemplars of *virtus* by which Chaucer measured his protagonists. My reading, on the contrary, follows the direction long ago indicated by C. S. Lewis in "What Chaucer Really Did to *Il Filostrato,*" *Essays and Studies* 17 (1932): "Chaucer approached his work as an 'Historial' poet contributing to the story of Troy. . . . The whole 'matter of Rome' is still a unity, with a structure and life of its own. That part of it which the poem in hand is treating, which is, so to speak, in focus, must be seen fading gradually away into its 'historial' surroundings" (59, 60–61).

108.   Un mio lavor sì doppio
       tra lo stil de' moderni e 'l sermon prisco

cient and modern preoccupations, between a historicizing desire to recover an "authentic" antiquity and a pressing interest in current issues, as well as between the demands of a historical narrative and the attractions of an erotic counterplot. Not surprisingly, doubleness is itself thematized within the poem. That this is not only Criseyde's famous duplicity but also the narrative's own salient characteristic is a crucial and often overlooked aspect of the poem's historiographical and philosophical program. Yet this doubleness has itself a double meaning. On the one hand, the circularity of the narrative is configured under the sign of Fortune and so endowed with the familiar valence of Boethian consolation; yet beneath this formulation dwells a darker, less accommodating interpretation in terms of the circularity embodied in Thebanness. These two possibilities are staged throughout the course of the poem and are finally brought together in one of its most remarkable moments, Troilus's dream of the boar and its interpretation by Cassandra.

The narrator introduces Book 4 as if it were the final book of the poem: the proem tells us that Fortune casts down Troilus and sets up Diomede, that Criseyde forsakes him, and that in "this ilke ferthe book" shall "the losse of lyf and love yfeere / Of Troilus be fully shewed heere" (4, 26–28). In fact, none of these things happens in Book 4: another book of almost two thousand lines must be traversed while the action draws to its slow, discouraging close. It is perhaps for just that reason that Book 4 bespeaks throughout a powerful desire for closure, and one the characters share with their narrator. Hence Troilus's continued demand for a tragic denouement: as soon as Criseyde's exchange has been decided he rushes to foreclose the very possibility of a future. "O deth, allas!" he cries, "why nyltow do me deye?" (4, 250), the first of many similar supplications.[109] Of course he wants more than merely extinction, in the sense of a simple loss of consciousness. He desires a conclusion appropriate to the experience it consummates, a closure that will shape his past so as to confirm his highest conception of himself and his beloved. Hence the invocation of literary models of tragic consequence, Oedipus (300–301), Proserpina (475–76), and especially Pyramus and Thisbe, star-crossed lovers who came to what the *Legend of Good Women* calls "a pitous ende" (904). These Ovidian lovers are invoked in the second half of Book 4, when Criseyde swoons into a trance that Troilus interprets as death. Provided with an opportunity

---

che (paventosamente a dirlo ardisco)
in fin a Roma n'udirai lo scoppio.
Robert M. Durling, ed. and trans. (Cambridge: Harvard University Press, 1976), 106–7.
109. For example, 4, 274–80, 501–4.

for suicide, Troilus declaims against "cruel Jove" and "Fortune adverse" (1192) and bequeaths his soul to his beloved: "Criseyde, o swete herte deere, / Receyve now my spirit!" (1209–10). But the story disappointingly fails to achieve its tragic resolution: Criseyde not only awakens from her faint at the climactic moment, but turns Troilus from heroic self-sacrifice to an erotic consolation—"lat us rise, and streght to bedde go" (1242)—that recapitulates in a neatly chiastic form the original consummation scene of Book 3, where it was Troilus who fainted. What had promised to be an ending, in short, is revealed instead as anticlimactic repetition.

For Troilus a tragic denouement would provide the pathos and intensity that could reaffirm the highest meanings of which the love affair is capable and demonstrate forever the nobility of the lovers' *entente*. For the narrator this kind of closure could provide all that, plus the opportunity to endow his romantic story with a sanctioned historical meaning as a tragedy of Fortune. Hence the first two stanzas of the proem to Book 4 follow Boccaccio by invoking a Fortune who presides over both this book and, by echoing the proem to Book 1, the poem as a whole. The narrative of Book 4 is shaped so as to accord with such a reading, recapitulating as it does the narrative events of Books 1 through 3. Both 1 and 4 open with invocations to Furies that are derived from Statius (1, 6–9; 4, 22–24),[110] and in both the war creates a crisis (Calkas's defection, Antenor's capture) that leads to a scene of pleading (Criseyde before Hector, Calkas before the Greeks) and then to a large public event (the feast of the Palladion, the Trojan Parliament) at both of which Troilus is stricken and retires alone. He is then in both cases visited by a consoling Pandarus, whereupon the scene shifts, again in both cases, to Criseyde, whom we find first with her ladies, then alone, and then with Pandarus. The first section of the poem moves toward its conclusion with Troilus and Criseyde in bed together and at accord, and so too does (with unhappy qualifications) Book 4.[111] The basic pattern is clear, and so is its ostensible meaning: Books 1 through 3 record Troilus's ascent on the wheel of Fortune, Book 4 the descending counterpart. Were the poem to end here, as both the narrator and Troilus want, its

---

110. For the Statian source, see Boyd Ashby Wise, *The Influence of Statius Upon Chaucer* (Baltimore: J. H. Furst, 1911), 13.

111. There are as well a large number of nonnarrative echoes between Books 1–3 and 4, echoes that have been well described by Donald W. Rowe, *O Love O Charite! Contraries Harmonized in Chaucer's Troilus* (Carbondale: Southern Illinois State University Press, 1976), 121–30. In accord with his sense of the sacramental quality of the poem, Rowe reads this circularity as expressing a divine stability in the midst of change.

structure would trace the hero's rise from the "sorwe" of courtship to the bliss of consummation and back to the "sorwe" of death, while the terms of his death would effectively protect him, and his beloved, from complicity. Noble of purpose and steadfast in their loyalty, both lovers could (like Romeo and Juliet) exhibit a high-minded pathos that only the most severe of judges would be prepared to criticize; they would be victims of historical circumstance who would exemplify the treachery of the world without being themselves subject to censure.

To designate *Troilus and Criseyde* a tragedy of Fortune, as Troilus, the narrator, and many modern critics seek to do, is to acknowledge its failure as a project of historical legitimization: to consign the narrative to the order of Fortune is to deny it all but a merely catalytic and private value.[112] But this loss, however absolute it may appear, nonetheless offers readers a powerful compensation. For the invocation of Fortune promises to circumscribe an otherwise dangerously inconclusive narrative with a stabilizing act of intellectual control. The idea of Fortune both provides the reader with a standpoint outside the whirligig world of events and, by privileging spiritual growth, preserves the notion of a purposive linearity by locating it within the ahistorical realm of the self. However miserable the events we are invited to observe, we are allowed the atavistic pleasure of knowing that it is not our misery and the self-protective gratification of knowing what it means.

That the idea of Fortune also functions in this way for both the characters and the narrator is suggested by the one major paradigm the poem presents of the interpretive process itself: Troilus's dream of the boar in Book 5 and Cassandra's interpretation. In the dream Troilus enters a forest, and while roaming in quest of either consolation or confirmation—"up and doun . . . he the forest soughte" (1237)—comes upon the central, fatal scene:

> He mette he saugh a bor with tuskes grete,
> That slepte ayeyn the bryghte sonnes hete.
> And by this bor, faste in his armes folde,
> Lay, kyssyng ay, his lady bryght, Criseyde. (5, 1238–41)

112. This interpretation appears in a pure form in Willard Farnham, *The Medieval Heritage of Elizabethan Tragedy* (Berkeley: University of California Press, 1936), for whom Troilus is culpable not for his specific behavior but for the larger and less narrowly moral mistake of having committed himself to the historical world in the first place (137–60). D. W. Robertson moralizes this reading by arguing that Troilus's initial error leads him into a series of blindnesses that leave him "a 'great natural,' who has no place to hide his bauble" (*Preface to Chaucer*, 499); see also "Chaucerian Tragedy," *ELH* 19 (1952): 1–37.

The force of this scene becomes clear when it is set beside the comparable passage in the *Filostrato*. There Troiolo is not in quest but merely a passive observer: hearing a tumult within a shadowed glade, he raises his eyes in time to see a charging boar, who is then seen drawing forth Criseida's heart with his "grifo" or snout (7, 23–24). In Boccaccio, the dream is all too easily interpreted. As Troiolo immediately realizes, the boar is Diomede, by token of the boar of Calydon that has become the family crest, and the action means that "he has taken from her her heart, that is, her love, with his speech"—"col parlare" (7, 27), hence the "grifo." But Chaucer's version is enigmatic. The context of search and discovery in which it is set defines the event as not just revelation but pedagogy: as in a *chanson d'aventure*, a pensive knight wanders through a suggestive landscape in quest of enlightenment. Similarly, the lesson is clearly more intricate than the mere fact of infidelity. The male sexuality that is implied in Boccaccio's scene is represented here in the explicit and threatening form of the "tuskes grete," and yet, oddly, the scene as a whole is less violent. The event has already taken place, passion is spent, the satisfied boar sleeps peacefully in the sun while Criseyde lavishes on it the affection for which the abandoned Troilus yearns. This is an allegory of neither female lust nor male seduction: Criseyde is not possessed by but in love with a boar, and the tenderness that she bestows on this gross representation of male sexuality is the true horror of the dream. We have here not simply a prophetic dream but a fully realized nightmare of the male erotic imagination, and it is as a nightmare that it serves to express the complicated feelings of envy, prurience, shame, and rage that possess the betrayed Troilus.[113]

That Troilus refuses to acknowledge this betrayal is understandable; but neither does the narrator offer any recognition of the detailed psychology that the dream represents. Troilus has a sense that the dream has revealed to him not only that "he hadde his lady lorn" but as well "the *signifiaunce* / Of hire untrouthe and his disaventure" (1445–48), and he turns to Cassandra for an explication. In her answer—an elaborate account of Theban history—Criseyde's infidelity is interpreted not in ethical or even chivalric terms but historiographically. This is unprecedented in the *Filostrato* or any other version of the story. Criseyde's behavior, Cassandra implicitly claims, is at once caused by and explicable in terms of the large movements of historical experience, patterns whose value is encapsulated in Theban history and expressed

---

113.   Chaucer carefully links the dream to Troilus's "malencolye" (5, 1216) in order to designate it as what Macrobius calls a *somnium naturale* and therefore open to psychological interpretation.

by the "figure" (1449) of the boar. Hence Cassandra's somewhat eccentric summary of the matter of Thebes both begins and ends with this bestial presence, and the repetitions of her concluding statement illustrate the replicating structure of her account as a whole:

> *This ilke boor* bitokneth Diomede,
> Tideus sone, that down descended is
> Fro Meleagre, that made *the boor* to blede. (5, 1513–16)

Meleager and Diomede are bound together by a line of descent whose value is betokened by the boar; and it is this value or "signifiaunce" that has come to dominate the poem.

Yet the meaning of representing a man, and a genealogical line, in these terms remains itself unexplained.[114] Cassandra presents Theban history as nothing more than a series of tragedies of Fortune: "Thow most a fewe of olde stories heere," she tells Troilus, "To purpos how that Fortune overthrowe / Hath lordes olde" (1459–61), and she insists throughout that her account is drawn from "olde bookes" that preserve a record of "gestes old" (1481, 1511). Cassandra's account, as Wetherbee rightly points out, "reduces the individuals she names to pawns, less important than the sequence of events in which they appear."[115] Wholly uninterested in the psychological values expressed so powerfully by both the dream and Theban history, Cassandra invokes a historiography that merely restates the problem of the relation of individuals to events without providing an answer. And far from explicating Troilus's dream, her interpretation simply replays its dark emotions and helpless compulsions in a historical key. A gloss that replicates its text, her "lesson" is necessarily doomed to rejection. As Diomede "down descended is" (1514) from Meleager, so Cassandra "descended down from gestes olde / To Diomede" (1511–12): history and the understanding of history run on

114. Such a mode of personal identification was of course common in Chaucer's time with the development and proliferation of the personal badge: Edward III, for example, had a boar as his personal *devise*, as did the de Vere family. For a possible relevance to Chaucer, see C. E. Pickford, "The Royal Boar and the Ellesmere Chaucer," PQ 5 (1926): 330–40.

115. Wetherbee, *Chaucer and the Poets*, 130. See also Monica McAlpine, *The Genre of Troilus and Criseyde* (Ithaca: Cornell University Press, 1978): "Here [Cassandra] eliminates all that makes an act human: the intention, the circumstances, the whole process of moral decision, the web of freedom and fate" (171). I cannot agree, however, with the conclusions that both of these critics draw from their shrewd observation. For McAlpine the limitations of Cassandra's interpretation impeach its authority and entitle us to ignore it; similarly, Wetherbee argues that because her account is "dehumanized and effectively meaningless, its symbolic potential [is] vast but finally incalculable" (131).

parallel lines of descent, but precisely because they never meet they remain always the same. The relationship between interpretation and event is not causal but specular: just as warriors and lovers perform the same acts, so do poets and historians tell the same stories, parallel events that share an analogous incomprehensibility. And by rejecting Cassandra as a prophetess, Troilus legitimizes her as a historian: denied an understanding of history, he will inevitably repeat it.

Cassandra's introduction of Theban history into the poem represents not the first reference to this material but rather the penultimate of its many appearances. For the poem is massively saturated with Thebanness.[116] When at the opening of Book 2 Pandarus discovers Criseyde and three of her ladies reading a book, he asks, "Is it of love?" and adds, "O, som good ye me leere!" (97). By way of answer Criseyde says that "this romaunce is of Thebes" (100) and mentions the killing of Laius and the engulfing of Amphiaraus. Pandarus impatiently brushes off her answer—"Al this knowe I myself, / Al th'assege of Thebes and the care" (106–7)—while pretentiously claiming knowledge of the original Latin version—"herof ben ther maked bookes twelve" (108)—although Criseyde is apparently reading the twelfth-century *Roman de Thèbes* or one of its prose *remaniements*.[117] But the Theban story cannot be so easily dismissed: the narrative continually reverts to it as if, in typically Theban fashion, to a guilty origin. The "double sorwe" of the poem's opening line derives, at least in part, from Jocasta's "doppia tristizia" in *Purgatorio* 22, 56, a phrase that Dante himself derived, with shrewd irony, from Augustine's *Confessions*.[118] The Theban story is in-

116.   The relation of Theban material to the *Troilus* has been previously discussed by Wise, *Influence of Statius*; Francis P. Magoun, "Chaucer's Summary of Statius' *Thebaid* II–XII," *Traditio* 11 (1955): 409–20; Alain Renoir, "Thebes, Troy, Criseyde, and Pandarus: An Instance of Chaucerian Irony," *SN* 32 (1960): 14–17; Paul M. Clogan, "Chaucer's Use of the *Thebaid*," *English Miscellany* 18 (1967): 9–31; John P. McCall, *Chaucer Among the Gods: The Poetics of Classical Myth* (University Park: Penn State University Press, 1979), 88–92; David Anderson, "Theban History in Chaucer's *Troilus*," *SAC* 4 (1982): 109–33; and Wetherbee, *Chaucer and the Poets*, 111–44. The common theme of these accounts is that the Theban precedent functions to provide an ominous analogy to the Trojan catastrophe, and hence offers a lesson that the protagonists willfully ignore.

117.   That Criseyde is reading the French *Roman* is suggested by her phrase "This romaunce is of Thebes" (on *roman* as "romaunce," see Strohm, "The Origin and Meaning of Middle English *Romaunce*"), by her mention of the death of Laius, which is recounted in the *Roman* but not in the *Thebaid*, and by the designation of Amphiaraus as a "bisshop."

118.   Augustine lamented his mother's death with a *duplicia tristitia* (9, 12, 31), sorrowing for both her loss to him and his weakness in not being able to celebrate a death that was in reality a translation to glory—a filial love that was thus an ambiguously redeemed version of the fatal Oedipal attraction. Versions of the phrase "double sorwe"

deed about love, as Pandarus in his presumption unwittingly suggested, and so has special relevance to a Trojan love story. Moreover, just as the opening line of the poem contains a Theban echo mediated through Dante and Augustine, so does the concluding description of Troilus's ascent to the spheres derive from Boccaccio's account of the ascent of the Theban Arcita in the *Teseida*, a rewriting of Statius's *Thebaid*.

Theban history also furnishes the narrative with a surprising number of its classical allusions, virtually all additions to the *Filostrato*.[119] Pandarus tells Troilus not to "walwe and wepe as Nyobe the queene" (1, 699) and later swears to Criseyde that if his intentions are not honorable he should be put "as depe . . . in helle / As Tantalus" (3, 592–93), both of whom are famous Theban victims.[120] Criseyde mentions in her summary to Pandarus how Amphiaraus "fil thorugh the ground to helle" (2, 105) and then in Book 4 promises to be true to Troilus or else "with body and soule synke in helle" (4, 1554); conversely, Pandarus tells Criseyde that if he is less than sincere, "To dethe mot I smyten be with thondre" (2, 1145), the notorious fate of Capaneus as he mounted the walls of Thebes. Criseyde has three ladies (perhaps the same three to whom she is reading the romance of Thebes) called Antigone (an explicitly Theban name);[121] Flexippe (which comes from Plexippus, one

---

also occur in other texts known to Chaucer. In the *Filostrato*, for example, when Criseida faints Troiolo thinks she is dead, and this is for him a "doppia doglia" (4, 118). But here the phrase seems to function simply as an intensifier, as in Chaucer's own usage in 4, 903, where Criseyde, hearing of Troilus's lament for her, says to Pandarus, "Iwis, his sorwe doubleth al my peyne." This is a not uncommon usage in Middle English: see, for example, Malory, *Works*, ed. Eugene Vinaver (Oxford: Oxford University Press, 1967), 3: 1185. More clearly relevant usages are also found in Joseph of Exeter's *Bellum*, 6, 771 and 6, 833. But what is significant for our purposes is that the phrase and its cognates appears in Chaucer's works only in his Theban poems: *Anelida and Arcite*, 87, 159, the "Complaint of Mars," 255, and the *Knight's Tale*, 1454. This also argues for the priority of a Theban usage, such as Jocasta's "doppia tristizia," as a source.

119.   Paul Clogan has argued that a number of these references are derived from the extensive glosses to the *Thebaid*; "Chaucer and the *Thebaid* Scholia," *SP* 61 (1964): 599–615 and "Medieval Glossed Manuscripts of the *Thebaid*," *Manuscripta* 11 (1967): 102–12. Although I have earlier argued that the name and epithet of "false Poliphete" is best explained by reference to Servius (see above, 109), since virtually all of Chaucer's allusions can be found in such elementary source books as Hyginus's *Fabulae*, Ovid's *Metamorphoses*, and the handbooks of the so-called Vatican Mythographers, it is unnecessary to posit extensive recourse to glosses.

120.   Tantalus is in fact Niobe's father, as Ovid has her boastfully and foolishly point out (*Metamorphoses* 6, 172–73).

121.   According to Hyginus, *Fabulae* 6, 5 (ed. H. I. Rose, 2d ed. [Leiden: A. W. Sythoff, 1963], 100) and the Second Vatican Mythographer 2, 179 (Georg Bode, ed., *Scriptores rerum*

of the uncles killed by Meleager);[122] and Tharbe (an otherwise unattested name just possibly derived from "Thebes" itself). She swears by Athamas (4, 1639–40), another Theban victim, and by her own mother "that cleped were Argyve" (4, 762), a variant form of Argia, the daughter of Adrastus and wife of Polynices.[123] When in Book 3 Pandarus needs a rival to act as the pretext for the attack of jealousy that has supposedly brought Troilus to see Criseyde in the middle of the night, he summons up "oon hatte Horaste" (3, 797), whose name is derived from Orestes. Impelled (according to the mythographers) to murder his mother through the influence of the fatal brooch of Thebes possessed by his wife Hermione, Orestes is also an appropriate name for a rival: classical mythographers told how he abducted Hermione from her husband Neoptolemus (a story retold, for instance, in Book 6 of Dictys' *Ephemeridos*).[124]

    In a more general sense, the continual invocation of the Fates and the Furies—figures inextricably linked in medieval mythography— locates the story in a Theban-like context of fatal passion.[125] The most

---

mythicarum latini tres romae, [Celle: Schulze, 1834], 1:55), Antigone is also the name of one of Laomedon's daughters. In the *Genealogie deorum gentilium* 6, 7 (ed. Vincenzo Romano [Bari: Laterza, 1951], 1:294), Boccaccio cites Servius as his authority for this information.

    122.   *Metamorphoses* 8, 440; see also Boccaccio, *Teseida* 8, 43, where he is called "Plesippo."

    123.   On Athamas, see *Metamorphoses* 4, 420, and Hyginus, ed. Rose, 1, 2, 5, 239; on Argyve as Argia, see Wise, *Influence of Statius,* 34–35, and Susan Schibanoff, "Argus and Argyve: Etymology and Characterization in Chaucer's *Troilus*," *Speculum* 51 (1976): 647–58.

    124.   For Orestes and the brooch of Thebes, see the Second Vatican Mythographer (Bode, ed., *Scriptores,* 1:101). As well as the Theban allusions enumerated in the text, one might also note the following: the invocation to Clio in the proem to Book 2 (2, 8) recalls Statius's similar invocation (*Thebaid* 1, 41; and see Dante's allusion to this Statian passage in *Purgatorio* 22, 58); Troilus's prayer before the consummation is saturated with classical allusions that derive from Theban poetry (3, 720–24; see notes in the *Riverside Chaucer,* Wise, *Influence of Statius,* 11, and Clogan, "*Thebaid* Scholia"); 5, 1–11 derive from the *Thebaid* and the *Tesedia*; Troilus's imagination of his funeral pyre in 5, 302–22 alludes to Arcita's similar imagination; the allusion to Manes at 5, 892–93 is probably derived from the *Thebaid* (these last three mentioned in the notes in the *Riverside Chaucer*); and the poet's instruction to his poem in the *licentia auctoris* to kiss the footsteps of the great *poetae* derives from *Thebaid* 12, 816–17. Wise's statement that, "with the exception of Ovid, and possibly of Boethius, Statius was Chaucer's most familiar Latin author" (141) is certainly right.

    125.   The three Furies and the three Fates are together inhabitants of the underworld, functioning as virtually identical agents of violence and disaster; see, for example, the *Roman de la Rose,* 16905–908 and 19802–808 (ed. Felix Lecoy, 3 vols, CFMA [Paris: Champion, 1965–70]), and Hans Liebeschütz, ed., *Fulgentius metaforalis* (Leipzig: Teubner, 1926), 108–14. Chaucer refers to the Fates as the "fatal sustren" (3, 733) and the

important instance is the narrator's opening invocation of "Thesiphone, . . . th[e] goddesse of torment" (1, 6–8), which discordantly but, as we come finally to understand, appropriately alludes to the curse with which Oedipus conjures up the same Fury at the beginning of the *Thebaid* (1, 46–87). For it is Oedipus, to whom Troilus explicitly compares himself and whose blindness he unwittingly imitates, who comes to function not just as the protagonist's most persistent Theban *alter ego* but as an emblem of the nature and conditions of historical action per se.[126] In reaction to the Trojan Parliament's decision to exchange Criseyde, Troilus avers that he will, "as Edippe," drag out "in derknesse / My sorwful lif, and dyen in distresse" (4, 300–301); he then enjoins his eyes to "wepen out youre sighte" (4, 312) now that Criseyde is gone—some medieval sources posit endless weeping as the cause of Oedipus's blindness[127]—and he, like Oedipus, retreats into a "derke chambre" (4, 354; cf. 232–33) to grieve.

These are, to be sure, melodramatic gestures.[128] But not only do they begin to confirm by their very extravagance the force of the analogy they posit, but Troilus makes his vow true in ways that are historically telling. In the *Canticus Troili* of Book 5, the double to the similar *Canticus* in Book 1 and, at the same time, an analogue to the *Planctus Oedipi* that the Middle Ages ascribed to the Theban protagonist, Troilus says that he moves toward his death "evere derk in torment, nyght by nyght" (5, 640).[129] When his "malencolye" (5, 1216) finally renders him so feeble that he must walk with a "potente" or staff (5, 1222), the Trojan lover, whose "hope alwey hym blente" (5, 1195), finally becomes a painfully exact replica of the blinded Oedipus. And like the Oedipus who was for

---

Furies as "Nyghtes doughtren thre" (4, 22). For Theban sources for his references to these trios, see notes in the *Riverside Chaucer* and the suggestions offered by Wise, *Influence of Statius*, and Clogan, "Chaucer's Use of the *Thebaid*."

126. This connection has been discussed in different terms by Julia Ebel, "Troilus and Oedipus: The Genealogy of an Image," *ES* 55 (1974): 15–21, and Chauncey Wood, *Elements of Chaucer's* Troilus, 153–63.

127. A late fourteenth- or early fifteenth-century prose version of the story, known as the *Roman d'Edipus* and included as part of the so-called *Histoire ancienne jusqu'à Cesar*, says both that "Edipus se creva les yeux par ennuy" and that he "plora tant que il en perdit la veue." Its renditions of Oedipus's laments also bear several striking resemblances to Troilus's complaints. This text is available in a nineteenth-century reproduction of a sixteenth-century printing (Paris: Collection Silvestre, 1858), from which the above phrases are taken (Biiiiʳ). The basic study is Leopold Constans, *La Légende d'Oedipe étudiée dans l'antiquité, au moyen âge et dans les temps modernes* (Paris: Maisonneuve, 1881); for the *Roman d'Edipus*, see 338–44. More recent bibliography is available in Lowell Edmunds, "Oedipus in the Middle Ages," *Antike und Abendland* 22 (1976): 140–55.

128. Wetherbee, *Chaucer and the Poets*, 210.

129. For the *Planctus Oedipi*, see above, 82 *n* 92.

the Middle Ages a figure of despair, Troilus calls on death to bear him away—"O deth, allas! why nyltow do me deye?" (4, 250)—and describes himself as a "combre-world, that may of nothyng serve, / But evere dye and nevere fulli sterve" (4, 279–80), language that inescapably recalls medieval discussions of despair.[130] Like Oedipus, he curses his gods, "his burthe, hymself, his fate, and ek nature" (5, 209)—curses phrased in language strikingly similar to that of the *Planctus Oedipi* and the complaints of the *Roman d'Edipus*—and in his dreams reenacts Oedipus's own inconclusive conclusion, an endless subsistence "allone / In place horrible, makyng ay his mone" (5, 249–50).

In the final analysis, however, the comparison between Oedipus and Troilus, like that between their cities, must be understood as an analogy between *forms* of behavior rather than simply between its content or ethical value. The sharp disparity between Troilus's infatuation with Criseyde and Oedipus's criminal lust for his mother cannot be overridden in the quest for common denominators, nor does Trojan society present anything equivalent to the catalogue of horrors of Theban history.[131] It is, rather, the recursive *shape* of Theban history, and its devastating effect upon the claim to linearity implicit in the assertion of Trojan foundation and the *translatio imperii* that follows from it, that is invoked by the Theban allusions. Moreover, if the affinity between Troilus and the blind Oedipus suggests that this fatal recursiveness is a function of ignorance, it also betokens more than ignorance: to reduce the story of either man to the truism *nosce teipsum* is to ignore the ineluctable power that moves each toward his fate. For the central topic of Chaucer's Theban poetry is the compulsion that lies beneath ignorance and that prescribes it as its *sine qua non*. In *Anelida and Arcite* Thebanness appeared as a fatally doubled self enabled by the self's ignorance of its own deepest desires. In the "Complaint of Mars" the "double wo and passioun" elicited by the Brooch of Thebes drives the uncomprehending if powerful protagonists—at once deities and planets—along their allotted paths. And in *Troilus and Criseyde* the self's compulsions are epitomized in Troilus's dream, its self-ignorance enacted in Cassandra's interpretation: an imagination possessed by double sorrow calls up the Theban story as a potential source of self-knowledge only to have the whole suppressed under the sign of Fortune.

130. For Oedipus and despair, see the discussion of the Old Man in the *Pardoner's Tale*, below, 412–18.

131. Indeed, as Mark Lambert persuasively argues in "*Troilus*, Books I–III: A Criseydan Reading," in *Essays on* Troilus and Criseyde, ed. Mary Salu (Cambridge: Brewer, 1979), 105–25, the besetting sin of Trojan society is triviality rather than any more strenuous vice.

VI: The Form of Subjectivity

The subjectivity represented in *Troilus and Criseyde* is as doubled, as duplicitous, as that of *Anelida and Arcite*. The love story the poem tells is about how two people strive, unsuccessfully, to become one; and their failure is a function of their own lack of oneness or integrity—a quality that must be understood in psychological as well as ethical terms. The condition to which both Troilus and Criseyde aspire in the poem is conceived as a love that overcomes difference—what the narrator calls, in reference to himself, "unliklynesse" (1, 16)—by establishing a unifying concord. As Pandarus, optimistically but finally inaccurately tells the lovers, "ye two ben al on" (4, 592).

"Love is he that alle thing may bynde" (1, 237), and as criticism has well shown, for Troilus this "holy bond" (3, 1261) not only unites him to Criseyde but "cercle[s] hertes alle" (3, 1767) in a universal, cosmic harmony.[132] Criseyde's aspirations are less philosophical, but criticism too rarely acknowledges that she also yearns for an unmediated mutuality, as the account of her inward conversion to love in Book 2 shows. First she listens to Antigone's song, which describes love as the reciprocal and unstinting exchange of hearts: the lady of the song loves a knight "In which myn herte growen is so faste, / And his in me, that it shal evere laste" (2, 872–73). Then she dreams a literal enactment of this exchange, with an eagle playing the role of Troilus. For Troilus Criseyde is firmly "iset" (3, 1488) in his heart, and for Criseyde Troilus is in turn "so depe in-with myn herte grave" (3, 1499) that he could (she says) never be turned out. "I am thyn, by God and by my trouthe" (3, 1512) she avers, and Troilus similarly tells Pandarus that "I thus am hires" (3, 1608)—a reciprocal self-surrender that allows for an apparently instinctive and equivalent mutuality: "ech of hem gan otheres lust obeye" (3, 1690). As the narrator says, "This is no litel thyng of for to seye" (3, 1688).

That Troilus and Criseyde posit as their goal unmediated mutuality and universal harmony both defines desire as privation and accounts for its inevitable unfulfillment. Both lovers are in search of a completeness that will minister to a sense of need that they differently but mutually express. For Troilus desire is experienced as the discomfort of absence: he burns with "the fyr of love" (1, 436), a metaphor invoked throughout the poem to articulate appetite as self-consumption. As he says at the outset, "at myn owen lust I brenne" (1, 407). For Criseyde

132. See, for example, Rowe, *O Love! O Charitee!*, passim. On the ambivalence of the imagery of binding in the poem, see Stephen Barney, "Troilus Bound," *Speculum* 47 (1972): 445–58.

the situation is more complicated, since the cultural constraints placed upon the representation of female sexuality allow it only a displaced expression. But in the one moment when her desire does emerge directly, it too adopts a metaphor of privation. Catching sight of Troilus returning from battle, she famously exclaims, "Who yaf me drynke?" (2, 651): the sight of Troilus is a love potion that quickens rather than slakes thirst. Love is an appetite that grows by feeding; lovers are driven by yearnings that cannot be relieved by each other.

This is an economy of desire that can easily be accommodated to traditional medieval paradigms. In Boethian terms the lovers are driven by an *amor conversus* that seeks to return to the *fons et origo* from which they originally derived but that has been misled into the false good of each other. In Christian terms the lovers are tormented by a *concupiscentia* that is the effect of the fall, an endless desire that they have, in the words of the *Parson's Tale*, "wrongfully disposed or ordeyned" so that they now "coveite, by coveitise of flessh, flesshly synne" (X, 336). But Chaucer is unusual in not allowing these absolutist positions either to foreclose his exploration of the dynamic of desire or to prescribe its terms. Much of the burden of the poem concerns the nature of the subjectivity that at once produces and is produced by the historical world; and while we are never allowed to forget its endemic insufficiencies, it is described with a particularity and intensity that frustrate appropriation by any essentializing interpretive scheme, whether medieval or modern.

Central to Chaucer's independence from absolutist schemes is his concept of *entente:* he transforms the Boethian concept of *intentio naturalis* into a historicized and therefore irreducibly complex notion of intention—part motive, part goal, part meaning. At the opening of the poem the audience is enjoined to "herk[en] with a good entencioun" (1, 52), and throughout the first three books we are encouraged to think that a similarly benevolent—and largely indeterminate—intention is shared by the characters as well. Pandarus assures Troilus at the outset that "myn entencioun / Nis nat to yow of reprehencioun" (1, 683–84) and tells Criseyde that "I speke of good entencioun" (2, 295), that "myn entent is cleene" (2, 580). He seeks to foreclose the very possibility of interpretation: his meaning is at once self-evident—"This al and som, and pleynly oure entente" (2, 363)—and benevolent: "What so I spak, I mente naught but wel" (2, 592). Criseyde is apparently persuaded. Troilus, she believes, "meneth in good wyse" (2, 721), Antigone's song was written "with . . . good entente" (2, 878), and she listens to the nightingale "in good entente" (2, 923). And like Pandarus, she wants to believe that her own intention is "pleyn": " 'For pleynly myn entente,' as seyde she, / Was for to love hym unwist, if she myghte" (2, 1293–94). When at Deiphoebus's house she asks Troilus "to telle [her] the fyn of his entente" (3, 125), Troilus outlines a program of courtly service that Criseyde accepts with the semicontractual and yet resolutely vague phrase, "as I wel mene, eke menen wel to me" (164).

Yet as the poem proceeds this vagueness is asked to bear an intolerable weight of implication. At the beginning of Book 3, for instance, Troilus and Pandarus struggle to articulate the nature of their relationship, with Pandarus finally sliding off the issue with a dismissive gesture: "Al sey I nought, thow wost wel what I meene" (256), he says, to which he later unhelpfully adds, "For wel I woot, thow menest wel, pardee" (337). In describing the consummation scene the narrator has continual recourse to bland, justificatory formulas. When Criseyde allows Troilus into the bedroom, we are told that, "Considered alle thynges as they stoode, / No wonder is, syn she did al for goode" (923–24); and then when she allows him into her bed, the formula reappears again, although now with an awkward qualification: "for every wyght, *I gesse*, / That loveth wel, meneth but gentilesse" (1147–48). Criseyde then explains to Troilus that "In alle thyng is myn entente cleene" (1166)—later she "Opned hire herte, and tolde hym hire entente" (1239)—while Troilus embraces her "as he that mente / Nothyng but wel" (1185–86) and then makes known his "clene entente" (1229). Finally, to complete this picture of well-meaning, "Pandarus with a ful good entente / Leyde hym to slepe" (1188–89).

What precisely is the content of this *entente?* The question becomes increasingly urgent as the narrative moves from its comic ascent in Books 1–3 to the tragic collapse of Books 4 and 5. When in Book 4 Pandarus is about to send Troilus to discuss their dilemma with Criseyde, he assures him that "by hire wordes ek, and by hire cheere, / Thou shalt ful sone aperceyve and wel here / Al hire entente" (655–57); and as Criseyde works her persuasions on Troilus the narrator hopefully adds that "al this thyng was sayd of good entente" (1416), that she "spak right as she mente" (1418). Yet we can doubt whether even Criseyde knows what she means, anymore than she did in Book 2. Even as she prepares in Book 5 to accept Diomede's proposal, she plaintively assures herself that "in conclusioun, / I mene wel" (5, 1003–4), and when she writes her final, unworthy letter to Troilus she concludes with a painfully self-revealing apology for its brevity: "Ek gret effect men write in places lite; / Th'entente is al, and nat the lettres space" (5, 1629–30). When Troilus sees his brooch on Diomede's armor he thinks that this *entente* is now clear, for he assumes that Criseyde meant to make a public profession of her love—"for that ye mente / Al outrely to

shewen youre entente" (5, 1693–94). The fact is apparently unargu-
able, but Criseyde (and the reader) may well feel that both more and
less was meant.

We are continually tempted toward irony and even cynicism by the
language of *entente,* which often seems simply a disguise for embarrassing motives. Yet such a reading is included within the poem in a form
that makes it increasing difficult to accept, since to do so requires us to
identify with the cynical Pandarus. Unable to understand that motives
(including his own) may be complex and even conflicted, Pandarus
focuses only on what the narrator calls "the fyn of his entente" (3, 553)
and seeks to foreclose the process by which that conclusion is to be
achieved as of no interest. As he himself says to Criseyde,

> Nece, alwey—lo!—to the laste,
> How so it be that som men hem delite
> With subtyl art hire tales to endite,
> Yet for al that, in hire entencioun,
> Hire tale is al for som conclusioun. (2, 255–59)

This conclusion is to bring Troilus and Criseyde to bed, after which
"Pandarus hath fully his entente" (3, 1582). But is it adequate to say,
with Pandarus, that the conclusion to which the lovers' *entente* is directed is the sexual act? And that in having it *they* have fully their
entente? And are the elaborate means by which that *entente* is brought to
fulfillment (the entire first half of a very long poem) simply a form of
erotic deferral, an elaborately extended foreplay?

To grant Pandarus's view interpretive authority is to reduce *Troilus
and Criseyde* to the *Filostrato.* For in that poem a lofty idealism—
compounded largely of Boethian and Dantean materials—is undercut
by a deeply misogynist cynicism about the nature of desire. This cynicism is, significantly, most explicitly voiced by Boccaccio's Pandaro:

> I believe indeed that every lady leads an amorous life
> in her wishes, and the only thing that restrains her is
> the fear of shame; and if for such yearning a full
> remedy can virtuously be given, he is foolish who does
> not despoil her, for in my opinion the distress vexes
> her little. My cousin is a widow, she desires, and
> should she deny it I would not believe her.[133]

133.   Trans. Nathaniel Edward Griffin and Arthur Beckwith Myrick (New York: Biblo
and Tannen, 1967 [1929]), 2, 27.

When Criseida shortly does deny it, Pandaro repeats his opinion with exasperation (2, 112), and Criseida instantly drops the pretense: she smiles in assent (113), and in her subsequent interior monologue admits to herself and to us her desire for a consummation: "would that I were now in his sweet embrace, pressed face to face!" (117)[134] According to the logic of Boccaccio's poem, these carnal impulses find their inevitable moral extension in her later infidelity, motivated as it is by the "lies, deceptions and betrayals" (53, 18) that lurk within her. The *Filostrato* must, therefore, end with a misogynist outburst ("Giovane donna è mobile" [53, 30]) qualified only by the claim that there does exist, somewhere, a "perfetta donna" who is at once amorous and faithful. Nor are these ambivalences absent from the dramatic frame in which Boccaccio's poem is set. Written to persuade the poet's own "donna gentil" of the intensity of his passive suffering, the poem also demonstrates the poet's active power as moral arbiter and propagandist. The lady is disingenuously advised to apply to herself only those "praiseworthy things" written about Criseida and to regard the "other things" as there just for the sake of the story—a selective reading that is meant to be impossible. Should she not return to her adoring poet, runs the clear implication, "la donna gentil" is in danger of becoming known as another "Criseida villana" (8, 28) through the agency of the same poet, now grown vengeful. His poem is, he tells us at the beginning, the "forma alla mia intenzione" (Proemio), and it accurately embodies the complex mix of emotions that women elicit from the men who are simultaneously their victims and masters.

Chaucer's poem, as C. S. Lewis argued many years ago, consistently excludes the misogyny that provides one pole for Boccaccio's amorous dialectic.[135] Pandaro's account of female desire is both sharply truncated in the corresponding speech by Chaucer's Pandarus and generalized into a human quality, characteristic of both men and women:

---

134. For Criseida's earlier expressions of desire, see Boccaccio's account of her meditation on Troiolo (2, 68–78).

135. In "What Chaucer Really Did to Il *Filostrato*," Lewis contrasted Boccaccio's "cynical Latin gallantries" with what he took to be Chaucer's commitment to the code of courtly love (75); but as Sanford Meech showed, what Chaucer was really doing was installing in the place of the *Filostrato*'s misogynist reductions a fully articulated conception of the self in the process of being in love (*Design in Chaucer's "Troilus"* [Syracuse: Syracuse University Press, 1959]). For moralizing readings of the *Filostrato*, however, see Robert P. apRoberts, "Love in the *Filostrato*," ChR 7 (1972): 1–26; and Chauncey Wood, *Elements of Chaucer's* Troilus, 3–37.

Was nevere man or womman yet bigete
That was unapt to suffren loves hete,
Celestial, or elles love of kynde;
Forthy som grace I hope in hire to fynde. (1, 977–80)

Similarly, Pandaro's second use of this Ovidian *topos* (2, 112) is wholly
revised by Chaucer to become a comment not on women's amorousness but on their *daunger* (2, 1149–52), and Criseida's answering smile
becomes in Criseyde both less knowing and less specific to Pandarus's
comment. Finally, the explicit antifeminism of Boccaccio's ending (8, 3)
is wholly excluded in Chaucer's poem. But Chaucer does more than
protect Criseyde from antifeminist reductions. His revisions also allow
into his poem a more capacious representation of subjectivity—the
whole inner world so inadequately designated by the single word
entente—than the *Filostrato* can accommodate. Boccaccio's poem remains within the generic confines of erotic literature, a typical if prominent example of the Ovidian tradition of the Middle Ages. His characters are defined by the genre: lovers and only lovers, they draw their
motivations from the store of recognized erotic impulses and define
their lives solely in terms of their amorous fates. But Chaucer's poem
expands these generic boundaries in order to explore the nature of subjectivity itself; and in doing so it shows how the notion of intention, as
defined by either philosophy (Boethius) or moral theology (the Parson), is inadequate to an account of human action.

To reduce the subjectivity of the *Troilus* to intentionality is to assume
that human beings exist as singular, self-identical, and self-present individuals, an assumption that the poem throughout calls into question.
Instead, we would do better to think of the subjectivity of the *Troilus* as
a site where not one but many intentions—in effect, many selves—are
in a ceaseless process of constitution. In one sense, the character who
most ostentatiously displays the multiplicity of selves that typifies this
subjectivity is the Janus-faced Pandarus. Mercurial in mood as in function, he alternates easily between modes of behavior that we usually
think of as distinct: as he shuttles visitors in and out of Troilus's
sickroom at Deiphoebus's house, for instance, he adopts and divests
himself of a wide variety of roles, and in his manipulation of the consummation scene he is equally adept at assuming—and perhaps even
experiencing—radically disparate forms of behavior. He is, moreover,
equally at home at Troilus's "beddes syde" (3, 236, 1589; 5, 294) or at
Criseyde's (3, 682, 1555–82), and he displays throughout the narrative
a sexual interest that is at once genderless and double-gendered, without specific affect and therefore capable of multiple cathexes. It is true

that the very facility that makes it possible for Pandarus to transfigure himself as he manipulates others might render his subjectivity less rather than more problematic: in defining him as less than fully invested in any of his roles, the poem invites us to understand him as an instance of a simple, in the sense of deliberate and therefore wholly controlled, hypocrisy. But even this kind of simplicity is delusive. The turmoil of selves that he displays comes finally to surround a strange emptiness at the center—we never finally do understand his own motivation, and neither, so far as we know, does he.

Just as Pandarus is more of a mystery than he may at first appear, so too are the lovers; and while we (and they) are tempted to stress their difference from him, the narrative insists that they are to an important degree equivalent. That Criseyde is changeable is the central fact about her: linked imagistically to the moon, to "slydynge fortune," and to the unstable world itself, she is an object of exchange whose subjectivity alters with her circumstances.[136] With Troilus she is a courtly lady anxiously aware that all worldly happiness is "fals felicitee" (3, 814), aggrieved and saddened by her lover's jealousy, and yet finally prepared to yield herself wholly to him: "And at o word, withouten repentaunce, / Welcome, my knyght, my pees, my suffisaunce!" (3, 1308–9). Yet immediately after this wholehearted yielding she engages in a notoriously ambiguous flirtation with Pandarus that causes even the narrator to turn away in embarrassment—"I passe al that which chargeth nought to seye" (3, 1576)—and she finally becomes the woman whose self-interest allows her to accept the matching selfishness of Diomede's brutal protection. It is all too easy to decide that the last of these Criseydes is the real one, but to do so requires us to impeach all the rest by assuming a self-consistency—a constancy of selfhood—that the poem itself shows to be an illusion.

For not even Troilus, endowed (as Criseyde herself recognizes) with "moral vertu, grounded upon trouthe" (4, 1672), is exempt from variableness. Two examples of his complexity—a complexity that he himself seeks to efface and that criticism has been equally reluctant to acknowledge—will suffice. After each of the dramatized meetings with his lady, Troilus engages in a conversation with Pandarus that reveals a sharply different self than had previously been in evidence. In the bedroom at Deiphoebus's house Troilus is a tongue-tied lover, unable to manage the elaborate game of role playing that Pandarus has fabricated: when Criseyde declines to be the courtly beloved but insists instead on acting the threatened victim pleading for protection, Troilus

136. For these comparisons, see Rowe, *O Love, O Charite!*, 57–91.

collapses into blushing silence (3, 78–84). Similarly, and even more drastically, at Pandarus's house the fiction of Horaste—and Criseyde's apparent belief in it—renders him not just silent but unconscious: unable to extricate himself from Pandarus's web, he faints.

But after each of these scenes he is a wholly different, and far less appealing, person. When Pandarus worries that he might be thought a bawd, Troilus provides not just the expected disclaimers but also an offer to be himself a bawd in return. Not only does this offer reinstate the sleaziness that he and Pandarus have been trying to deny, but it is delivered in a language far more blunt that any that Pandarus would use:

> I have my faire suster Polixene,
> Cassandre, Eleyne, or any of the frape—
> Be she nevere so fair or wel yshape,
> Tel me which thow wilt of everychone,
> To han for thyn, and lat me thanne allone. (3, 409–13)

Similarly, when after the lovers' night together Pandarus again comes to Troilus, not only does Troilus "telle hym of his glade nyght" (3, 1646) but he is "nevere ful to speke of this matere" (1661). "This tale ay was span-newe to bygynne, / Til that the night departed hem atwynne" (1665–66): for an entire day Troilus rehearses with his friend the night they have *together* (we unhappily remember) spent with Criseyde— men discoursing together about a woman they have, in some indefinable but nonetheless real way, already shared. Here it is Criseyde who is the mediating third term: at once present in memory and absent in fact, she is the means by which two men spend a day together—and a day apparently spent, moreover, in bed.[137]

We can, if we wish, draw a moral distinction between Criseyde's abandonment of Troilus and Troilus's talking about Criseyde with Pandarus, but we should not allow it to obscure the similarity between the two lovers. In fact, Chaucer continually insists that not one but both the lovers are simultaneously knowing and unknowing, at once conscious of the nature of their desire and the means of its fulfillment and yet profoundly, and necessarily, unaware. Criseyde must know, for example, that the meeting at Deiphoebus's house is not required by

---

137. When Pandarus first arrives he sits on the "beddes syde" (1589) to talk with Troilus, but Troilus leaps up and gets on his knees in thanksgiving. Then, however, "down in his bed he lay" (1615), and we never hear of him getting up again: just as the first conversation takes place with Pandarus on the "beddes syde" (3, 236) and Troilus lying down, so too does this one.

Poliphete's threat—which she herself has dismissed (2, 1477–78)—and both the secret pleasure she takes at the discussion of Troilus's illness and virtues ("For which with sobre cheere hire herte lough" [2, 1592]) and her lack of surprise at the absence of Helen and Deiphoebus in his bedroom certainly suggest that she knows the true purpose of the meeting. But does this mean that her continued playing of the role of threatened victim is simply hypocrisy, an empty gesture toward conventions of seemliness? Or does it not rather express hesitations and anxieties that are deeply a part of her character? Similarly, the night at Pandarus's house where the lovers will, as the narrator delicately says, "leiser have hire speches to fulfelle" (3, 510) is prepared for by innuendo and even outright suggestion (see, e.g., 3, 566–67); indeed, the very pretext that keeps Criseyde from going home—that it is raining—is itself empty, since it was raining not only before she came but when the invitation was first accepted (see 3, 562). Yet does that mean that Criseyde's shock on being awakened by Pandarus, and her protestations about receiving Troilus, are meaningless? If they are, why does Pandarus confect the story about Horaste in the first place? The fact is that this semiawareness is a necessary condition for the love affair. No doubt Criseyde is in Pandarus's house because she wants to make love with Troilus: as she finally says to him, "Ne hadde I er now, my swete herte deere, / Ben yolde, ywis, I were now nought here!" (3, 1210–11). But because her world proscribes the explicit representation of female sexual desire, she cannot admit this want either to others or to herself. Indeed, the obsessive secrecy that surrounds and perhaps even dooms the affair is best understood as a metaphoric displacement of this need for *self*-concealment: it is less "every pie and every lette-game" (3, 527) who threaten the affair than the guilt and shame with which sexuality, and specifically female sexuality, is invested.

When Chaucer describes how Criseyde falls in love, he shows not only that desire is experienced by her as an external force that comes upon her, but that even when it has become a part of her—when it has become *her* desire—she is unable to represent it to herself as her own. Aroused first by Pandarus's words, her feelings are intensified by the sight of Troilus returning from battle to the point where she can understand them only as a form of almost chemical change: "Who yaf me drynke?"[138] Retreating into her closet, she then retreats yet further into

138. That Criseyde has been prepared by Pandarus's words is suggested by the description of "al hir meyne" rushing to welcome him with a cry of remarkably sexual suggestiveness: "cast up the yates wyde! / For thorwgh this strete he moot to paleys ride" (615–16).

her own mind: by debating the question of love she hopes to gain a conscious purchase upon it. This process is not resolved but merely sealed by a series of symbolic events (all of them Chaucer's invention) that serve to present love, and specifically passion, as an entity at once a part of and apart from the female subject who experiences it. First there is the overhearing of the *Canticus Antigoni* (as several manuscripts call it). A song of love as mutuality, it alienates Criseyde's desire from itself by its double vicariousness: it is not even Antigone's own song much less Criseyde's (and hence its difference from the *Canticus Troili* of the previous book) but the song of the unnamed "goodlieste mayde / Of gret estat in al the town of Troye" (880–81). Then there is the "lay / Of love" (921–22) sung by the nightingale in the cedar tree, a wordless song that by its oblique allusion to Philomela images passion as a function only of the rapacious male and so simultaneously invokes and mutes the female fear of desire. And finally there is the dream of the bone-white eagle with his "longe clawes" (927), who in rending from her her heart and replacing it with his own fulfills the promise of mutuality offered in Antigone's song and so redeems the violence of the means: "she nought agroos, ne nothyng smerte" (930). Criseyde remains the passive recipient of actions performed not only upon her body but with her will—and yet at no point does either body or will find representation. By this point, Criseyde has, as she will later, passively say, "ben yold" (3, 1210), but her accession to that yielding— much less her desire for it—remains unspoken and unacknowledged. She knows and doesn't know that she desires: she has heard it and dreamed it, and the knowledge is at once part of and apart from her.

The unreflective, subterranean way in which love comes upon Criseyde is a function not of moral failure but of cultural necessity: all we need do to demonstrate this to ourselves is to try to imagine in what terms she might acknowledge her own sexuality. For then she immediately turns into a character like the Miller's Alison, or Alison of Bath— and she perforce exits from the world of this poem. The precondition of Criseyde's existence as Criseyde, in other words, is that she *not* know the burden of that name.

Troilus's Oedipean blindness is also prescribed by cultural imperatives. After his sight of Criseyde in the temple he composes the *Canticus Troili*, asserting his utter passivity before the transcendent force that has possessed him. So too does Chaucer assert his passivity in receiving the translation of this song from "myn auctour called Lollius" (1, 394). But just as the "tonges difference" (1, 395) that is the condition of all writing subverts the disingenuous claim of the poet, so do the circumstances of the lover's song call into question the singleness of his *entente*: it is one of the means by which Troilus will *"arten* hire to love" (1, 388), and its strategic value stands in awkward opposition to its transcendent claims.[139] Neither poet nor lover is in touch with an origin (Love, Lollius) that legitimizes their analogous projects. Indeed, as soon as the metaphor of Cupid shooting lovers with his arrows is invoked in the temple scene in Book 1 (206–10) it is immediately undone by the heavily sexualized eye play in which Troilus and Criseyde then engage. Troilus's "eye percede, and so depe it wente, / Til on Criseyde it smot, and ther it stente" (1, 272–73); but when she responds with her "somdele deignous" glance, "He was tho glad his hornes in to shrinke" (300). Rather than proceeding from a transcendent source, desire is a function of human sexuality, and the metaphor of Cupid's arrows is revealed as a mystification of its physical source.

But if sexuality is the ground of Troilus's desire, it is in no sense its whole content. Indeed, if it were, the loss of Criseyde would be easily consoled. To "arten" Criseyde solely for the purposes of sexual gratification would be as much a betrayal of Troilus's *gentilesse* as it would be to "ravisshe" her out of Troy. Hence the necessity of Pandarus, whose function for Troilus is to enact those aspects of his *entente* to love that he cannot acknowledge. It is because Pandarus is available not only to handle the embarrassing details of the consummation but actually to undress Troilus and install him in Criseyde's bed that Troilus can afford to faint. The point is not, as D. W. Robertson has memorably said, that Troilus loves Criseyde for nothing more "than her pleasing 'figure' and surpassing competence in bed," but that his desire is initiated by and necessarily includes a sexuality that he wishes both to enact and, for reasons we are surely meant to admire, to disavow.[140]

Willful ignorance is thus the condition of the lovers' very existence. Endowed with a subjectivity that is irreducibly complex, and driven by a desire that at once includes sexuality and aspires to a satisfaction that sexual possession can never provide, their unification can only be accomplished by means of a go-between whose very presence necessarily betrays, and betrays it to, its own multiplicity. To acknowledge that Pandarus represents the mediated and therefore unsatisfactory gratification at which all desire arrives is not, however, to establish him as the cause of the failure. On the contrary, the tragedy of desire is that its efforts to recover that which has been lost serve to confirm how truly

139. The verb *arten* is derived, according to the *MED*, from *arctare* and means to compel, force, or induce; but it also absorbs ominous connotations from its homonym, *art*.

140. Robertson, *Preface to Chaucer*, 496.

lost it is: the condition of desire is always to rebegin. This rebeginning is enacted by the lovers in Book 4, which repeats (as we have seen) the structure of the action of Books 1–3. An effort at closure, Book 4 not only, and necessarily, fails of its desire but then opens onto the saddest act of repetition of all, the parodic reenactments of the past that occupy Book 5. With Diomede Criseyde not only engages in a foreshortened and debased reenactment of her courtship with Troilus, but as the poem leaves her she recognizes that her fate is to be "rolled . . . on many a tonge" (5, 1061) by historians who are the literary equivalent of Diomede with his "tonge large" (5, 804). This is both a Dantesque vision of the endless historiographical recording in which she is condemned to reenact her original crime and, with Chaucer's invocation of the "tonge" with which both Diomede and historians like himself manipulate her, a disturbingly vivid reminder of the sexual abuse implicit in misogynist writing.

In describing Criseyde's betrayal, as with the other decisive moments of his poem, the narrator insists that the process by which actions unfold is so imperceptibly gradual and so compounded of motives and circumstances that the search for a single or simple explanation—"the cause whi"—is inevitably thwarted. At the conclusion of Diomede's interview with Criseyde in her tent, "he roos and tok his leve."

> The brighte Venus folwede and ay taughte
> The wey ther brode Phebus down alighte;
> And Cynthea hire char-hors overraughte
> To whirle out of the Leoun, if she myghte;
> And Signifer his candels sheweth bright
> Whan that Criseyde unto hire bedde wente
> Inwith hire faders faire brighte tente,
>
> Retornyng in hire soule ay up and down
> The wordes of this sodeyn Diomede,
> His grete estat, and perel of the town,
> And that she was allone and hadde nede
> Of frendes help; and thus bygan to brede
> The cause whi, the sothe for to telle,
> That she took fully purpos for to dwelle. (5, 1016–29)

The astronomical machinery represents not only the relentless passage of time—Criseyde had promised Troilus she would return "Er Phebus suster, Lucina the sheene, / The Leoun passe out of this Ariete" (4,

1591–92)—but also the workings of forces that operate in ways that are necessarily not fully available to self-reflection. Now as the moon leaves Leo so does Criseyde leave the lover who has just been described as "Yong, fressh, strong, and hardy as lyoun" (5, 830).[141] Venus is somehow in Diomede's train here, and she in turn dominates Phoebus Apollo: to say that love overcomes wisdom is a not inaccurate translation of the astronomical symbolism, but neither is it fully adequate as an account of Criseyde's decision. The Zodiac bears signs, but their meaning is not available to Criseyde, an ignorance that is both the condition of her very existence and a key constitutive of her decision— if "decision" is the right word. Lying in bed, Criseyde "returns" Diomede's words as the heavens turn, a scene that itself returns to the night some three years before when "lay she stille and thoughte" (2, 915) of Troilus's words, of Pandarus's, and of Antigone's. Then she had heard the "lay / Of love" sung by the nightingale, had dreamed the dream of the eagle, and had awakened (we were prepared to believe) in love.[142]

In deciding to stay with Diomede and abandon Troilus, Criseyde not only continues her earlier behavior but reveals her life to be a continuous process that cannot be endowed with a precisely demarcated beginning and ending, in the sense of either a single motive or an intended goal. If it were true, as Pandarus had said, that "th'ende is every tales strengthe" (2, 260), now that we reach that conclusion we should be able retrospectively to evaluate the meaning of the events that have occurred: "But natheles men seyen that at the laste, / For any thyng, men shal the soothe se" (5, 1639–40). Criseyde's liaison with Diomede ought then to tell us what her liaison with Troilus meant: at the end of her career in the poem her actions will have made clear what she meant at the beginning, just as when Troilus and Criseyde ended up in bed we knew (apparently) that this had always been "the fyn of hir entente." But in fact, far from clarifying the enigma of her character and motivation, much less of human actions in general, Criseyde's behavior in

141. And see also 1, 1074, where we are told that "in the feld [Troilus] pleyde tho leoun." The symmetry between Troilus the lion and his rival Diomede the boar perhaps derives from the *Thebaid*, where Adrastus is given a prophecy that his two daughters will be married to a lion (Polynices) and a boar (Tydeus); see *Thebaid* 1, 395–400.

142. For an account of the symmetry between Criseyde falling in and out of love with Troilus, see Donald R. Howard, "Experience, Language, and Consciousness: *Troilus and Criseyde,* II, 596–931," in *Medieval Literature and Folklore Studies: Essays in Honor of Francis Lee Utley,* ed. Jerome Mandel and Bruce A. Rosenberg (New Brunswick: Rutgers University Press, 1970), 173–92.

Book 5 serves to compound the difficulty: her end does not gloss but replicates her beginning.[143]

It seems that the narrator himself finds this narrative inconclusion painful. So, at least, we might judge from his last-minute attempt to suppress it. In the midst of Diomede's second and successful assault on Criseyde, he suddenly introduces into the poem portraits of the three protagonists. Technically, the presence of these portraits is sanctioned by the historiographical tradition: Dares, Benoît, and Joseph of Exeter all include similar passages in their histories, and Chaucer's version may owe some details specifically to Joseph.[144] But the point about their late appearance in *this* version of the story is that they evade the very problem of interpretation on which Chaucer has hitherto insisted. By substituting for the detailed representation of subjectivity woodenly externalized *effictiones* ornamented with brief judgments—Diomede has the reputation of being "of tonge large" (804), Criseyde is, notoriously, "slydynge of corage" (825), Troilus is "trewe as stiel in ech condicioun" (831)—the narrator suddenly implies that the relation of character to action has become self-evident. But the very narrative that these portraits mean to gloss belies such interpretive confidence.

The circularity traced by Criseyde in Book 5 is traced as well by Troilus, who pathetically (and, for many readers, irritatingly) repeats the lovesick behavior he originally performed in Book 1. When in Book 1 Troilus returned from the temple he made "a mirour of his mynde, / In which he saugh al holly [Criseyde's] figure" (1, 365–66), and in Book 5

---

143.   As we would expect of a Troy poem, *Troilus and Criseyde* is saturated with the language of beginnings and endings: see, for example, 1, 377–78; 1, 973; 2, 671–72; 2, 790–91; 2, 1234–35; 2, 1565–66; 2, 1595–96; 3, 462; 4, 1282–84; 5, 764–65; 5, 1003–4; and 5, 1828–33.

144.   Ever since R. K. Root's essay on "Chaucer's Dares," *MP* 15 (1917–18): 1–22, it has been assumed that Chaucer knew Joseph of Exeter's *Ilias Daretis Phrygii* and used it in these portraits. But the evidence is very slight. There is also no firm evidence that Chaucer knew either Dares or Dictys directly, but given their assimilation into Benoît and Guido it is unlikely that we would be able to recognize their direct presence in Chaucer's poem in any case. It is possible, however, that his reference to Geoffrey of Monmouth as a Trojan historian in the *House of Fame* (1470) shows that Chaucer was misled by one of the several manuscripts of Geoffrey's *Historia* that was prefaced with Dares' *Historia* into thinking that Geoffrey was the author of the entire Trojan-British compilation. He may have read Dares' *Historia*, in other words, thinking it was by Geoffrey, and assumed that Dares' work was something else again. *Pace* Root, it seems unlikely that he would have thought that Joseph of Exeter's tortuously stylized poem, with its several references to twelfth-century events, was Dares' eyewitness history. For a fourteenth-century version of this technique, see George B. Stow, ed., *Historia vitae et regni Ricardi Secundi* (Philadelphia: University of Pennsylvania Press, 1977), in which the author includes a portrait of Richard II just after his death but prior to the end of the book (161).

he reactivates the imaginative faculty as a cushion against the intrusion of the historical world. "Refiguryng hire shap, hire wommanhede, / Withinne his herte" (5, 473–74) and revisiting the "places of the town / In which he whilom hadde al his plesaunce" (5, 562–63), including her darkened palace, he deliberately tries to recreate the past. And he recreates it in less self-aware ways as well. As soon as he was stricken with love in Book 1 Troilus adopted a series of mortal poses. He was "refus of every creature" and devoted to death; overwhelmed by "sorowe and thought," he "mot nedes deye," to "sterve, unknowe, of [his] destresse," and even Pandarus admitted that he endured "wo / As sharp as doth he Ticius in helle" (1, 570, 579, 573, 616, 785–86). In Book 5 both the suffering and the theatricalization of suffering return. Troilus cries out for death (e.g., 5, 206) and prescribes both his funeral arrangements and his final memorial (the ashes of his heart are to be conserved in a golden urn and bequeathed to Criseyde "for a remembraunce" [5, 315]).[145] "Of hymself ymagened he ofte / To ben defet" (5, 617–18), and he is soon "so defet" (5, 1219) that he has to walk with a stick. When asked the nature of his illness, Troilus is stoically (and gallantly) vague but then meaningfully adds that "he felte a grevous maladie / Aboute his herte, and fayn he wolde dye" (5, 1231–32); and he now confirms Pandarus's original account of his infernal sufferings by retreating to his bed where he "torneth / In furie, as doth he Ixion in helle" (5, 211–12). The torments of the unacknowledged lover in Book 1 become the anguish of the rejected lover in Book 5 and are in both cases an inextricable compound of deep feeling and play acting, the authentic and the theatrical. As does Criseyde, Troilus in his ending returns to his beginning, and nowhere with more poignance than in the scornful laughter from the spheres that echoes the scornful laughter in the temple when he first entered upon his circular course.

Telling the story of Troilus's "double sorwe," the narrative of *Troilus and Criseyde* is itself pervaded with doubleness. In revising Boccaccio, Chaucer consistently added replicating counterparts to what are in the *Filostrato* single incidents. Troilus is seen from Criseyde's window not once but twice; Criseyde gives Troilus a brooch and Chaucer has Troilus reciprocate; love letters are exchanged twice, an event that is then itself repeated in the less amiable exchange of Book 5; Troilus's self-revelation to Pandarus is represented twice, first by the narrator and then by Pandarus himself, who characteristically doubles the incident into two acts of revelation (first in the garden, then in Troilus's room);

---

145. Significantly, Troilus's imagination of his death derives from Arcita's similar imagination in the *Teseida*; see the note in the *Riverside Chaucer* to 5, 280.

the added meeting at Deiphoebus's house prefigures the consummation scene; and Criseyde not only has two lovers but has the second
woo her twice. So too does the Theban story appear in Book 2 in two
versions, in both its French and Latin forms, and it then reappears in
Cassandra's discourse in Book 5. Nor is the habit of repetition confined
to details. As the narrative proceeds it gradually reveals itself to be
organized by a whole armature of repeating structures, the most obvious being the recapitulation of Books 1–3 in Book 4 and then, as we
have just seen, the further matching of Book 1 and Book 5. And the
poem as a whole opens with a Theban phrase ("double sorwe") derived
from Dante's rewriting of Augustine in *Purgatorio* 22 and closes with a
Christian prayer addressed to "Thow oon and two and thre, eterne on
lyve, / That regnest ay in thre and two and oon" (5, 1863–64) that echoes Dante's account of the singing of the "holy circles" in *Paradiso* 14.

The doubleness of the narrative is a symmetrical counterpart to the
equivocal subjectivity that is so much the poem's center of attention. A
doubled self—in a sense that includes both moral duplicity and the
endless psychological multiplicity that defines subjectivity itself—is at
once encased within and enacted as a doubled history. Yet the meaning
of this symmetry remains enigmatic. We can establish clear causal lines
in neither direction: the poem will not allow us to say that the failed
love of Troilus and Criseyde causes the fall of Troy nor that the fall of
Troy causes the failure of the love affair. Lacking "the cause whi," all we
can remark upon is the symmetry itself. The public world of history and
the private world of the self stand as mirror images of each other, a
specularity that itself reduplicates the doubleness of which they are
constituted. And as an act of historiographical analysis the poem itself
becomes what Petrarch called a *lavor doppio*, a doubling of the "original
speech" or *sermo prisco* of the ancients by a modern respeaking. Past
and present become hopelessly intermingled, and the original story
disappears in the act of its recovery.

In the *Boece* Lady Philosophy describes man as a being helplessly
caught in the middle of a process that he can neither evade nor understand. "Certes," she says, "ye men, that ben erthliche beestes, dremen
alwey your bygynnynge, although it be with a thynne ymaginacioun;
and by a maner thought, al be it nat clerly ne parfitely, ye loken from
afer to thilke verray fyn of blisfulnesse" (3, 3, 1–6). It is this world of
mediation, of replicated acts that foreclose the quest for either beginning or end, that Chaucer represents in *Troilus and Criseyde*. Boethianism offers to its believers the knowledge of a *fons et origo* that is not
only itself unmediated but identical with the "oon ende of blisfulnesse"
(3, 2, 8) to which man's *intentio naturalis* instinctively converts him. Yet

for all their striving, not only does this consoling vision finally elude the poem's protagonists, but the terms of its relationship to the historical world requires that it should. Invoked throughout the poem by an elaborate set of allusions, Boethianism functions not as a mode of being available to them and willfully ignored but as a norm of judgment that stands outside and apart from a historical world it weighs in the philosophic balance and finds wanting.[146] When Troilus does finally escape from his own historicity by an ascent through the spheres, the Boethian "ful avysement" (5, 1811) at which he arrives is a scornful dismissiveness that condemns all historical experience to "blynde lust" (5, 1834). Yet by drawing his account of Troilus's ascent from the *Teseida*, Chaucer manages to locate even this apparently definitive Boethian moment within a Theben context, and by correlating Troilus's final enlightenment with his youthful ignorance, Chaucer manages to suggest the ultimate impotence, even irrelevance, of Boethianism. Rather than a mode of understanding that is fully aware of the experiential world it presumes to judge, the poem implies, Boethianism is an ideal dream of order that is not only continually belied by experience but is itself motivated by recursive yearnings. Far from prescribing how history either should or could be, Boethianism yearns for a utopian world in which origin and end are simultaneously possessed—a world, that is, from which the embarrassment of history has been entirely banished. In the course of urging Troilus not to despair at the news of Criseyde's exchange, Pandarus offers him (in a stanza original with Chaucer) good Boethian advice about the dangers of trusting in a world governed by Fortune (4, 386–92). This advice is, however, not only impeached both by its source in the poem and by its accompanying proposal that Troilus should transfer his affections to another woman, but Troilus's reply itself offers the definitive statement about the limitations of Boethian transcendence: "O, where hastow ben hid so longe in muwe, / That kanst so wel and formely arguwe?" (4, 496–97).

We remember that in his *Scalacronica* Sir Thomas Gray founded the

---

146. For these allusions, and various Boethian readings of the poem, see Theodore A. Stroud, "Boethius' Influence on Chaucer's *Troilus*," *MP* 49 (1951–52): 1–9; John P. McCall, "Five-Book Structure in Chaucer's *Troilus*," *MLQ* 23 (1962): 297–308; three important articles by Alan Gaylord, "Uncle Pandarus as Lady Philosophy," *Papers of the Michigan Academy of Science, Arts, and Letters* 46 (1961): 571–95; "Chaucer's Tender Trap: The *Troilus* and the 'Yonge, Fresshe Folkes,'–" *English Miscellany* 15 (1964): 25–45; and "Friendship in Chaucer's *Troilus*," *ChR* 3 (1968–69): 239–64; John M. Steadman, *Disembodied Laughter: Troilus and the Apotheosis Tradition* (Berkeley: University of California Press, 1972); McAlpine, *Genre of* Troilus and Criseyde; Rowe, *O Love O Charite!*; and Wood, *Elements of Chaucer's* Troilus.

ladder of history upon two books, the Bible and "la gest de Troy." Yet in Chaucer's retelling the Trojan source gives way to reveal beneath it yet another source, and one that compulsively insists that beginnings are always rebeginnings, that action is always repetition. Just as Lollius is revealed upon inquiry to be a mumbling together of sources, disparate and even contradictory;[147] and just as the lovers' *entente* is shown in enactment to be a tangled and finally unfathomable compound of idealism, self-regard, and appetite; so the Trojan origin becomes equally inextricable from its own, unacknowledged past. The poem defines historical experience in Theban terms as iterative and compelled, and like Troilus before Cassandra, habitually—and necessarily—blind to its own meaning. This message preempts not only local lessons about the meaning of Criseyde's betrayal and Troilus's disillusionment but large-scale historical hypotheses about the fall of Troy and the meaning of history itself

If history has no meaning, or at least none available to human understanding, then Chaucer's essay in the philosophy of history must end as inconclusively as both Criseyde's career and Troilus's life. Criticism has often described what Lowes long ago called "the tumultuous hitherings and thitherings of mood and matter in the last dozen stanzas of the poem," descriptions that provide vivid evidence of the interpretive impasse to which the poem brings both its narrator and its readers.[148] The final stanza is a tacit admission of this abandonment of authorial control. It is a prayer directed to God, the divine *scriptor* who is "Uncircumscript and al maist circumscrive" (5, 1865), and it expresses

147. As Kittredge pointed out in "Chaucer's Lollius," *Harvard Studies in Classical Philology* 28 (1917): 47–133, Chaucer almost certainly got the idea that Lollius was a Trojan historian from Horace's *Epistle* 1, 2, probably as (mis)cited by John of Salisbury in the *Policraticus*. But he could not have been ignorant of the fact that the ME verb *lollen* meant to mumble or to sing (which is one of the modern explanations offered for the term Lollard: see Malcolm D. Lambert, *Medieval Heresy: Popular Movements from Bogomil to Hus* [London: Edward Arnold, 1977], 302). A native word for indistinct singing then endowed with a classical suffix, "Lollius" is an economical representation of the situation of the vernacular poet who combines a wide variety of postclassical materials (the *Filostrato*, Petrarch, the *Roman de la Rose*, Guido delle Colonne, Benoît de Sainte-Maure, et al.) in an effort to recreate an unavailable classical origin. It was a commonplace of Trojan historiography to complain at the outset of each retelling of the story about the inadequacies and inaccuracies of previous tellings, and in particular to berate Homer for his Greek bias and his predilection for fabling; see, for example, the Prologus to Guido's *Historia* and Chaucer's own account of the rivalry among the Trojan historians in the *House of Fame* (1475–80).

148. *Geoffrey Chaucer and the Development of his Genius* (Boston: Houghton Mifflin, 1934), 153. An exemplary account is given by Donaldson, *Speaking of Chaucer*, 84–101.

both distance from this divine source and faith in its availability. The stanza itself speaks to the Creator largely through the mediation of others' language: it is Chaucer's version of Dante's version of a hymn by Bernard of Clairvaux; and as spoken by a man threatened by "visible and invisible foon" (5, 1866), it is an evening prayer that corresponds to the bidding prayer with which the poem opens. But this sense of distance, of a speaker mired in the historical world and alienated from the divine origin, is both enforced and countered by the prayer's content. On the one hand, it begins with a circularity that includes, and presumably transcends, the recursions of both Thebes and Boethius, addressing itself to "Thow oon and two and thre, eterne on lyve, / That regnest ay in thre and two and oon" (5, 1863–64). And on the other, it concludes with a reference first to the human member of the Trinity, who can mercifully make His creation worthy of Him—"for thi mercy, digne" (5, 1868)—and then to the fully human Mary, "mayde and moder thyn benigne" (5, 1869). In thus coming to rest on the Mother of God, who (as the Second Nun, citing the same Dantean source, says) "nobledest . . . oure nature" (VIII, 40), perhaps the poem means finally to acknowledge that the enigma of the historical world encompasses at least the possibility of a divine sanction. And yet the consolation here offered remains wholly private, a gesture of inclusion spoken out of faith rather than hope.

VII: *Trojan History and the History of* Trinovantum

The impasse at which the poem's historical interrogation thus arrives is, as I have tried to show, partly determined by the terms of reference—the shape of the materials and the available analytic paradigms—in which that interrogation had inevitably to take place. Only by fending off a culturally prescribed transcendentalism could Chaucer's microscopic exploration of the dialectic between the self and history be enabled at all, and with the project finally in ruins he embraced the Christian spiritualism that his secular poem had previously held in abeyance. But as well as expressing this general cultural dilemma, *Troilus and Criseyde* also witnesses to the English and specifically Chaucerian experience of the 1380s, and it is with a brief account of this experience that I shall bring this discussion to a close. For here we discover conditions sufficient in themselves to explain Chaucer's purpose in eliciting both this powerfully tragic poem and its dismissive counterpart, the *Knight's Tale*—a poem in which Chaucer both sums up and sets aside the entire historical project that had preoccupied him throughout the first part of his career.[149]

The 1380s were a time of disheartening turbulence for England, and *Troilus and Criseyde* is addressed to a nation threatened by enemies from without and dissension from within. Throughout the decade the war with France went badly, and from 1385 through 1388 the country was threatened by invasion from the Scots in the north and the French in the south.[150] In the summer of 1386 the French gathered a huge invasion fleet at Sluys—one chronicler compared it to the Greek fleet that invaded Troy—and in London and along the southern coast anxiety became panic.[151] Domestic political life was equally distressing. The suppression of the Rising of 1381—an event described by Gower in terms of the collapse of antique, and especially Trojan, chivalry—was

149.   The following discussion assumes that Chaucer wrote the *Troilus* in the mid-1380s, and that he was probably still working on it through 1387—although nothing in the discussion in fact requires so late a date for the poem's completion. The standard date for the *terminus ad quem* has been late 1386 or early 1387, for two reasons. One is the putative use made of the poem by Usk in his *Testament of Love*. Usk may have written that work prior to October 7, 1387, the date of his appointment by the king as Under-Sheriff of Middlesex, since the *Testament* seems to have been written at least in part in hope of preferment; or he may have written it while awaiting his execution, which took place on March 4, 1388. In addition to this uncertainty is the fact that the instances of his use cited by Skeat in *Chaucerian and Other Pieces* (Oxford: Oxford University Press, 1897), xxvii, and by Root in the introduction to his edition of the *Troilus* (Princeton: Princeton University Press, 1926), xv, show that Usk had certain knowledge only of Troilus's predestination soliloquy in Book 4, a passage that has an odd textual history and that, if Usk knew it in the form in which it appeared in the *Troilus*, he misunderstood. He may also have known a few other lines, but with one exception—an allusion to Lachesis (see Skeat's first example, xxvii)—these other echoes are all either proverbial or so fleeting as hardly to provide decisive evidence for Usk's familiarity with the poem as a finished piece of work. In sum, the evidence provided by the *Testament of Love* for date is ambiguous at best. The other reason for the traditional *terminus ad quem* is the dedication to "philosophical Strode:" a Ralph Strode who was a London lawyer and associate of Chaucer died in 1387. But it is not certain that this is the same Strode as the Fellow of Merton who could with more justice be addressed as "philosophical"; see John Hurt Fisher, *John Gower: Moral Philosopher and Friend of Chaucer* (New York: New York University Press, 1964), 61. Finally, J. D. North has shown that according to the astronomical references the fictional action of the poem begins in April 1385 and concludes three years later, with Criseyde leaving Troy on 3 May 1388 and deciding to remain with the Greeks on 13 May; see J. D. North, "Kalenderes Enlumyned Ben They: Some Astronomical Themes in Chaucer," *RES*, n.s. 20 (1969), 142–49.

150.   On the English sense of being under seige—"sorrounded by enemies bent on the kingdom's destruction" (55)—throughout the 1380s, see Barnie, *War in Medieval English Society*, 33–55.

151.   On these fears, see J. J. N. Palmer, *England, France and Christendom, 1377–99* (London: Routledge and Kegan Paul, 1972), 67–87; for the Trojan allusion, see 74.

followed not by a period of national healing but by a bitter and finally bloody struggle between the king and his nobility. In the first half of the decade Richard sought to deprive the great magnates of their customary role as advisors to the crown by replacing them with a new "courtier nobility" that he had himself created from the ranks of his vastly increased household.[152] Then in the so-called Wonderful Parliament of October 1386 the magnates struck back, and Gloucester and Arundel persuaded Parliament to establish "a great and continual council" to govern the country, and, in effect, the king as well.

They also sought to establish the principle that the king was constitutionally subject to Parliament, a principle that Richard contested the subsequent August by obtaining judicial opinions that he was *supra jure*.[153] Also in dispute between the crown and its nobility—and perhaps the primary issue between them—was the question of the war. Richard and his chancellor Michael de la Pole had sought to obtain a more or less permanent peace with France, a policy that was intensely unpopular with the nobility. But even with the impeachment of de la Pole in the Parliament of 1386, Richard did not abandon his peace policy, and throughout 1387 he continued to conduct secret negotiations with Charles V of France. With the Merciless Parliament of February through June 1388, however, the Lords Appellant (Gloucester, Arundel, Warwick, Derby, and Nottingham) brought these efforts to an end: in wreaking their vengeance upon the king's supporters, they made it clear that high on their list of treasons was the charge of having conspired with the king of France, and they condemned all those whom they could accuse of having had dealings with the enemy on the king's behalf.[154] Free to prosecute the war with unfettered enthusiasm, however, all that Gloucester and Arundel could produce, despite massive expenditures and great expectations, was a bungled and militarily insignificant campaign in Gascony in the summer of 1388, and with this failure their credi-

152.   This process is described by Anthony Tuck, *Richard II and the English Nobility* (New York: St. Martin's Press, 1974): "A new courtier nobility was coming into existence which took precedence over the established aristocracy in access to the king, in patronage, and even to some degree in influence in the localities" (86).

153.   On the constitutional issue, see J. J. N. Palmer, "The Parliament of 1385 and the Constitutional Crisis of 1386," *Speculum* 46 (1971): 477–90.

154.   As Palmer shows, "The king's advisers were accused with arranging a meeting between the two kings, planning to conclude a five year truce, and formulating peace proposals which involved certain territorial concessions. . . . By presenting [this policy] as a conspiracy whose sole purpose was to destroy the council, the Appellants secured its condemnation as treason" (*England, France and Christendom*, 117). In *Richard II*, Tuck discusses the massive unpopularity of Richard's peace policy and the execution of the chamber knight John Salesbury for his role in the negotiations (61–62).

bility as a government collapsed and the king regained control in the spring of 1389 with his own declaration of majority.

What makes these events relevant to a discussion of *Troilus and Criseyde* is the fact that Chaucer was himself deeply, and dangerously, involved. He was a member of the king's party in the so-called Wonderful Parliament of 1386, and the account of the Trojan Parliament of Book 4, in which Criseyde is exchanged for Antenor, serves as a mordant commentary, albeit one delivered from a narrowly royalist perspective.[155] In 1386 Arundel and Gloucester harnessed the dissatisfactions of the Commons to their purpose, exploiting its anger at the prosecution of the war and the general collapse of governmental authority to win from Parliament the decision to establish the Council of magnates.[156] In Chaucer's Trojan Parliament it is also "the noyse of peple" (4, 183) and "the folk" (4, 198, 202), as they are dismissively called, who demand the exchange of Criseyde.[157] The innocent victim of the Parliament of 1386—innocent at least from the king's point of view—was Michael de la Pole, earl of Suffolk. Since his appointment as chancellor in 1384 de la Pole had assiduously fostered Richard's authoritarian tendencies,[158] and when Parliament demanded his dismissal Richard defended him by invoking his royal prerogative: he told the Commons that he "would not remove from office for their sake the least scullion of his kitchen."[159] In the Trojan Parliament the victim was defended by Hector in more high-minded but equally uncompromising terms: "We

155. For Chaucer as one of the king's knights in the Parliament, see T. F. Tout, *Chapters in the Administrative History of Mediaeval England* (Manchester: Manchester University Press, 1928), 3:413 n. 3; Margaret Galway, "Geoffrey Chaucer, J.P. and M.P.," *MLR* 36 (1941): 1–36. The relevance of the Trojan Parliament to that of 1386 was first pointed out by McCall and Rudisill, "Parliament of 1386," although they argued the analogy only in general terms. Their claim has been disputed, for example, by Robertson, "Probable Date and Purpose," 153.

156. J. S. Roskell, *The Impeachment of Michael de la Pole, Earl of Suffolk in 1386* (Manchester: Manchester University Press, 1984), 18; Richard H. Jones, *The Royal Policy of Richard II: Absolutism in the Later Middle Ages* (Oxford: Blackwell, 1968), 34–35; Anthony Goodman, *The Loyal Conspiracy: The Lords Appellant under Richard II* (London: Routledge and Kegan Paul, 1971), 14–15.

157. "The noyse of peple up stirte thanne at ones, / As breme as blase of straw iset on-fire" (4, 183–84): if the second line contains an allusion to Jack Straw and the Rising of 1381—as was argued by Carleton Brown, "Another Contemporary Allusion in Chaucer's *Troilus*," *MLN* 26 (1911): 208–11—then the representation of the Commons becomes even more contemptuous.

158. Roskell, *Impeachment*, 34–35.

159. This is the report given by Knighton: the king said "se nolle pro ipsis nec minimum garcionem de coquina sua amovere de officio suo" (Joseph Rawson Lumby, ed., *Chronicon*, Rolls Series [London: HMSO, 1895], 2:215).

usen here no wommen for to selle" (4, 182). Yet in both cases the defender had to yield: "every lord and burgeys" (4, 345) of Troy agreed to exchange Criseyde for Antenor, while the members of the Wonderful Parliament—"proceres et domini atque totus populus communitatis parliamenti," as they referred to themselves—handed de la Pole over for impeachment.[160] And what both parties received in return—again, from a narrowly royalist view—were traitors: the Trojans welcomed back Antenor, Parliament handed the country over to Gloucester and Arundel. That Richard thought of these men specifically as *traitors* is shown by the way in which, when he asked the judges to rule on the legality of Parliament's actions, he so phrased his questions as to lead them to conclude that those who had provided leadership to the Parliament should be punished "ut *proditores.*"[161] The word rings throughout the judges' replies: just as Antenor was "traitour to the town" (4, 204), so Arundel and Gloucester were traitors to their king.

Chaucer was also a victim of the 1386 Parliament. He lost his two positions in the Custom, gave up the rent-free lease on his house over Aldgate, and over the next two years continued to be harrassed by both the aristocratic opposition and by financial insecurity.[162] He nonetheless remained loyal to the king, and at the end of June 1387, received a Letter of Protection that would permit him to go to Calais "in the king's ser-

---

160. For Parliament's self-designation, see Knighton, *Chronicon,* 2:216.

161. See S. B. Chrimes, "Richard II's Questions to the Judges, 1387," *Law Quarterly Review* 72 (1956): 365–90.

162. For the documents relating to the loss of the Customs positions and the lease of the house, see Martin M. Crow and Clair C. Olson, eds., *Chaucer Life-Records* (Oxford: Oxford University Press, 1966), 145–46, 268–69. For details of Chaucer's loans, and his sale of his annuity, see ibid., 330 (a loan of 20s. on 21 December 1387), 384–86 (he is sued for the recovery of a debt on 25 April 1388), 336–38 (surrender of his annuity to John Scalby on 1 May 1388), 388–90 (sued for another debt in the autumn of 1388). On 20 January 1388 Chaucer was asked to account for money he took in as controller of customs prior to his dismissal of 4 December 1386 (ibid., 245–46). Crow and Olson suggest that these events are not connected to the parliamentary events, and the claim that Chaucer's move to Kent was motivated not by political factionalism but a desire for retired country living is also promoted by F. R. H. DuBoulay, "The Historical Chaucer," in Derek Brewer, ed., *Geoffrey Chaucer* (London: G. Bell, 1974), 49–52. But the Parliament established a commission to investigate corruption by officials appointed by Richard, and there seems little reason to avoid the obvious inference that Chaucer was, along with other royalists, a victim of Gloucester's triumph. This is also the conclusion at which Tout arrived: "It was doubtless the result of the commissioners' activity that in December 1386 Geoffrey Chaucer, king's esquire, who had sat for Kent in the recent parliament, was removed from his two posts in the customs" (Tout, *Chapters,* 3:417). For further arguments linking the dismissal to the Appellants' program, see Robertson, "Probable Date and Purpose."

vice."[163] While we cannot know the exact nature of this business, Chaucer's journey took place at a time when there was much traveling to and from the continent by royal agents engaged in Richard's secret peace negotiations with the French. Indeed, on 5 July 1387 Charles V sent an embassy from Paris to meet with the English, and it is not improbable that this meeting took place at Calais.[164] Furthermore, the Lords Appellant subsequently claimed that Richard conducted the negotiations "through persons of low estate" in order to avoid surveillance—a description that certainly fits Chaucer.[165] And even if this speculation about the reason for Chaucer's trip to Calais is unprovable, the trip itself nonetheless fell under suspicion. For in January 1388 the Lords Appellant ordered the constable of Dover "to collect 'all writs; writings, orders and commands from 20 November 1386 until 14 January 1388 . . . on behalf of the king . . . for passage for all who have passed from the realm over the sea for whatsoever cause.' "[166] The result of this investigation was the condemnation of a number of Richard's agents for negotiating with the French, and the execution of one of them—the chamber knight John Salesbury, who fifteen years earlier had been a squire with Chaucer in the household of Edward III.[167] Low as his estate may have been, in other words, Chaucer's journey must have made him vulnerable to factional violence, and it was not until Richard assumed his majority on 3 May 1389—and appointed Chaucer clerk of the king's works on 12 July of the same year—that the poet could have felt himself, at least for the moment, in a secure position.

Whether or not this explanation for Chaucer's trip to Calais is correct, his presence in the Parliament of 1386, and its effect upon his

163. Crow and Olson, *Life-Records*, 61–62.
164. Palmer, *England, France and Christendom*, 107.
165. Ibid., 107–8.
166. Ibid., 115. Palmer adds: "The information thus acquired was put to effective use in the parliament—deservedly known as the Merciless Parliament—which met on 3 February 1388 to try the king's friends, advisers and agents. Prominent among the charges then made against them was a group of articles which accused them of treasonable dealings with France" (ibid.).
167. For Salesbury's execution, see ibid., 118; and for his presence with Chaucer in the household of Edward III, see Crow and Olson, *Life-Records*, 100–102, 107, 109. Margaret Galway suggests, on no clear evidence, that Chaucer did not in fact go abroad at all, but that the permission to go was a ruse obtained to protect him from his creditors ("Geoffrey Chaucer," 31); while Paul Olson asserts, also without adducing further evidence, that Chaucer went to Calais with Sir William Beauchamp "to reestablish peace talks with the King of France" (*The* Canterbury Tales *and the Good Society* [Princeton: Princeton University Press, 1986], 8; see also 52). Olson does not discuss the political dangers attending such a trip nor the Appellants' subsequent investigation. Robertson, "Probable Date and Purpose," says that Chaucer "probably" accompanied Beauchamp.

career, showed him to have been deeply, and unhappily, involved in the factionalized political world of the mid-1380s. Nor should we too quickly assume that the writing of *Troilus and Criseyde* was not itself an act that carried with it important, and even dangerous, political consequences. We have already seen how the Troy story always carried political implications, implications that were exploited by propagandists throughout the war years of the later fourteenth century. In the 1350s, for example, Richard of Bury invoked the linked ideas of *translatio studii* and *translatio imperii* to predict an English victory, while across the channel Jean de Roquetaillade was simultaneously bolstering morale after the defeats of the 1340s and 1350s with the claim that the Trojan *imperium* would inevitably pass to France.[168] Later in the century, in the *Débat des Hérauts de France et d'Angleterre,* representatives of the warring nations argued over which was the true descendant of Troy and so entitled to the future.[169] And at the end of his *Troy Book* Lydgate sought to redeem the Trojan past with the hope that a triumphant Henry V would bring peace to France and England.[170] Nor were the political implications of the Trojan story confined merely to nationalist propaganda. We remember that among the accusations brought by the Appellants against Nicholas Brembre—the mayor of London, a supporter of the king, and, as collector of customs, a close business associate of Chaucer's—was that he wanted to change the name of London to New Troy and to designate himself as duke of Troy. One thing this improbable accusation tells us is just how deeply possessive was the warlike aristocracy of its Trojan heritage: one of the worst things they could say about a merchant like Brembre—who was described throughout the bill of accusation as the "faulx Chivaler de Londres"[171]—was that he was trying to appropriate the imperial legend of a martial Britain for his own, no doubt mercantile, purposes. But it also serves as a snide attack on Richard's attempt to create a "courtier nobility" by implying that he would debase even the royal myth of Troy in order to ennoble a grocer.

What then of a mere controller of customs who had the effrontery to set himself up as the purveyor of Trojan history? As European monarchs (including England's Henry II and the future Henry V) knew, the Trojan myth provided above all a typology of monarchical legitimacy:

168. Richard of Bury, *Philobiblon,* ed. and trans. E. C. Thomas (Oxford: Basil Blackwell, 1970), 107. For Jean de Roquetaillade, see Marjorie Reeves, "History and Prophecy in Medieval Thought," *M&H* 5 (1974), 69.

169. Bernard Guenée, *States and Rulers in Later Medieval Europe,* trans. Juliet Vale (Oxford: Blackwell, 1985), 60–61.

170. Benson, *History of Troy,* 118.

171. *Rot. Parl.,* 3:228–38.

as empire descended from the Trojans, so too monarchy enjoyed a genealogical authority. The Richard of the 1380s, threatened with deposition and denied his full authority, could not have been insensitive to these meanings. Moreover, throughout the 1380s, as into the 1390s, Richard made great efforts to fashion for himself a fully chivalric identity: he led his army into the field in the Scottish campaign of 1385—the first time an English monarch had done so since Edward III's last campaign of 1369, he sponsored and even participated in tournaments, and he adapted both the insignia and the habits of his illustrious father and grandfather to his own purposes.[172] A fully chivalric poem recalling to his subjects their glorious Trojan past would certainly have been consistent with these strategies—especially for a king who, in his self-composed epitaph, compared himself to Homer, the author of all Trojan histories.[173]

Yet of course *Troilus and Criseyde* is not really that kind of poem. Despite the royalist attitudes that govern its account of the Trojan Parliament, despite the generally affirmative effect that any Trojan narrative has upon royal authority, *Troilus and Criseyde* cannot really be aligned with specific monarchical interests. On the contrary, its meditations on history are both too general and too profound to be contained by any narrowly partisan purpose. It is neither a militarist nor a pacificist poem: unambiguously celebrating martial achievement, it also measures the cost of war upon the amorousness that is the other crucial element of the chivalric life-style, and it shows the noble life at odds with itself, fulfilling its deepest romantic needs in a context that dooms them to extinction.[174] If we read the poem topically, we can see that its representation of a society under seige that undoes itself through parliamentary miscalculation has a general rather than specific and partisan relevance. The 1380s were a time of disputed sovereignty, conspiratorial factionalism, and disastrous militarism—all issues upon which *Troilus and Criseyde* reflects. The poem's continual concern with authority, as both literary source and metaphysical foundation, is a textual ana-

172. For further on Richard's chivalric identity, see below, 187–89.

173. Richard said he was "lyke to Homer" (cited by George B. Stow, "Chronicles versus Records: The Character of Richard II," in *Documenting the Past: Essays in Medieval History Presented to George Peddy Cuttino,* ed. J. S. Hamilton and Patricia J. Bradley (Woodbridge: Boydell, 1989), 165.

174. It should be added that the poem's emphasis upon the intensity of personal feeling must have seemed relevant to Richard's own capacity for passionate engagements, first with Robert de Vere, the Earl of Oxford, then with Anne of Bohemia. For the evidence, see Stow, "Chronicles versus Records," 161 n. 33, 163.

logue to the troubled, and finally unresolved, constitutional debate over sovereignty. Similarly, the figure of Pandarus is a comic version of the malign conspiratorial manipulator who pervaded the poet's historical world, while the poem's privileging of *trouthe*, even when the object of loyalty is unworthy, reflects a time of broken commitments and dark betrayals.[175]

And Chaucer's meditations on history go even deeper than these general analogies, opening up disquieting profundities. For the poem's deepest message is not about the failure of any particular historical moment but about the failure of history, and of historical understanding, per se. Telling a story of complicity and victimization, it shows us a historical world that is simultaneously created by and yet set apart from the men and women who seek to live their lives within it. The final message is one of bafflement before a narrative—and a world—that defies understanding and forecloses consolation: we could hardly expect a poem that stands silent before the tragedy of secular history to offer anything more than an uncommitted reflection on its own historical moment. Deriving from and speaking to the unhappy world of the 1380s, the *Troilus* refuses to offer any clear message; and this lack of clarity itself expresses the dilemma the poem represents. All engagement in the world of history is dangerous and finally disappointing, and yet engagement cannot be avoided; the act of representation is itself an act of loyalty, but the results are both of uncertain authenticity and hardly worth the risk; survival is an imperative, but what of *trouthe?* And to what—or to whom—should

175. In fact, in Book 4 Pandarus's conspiratorial instincts become less comic as he tries to persuade Troilus to violate the parliamentary decision, ratified by the king, to exchange Criseyde for Antenor. That Pandarus is here initiating a factional dispute is made clear when he pledges his loyalty to Troilus in terms that assume civil disorder:

> I wol myself ben with the at this dede,
> Theigh ich and al my kyn upon a stownde,
> Shulle in a strete as dogges liggen dede,
> Thorugh-girt with many a wid and blody wownde,
> In every cas I wol a frend be founde. (624–28)

An earlier version of this factionalism is implied in Pandarus's mobilization of the royal family (Hector, Helen, Deiphoebus, and Troilus) against Polyphete and his supporters, Aeneas and Antenor. To a governing class riven by internecine rivalry, these conspiracies must have seemed painfully relevant. Lines that also have a powerfully contemporary relevance in the context of the 1380s are Criseyde's suggestion in Book 4 that the war will soon be over because "men purposen pees on every syde" (1350; and see 1352–58). Both passages are either added to Boccaccio or revised in the direction of contemporary relevance.

one be true? These are the questions that Chaucer's experience in the 1380s must have forced upon him, and his poem asks them as both fictive form and historical act. But the very conditions that entail their asking foreclose the possibility of an answer: stranded before the enigma of his own and his nation's history, Chaucer's final response is to offer up a prayer for release.

Chapter Three

The Knight's Tale *and the Crisis of Chivalric Identity*

"These were men who believed history was in their care."

The critical history of the *Knight's Tale* is both extensive—in 1950 one interpreter could already wryly entitle his article *"Knight's Tale 38"*— and exemplary, providing an account *in parvo* of the central debates of modern Chaucer studies.[1] It was also in 1950 that Charles Muscatine published the article that redefined the issues in terms that have continued to govern critical discussion until the present moment. As a New Critic, Muscatine insisted that the *Tale* was above all a literary artifact, a verbal "organization whose fullest meaning is dependent on the interplay of a variety of elements."[2] Thus the theme of the poem, defined by Muscatine as "the struggle between noble designs and chaos," expressed the very dynamic of both poetry and criticism itself. In effect, by applying to the poem the New Critical "reduction terms" of order and disorder, Muscatine showed that the *Knight's Tale* enacted, in both theme and form, the struggle in which he was himself engaged as a critic: the *Tale* became not merely a subject of New Critical practice but an exemplification of New Critical ideology.[3]

Accepting Muscatine's definition of order and disorder as the central theme of the *Tale*, the numerous formalist readings that have followed have debated whether it endorses or subverts regulation, whether it is an optimistic account of the civilizing process or whether it

---

1. Edward Ham, *"Knight's Tale 38,"* ELH 17 (1950): 252–61.

2. Charles Muscatine, "Form, Texture, and Meaning in Chaucer's *Knight's Tale,"* PMLA 65 (1950): 911–29; repr. Edward Wagenknecht, ed., *Chaucer: Modern Essays in Criticism* (New York: Oxford University Press, 1959), 63.

3. For the "reduction terms" of New Criticism, see the acute critique of R. S. Crane, *The Languages of Criticism and the Structures of Poetry* (Toronto: University of Toronto Press, 1953), 123–24.

bespeaks an ironic, or tragic, attitude.[4] Muscatine, breathing New Critical enthusiasm for art's ability to endow experience with a coherent shape, had promoted an optimistic reading of the *Tale*. Theseus is to be admired for his continued commitment to the idea of order in the face of Saturn's depredations, and the "subsurface insistence on disorder" was to be seen as the *Tale*'s "crowning complexity, its most compelling claim to maturity":

> The impressive, patterned edifice of the noble life, its dignity and richness, its regard for law and decorum, are all bulwarks against the ever-threatening forces of chaos, and in constant collision with them. . . . When the earthly designs suddenly crumble, true nobility is faith in the ultimate order of all things. Saturn, disorder, nothing more or less, is the agent of Arcite's death, and Theseus, noble in the highest sense, interprets it in the deepest perspective. (80–81)

The *Tale* could thus be read as expressing issues relevant not merely to the noble life of the late Middle Ages but to all forms of historical engagement; and it was thereby accommodated both to the great tradition of English literature and to the ideals of a cold-war American liberalism that often wanted to understand all of history as nothing more or less than a struggle between noble designs and chaos.

But both the formalist desire to stress the *Tale*'s literariness and the liberalism that is its political analogue have been challenged by an opposing attitude—itself divided into two camps—committed instead to the historicity of cultural value. In camp one are ranked, under the banner of D. W. Robertson, those who believe that all medieval writing was governed by a fully coherent and hierarchically organized world view. In this view disorder is not a structural fault in the nature of things but an effect of human blindness and immorality; and what Theseus confronts is moral weakness as embodied in the eroti-

---

4. See, for example, Richard Neuse, "The Knight: The First Mover in Chaucer's Human Comedy," *University of Toronto Quarterly* 31 (1962); reprinted in J. A. Burrow, ed., *Geoffrey Chaucer: A Critical Anthology* (Harmondsworth: Penguin Books, 1969), 242–63; Elizabeth Salter, *Chaucer: The Knight's Tale and the Clerk's Tale* (London: Edward Arnold, 1962), 9–36; Joseph Westlund, "The *Knight's Tale* as an Impetus for Pilgrimage," *PQ* 43 (1964): 526–37; Jeffrey Helterman, "The Dehumanizing Metamorphoses of *The Knight's Tale*," *ELH* 38 (1971): 493–511; Kathleen A. Blake, "Order and the Noble Life in Chaucer's *Knight's Tale*?" *MLQ* 34 (1973): 3–19; and V. A. Kolve, *Chaucer and the Imagery of Narrative* (Stanford: Stanford University Press, 1984), 85–157. One of the best of these readings is Robert Hanning, "'The Struggle between Noble Designs and Chaos': The Literary Tradition of Chaucer's Knight's Tale," *The Literary Review* 23 (1980): 519–41, an essay that takes as its title Muscatine's key phrase.

cally obsessed Theban cousins, a disordinance that his harsh measures succeed in transforming into the marital harmony with which the *Tale* concludes. There can thus be no ambivalence or pathos in the regulatory effort but only a righteous indignation.[5] In camp two, however, is an iconoclastic criticism, smaller but equally militant, for which the *Tale* records the guilt of the regulator himself. Theseus becomes not even a well-meaning failure but a cruel tyrant, a Chaucerian commentary on the decline of medieval chivalry into brutal exploitation.[6] For the conservatives, the idea of order is medieval, and what is medieval is always moral; for those on the left, the order that Theseus imposes is specific to fourteenth-century chivalry, and the *Tale* stands as Chaucer's polemical attack upon aristocratic privilege.

I too must work both with a concept of order and with history in this chapter—specifically the medieval concept of order with which the *Tale* is most obviously allied, the Order of Chivalry.[7] But I do not believe that Chaucer's engagement with chivalry took the form of either moral or social polemic. In part, this is because Chaucer habitually eschewed direct commentary: his characteristic relation to the world was analytic rather than rhetorical. But in larger part this is because his analysis

5. For this tradition of reading, see Robertson, *A Preface to Chaucer* (Princeton: Princeton University Press, 1962), 260–66, 370–73, 466-68; John Halverson, "Aspects of Order in the *Knight's Tale*," *SP* 57 (1960): 606–21; Douglas Brooks and Alastair Fowler, "The Meaning of Chaucer's *Knight's Tale*," *MAE* 39 (1970): 123–46; Alan Gaylord, "The Role of Saturn in the *Knight's Tale*," *ChR* 8 (1973–74): 172–90; Patricia M. Kean, *Chaucer and the Making of English Poetry,* 2: *The Art of Narrative* (London: Routledge and Kegan Paul, 1972), 1–52; John P. McCall, *Chaucer Among the Gods* (University Park: Pennsylvania State University Press, 1979), 63–86; and Paul A. Olson, "Chaucer's Epic Statement and the Political Milieu of the Late Fourteenth Century," *Mediaevalia* 5 (1979): 61–87; see also Olson's *The* Canterbury Tales *and the Good Society* (Princeton: Princeton University Press, 1986), 51–66.

6. Terry Jones, *Chaucer's Knight: The Portrait of a Medieval Mercenary* (Baton Rouge: Louisiana State University Press, 1980); David Aers; *Chaucer, Langland and the Creative Imagination* (London: Routledge and Kegan Paul, 1980), 174–95; Aers's review of Jones's book in *SAC* 4 (1982): 169–75; and Stephen Knight, *Geoffrey Chaucer* (Oxford: Basil Blackwell, 1985), 83–90. But compare Maurice Keen, "Chaucer's Knight, the English Aristocracy and the Crusade," in *English Court Culture in the Later Middle Ages,* ed. V. J. Scattergood and J. W. Sherborne (London: Duckworth, 1983), 45–61; and G. A. Lester, "Chaucer's Knight and the Earl of Warwick," *N&Q* 28 (1981): 200–202; Lester, "Chaucer's Knight and the Medieval Tournament," *Neophilologus* 46 (1982): 460–68.

7. For previous discussions of the *Tale* in relation to chivalry, see, in addition to the works cited in note 6, Thomas J. Hatton, "Chaucer's Crusading Knight: A Slanted Ideal," *ChR* 3 (1968–69): 77–87; Olson, "Chaucer's Epic Statement"; C. David Benson, "The *Knight's Tale* as History," *ChR* 3 (1968–69): 107–23; Bruce Kent Cowgill, "The *Knight's Tale* and the Hundred Years' War," *PQ* 54 (1975): 670–79; Stuart Robertson, "Elements of Realism in the *Knight's Tale*," *JEGP* 14 (1915): 226–55; Judith Scherer Herz, "Chaucer's Elegiac Knight," *Criticism* 6 (1964): 212–24.

focused, finally, neither on moral standards nor on social conditions but on attitudes; that is to say, on socially determined and therefore historically contingent values and beliefs. Ultimately, this is the more radical critique. By making the central issue of the *Tale* not the idea of order per se but the *chivalric* idea of order, Chaucer himself historicized his world. Chivalry's seemingly ubiquitous and transhistorical claims were revealed as merely local currency, a demystification that permitted Chaucer to explore chivalry's contradictions both in its contemporary practices and, more profoundly, in the idea of chivalry itself.

In this historical siting Chaucer was of course greatly assisted by the central formal device of the *Canterbury Tales* as a whole, the tale-telling game that grounds each discourse in the specifics—vocational or psychological—of a speaker. By the very conditions of their expression a knight's concerns as understood by a knight, the contents of the *Knight's Tale* become the substance of chivalric identity. Although it has received relatively little attention, the drama of narration itself provides the most profound analysis of the form of consciousness it represents.[8] The Knight means his *Tale* to celebrate an ideal of order, but its most powerful and enigmatic moments derive from a struggle between the *Tale* and its teller, between the unsettling meanings it insistently expresses and those other, more confirmatory assertions the Knight seeks to promote.

At the heart of this struggle is the nature of chivalric identity. It is essential to grasp, as our initial premise, that chivalry entailed a form of selfhood insistently, even exclusively, public. It stressed a collective or corporate self-definition and so ignored the merely personal or individual. It sought, as a code of behavior, at every turn to foreclose self-reflection and critical distance. The Knight's portrait in the *General Prologue* conforms to this model of identity formation. As we have seen, it is governed both by rhetorical prescription and social injunction, its formulae those of a highly conservative, apparently seamless literary and social ideology.[9] But precisely in its effacement of the subject this portrait stands in opposition to those characterizing procedures of the *General Prologue* as a whole that it sets in motion; and by the time he comes to tell his *Tale*, the Knight has been released from his formulaic

8. Robert Hanning has posited an analogy between Duke Theseus and the tale-telling Knight as ordering figures, and he has provocatively related the "tale's ambivalence about the possibility of order in the world" to "the problematic view of life implicit in a [chivalric] code that seeks to moralize and dignify aggression" ("Struggle," 537, 540).

9. See Introduction, 30–31.

enclosure into the unstable territory where questions are asked—into the problematic of self-definition that motivates the *Canterbury Tales.* This problematic is expressed by the Knight through his self-conflicted mode of narration. This is, I shall argue, a rhetorical version of the struggle at the heart of chivalry itself, and it enacts the same kinds of suppressions and elisions that enabled chivalry to function as both an ideology and a form of practice. The economy of the *Knight's Tale,* as of chivalry, is an oscillation between knowing and unknowing, between the simultaneous recognition and suppression of reality. The *Knight's Tale* shows us the chivalric mind engaged in an act of self-legitimization that simultaneously and secretly undoes itself. The severity of the control that the Knight imposes upon his narrative is in fact the unwilling agent of control's subversion; and the harder he tries to civilize his materials and make them exemplify chivalry's belief in progress, the more evidently he produces formal stasis and moral incoherence.

In *Troilus and Criseyde* Chaucer also dealt with the problem of history by returning to classical story. In the earlier poem, he acknowledged that the modernist desire for originality, for a new beginning founded on an antique moment of *true* beginning, was impossible of fulfillment; and that the notion of the self as an analogously ahistorical entity, self-identical and socially autonomous, was equally illusory. The *Knight's Tale* is then the next step in historical understanding, for it defines the desire to escape from history as itself class specific and socially determined, as itself, in other words, historical. By ascribing the *Tale* to a narrator who is not some version of himself (that is, a servant of the noble society he investigates) but an authoritative representative of that society, Chaucer broadens and deepens his cultural analysis, entering as it were the collective consciousness of the second estate and showing, despite its resistance, what dark fears it harbored. And he also begins the process by which he will objectify and finally alienate a point of view with which he once identified himself. As we shall see, the *Knight's Tale* functions in an important sense as the other against which the project of the *Canterbury Tales* is ultimately defined; and it therefore appropriately begins the game of *quiting* that will at once include and counter it. The *Tale* is an act of both cultural investigation and aesthetic self-reflection, and it serves as both a critique of social practices and a form of authorial self-definition.[10]

10. What are the chronological relations of the *Troilus* and the *Knight's Tale?* The *Knight's Tale* used to be dated in the early 1380s on the grounds of presumed contemporary allusions and the mention of a poem on "al the love of Palamon and Arcite" in the

In what sense is the *Knight's Tale* a tale of chivalry's interior? To ask such a question is inevitably to enter into the twentieth-century debate over chivalry's character as an institution. The terms of the debate were defined by Johan Huizinga, whose classic *Waning of the Middle Ages* (1924) argued that late-medieval chivalry represented above all an attempt by the nobility to escape from a threatening and incomprehensible reality. While acknowledging that noble practice often demonstrated "the political and military value of chivalrous ideas," and while agreeing that chivalry formed the basis for the later development of "clemency and right" and "all the best elements of patriotism," Huizinga nonetheless delivered a stinging critique. "In order to forget the

---

Prologue to the *Legend of Good Women*. Johnstone Parr, however, showed that the allusions could quite easily refer to the events of 1386–88—and, indeed, as his argument implied, but for its own purposes could not make explicit, to virtually any events whatsoever ("The Date and Revision of Chaucer's *Knight's Tale*," *PMLA* 60 [1945]: 307–24). Parr supported his claim for a later date with two other arguments. When Saturn said, "I do vengeance and pleyn correcioun, / While I dwelle in the signe of the leoun" (2462–63), he was describing the state of the skies from July 1387 through August 1389, and especially from late November 1387 through mid-April 1388—which would include the time of the Merciless Parliament. The other argument was the striking similarity between the description of Theseus's tournament and two contemporary accounts, by Froissart and Christopher Okland, of Richard's famous tournament at Smithfield in October, 1390—a tournament that Chaucer, as clerk of the king's works, helped to prepare. On this latter point, Parr was taken to task by Robert A. Pratt for underestimating the amount of the description that derived from the *Teseida* ("Was Chaucer's *Knight's Tale* Extensively Revised After the Middle of 1390?" *PMLA* 63 [1948]: 726–36). But despite Pratt's corrections, enough remains of Parr's argument—as he himself pointed out in reply (*PMLA* 63 [1948]: 736–39)—to leave open the possibility that Chaucer meant his audience to see a parallel between Theseus's tournament and Richard's. Perhaps the most striking details shared by Froissart and Chaucer are the dates—in both cases the festivities start on Sunday, with the main combats on Tuesday—and the organization of the participants into two companies. Similarly, although this is not an argument made by Parr, while Froissart's account restricts the tourney to jousts, Okland's description makes it clear that a "feat of arms" between the two companies was also involved, a form of tourneying that became popular only in the last decades of the fourteenth century: see Raphael Holinshed, *Chronicles* (London: Johnson, 1807), 2:312 (Holinshed's source is Okland's Latin poem, which has subsequently disappeared); Juliet R. V. Barker, *The Tournament in England, 1100–1400* (Woodbridge: Boydell, 1986), 158. Finally, J. D. North's astronomical investigations have shown that the fictive events of both the *Troilus* and the *Knight's Tale* take place contemporaneously: Pandarus begins the wooing of Criseyde on May 3, 1385, and Criseyde leaves Troy exactly three years later, on May 3, 1388; meanwhile, Palamon escapes from prison on May 3, 1387, and the fatal tournament begins a year later, on May 5, 1388: "Kalenderes Enlumyned Ben They: Some Astronomical Themes in Chaucer," *RES*, n.s. 20 (1969), 42–53. The upshot of this evidence, then, is that it is likely that the *Troilus* and the *Knight's Tale* were being written at about the same time but that the *Knight's Tale* continued to be worked on after the *Troilus* was completed.

painful imperfection of reality, the nobles turn to the continual illusion of a high and heroic life. They wear the mask of Lancelot and of Tristram. It is an amazing self-deception."[11] But the realities of late-medieval warfare—its financial structure and rationale, its "endless treasons and brutalities," and its technical development that rendered the aristocratic cavalryman vulnerable to the archer, the pikeman, and the gunner—"were bound to open the eyes of the nobility and show the falseness and uselessness of their ideal" (90). For Huizinga chivalry had always been essentially cosmetic; but what distinguished its late-medieval form was that the fraudulence could no longer be disguised, and not even the aristocracy itself could fully credit its chivalric play acting: "a blasé aristocracy laughs at its own ideal" (81) with a brittle, *fin de siècle* sophistication.

Huizinga's successors first softened and then sought to overturn his analysis. In *The Decline of Chivalry* (1937), as its title proclaims, Raymond Kilgour's survey of the fourteenth- and fifteenth-century criticisms of aristocratic behavior concluded that "all the vices which had been latent in chivalry [then] appeared in the open."[12] But Kilgour worked from premises his master had never accepted—that chivalric ideals had once been upheld, that the late Middle Ages saw a decline from an authentic chivalry, and that it was this decadence that contemporary writers were criticizing. Similarly, in *The Indian Summer of English Chivalry* (1960), Arthur Ferguson took fifteenth-century writers at their word when they said, as they persistently did, that they were trying to restore a virtue now fallen on evil days.[13]

The final step in this process of revision was to suggest that not only had chivalry once been a legitimate ideal of life but that it remained so throughout the later Middle Ages. Malcolm and Juliet Vale, and especially Maurice Keen, have argued that the ideals of chivalry remained, from the beginning of the Middle Ages to the end, both credible and in touch with reality.[14] Keen, for instance, claimed that the proliferating

11. Johan Huizinga, *The Waning of the Middle Ages*, trans. F. Hopman (London: Edward Arnold, 1924), 82, 93, 69. Further citations will be included in the text.

12. Raymond Lincoln Kilgour, *The Decline of Chivalry as Shown in the French Literature of the Late Middle Ages* (Cambridge: Harvard University Press, 1937), 14.

13. Arthur B. Ferguson, *The Indian Summer of English Chivalry: Studies in the Decline and Transformation of Chivalric Idealism* (Durham: Duke University Press, 1960).

14. Malcolm Vale, *War and Chivalry: Warfare and Aristocratic Culture in England, France and Burgundy at the End of the Middle Ages* (London: Duckworth, 1981); Juliet Vale, *Edward III and Chivalry: Chivalric Society and Its Context, 1270–1350* (Woodbridge: Boydell, 1982); Maurice Keen, *Chivalry* (New Haven: Yale University Press, 1984); see also Keen's "Huizinga, Kilgour and the Decline of Chivalry," *M&H*, n.s. 8 (1977): 1–20. For useful selections from the huge bibliography on chivalry, see the titles listed by Richard Barber, *The*

secular orders of knighthood—the Garter, the Star, the Golden Fleece, and so forth—were not just aristocratic men's clubs but important political initiatives; crusading, while serving secular purposes, also retained its religious legitimacy and expressed a genuine knightly piety; and tournaments were not simply empty ceremonies but tough exercises that trained knights for the business of war. Indeed, for Keen the crucial social and political reality that legitimized chivalry was precisely warfare, which not only required a code to dignify and ritualize its agents but also simultaneously generated and reconciled the central contradictions of chivalry; between the individualism of knight errantry and the collectivism of the chivalric community, between disruptive competitiveness and self-effacing service, war was the link. Because the nobility bore the cost of arming and training themselves as warriors, the individualist idea of knight errantry had to be maintained as a spiritual return for that outlay. "These social facts and forces," wrote Keen, "underpinned the medieval cult of the well-born warrior, and assented to his seeking justification in the eyes at once of his God, his ruler, and his beloved lady in following the profession of arms" (227). And if the ideals of chivalry were always beyond reach, if chivalry always battled against "its own distorted image" (237) in the behavior of those who betrayed its high-minded precepts, "there is nothing very surprising about this, really; . . . [it is] a permanent feature of the human situation" (233). The fact that ideals are always contaminated by the impurity of history does not make them any the less deserving of admiration or less worthy of belief.

In effect, Keen reinvoked, as a timeless paradigm, the struggle between noble designs and chaos. But we may now legitimately ask whether the chivalry of the late Middle Ages is best understood in these essentially—and essentializing—liberal terms. For one thing, Keen's account underestimates the extent to which service in warfare was, quite apart from booty and ransoms, a profitable enterprise for the knight, and especially for the noble commander. If the knight took the time and expense to prepare himself for war, it was less because he wanted to respond to "the needs of service" than because he knew it made good financial sense.[15] Second, and more seriously, Keen's ac-

---

Knight and Chivalry, 2d ed. (Ipswich: Boydell, 1974), and by Arno Borst, ed., *Das Rittertum im Mittelalter* (Darmstadt: Wissenschaftliche Gesellschaft, 1982).

15.   For a detailed demonstration that "an attitude towards war as a speculative, but at best hugely profitable trade . . . was shared by all who joined the mercenary armies of Edward III and Henry V," see K. B. McFarlane, *The Nobility of Later Medieval England* (Oxford: Clarendon Press, 1973), 19–60; the citation is from 21. See also Vale, *War and*

count assumes that warfare is somehow a natural phenomenon, a state of affairs that comes into being apart from human agency and against human interests, a natural disaster that requires the services of military men and whose harshness legitimizes their martial ethic. But of course wars are made by men, and in the late Middle Ages they were made by the very men whose social status and financial well-being most depended on them. The *condottiere* Sir John Hawkwood knew this very well: according to a famous story that Keen himself repeats, when two passing friars wished him peace, Hawkwood complained that this was an ugly greeting, since peace would put him out of business.[16] A less bald instance of the same understanding is provided by Commynes' comment on Charles the Bold of Burgundy: "He desired great glory, which more than anything else led him to undertake his wars; and he longed to resemble those ancient princes who have been so much talked of after their death."[17] Similar contemporary comments on the heroes of late-medieval chivalry could be reproduced virtually *ad libidum:* the knight sought above all a field of action upon which, in the words of Marshall Boucicaut's biographer, "to employ his youth," a quest that found its most satisfying goal in warfare.[18] Then as now, it was not wars that made soldiers but the other way around. And of no war was this more true than the Hundred Years War between France and England, a dynastic squabble in large part generated and perpetu-

---

Chivalry, 28, and for an earlier period, Philippe Contamine, *War in the Middle Ages,* trans. Michael Jones (Oxford: Blackwell, 1984), 90–101. According to Contamine, "Money was the almost obligatory link between authority and soldiers. According to contemporaries themselves, this phenomenon accelerated from the mid-twelfth century" (90).

16. Keen, *Chivalry,* 227.

17. Cited by Huizinga, *Waning,* 60.

18. Because of a truce, "it seemed to Boucicaut that there was little necessity for warmaking in France, and so as to continue to employ his youth usefully he returned for a second time to Prussia, where it was said that this season there would be good warfare. He stayed there for a time, and then returned to France" (*Le Livre des faicts du Mareschal de Boucicaut,* in *Nouvelle Collection des mémoires relatifs à l'histoire de France,* ed. Joseph F. Michaud and J. J. F. Poujoulat [Paris: Féchoz et Letouzey, 1881], 224: "il luy semble que on ne bensongnoit mie moult adonc en France en faict de guerre, pour tousjours employer sa jeunesse en bien faire, s'en retourna la deuxiesme fois en Prusse, où l'on disoit que celle saisaon devoit avoir belle guerre. Là demeura un temps, puis s'en revient en France"). See also Froissart's account of Edward III's motives for going to Normandy in 1346, where as it happened he won the battle of Crécy: the king of England was then "in the flower of his youth . . . and desired nothing but to follow arms and search out his enemies" (*Chroniques,* ed. Siméon Luce [Paris: Reynouard, 1869], 3:131: "en la fleur de sa jonèce et . . . ne desiront fors à trouver les armes et ses ennemis").

ated by chivalric ambition.[19] Nor is it some impersonal "society," as
Keen says, that "sought to do justice to its conception of [the knight's]
dignity through elaborate rituals," a grateful populace applauding its
saviors. Rather, it was knighthood itself that continually reinforced its
own sense of its own dignity through rituals that it staged by and for
itself—an early instance of the apparently endless capacity of the military for self-congratulation.

Given our contemporary appreciation for the ability of the self to
sustain contradictions, we will want to modify Huizinga's argument
that late-medieval chivalry was an empty cultural form that not even
the nobility could fully credit. But by the same token, Huizinga's account of courtly chroniclers and their patrons seems now all the more
perspicacious:

> The confused image of contemporaneous history being much too
> complicated for their comprehension, they simplified it, as it were,
> by the fiction of chivalry as a moving force. . . . By this traditional
> fiction they succeeded in explaining to themselves, as well as they
> could, the motives and the course of history, which thus was reduced
> to a spectacle of the honour of princes and the virtue of knights, to a
> noble game with edifying and heroic rules. (59)

In other words, from ethical confusion and discomfort arise, first, the
need to insist on honor as chivalry's guiding principle; and, second, the
need to convey that message by exterior symbols, whose glittering surface would distract attention from the dark contradictions beneath. The
term "honor" became its own verbal symbol, a shorthand for motives
that would not bear further inspection.

According to Froissart, the wars between France and England were
undertaken by "brave men . . . in order to advance their bodies and
increase their honor."[20] Guillaume Machaut, the biographer of Peter of
Cyprus, tells us that when Peter urged his men to undertake the assault
of Alexandria he encouraged them not because it was the first step in

---

19. This is not to say that there were not social and political instabilities in the relationship between France and England, and within each country, that made war possible;
but it required the desire for war to make it happen. The fact that the precise war aims of
England's two warrior-kings—Edward III and Henry V—were never made explicit, and
continue to puzzle modern historians, is persuasive evidence that it was war itself that
was the primary goal; see Christopher Allmand, *The Hundred Years War: England and
France at War c. 1300–c. 1450* (Cambridge: Cambridge University Press, 1988), 7–12, 57.

20. Froissart, *Chroniques*: "li vaillant homme . . . pour avancier leurs corps et
acoistre leur honneur" (2:179).

the reconquest of the Holy Land but because they would win "such honor that a more honorable thing would never happen to any of them"; and when they abandoned him after the assault and returned to Cyprus, Peter lamented not the failure of the expedition but the dishonor that had befallen him: "Honor, now you are dead!"[21] And when the Black Prince entered the Spanish War on the side of Pedro the Cruel, he justified his action on the grounds that Pedro was a lawful king and Henry a bastard; but the Chandos Herald understood his motive to be rivalry with Bertrand du Guesclin over the title of most honorable knight. As the Herald has Edward say before the decisive battle of Najera, "My heart summons and draws me to conquer a life of honor."[22] Not, of course, that honor depended on victory: after the battle of Poitiers, the Black Prince awarded "the prize and the garland" to the captured King John, telling him, according to Froissart, that although he had lost the battle he had "conquered the high name of prowess."[23]

By defining its values almost entirely in terms of personal worth, chivalry tended to privatize all historical action. For all the claims of social improvement made by its more highminded apologists (and they are fewer than we might expect), its deepest ambition was to produce not a better world but a perfect knight. It was committed to codes of behavior not as programs of action but techniques of self-fashioning: the chivalric life was its own goal. Becoming ever more elaborate in its self-articulation, chivalry sought to create a form of life that was autonomous and self-sustaining, complete in itself and requiring no authentication from outside. Acknowledging no goal other than its own enactment, chivalry justified itself by the very absolutism of its self-commitment and the intricacy and elegance of its performance; and by understanding itself only in its own terms, it preempted the critical thought that a more strategically self-aware engagement with the world might have prompted.

Hence the insistence throughout chivalric writing on the simplicity of chivalric selfhood. Chivalric heroes are represented as driven by a single, all-compelling desire. Peter of Cyprus is inspired by a youthful vision to found the Order of the Sword, "and this was the goal of all his

21. Guillaume Machaut, *La Prise d'Alexandrie*, ed. M. L. de Mas Latrie (Geneva: Flick, 1877): "tele honnour . . . / Qu'onques chose plus honnourable / N'avint a nul de nous" (2714–17); "Honneur, or yes tu morte!" (3583)

22. Diana B. Tyson, ed., *La Vie du Prince Noir by Chandos Herald* (Tübingen: Max Niemeyer, 1975): "mon coer semonte et attise / De conquestre vie de honour" (3180–81).

23. Froissart, *Chroniques*: "vous avés conquis au jour d'ui le haut nom de proéce, et avés passet tous les mieulz faisans de vostre costet"; "le pris et le chapelet" (5:64).

efforts."²⁴ Geoffroi de Charny, a preeminent chevalier who died defending his king's *oriflamme* at Poitiers, tells us in his authoritative *Livre de Chevalerie* that the youths who will become successful soldiers are those who have haunted the *mestier d'armes* from their earliest days and are driven solely by the desire "to have the high honor of prowess."²⁵ All other interests are weaknesses. The biographers of both du Guesclin and Boucicaut stress the violence of the heroes' *enfances* as evidence of their single-mindedness, their unconditional commitment to a mode of life that is itself not only beyond all questioning but so deeply embedded in the hero's consciousness as to have become the only content of his character.²⁶ Knighthood is not a vocation elected by these men but their very mode of being, an ideological conditioning that precludes critical self-reflection because it wholly conditions self-construction.

A well-known example of the contradictions chivalric discourse was able to support is its assertion that the knightly desires for honor and wealth are entirely compatible. Machaut, for example, explains Peter of Cyprus's adoption of the sword as the emblem of his crusading order in these terms: "For when an eminent prince conquers by the sword, he acquires glory—honor and profit together—and a good name."²⁷ Certainly the chivalric mind was capable of distinguishing between *honneur* and *profit*—Geoffroi de Charny, for example, was quite aware that the purity of the chivalric impulse could be corrupted by acquisitiveness— but it habitually avoided such an analysis.²⁸ Similarly, chivalric piety is a

24. Machaut, *Prise:* "et c'estoit la conclusion / De toute son entencion" (283–84). Machaut later adds: "And he never cared anything for dogs, or hawks, nor pretty women; only to injure his enemies—that was where he put all his effort" ("Si ne metoit mie s'entente / En chiens, n'oisiaus, n'en dame gente, / Fors en ses anemis grever. / Là vuet il mettre et esprouver / Cuer, corps, vigour, vie et puissance, / Son tans et toute sa chevance" [lines 4340–45]).

25. The *Livre de Chevalerie* is printed by Kervyn de Lettenhove, ed., *Les Oeuvres de Froissart*, t. 1, pt. 3 (Brussels: Devaux, 1873): "pour avoir la haute honnour de proesse" (472–73).

26. For du Guesclin, see E. Charrière, ed., *Chronique de Bertrand du Guesclin par Cuvelier* (Paris: Didot, 1839), 10–11 (lines 154–94); for Boucicaut, see Michaud and Poujoulat, *Nouvelle Collection*, 217–19.

27. Machaut, *Prise:*
Car quant uns haus princes conquiert
Par l'espee, gloire en acquiert,
Honneur et profit tout ensambla,
Et bon memoire, ce me samble. (479–82)

28. For de Charny, those who go to war solely in order to gain booty (although it is acceptable as a side effect) are less worthy than those who fight for honor: "And so one ought to engage in warfare more for honor, which lasts for ever, than for profit and gain, which one can lose in an hour" ("Et pour ce doit-l'en mettre en ce mestier plus son cuer et

blend of sacred and secular values, in particular the desire for fame in this world and salvation in the next, that can easily be distinguished and ranked by nonchivalric writers but that in chivalric discourse remain undiscriminated.[29]

But for modern readers the most striking dissonance is the capacity of chivalric writers to accommodate the brutality of medieval warfare to the idealistic vocabulary of the chivalric lexicon. While Froissart, for instance, was able to deplore the Black Prince's notorious sack of Limoges, his interest in the equally horrifying sack of Caen by Edward III some twenty-five years earlier focused almost entirely on a single gesture of chivalric generosity: two French knights were rescued from English men-at-arms by Sir Thomas Holland, whom they recognized "because they had once known and accompanied each other at Granada and in Prussia and on other trips, as is common among knights."[30] The class solidarity of chivalry finds its perfect literary analogue in the narrowness of Froissart's interests, who almost always averted his eyes from the universal practice of pillaging. As John Barnie has said,

> Although the military elite were committed to a general strategy involving rapine and slaughter on the part of the men-at-arms under their command, they comprehended their own role in very different terms. . . . The soldiery were essential to the war effort, but in a sense they fought a different war based on different assumptions.[31]

Throughout their writings the social and ethical problems chivalry fostered are alienated as the other it is designed to repress. For chivalric theorists like Ramon Lull and Christine de Pisan, there are not good and bad knights but only true and false ones, knights and non-

---

s'entente a l'onneur, qui tous temps dure, que a proffit et gaing que l'en peut perdre en une seule heure" [*Livre*, 471–72]).

29. See Keen, *Chivalry*, 44–63. Keen argues throughout his book that medieval chivalry had an essentially secular inspiration that absorbed and made use of religious values rather than vice versa.

30. Froissart, *Chroniques*: "car il s'estoient aultre fois veu et compagniet l'un l'autre à Grenade et en Prusse et en aultres voiages, ensi que chevalier se treuvent." Holland then tried to control the English soldiers, and Froissart admiringly tells us that several "gentilz chevaliers d'Engleterre" prevented many townswomen and nuns from being raped (3:144–45).

31. Barnie, *War in Medieval English Society: Social Values in the Hundred Years War, 1377–99* (London: Weidenfield and Nicolson, 1974), 72.

knights.[32] The medieval soldier is either a knight within the Order of
Chivalry or he is "disordinant" and no knight at all; and the excesses of
the battlefield are the acts of the unchivalrous rather than an inevitable
consequence of chivalry itself.[33] Hence chivalry's fascination with aestheticized and theatricalized self-representations, whether as heraldry
or in the more elaborate displays of literary role playing. That these
mannerisms were in fact coextensive with a severe martial vigor—and
with a brutality that can match anything the earlier Middle Ages has to
offer—is not a contradiction at all but precisely what we should expect.
For if one kind of material reality is not to be acknowledged, another
must take its place.

In recuperating chivalry by stressing its political and military efficacy, Keen's account inevitably underestimated its function as an ideological refiguring of an unacceptable reality. It also underestimated the
degree to which chivalry functioned not simply as a martial ethic but as
a form of class consciousness. In the too-easily forgotten words of the
nineteenth-century radical historian E. A. Freeman, "The chivalrous
spirit is above all things a class spirit."[34] For its force and meaning to be
grasped, chivalry must be understood as the central form of self-
definition by means of which the noble class situated itself within medieval society. The question is not only whether the ideals of chivalry

32.   Lull's *Libro del ordre de cavayleria*, written in the last quarter of the thirteen century,
was translated into French as *Le Livre de l'ordre de chevalerie*, ed. F. Minervini (Bari: Adriatica,
1972) and from the French into English by Caxton as *The Book of the Ordre of Chyualry*, ed. A.
T. P. Byles, EETS, OS 168 (London: Oxford University Press, 1926). Christine's *Le Livre des
fais d'armes et de chevalerie*, a compilation of texts by Vegetius, Frontinus, Valerius Maximus,
and Honoré Bonet, is largely concerned with military strategy and the rules of war; there is
no modern edition but it was also translated into English by Caxton as *The Book of Fayttes of
Armes and of Chyualrye*, ed. A. T. P. Byles, EETS, OS 189 (London: Oxford University Press,
1932). For the "disordinate knyghte," see *The Book of the Order of Chyualry*, 10. In Lull's
absolutist conception, chivalry is a defining condition—"chyualrye gyueth to a knyghte
alle that to hym apperteyneth" (12)—and hence, if all who violate the order are
"disordinate," that is, not knights, so then, by a logical error that makes natural sense, all
who are indisputably knights must similarly partake of that moral superiority.

33.   In his earlier and more critical "Chivalry, Nobility and the Man-at-Arms," in *War,
Literature, and Politics in the Late Middle Ages*, ed. C. T. Allmand (Liverpool: Liverpool
University Press, 1976), 32–45, Keen showed how the idealism of chivalry legitimized
not simply the pitched battles of the Hundred Years War but also the depredations
wreaked upon the defenseless inhabitants of France and Italy by the *routiers*. For a
fourteenth-century example, see the comments of Walter Bentley, who said that the men
ravaging Brittany were "not knights or squires . . . [but] fellows of low degree" (H. J.
Hewitt, *The Organization of War under Edward III, 1338–62* [Manchester: Manchester University Press, 1966], 136).

34.   E. A. Freeman, *The Norman Conquest*, 5:482; cited by Kilgour, *Decline of Chivalry*,
15.

conformed to the military reality of the later Middle Ages. Rather, it is what was entailed, psychologically as well as socially, by this self-definition, and also what was left out. Insofar as the nobleman restricted his self-understanding to a chivalric identity, to that extent he excluded from his view the economic, social, and political forces that were challenging his dominance. There is considerable evidence to suggest that in the late fourteenth century chivalric identity was beginning to be seen as inadequate even to the governing class; and to an observer like Chaucer, who was seeking detachment, the rifts in the construct must have been of particular interest.

I

The portrait of the Knight in the *General Prologue* presents a man who seems wholly unconnected to the public life of late fourteenth-century England. So far as we can tell he has participated in none of the numerous French campaigns of the preceding forty years, nor has he joined with either John of Gaunt or Edward the Black Prince in their Spanish adventures. Only one ambiguous mention of "his lordes werre" (I, 47) and an allusion in the Squire's portrait to *his* participation in the Despenser Crusade of 1383 (85–86) provide any reference to the most consequential military events of the time. Nor are we given any sense of the Knight's role in the governance of England: "He was late ycome from his viage" (77), and the roll call of exotic locales where he has fought distances him from the tumultuous English politics of the 1370s and 1380s. Moreover, as commentators have pointed out, his crusading campaigns that can be clearly dated took place in the 1360s, and Donald Howard is surely right to stress the aura of "obsolescence" that clings to the portrait.[35] The *Tale* he tells continues this sense of historical irrelevance: its narrative about the romantic rivalry of two young men and its resolution by a powerful ruler explicitly exemplifies classical and not medieval chivalry, while its celebration of the ostentatious inessentials of the chivalric life-style seems dramatically at odds with what the *General Prologue* has suggested of the Knight's personal austerity. But it may be that the *Tale*'s components are, after all, materially related to the Knight's experience and merely displaced (according to the rhetorical habits of chivalry itself) into a more ornamental vision of themselves.

Rivalry and governance: the two central topics of the *Tale* are also at the center of the problematic of the noble life in the England of the late

---

35. Donald Howard, *The Idea of the* Canterbury Tales (Berkeley: University of California Press, 1976), 94–97.

fourteenth century. We can understand both the competitive economy of the honor system and its effect on the political authority of the aristocracy if we can trace the logic of displacement that governs the Knight's oblique representation of his world. In order to show this displacement at work, we will first need to consider an exemplary instance of the relation between honor and competition, rivalry and governance, an instance especially pertinent because Chaucer himself was a spectator, and to some extent a participant, in the contest. I refer to the famous dispute between Sir Richard Scrope and Sir Robert Grosvenor over the right to bear the arms *azure* with *bend d'or.* The dispute began on August 14, 1385: while King Richard was leading a huge army toward an anticipated battle against invading French troops and their Scottish allies, two of his knights suddenly discovered that they were both endowed, apparently quite by accident, with the same armorial bearings. Over the next six years their suit was adjudicated by the Court of Chivalry, the tribunal presided over by the constable and marshal of England to deal with "deeds of arms and of war" at home and abroad.[36] The court conducted its inquiry both by examining material evidence—muniments, tombs, windows, paintings, vestments—and by receiving almost 450 depositions, some 300 of which survive. These depositions were delivered by, in the words of the court, "abbots, priors, and others of Holy Church and . . . lords, knights, and esquires of honor, and gentlemen having knowledge of arms, and"—a point important enough to make explicit—"from no man of the commons or any other estate."[37] One of the "esquires of honor" who gave testimony, on October 15, 1387, in the Church of St. Margaret, Westminster, was Geoffrey Chaucer.[38]

36. These are the terms of reference laid down by Parliament in 1389, cited by Anthony Wagner, *Heralds of England* (London: Stationery Office, 1967), 38; see Maurice Keen, "The Jurisdiction and Origins of the Court of Chivalry," in *War and Government in the Middle Ages: Essays in Honour of J. O. Prestwich,* ed. John Gillingham and J. C. Holt (Woodbridge: Boydell, 1984), 159–69, and the still valuable G. D. Squibb, *The High Court of Chivalry* (Oxford: Clarendon Press, 1959).

37. Nicholas Harris Nicolas, ed., *The Controversy between Sir Richard Scrope and Sir Robert Grosvenor* (London: Samuel Bentley, 1832), 1:40. The translation is taken from John Gough Nichols, ed., *The Herald and Genealogist* 1 (1863), 390. An account of the controversy is provided by Ronald Stewart-Brown, "The Scrope and Grosvenor Controversy, 1385–1391," *Transactions of the Historic Society of Lancashire and Cheshire* 89 (1937): 1–22; a brief discussion may also be found in Noel Denholm-Young, *The Country Gentry in the Fourteenth Century* (Oxford: Clarendon Press, 1969), 133–35.

38. Chaucer's deposition is printed in Nichols, *Controversy,* 1:178–79, and in Martin M. Crow and Clair C. Olson, eds., *Chaucer Life-Records* (Oxford: Oxford University Press, 1966), 270–73. See also Donald R. Howard, *Chaucer: His Life, His Works, His World* (New York: Dutton, 1987), 390–93.

We shall in due course examine Chaucer's deposition, but for the moment the dispute itself, and especially its remarkable denouement, will sufficiently repay attention. For it neatly embodies the ideology that governed the honor world of chivalry, just as the Scottish campaign that was its occasion encapsulates, as we shall see, the specific difficulties faced by both the monarchy and the nobility in the last decades of the fourteenth century. This is the chivalric community to which Chaucer was attached for much of his life, that provided the social context for the courtly *makyng* that comprised the first two-thirds of his literary career, and that supplied both the setting and the subject of the *Knight's Tale*. But as his deposition in the Scrope-Grosvenor case suggests, and as the details of his career make clear, he did and did not belong here—an ambiguity crucial both to the *Knight's Tale* and to the larger project it initiates.

Scrope's dispute with Grosvenor was not the first time he had been compelled to defend his right to the arms *azure* with *bend d'or*. During John of Gaunt's campaign of 1373, Scrope had discovered that a Cornish knight called Thomas Carminowe was bearing identical arms. On that occasion, the dispute was referred not to the Court of Chivalry but to an informal tribunal of seven knights presided over by Gaunt himself. Scrope swore that his family had borne the arms since the time of the Conquest; but Carminowe claimed that they had been granted to his lineage by none other than King Arthur. The tribunal decided— apparently on the grounds that the two families derived from what it decided were two different countries, Britain and Normandy—that both grants were legitimate.[39] Nor was Scrope's difficulty particularly unusual: there are records of at least seven similar disputes in the period 1300–1410, and there must have been many others that have left no trace.

The fact is that there was no way to control the assumption of coats of arms, despite their social importance. For the nobility, arms were nothing less than "tokyns of nobleness," *insignia nobilitatis.* Far more than simply a means of identification for the tournament or battlefield, they were a statement both of identity understood genealogically and of social privilege justified by heredity. They both defined the self in terms of the current social order and were a constant reminder that that order was legitimate. As Brigitte Rezak has explained, knight's seals had originally carried the image of a mounted warrior because "it was the military function which had allowed their assimilation into the noble group." But at a later stage this image seemed rather a "reminder of

39. The story is told in the course of testimony given by John of Gaunt in the later dispute (Nicolas, *Controversy*, 1:49–50).

their servile origins," and was therefore replaced by the coats of arms that symbolized "the identity of a family which, having freed itself from the status of domestic retainer, had developed personal power and judicial privileges, genealogical consciousness and hereditary transmission: a family constituted as a dynastic lineage."[40]

Given this valence, there was an inevitable proliferation of arms throughout the chivalric class. One roll of arms, prepared about 1380, contains 1,611 painted coats of arms, almost all English, and another, slightly later, contains, 1,595; since the nobility of late-medieval England included over 3,000 families, there must have been many more arms that escaped heraldic notice.[41] Far more unsettling, however, was the extension of the system beyond the nobility. By the mid-thirteenth century urban merchants and craftsmen began to assume coats of arms, and in the fourteenth century the fashion spread not just to corporations but—the ultimate affront—to peasants.[42] While heraldic writers recognized that the proliferation of arms could not be stopped, they also urged some form of control.[43] In 1417 Henry V sent letters to the sheriffs of four counties ordering them to supervise the assumption of arms, and between 1417 and 1420 his brother the duke of Clarence issued ordinances providing for heraldic visitation and the registration of armorial bearings.[44] Nonetheless, only the Tudors were finally able to centralize the honor system, as with so much else, and establish the monarchy as the "fount of honor."[45]

---

40. Brigitte Bedos Rezak, "The Social Implications of the Art of Chivalry: The Sigillographic Evidence (France 1050–1250)," in *The Medieval Court in Europe*, ed. Edward E. Haymes (Munich: Wilhelm Fink, 1986), 159.

41. For heraldic rolls, see Anthony Richard Wagner, ed., *A Catalogue of English Mediaeval Rolls of Arms* (Oxford: Oxford University Press, 1950), 69–71, 73–78; for the size of the nobility, Chris Given-Wilson, *The English Nobility in the Late Middle Ages* (London: Routledge and Kegan Paul, 1987), 18–19.

42. See Michel Pastoureau, *Les armoiries*, Typologie des sources du moyen âge occidental 20 (Turnhout: Brepols, 1976), 29–31; for the special circumstances in England, Wagner, *Heralds of England*, 35.

43. Rodney Dennys, *The Heraldic Imagination* (London: Barrie and Jenkins, 1975), 63. The heraldic treatise written in 1434 by Jean Courtois, the Sicily Herald, describes the conditions that must be met for entrance to knighthood and includes an emotional plea that the elaborate dubbing ceremony be reinstituted (Ferdinand Roland, ed., *Parties inédites de l'oeuvre de Sicile*, Société des Bibliophiles Belges de Mons 22 [Mons: DeQuesme-Masquillier, 1867], 72–78).

44. Anthony Richard Wagner, *Heralds and Heraldry in the Middle Ages* (London: Oxford University Press, 1956), 59–64.

45. Mervyn James, *English Politics and the Concept of Honour, 1485–1642*, Past and Present, Supplement No. 3 (Cambridge: Cambridge University Press, 1978); reprinted in James, *Society, Politics and Culture: Studies in Early Modern England* (Cambridge: Cambridge University Press, 1986), 308–415.

This uncontrolled dispersion of heraldic arms made the assertion of proprietary rights both essential and impossible. Within the chivalric community of honor, personal identity was both public—you were what you were seen to be—and corporate—you were your family. Any infringement on the secure possession of one's arms was an infringement on one's very being and an attack on the foundation of the honor system—on the stalwart, sovereign will as the final ground of value. Since the coat of arms represented each family as an independent dynastic lineage, the coexistence of identical arms subverted the autonomy and sovereignty of the family and hence of the individual who derived his identity from it. Such an embarrassment naturally ignited rivalry, that aggressive self-assertiveness and competitive desire to excell over others that simultaneously animated and endangered the community of honor. And since, as the anthropologist Julian Pitt-Rivers has memorably said, "the ultimate vindication of honor lies in physical violence," the Scrope-Grosvenor dispute seemed as likely to end in knightly combat as did the equally irreconcilable confrontation between the Knight's fictive protagonists, Arcite and Palamon.[46]

It was only thanks to the extraordinary measures taken by the Court of Chivalry that the "bataille" that Scrope and Grosvenor offered to fight was in fact avoided, and even then the formal procedures almost came to nought.[47] In November 1390 the court (which by this time included Chaucer's friend, the chamber knight Lewis Clifford) decided that Scrope was entitled to the arms but that Grosvenor could continue to use them if he added a plain silver bordure. Not surprisingly, this judgment satisfied neither party, and both appealed to the king. Although he had no reason to esteem Scrope, whom he had intemperately removed as chancellor in 1382 and who had subsequently supported the Lords Appellant in the crisis of 1386–88, Richard nonetheless ruled in his favor on May 1, 1391.[48] Grosvenor was required not

46. Julian Pitt-Rivers, "Honour and Social Status," in *Honour and Shame: The Values of Mediterranean Society*, ed. J. G. Peristiany (London: Weidenfeld and Nicolson, 1965), 29.

47. Nicolas, *Controversy*, 1:48.

48. Scrope did, however, unsuccessfully defend Michael de la Pole against impeachment in 1386: see Anthony Tuck, *Richard II and the English Nobility* (New York: St. Martin's, 1974), 77. But in 1399 Scrope was one of those who signed the order for Richard's deposition. For an account of his administrative career, his new-made wealth, and his litigiousness, see T. F. Tout, *Chapters in the Administrative History of Mediaeval England* (Manchester: Manchester University Press, 1920–33), 3:276–77; for further details, see Chris Given-Wilson, *The Royal Household and the King's Affinity* (New Haven: Yale University Press, 1986), 74, 142, 158. Grosvenor was supported almost exclusively by the Cheshire gentry: see Michael J. Bennett, *Community, Class and Careerism: Chesnire and Lancashire Society in the Age of* Sir Gawain and the Green Knight (Cambridge: Cambridge University Press, 1983), 16.

only to adopt new arms but to pay costs to Scrope, costs that amounted to the staggering sum of £466 13s 4d. Although this amount was later reduced to 500 marks (£333 6s 8d), Grosvenor must still have faced ruin when, at the Parliament held in November, Scrope confronted him in the parliament chamber and, in the presence of John of Gaunt, demanded payment.[49]

Grosvenor's defiance crumbled. According to an extraordinary record preserved, for reasons that will shortly become clear, as a writ in the Close Rolls, "Sir Robert [Grosvenor] with his own mouth said that Sir Richard had recovered of him 500 marks for costs and damages, that he had not the money to pay it, and that he would pay it if he had, wherefore he requested Sir Richard to forgive him the money and for his friendship."[50] Scrope said that he would give his answer in the presence of the king, and on November 13,

> before the king in his palace at Westminster, in presence of my lord of Guienne [i.e., Gaunt], the archbishop of Dublin, the bishops of London, Chester and Chichester, the earls of Derby, Rutland, March, Arundel, Huntingdon, and Northumberland, the lords Roos, Neville, and Cobham, Sir Matthew de Gourney, and knights and esquires in great number, Sir Richard and Sir Robert being there in person, Sir Richard by word of mouth rehearsed the request of Sir Robert, . . . and then told him that the highest and the most sovereign things a knight ought to guard in defence of his estate are his troth and his arms, and that in both of them Sir Robert had impeached him.

He went on to say that "concerning his arms he had a good issue, thanks to God and the king's righteous judgment," but that in the course of the dispute Grosvenor "had averred against him falsehood, fraud, and deceit." Grosvenor replied that "what he did was by advice of his counsel, instructing him that otherwise he might not prosecute his appeal, and that he had no knowledge of such defaults to the re-

49. For the financial implications, compare the dispute between Lord Grey of Ruthyn and Sir Edward Hastings over the right to inherit the arms of John, Lord Hastings. Hastings lost the case in 1410 and was assessed £987, was thrown into the Marshalsea in 1417, and spent the next twenty-six years writing pathetic letters to the king maintaining the justice of his cause (Charles George Young, ed., *An Account of the Controversy between Reginald Lord Grey of Ruthyn and Sir Edward Hastings* [London: Privately Printed, 1841]).

50. An English translation of the record is printed in the *Calendar of Close Rolls, 1389–92*, 518–19, from which all citations are taken. I have modernized the spelling of the names.

proach of Sir Richard." Scrope insisted, however, that "he ought not and would not ever be friends with Sir Robert . . . unless due amends were made him to save his honor." Grosvenor then repeated his statement that "he had no knowledge of falsehood, fraud, deceit or reproach of Sir Richard." Scrope now softened, and requested that since "the villanies and reproaches aforesaid were entered of record in the process, these words should be clearly entered likewise, to remain for making manifest his truth and honor" ("cestes motes & paroles devroiont clerement entres & de record a devinner en declaration de vite loialte et de soun honour").[51] The king granted the request, Scrope and Grosvenor were reconciled, and the costs were waived.

But this was not the final act. Three days later Scrope and Grosvenor appeared "in full parliament" with John of Gaunt presiding. Scrope "bore in his hand a schedule containing the whole tenor of the foregoing memorandum," and the substance of this document was "laid before Sir Robert in his mother tongue" by Gaunt. Gaunt then asked Grosvenor yet again whether he knew of "any falsehood, untruth or reproach now or at any time past in or against the person of Sir Richard; with a calm countenance Sir Robert confessed"—for, be it noted, the third time—"that he knew or heard of none in word or deed, and further averred that the dishonorable words in the schedule contained were spoken not out of his own head but merely at the instigation of his counsel." And Grosvenor further agreed that it "was his will and petition . . . that his confession should be enrolled upon the chancery rolls . . . for a record in time to come"—the record that we have just summarized.

I have cited this document at length in order to stress not just the highly public, ceremonial nature of the honor exchanges that constituted chivalric culture but the wholly social, even material sense of selfhood that it presupposed. Scrope demanded that his *loialte et honour* be made whole and be made manifest, placed *en declaration*. Visibility, even palpability, was required. Usually this could be accomplished only by a physical act: a knight made good a reproach "with his body" and "on the body" of his enemy. But if violence were to be avoided, then another form of tangible, concrete reclamation was necessary. Hence the act of public recantation. Moreover, and perhaps most strikingly, this act must then be itself legitimized—made real—by being ritualized as a theatrical performance. The efficacy of the event depended on its ceremonial enactment: theatricality, far from impeaching the validity of an event, was a warrant of its authenticity. Not only

---

51. The French original is cited from PRO C54/233/27d.

Scrope's damaged selfhood but the chivalric community as a whole were thereby declared whole: the ceremony of reparation was performed before the assembled nobility of England in Parliament and the destructive act itself was removed from the repertoire of chivalric behavior and ascribed to the nonchivalric lawyer. And the final warrant was the material document itself, a piece of parchment that Scrope held in his hand, that Gaunt read, and that Grosvenor, in the presence of the Parliament of England, acceded to "with a calm countenance" that bespoke his wholehearted accord. Things were not merely what but *as* they seemed.

Yet the very ritual aspect of the case, its insistence that legitimacy is located in the material sign, was an indication of chivalry's lack of confidence in itself, of a gap where the signified essence ought to be. Such ceremonies are necessary because noble identity depends upon a system of signification—in this case, coats of arms—that is always open to misuse. Both the palpability of chivalric identity and its collective nature require that it be jealously guarded and relentlessly asserted. Because of its visibility, its location in the contingency of the material sign, rather than in an intangible, inner realm, it is always vulnerable to depredation and decay. Insisting upon the self-evidence of his identity, the nobleman found himself in the paradoxical position of constantly having to reaffirm its existence; the very absoluteness of his superiority forced upon him the need of endless reconfirmation. This was all the more so when, as was the case with Scrope and, at one time or another, with every nobleman, he felt himself vulnerable to the charge of being a parvenu. Despite his distinguished military career, Scrope was the first member of a family that had only recently become prominent to achieve eminence.[52] Moreover, his wealth was derived not from his war service but from his tenure of a wide range of administrative offices, a source that was no doubt reflected in his decision to build his manor at Bolton in an ostentatiously militaristic style.[53]

Scrope's sensitivity to slight had sources other than his own social insecurity. For the decades of the 1370s and 1380s were a time of crisis for the governing class of England in general. While this crisis was both extensive and profound, its salient features can be seen in the paradigmatic Scottish campaign of August 1385. The initial motivation for the campaign was to provide the eighteen-year-old king with an opportu-

52. McFarlane, *Nobility*, 22; his military career is briefly described by Denholm-Young, *Country Gentry*, 132–33. According to Given-Wilson, the Scropes were one of "the 'new' families thrown up by the fourteenth century" (*English Nobility*, 64).

53. Given-Wilson, *English Nobility*, 157; Tout, *Chapters*, 3:276–77.

nity to come into his own not only as monarch but as the leader of the chivalry of England, a warrior king worthy of his glorious father and grandfather. Parliament granted money for the campaign only on condition that the king lead the army himself, and it noted that this was "le primer Viage nostre dit Seigneur le Roy."[54] In fact, throughout the early years of his reign Richard had made considerable efforts to assume a fully chivalric identity. He was, in Juliet Barker's words, "a lavish patron" of the quintessentially chivalric sport of tourneying, and he appeared at tournaments in 1378–79, and again in 1386, in armor decorated with Edward III's famous sun badge.[55] Also in the mid-1380s the Chandos Herald wrote the biography of Richard's heroic father, *La Vie du Prince Noir*, which scholars have plausibly seen as having been commissioned by the king.[56] Similarly, in 1389 the king's uncle Gloucester wrote "An Ordenaunce and Fourme of Fightyng within Listes" for him, and a *Tractatus de Armis*, a book on heraldry, was written in about 1394 for Queen Anne.[57] Later in the 1390s Richard turned away from his martial lineage and adopted the disgraced Edward II and the unwarlike Edward the Confessor as his political patron saints.[58] But in this earlier period, which would include the famous tournaments at Smithfield in 1390 (for both of which Chaucer erected scaffolds), Richard was engaged in the process of fashioning a chivalric identity.

Such a course was in large part dictated by political necessity, a deliberate response on Richard's part to his troubled relations with his barons. In the Parliament of 1384 the earl of Arundel had openly threatened the king with Edward II's fate, there were rumors that Richard had ordered Gaunt's assassination, and at a tournament in February 1385 there perhaps really was a plot against Gaunt's life initiated by some of the young men around the king. The Scottish campaign of 1385

---

54. *Rot. Parl.*, 3:185.

55. Juliet R. V. Barker, *The Tournament in England, 1100–1400* (Woodbridge: Boydell, 1986), 69 and 185. Richard was the first English monarch to employ someone with the title "king's painter," a man named Gilbert Prince, much of whose work was done "in connection with tournaments, devices on banners, etc." (J. J. G. Alexander, "Painting and Manuscript Illumination for Royal Patrons in the Later Middle Ages," in Scattergood and Sherborne, *English Court Culture*, 155).

56. See Tyson, *Vie du Prince Noir*, 30–33; and Alexander, "Painting and Manuscript Illumination," 157. Froissart says that at his coronation in 1377 Richard made the Chandos Herald King of Arms of England (Wagner, *Heralds and Heraldry*, 36).

57. The "Ordenaunce" is printed in Sir Travers Twiss, ed., *The Black Book of the Admiralty*, Rolls Series, 55 (London: Longman, 1871), 1:300–329; for the *Tractatus*, see Evan John Jones, *Medieval Heraldry: Some Fourteenth-Century Heraldic Works* (Cardiff: William Lewis, 1943), 95–212.

58. May McKisack, *The Fourteenth Century* (Oxford: Clarendon Press, 1959), 498.

was thus an attempt to reunite the governing class in its ancient role as defender of the kingdom, to heal the rivalries among self-assertive and easily affronted nobles.[59] Richard sought to raise his army, "possibly the largest English army of the entire war,"[60] by invoking, for the first time in almost a century and for the last time in English history, the ancient feudal levy. There were probably financial motives behind this move, since Richard would have profited from the scutage involved,[61] but the ideological interests were also very real. By invoking the levy, Richard at least asserted, even if he could not in the event enforce, his role as the feudal overlord of England, the personal seigneur of all those who followed him to war.

Yet such a program was bound to fail. The nobility were naturally not disposed to forego the financial rewards of campaigning, and the chivalric code itself was inimical to real-world centrism, as distinct from symbolic incorporation. As Richard Kaeuper has rightly said, "chivalry by and large represented a countercurrent to the movement toward the Western form of state" so evident in the later Middle Ages: the culture of honor was inimical to all *étatist* notions and especially to the idea of a centralized authority. This opposition was all the more intense when it became internalized in the monarch himself, who was at once chivalric knight and Crown, at once an honorman in a dispersed field of autonomous competitors and, as the sovereign, the locus of authority.[62] Not surprisingly, the campaign of 1385 failed to achieve its purpose. The dispute between Scrope and Grosvenor may have been one of the longest lasting of the problems associated with it, but there were other, far more serious conflicts. The king's half-brother, John Holland, killed Ralph Stafford, the heir to the earl of Stafford, in a brawl that outraged the king and, according to the chroniclers, killed with grief the Dowager Princess Joan, Richard's and Holland's mother. And, crucially, the campaign set Richard himself in conflict with Gaunt, who urged continuing the *chevauchée* deep into Scotland, whereas Richard, for whatever reason, decided to withdraw and return home, having accomplished little

59. See Anthony Tuck, *Richard II and the English Nobility* (London: Edward Arnold, 1973), 96–98.

60. For the size of the army, see J. J. N. Palmer, *England, France and Christendom, 1377–99* (London: Routledge and Kegan Paul, 1972), 60.

61. J. J. N. Palmer, "The Last Summons of the Feudal Army in England," *EHR* 83 (1968): 771–75; Anthony Tuck, *Crown and Nobility, 1272–1461: Political Conflict in Late Medieval England* (London: Fontana Press, 1985), 184–85.

62. Richard Kaeuper, *War, Justice and Public Order* (Oxford: Clarendon Press, 1988), 195; see also 382.

more than the burning of two abbeys.[63] The hostility between him and his nobility remained as intense as ever: the next year Gaunt left for Portugal and Richard had to face the wrath of the Appellants alone.

The military failure of the expedition was a particularly bitter disappointment for both Parliament and the country as a whole. For the previous fifteen years or so England's military position had been growing progressively more precarious, and by 1385 it was reaching crisis proportions. Both the Scots and the French were harrying large parts of the country, and France was preparing for a major invasion, a catastrophe that in the event England only barely avoided. The campaign of 1385 was to reverse English fortunes. No English king had led his army into the field for a quarter of a century, since Edward's final, disappointing campaign of 1359–60 (in the course of which, incidentally, Chaucer had been captured).[64] The previous war effort had been the shameful Despenser Crusade of 1383, an inconclusive if brutal *chevauchée* that had brought discredit to everyone involved. If it was becoming increasingly apparent that the knighthood could not defend the kingdom from its enemies—and as John Barnie has shown in detail, the ineffective nobility was treated to a rising storm of criticism throughout the 1370s and 1380s—the campaign of 1385 did nothing to dispel the sense of chivalric impotence.[65]

There was, moreover, a larger crisis of governance within the kingdom as a whole. The Rising of 1381 was only the most spectacular instance of the breakdown of law and order, of the inability of the knighthood to perform its role of policeman to society.[66] But the Rising represented a deeper malaise, one visible to thoughtful observers. It was ignited by resistance to the progressively heavier taxation that the war required, money that quickly found its way into the coffers of the noble-

63. Palmer argues that the very idea of the campaign was ill-advised: what most needed doing at this critical time was shoring up Ghent, a crucial ally. But by being distracted northwards by the arrival of the French in Scotland, the English forced Ghent to sign a truce with France that removed her from the war (*England, France and Christendom*, 60–61).

64. Edward had tried to mount a campaign in 1374, but after waiting on shipboard for almost three months for favorable winds he canceled the effort.

65. Barnie, *War in Medieval Society*, 108–10, 117–27, 142–45. In his address to Parliament in 1377, Peter de la Mare described how "Chivalrie ad este rebuquiz et tenuz en viletee" (*Rot. Parl.*, 3:5).

66. Caxton's *Book of the Ordre of Chyvalry* presented this chivalric responsibility in blunt terms: "Thoffyce of a knyght is to mayntene the londe for by cause that the drede of the comyn people haue of the knyghts they labour & cultyue the erthe for fere leste they shold be destroyed. And by the drede of the knyghtes they redoubte the kynges, prynces, and lordes, by whome they [the knights] haue theyr power" (32).

men who were the most insistent proponents of taxes. Some 75 percent of the money raised for war was spent on wages, the largest share of which was paid to the noble contractors who provided the troops.[67] If noblemen were growing rich on war profits, it was at least as much because they were bleeding their own country as because they were ravaging France. Indeed, the most pervasive economic effect of the war was to transfer wealth from the most productive sectors of society—the ecclesiastical manors, the wool and cloth producers, the urban merchants, and, above all, the steadily developing small commodity producers among the peasantry—into the least productive sector, a spendthrift aristocracy obsessed with buying the luxury goods necessary to ratify a life-style, and a social superiority, that was becoming progressively more difficult to justify.[68] It was above all resistance to this transfer of wealth, most explicitly in the form of taxation but also through the wide variety of means by which the medieval seigneur extracted surplus value from the agricultural producers, that sparked the Rising.

We should also note that the economic position of the seigneur was becoming, in the decades of the 1370s and 1380s, increasingly conflicted. The shift in economic power accomplished by the Plague, with its redistribution of the balance of land and labor, had been fended off by the Statute of Laborers and a range of local seigneurial countermeasures. But by the last third of the century these defenses were no longer effective. As the economic historian J. L. Bolton has shown, in the years 1370–90 "the tide turned full against" the landlord.[69] The result was that only the best-managed estates could prosper in what had become a fully rentier economy.[70] This placed another strain upon noble identity, since the warrior class was not supposed, ideologically, to soil its hands

---

67. Kaeuper, *War, Justice and Public Order*, 105. He argues strongly for the destructive effects of the war on the English as well as the French economy (32–133).

68. For a detailed account of this process, see ibid. For an account of the development of a system of public finance in response to the needs of war, and the growing centralization of government and growth of monarchical authority, see G. L. Harriss, *King, Parliament, and Public Finance in Medieval England to 1369* (Oxford: Clarendon Press, 1975). For the aristocratic appetite for luxury goods in the last half of the fourteenth century, see Harry A. Miskimin, *The Economy of Early Renaissance Europe 1300–1460* (Cambridge: Cambridge University Press, 1975), 90–92, 99–105, 127–28, 135–38, 141–42, and McFarlane, *Nobility*, 96. There is a fuller account of these economic issues, and especially of the condition of the peasantry, in chapter 5, below.

69. J. L. Bolton, *The Medieval English Economy 1150–1500* (London: Dent, 1980), 214.

70. On this point, in addition to Bolton, see McFarlane, *Nobility*, 41–60, 213–27, whose focus on the peerage leads him to take a more sanguine view of the economic condition of the nobility.

with agriculture, even at the level of estate management.[71] According to the chivalric theorist Honoré Bonet,

> the laws say that a knight must not till the soil, or tend vines, or keep beasts, that is to say, be a shepherd, or be a matchmaker, or lawyer; otherwise he must lose knighthood and the privileges of a knight. And he should never, if he is a paid soldier, buy land or vineyards while he is in service, and what he does buy must belong to his lord. If you wish to know why this was so ordained, I tell you that it was that knights should have no cause to leave arms for desire of acquiring worldly riches.[72]

War, then, might ease the knight's ideological and financial difficulties but only by generating new contradictions. At the simplest level, violence—whether martial or recreative—may have legitimized the knight's social identity, but it was also a highly destructive practice for both individuals and the class as a whole: between 1351 and 1400, about 25 percent of all the peers who died succumbed to violence in one form or another, a fact that was not unrelated to the failure of the direct male line in a quarter of the noble families every twenty-five years throughout the fourteenth and fifteenth centuries.[73] Maintaining noble status meant risking both one's life and the survival of the very class one was seeking to preserve. War also exacerbated the problem of law and order, specifically through the system of retaining. This began as a strategy for raising troops: a nobleman would sign indentures of service with retainers, whom he would equip and for whom he was then paid by the king. But the system soon developed into what has been called bastard feudalism: the lord would contract for the loyalty of paid retainers who constituted his affinity, some of whom would wear his livery and all of whom could be counted on to support his interests.[74]

71. See, for example, Georges Duby, *Rural Economy and Country Life in the Medieval West*, trans. Cynthia Postan (Columbia: University of South Carolina Press, 1968), 231. This is not to say that the nobility was not concerned to exploit its rights with ruthless efficiency and did not also, at various times and places throughout the Middle Ages, show a keen interest in argicultural productivity (see 72, 88–89, 200–202).

72. Honoré Bonet, *The Tree of Battles*, trans. G. W. Coopland (Liverpool: Liverpool University Press, 1949), 131.

73. Joel Rosenthal, "Mediaeval Longevity and the Secular Peerage, 1350–1400," *Population Studies* 27 (1973): 287–93. As McFarlane says, "It is not generally realized how near to extinction most families were; their survival was always in the balance and only a tiny handful managed to hang on in the male line from one century to another" (*Nobility*, 78).

74. See K. B. McFarlane, "Bastard Feudalism," *BIHR* 20 (1945): 161–80, reprinted in *England in the Fifteenth Century: Collected Essays* (London: Hambledon Press, 1981), 23–43.

The effect was to create multiple private armies, and throughout the latter part of the fourteenth century and into the fifteenth there were continual complaints about the inevitable abuses; Parliament even designated retaining as one of the causes of the Rising of 1381.[75] Perhaps the most ubiquitous complaint was of the corruption of the legal system through "maintenance-at-law," in which the loyalty of the officers of the king's courts was bought by a local magnate, with the result that justice was denied the ordinary suitor.[76] Far from serving as the dispensers of justice, as their codes of chivalry constantly asserted, and as the social function that legitimized their economic superiority required, the nobility was too often engaged in disabling the system they were supposed to uphold.[77]

Retaining also exploited and made still more materially evident the public nature of chivalric identity. Not only were retainers often dressed in the livery of their masters, but there developed in the later fourteenth century, as an adjunct to the heraldic system of coats of arms, the personal *devise* or badge.[78] The badge system absorbed the individual into a collectivity by making fully visible the bonds of affiliation; it also kept constantly on view a peculiar form of reification, whereby the names of the nobility were related totemically to the natural world, especially to animals. Thus Richard's own white hart "gorged" (i.e., crowned) materialized his name as "riche-hart."[79]

---

75. See, for example, R. L. Storey, "Liveries and Commissions of the Peace, 1388–90," in *The Reign of Richard II: Essays in Honour of May McKisack*, ed. F. R. H. Du Boulay and Caroline Barron (London: Athlone, 1971), 131–52, and Kaeuper, *War, Justice and Public Order*, 181–83.

76. See Anna Baldwin's demonstration that Langland's Lady Meed is "a lifelike example of the kind of person who used such reward [i.e., meed] in order to sustain and protect an unscrupulous retinue, and so increase her own power" (*The Theme of Government in* Piers Plowman [Cambridge: Brewer, 1981], 27).

77. For a recent survey, see J. G. Bellamy, *Bastard Feudalism and the Law* (London: Routledge, 1989).

78. "The fourteenth-century saw a gradual eclipse in the popularity of the coat of arms in favour of the personal device or badge on tournament clothing" (Barker, *Tournament*, 183). Richard's white hart badge was apparently first displayed at the Smithfield tournament in October, 1390.

79. Devising a badge from a pun on the name—"canting heraldry," as modern writers have called it—may also have been used by Edward III, whose sun bursting from a bank of clouds was perhaps meant to represent Windsor as "golden winds." For this suggestion, and others (the de la Veres' blue boar derived from the Latin *verres*, the Lancastrian falcon from a pun on Fulk, the name of Geoffrey of Anjou's father), see H. Stanford London, *Royal Beasts* (East Knoyle: Heraldry Society, 1956), 35, 18–19, 57. Another example is the use of a leg (*folle jambe*) as a crest by Sir Godfrey Foljambe (d. 1376); see *Age of Chivalry: Art in Plantagenet England 1200–1400*, ed. Jonathan Alexander and Paul

When disseminated throughout the elaborately detailed object-world of the late-medieval court, the badge served to obscure the distinction between the king and his possessions—in this case, the people in his service. The modern conception of the name as the arbitrary sign of a subject—of a selfhood that exists in a private realm apart from the public arena in which the name circulates—was in this case replaced by a "natural" signification. The names of the nobility, no less than the political and economic dominance that the badge asserted and even enacted, were thus seen to be ordained by the natural order of things. That Chaucer found this semiotics both intriguing and disturbing is registered in the two most significant examples in his work: Diomede's boar in *Troilus and Criseyde* and Theseus's Minotaur (to which we shall return).

Badges, like retaining itself, asserted the exclusivity of the aristocratic community and were intensely unpopular among the populace at large, as is clear from the bitter complaints against men in livery and the parliamentary and even royal attempts to control the practice.[80] Retroactively, we can now see them as one of the marks of honor by which the nobility sought to reconfirm, to itself and to the nation, its own solidarity and superiority. As Given-Wilson has said, social distinctions became in Chaucer's England "more rigidly defined, more blatantly advertised, and more jealously guarded" than in earlier centuries.[81] And what was true of the peerage, which gradually drew apart from the lower ranks of the nobility in both wealth and prestige, was of course even more true of those lesser nobles who were threatened by the prospect of slipping into the ranks of the nonnoble. Hence we find in the later Middle Ages a growing insistence upon the priority of lineage as a definition of nobility, a persistent effort to stratify society as a whole and to fix the precedence of its ranks, and a jealous guarding of forms of dress, recreative habits (like hunting), and social rituals (like

---

Binski (London: Royal Academy of Arts, 1987), 210. For a particularly intricate and fascinating instance, see Ann Claxton, "The Sign of the Dog: An Examination of the Devonshire Hunting Tapestries," *JMH* 14 (1988): 127–79.

80. Storey, "Liveries and Commissions of the Peace," details the parliamentary complaints about liveries in the 1380s; in the Parliament of 1389 Richard offered to abolish his badges, but the nobility would not reciprocate (131–35). As for the attitude toward liveries of the populace at large, according to G. R. Owst, *Literature and Pulpit in Medieval England* (Oxford: Blackwell, 1961),

> Page after page of the fiercest denunciation will be found in the sermons against . . . "officers of gret men that wereth her lyverethes; the wiche, by colour of lawe and aȝens lawe, robbeth and dispoyleth the poure peple, now betynge, now sleyinge, now puttynge hem from hous and landes. Like as thei here there lordis saile blowe, so thei be meved" (324, citing MS B.L. Roy.18.B.xxiii, fol. 142).

81. Given-Wilson, *English Nobility*, 57.

tournaments) that were thought to be the traditional elements of a noble life-style—the very elements, as we can now more understandably see, with which Chaucer's Knight filled the borders and ornamented the surface of his *Tale.*[82]

Before turning to the *Knight's Tale* itself, however, something must be said about Chaucer's own relation to the community of honor so vividly on display in the Scrope-Grosvenor dispute. He was, after all, a king's esquire all his life, a member of the *gentil* class entitled to bear arms, an apparently close friend of several highly placed chamber knights who were all, in McFarlane's words, "career soldiers who had seen much campaigning" and "belonged to the international chivalrous class and spoke its lingua franca," and a producer of texts, at least up until the late 1380s, that were designed for a courtly, chivalrous audience.[83] He was also a witness in the Scrope-Grosvenor proceedings: according to Keen, his "substantial testimony" shows us "Chaucer in the company of the knighthood of his time, speaking in *propria persona* not as poet or diplomat or controller of the customs but as one who had seen honourable war service and could recall what old knights and squires worthy of credence in points of chivalry had retailed in his hearing."[84]

But in fact Chaucer's testimony is by no means as unproblematically embedded within the norms and conventions of the community of honor as this description implies. The vast majority of the almost three hundred surviving depositions are resolutely impersonal: the witness recites the campaigns on which he saw Scrope bearing the arms in question and closes with a formula to the effect that (to cite one taken at random) "he had indeed heard from nobles and valiant knights and squires that the aforesaid arms were descended by direct line to Sir Richard from beyond memory, as public opinion and fame had always said and continued to say."[85] On only a very few occasions does the witness volunteer any details about himself, and when asked about

82. On the fifteenth-century emphasis on lineage as a requirement for nobility, see Mervyn James, "English Politics and the Concept of Honour," who discusses Caxton's revision of Lull's *Book of Chivalry* in order to stress the importance of descent, and the same emphasis in the fifteenth-century *Boke of St. Albans* (310, 319). On the growing exclusivity of the tournament in the later Middle Ages, see Barker, *Tournament*, 112–17, 134–35, 188.

83. K. B. McFarlane, *Lancastrian Kings and Lollard Knights* (Oxford: Clarendon Press, 1972), 160, 179. For an account of Chaucer's social position, see above, 32–39.

84. Maurice Keen, "Chaucer's Knight, the English Aristocracy and the Crusades," in *English Court Culture*, ed. Scattergood and Sherborne, 50.

85. This passage is from the testimony of Sir Miles de Boys, in Nicolas, *Controversy*, 1:68.

Grosvenor the vast majority say that they have never heard of him or heard of him only during the Scottish campaign of 1385 when the dispute arose. Chaucer's testimony is different in two respects. First, he adds an unusual detail to his account of his service in the French campaign of 1359–60: "He saw [Richard Scrope and his cousin Henry] thus armed throughout the entire campaign until the said Geoffrey was captured." Of all the depositions given, this is, to my knowledge, the only one in which a witness not only describes a specific event from his war experiences but admits to the indignity of capture.[86]

Second, when asked about Grosvenor, Chaucer takes it upon himself to provide a brief narrative:

> He said that one time he was in Friday Street in London, and as he went along the street he saw a new sign hanging outside made of the aforesaid arms. And he asked what inn was this that had hung out the Scrope arms. And another person answered him and said, "No sir, they are not hung out as the Scrope arms nor painted there for those arms. But they are painted and put there for a knight of the county of Chester who is called Sir Robert Grosvenor." And this was the first time that he had ever heard of Sir Robert Grosvenor or of his ancestors or of any other person bearing the name of Grosvenor.[87]

What is striking about this passage, and all the more so within its chivalric context, is its urban setting, its circumstantial detail, and especially its narrative form. The Grosvenor arms are discovered neither on a battlefield nor at a tourney but on a city street so familiar to this witness that he wished to specify its name. Similarly, the sign gives up its meaning only in response to a question; not only is its significance not self-evident, but it can only be explained by an account of the way in which the witness discovered it. The witness is unavoidable throughout this testimony: in order to learn about the arms *azure* with *bend d'or* we must also hear about Chaucer's capture by the French and his conversation

---

86. The other witnesses simply list the campaigns during which they saw the Scrope arms, for example, "devant Parys en compaignie de Roy [and] a Balynghawhill & en Caux & en Escoce" (ibid., 1:173). That capture could be considered an indignity is illustrated by the comments of the Sicily Herald, who insists that a knight should prefer death before the servitude of imprisonment; see Roland, *Parties inédites*, 70.

87. Friday Street ran north-south just to the east of St. Paul's. According to Stow, its name derived from the fact that fishmongers dwelled there who served "Frydayes market;" see Charles Lethbridge Kingsford, ed., *A Survey of London by John Stow* (Oxford: Clarendon Press, 1908), 1:351. It is pleasant to report that a bit of Friday Street survives, one side occupied by a Danish bank, the other by the offices of the *Financial Times*.

in Friday Street. Not only are these details unchivalric, but they can only be released by a subjectivity, only be described from the perspective of a specific individual: we have not only a narrative but a narrator, not only a tale but a teller. If within the culture of honor identity is typically conceived in corporate and social terms, Chaucer's insistence upon the experiencing subject, especially in relation to a chivalric dispute, represents a strikingly different form of self-understanding.

But there is another aspect of the Scrope-Grosvenor testimony that can help us to specify Chaucer's relation to the community of honor. In his reply to Grosvenor before John of Gaunt, Scrope had said, we remember, that "the highest and the most sovereign things a knight ought to guard in defence of his estate are his troth and his arms, and that in both of them Sir Robert had impeached him" ("les plus hautes & sovergnes choses que chivaler deust garder en salvacioun de son estat ceux sount sa loialte & ses armes et en ambideux yceux le dit monsieur Robert luy avoit empesche").[88] As every Chaucerian will recognize, Scrope's statement strikingly prefigures Arveragus's similar dictum in the *Franklin's Tale:* "Trouthe is the hyeste thyng that man may kepe" (V, 1479). But Arveragus cites this chivalric formula—whether specifically from Scrope or whether, as is more likely, from chivalric discourse in general—in order to express a very different ethic. For Arveragus, *trouthe* is an internal condition, a sense of integrity specific to the individual and wholly within his or her own keeping. Dorigen must keep her *trouthe* to Aurelius despite the fact that to sleep with him will, in society's (and Scrope's) terms, dishonor both her and her husband. For Arveragus, if she breaks her promise, regardless of who knows, she violates her inner integrity as a person. Derek Brewer has rightly said that in the *Franklin's Tale* "to *be* honorable is to love *trouthe,* not to love *honor.*" He adds:

> *Trouthe* is loyalty, and in the cluster of notions that compose the sentiment of honor, the keeping of *trouthe* must be isolated as so much the superior inner moral value as to be positively hostile to social relationship and reputation. . . . Honor as social virtue, and honor as chastity or possession, are subordinated to honor as obedience to a high moral ideal, perforce an inner, indeed, a spiritual value.[89]

88. The French original is cited from PRO C54/233/27d.

89. D. S. Brewer, "Honour in Chaucer," *Essays and Studies* 26 (1973), 4, 17–18, who draws the relevant contrast with Criseyde. For further on this topic, see Alcuin Blamires, "Chaucer's Revaluation of Chivalric Honor," *Mediaevalia* 5 (1979): 245–69.

Given Chaucer's promotion of *trouthe* as a central moral value throughout his work, from *Troilus and Criseyde* through to the "*Balade de Bon Conseyl*," we can hardly doubt that Arveragus's ethic represents his author's own opinion. Moreover, in the *House of Fame* Chaucer stages his distance from the community of honor almost *in propria persona*. With considerable justice, contemporary criticism has read that poem as a demystification of medieval logocentrism. But it contains as well a biting social satire of the honor world of chivalry, the conditions of chivalric identity, and the role of the writer as mere agent of renown. Fame's temple is filled with "pursevantes and heraudes" wearing "cote-armure" and paid to celebrate the glory of "chevalrie" (1308–40), while the capricious Lady Fame herself bears up "Bothe th'armes and the name / Of thoo that hadde large fame" (1411–12), beginning with two of the founders of chivalry, Alexander and Hercules. The great historians and *poetae* of antiquity (Josephus, Statius, Homer and the Trojan historians, Virgil, Ovid, Lucan, and Claudian) then follow, each bearing up the fame of peoples and the names of heroes. These poetic masters are here reduced to "rokes nestes": "hit a ful confus matere / Were alle the gestes for to here / That they of write, or how they highte" (1516–20). Not surprisingly, Chaucer then makes clear his own desire for independence from this world of aristocratic self-promotion. Asked if he has come to achieve fame for himself, he replies, "Nay,"

> Sufficeth me, as I were ded,
> That no wight have my name in honde.
> I wot myself best how y stonde;
> For what I drye, or what I thynke,
> I wil myselven al hyt drynke. (1876–80)

Beyond a general writerly desire for autonomy, inevitably felt most intensely in a patronage system, Chaucer here separates himself from the value system of the noble class for whom his work is produced. In the words of a Renaissance theorist of honor, "Honor is not in his [own] hand who is honored, but in the hearts and opinions of other men."[90] But Chaucer will not have his name "in [the] honde" of anyone, and his worth depends not on others' opinions but on his own: "I wot myself best how y stonde."

This has been a long preamble to a *Tale*. But if we are fully to understand the *Knight's Tale*, both as a text in its own right and as the initiat-

---

90. James Cleland, *Propaideia, or the Institution of a Young Noble Man* (1607), cited by James, "English Politics and the Concept of Honor," 312.

ing movement of the *Canterbury Tales,* we must recognize it as the fictive expression of an aristocratic self-understanding typical of the late
fourteenth century. Both the issues with which it deals—the obsessive
rivalry of willful aristocrats, the self-defeat of authority—and the
thwarted self-understanding that it simultaneously represents and expresses are derived from the honor world of the contemporary English
nobility. Chaucer's relation to this world, both biographically and ideologically, was not oppositional but oblique, a little off to the side; and in
the *Knight's Tale* he provides the kind of shrewd assessment that is
possible only for the slightly distanced insider.

II

Whatever final meaning the *Knight's Tale* may bear, it is clear that the
Knight himself intends it to celebrate both Theseus as a model of rational governance and chivalry as a force for civilization.[91] The narrative opens with Theseus celebrating his triumph over Hippolyta and
her Amazons, an imposition of male authority upon the unnatural
"regne of Femenye" (877) that the Knight presents as an act of pacifica-
tion: the "grete bataille" (879) of conquest has given way to a festal
wedding (883) that transforms victor and vanquished into husband
and wife. Moreover, with the colloquy between Theseus and the black-
clad women who interrupt his victory parade the Knight assures us
that his hero represents a chivalry aware not only of its reponsibilities
but of the dangers that attend eminence. Revealing themselves to be
the widows of Argives who fell in the Theban war between Eteocles
and Polynices, the women beseech Theseus to repress the tyrannical
Creon who has denied to their husbands' bodies the burial rites that
religious custom requires. After an initial burst of anger at what he
takes to be an envious assault upon his honor, Theseus soon becomes
deeply moved by their plight and accedes to their wishes. Immediately
reversing his course, he directs his army to Thebes where he personally
slays Creon, destroys the city, and restores the bones of the dead warriors to their wives "to doon obsequies, as was tho the gyse" (993).

91.   This is also the position of many Chaucerians. See Robertson, *Preface to Chaucer,*
105–10, 260–66; Kean, *Chaucer and the Making of English Poetry,* 2:1–52; Gaylord, "The Role
of Saturn," 171–90; Alastair Minnis, *Chaucer and Pagan Antiquity* (Cambridge: Brewer,
1982), 121–25; and Traugott Lawler, *The One and the Many in the* Canterbury Tales (New
Haven: Archon, 1980), 89–94. Others have countered with unflattering accounts of Theseus's character: Henry J. Webb, "A Reinterpretation of Chaucer's Theseus," *RES* 23
(1947): 289–96; Neuse, "The Knight: The First Mover in Chaucer's Comedy"; Aers, *Chaucer, Langland, and the Creative Imagination,* 174–95; and Jones, *Chaucer's Knight.*

While their inappropriate dress, weeping, and aggressive intervention into Theseus's triumph—"they nolde nevere stenten / Til they the
reynes of his brydel henten" (903–4)—might seem to mark the Argive
widows as disruptive, they in fact follow the same protocols as the
triumph they interrupt. They appear before Theseus in a reassuringly
hieratic form, keeping "tweye and tweye, / Ech after oother, clad in
clothes blake" (898–99), their spokeswoman is the widow of Capaneus,
"the eldeste of hem alle" (912), and they are motivated not by a disruptive envy, as Theseus initially feared, but by the desire to perform their
wifely and religious duty. Similarly, the scene as a whole is a familiar,
and reassuringly moral, medieval literary event. The procession enters
Athens "with muchel glorie and greet solempyntee" (870), and the triumphant Theseus—"in al his wele and in his mooste pride" (895)—is
evidently vulnerable to the dangers attendant upon earthly success.
The analogous procession of the Argive widows thus functions as a
cautionary *exemplum*, a warning against overconfidence. The widow of
Capaneus describes Theseus as one to whom "Fortune hath yiven /
Victorie, and as a conqueror to lyven" (915–16), while the widows are
"wrecched wommen" (921) and "caytyves" (924) subject to "Fortune
and hire false wheel, / That noon estaat assureth to be weel" (925–26).
We are presented, in short, with a familiar medieval confrontation, between a man in the pride of life and cautionary figures who by both
example and speech warn him that pride goeth before a fall.[92]

What appeared at first to be a rupture in the progress both of Theseus's triumph and of the narrative is thus a necessary adjustment designed to keep that progress secure. Fully cognizant of the threat that
Fortune poses to the conqueror, Theseus's campaign against Creon acknowledges that chivalric arms derive their most powerful legitimacy,
and perhaps even a measure of security, from their support of the unfortunate. "Thus rit this duc, thus rit this conquerour, / And in his hoost of
chivalrie the flour" (981–82) concludes the episode, the anaphora ex-

---

92. The closest analogue to this scene in Middle English poetry is the meeting, in a
dream, of Arthur "þe conquerour" with a Dame Fortune who prophecies his coming
downfall in the *Alliterative Morte Arthure* (Mary Hamel, ed. [New York: Garland Press,
1984], lines 3218–393). There are also numerous texts, like *Winner and Waster, The
Parlement of the Three Ages*, and "The Bird with Four Feathers" (in *Religious Lyrics of the
XIVth Century*, ed. Carleton Brown [Oxford: Clarendon Press, 1924], 208–15), that locate
their pedagogy within the context of a *chanson d'aventure,* or the widespread legend of
Three Living and Three Dead (for which see the comments and bibliography provided
for Henryson's "Thre Ded Polis" by Denton Fox, ed., *The Poems of Robert Henryson* [Ox-
ford: Clarendon Press, 1981], 487). The meeting of the Pardoner's three rioters with the
cautionary figure of the Old Man is another Chaucerian instance of this motif.

pressing a forward progress empowered by its ability to disarm a hostile criticism, and with it a hostile fate.

Equally clearly, the Creon "digression" connects the *Knight's Tale* to Chaucer's previous investigation of the Theban legends, first in *Anelida and Arcite* and then in the *Troilus*. Creon would not let the dead be buried, and neither, it turns out, can the fatal quality of Thebanness be definitively interred. It is from the "taas of bodyes dede" created by Theseus that Arcite and Palamon, "nat fully quyke ne fully dede," are "torn." Unnaturally brought back to life from a Theban past Theseus is seeking to suppress, the cousins are reborn into an Athenian present they continue to disrupt; and from the Knight's perspective, they embody an irrationality that Theseus must chasten into civilization. Chaucer had earlier defined Thebanness as having two destructive patterns: the one a fratricidal and self-destructive rivalry that gives full rein to the violence of the appetitive self; the other a fatal recursiveness that undermines all progressivity upon which the ideals of secular history are based and condemns chivalric ambition, whether antique or modern, to an endless repetition. It is in order to disarm this double Theban threat that the new hero Theseus undertakes his campaign against the "olde Creon" (938) who would continue the course of Theban barbarity. So too, it is in order to contain Theban self-destructiveness that he first imprisons Arcite and Palamon "for everemoore" (1032) and then, when they are at large in the Athenian world, seeks to channel their violence into the culturally sanctioned form of a tournament that Chaucer's contemporaries would have recognized as a "duel of chivalry" or "feat of arms."[93]

Theseus aims throughout to bring Theban self-replication to a definitive end—an aim that his language constantly thematizes. When he discovers the rivals fighting in the grove he prescribes the "short conclusioun" (1743) of immediate execution; persuaded to a more merciful course by the ladies, he then establishes the tournament as a "plat conclusioun, / Withouten any repplicacioun" (1845–46).[94] The finality of this disposition is twice stressed: "Lo heere youre ende of that I shal devyse" (1844); "This is youre ende and youre conclusioun" (1869). When, by the intervention of the Fury, resolution continues to evade him, Theseus once again reinvokes the capacity of cultural forms to civilize savagery. The offending grove is burned, and Arcite's arbitrary

---

93. George Neilson, *Trial by Combat* (Glasgow: William Hodge, 1890), 74; Barker, *Tournament*, 158.

94. There is probably a pun on "repplicacioun" here; for a very similar use, also in the context of courtly rivalry, see the *Parliament of Fowls*, 536.

death is accorded elaborate funeral rites. Theseus's final act of settlement is then the marriage of Palamon and Emily, marked (and justified) by the famous "First Movere" speech; and when the speech "conclude[s] . . . this longe serye" (3067) of events with the assertion that the marriage will "make of sorwes two / O parfit joye, lastynge everemo" (3071–72), this at last is an outcome, we are assured, that is truly conclusive: "Thus *endeth* Palamon and Emelye," says the Knight, "And God save al this faire compaignye!" (3017–8)

The Knight means his narrative to record the disarming of an aboriginal Theban ferocity by Athenian civilization, the replacement of a regressive Theban repetitiveness with the purposive linearity of the Athenian *mission civilisatrice*. This narrative is, in turn, intended by him as an allegory of the progress of chivalry, a secular fraternity that imposes order first upon itself—the Order of Chivalry—and then upon an unruly world. We can see this most sharply by comparing his *Tale* with *Anelida and Arcite*, which shares the same matrix of medieval classicism but neither the same literary mode nor the same philosophical agenda.

Although doubtless we will never know with certainty the precise historical relation of the *Knight's Tale* to *Anelida and Arcite*, criticism has plausibly maintained that the *Anelida* represents Chaucer's first attempt to come to terms with the Boccaccian classicism of the *Teseida*, and both internal chronology and thematic development support its placing before the *Knight's Tale*.[95] *Anelida and Arcite* begins with the same opening as in the *Knight's Tale*: Theseus has conquered Hippolyta and is on his way home to Athens in triumph but the poet then swerves away and temporally back from this narrative progress—"Let I this noble prince Theseus / Toward Athenes in his wey rydinge" (45–46)—to describe the world of Creon's Thebes:

> And founde I wol in shortly for to bringe
> The slye wey of that I gan to write,
> Of quene Anelida and fals Arcite. (47–49)

The rest of the poem, as we have seen, is an exploration of the Theban condition refracted through the tropes of Ovidian eroticism, a condition in need of Athenian redemption.

The events of the *Anelida* at once precede and justify the campaign against Thebes that Theseus, having by now arrived home, launches at the beginning of the *Knight's Tale*. But generically, the movement from

95. The best general discussion of this topic remains Robert A. Pratt's important article, "Chaucer's Use of the *Teseida*," *PMLA* 62 (1947): 598–621.

the *Anelida* to the *Knight's Tale* is from lyric to narrative: and if the structure of the *Anelida's* lyric complaint allows no formal solution to recursiveness, to the barren doubling back upon itself that defines the Theban pattern of experience, the turn to narrative promises to endow experience with a linear and purposive beginning, middle, and end. Indeed, the Knight's narrativity is persistently brought to our attention in ways that suggest that it stands in allegorical relationship to experience, that he tells his *Tale* in the image of the way he believes that life is, or can be, arranged. Hence the patterns of symmetry, balance, and homology that pervade his *Tale* and that criticism has so often, and so well, described—patterns that testify to his desire to represent a world totally organized by the order, and Order, of chivalry.[96] However, if elsewhere in the *Tales* (as also in Chaucer's deposition in the Scrope-Grosvenor case) narrative is the model of communication by which discourse acknowledges the inevitable presence of the subject—of the interests and needs that connect the tale to the teller—the Knight's narrativity cannot be exempt from this function, however much he would like it to be so. If the Knight's project is to absorb the local and contingent into the universal and permanent, Chaucer's is to show how local and contingent is the civilizing claim itself. If the Knight displaces his own anxieties and those of his class onto the romantic foolishness of Palamon and Arcite, and insists on a Thesean superiority to that foolishness, Chaucer undoes that superiority. For he gives him a *Tale* (like his world) too complex for his rhetorical management.

III

This may also help to explain the struggles of Chaucer's readers subsequently. But I shall here offer an account of the *Tale's* complexities that makes textual difficulty the sign of genuine perplexity—the sign of how profound are the contradictions the Knight seeks to mediate and how penetrating is the thought with which Chaucer meditated chivalry's condition and its metaphysical claims. And I shall begin by refocusing on several crucial moments in the *Tale* that criticism has seen as decisive in evaluating the success or failure of Theseus as a noble designer. One of these is, of course, the "First Movere" speech with which Theseus justifies not only the marriage between Palamon and Emelye but the benevolence and effectiveness of his rule. We have seen that Theseus has undertaken a mission to disarm Thebanness with fi-

96. See, for example, Halverson, "Aspects of Order," and Helen Cooper, *The Structure of the* Canterbury Tales (Athens: University of Georgia Press, 1983), 93–101.

nality: he seeks to bring a self-replicating process of violence to a definitive conclusion. The "First Movere" speech is thus an explanation of
how closure is possible within the historical world, an explanation that
inevitably and appropriately invokes a transhistorical authority—in
this case, "Juppiter the kyng" (3035), who corresponds on the level of
divinity to Duke Theseus himself. And although Theseus acknowledges that "al this thyng moot deye" (3034), he adds the comforting
vision of an encompassing providential care:

> What maketh this but Juppiter, the kyng,
> That is prince and cause of all thyng,
> Convertynge al unto his proper welle
> From which it is dirryved, sooth to telle? (3035–38)

All things, we remember from Boethius, are "constreynede . . . into
roundnesses" (4, vi, 56), and Jupiter's "welle" is that "clere welle of
good" (3, xii, 1–2) that is at once *fons et origo* and *finis*, both "the
begynnynge of alle thinges" (3, 10, 100) and the "oon ende of
blisfulnesse" (3, 2, 8). This Boethian vision stands as the antithesis to the
Theban *revolutus in ortus* and here makes its most vigorous assertion.

Yet the "First Movere" speech is deeply problematic, not least in its
philosophical consolations. We remember that the world over which
Theseus presides has in fact allowed no room for the Jupiter whom he
invokes but was driven instead by rivalries that only the malevolent
Saturn could resolve; that Arcite himself foresaw his final resting place
as "his colde grave" (2778)—even the Knight, refusing to speculate,
admitted that "Arcite is coold" (2815) and handed his soul over to the
grimly imagined Mars; and that while Theseus blandly asserts that the
marriage of Palamon and Emily institutes a "parfit joye, *lastynge
everemo*," the aged Egeus knows that nothing in this world lasts forever, that no conclusion is conclusive. He "hadde seyn it chaunge
bothe up and doun, / Joye after wo, and wo after gladnesse" (2840–41),
and after Arcite's death he "shewed [the Athenians] ensamples and
liknesse" (2842) of this lugubrious truth. Not surprisingly, Theseus
seeks to efface Egeus's bleak wisdom: a vision of life as constant
"transmutacioun" (2839), a wandering "to and fro" that falls into the
cyclic patterns of return, can hardly sustain the Thesean mission of
purposive change. But nothing in the *Tale* suggests that he is right and
Egeus wrong.

In fact, the generational pattern that Chaucer adds to Boccaccio's
narrative not only makes Arcite and Palamon younger versions of Theseus, as he himself acknowledges (1811–17), but places him down the

line from Egeus, who represents the bleak wisdom of old age to which he must himself in time come.[97] And also in Theseus's future is the death of his son Hippolytus, an event that will force upon him the inescapability of the very structure of events he is even now seeking to render definitively concluded. For when Theseus is later betrayed by Phaedra, he calls upon Neptune to send a monster up from the sea to startle Hippolytus's horses, who plunge over a cliff and into the sea. The emergence of a subterranean Fury as the agency of Hippolytus's death not only echoes Arcite's fate but also recalls both the chthonic act that initiated Theban history, the emergence of the dragon warriors from the bloody field, and the opening scene of the *Thebaid*, in which Oedipus summoned up a Fury to inflame his sons with the self-destructive rage that will be their undoing.[98] Indeed, Hippolytus's death even imitates that of Egeus himself, who seeing the black sails on Theseus's ship as it returned from Crete threw himself into the sea from the cliffs.

If the "First Movere" speech unsettles the enterprise to which it is supposed to provide stability, there are other narrative moments even more explicitly disturbing. Perhaps the most vivid is the scene of Arcite's accident and subsequent death, for which the narrative has insidiously prepared us in the description of his lovesickness. Whereas before "heroic" love and melancholy had turned "al up so doun / Bothe habit and disposicioun" (1377–78), Arcite is now tossed from his horse onto the top of his head ("He pighte hym on the pomel of his heed" [2689]), the blood rushes from his liver into his face ("As blak he lay as any cole or crowe, / So was the blood yronnen in his face" [2692–93]), and his crushed chest contains a literally broken heart ("herte soor" [2695]). His "up so doun" condition worsens and his spirits become congested: "Swelleth the brest of Arcite, and the soore"—both the wound and the sorrow—"Encreeseth at his herte moore and moore" (2743–44). Arcite is thus both literally and metaphorically killed by love.[99]

---

97. This generational pattern is stressed by Neuse, "The Knight: The First Mover in Chaucer's Human Comedy," and, with important revisions, by J. A. Burrow, "Chaucer's *Knight's Tale* and the Three Ages of Man," in his *Essays on Medieval Literature* (Oxford: Clarendon Press, 1984), 27–48.

98. That the irruption of the fury is a specifically Theban phenomenon is also pointed out by Robert Haller, "The *Knight's Tale* and the Epic Tradition," *ChR* 1 (1966), 75.

99. This point has also been made by Edward C. Schweitzer, "Fate and Freedom in *The Knight's Tale*," *SAC* 3 (1981): 13–45, although as part of a very different argument. See also E. Talbot Donaldson, "Arcite's Injury," in *Middle English Studies Presented to Norman Davis in Honour of his Seventieth Birthday,* ed. Douglas Gray and E. G. Stanley (Oxford: Clarendon Press, 1983), 65–67.

This account makes both perfect sense and yet no sense at all. Arcite's death is rhetorically represented as fulfilling the fate that he had himself prefigured when he initially fell in love: "I nam but deed, ther nys no remedye" (1274). But the Knight never explains why such hyperboles *ought* to be fatal, nor why, if indeed a judgment is involved, Palamon should be exempted. It is this metaphysical incoherence that Arcite laments in his famous and understandably baffled farewell:

> What is this world? What asketh men to have?
> Now with his love, now in his colde grave
> Allone, withouten any compaignye. (2777–79)

Certainly we can invoke Boethian wisdom as an answer to Arcite's questions, and like all sapiential systems it can render the incoherent supportable, if scarcely more coherent. But many readers of the *Tale* continue to balk at the previously exact *equivalence* between Arcite and Palamon, an equivalence that suddenly vanishes, leaving Arcite alone in the cold grave and Palamon in "blisse and melodye" (3097) with Emily.[100]

Of course, we *can* draw distinctions between the lovers in terms of the casuistry of love, whether understood in terms of the details of love service—who saw her first? (Palamon); who loved her first as a woman rather than as a goddess? (Arcite)—or of service to the presiding deities of Venus (Palamon) and Mars (Arcite). And within the cultic game of chivalric love, there may even be a certain logic in awarding Emelye to Palamon on these grounds. But they are grounds that have force *only* within the game of love: immense consequences that are both ethical and philosophical are allowed to flow from the morally trivial decision whether to pray either to Mars for the victory that will win Emelye (Arcite) or to Venus for Emelye herself (Palamon). That a life-or-death choice should present itself in so casuistical a form is particularly offensive in view of the Knight's insistence on morally decisive action. If the poem can finally be explained only as a courtly *demande d'amour*, the Knight's belief in purposive change must be seen as empty.[101] And

---

100. Criticism has often tried to distinguish between the two; the early attempts—and their contradictory results—have been surveyed by Muscatine, "Form, Texture, and Meaning." More recent, representative attempts include Halverson, "Aspects of Order"; Brooks and Fowler, "The Meaning of Chaucer's *Knight's Tale*"; McCall, *Chaucer Among the Gods*, 73–76; A. V. C. Schmidt, "The Tragedy of Arcite: A Reconsideration of the *Knight's Tale*," *EIC* 19 (1969): 107–17; and Derek Pearsall, *The Canterbury Tales* (London: Unwin, 1985), 129–30.

101. For an argument that the poem is a *demande d'amour*, see J. R. Hulbert, "What was Chaucer's Aim in the *Knight's Tale*?" *SP* 26 (1929): 375–85.

even for those readers who believe they can distinguish between the protagonists in terms of their martial or venerean dispositions, these differences do not have *moral* value. As one of them admits, the two cousins are "equally honorable and brave as knights, equally ardent as lovers, and equally limited as pagans."[102]

What is particularly striking is that the Knight himself insists upon their perfect equivalence. When, for instance, Arcite's release from prison renders their conditions incommensurate, the Knight reestablishes a formal balance by having them lament their situations in virtually identical terms. Again, the action in part 2 seems to divide the lovers by placing Arcite in "blisse" (1449) and leaving Palamon in "martirdom" (1460); but it shortly brings them back together again in the grove, where the brutality of their struggle renders them indistinguishable:

> Thou myghtest wene that this Palamon
> In his fightyng were a wood leon,
> And as a crueel tigre was Arcite;
> As wilde bores gonne they to smyte,
> That frothen whit as foom for ire wood. (1655–59)

And when the lovers next confront each other, in the amphitheatre, their two bands of supporters are described as being of identical value:

> In al the world, to seken up and doun,
> So evene, withouten variacioun,
> Ther nere swiche compaignyes tweye,
> For ther was noon so wys that koude seye
> That any hadde of oother avauntage
> Of worthynesse, ne of estaat, ne age,
> So evene were they chosen, for to gesse. (2587–93)

Similarly, Lygurge may be, as the scholars tell us, Saturnian in complexion, and Emetreus Martian, but this distinction is overridden by a host of theatrical and sumptuous details.[103] Indeed, what makes no sense in a

---

102. Minnis, *Chaucer and Pagan Antiquity*, 135–36.
103. This initial identification of Lygurge and Emetreus was made by Walter Clyde Curry, *Chaucer and the Mediaeval Sciences*, 2d ed. (New York: Barnes and Noble, 1960), 131–37. The details that did not fit into Curry's scheme have been reanalyzed by Brooks and Fowler, "Meaning of Chaucer's *Knight's Tale*," 130–34, who seek to demonstrate that in a scheme of the Four Ages of Man Lygurge represents maturity and Emetreus youth, thus accounting for the victory of Palamon. Brooks and Fowler acknowledge, however, that

moral iconography (Lygurge's black beard, gryphon look, chair of gold and four white bulls, black bear skin with golden studs, jewel-studded golden wreath, and white hunting dogs are matched by Emetreus's pearl-studded white "cote-armure," lion look, laurel wreath, white eagle, and tame lions and leopards) makes perfect sense as a celebration of chivalric badges and conspicuous consumption generally—a celebration silently undercut by our awareness that such details are ethically meaningless. The point is, in short, that since Arcite and Palamon are indistinguishable at the level of worth, the choice must be made between them on other, arbitrary grounds. And just as their initial argument over Emily turned on hair splitting, so does (and must) the final judgment depend on legalistic distinctions. If we read this message out from the *Tale* to the fourteenth-century honor community, its critique of the procedures of chivalric identity formation (as they can be seen at work in the Scrope-Grosvenor armorial dispute, for instance) is truly devastating.

"The rhetoric of symmetry and balance has the effect of proposing everything in terms of alternatives; alternatives cry out for choice; but grounds for reasoned choosing are remarkably scant."[104] Kathleen Blake's description of the *Tale* as a whole speaks also to Theseus's efforts at composing differences on the level of action. For Theseus the irrational suddenly emerges in the symbolic manifestation of the Fury, a pointed expression of chthonic Theban primitiveness. As a narrator the Knight displays an analogous commitment to coherence, and yet it too is undone. But in his case the destructive forces cannot pretend, like the Fury, to have entered his world from outside the system of chivalric supervision. On the contrary, as a survey of the Knight's narrative habits will make clear, it is a function of the system in which he believes, and of the dark shape of his own drive for order.

IV

The *Knight's Tale* is driven by a passion for order whose narrative enactment, through an equal passion for formal balance, symmetries, and homologies, brings about a profound thematic disarray.[105] This self-canceling narrative rhetoric is visible throughout the *Tale*, but it can be

---

all the details still do not quite fit, and they finally confess that "it may well be that [the two kings] are not to be fully understood" (134).

104. Blake, "Order and the Noble Life," 7.

105. I have been anticipated in this point by Dale Underwood, "The First of *The Canterbury Tales*," *ELH* 26 (1959): 455–69, although he finally acquiesces in the view that the poem's resistance to its narrator's patterning is only apparent, and implies "the universe of divine order."

most economically examined in the stretch of narrative that extends
from the Theban cousins' imprisonment, when they fall in love with
Emily, to the establishment of the tournament that promises to resolve
their rivalry (1033–880). The Knight's objective is to show that while
Arcite and Palamon, as embodiments of the forces of disorder, may
escape from Theseus's prison, they can nevertheless be contained by
the regulatory effect of cultural forms of which he himself is the super-
visory agent. We are treated first to a series of accidents and reversals.
Arcite's "perpetuel" imprisonment is unexpectedly alleviated first by
the sight of Emily and then by the intervention of Pirithous—events
that serve, unexpectedly, not to alleviate his distress but to increase it;
then he returns from Theban exile to Theseus's court through the miraculous intervention of Mercury, which transforms the "crueel torment" (1382) of exile into the "blisse" (1449) of service; Palamon, although also "a prisoner / Perpetuelly" (1457–58), manages to escape;
Arcite leaves the court to celebrate his joy in a grove but finds, unexpectedly, first that his exhilaration is transformed into melancholy, then
that Palamon is lurking in malevolent wait for him; and when they try
to settle their differences through knightly battle they are interrupted
by Theseus. The narrative of this part of the *Tale* evidently proceeds
entirely "by aventure or cas" (1074), words that echo and reecho
throughout the *Tale* as a whole (e.g., 1160, 1186, 1235, 1288, 1465, 1506,
1516, 2357, 2703, 2722 [aventure]; 1242, 1780, 2110, 2357, 2822 [cas]).
And yet its final configuration—Arcite and Palamon submissive before
Theseus, the ladies tearfully intervening on their behalf, and Theseus
regally instituting a sanctioned solution to an otherwise intractable
impasse—declares that the narrative has arrived, almost magically, at
an appropriate "conclusion." Put metaphysically, the shape of the narrative argues that what appears to be "aventure" or "cas" is in fact
"destynee" (1465). Events that might in other stories be considered to
be random are here revealed to be part of a master plan that has been,
we are encouraged to think, in force from the beginning.

In even smaller details the Knight's way of telling his *Tale* insists on
his power to contain disruptive energies and make them part of a pattern. Take, for example, the description of Palamon and Arcite falling in
love with Emily, a scene whose very conventionality represents the
cultic values of the courtly world in a seemingly innocent form: a lady
performs her springtime observances in a garden. Yet, if we look
closely, Emily and her garden prove to be identical, each mirroring the
other and thereby excluding the world: on "a morwe of May" (1034),
Emily, "fressher than the May with floures newe" (1037) and with the
roses in her cheeks vying with the lilies over "which was the fyner of

hem two" (1039), gathers from the garden "floures, party white and rede" (1053) with which to weave "a subtil gerland" (1054) for herself. First Palamon, and then Arcite taking his cue from Palamon, gaze upon Emily, with the result that the earlier rivalry between the rose and the lily in Emily's complexion is now transferred to the Theban cousins. What was at first a lyrical specularity now reveals itself as a form of narrative narcissism: we are presented with a single scene, the lady mirroring and mirrored by her garden, that unfolds into events that themselves mirror this original configuration.

The effect of such meticulous management is to rob the project of both an oppositional force by which it can be tested and, more seriously, to render narrative events so utterly homologous as to freeze the narrative. As critics have often noted, the *Knight's Tale* is a tableau, a frieze, a set of static images, a pageant; at its most dynamic, a procession.[106] For all their apparently unlooked-for arbitrariness, the events of the narrative are so patterned that what we have seen we will see again. There are, for instance, three scenes of springtime observances; Emily's in the garden is followed by Arcite's "observaunce to May" (1500) in the grove and then, most tellingly, by Theseus's hunt "at the grete hert in May" (1665). The argument in the prison becomes the battle in the grove and then the tournament in the amphitheater. Theseus disarms a series of challenges: Hippolyta's, Creon's, Arcite's and Palamon's, and finally (so he thinks) that of death itself. The effect of these patterns is to shift the narrative itself from the mode of purposive development—a problem is encountered and resolved—to one of repetition, in which all narrative actions assume the same configuration, one that perfectly expresses both the self-congratulation of chivalric ideology and the inconclusiveness of chivalric practice.

In addition to creating these patterns, the Knight constantly interjects reminders not just of his narratorial presence but of his persistent supervision of his *Tale*. These interjections include not only conventional transitional passages (e.g., "And in this blisse lete I now Arcite, / And speke I wole of Palamon a lite" [1449–50]), but also a series of interpretive comments designed to contain events within familiar categories. After Palamon escapes from prison and hides in the grove, the Knight turns to Arcite "that litel wiste how ny that was his care, / Til that Fortune had broght him in the snare" (1489–90). And as Arcite roams within the fatal grove, the Knight offers another, more extended warning, this time adorned with a proverb:

106. This critical topic is best expressed, and developed, by Kolve, *Chaucer and the Imagery of Narrative*, 85–157.

But sooth is seyd, go sithen many yeres,
That "feeld hath eyen and the wode hath eres."
It is ful fair a man to bere hym evene,
For al day meeteth men at unset stevene.
Ful litel woot Arcite of his felawe,
That was so ny to herken al his sawe,
For in the bussh he sitteth now ful stille. (1521–27)

We recognize here the voice of the professional soldier who knows the
world to be a dangerous and unpredictable place and never lets down
his guard. But this anxious sense of perpetual surveillance, graphically
represented by the image of watching fields and listening woods, is in
fact helpless to *prevent* what happens. Its warnings are intended only
for the reader. Arcite blindly wanders in the woods while the Knight
exempts himself from a similar blindness by drawing the appropriate
lesson. And so on throughout part 2: when Arcite's mood abruptly
changes, the Knight provides an extended account of lovers' typical
behavior, which he ascribes to the supervision of the planet Venus
(1531–39); when Palamon and Arcite agree to fight for Emily, the
Knight ascribes their intransigence to Cupid (1623–26); as each knight
nervously awaits the other, the Knight compares them to Thracian
hunters awaiting the charge of their prey, and they then become that
prey themselves by being compared to lions, tigers, and boars; and as
Theseus enters upon his own hunt, the Knight accounts for his propi-
tious presence by again invoking a destiny that seems to work through
astral influence. Once more narrative configurations echo each other
(Venus, Cupid, and Diana are separately but analogously invoked,
Arcite's observance is matched by Theseus's, the Theban lovers are like
the hunters whom Theseus then leads out and are themselves the prey
he captures); and we are aware throughout of the way these strategies
contain and homologize events that would otherwise seem disjunctive
and destabilizing. In every case the Knight remains apart from and
above his *Tale*, fully in control not only of its narrative elements but of
its meaning, secure in the possession of interpretive categories that can
assimilate the events to a supervening ideology that is itself invulnerable to analysis.

Finally, one of the Knight's most common strategies of narrative
containment is, literally, to build containers: it will help us to see how
his version of narrative is in fact antinarrative by thinking of it as
construction, as architectonics. Each narrative event is carefully
sealed off from the others with a statement of finality: "ther is
namoore to telle" (974); "what nedeth wordes mo?" (1029); "This is

th'effect" (1487); "This is the'effect; ther is namoore to seye" (2366); "there is namoore to seyn" (2601). Indeed, at the very outset of the *Tale* this instinct threatens to annul the story before it begins. For once Theseus has imprisoned the cousins "perpetuelly" (1024), the Knight declares the narrative finished:

> And whan this worthy duc hath thus ydon,
> He took his hoost, and hoom he rit anon
> With laurer crowned as a conquerour;
> And ther he lyveth in joye and in honour
> Terme of his lyf; what nedeth wordes mo?
> And in a tour, in angwissh and in wo,
> Dwellen this Palamon and eek Arcite
> For everemoore; ther may no gold hem quite. (1025–32)[107]

Nevertheless, the story does proceed, if somewhat jerkily. For the method of construction leaves its traces in the large number of transitional passages that staple the narrative together. An example already familiar to us is when the Knight "lete . . . this noble duc to Atthenes ryde" (873) while he circles back over the campaign against Hippolyta and then ostentatiously reenters the narrative line: "And ther I lefte, I wol ayeyn bigynne" (892). There are many other instances:

> Now wol I stynte of Palamon a lite,
> And lete hym in his prisoun stille dwelle,
> And of Arcita forth I wol yow telle. (1334–36)

> And in this blisse lete I now Arcite,
> And speke I wole of Palamon a lite. (1449–50)

> Now wol I turne to Arcite ageyn. (1488)

> And in this wise I lete hem fightyng dwelle,
> And forth I wole of Theseus yow telle. (1661–62)

---

107. I have here replaced line 1031 in the *Riverside Chaucer*—which is Ellesmere's ungrammatical "This Palamon and his felawe Arcite"—with Hengwrt's reading. See John M. Manly and Edith Rickert, *The Text of the Canterbury Tales* (Chicago: University of Chicago Press, 1940), 3:427; Hengwrt's reading is also adopted by E. T. Donaldson, ed., *Chaucer's Poetry*, 2d ed. (New York: Ronald Press, 1975), and by Robert A. Pratt, ed., *The Tales of Canterbury* (Boston: Houghton Mifflin, 1974).

But stynte I wole of Theseus a lite,
And speke of Palamon and of Arcite. (2093–94)

Now wol I stynten of the goddes above,
Of Mars, and of Venus, goddessse of love,
And telle yow as pleynly as I kan
The grete effect, for which that I bygan (2479–82)

Of this bataille I wol namoore endite,
But speken of Palamon and of Arcite. (2741–42)

Now wol I speken forth of Emelye. (2816)

The seamlessness of narrative time is thus fragmented into discrete units that are disposed into what the Knight believes to be a well-proportioned story; and the goal is to claim an ascendancy over time itself, a position at once outside and above the onward motion that is the condition of storytelling, as it is of life.

But the very temporality that the Knight seeks to dominate continues to harrass him. This, too, is acknowledged from the *Tale*'s opening movement, where, "if it nere to long to heere" (875), the Knight would have provided the details of Theseus's conquest of Hippolyta—"but al that thyng I moot as now forbere" (885). Further acts of forbearance follow: "But shortly for to speken" (985), "But shortly for to telle" (1000), "If that I hadde leyser for to seye" (1188), "To telle it yow as shortly as I may" (1190), "And shortly to concluden" (1358, 1895), "As shortly as I kan, I wol me haste" (2052), "But shortly to the point thanne wol I wende, / And maken of my longe tale an ende" (2965–66)—these are phrases, and sentiments, that are ubiquitous throughout his performance.[108] This anxiety about temporality is perfectly articulated in the Knight's most ostentatious stylistic characteristic, the *occupatio*. For the *occupatio* is a figure that asserts simultaneously that there is not enough time to describe an event (Theseus's feast, Arcite's funeral) and yet time enough for a detailed description (2197–208, 2919–66). Witnessing both to the pressure of time and yet to its pliability, the *occupatio*

---

108.   For example: "And shortly" (1377); "What sholde I al day . . . endite?" (1380); "I passe as lightly as I may" (1461); "Suffiseth heere ensamples oon or two" (1953); "Suffiseth oon ensample" (2039); "Of al this make I now no mencioun, / But al th'effect, that thynketh me the beste" (2206–7); "Al telle I noght as now his observaunces" (2264); "What helpeth it to tarien forth the day / To tellen how . . . ?" (2820–21).

expresses the uncertainty of the Knight's relation both to temporality and to the historical life in time.

The meaning of these narrative (or antinarrative) routines goes far beyond the rhetorical management of one's audience. At issue is an unresolved struggle that inhabits, and in part defines, the chivalric imagination. It is a dialectic between a conception of historical reality as already accomplished, and hence fixed within an order of destiny, and a conception of history as radically prospective, and hence subject to randomness and accident—a dialectic, in short, between "destynee" and "aventure." These are the polarized extremes that the *Knight's Tale* articulates but that it can never mediate; and they express a similarly unresolved dialectic between the chivalric will to dominate the world and its equally profound, even unbearable sense of weakness and impotence. In his efforts to assimilate a threatening arbitrariness to preexisting patterns of significance, the Knight tries to articulate a world from which temporality and contingency have been banished; iteration and sectioning hold back narrative or package it into manageable units; *occupatio* raises this impulse to the almost conscious level of a ruse. But uncertainty enters the story nevertheless.

V

The form this uncertainty takes is astrology. All readers of the *Knight's Tale* find their attention is at some stage irresistibly drawn to the description of Theseus's oratories, where the pagan gods are represented in their planetary forms. In placing astrology at the center of his representation of the chivalric life, Chaucer was not merely responding to a personal interest but also invoking a central practice of late-medieval noble culture. It was, perhaps, also *the* practice that best expressed chivalry's central contradictions.

Although committed to a resolutely optimistic and progressive view of its role in the world, chivalry habitually represented itself in sorrowful, even tragic terms. The profound sense of the pathos of the noble life is fully registered in chivalric chronicles and biographies. For example, the careers of both Peter of Cyprus and Edward, the Black Prince are, as narrated by their admiring biographers, deeply disappointing. Peter began his crusading with the brilliant capture of Alexandria but had immediately to yield it up, and he spent the rest of his life engaged in inconclusive negotiations and watching minor victories turn into major defeats—an unhappy pattern fulfilled by his murder at the hands of his own nobility. Possessed by a restless idealism, he achieved only disappointment and anticlimax. "I have failed in my purpose,"

Machaut has him say after the abandonment of Alexandria, "I have lost my way" (3013, 3042)—comments that could with equal justice be applied to his life as a whole.[109] Machaut's summarizing conclusion is appropriately bleak: "For truly I never saw such a piteous end to such a fine beginning."[110]

While Edward's life had greater rewards—victory at Poitiers and at Najera, a love match with a beautiful wife, dominion over Gascony—it too traced a tragic course. The triumph over du Guesclin at Najera was tainted by Pedro's subsequent refusal to recompense Edward for his efforts, and upon his return from Spain the Prince was stricken with both the "treasons and falsehoods" that cost him Gascony and the illness that eventually killed him.[111] He bore his sufferings with stoic endurance—"everything has its place," he says—and maintained hope in the future: "If I can overcome this I will indeed take my revenge," a vengeance he did indeed take on the faithless Limoges.[112] But the final years of his life were marked by decline and loss: his companions Audelay and Chandos and his eldest son died, he lost La Rochelle and an expedition for its recovery was canceled for lack of wind, and his illness finally overmastered him. The deathbed speech to his companions that the Chandos Herald gives him is only slightly less baffled than Arcite's: "We are not lords here. Everything is inevitable that takes place here, and no man can turn it aside."[113] The epitaph that concludes the narrative, and that was probably added to the first version by a later scribe, goes further still. Like Arcite, "allone, withouten any compaignye" (2779), the Black Prince in his grave is also isolated, cut off from the chivalric community: "My house is very narrow, there are with me only worms."[114] At the very

109.   Machaut, *Prise:* "J'ay failly à m'entente" (3013); "J'ay erré" (3042).
110.   "Car onques mais certeinnement / De si très bon commencement / Je ne vi si piteuse fin" (8868–70).
111.   Tyson, *Vie:* "traisons et fauxetées" (3909).
112.   "Tut avera son lieu, / Et si de cy lever me purroie / Bien la vengeance em prenderoie" (3964–66).
113.   "Nous ne sumes pas seigniour cy. / Tut coviendra par ci passer, / Nulle homme ne s'en poet destourner" (4114–16).
114.   "Moult est estroit ma maisoun, / Ove moi n'ad si vermin noun" (4269–70). The importance of companionship to the chivalric warrior can hardly be overstated (see, e.g., the passage from Jean de Beuil's *Le Jouvencel* cited by Vale, *War and Chivalry*, 30), and its loss is a large part of the fearfulness of death. In *Le Livre de Bon Jehan, Duc de Bretagne*, Guillaume de Saint-André expressed the loneliness of death in terms that are strikingly reminiscent of the Chandos Herald: "It's a great misery and pity that in death there is no friendship either of companion or kinsman" ("C'est grant misare et grant pitié / Qu'en la mort n'a nulle amitié / Ne de voesin ne de parent" [4254–56]). Guillaume's biography is printed in Carrière, *Chronique de Bertrand du Guesclin*, 2:425–560.

outset of his treatise on chivalry Honoré Bonet expresses the same understanding with pungent and poignant directness: the Tree of Battles is a Tree of Mourning.[115]

These are not merely religious commonplaces but a specifically chivalric metaphysic underwritten by a deep pessimism. The dark figure of Fortune is a common presence: according to Mervyn James, "Perhaps the most fundamental tenet of honour belief is that Fate, irrational, incomprehensible and uncontrollable, rules over human history."[116] While languishing in prison in the winter of 1394–95, Thomas of Saluzzo composed a long allegorical poem called the *Chevalier Errant* in which a number of prominent contemporary knights are found in attendance at the court of a capricious Lady Fortune.[117] When Bonet attempts to explain the unhappy fate of chivalric heroism he inscribes into his prose text verses that describe "comment Fortune l'a du tout reversée"; and while he acknowledges that all events derive from "la voulenté de Dieu" it is "Fortune variable" who performs the mysterious divine decrees and to whom even the most pious of knights is subject.[118] Throughout the *Prise d'Alexandrie* Machaut has recourse to Fortune as the only explanatory principle that can account for Peter's various failures, and the Chandos Herald invokes her for similar purposes.[119] Indeed, the Chandos Herald organizes his *Vie du Prince Noir* according to a five-part structure that imitates the turning of the Wheel of Fortune. Two ascending narrative elements—marked, respectively, by the Battle of Crécy and the Battle of Poitiers—lead to Edward's marriage with Joan of Kent and seven years of triumphant and joyful overlordship in Gascony; but this climax is in turn followed by two descending movements, first the war in Spain, then the final collapse.

Yet it is de Charny who provides, for our purpose, the most interesting use of Fortune. He was not only directly familiar with the Boethianism that inflects these texts; he also deforms it in ways that are

115. Bonet, *Tree of Battles,* 79. The more unambiguously celebratory biographies of du Guesclin and Boucicaut are able to suppress this sense of doom only by ostentatiously rewriting history. Cuvelier, for example, erases many of du Guesclin's failures; and while Boucicaut's biography includes the disaster of Nicopolis, it is able to achieve a happy ending only because it was written in the first decade of the fifteenth century while Boucicaut was still governor of Genoa and before his capture at Agincourt and his death, while still in captivity, in 1421.

116. James, "English Politics and the Concept of Honour," 315.

117. Keen, *Chivalry,* 18–19.

118. On the verses, see Bonet, *Tree of Battles,* 297 and 113; on Fortune and the will of God, see 296.

119. For Machaut, see *Prise,* 5, 11, 18, 23, 110, and 113–14; for the Chandos Herald, see Tyson, *Vie,* 3565–97 (146–47).

strikingly similar to the *Knight's Tale.* De Charny's understanding of chivalry was absolutist in conception, for the most part closed to troubling recognitions. His knight lives in a universe that is not just morally coherent but transparently so: "For our Lord assigns and endows his goods there where he sees that they are best employed, and also shameful dishonor on those who think to have goods and honors for themselves without thinking of him."[120] Given this kind of universe, how then do we account for the fact that victory so often goes to the less worthy opponent? "This fortune is good," says de Charny, in true Boethian fashion, and he begins the Boethian argument that an unjust victory is more burdensome to the victor than the vanquished. Yet after broaching this argument he immediately retreats into radically un-Boethian claims: that the confrontation of the worse and the better cannot long continue without a victory for the better because reason will not allow it, that "those goods which have come by the grace of God are not goods of Fortune at all," that it is only those who have unjustly mounted up who are brought low by Fortune.[121] In short, de Charny both invokes and misrepresents the Boethian challenge to the life of worldly engagement, seeking to evade chivalry's central paradox—that the worldy power with which it is invested is not only not a protection against disaster but actually renders it more than usually vulnerable to catastrophe.

This tragically riven and logically incoherent metaphysic is structurally related to the chivalric obsession with astrology. Throughout the later Middle Ages astrology was very much at home in princely courts throughout Europe. Emperor Frederick II employed the famous Michael Scot, Guido da Montefeltro patronized the equally well-known Guido Bonatti, Emperor Charles IV had an official astrologer, and Boccaccio recommended Andalò di Negro to Hugh IV of Cyprus.[122] During

120.   De Charney, *Livre:* "Car Nostre-Seigneur assiet et met ses biens là où il voit qu'il est miex emploïe et aussi les hontes et les maulx sur yceuls qui cuident avoir les biens et les honnours d'euls-meismes sans souvenir de lui" (528).

121.   "Car la raison est tousjours plus segure et plus ferme et de longue durée que les fortunes"; "ycils biens qui par la grâce de Dieu sont ainsi venus, ne sont mie bien de fortune" (494).

122.   Dante places both Michael Scot and Guido Bonatti in the bolgia of the soothsayers in *Inferno* 20, and in *Decameron* 8, 9 Boccaccio has Michael Scot characterized as a "gran maestro in nigromantia" (*Opere*, ed. Cesare Segre [Milan: Mursia, 1963], 545). On Charles IV's astrologer, see Petrarch's *Familiares* 23, 2 and Lynn Thorndike, *A History of Magic and Experimental Science* (New York: Columbia University Press, 1934), 3:220; and for Boccaccio's recommendation of Andalò di Negro, see his *De geneologie deorum*, 15, 6. Much of Boccaccio's mythographic material in the *De genealogie* is in fact derived from Andalò; see Charles Osgood, *Boccaccio on Poetry* (Indianapolis: Bobbs Merrill, 1956), 188 n. 2. On Chaucer and Andalò, see below, note 124.

Chaucer's lifetime, the French monarchy had a special commitment to astrology: Charles V brought Christine de Pisan's father Thomas from Italy to Paris to join his band of astrologers, and according to contemporaries his sons Charles VI and Louis of Orleans were both deeply involved in various forms of astrological divination.[123] Even in England, where evidence of astrological activity among the ruling classes is less plentiful, there does survive an extensive geomantic and astrological book commissioned by Richard II and written in March 1391 and a deluxe manuscript of Guido Bonatti's *Liber astronomicus* made for Henry VII.[124] In fact, Gervase Mathew was so impressed by the "trust in the power of the planets" that pervades Richard's *Libellus Geomancie* that he suggested that "a study of planetary conjunctions might provide a clue to several of Richard's actions in the political crises of his reign."[125] Indeed, after Richard's deposition in 1399 it was reported in Parliament that a king's clerk named Maudeleyn was found with a scroll belonging to Richard on which were written magic incantations.[126]

123. The best evidence of Charles V's interest in astrology is the closely reasoned attack launched by Nicole Oresme in his *Livre de divinacion,* written for Charles shortly after 1361; see G. W. Coopland, ed. and trans., *Nicole Oresme and the Astrologers* (Cambridge: Harvard University Press, 1952). For Charles VI, see the extensive (and egregious) defense of free will against astral determinism in Deschamps' *Fiction du lion,* a beast fable directed to Charles, and Philippe de Mézière's *Songe du vieil pelerin,* which incorporates Oresme's *Livre* in a book meant now for the son rather than the father; see also Thorndike, *History of Magic,* 3:590–91. Similarly, Deschamps' *Contre les sortileges* draws heavily upon Oresme in order to warn Louis of Orleans against judicial astrology.

124. Richard II's book survives in two manuscripts, MS Bodley 581 and BL MS Royal 12.C.V. For descriptions, see Philippe Genet, ed., *Four English Political Tracts,* Camden Society, 4th ser., 18 (1977), 22–39; V. J. Scattergood, "Literary Culture at the Court of Richard II," in Scattergood and Sherborne, *English Court Culture,* 29–43; several of the illuminations are reproduced in Roger Sherman Loomis, *A Mirror of Chaucer's World* (Princeton: Princeton University Press, 1965), 121–22. For Henry VII's ownership of a copy of Guido's book, see Thorndike, *History of Magic* (New York: Macmillan, 1923), 2:827. In Theseus's oratory of Mars in the *Knight's Tale,* the geomantic signs Puella and Rubeus are inscribed over the head of the statue. In *The Medieval Anadyomene: A Study in Chaucer's Mythography* (Oxford: Blackwell, 1972), Meg Twycross argues that these signs "so strongly suggest the Oriental-derived Mars of the Michael Scot manuscripts that I think we must claim the Scot illustration as a 'source' in their own right" (50–51). Twycross also shows that Venus's "citole" derives from the astrological tradition and suggests that Chaucer might have found this detail in either Arabic treatises or in the writings of Andalò di Negro. So far as I know, there has as yet been no effort to compare Chaucer's use of astrological and geomantic materials in the *Knight's Tale* with Richard's *Libellus Geomancie.*

125. Gervase Mathew, *The Court of Richard II* (London: John Murray, 1968), 40. Nancy and Ronald Reagan have shown that the princely habit of consulting astrologers before important undertakings is not confined to prescientific ages.

126. Given-Wilson, *Royal Household,* 181.

To judge from the complaints of the antiastrological writers, temporal lords were almost irresistibly drawn to astrologers, no matter how
dubious their results.[127] In his *Recueil des plus celebres astrologues,* Symon
de Phares represents the unhappy recent history of France and England as a chronicle of predictable (and predicted) disasters: for each
battle of the Hundred Years War he provides an astrologer who foresaw
its outcome, and each chivalric hero is similarly accompanied by an
astrologer.[128] Indeed, the influential *Tractatus de bello* by John of
Legnano actually presented war as brought about by God working
through the celestial bodies upon man's corporeal nature.[129] When
Honoré Bonet popularized Legnano's treatise in his *Tree of Battles,* he
put the issue clearly:

> Aristotle says that, of necessity, in this world earthly bodies derive
> their condition and nature from the disposition of the stars. But it is
> plain that among the stars there is by nature rebellion and contra-
> riety, for one engenders heat, another cold; one love, another dissen-
> sions; one luxury, another chastity; one blood, another melancholy.
> Then since there is contradiction between these heavenly bodies it
> most certainly exists among earthly bodies, which are governed by
> their movements.[130]

Finally, there is tangible evidence of the role played by astrology in the
life of the nobility in the numerous talismans that have survived. These
are gems and jewelry that were engraved with representations of the
planetary deities—engravings that followed the same mythographical

127.   For Lull's and Hesse's criticism of the relationship between astrologers and
their royal patrons, see Thorndike, *History of Magic,* 2:868 and 3:498. In *Seniles* 3, 1, Petrarch poured scorn upon the princely fascination with astrology, although his own attitude was by no means unambiguous; see Theodore Otto Wedel, *The Medieval Attitude
Towards Astrology* (New Haven: Yale University Press, 1920), 82–86.

128.   Symon de Phares, *Recueil des plus celebres astrologues,* ed. Ernest Wickersheimer
(Paris: Champion, 1929); see especially 222–61. Symon's treatise, which he wrote to defend himself against the charge of heresy, should be contrasted to Thomas Bradwardine's
well-known *Sermo Epicinus,* which he preached in October 1346 to Edward III and his
victorious troops after the battle of Crécy. Bradwardine's theme is that victory belongs to
God alone, and he bitterly attacks the "vani astrologi" who have revived the astral super-
stitions of the "antiqui gentiles" by worshipping "ymagines stellarum." See Heiko A.
Oberman and James A. Weisheipl, "The *Sermo Epicinus* Ascribed to Thomas Bradwardine
(1346),"*AHDLMA* 25 (1958): 295–329; the citations are from 308.

129.   Thomas Erskine Holland, ed., *Tractatus de bello, de represaliis et de duello,* with a
translation by J. L. Brierly (Washington: Carnegie Institution, 1917); see 209–11, 224–29.

130.   Bonet, *Tree of Battles,* 118.

programs as guided Chaucer's Knight in his account of Theseus's oratories.[131] And they were doubtless used with the kinds of prayers to the
planets that Michael Scot provides in his *Liber introductorius* and that are
also offered up by the Knight's protagonists.[132]

Clearly there is a highly contemporary relevance in the astrology of
the *Knight's Tale;* but what, precisely, was Chaucer's point? Most discussions of astrology, both medieval and modern, focus almost entirely
upon its heterodoxy. It might be possible to read Chaucer's interest in
the topic as also primarily judgmental, were it not that the extent and
subtlety of his explorations show that astrology provides him with opportunities for more than just censure.[133] In narratives that have either
a non-Christian setting ("Complaint of Mars," the "Legend of Hypermnestra," *Troilus and Criseyde,* the *Knight's Tale,* the *Squire's Tale*) or op-
pose Christian to non-Christian values (the *Man of Law's Tale,* the *Franklin's Tale*), an astrological blueprint or subtext serves as a cosmological
analogue to the protagonists' sense that they are trapped within a situation from which there is no escape.[134] More than simply a way of thrusting responsibility upon the stars, astrology expresses the protagonist's
sense of having become so inextricably engaged in a course of events
that the self can no longer think of itself apart from the action in which it
finds itself absorbed. This meaning is most radically expressed in "The
Complaint of Mars." The protagonists of the poem are at once victims
of a predetermined structure of action and planets that themselves create this structure: they are themselves the fate of which they complain.
Moral judgment is thus beside the point: to argue that they have behaved foolishly is in effect to argue that they should be different beings

131. Engraved gems and jewelry are discussed by Joan Evans, *Magical Jewels of the
Middle Ages and the Renaissance, Particularly in England* (Oxford: Clarendon Press, 1922).
The mythographical programs that governed the engraving of the planetary deities are
described in the widely read astrological manual *Picatrix;* although this text has never
been printed, a German translation of the Arabic original is available: Hellmut Ritter and
Martin Plessner, trans., *"Picatrix": Das Ziel des Weisen von Pseudo-Magriti* (London: The
University of London Press, 1962); see especially lxv. See also on this topic Thorndike,
History of Magic, 2:820–21 and Jean Seznec, *The Survival of the Pagan Gods: The Mythological
Tradition and Its Place in Renaissance Humanism and Art,* trans. Barbara Sessions (New York:
Pantheon Books, 1953), 53–56. As Seznec points out, the *Picatrix* also contains prayers to
the planetary deities. These engravings are probably what Bradwardine meant when he
attacked the worship of "ymagines stellarum" (see above, note 128).

132. For Michael Scot, see Thorndike, *History of Magic,* 2:235–27.

133. This is the reading offered most extensively by Chauncey Wood, *Chaucer and the
Country of the Stars* (Princeton: Princeton University Press, 1970).

134. The astrological situations that these texts describe have been discussed in detail by J. D. North, "Kalenderes Enlumyned," 129–54, 257–83, 418–44.

than they are. Not coincidentally, Chaucer explicates here the meaning of the Broche of Thebes, establishing an analogy among astral compulsion, the obsessions of the self, and historical repetition. The almost incomprehensible complexity of celestial cycles and epicycles, and the arcane learning through which they are known, thus become a metaphor for an equally complex subjectivity.

The medieval debate over astrology in fact repeated, in a different register, the contradictions within chivalry. Virtually every writer on astrology agrees on two incompatible propositions. True, man is an *imago Dei* and therefore endowed with an immortal soul unconstrained by any merely physical force, however superior. Hence astrological discussions insist, commonly by invoking the ubiquitous Ptolemaic adage, "Vir sapiens dominabitur astris," that celestial influence can always be resisted or overcome.[135] But equally true, man is a composite being, endowed with a rational soul but burdened as well with both a physical body and a lower and passionate self, and hence subject to celestial influence.[136] This split is reflected throughout medieval discussions of astrology. "There is in man a double spring of action," says Albertus Magnus, "namely, nature and the will; and nature for its parts is ruled by the stars, while the will is free; but unless it resists, it is swept along by nature and becomes hardened [*induratur*]."[137] Such induration, however unfortunate, enables astrological prediction. As Aquinas, among many others, points out, "The majority of men are in fact governed by their passions, which are dependent upon bodily appetites; in these the influence of the stars is clearly felt. Few indeed are the wise who are capable of resisting their animal instincts. Astrologers, consequently, are able to foretell the truth in the majority of cases, especially when they undertake general predictions."[138] The wise man

---

135. Despite its ascription to Ptolemy, this adage does not appear in his works, although there are analogous phrasings; see the discussion in Coopland, *Nicole Oresme*, 175–77.

136. Thorndike provides many medieval statements of the power of the stars over the natural world; for two examples, see the citations from Grosseteste (*History of Magic* 2:445) and Vincent of Beauvais (ibid., 2:468). Even Oresme, in his powerfully argued and uncompromisingly hostile *Livre de divinacions*, defines the scope of celestial influence as including the condition of the physical body and "la complexion et inclinacion de la personne" (Coopland, *Nicole Oresme*, 56).

137. Thorndike, *History of Magic*, 2:584; Thorndike translates *induratur* as "mechanization," an attractive suggestion I have rejected only because of its anachronism.

138. Cited and translated by Wedel, *Medieval Attitude Towards Astrology*, 68. Aquinas continues (in Wedel's translation): "In particular predictions, they [i.e., astrologers] do not attain certainty, for nothing prevents a man from resisting the dictates of his lower faculties. Wherefore the astrologers themselves are wont to say 'that the wise man rules

can indeed rise above the stars, but since so many of his fellows do not he had best understand the terms of their subjection.[139] According to Honoré Bonet, it may be that the wise man rules the stars, but "the number of wise men is small and of fools great, and because the simple are unable to be lords of the planets or of the heavenly influences, by the inclination of nature and of the flesh they often raise wars in the world."[140] Gower's *Vox Clamantis* defines the *vir sapiens* as he who rises above the stars;[141] but his *Confessio Amantis* defines a "lawe original" by which the planets work their influence and provides the elementary astronomical and astrological doctrine for that law's understanding. In short, the *vir sapiens* will either ignore the stars entirely or become a master astrologer—contradictory advice that witnesses to profound contradictions within medieval culture as a whole.[142] And it also witnesses to the profound pessimism that haunted chivalry: according to the Sicily Herald, when Ulysses discovered that he had been mortally wounded by his son Telegonus, "He forgave him his death, knowing that he was doomed to die because of the influence of celestial bodies, . . . as were many other great lords and princes."[143]

---

the stars,' forasmuch, namely, as he rules his own passions." Thorndike cites Scotus to the same effect: "We are told that it is rash for 'astronomers' to predict war for one conjunction of the planets and peace for another, or to say that persons born under a certain constellation will necessarily be dissolute. But the will is prone to follow the inclination of the appetite, so that in many cases it so happens, and someone has said that if you want to be a successful prophet, prophesy all evil . . ." (*History of Magic*, 3:5).

139.   Even aggressively antiastrological writers, such as William of Auvergne and Nicole Oresme, have to admit that, as William says with characteristic intolerance, "the multitude and populace from want of intelligence and other evil dispositions live almost after the manner of brutes" and that therefore generalized astrological predictions have a fair degree of accuracy (Thorndike, *History of Magic*, 2:368–69, citing *De universo*). Oresme admits that the great events of history are indeed controlled by the stars and can even be predicted in general terms—a large concession (Coopland, *Nicole Oresme*, 54–56).

140.   Bonet, *Tree of Battles*, 119.

141.   Gower, *Vox clamantis*, 2, 5, 239–41; 2, 9, 442–53; in Eric W. Stockton, trans., *The Major Latin Works of John Gower* (Seattle: University of Washington Press, 1962), 103, 108.

142.   G. C. Macauley, ed., *The English Works of John Gower*, EETS, ES 81–82 (London: Oxford University Press, 1901), 2:250. Hence Gower's Latin verses cite a version of the Ptolemaic adage—*Vir mediante de sapiens dominabitur astris*—to mean that "with the help of God the man wise [in astronomy] will dominate the stars." This instrumental meaning is in fact consistent with the Ptolemaic texts from which the adage originally derived, and it is the meaning that antiastrological writers like Oresme and Deschamps ascribed to it; see Coopland, *Nicole Oresme*, 66–68; Deschamps, *Oeuvres Complètes*, ed. Le Marquis de Queux de Saint-Hilaire (Paris: Didot Firmin, 1880–82), 2:144–45, 3:123–25.

143.   "Si luy pardonna sa mort, sachant que par l'influence des corps célestes il estoit menacié de finer ainsi, et jasoit ce qu'il en feust préadverti, si ne le sceut-il évader, nés que ont fait pluiseurs aultres grans princes et seigneurs" (Roland, *Parties inédites*, 38).

Astrology ought not to work, but in fact it does; a wise man ought to ignore the stars, but the requirements of the practical world demand that he understand them. It was thus as a form of worldly wisdom that astrology appealed to medieval secular rulers.[144] Apparently unpersuaded by or (more likely) uninterested in the clerical arguments about free will and astral determinism, they saw astrology as a means of manipulating a reality that was intractable in the best of circumstances. One of the most popular of the astrological handbooks, the *Speculum astronomiae*, argued that "in entering upon great undertakings, it is rashness not freedom of the will to despise election of the hour"; and Guido Bonatti said that only astrology made it possible for men to withstand the attacks of a malevolent Fortune.[145] And yet for all its assertion of the power of man to grasp and control his own historical destiny, astrology simultaneously witnessed to a profound sense of helplessness. As Aby Warburg long ago pointed out, "astrology, from its very inception, presents a double intellectual front. As a theory, it seeks to place before us the eternal laws of the universe in clear outline; whereas its practice stands under the sign of the fear of demons, the 'most primitive form of religious causation.'"[146] Located irresolutely between the critical thought of the future and the ancient atavism of the past, and witnessing simultaneously to a desire for control and a feeling of helplessness, astrology articulates with unusual economy the contradictions at the heart of the aristocratic culture of the later Middle Ages.

VI

With the reinstallation of Theseus in his dominant position at the end of part 2, narratorial authority is reaffirmed; and the displays of chivalric and aesthetic power that the Knight offers us at the beginning of part 3 serve to consolidate this. As commentators have rightly noted, the construction of the amphitheater is the most explicit statement of Theseus's power, one with which the Knight eagerly identifies himself.[147] Throughout this elaborate description we are made aware of

144. See Ernst Cassirer, *The Individual and the Cosmos in Renaissance Philosophy*, trans. Mario Domandi (New York: Harper Torchbooks, 1964 [1927]), 98–122.

145. Thorndike, *History of Magic*, 2:700, 830–31.

146. Cited by Cassirer, *Individual and the Cosmos*, 105.

147. Compare Halverson:

In an artifical *temenos* of precise dimensions and construction, the combat becomes rationalized; it is contained in the perfect circle of the stadium; it is bound by strict rules reducing potential violence; . . . Crude and heedless passion submits to the formal containment of rational law. In all this The-

the artifactual quality not merely of the amphitheater and its attendant oratories but, more tellingly, of the representations of the pagan
gods on the oratory walls. This is the result of Chaucer's revision of
Boccaccio. In the *Teseida* the gods' dwelling places are actual temples
on Mount Cithaeron and in Thrace, but for the Knight they are pictures on the walls of Theseus's oratories. Whereas Boccaccio had established a distance between the human and the divine that could be
bridged only by the sanctified language of the lovers' *orazioni*, Chaucer brings the gods down from their heavens and installs them within
man-made oratories.

The fact that we are seeing the gods at two removes—through a
poetic description of their painted portraits—is stressed throughout
the Knight's account: Theseus has hired every available "portreyour
[and] kervere of ymages" (1899) to "maken and devyse" (1901) the
oratories, and the Knight is in turn careful "to devyse" (1914) for his
audience

> The noble kervyng and the portreitures,
> The shap, the contenaunce, and the figures
> That weren in thise oratories thre. (1915–17)

The objects of his attention are not the gods themselves but scenes
"wroght on the wal" (1919), "portreiture" (1914, 1968) that is "with
soutil pencel . . . depeynted" (2049; and see also 1934, 1938, 1970,
1975, 1995, 2036, 2037, 2054, 2060, 2069); and the Knight actually concludes his account with a reminder of the relation between art and patronage: "Wel koude he peynten lifly that it wroghte; / With many a
floryn he the hewes boghte" (2087–88). In sum, both the oratories and
the amphitheater of which they are part witness to the power not of the
deities who are there represented but of the duke who has brought
those representations into being (and will later reign over this edifice
"as he were a god in trone" [2529]). A more complex authority accrues
to the Knight: in tracing in words the pictures Theseus has commissioned, the Knight assumes the role of both artist and patron—he who
conceives the iconographic program as well as he who achieves it. The
ecphrasis of each of the three oratories unfolds in three identical movements: first a series of quasi-allegorical figures are described "by ordre"

---

seus is the guiding spirit, a role which the fine balance of his character
enhances.
"Aspects of the Order in the *Knight's Tale*," 615; see also Kolve, *Chaucer and the Imagery of
Narrative*, 105, 112.

(Venus [1918–35], Mars [1995–2030], and—in a vestigial and thus all the more significant gesture toward symmetry—Diana [2054–55]); a series of mythographical victims then follows (of Venus [1936–54], of Mars [2031–40], and of Diana [2056–74]; and each description concludes with an account of the deity's statue (Venus [1955–66], Mars [2041–50], Diana [2075–99]). As before, a symmetrical pattern serves to assert an unqualified narratorial control—the creation of a pantheon by a master artificer who can make the gods sit still in their proper places.

Yet as we should expect, this self-confidently architectonic account of the *theatrum mundi* in fact reveals the chivalric dynamic we have been describing: a will to power that brings into existence the powerlessness it seeks to avoid. For it is exactly here, in Theseus's amphitheater, that the forces will emerge to overwhelm Theseus, his world, and his authority. And while the form of the amphitheater and its oratories bespeaks human control, as well as the propitiation implied by distinguishing the powers from each other and regulating their cults, the actual descriptions of the planetary deities witness instead to their implacability. As criticism has often noted, the relentlessly negative quality of the divine representations, with their focus upon the "care and wo" (2072) that each figure brings down upon the children of its "divisioun" (2024), stands in sharp and disturbing contrast to the celebratory purpose they are designed to serve.[148] Endowed with the power to imagine his own gods, Theseus is nonetheless able to imagine only his own helplessness: power portrays itself as weakness.

A similar contrast is enacted at the level of the Knight's narration. Although his careful ecphrasis asserts his control over the painted scenes of the oratories, as his account proceeds he falls more and more thoroughly under the domination of the images he describes. What is first presented as an afterthought ("But yet hadde I foryeten to devyse / The noble kervying and the portreitures" [1914–15]) becomes first an investment and then an obsession. The images in Venus's oratory are "ful pitous to biholde" (1918), but they are held at bay by a moralizing commentary on the deity represented.

Thus may ye seen that wysdom ne richesse,
Beautee ne sleighte, strengthe ne hardynesse,
Ne may with Venus holde champartie,
For as hir list the world than may she gye.

148.   Kolve, for example, points out that Chaucer places "nearly exclusive emphasis on all that is destructive or unhappy" (*Chaucer and the Imagery of Narrative*, 121).

Lo, alle thise folk so caught were in hir las,
Til they for wo ful ofte seyde "allas!" (1947–52)

Consistent with the major traditions of medieval mythographic writing, the Knight places Venus in the category of moral allegory, while admiring his own mastery of mythographic materials: "Suffiseth heere ensamples oon or two, / And though I koude rekene thousand mo" (1953–54).[149]

Relaxed and confident (perhaps overconfident) the Knight turns to the temple of his own personal deity, Mars; but suddenly losing his interpretive distance, he begins to speak of the pictures as if he had himself actually witnessed them: the phrase "I saugh" enters the narrative (1995) and pervades the Knight's account throughout both Mars's (2005, 2011, 2017, 2028) and Diana's (2056, 2062, 2065, 2067, 2073) oratories. In fact, the dislocation of narrative conventions is even more extreme than is usually acknowledged. The Knight begins with a description of a barren forest that was "peynted" on the wall, and then tells us that in the middle of this forest "ther stood the temple of Mars armypotente" (1982). It is within *this* temple that the descriptions that then follow are located: the Knight has, as it were, moved *through* the picture and into a world of images that have a wholly mental location.

Hence it remains for many lines unclear whether the objects of his account are pictures, visions, or actual enactments of the horrific scenes he describes. Does the "derke ymagyning / Of Felonye" refer to an image of Felony, one comparable to the quasi-allegorical pictures of "Plesaunce and Hope, Desir, [and] Foolhardynesse" (1925) that we find in the oratory of Venus? Or is Felony the dark imaginer of the scenes that then follow—"The smylere with the knyf under the cloke; / The shepne brennynge with the blake smoke" (1999–2000)? The acts of violence that the verse here records are eerily depersonalized and generalized by the staccato repetition of the anaphoric article:

149. Chaucer's immediate source for his accounts was probably a version of Pierre Bersuire's *Ovidius moralizatus;* see Twycross, *Medieval Anadyomene,* 14. Boccaccio included a moralized reading of the gods in the *Teseida,* although not in his text but in his *chiose,* which were in only a few instances included with the poem (see Twycross, 67 n. 157). Earlier scholarship argued that Chaucer's source was the so-called *Libellus de imaginibus deorum,* a compendium of mythographic descriptions taken from the *Ovidius moralizatus* minus the moralizing; Twycross provides a careful account before opting for Bersuire. For a survey of this mythographic material, and the relationships among the various texts, see Seznec, *Survival of the Pagan Gods,* 170ff.; the *Libellus* is printed by Hans Liebeschütz in *Fulgentius metaforalis* (Leipzig: Teubner, 1926), 117–28; a 1543 printed edition is reproduced by Stephen Orgel, although wrongly ascribed to Bersuire (New York: Garland Press, 1979).

The tresoun of the mordrynge in the bedde;
The open werre, with woundes al bibledde; . . .
The sleere of hymself yet saugh I ther—
His herte-blood hath bathed al his heer—
The nayl ydryven in the shode anyght;
The colde deeth, with mouth gapyng upright. . . .
The careyne in the busk, with throte ycorve;
A thousand slayne, and nat of qualm ystorve;
The tiraunt, with the pray by force yraft;
The toun destroyed, ther was no thyng laft. . . .
The hunte strangled with the wilde beres;
The sowe freten the child right in the cradel;
The cook yscalded, for al his longe ladel. (2001–20)

And despite a grim specificity, the allegorizing "the" designates these disasters as representative instances, emblems of what happens when Mars is in the ascendancy, nightmare visions of a world governed by disaster.

The effect of this ubiquity is to raise the problem of supervision. Insofar as the Knight truly does *see* these images, they witness to his repressed knowledge of military chivalry's darker, more malevolent valence. And many of the items in this catalogue of disasters could be applied, with only minor adjustments, to his own *Tale:* "The crueel ire, reed as any gleede" (1997), "The open werre, with woundes al bibledde" (2002), "A thousand slayn, and nat of qualm ystorve" (2014), "The tiraunt, with the pray by force yraft" (2015), "The toun destroyed, ther was no thyng laft" (2016). In a "derke ymagyning" we could recognize here the campaign against Thebes, the mindless rivalry between Palamon and Arcite, and even the upcoming tournament.

Yet what follows is still more revelatory. For the Knight images a fully allegorical version of Theseus, the "noble conquerour" (998, and see also 862, 866, 916, 981, 1027) who shall himself shortly be "set . . . ful riche and hye" (2577) in the very amphitheater where this image is painted as the figure of supervision who presides over the martial world as a whole:

And al above, depeynted in a tour,
Saugh I Conquest, sittynge in greet honour,
With the sharpe swerd over his heed
Hangyng by a soutil twynes threed. (2027–30)

What this ancient emblem of the sword of Damocles tells is no less alarming for being familiar: that the central source of stability in the world conceived by chivalry is himself permanently at risk. Yet while the Knight is apparently prepared to recognize this emblem, and with it the irony that attaches to Theseus, he is not able or willing to recognize *himself* in the Damoclean posture. Indeed, the catalogue that follows of conqueror figures from classical history is so arranged as to give him the utmost protection from self-application:

> Depeynted was the slaughtre of Julius,
> Of grete Nero, and of Antonius;
> Al be that thilke tyme they were unborn,
> Yet was hir deth depeynted ther-biforn
> By amansynge of Mars, right by figure.
> So was it shewed in that portreiture,
> As is depeynted in the sterres above
> Who shal be slayn or elles deed for love.
> Suffiseth oon ensample in stories olde;
> I may nat rekene hem alle though I wolde. (2031–40)

The Knight establishes here an equivalence between astral and artistic determinism. As the deaths of mighty conquerors are painted on the walls, so are they painted in the stars; as artists depict the fall of the great in images (or in words that work like images), so do the stars in history; as the stars know the future of the world over which they preside, so too does he. And suddenly we realize (retroactively) that this applies also to his own *Tale* and its protagonists. For he "who shal be slayn . . . for love" can be none other than Arcite; it is he who is the "oon ensample in stories olde," and the *Knight's Tale* itself is the very "olde storie," as he had called it in his opening line (859). We have here an almost instinctive gesture of narrative power, but one that must ultimately be seen as trivial in the face of the real-world helplessness that motivates it, its mimetic magic unable to solve the very questions of justice and causality the story itself raises.

At every level, then, the *Knight's Tale* demonstrates Chaucer's analysis of chivalry, not so much as a misplaced ideal or as a destructive sociopolitical practice (although both are implied) but as a failure of self-understanding. At the first and simplest level, the impasse of late fourteenth-century chivalry is represented in the Palamon-Arcite complex, the story of meaningless competition conducted in terms of a chivalric selfhood that prevents individual development and submerges the self in a surface pattern of ritual and replication. In these young men Chaucer represents the selfhood of the honorman that he witnessed in the Scrope-Grosvenor controversy. By definition incapable of change, they are bound to the stake of their fixed purpose. When Palamon confronts Arcite in the grove he presents their rivalry in terms that allow for no compromise:

> I wol be deed, or elles thou shalt dye.
> Thou shalt nat love my lady Emelye,
> But I wol love hire oonly and namo. (1587–89)

And the subsequent *prosopopeia* of the Thracian hunter imagined by the Knight serves to reinforce these terms:

> Here cometh my mortal enemy!
> Withoute faille, he moot be deed, or I,
> For outher I moot sleen hym at the gappe,
> Or he moot sleen me, if that me myshappe. (1643–46)

Either/or: committed irrevocably, loving unconditionally, they reject the idea of compromise as inconceivable. The *Tale* contrasts their unchanging passion to a series of changing geographical locales—the prison, the grove, the amphitheater, the funeral pyre. But the spatial alteration makes no difference: given the intensity of their ardor and the narrowness of their consciousness, they remain as psychologically imprisoned as if they had never left the tower where the action began.[150] Bleakly submissive before a fatality that has (so they think) overwhelmed them, they are equally passive before a desire that they experience as wholly absolutist in its demands.

The result is a self-fulfilling desire for conclusiveness and finality that recalls nothing so much as the Theban-like Troilus of Books 4 and 5—unless it be the noble rivals for the coat of arms *azure* with *bend d'or.* "And but I have hir mercy and hir grace, . . . / I nam but deed; ther nis namoore to seye" (1120–22), affirms Arcite at the outset, an extremity he reaffirms when exiled: "Syn that I may nat seen you, Emelye, / I nam

---

150. As Peter Elbow says, "Arcite and Palamon sometimes engage in what might look like thinking: making logical distinctions and drawing inferences (1152–86, 1223–74, and in particular 1280–333). But in every case they are using words and thoughts to justify a mood and point of view they already hold: anger and self-justification in the first case and despair in the other two. They use the ingredients of thought not for flexibility but to avoid flexibility" ("How Chaucer Transcends Oppositions in the *Knight's Tale,*" *ChR* 7 [1972–73], 108).

but deed; ther nys no remedye" (1273–74). And Palamon's words to Theseus when the lovers are surprised in the grove assert this yearning for finality in uncompromising terms:

> Sire, what nedeth wordes mo?
> We have the deeth disserved bothe two.
> Two woful wrecches been we, two caytyves,
> That ben encombred of oure owen lyves;
> And as thou art a rightful lord and juge,
> Ne yif us neither mercy nor refuge,
> But sle me first, for seinte charitee!
> But sle my felawe eek as wel as me. (1715–22)

The real awfulness of this request—emphasized by the interjected anachronism, "for seinte charitee!"—bespeaks a chivalric conscious-ness so narrowed in scope as to have become frozen within a double posture of erotic need and martial violence. And such a posture entails a spiritual emptiness that yearns for release even at the cost of self-extinction: "Two woful wrecches been we, two caytyves, / That been encombred of oure owene lyves."[151]

At a second level, chivalry's dilemma is anatomized in the figure of Theseus, seen by the Knight as providing an alternative to the self-destructive Theban lovers and exemplifying the civilizing process. Yet, as we have seen, this reading ignores both the threads of legend, plot, and character that link Theseus to Arcite and Palamon and, more impor-tant, the moral incoherence of the *Tale* itself. In his revisions of the *Teseida* Chaucer seems to have been concerned to soften the polariza-tions that would set Theseus against the Thebans. Boccaccio's reiter-ated invocation of the Theban story as the single explanation for the young lovers' behavior is here diminished to a subtheme, while Chau-cer adds, as we have seen, a generational pattern to Boccaccio's narra-tive. Arcite and Palamon are younger versions of Theseus, as he him-self acknowledges (1811–17), and his own vigorous optimism loses much of its authority in the presence of Egeus, who represents the bleak wisdom of old age to which Theseus must himself in time come.[152] And both the future that awaits him and, as we shall see, his

---

151. For examples of the way in which the language of wretches, caitiffs, and encum-berment invokes the concept of despair, see *Troilus and Criseyde*, 4, 279–80, the *Pardoner's Tale*, 728, and the *Parson's Tale*, 344; and see below, chapter 8.

152. See, for example, *Teseida*, 3, 65–66; 4, 11–17; 5, 55–60; and especially 10, 96–98. In *Chaucer and Boccaccio* (Oxford: Society for the Study of Mediaeval Languages and Litera-

legendary past inscribe him within the pattern of repetition that controls the young cousins.

Most important, Chaucer shows that the narrowed consciousness and obsessive fixation of Arcite and Palamon are not the other against which Theseus's and the Knight's rationality is to be defined but a dark version of that very rationality itself. The same ambivalent vacillation between utter helplessness and unconstrained desire that characterizes the Theban lovers marks both the cultural order imposed by Theseus and the narrative organization articulated by the Knight. In their narrow repetitiveness and yearning for finality both Theseus and the Knight unavoidably witness to the form of consciousness that characterizes the Theban lovers. The suicidal rhetoric of the Theban lovers is more subtly reenacted in Theseus's hapless decision making and still more subtly in the narrative strategies of the Knight. And what links all three levels of analysis is the gap between structures of belief and historical experience, between late fourteenth-century chivalric ideology and the facts of life in Chaucer's England. It was noble culture's inability to come to self-consciousness, to rewrite its own ideology in relation to socioeconomic change, that the *Knight's Tale* records. And as the opening premise of a major work conceived in entirely new cultural terms, it is both Chaucer's farewell to the chivalric context of his earlier writing and his promise to himself that what chivalry had repressed—the individual subject in time and motion—was now about to return.

---

ture, 1977), Piero Boitani rightly says that "of Thebes, Boccaccio tells us almost everything that pertains to its myth" (21). Oddly enough, however, Boitani maintains that these allusions are unhelpful in trying to explain the lovers' situation.

Chapter Four
From Tragedy to Comedy through the Legend of Good Women

"He thought the only end to isolation was to reach the point where he was no longer separated from the true struggles that went on around him. The name we give this point is history."

As we saw in relation to *Troilus and Criseyde*, scholarship has generally regarded Chaucer's classicism as a somewhat backward English instance of the general fourteenth-century development we now call humanism.[1] Its roots are understood to reside in both the recuperative movement initiated by Petrarch and, especially, Boccaccio and in the somewhat earlier and more recognizably medieval explorations of the so-called classicizing friars. Its motivating factor is usually taken to be either a disinterested effort to understand the past in its own terms or a more polemical desire to elicit from the reader an awareness of the saving Christian difference that separates him or her from a benighted pagan world.[2]

Neither of these accounts, despite their strengths, is wholly adequate. On the one hand, the argument of historical authenticity must slight the crucial difference—rightly insisted upon by earlier scholarship—between Chaucer's classical poems and those of his Italian models. Compared to the deliberate classicizing of Boccaccio's *Teseida*, for instance, the *Knight's Tale* is egregiously medieval: it con-

1. See chapter 1, above, 59–61, 78–83, for a more complete version of the argument of this paragraph.

2. For Alastair Minnis Chaucer's intention in the *Troilus* and the *Knight's Tale* is "to show how [the classical pagans] thought and behaved in their historical time and place" (*Chaucer and Pagan Antiquity* [Cambridge: Brewer, 1982], 6). For a similar argument, see V. A. Kolve, *Chaucer and the Imagery of Narrative* (Stanford: Stanford University Press, 1984), 86. For the argument of historical difference as a spur to religious reflection, see John R. McCall, *Chaucer Among the Gods* (University Park: Pennsylvania State University Press, 1979), 41.

tinually declares, as both my discussion and many others have sought to demonstrate, its contemporary interest.[3] While the *Teseida* is a medieval imitation of a classical poem, the *Knight's Tale* is a historical description designed to demonstrate not difference but continuity: its deliberate anachronisms reveal the deep historical imperatives that refigure the present into the form of the past. On the other hand, as the "humanist" critics have pointed out, the argument of religious difference must slight the intensity of the dilemmas in which Chaucer's protagonists find themselves, reducing them to moves in an interpretive game in which the Christian reader holds all the cards. While these poems do not mean to challenge either Christian truth or Boethian philosophy, they do put in question the self-justification of the historical life itself. Can history be founded upon a basis that will legitimize the human commitment to an earthly course? Or must we finally turn to a spiritual transcendence that annuls the historical life as a value in and of itself?

What must be added to this version of humanist inquiry is that, for Chaucer, the philosophical interrogation of history did not itself appear in a historically neutral form; on the contrary, it was the intellectual property of a specific social class. As *Troilus and Criseyde* implies, and as the *Knight's Tale* makes absolutely clear, the subject of history entered Chaucer's poetry in terms that were defined by noble culture. Put most simply, historical action is figured in these poems in the terms—love and war, Venus and Mars—in which the nobility habitually represented its central concerns to itself. But in a deeper sense, to understand history as a philosophical problem is to decide not to understand it in other, more socially specific and politically charged ways. The universalizing and essentializing impulses that motivate the philosophical understanding of history efface, as critics of humanism never tire of pointing out, history as local and particular, as a site of material practice and political action. This is, moreover, the kind of history in which the *Canterbury Tales* as a whole grounds itself.

In understanding Chaucer's poems of classical history as aristocratic productions, we should realize that antiquity was most insistently present to him as a central element of noble culture. I do not mean to argue that Chaucer did not read and learn from a wide range of materials dealing with the classical past, including the classicizing friars, the Italian humanists, and the classical poets themselves; nor do I wish to promote medieval historical texts like the *romans d'antiquité* as primary

3. For discussions of the contemporary relevance of the *Knight's Tale*, see chapter 3, note 7.

influences: Chaucer's poems are, after all, rewritings not of the *Roman de Troie* and the *Roman de Thèbes* but of the *Filostrato* and the *Teseida*. But I do mean to propose that within the social environment within which Chaucer wrote, classical history, whatever its sources, had become a form of knowledge that was marked as aristocratic; and that the *Knight's Tale* serves to foreground this class-specific character. Finally, by making explicit, perhaps as much to himself as to his reader, the social meaning of historiography Chaucer set aside a preoccupation that had absorbed him throughout the first part of his career as a writer, a liberating gesture that stands as the first step in the counterdefinition of the *Canterbury Tales*.

That Chaucer could have thought of classical history as a socially specific form of knowledge is an effect of its immense popularity with the late-medieval aristocracy. Not that such a use of the classical past is not visible in earlier periods: Einhard's *Vita Caroli*, for instance, was modeled on Suetonius's *De vita Caesarum*, and William of Poitiers described the Norman conquest of England in terms drawn from classical accounts of the Fall of Troy.[4] But it was in the second half of the twelfth century, with the writing of the *romans d'antiquité* and the Alexander romances, that medieval chivalry began fully to appropriate antiquity to its own ideological needs. This process accelerated in the early thirteenth century with the production of two huge prose histories that were to remain popular throughout the later Middle Ages. *Li Faits des Romains*—a work that Jacques Monfrin has called "one of the basic books of lay culture throughout the Middle Ages"—was composed in 1213–14; it is a rewriting of Caesar's *Commentaries* with liberal extracts from Suetonius, Sallust, and Lucan.[5] Similarly, the text scholars now call the *Histoire ancienne jusqu'à César*, written in its first form between 1223–30, used Orosius's chronology as the framework for a compilation from many different sources, including prose versions of the *ro-*

4.   On Einhard, see Lewis Thorpe, trans., *Two Lives of Charlemagne* (Harmondsworth: Penguin Books, 1969), 37–39; for the classicism of William of Poitiers's *Gesta Guillelmi Ducis Normannorum et Regis Anglorum*, see Ralph H. C. Davis, "William of Poitiers and His History of William the Conqueror," in *The Writing of History in the Middle Ages: Essays Presented to Richard William Southern*, ed. R. H. C. Davis and J. M. Wallace-Hadrill (Oxford: Clarendon Press, 1981), 78–100. A good survey of the chivalric appropriation of the classical past is provided by Maurice Keen, *Chivalry* (New Haven: Yale University Press, 1984), 107–13.

5.   Jacques Monfrin, "Les traducteurs et leur public en France au Moyen Age," in *L'humanisme médiéval dans les littératures romanes du XIIᵉ au XIVᵉ siècles*, ed. Anthime Fourrier (Paris: Klincksieck, 1964), 249.

mans d'antiquité.[6] Both these works were especially popular in the four-teenth and fifteenth centuries: Charles V of France owned five manu-scripts of the *Faits,* three of which also contained the *Histoire ancienne;* and it was during his reign, and probably under his patronage, that a second redaction of the *Histoire ancienne* was made.[7] Charles's father, John, had Livy translated (by Pierre Bersuire), and when Charles VI made a visit to Mont St. Michel in 1393, he took with him a book enti-tled "des Faiz de Troye, des Roumains, de Thèbes, de Alixandre," a collection that covered the full range of classical history.[8] We have al-ready seen how widespread knowledge of the Troy story was among the nobility in the later Middle Ages: to add three widely scattered examples, Troy books were owned by Guy of Warwick (d. 1315), by Isabelle of France, Edward II's queen (d. 1358), and by Philip the Bold (d. 1404)—and apparently by most other aristocrats as well.[9]

But it was not just the Troy story or the large compilations that at-tracted aristocratic interest. Charles d'Orleans was doubtless more bookish than most of his noble colleagues, but his library contained items that accurately reflect what Guenée has called "the historical cul-ture of the nobility."[10] He owned a book of *Julius Caesar* (probably Jean de Tuin's *Roman de Jules César,* a prose account based on Lucan), the *Chronique martinienne* in both Latin and French, the *Faits des Romans,* a *Histoire d'Alexandre,* "Le livre de Josephus des antiquitez et plusiers histoires des le commancement du monde, de Thebes et de Troyes" (a translation of Josephus's *Antiquities* had been begun under Charles V in

6.   For the *Histoire ancienne,* see Paul Meyer, "Les premières compilations françaises d'histoire ancienne," *Romania* 14 (1885): 36–76; for its use of the *romans d'antiquité,* see Guy Raynaud de Lage, *Le Moyen Age* 63 (1957): 267–309.

7.   Bernard Guenée, "La Culture historique des nobles: le succès des *Faits des Romains* (XIIIᵉ–XVᵉ siècles)," in *La Noblesse au Moyen Age,* ed. Philippe Contamine (Paris: Presses universitaires de France, 1976), 261–88; for Charles V's ownership, see 279–80. Manuscripts of the *Faits* were also owned by the Ducs de Berry, Orleans, and Burgundy, and the Duke of Bedford owned a copy when he died in 1435 (281).

8.   On John's patronage of Bersuire's translation, see Jacques Monfrin, "La traduc-tion française de Tite-Live," *Histoire littéraire de la France* (Paris: Imprimerie Nationale, 1962), 39:359–60. For Charles VI's book, see Richard Firth Green, *Poets and Princepleasers: Literature and the English Court in the Late Middle Ages* (Toronto: University of Toronto Press, 1980), 137.

9.   For aristocratic interest in the Troy story, see above, chapter 2, notes 19–34; for Guy, see Madelaine Blaess, "L'Abbaye de Bordesley et les livres de Guy de Beauchamp," *Romania* 78 (1957), 513; for Isabelle, see Tout, *Chapters in the Administrative History of Eng-land* (Manchester: Manchester University Press, 1933), 5:249; for Philip, Muriel J. Hughes, "The Library of Philip the Bold and Margaret of Flanders, first Valois Duke and Duchess of Burgundy," *JMH* 4 (1978): 145–88.

10.   See above, note 7.

1380 and completed under the patronage of Jean, Duc de Berry in 1404), Lucan (perhaps another version of Jean de Tuin's *Roman*, which was loosely based on the *Pharsalia*), Sallust's *Jugurtha* and *Cataline*, a French and a Latin Valerius Maximus (the Latin original was by far the most popular history of the Middle Ages, surviving in at least 419 manuscripts),[11] and four manuscripts of Virgil, one of which included Juvenal and another Statius's *Thebaid*.[12]

Charles was probably unusual, and it may also be true that the French aristocracy was better read than the English.[13] But perhaps not: Richard Green has pointed out the quite disproportionate number of works of classical history among the books of Edward IV now owned by the British Library.[14] It is clear that the late-medieval nobility as a whole were deeply interested in classical history, and that they regarded antiquity as the legitimizing origin of their own nobility. A striking instance of this genealogical imperative can be found in a passage from the funeral panegyric for Edward I, which has the knights of the realm lament their lord in the following terms:

> Once with Alexander, king of Macedon, we defeated the kings of the Medes and Persians and subdued the provinces of the East. Now, at the end of time, with great King Edward, we have borne a ten-year war with Philip, famous king of France; we have won back Gascony, taken by guile, with force of arms; we have got Wales by slaughter; we have invaded Scotland and cut down her tyrants at the point of the sword.[15]

11. Bernard Guenée, *Histoire et culture historique dans l'occident médiéval* (Paris: Aubier, 1980), 250.

12. Pierre Champion, *La Librairie de Charles d'Orléans* (Paris: Champion, 1910), 30, 32–33, 45, 55, 64, 70, 95–97, 107, 108, 112–14.

13. But see K. B. McFarlane, *The Nobility of Later Medieval England* (Oxford: Clarendon Press, 1973), 228–47.

14. Green, *Poets and Princepleasers*, 135–36; see also Margaret Kekewich, "Edward IV, William Caxton, and Literary Patronage in Yorkist England," *MLR* 66 (1971), 484–85.

15. "Commendatio lamentabilis in transitu magni regis Edwardi," *Chronicles of the Reigns of Edward I and Edward II*, Rolls Series, ed. W. Stubbs (London: Longmans, 1883), 2:14; cited and translated by Beryl Smalley, *English Friars and Antiquity in the Early Fourteenth Century* (Oxford: Basil Blackwell, 1960), 9. For the beginning of heraldry at Troy, see an English "Tretis of Armes" written about 1400 (Evan John Jones, *Medieval Heraldry: Some Fourteenth-Century Heraldic Works* [Cardiff: William Lewis, 1943], 213–14); the Sicily Herald designates Antenor as the first herald (Ferdinand Roland, ed., *Parties inédites de l'oeuvre de Sicile*, Société des Bibliophiles Belges de Mons 22 [Mons: DeQuesme-Masquillier, 1867], 121). Christine de Pisan's *Epistre d'Othea* is an elaborate moralization of chivalry by means of classical precedents: see George F. Warner, ed., *The Epistle of Othea to Hector*, trans. Stephen Scrope (London: Roxburghe Club, 1904), 94–95.

The classical past and the medieval present are seamlessly continuous, tied together by the shared virtues of chivalry: as knights did in the past, so do they now, and so they shall continue to do (as Theseus says) "for everemo."[16]

Chaucer's two major essays in classical historiography were both, as we have seen, an investigation at the level of philosophical generality of the perils of the aristocratic historical consciousness, the danger hidden in the genealogical presupposition that value descends from an omnipotent past. In both the *Troilus* and the *Knight's Tale* the present is not empowered but subverted by its inheritance from the past, and the purposive line of history twists back into an imprisoning circle: first Troy and then Athens is undone by a specular Theban subtext. And the historical moment that Chaucer used to represent the past in these poems is the antiquity that the aristocratic world took as its own. In the *Troilus* this social location is assumed; in the *Knight's Tale* it becomes part of the meaning of the text.

If we are fully to understand the complexity of Chaucer's relation both to classicism and to nobility, and the role of both in the initiation of the *Canterbury Tales*, we must turn briefly to one other poem, the *Legend of Good Women*. As we have seen, the *Legend* is the road not taken after the *Troilus:* in its representation of character (the self as object), principle of organization (an externally imposed homology), historical siting (antiquity), and social valence (aristocratic) it represents all that the *Canterbury Tales* is not. And in its account of the relation of the poet to the aristocratic audience presupposed by his early poetry, and in its version of the Thesean virtue that serves the *Knight's Tale* as its central value, it can help us to see how the *Knight's Tale* serves the *Canterbury Tales* as that which it must summon up and then reject in order to be itself.[17]

---

16. In fact, in some accounts Theseus himself was the founder of chivalry: see Ranulf Higden, *Polychronicon*, ed. Churchill Babington, Rolls Series (London: Longmans, 1885), 2:381–95; and John Lydgate, *Fall of Princes*, ed. Henry Bergen (Washington: Carnegie Institution, 1923–27), Book 1, line 4400 (1:122).

17. While the *Legend* is traditionally dated 1386–88, there are no certain grounds for that assertion; all we can be reasonably sure of is that it was after the *Troilus* was finished and had been circulating within court circles. J. D. North dates the horoscope in the *Legend of Hypermnestra* January 3, 1391; and he dates the *Man of Law's Tale*, whose *Prologue* mentions the *Legend*, May 13, 1394: "Kalenderes Enlumyned Ben They: Some Astronomical Themes in Chaucer," *RES*, n.s. 20 (1969), 268–69, 426–31. John Tatlock's arguments for a date for the *Prologue* before Usk's death in March 1388 are not especially persuasive: see *The Development and Chronology of Chaucer's Works*, Chaucer Society, 2d ser., 37 (London: Trübner, 1907), 22–23. Chaucer was evidently still working on the *Prologue* after June 1394, when Queen Anne died; and in the revision he did not

I

The *Legend of Good Women* registers Chaucer's desire to escape from subjection to a court, and to aristocratic values generally, that are felt as increasingly tyrannical. The waking section of the *Prologue* establishes a set of oppositions: "joy in hevene" versus "peyne in helle" (2), the "brightnesse" of daylight versus the "derknesse" of night (63–64), "th'attempre sonne" of spring versus winter's "sword of cold" (127–28).[18] These oppositions are aligned with another, familiar Chaucerian distinction: things that "men han sen with ye" (11) versus "olde appreved stories" (21), the "reverence" (52) lavished on the daisy versus the "reverence" and "devocioun" (39) due to books. In the waking segment this opposition is resolved in favor of the first, experiential term. Books are set aside in order to indulge in daisy worship, and songs invoked as authorities give way before the poet's instinctive, untutored hymn of praise: "As an harpe obeieth to the honde / And maketh it soune after his fyngerynge" (90–91), so is the poet's heart inspired by the daisy to an act of instinctive poeticizing (92–96). Indeed, he stages this inspiration in the very act of speaking the poem, insisting that even now he remains possessed by the recollected emotion of his love. "I may not al at-ones speke in ryme," he says breathlessly:

> My besy gost, that thursteth alwey newe
> To seen this flour so yong, so fressh of hewe,
> Constreyned me with so gledy desir
> That in myn herte I feel *yet* the fir
> That made me to ryse er yt were day. (102–7)

The power of his desire preempts both books and talk about books: what absorbs his attention are not "olde appreved stories" but the "resureccioun / Of this flour" (110–11).

The poet's fervent experience of daisy worship thus fends off appropriation by the authority of literary tradition and especially by the courtly rivalry between the flower and the leaf (188–96). Chaucer takes

---

remove the reference to the poem about Palamon and Arcite, despite the likelihood that he had long since initiated the *Canterbury Tales,* in which it became the *Knight's Tale:* see Charles A. Owen, *Pilgrimage and Storytelling in the* Canterbury Tales (Norman: University of Oklahoma Press, 1977), 35–36.

18. All citations from the *Prologue* are from the earlier, pre-1394 F-version.

pains to stress the independence of his daisy worship from the cultic practice of courtly game. His experience is prior to these social forms; an event that took place "er swich stryf was begonne" (196), it is represented as presocial if not pretextual, an instinctive, unmediated, almost prelapsarian affinity between man and the natural world. Yet once he enters the world of the dream—the traditional locale for courtly poetry—just this feared absorption into contemporary social and textual forms occurs. The heliotropic calling of daisy to sun that he celebrated while awake is now refigured as the sovereignty of the tyrannical God of Love over his sacrificial consort Alceste. What was before an instinctive symbiosis here becomes hierarchy, and the "gledy desire" that moved the poet is now absorbed into "the craft of fyn lovynge" (544). The poet is arraigned for his crimes against *gentillesse* and condemned to return to the "bookes" (556) and "olde auctours" (575) from which his holiday mood had turned him. For it is there that he will find his subject matter, in the pantheon of classical heroines who are the female counterparts to the antique models of martial heroism that inspire contemporary knights. Once again he must glean the field of classical history.[19]

In the event he enacts his revenge upon authority in a number of ways: by radically deforming his *auctores*, by unmasking the misogynist violence that underwrites Alceste's version of feminine virtue, by simply refusing to fulfill his commission. But the form of resistance of most interest to us now is the irony with which he treats the noble cult of "fyn lovynge": subject to the intransigent and uncomprehending demands of a *gentil* audience, the poet in turn subjects *gentillesse* itself to relentless critique. Throughout the *Legends* the promise of *gentillesse* is one of the attractions that men use to deceive their feminine victims. Antony, despite forsaking Octavia, is "a ful worthy gentil werreyour" (597) endowed with a "gentillesse" (610) that, among other things, makes him irresistible to Cleopatra. Aeneas seems to Dido "lyk to ben a verray gentil man" (1068): he "hadde a noble visage for the nones" (1070), "wel a lord he semede for to be" (1074), and her pity is aroused by the thought "that evere swich a noble man as he/ Shal ben disherited in swich degre" (1964–65). Hence when she is abandoned she plaintively protests that "*I* am a gentil woman and a queen" (1306), while the

19. That the *Legend* is conceived as a work of history is made clear by Chaucer's repeated use of the word "storie" to describe its form: see, for instance, 21, 98, 421, 576, 618, 1153, 1161, 1684, 1825, 1888, 2239, 2243, 2257, 2364, and 2484. And that when used generically the Middle English word "storie" means "history" is demonstrated by Paul Strohm, "*Storie, Spelle, Geste, Romaunce, Tragedie:* Generic Distinctions in Middle English Troy Narratives," *Speculum* 46 (1971): 348–59.

supportive narrator scornfully comments on the behavior "of this grete gentil-man" (1264), Aeneas. When Hypsipyle first observes Jason and Hercules she carefully notes that they are "gentil-men of grete degree" (1506); and she then falls prey to Hercules' account of Jason as "so gret a gentilman . . . / And of Thessalye likly kyng to be" (1532–33)—a gross exaggeration of his future prospects. Jason's villainy is directed specifically against "gentil women" (1370)—"To don with gentil women his delyt, / This is his lust and his felicite" (1587–88)—for strategic reasons: as the examples of both Medea (who is attracted to "his lok as real as a leoun" [1605]) and Hypsipyle show, they are easily deceived by a man who fulfills their social expectations.

In the world of the legends *gentillesse* designates not nobility of spirit but social advantage, a superiority of place that unprincipled men use to victimize grasping women. This biting attitude toward aristocratic pretensions is most explicit, significantly, in the section of the poem that bears most directly on the *Knight's Tale,* the *Legend of Ariadne.* Ariadne's pity for Theseus—the "pite" that "renneth soone in gentil herte" in the *Prologue* (503)—is aroused by the idea of "a kynges sone . . . in swich prysoun" (1975), of a "woful lordes sone" (1979) who has fallen into "povre estat" (1981). Theseus himself assures Ariadne that in return for her help he will serve her as a page, even though he is "a kynges sone and ek a knyght" (2055), a phrase that she repeats back to him in assuring him that "a kynges sone and ek a knyght" (2080) should not abase himself "to ben my servant in so low degre" (2081). "Ye ben as gentil born as I" (2090), she carefully notes, a *gentillesse* that, in its most thoroughly materialized form, then persuades her and Phaedra to commit themselves to Theseus's escape. For Theseus offers to make her duchess of Athens and to betroth her sister to his son, an offer that Ariadne enthusiastically accepts. "Now syster myn," she says,

Now be we duchesses, bothe I and ye,
And sekered to the regals of Athenes,
And bothe hereafter likly to ben quenes;
And saved from his deth a kynges sone,
As evere of *gentil* women is the wone
To save a *gentyl* man, emforth hire myght,
In honest cause, and namely in his ryght. (2127–33)

"Pite" does indeed "renneth soone in gentil herte": *gentillesse* is a claim to social superiority that tries and fails to dignify the appetite by which the inhabitants of this world are at once driven and undone.

The *Legend of Ariadne's* sardonic critique of *gentillesse* is absent from the *Knight's Tale,* since the *Tale* does not allow for a perspective outside its own ideology. But it is present, of course, in the *Miller's Tale* and elsewhere in the *Canterbury Tales:* in that sense, the *Legend of Ariadne* is Chaucer's own commentary on the assumptions that make the *Knight's Tale* possible but which it cannot itself make visible. This does not mean, however, that the relevance of the *Legend* to the *Tale* is only by implication. While it is impossible to specify the chronological relationship between these two poems with certainty, they have clear textual affinities that suggest that Chaucer thought of them together. For one thing, Theseus's prison "was joynynge in the wal to a foreyne" (1962) or privy, from within which Ariadne and Phaedra overhear his complaints—a mocking prefiguration, or echo, of Arcite's and Palamon's prison tower "evene joynant to the gardyn wal / Ther as this Emelye hadde hir pleyynge" (1060–61). For another, Theseus promises to serve in Minos's court as a "page" (2037) if the sisters will help him, and actually claims to have loved Ariadne "this sevene yer" (2120) even "thogh ye ne wiste it nat" (2116)—empty assertions that Palamon and Arcite make good.[20] More important, in the *Legend of Ariadne* Chaucer applies directly to Theseus the fatal pattern of recursiveness that is in the *Knight's Tale* embodied in the Theban cousins and attributed to him only by implication; and in the *Tale* itself he changed the chronology of Theseus's career as Boccaccio had presented it in order to stress the relevance of the events of the *Legend* to the action of the *Tale.*

The *Legend of Ariadne* is structured according to a pattern of betrayal and revenge. The story Chaucer tells begins with the death of Androgeos, an innocent victim of Athenian "envye" (1899) whose murder ignites a cycle of vengeance. When in order "to wreke" (1901) his son's death Minos invades Greece and besieges Nisus's Megara, the citadel is handed over by Nisus's daughter Scylla, who is then herself discarded by Minos. Minos is then in turn deceived by *his* daughters Ariadne and Phaedra, only for Ariadne to be abandoned by Theseus; and Theseus, albeit inadvertently, misleads his father

20. John Livingstone Lowes argued that the passages in the *Legend of Ariadne* that seem to allude to the *Knight's Tale* were derived directly from the *Teseida,* that the *Legend* was written before the *Knight's Tale,* and therefore—since he identified the "Palamon and Arcite" mentioned in the *Prologue* with the *Knight's Tale*—before the *Prologue.* Quite apart from this improbable sequence of composition, Lowes's argument assumes that Chaucer's courtly sensibility would not have allowed him to write the ugly scene of Ariadne and Phaedra overhearing Theseus from a privy after writing the beautiful scene of Emily being seen by Palamon and Arcite in the garden ("The Prologue to the *Legend of Good Women* Considered in its Chronological Relations," *PMLA* 20 [1905]: 749–864).

Aegeus by forgetting to change his black sails to white and so causing Aegeus to plunge into the sea in despair—a forgetfulness by which the gods avenge (1892) Theseus's rejection of Ariadne. Thus we have a series of betrayals: Androgeos–Athenians, Nisus–Scylla, Scylla–Minos–Ariadne, Ariadne–Theseus, Aegeus–Theseus—a repeated pattern in which Theseus is inextricably entangled and that will continue into the future. For as we have already seen, when his wife Phaedra seeks to deceive him with his son Hippolytus, he is persuaded to betray Hippolytus as well, who dies in a manner that recalls Aegeus's earlier death and even prefigures Theseus's own betrayal at the hands of Lycomedes, who cast him down into the sea from a cliff.

The compulsions of this pattern and its thematic relevance to the *Knight's Tale* are clear enough; and if in the *Tale* Theseus himself seems at first sight to have left the darker aspects of his legend behind him, on closer inspection it appears that Chaucer undid that Boccaccian reformation. Mythographers generally agreed that Theseus's Cretan adventure, and the abandonment of Ariadne and marriage with Phaedra, occurred in his youth, preceding both his campaign against the Amazons and the birth of Hippolytus. Boccaccio, however, wanting to suppress both the abandonment of Ariadne and the extramarital relationship with Hippolyta because they undermined his celebratory purpose, placed the campaign against the Amazons before the Cretan adventure. Thus he carefully included Minos as one of the guests at the tournament, "for he had not yet felt grief for his comely Androgeos," the son whose death in Athens initiated the sacrifice of Athenian youths that Theseus's killing of the Minotaur ended.[21] But Chaucer returned to the traditional order by ostentatiously invoking Theseus's Cretan prehistory at the beginning of the *Tale:* when he rides off against Creon, Theseus unfurls the banner of "the Mynotaur, which that he slough in Crete" (980). Duplicitous in character as in fate, Theseus does indeed march under the sign of the Minotaur, the *monstrum biformis* (as both Virgil and Ovid called him) that expresses dou-

21.   Bernadette McCoy, trans., *The Book of Theseus* (New York: Medieval Text Association, 1974), 153. In another place, however, Boccaccio makes an error in Teseo's career: when Teseo leaves for Thebes he says that he is not seeking to conquer the kingdom as a patrimony for Demophoon, who was Phaedra's son and therefore not yet born. That Theseus's highly syncretic myth caused chronological problems is also shown by an error in the First Vatican Mythographer, who has the plan by which Hippolytus was killed concocted by Aegeus, who was usually said to have committed suicide when Theseus returned from Crete with black sails (Georg Bode, ed., *Scriptores rerum mythicarum Latini tres Romae nuper reperti* [Celle: Schulze, 1834], 1:17)—that is, long before Hippolytus was born.

bleness in a single figure.[22] And as a manifest example of a late-medieval heraldic *insignum* or "tokyn of nobleness," the Minotaur provides a dark commentary on contemporary habits of self-identification.

Alceste's penance in the *Prologue* sought to return Chaucer himself to an earlier state, back to the antiquity that had provided the subject of *Troilus and Criseyde* and the historical form for noble self-understanding. In both the *Legend of Ariadne* and the *Knight's Tale* he meditates on and finally rejects this return; in the remainder of the *Canterbury Tales* he marks out a way forward. The road not taken in the Chaucerian career is the way of historical tragedy that reaches its climax in the *Troilus* and that in the *Knight's Tale* and the *Legend of Good Women* is definitively set aside. At the end of the "tragedye" (5, 1786) of the *Troilus* the poet designated an alternative way when he prayed God to "sende som myght to make in som comedye" (5, 1788). It is with the *Canterbury Tales* that this prayer was answered.[23]

In the Middle Ages the contrast between tragedy and comedy turned on three variables: the high style of tragedy versus the mixed style of comedy, the tragic curve from "wele to wo" versus the ascending curve of comedy, and the difference in subject matter.[24] While all three of these criteria are relevant to the *Tales*, the last distinction is perhaps most central. Tragedy deals with the world of public events— of history—in which the socially exalted enact their inevitable fate: according to Donatus, "tragedy aspires to historical truth" (29), and as the Monk succinctly says, "tragedie is . . . a certein *storie*" (1973), that is, a history. Comedy, on the other hand, describes not events but, as one medieval description of Terence puts it, the "mores hominum, iuvenumque senumque" (34). In effect, the subject matter of comedy is character: it seeks to represent men and women not in terms of their social existence but as individuals. According to the schoolbook definitions, it concerns itself with *privatae personae, privati homines, res*

22. Virgil, *Aeneid* 6, 25; Ovid, *Metamorphoses* 8, 156. Theseus's doubleness and its connection to the Minotaur in the doubled labyrinth is the theme of Ariadne's letter in *Heroides* 10 (see especially lines 102, 127–28).

23. For the *Tales* as a comedy, see Paul Theiner, "The Medieval Terence," in *The Lerned and the Lewed*, ed. Larry Benson (Cambridge: Harvard University Press, 1974), 231–48. In the Prologue to the *Fall of Princes* Lydgate refers to Chaucer's "comedyes" (line 246).

24. Wilhelm Cloetta, *Beiträge zur Literaturgeschichte des Mittelalters und der Renaissance*, 1: *Komödie und Tragödie im Mittelalter* (Halle: Niemeyer, 1890), 28; subsequent references will be included in the text. See also Strohm, "*Storie, Spelle, Geste, Romaunce, Tragedie*," 356.

privatorum et humilium personarum.[25] And perhaps because it conceives of the person apart from social role, comedy is typically understood by the Middle Ages as a socially antithetical form. According to some medieval commentators, it is a peasant's song or *cantus villanus;* Vincent of Beauvais's *Speculum historiale* claims that the form is derived originally from rustic harvest festivals at which each laborer would describe "the condition of his life"; and another medieval text calls it a "carmen aptum comestioni"—a song for feasting.[26] In sum, comedy is socially humble, realistic in its mode of representation, and festive in its occasion; and its subject matter is the private person—what we would call the individual or perhaps even, as does Chaucer in *Troilus and Criseyde,* the "hertes privete" (4, 1111).

A tale-telling game that invokes a wide range of festive forms, an insistently "voiced" text that foregrounds character at every turn, a collection organized according to intrinsic and self-generating formal principles, and a contest that gives full play to social antagonisms and grants unexpected authority to the voices of the socially ignoble: the *Canterbury Tales* is a comedy that declares its difference from historical tragedy at every turn. This does not mean, however, that it is itself an ahistorical form. On the contrary, its definition as socially oppositional firmly situates it within a historical world conceived not as the past but the present, and not philosophically but materially, as the site of specific and surprisingly antagonistic practices. As the next chapter will argue, when Chaucer comes to define a mode of writing that can serve as the alternative to the noble discourse of the *Knight's Tale,* it is to the highly politicized *cantus villanus* of the *Miller's Tale* that he turns. That this alternative should prove in the event to be far too explicitly oppositional for Chaucer should again not surprise us, and in the rest of the opening movement of the *Tales* he seeks out a placement from which he can observe his world. "I wot myself best how y stonde" (1878), he had said in the *House of Fame;* the *Canterbury Tales* records the process of turning that sense of independence into a poetic program.

25. These definitions come, respectively, from Donatus, Isidore, and Lactantius Placidus; all are cited from Cloetta, *Komödie und Tragödie,* 28, 19, and 21.

26. See Cloetta, *Komödie und Tragödie,* 34, 46–47. This social definition is also important to Dante, who uses the terms "tragedy" and "comedy" in contexts that might well have attracted Chaucer's attention. In the *Letter to Can Grande,* Dante derives comedy "from *comus,* 'a village,' and *oda,* which is, 'song'; whence comedy is, as it were, 'rustic song' " (10). In *Inferno* 20 Virgil refers to "l'alta mia tragedìa" (113) and in canto 21, Dante counters by calling his own poem "la mia comedìa" (2): canto 20 deals with the classical world of soothsayers, while canto 21 introduces the travelers into the world, wholly foreign to Virgil, of the slangy, vulgar devils.

Chapter Five
The Miller's Tale *and the Politics of Laughter*

"Facts, words, historic ideas. He struggled against his fate, yes, exactly, like someone in the social universe of Marx. He believed genuinely in high principles and aims even if he was not yet assured of a sense of perspective."

The *Knight's Tale* represents in its narrative and exemplifies by its mode of narration the crisis of governance experienced by the fourteenth-century aristocracy. With the Miller's drunken interruption, we know that this crisis has encroached upon the tale-telling game of the Canterbury pilgrims. When Harry Bailly calls upon the Monk to tell "somewhat to quite with the Knightes tale" (3119), his choice shows that he is dutifully organizing the game according to the conservative program of the three orders: first the *miles*, then his clerical counterpart, the *monachus*.[1] But the Miller will have none of it, and by his intervention not only subverts the social hierachy but substitutes his own principle of order. "I kan a noble tale for the nones," he says, "with which I wol now quite the Knyghtes tale" (3126–27), and his tale enacts the very "quitting" it narrates. What happens to Absolon, Nicholas, and John *in* the *Miller's Tale*, in other words, happens to the Knight *by means of* the *Miller's Tale*. Indeed, in his aggressive misreading of the Host's words, whose "quite" means "reward" but which the Miller reinterprets as "retaliate," he allows into the tale-telling game the linguistic subversion that characterizes his own *Tale*, in which words such as "derne," "hende," "pryvetee," and "berd," and even the innocuous "water," are all revealed to have meanings that subvert or "quite" their conven-

---

1. For the relation of the Knight to the Monk, see Robert A. Kaske, "The Knight's Interruption of the *Monk's Tale*," *ELH* 24 (1957): 249–68.

tional and intended meanings.[2] So too is his interruption a subversion of form. The principle of hierarchy derived from the three orders is set aside in favor of an internally generated and self-sustaining principle of "quiting." The tale-telling game, in short, becomes itself a fabliau and is apparently henceforth to be governed by the fabliau principle— explicitly announced by the Reeve—of *ars ut artem falleret*.[3]

With the Miller's interruption, Chaucer thus sets aside a principle of order sanctioned by social authority in favor of one derived from a literary form that continually proclaims its own marginality. More generally, he asserts that the dynamic of the *Canterbury Tales* will be self-generating rather than derivative, that in its spontaneity and self-discovery it will resist mechanical and externally imposed structural dispositions, and especially those—such as estates satire—expressive of the established institutions of social authority. And yet as soon as this experiment in form is proclaimed it begins to be called into question. In its bitter "quiting" of the Miller the Reeve's "jape of malice" (4338) indulges the fabliau's dark undercurrent of violence and victimization that the *Miller's Tale* managed to contain if not fully to efface, while the Cook then introduces a tale in which the Reeve's "cherles termes" now delineate a world of *Lumpenproletariat* squalor and moral anarchy. With his interruption the Miller seems to have allowed entrance into the pilgrimage of a "harlotrie" (3184) and "ribaudye" (3866) that has debased the "game and pley" (4335) of tale telling itself.

But despite this apparent failure, Chaucer provocatively returns to precisely the same structure in the second movement of the *Tales* (Fragments II–III), and now with the Wife of Bath as his revisionary agent. After the Man of Law has completed his "thrifty tale" (1165) of Constance, the Host calls upon the Parson to continue. "I se wel," he says, "that ye lerned men in lore / Can moche good" (1168–69), and despite the Parson's censoriousness the Host encourages him in his "predicacioun" (1176). But the Wife of Bath now reenacts the Miller's earlier subversion: " 'Nay, by my fader soule, that shal he nat,' / Seyde the [Wyf of Bathe],

2. For some of these puns, see E. Talbot Donaldson, "The Idiom of Popular Poetry in the *Miller's Tale*," *English Institute Essays*, 1950 (New York: Columbia University Press, 1951), 116–40.

3. As Alfred David says, "A case could be made that the whole pilgrimage had to be invented for the sake of the fabliaux" (*The Strumpet Muse: Art and Morals in Chaucer's Poetry* [Bloomington: Indiana University Press, 1976], 106.) See also Traugott Lawler's argument that the *Canterbury Tales* as a whole is "a kind of meta-fabliau" (*The One and the Many in the* Canterbury Tales [Hamden: Archon Books, 1980], 39).

'schal he nat preche'" (1178–79), and she herself becomes the "noble prechour" (III, 165) whom she has displaced.[4] And with her interruption the Wife initiates a line of development—both in the limited scope of the so-called Marriage Group and in the extended pattern of binary opposition that governs the articulation of the *Tales* throughout—that will continue until the definitive cancellation of the *Canterbury Tales* finally accomplished by the long-deferred Parson.

Why does the Wife of Bath's interruption succeed while the Miller's fails? The answer to this question is, I believe, best framed in political terms: the Miller's challenge is articulated in explicitly class terms and is as a result too explicitly threatening, while the Wife's is deflected into a traditional mode of ideological opposition—that is, into promoting the claims of a socially undetermined subjectivity, traditionally thought to be possessed by women, that stands apart from *all* forms of class consciousness. In other words, Chaucer begins by posing his opposition to the dominant ideology in terms of class antagonism, but then retreats by setting up as his privileged category subjectivity per se, the free-floating individual whose needs and satisfactions stand outside any social structure. The Miller's peasant self-assertiveness is immediately registered as threatening, and the subsequent development of Fragment I serves to contain this threat by stigmatizing it as not merely disruptive of social order but destructive of its own holiday gaiety. Then in Fragments II–III this containment is given a definitive form first by the Wife of Bath, with her privileging of a subjectivity that is presented as politically inert, and then in the complementary tales of the Friar and Summoner, in which peasant self-assertiveness is both dissipated into internecine squabbling among ecclesiastical agents and appropriated, at the end of the *Summoner's Tale*, by seigneurial authority. And while we may see this move as politically timid, it was nonetheless crucial to Chaucer's subsequent dominance of our literary tradition. For it is as the great champion of the individual that Chaucer has displaced his rivals (like Gower and, especially, Langland—both of whom haunt the *Canterbury Tales* as rejected possibilities) in order to established himself as the Father of English Poetry.

4. I have adopted the emendation proposed by E. Talbot Donaldson, ed., *Chaucer's Poetry*, 2d ed. (New York: Ronald Press, 1975), 190. Donaldson has defended this emendation in "The Ordering of the *Canterbury Tales*," in *Medieval Literature and Folklore Studies: Essays in Honor of Francis Lee Utley*, ed. Jerome Mandel and Bruce A. Rosenberg (New Brunswick: Rutgers University Press, 1970), 201–3. For my reliance on the Ellesmere order, which entails accepting the authenticity of the *Man of Law's Endlink*, see above, Introduction, 41–44.

I

If we are fully to understand the social meaning of the first eight *Canterbury Tales*, we must revise our conventional understanding of the shape of fourteenth-century society. Specifically, we must dispense with the ideas that the most dynamic element of late-medieval English society was the city and that the agents of historical progress were merchants. On the contrary, we must realize that the most powerful forces for economic and social change were generated in the country, and that the agents of these changes were agrarian workers (like the Miller) and rural small-commodity producers (like the Wife of Bath). For literary critics, this is an understanding that requires a shift in assumptions. For we have instinctively assumed that medieval society can still be understood in terms of an opposition between the *Naturalwirtschaft* of an economically inert, socially repressive, and culturally backward country and the *Geldwirtschaft* of an innovative, mobile, and avant-garde town. But this account has come under attack both for its political assumptions and for its simplification of the historical evidence.

What underwrites the traditional account is the assumption that the town—and the open market that is its raison d'être—is the solvent of the feudal mode of production: urban freedom from the reciprocal dependencies of feudalism allows for the creation of a free-floating individual, capable of entering into contractual relations; labor is divided into the specializations necessary for the eventual triumph of industrialization; and an emergent civic humanism provides the foundations for the development of parliamentary democracy. What has been widely if tacitly accepted, in other words, is the familiar and oddly inescapable Whig interpretation of history, with the heroic bourgeoisie, here instantiated in the form of the medieval merchant adventurer, as history's prime mover.[5] As R. J. Holton has recently pointed out, this account depends upon the classic Enlightenment notion that history proceeds "in terms of the progressive realisation of a system of 'natural liberty' achievable through free market relations. . . . The assumption is that given the removal of barriers economic freedom (or 'capitalism') becomes established of itself."[6]

    5. Herbert F. Butterfield, *The Whig Interpretation of History* (London: G. Bell, 1931).
    6. R. J. Holton, *The Transition from Feudalism to Capitalism* (New York: St. Martin's Press, 1985), 35, 38–39. For a recent version of the orthodox account, see Carlo M. Cipolla, *Before the Industrial Revolution: European Society and Economy, 1000–1700*, 2d ed. (New York: Norton, 1980 [1976]), for whom "the urban movement of the eleventh to thirteenth centuries [was] the turning point of world history. . . . The urban revolution of the eleventh and twelfth centuries was the prelude to, and created the prerequisites for, the Industrial Revolution of the nineteenth century" (146, 149).

Even if one reads the changes brought about by the rise of a money economy negatively, the essential terms of the analysis do not change. Rather than arguing that individuals are now free to determine their own economic fates for themselves, with a consequent increase in innovative entrepreneurialism and technological development, we could instead, in a quasi-Marxist way, describe these changes in terms of the infection of personal relations with the cash nexus, the subjection of natural value to the relentless commodification of the market, and the transformation of the worker, who under feudalism was either himself part of the means of production or, better yet, possessed them, into an alienated wage laborer. But such a neo-Smithian Marxism, as it has been cogently termed, still sees the agency of economic and social transformation as the town-based market economy—and still stigmatizes the country as a regressive brake upon the productive forces.[7]

In fact, political interests quite apart, the idea that the dynamic of late-medieval society can be understood in terms of the opposition between a feudal natural economy and a capitalist money economy has been for many years under attack by medieval historians.[8] Over forty years ago, M. M. Postan called the rise of the money economy "one of the residuary hypotheses of economic history: a *deus ex machina* to be called upon when no other explanation is available"—cautionary words that have had too little impact upon literary critics.[9] Similarly

---

7.   Robert Brenner, "The Origins of Capitalist Development: A Critique of Neo-Smithian Marxism," *New Left Review* 104 (1977): 25–82. This is not to say that Marx himself does not provide the materials for such an analysis, as in the chapter on money in the *Grundrisse: Foundations of the Critique of Political Economy*, trans. Martin Nicolaus (Harmondsworth: Penguin Books, 1973 [1857–58]), especially 156–58. For Marx's varying views on the transition from feudalism to capitalism, see Holton, *Transition*, 64–102; J. S. Neale, "Introduction," in *Feudalism, Capitalism and Beyond*, ed. Eugene Kamenka and J. S. Neale (Canberra: Australian National University Press, 1975), 3–27; and Jon Elster, *Making Sense of Marx* (Cambridge: Cambridge University Press, 1985), 301–17.

8.   See especially M. M. Postan, *Medieval Trade and Finance* (Cambridge: Cambridge University Press, 1973); *Essays on Medieval Agriculture and General Problems of the Medieval Economy* (Cambridge: Cambridge University Press, 1973); *The Medieval Economy and Society* (Harmondsworth: Penguin Books, 1975 [1972]); and Georges Duby, *Rural Economy and Country Life in the Medieval West*, trans. Cynthia Postan (Columbia: South Carolina University Press, 1968).

9.   M. M. Postan, "The Rise of a Money Economy," *Economic History Review* 14 (1944), reprinted in *Essays on Medieval Agriculture and General Problems of the Medieval Economy* (Cambridge: Cambridge University Press, 1973), 28. Chaucerians for whom the rise of the money economy is a central interpretive category include R. A. Shoaf, *Dante, Chaucer, and the Currency of the Word* (Norman: Pilgrim Books, 1983) and Stephen Knight, *Geoffrey Chaucer* (Oxford: Blackwell, 1985).

oversimple is the notion that the changes in late-medieval English society can be understood as a struggle between progressive urban centers dominated by a mobile bourgeoisie and free citizenry and, ranged against them, a hierarchical and static rural feudalism dominated by a conservative nobility and Church. It is clear, for example, that the agrarian economy was thoroughly monetized and exchange oriented throughout the Middle Ages, that peasant society had been for many centuries highly stratified and differentiated, and that there existed since at least the twelfth century a vigorous, monetized, and even credit-based peasant land market, a market for agricultural wage labor, and small-scale but essential rural industry and commodity production.[10] Similarly, both lay and ecclesiastical landlords were engaged in sophisticated techniques of estate management and in the calculative pursuit of profit maximization,[11] many members of the seigneurial class were deeply involved in the world of international trade,[12] and even the quintessentially noble activity of warfare was pervaded with the values of the cash nexus.[13] Finally, the notion that medieval cities were "non-feudal islands in a feudal sea"—while pointing to an important truth—can too easily be exaggerated.[14] If in theory *Stadtluft machts frei*, in practice a city like London tightly restricted access to citizenship, while civic life as a whole was dominated by a conservative merchant patriciate that imposed upon the city much the same structure of domi-

10. Rodney H. Hilton, *The English Peasantry in the Later Middle Ages* (Oxford: Clarendon Press, 1975); and Hilton, *Class Conflict and the Crisis of Feudalism* (London: Hambledon Press, 1985); see also P. D. A. Harvey, ed., *The Peasant Land Market in Medieval England* (Oxford: Clarendon Press, 1984).

11. For the role of monasticism in the development of the calculative pursuit of profit maximization that, following Sombart and Weber, is usually regarded as the central characteristic of capitalism, see H. E. Hallam, "The Medieval Social Picture," in Kamenka and Neale, *Feudalism, Capitalism, and Beyond*, 29–49. On landlords' adaptation to changed circumstances, see the general account given by Harry A. Miskimin, *The Economy of Early Renaissance Europe, 1300–1460* (Cambridge: Cambridge University Press, 1975 [1969]), 32–47; and K. B. McFarlane, *The Nobility of Later Medieval England* (Oxford: Clarendon Press, 1973): "All the evidence suggests that most of the landowners of our period—*all* who have left any records—were well able to take care of their property, and if they got the chance, of their neighbours' also. The indolent, the vacillating, or the feebly good-intentioned would not long have had any estates to enjoy" (53).

12. On the aristocratic participation in trade, see Sylvia Thrupp, *The Merchant Class of Medieval London* (Ann Arbor: University of Michigan Press, 1962 [1948]), 243–44, 256–63; T. H. Lloyd, *The English Wool Trade in the Middle Ages* (Cambridge: Cambridge University Press, 1977) entitles his fifth chapter, "Edward III—Woolmonger Extraordinary."

13. See above, chapter 3, 172–74.

14. Postan, *Medieval Economy and Society*, 239.

nance and subordination as was in force across the feudal world as a whole.[15]

It has been argued that what this revisionary history demonstrates is that feudalism was really capitalism writ small, a variant on the Whig thesis that capitalism represents the natural condition of economic man.[16] The most vigorous alternative to this account is that offered by recent Marxist historians, for whom the key component of *all* nonsocialist economies is the governing classes' exploitation of the producers in order to extract surplus value.[17] These historians understand feudalism not simply as an inefficient means by which the individual seeks to fulfill his economic destiny but as a mode of production characterized by the *direct* rather than indirect exploitation of labor by the ruling classes. Similarly, markets—and the cities that developed around them—represent not an alternative to the feudal mode of production but, given the need of the exploiting class to extract surplus value in the form of money, an element necessary for the proper functioning of the feudal economy.[18] For Marx, medieval merchant capital was never itself progressive or transformative but remained parasitic upon the truly productive forces of society—forces that had always been and

15. See below, chapter 7, 329–30.

16. This argument has been most vigorously advanced by Alan Macfarlane, *The Origins of English Individualism* (Oxford: Blackwell, 1978), and in his subsequent work. For a useful analysis, see K. D. M. Snell, "English Historical Continuity and the Culture of Capitalism: The Work of Alan Macfarlane," *History Workshop* 27 (1989):154–63.

17. The crucial figures here are Rodney Hilton (see note 10), Maurice Dobb, and Robert Brenner. The central topic of their work is the nature of the transition from feudalism to capitalism: see Rodney Hilton, ed., *The Transition from Feudalism to Capitalism* (London: Verso, 1978)—a collection of essays, mostly from the 1950s, concerned with the seminal book by Dobb, *Studies in the Development of Capitalism* (New York: International Publishers, 1947), and including an important introduction by Hilton; see also John E. Martin, *Feudalism to Capitalism: Peasant and Landlord in English Agrarian Development* (Atlantic Highlands: Humanities Press, 1983); Kamenka and Neale, *Feudalism, Capitalism and Beyond*, and Holton, *Transition*. For theoretical comments as well as empirical studies, see also Hilton, *Class Conflict*, and Guy Bois, *The Crisis of Feudalism: Economy and Society in Eastern Normandy c. 1300–1550* (Cambridge: Cambridge University Press, 1984). The work of Dobb and Hilton is discussed by Harvey J. Kaye, *The British Marxist Historians* (London: Polity Press, 1984). For the reemergence of these issues in the work of Robert Brenner, see T. H. Aston and C. H. E. Philpin, eds., *The Brenner Debate* (Cambridge: Cambridge University Press, 1985).

18. For a recent discussion, with extensive bibliography, see R. J. Hilton, *Cities, Capitalism and Civilization* (London: Allen and Unwin, 1986); see also Rodney Hilton, "Towns in Societies—Medieval England," *Urban History Yearbook* (1982): 7–13, and Hilton, "Medieval Market Towns and Simple Commodity Production," *Past and Present* 109 (1985): 3–23.

(until at least the eighteenth century) remained agricultural.[19] In sum, the prime mover in feudal society was not proto-capitalist trade but the growing surplus value that the landowning class was able to extract from the agrarian economy. Thus it is that contemporary medieval historians have discovered, to cite the title of Robert Brenner's recent, highly influential article, "The Agrarian Roots of European Capitalism"—a discovery that sees the agricultural sector as being the locus for Marx's "really revolutionizing path" of transition by which the producer becomes himself a capitalist.[20]

Understanding economic life in terms of class struggle, these historians have argued that what brought about the collapse of feudalism and the transition to capitalism was the growing ability of the late-medieval peasant to withhold surplus value and turn it to his own, independent economic uses. Thus historians such as Maurice Dobb and, especially, Rodney Hilton have followed Marx's lead in describing the period 1350 to 1450 as the golden age of the English peasant.[21] As Hilton has pointed out, "Medieval peasants were quite capable, in economic terms, of providing for themselves without the intervention of any ruling class. In this they differed from ancient slaves, and from modern wage workers who have to work on the means of production in order to gain their living."[22] Since it always possessed (even if it did not yet own) the means of production, when the medieval peasantry developed sufficient strength to resist the grossest forms of seigneurial exaction it was able to retain the surplus value of the agrarian economy, which had up to this time been appropriated by the ruling classes. Hilton describes the results in the following terms:

> Between 1350 and 1450 . . . we find that relative land abundance was combined, for various reasons, with a relaxation of seigneurial domination and a notable lightening of the economic burden on the peasant economy. Peasant society, in spite of still existing within (in broad terms) a feudal framework, developed according to laws of motion internal to itself. The village community was dominated by the richer

19. Marx's attack on merchant capital as not being what he calls in the first volume of *Capital* "the really revolutionizing path" of transformation can be found in chapters 20 and 47 of *Capital* III.

20. Brenner's article appeared first in *Past and Present* 97 (1982): 16–113, and is now reprinted in Aston and Philpin, eds., *Brenner Debate*, 213–327.

21. Hilton is here following the lead of both Postan and of the great economic historian and political radical, J. E. Thorrold Rogers, *A History of Agriculture and Prices in England*, 7 vols. (Oxford: Oxford University Press, 1866–1902).

22. Rodney Hilton, *Bond Men Made Free* (London: Methuen, 1977 [1973]), 41.

peasant families, who ran the manorial court in its jurisdictional, pu-
nitive and land-registration functions. The limits on rents and services were firmly fixed well below what the lords wanted.[23]

Hence, concludes Hilton, "it is possible that the century after the Black
Death was the golden age of the middle rather than of the rich peasantry (the yeoman)."[24] But it is also the case that this rural economy is
the seedbed for later capitalist development. As Dobb pointed out, and
as Hilton and Brenner have shown in detail, "It is then from the petty
mode of production (in the degree to which it secures independence of
action, and social differentiation in turn develops within it) that capitalism is born."[25]

The effect of these arguments is to present a very different picture of
late-medieval English society than we are used to seeing. Rather than
the merchant class and the city functioning as the agents for change,
they are instead to be understood as dependent upon a seigneurial
class addicted to luxuries but under increasing economic pressure.[26]
Conversely, however, the agricultural economy remains strong but always at a local level: while the increased agricultural productivity of the
postplague years does not, because of the decline in demand, lead to a
substantial increase in money income, the small agricultural producers
are able to keep more of their product and to expand their holdings, an
expansion that takes place at the expense of both the large landholders
and, on the other side, of their less successful peasant neighbors.[27] It is
thus the *rural* sector of the economy that is dynamic, and the solvent of
feudal relations is neither merchant capital nor the trading activity it
finances but a vigorous peasant economy; and the crucial element in
the collapse of feudalism is peasant resistance to the seigneurial extrac-

23. Rodney Hilton, "Reasons for Inequality Among Medieval Peasants," *Journal of
Peasant Studies* 5 (1978): 271–83, reprinted in *Class Conflict,* 149.

24. Hilton, "Reasons for Inequality," 149. Hilton's *The English Peasantry of the Later
Middle Ages* provides a description of this golden age.

25. Maurice Dobb, "A Reply," in Hilton, *Transition from Feudalism to Capitalism,* 59.

26. The growth of the luxury trade, and its impoverishing effect upon seigneurial
fortunes, is discussed by Miskimin, *Economy of Early Renaissance Europe,* 135–37; see
above, chapter 3, note 68. For a detailed picture of aristocratic consumption as well as an
account of how the nobility met the economic crises of the later Middle Ages, see Christopher Dyer, *Standards of Living in the Later Middle Ages* (Cambridge: Cambridge University
Press, 1989), 27–108.

27. Both the existence and the nature of the late-medieval improvement of peasant
conditions remains a controversial issue among medieval historians; for alternative accounts, see Postan, *Medieval Economy and Society,* 201–2, and Miskimin, *Economy of Early
Renaissance Europe,* 50–51, 56–57.

tion of surplus profit from the agrarian economy. What we have, then, to conclude this discussion with a highly schematic description, is a feverish consumer boom in luxury goods masking irreparable structural weaknesses and set against a powerful, self-confident peasant economy—a self-confidence visible throughout the later-medieval period and nowhere more dramatically than in the Rising of 1381. For the Rising was much less the *cri de coeur* of an unbearably downtrodden peasantry than the outraged reaction of independent peasant producers to the seigneurial attempt to contain their growth.[28]

This account should encourage us to recognize that the distinction between noble and bourgeois, feudal and urban, while real and visible, does not describe the central opposition within fourteenth-century English society. On the contrary, both sets of values, however different one from the other, are *together* part of the dominant ideology, and both are to be set against the largely inarticulate but nonetheless insistent pressure of rural commodity production and the political resistance it spawned. The crucial ideological opposition is not between the seigneurial nobility and the urban merchant class but between both of these elements of the exploiting class and the increasingly independent and self-sufficient productive classes in the country.

The unity of the ruling classes, whether seigneurial or mercantile, is especially visible in the case of Chaucer himself. Far from being simply an ordinary London citizen (itself a privileged category, to be sure), Chaucer was the son of one of the members of the mercantile patriciate who controlled the city, a position that is certainly reflected in his early entrance into the household of the Duchess of Ulster and in his successful career within the courts of Edward III, of John of Gaunt, and of Richard II. Moreover, as one of Richard's royal servants the poet did not, as we have seen, disclaim any interest or role in politics; on the contrary, he was very much the king's man in the crucial Parliament of 1386, suffered for his allegiance when the king's party failed, and was finally rewarded for his loyalty when the king regained power in 1389.[29] In other words, to see Chaucer as somehow caught between two worlds and therefore free of both is both to misunderstand the structure of late-medieval English society and to underestimate the strength of the poet's political commitments, whether freely chosen or not. What this ultimately means, then, is that whatever signs of a turn-

28. Christopher Dyer, "The Social and Economic Background to the Rural Revolt of 1381," in *The English Rising of 1381*, ed. R. H. Hilton and T. H. Aston (Cambridge: Cambridge University Press, 1984), 9–42.
29. See above, 32–39, 155–162.

ing away from the forms and values of aristocratic culture that we recognize in the *Canterbury Tales*—and I believe there are a great many—should be understood not as a function of the instinctive pull of a natural origin (Chaucer returning to his bourgeois roots) but as a conscious and deliberate decision. Moreover, given the fact that the most powerful alternative to this dominance was embodied in a rebellious peasantry that we might expect Chaucer to have regarded with little natural sympathy, we can anticipate that any turn toward alternative values will be marked with a powerful ambivalence.

II

One could argue that Chaucer chose a miller as his initial agent of disruption simply in order to set up the hostile Reeve's use of the traditional tale of The Miller and Two Clerks. But in fact millers played a crucial if still somewhat obscure role in the medieval rural economy. The millsoke—the toll paid by peasants who were required to have their grain ground at the seigneurial mill—was not only a significant source of income for the landlord but a bitterly resented imposition upon the rural producer and a central focus of peasant resistance to seigneurial authority.[30] But if the disruptive energy with which Chaucer endows his Miller derives from this general condition, we remain uncertain about the particular role that millers themselves played in the struggle for peasant advancement. Since they are neither tenants of land nor tillers of soil they cannot technically be considered peasants. Rather, their vocation locates them within the artisanal class, like the Miller's John the carpenter. But their actual functioning within the village community, like their economic status, remains uncertain. Were they agents of seigneurial control, like bailiffs? Were they mediatory agents, as reeves were supposed to be? Or were they themselves part of the resistant village community, underlings who had their own grievances? We know that from at least the twelfth century mills were leased out by landlords for a fixed rent, but to what extent the leasees were

---

30. See Richard Holt, "Whose Were the Profits of Corn Milling," *Past and Present* 116 (1987): 3–23; Richard Bennett and John Elton, *The History of Corn Milling*, 4 vols. (London: Simpkin Marshall, 1898–1904), 1:20–21 and 4:40–53; Marc Bloch, *Land and Work in Medieval Europe*, trans. J. E. Anderson (Berkeley: University of California Press, 1967), 157. For an account of what Bloch calls "a veritable milling epic" at St. Albans during the Rising, see Rosamond Faith in "The 'Great Rumour' of 1377 and Peasant Ideology," in Hilton and Aston, *English Rising*, 66.

themselves the millers is by no means clear.[31] We also know that throughout the thirteenth century most of the previously "free" mills that had been owned by nonseigneurial proprietors were brought back under manorial control.[32] So too, that millers stole is confirmed by both numerous documents and popular reputation, but were their victims primarily the peasants or the lord?[33] Similarly, we do not really know how relatively prosperous millers were. There is some evidence to support the widespread opinion that "the miller was commonly one of the most considerable men in the village," and the sharp decline in mill rents in the postplague period suggests that millers were, like the other members of the peasant community, able to drive better bargains with mill owners—a sign of growing strength that doubtless contributed to their unpopularity.[34] Not coincidentally, then, millers were included in

31. For the leasing of mills, see Evgeny A. Kosminsky, *Studies in the Agrarian History of England in the Thirteenth Century,* trans. Ruth Kisch, ed. Rodney H. Hilton (Oxford: Blackwell, 1956), 52. For an example of the miller as himself the leasee, see Herbert P. R. Finberg, *Tavistock Abbey: A Study in the Social and Economic History of Devon* (Cambridge: Cambridge University Press, 1951), 195; a recent study of medieval milling reportedly claims that "mills became part of peasant holdings by the thirteenth century rather than monopoly tools of exploitation by the lords" (a summary by J. Ambrose Raftis, "Social Change versus Revolution: New Interpretations of the Peasants' Revolt of 1381," in *Social Unrest in the Late Middle Ages,* ed. Francis X. Newman [Binghamton: Medieval and Renaissance Texts and Studies, 1986], 7, of Christopher Dyer and John Langdon, "English Medieval Mills," *Bulletin of the University of Birmingham* [23 January 1984]: 1–2—a paper I have been unable to consult). But for examples of the leasee as a nonresident, who then either pays the miller a salary or allows him to reimburse himself by taking a portion of the toll, see the discussion by Bennett and Elton, *History of Corn Milling,* 4:67–84, 136–43; and Tim Lomas, "Southeast Durham: Late Fourteenth and Fifteenth Centuries," in Harvey, *Peasant Land Market,* 323. The mill that Margery Kempe bought in the early fifteenth century must have been operated by a hired miller; see *The Book of Margery Kempe,* trans. Barry Windeatt (Harmondsworth: Penguin Books, 1985), 44.

32. For this "reassertion of seigneurial monopoly," see Holt, "Whose Were the Profits," *passim.*

33. On the distasteful reputation of millers, see George Fenwick Jones, "Chaucer and the Medieval Miller," *MLQ* 16 (1955): 3–15, and Bennett and Elton, *History of Corn Milling,* vol. 3, *passim.* There is also evidence that millers stole from mill owners: among the many accusations laid against millers in the legal records, there are a number that charge them with stealing mill parts; see Barbara Hanawalt, *Crime and Conflict in English Communities, 1300–1348* (Cambridge: Harvard University Press, 1979), 135. When the miller's "popular" image as a thief is invoked, it should also be remembered that the custodians of the documents that record this description were not the peasants whose grain was being ground but the governing classes who were extracting profit from the process over which the miller presided.

34. The common opinion is cited from George C. Homans, *English Villagers of the Thirteenth Century* (Cambridge: Harvard University Press, 1941), 285, who unfortunately offers no evidence. According to William G. Hoskins, *The Midland Peasant: The Economic*

the various Statutes of Labourers whose fees the government sought to control.[35]

One thing we do know for certain, however, is that millers were participants in the Rising of 1381. One John Fillol, for instance, a miller from Hanningfield, Essex, was hanged for his part in the revolt, and the records indicate that other millers played a prominent role.[36] Furthermore, if names are any indication of occupation, it is significant that a John Millere of London was charged with being one of those who stole wine from the Vintry, another John Meller of Ulford was hung and his goods confiscated, and the eloquent leader of the rebels at St. Albans was William Grindecobbe.[37] Moreover, when the rebels of Bury St. Edmonds beheaded John Cavendish, a king's justice who had enforced the Statute of Labourers with particular severity, the executioner was named Matthew Miller; given both the physical strength of millers

---

and Social History of a Leicestershire Village (London: Macmillan, 1957), "Among the tradesmen of Wigston in the sixteenth century the miller was pre-eminent" (169); and in "Debt Litigation in a Late Medieval English Vill," in *Pathways to Medieval Peasants*, ed. J. Ambrose Raftis (Toronto: Pontifical Institute of Mediaeval Studies, 1981), Elaine Clark shows that in at least one instance millers served as village money lenders. On the other hand, in "Berkshire: Fourteenth and Fifteenth Centuries," in Harvey, *Peasant Land Market*, Rosamond Faith provides a custumal drawn up in 1221 for the village of Woolstone that seems to show that the three millers living in the village were considered among the least substantial of the inhabitants (122–23). Holt, "Whose Were the Profits," tells of the prosperity of one Leuric the Miller on a Glastonbury estate, but it appears that Leuric did not do the milling himself but simply leased the mill and then hired a servant to do it for him (18–19). On mill income, Finberg points out that for the mills on the manors of Tavistock Abbey "the farm was appreciably lower in the fifteenth century than it had been before the Black Death" (*Tavistock Abbey*, 195). The fact that the mills were not farmed during the period 1350–1450 suggests that no tenants could be found. For other examples of falling rents from mills, see J. Ambrose Raftis, *Warboys: Two Hundred Years in the Life of an English Mediaeval Village* (Toronto: Pontifical Institute of Mediaeval Studies, 1974), the table on 260, and especially Bois, *Crisis of Feudalism*, 226–34.

35. Bertha Haven Putnam, *Enforcement of the Statute of Labourers* (New York: Columbia University Press, 1908), 81.

36. For John Fillol, see Christopher Dyer, "The Social and Economic Background," 38; for another anonymous miller, see Dyer, 16. In his hysterical account of the rebellion in *Vox clamantis*, John Gower also contemptuously testifies to the presence of millers among the rebels: "nor did the dog at the mill stay home" (*The Major Latin Works of John Gower*, trans. Eric W. Stockton [Seattle: University of Washington Press, 1962], 59). Francis R. H. Du Boulay, *The Lordship of Canterbury: An Essay on Mediaeval Society* (London: Nelson, 1966) mentions that one of the ringleaders of "Cade's" rebellion in the mid-fifteenth century was a "malt-miller" (191).

37. On the two John Millers, see André Réville and Charles Petit-Dutaillis, *Le Soulèvement des Travailleurs d'Angleterre en 1381* (Paris: Picard, 1898), 224 and 232; on William Grindecobbe, and his famous speech, see R. B. Dobson, ed., *The Peasants' Revolt of 1381* (London: Macmillan, 1970), 269–77.

and their reputation for violence, the name seems likely here to coincide with vocation.[38]

Most important, however, is the fact that the peasants themselves seem to have seen the figure of the miller as capable of embodying both their grievances and their desire for an almost apocalyptic reckoning. Two of John Ball's famous letters that circulated during the Rising refer specifically to an allegorized miller:

> Johan the Mullere hath ygrownde smal, smal, smal;
> The Kyngis sone of heuene shalle pay for alle.
> Be war or ye be wo;
> Knoweth ʒour frend fro ʒoure foo,
> Haveth ynowe and seyth "Hoo":
> And do welle and bettre, and fleth synne,
> And seketh pees and holde therynne.

> Jakke Mylner asketh help to turne hys mylne aright. He
> hath grounden smal smal; the kings sone of heven he
> schal pay for alle. Loke thy mylne go aright, with the
> foure sayles, and the post stands in stedfastnesse.
> With ryght and with myght, with skyl and with wylle,
> lat myght helpe ryght, and skyl go before wille and
> ryght before myght, than goth oure mylne aryght. And
> if myght go before ryght, and wylle before skylle, than
> is oure mylne mys adyght.[39]

38. Edgar Powell, *The Rising in East Anglia in 1381* (Cambridge: Cambridge University Press, 1896), 13–14. In fact, perhaps because of their social location at one of the pressure points of the feudal system, millers do seem to have been involved in violence more than other peasants: see James Buchanan Given, *Society and Homicide in Thirteenth-Century England* (Stanford: Stanford University Press, 1977), 87.

39. The verse letter is cited from Thomas Walsingham, *Historia anglicana*, ed. Henry Thomas Riley (London: Longman, 1864), 2:34; the second, from Knighton's *Chronicon*, is cited from Dobson, ed., *Peasants' Revolt*, 381–82. For a bibliographical account of the various versions of these letters, see Rossell Hope Robbins, "Poems on Contemporary Conditions," in *A Manual of the Writings in Middle English 1050–1500*, ed. Albert E. Hartung (New Haven: Connecticut Academy of Arts and Sciences, 1975), 5:1513–14. For further discussion of John Ball's Letters, see Rossell Hope Robbins, "Dissent in Middle English Literature: The Spirit of (Thirteen) Seventy-Six," *M&H*, 9 (1979): 25–51; and Russell A. Peck, "Social Conscience and the Poets," in Newman, *Social Unrest*, 113–48. These two texts have been recently put in relation to the *Miller's Tale* by Paul A. Olson, *The Canterbury Tales and the Good Society* (Princeton: Princeton University Press, 1986), 54–55, who presents the Miller as "cousin to the revolt's 'Jack the Miller' but seen through [Chaucer's] elite court eyes" (75). A reading similar to Olson's may be found in the excellent article by Robert P. Miller, "The *Miller's Tale* as a Complaint," *ChR* 5 (1970–71): 147–60; see also Knight, *Geoffrey Chaucer*, 90–93.

No doubt there is a scriptural subtext to these threatening words (see, e.g, Matthew 21:44, Luke 20:18), but they more immediately witness to the long history of peasant anger toward the seigneurial monopoly of the power of the mill—a power that the rebels of 1381 here seek to appropriate and turn to their own, retributive uses. Chaucer's Robin the Miller would have called such retribution *quiting,* and lest we think the analogy with John Ball's Jack the Miller is arbitrary, let us remember at the outset that Jack's message includes an ambiguous injunction— "Haueth y-now, and seith 'Hoo' "—that is also at the center of Robin's lesson:

> I have a wyf, pardee, as wel as thow;
> Yet nolde I, for the oxen in my plogh,
> *Take upon me more than ynogh.* . . .
> So he may fynde Goddes foyson there,
> Of the remenant nedeth nat enquere. (3158–66)

Part of the peasant's claim to freedom, and what sets him apart from the extortionate lord who would bind him, is that he understands the natural fitness of things, and knows both when he has (and when he has had) enough.

III

There is a specifically political appropriateness to the fact that the *Miller's Tale* is a narrative staging of the vitality and resourcefulness of the natural world. In part, these values are embodied in Alisoun, whose vernal beauty serves to elicit the male desire that motivates the *Tale.* All three of the men attempt, with varying degrees of success, to constrain her to their needs: John holds "hire narwe in cage, / For she was wylde and yong, and he was old" (3224–25);[40] to Absolon she is a prey to be caught—"if she hadde been a mous, / And he a cat, he wolde hire hente anon" (3346–47);[41] and if Nicholas does manage to seize her,

40. Implicit in this metaphor is the Boethian image of the caged bird who yearns for its woodland home—an allusion that serves to legitimize Alisoun; see George D. Economou, "Chaucer's Use of the Bird in the Cage Image in the *Canterbury Tales,*" PQ 54 (1975): 679–84.

41. Absolon's attack with the coulter takes on a telling configuration in this context: in thinking to brand Alisoun he means both to efface the hairy sexual reality that she has forced upon him and to force her to the sexual cultivation appropriate to her femaleness (hence the coulter); but in instead branding/plowing Nicholas he reveals what a Boethian philosopher would call his true "ende." I take it that the Miller's purpose in establishing

it is only for a moment: "she sproong as a colt dooth in the trave, / And with hir heed she wryed faste awey" (3282–83). Yet the *Miller's Tale* does not in fact articulate an opposition between natural freedom and social constraint; on the contrary, it presents this opposition as mediated by a moderation that bespeaks a calm confidence in the just workings of natural law. The *Tale* everywhere displays an apparently flawless orderliness: not only does the apparently random aimlessness of the plot reveal itself to be ordered by an exquisite logic, but the unthinking hedonism of the action leads to judgments of an impeccable exactness. The dandified Absolon suffers a scatological humiliation, the too-clever Nicholas—who "thoughte he wolde amenden al the jape" (3799)—becomes himself the butt of a jape executed by his intended victim, and the arrogantly know-nothing John is victimized by his violation of the natural law that "man sholde wedde his simylitude" (3228). Compared to the moral anarchy over which the Knight has (however unwittingly) presided, the *Miller's Tale* seems to articulate a world of perfect moral sense: in a famous comment, E. M. W. Tillyard described the climax of the *Tale* as arousing "feelings akin to those of religious wonder."[42] Although the Miller's ludic festivity bursts into the pilgrimage with rude insistence, it appears to contain its own self-regulation. To attempt to control it is at once unavailing and unnecessary. The natural and the supernatural are in perfect harmony, the *Tale* tells us, and the "belle of laudes" (3655) that rings while the lovers are enjoying their sexual frolics harmonizes the "melodye" (3652) in Alisoun's and Nicholas's bed of love with the song of the friars in the chantry. The result is an unstinted hymn of praise: "what wol ye bet than weel?" (3370).[43]

Criticism has traditionally read this claim as either an end in itself—an effect of the benign naturalism of the *fabliau*—or as an expression of the Miller's philosophical naivete and spiritual culpability.[44] But in fact, I believe, the Miller's celebration of the natural—as a world of beauty, as a source of glad animal spirits, and (most important) as a principle of order—is best understood as a political statement that is consistent

this pattern is to mock what he takes to be a homerotic rivalry that binds Arcite and Palamon together in the *Knight's Tale.*

42. E. M. W. Tillyard, *Poetry Direct and Oblique* (London: Chatto and Windus, 1945), 92.

43. See David, *Strumpet Muse*, 103.

44. For the first, see V. A. Kolve, *Chaucer and the Imagery of Narrative* (Stanford: Stanford University Press, 1984), 158–216; for the second, Morton Bloomfield, "*The Miller's Tale*—an unBoethian Interpretation," in Mandel and Rosenberg, *Medieval Literature and Folklore Studies*, 205–11.

with the deeply political nature of the *Tale* as a whole.[45] Criticism has shown how the *Tale* launches a pointed attack upon the chivalric ideology so thoroughly, and critically, represented in the *Knight's Tale*. The heroic *Theseus artifex* is here represented by John the carpenter, his astrological credulity inciting him, to his cost, to pry into "Goddes pryvetee" (3454, 3558), just as Theseus's hubric oratories invoked planetary gods who then brought disasters down upon the world that worshipped them; and in its largest sense, the *Tale* teaches a lesson about the impossibility of constraining either people or events to the kind of overmastering will that characterizes chivalry. Similarly, Nicholas and Absolon travesty two forms of the chivalric love ethic that underwrites the *Knight's Tale:* Nicholas is the predatory seducer who deploys the forms of courtly wooing in order to gratify his appetites, Absolon the narcissistic, inefficient dandy who plays at lovemaking without understanding how to do it. And here too the critique is not only mocking but includes as well a sharp sense of grievance: in directing their attentions to Alisoun, after all, Nicholas and Absolon seek to enact a characteristically seigneurial appropriation:

> She was a prymerole, a piggesnye,
> For any lord to leggen in his bedde,
> Or yet for any good yeman to wedde. (3268–70)

Yet it is not only or even primarily the seigneurial class that is the target of the Miller's *quiting*. If the representations of Nicholas and Absolon serve to mock and subvert the Knight's chivalric culture, they are also vehicles for an attack upon an ecclesiastical establishment that is perceived as equally overbearing and exploitative; and given the fact, as Hilton has pointed out, that "the great ecclesiastical landlords [were] notorious for their bad relations with their tenants," the anticlericalism of the *Tale*, as of medieval peasant movements as a whole, is not to be wondered at.[46] To be sure, in the figure of the inefficient Absolon, a parish clerk who puts on snobbish airs, theatrically displays (in his role as Herod) a ferocity he clearly lacks in life, and laughably deforms the

---

45. See Olson, *The* Canterbury Tales *and the Good Society,* 75–80.

46. Rodney Hilton, *A Medieval Society: The West Midlands at the End of the Thirteenth Century* (London: Weidenfeld and Nicolson, 1966), 156. For the anticlericalism of peasant movements, see Hilton, *Bond Men Made Free,* 50–52, 101–3, 106–8, 124–25, 167–68, 198–206; Michel Mollat and Philippe Wolff, *Ongles bleus, Jacques et Ciompi: les révolutions populaires en Europe aux XIVe et XVe siècles* (Paris: Calman-Lévy, 1970), 288. One episode in the Rising particularly relevant to the *Miller's Tale* is the attack at Cambridge against the manor held by Corpus Christi College; for an account, see Dobson, *Peasants' Revolt,* 240–42.

biblical text for seductive purposes, the Miller's critique is essentially mocking and contemptuous. But even here more than mockery is at issue. For by having Absolon use the *Song of Songs* as his text, the Miller is calling attention to a tradition of interpretation in which is visible perhaps more than in any other the coercive manipulation inherent in the institution of biblical exegesis per se. As the very frequency with which it was discussed suggests (it was by far the most commonly interpreted book of the Bible throughout the Middle Ages), the *Song of Songs* was an especially provocative text to medieval exegetes, challenging them to rewrite a Hebrew love song into the dogmatic terms of church doctrine.[47] And yet, implies the Miller, if their fascination bespeaks an awareness of the *Song*'s destabilizing potential, it also witnesses to an unacknowledged pleasure in its seductive literality, a literality that Absolon here turns precisely to the purposes of seduction. In other words, the Miller is arguing that Absolon's misuse of the *Song of Songs* is a characteristically clerical misappropriation: what exegetes typically do *to* the *Song of Songs*, Absolon here seeks to do to Alisoun *by means of* the *Song of Songs*.[48]

If in the figure of Absolon clerical *dominium* is revealed as hypocritically self-regarding and yet comically ineffective, in the figure of Nicholas the ecclesiast is represented as a far more proficient manipulator. Here the instruments of manipulation are other forms of clerical culture—astrology to be sure but also, and most tellingly, the mystery plays to which allusion is made throughout the *Tale*. For it is Nicholas who stages the entire production, using as his primary text the Noah

47. Jean Leclercq, *The Love of Learning and the Desire for God*, trans. Jean Misrahi (New York: New American Library, 1962), 90–93. The inescapable ambiguity of the *Song* is well demonstrated by Tony Hunt, "The *Song of Songs* and Courtly Literature," in *Court and Poet*, ed. Glyn S. Burgess (Liverpool: Francis Cairns, 1981), 189–96, and by Theresa Coletti, *Naming the Rose: Eco, Medieval Signs, and Modern Theory* (Ithaca: Cornell University Press, 1988), 47–53.

48. For telling instances of the ambivalence with which the "plaisir du texte" of the *Song of Songs* was regarded by medieval exegetes, see Augustine, *De doctrina christiana* 2, 6, and the Preface to Origen's *Commentary*, in which he warns "everyone who is not yet rid of the vexations of flesh and blood and has not ceased to feel the passion of his bodily nature, to refrain completely from reading this little book and the things that will be said about it" (*The Song of Songs: Commentary and Homilies*, trans. R. P. Lawson [Westminster: The Newman Press, 1957], 23). As a castrate, Origen was of course protected from this threat, which is perhaps why it is the effete Absolon who purveys the *Song* in the *Miller's Tale*. For modern exegetical readings of the Miller's allusions, see Robert E. Kaske, "The 'Canticum Canticorum' in the 'Miller's Tale'," *SP* 59 (1962): 479–500; James Wimsatt, "Chaucer and the Canticle of Canticles," in *Chaucer the Love Poet*, ed. Jerome Mitchell and William Provost (Athens: University of Georgia Press, 1973), 66–90.

play.[49] It is the appropriateness of this choice that I wish to examine. In one sense, since the play focuses on the theme of *maistrye* in the relationship of Noah to his wife, it has a natural affinity for "maister Nicholay" (3437, 3579)—who, as his unnecessarily elaborate plot shows, is seeking not just to seduce Alisoun but to demonstrate in particularly spectacular fashion his superiority over "men that swynke" (3491).[50] But it has as well, I believe, another, deeper relevance to the political dynamic that controls the *Miller's Tale*, the exploration of which will return us to the question of peasant consciousness and the nature of nature.

IV

When Richard II revoked his charters of manumission and suppressed the rebellion, he told the peasants, "Rustics you were and rustics you are still; you will remain in bondage, not as before but incomparably harsher."[51] Behind these chilling words lies what Rodney Hilton calls "the caste interpretation of peasant status"—the idea that serfdom is a permanent condition of moral inferiority inherent in the peasant's very being rather than a social status capable of being both assumed and (at least in theory) left behind.[52] The common medieval opinion that the grossly inequitable social order was a consequence of man's sinful nature, while implying a passive acquiescence in injustice, was not in a crudely direct way an instrument to enforce specific class interests: for Augustine, the distinction between Cain, the founder of the *civitas terrena* (in which we all live) and Abel, the precursor of Christ and thus founder of the *civitas Dei* (to which we all aspire), was less historical than moral and spiritual, an opposition fought out within the soul of each Christian.[53] But later writers gave the distinction a specific social

49. For an excellent account of these allusions, see Sandra Pierson Prior, "Parodying Typology and the Mystery Plays in the Miller's Tale," *JMRS* 16 (1986): 57–73.

50. For the Noah play as about *maistrye*, see V. A. Kolve, *The Play Called Corpus Christi* (Stanford: Stanford University Press, 1966), 146–51.

51. This is Walsingham's account, as translated in Dobson, *Peasants' Revolt*, 311. For the original, see Walsingham, *Historia anglicana*, 2:18. Dobson also prints a contemporary account of the revolt of the villeins of Darnall and Over in 1336, who are forced to swear to the Abbot of Vale Royal "that they were villeins, they and their sons after them to all eternity" (81).

52. Hilton, *Class Conflict*, 138.

53. Augustine explained that before the fall there was no mastery or servitude because God "did not wish the rational being, made in his own image, to have dominion over any but irrational creatures, not man over man, but man over the beasts." But with the entrance of sin into the world all was changed: "The first cause of servitude is sin,

instantiation: as one late-medieval cleric misleadingly claimed, "Augustine said that the miserable calamity of bondage hath reasonably been brought into the world because of the demerits of the peoples, so that bondage is now fitly rooted among peasants and common folk."[54] And this distinction could then be scripturally authorized by identifying Abel as the father of all nobility, Cain as the first *servus*.[55] The ultimate effect of this line of argument was not only to explain the peasant's subjection as a function of his sinfulness but to define the peasant as in effect belonging to another order of being, as a member of a different species, a nonhuman. Hence when Gower says, in Book 5 of the *Vox clamantis*, that the peasantry "is a race without power of reason, like beasts," he is not only repeating a ubiquitous vilification but characterizing the peasantry as subhuman creatures whose fallen nature requires subjection.[56]

---

whereby man was subjected to man in the condition of bondage" (*City of God* 19, 15; trans. Henry Bettenson [Harmondsworth: Penguin Books, 1972], 874–75). For the medieval justification of social inequality, and specifically of sin as the source of the class of *laboratores*, see Georges Duby, *The Three Orders: Feudal Society Imagined*, trans. Arthur Goldhammer (Chicago: University of Chicago Press, 1980), 52 and passim.

54. Balthasar Reber, *Felix Hemmerlin von Zurich* (Zurich, 1846), cited by G. G. Coulton, *The Medieval Village* (Cambridge: Cambridge University Press, 1925), 522.

55. David Williams, *Cain and Beowulf* (Toronto: University of Toronto Press, 1982); see also Coulton, *Medieval Village*, 21, 247; and for the representation of Cain in the Towneley *Mactatio Abel* as a husbandman, see G. R. Owst, *Literature and Pulpit in Medieval England*, 2d ed. (Oxford: Blackwell, 1961), 491–92. It is this enrollment of the peasant in the damned race of Cain that accounts for his designation in antipeasant writings as a Jew (see Paul Lehmann, *Parodistische Texte* [Munich: Die Drei Masken, 1923], where the peasant is described as being "ineptus et turpis ut Judeus" [21]), as a Christ-killer (see Francesco Novati, *Carmina Medii Aevi* [Florence: Libreria Dante, 1883], for a poem that asserts that "Christo fu da villan crucificò, / e stogom sempre in pioza, in vento e in neve, / perchè havom fato così gran peccò" [27 n. 1]), and as an *alter Judas* (Novati, 45).

56. *Major Latin Works*, trans. Stockton, 210; this is an identification that he later enforced by depicting the Peasants' Revolt as a rising of maddened animals. For other instances of the use of animalistic language to describe the participants in the events of 1381, see Dobson, *Peasants' Revolt*, 138, 173, and passim. For examples of antipeasant writings that stress the animal nature of the peasant, see Novati, *Carmina Medii Aevi*, 32 n. 1, 34–38; as Matteo Vegio said in the early fifteenth century, a peasant's ox has a more human appearance than does the peasant himself (31 n. 1). See also the medieval proverb, "Rusticus asello similis est, hoc tibi dico" (Hans Walther, *Lateinische Sprichwörter und Sentenzen des Mittelalters und der Frühen Neuzeit*, ed. Paul Gerhard Schmidt [Göttingen: Vandenhoeck und Ruprecht, 1986], 9:511 [item 223]). The notion of the peasant as a creature capable not of love but only of lust is part of this identification of his fallen nature: as Andreas Capellanus famously said in his *De amore*, rustics "are impelled to acts of love in the natural way like a horse or a mule, just as nature's pressure directs them" (ed. and trans. P. G. Walsh [London: Duckworth, 1982], 223). See also the treatise on love included within *Li Hystore de Julius César*: "Volentei d'amer ki en vilain se met estriner le

It was this definition of serfdom as an intrinsic and permanent condition of sinfulness, and not simply certain economic disadvantages that attached to villeinage, that the 1381 rebels sought to efface. Froissart's well-known summary of the peasants' demands makes this abundantly clear:

> These unhappy people . . . said that they were kept in great servage, and in the beginning of the world, they said, there were no bondmen, wherefore they maintained that none ought to be bond without he did treason to his lord, as Lucifer did to God; but they said that they could have no such battle for they were neither angels nor spirits, but men formed to the similitude of their lords, saying why should they then be kept so under like beasts.[57]

As Hilton has said, the rebels "strove not merely for a reduction of rent but for human dignity"[58]—a statement that can also be applied to virtually every late-medieval peasant revolt.

For all its comic tolerance, the *Miller's Tale* takes part in this struggle, and not least by subverting and mocking the very terms with which the reigning ideology sought to stigmatize and oppress peasants. For one thing, the Miller's witty, even elegant *Tale*—an achievement that not even modern critics, who continue to wonder at the presence of so intelligent a tale in the mouth of so obviously brutish a teller, have been quite prepared to grant him—proves that the peasant is not the inarticu-

---

fait ausi *comme une beste salvage,* ne il ne poet son corage aploiier a nule cortoisie ne a nule bonté, ains aime folement et sans coverture. Et che n'est mie amours, ains est ensi comme rage, quant vilains s'entremet d'amer" (ed. A. Långfors, *Romania* 56 [1930], 367).

Two well-known representations of the peasant as a subhuman, animal creature can be found in Chrétien de Troyes' *Le chevalier du lion* and in *Aucassin et Nicolette;* a particularly bestial visual image of a miller may be found in the margins of the Luttrell Psalter, conveniently reproduced on the cover of the paperback edition of Postan's *Medieval Economy and Society.* Less prejudicial pictures that serve to link the peasant to the natural world can be seen in late-medieval calendar illustrations, where the peasant serves as virtually a marker of the passage of the year. For examples, see Henrik Specht, *Poetry and the Iconography of the Peasant: The Attitude to the Peasant in Late Medieval English Literature and in Contemporary Calendar Illustration* (Copenhagen: Akademisk Forlag, 1983). Duby is by and large correct when he points out that the medieval world "still recognized only one value in manual labor: that of salutary punishment. Work was servitude. It debased, degraded" (*Three Orders,* 325–26). As Hilton says, "The gentry and the nobility regarded peasants as different creatures from themselves, almost as a different race" (*Bond Men Made Free,* 35).

57.   Dobson, *Peasants' Revolt,* 370; the translation is by Lord Berners. For the original, see Kervyn de Lettenhove, ed., *Oeuvres de Froissart* (Brussels: Devaux, 1869), 9:387.

58.   Hilton, *Class Conflict,* 138.

late figure that hostile representations had depicted. It also establishes an alternative version of the natural world. In place of the Knight's paranoid insistence on the continual need for supervision and constraint, the Miller describes (as we have seen) a world that shatters all efforts at confinement but that nonetheless contains its own principle of equilibrium, a natural sense of fitness and decorum. In locating at the thematic center of his *Tale* this benign, virtually prelapsarian *lex naturalis*, the Miller is thus reversing the terms of antipeasant defamation. Far from being fallen and degraded, nature here serves as a beneficient and supportive principle; far from being in need of compensation by the *lex positiva* created by men, the *lex naturalis* is seen as providing an unerring standard.

The Miller's rehabilitation of nature as a principle of moral order is itself profoundly expressive of his class consciousness. For he promotes a view of the natural world that was—so far as we can tell from the fragmentary evidence—common to rural movements throughout the late Middle Ages. That nature provides a self-evident norm of fairness, an originary and still authoritative principle of equality, is implicit in the famous couplet of 1381, "Whan Adam dalf, and Eve span / Wo was thanne a gentilman?"[59] And in their political program the rebels sought to return England to a similarly prelapsarian condition, in which both a people's monarchy and a people's church could subsist without any intervening hierarchy.[60] Furthermore, both here and throughout the Middle Ages, one of the goals of peasant resistance was to achieve access to the bounty of the natural world—the woods, fish, and game—that they felt was theirs by right of being natural creatures like their lords.[61] In sum, stigmatized by their opponents as beings who expressed with special and culpable directness the fallenness of nature—"they so till the earth, they are so utterly earthly, that we may

---

59. Walsingham, *Historia anglicana*, 2:32. That this couplet was a traditional homiletic saying long before 1381 does not affect its utopianist meaning within the context of political rebellion; see Owst, *Literature and Pulpit*, 291–94.

60. For the program of the Peasants' Revolt, see Hilton, *Bond Men Made Free*, 229.

61. For examples, going back as far as the tenth-century peasants' war in Normandy, see Hilton, *Bond Men Made Free*, 71, 230; and for the peasant sense that the natural world should not be subjected to the tyrannical control entailed by private ownership, see 40. As the German peasants of 1525 said in the Fourth of their Twelve Articles, "When the Lord God created man, he gave him dominion over all animals, over the birds of the air, and the fish in the waters" (Peter Blickle, *The Revolution of 1525: The German Peasants' War from a New Perspective*, trans. Thomas A. Brady and H. C. Erik Midelfort [Baltimore: Johns Hopkins University Press, 1981], 198). Similarly, as Hilton points out, the Robin Hood ballads express a "Utopian vision of free communities of hunters eating their fill of a forbidden food" (*Bond Men Made Free*, 72).

truly say of them: They shall lick the earth and eat it," as one particularly vicious prelate put it, while an English celebrant of peasant humil-
ity described them as "grobbyng aboute the erthe"—peasants not only
accepted this "natural" identity but redeemed it by insisting, like the
Miller in his *Tale,* upon nature's essential goodness.[62]

Far from being the result of either misguided optimism or spiritual
turpitude, then, the Miller's rehabilitation of nature is part of a political
program that turns against the governing classes one of its own instruments of ideological control. The same thing can be said about his use
of the Noah story. We have already seen how the distinction between
Cain and Abel was used as an aristocratic *Gründungsage* to justify the
subjection of the peasant. The story of Noah was upon occasion used
for the same purpose. When human history was refounded after the
flood, the original division of peoples established by Cain and Abel
now became a threefold distinction to be drawn among Noah's three
sons, Japhet, Ham, and Shem. Once again, a distinction that for
patristic writers existed at the level of the spiritual and ecclesiastical life
became defined in the later Middle Ages in terms of social opposition.
The first writer to make this definition explicit was, it seems, Honorius
of Autun in his *De imagine mundi* (1133): "At this time humankind was
divided into three: into freemen, knights, and serfs [*servos*]. Freemen
[are descended] from Shem, knights from Japhet, serfs from Ham."[63]
Ham's subjection was to be explained by the curse laid upon Ham's son
Canaan by Noah when Ham mocked his drunken father's nakedness:
"Cursed be Canaan, a servant of servants [*servus servorum*] shall he be
unto his brethern" (Genesis 9:25). As exegetes had always insisted,
Ham was of the race of Cain, and now this text identified that race with
the *servi* who were so visible a part of medieval life.[64] Needless to say,

---

62. Roderigo, Bishop of Zamorra, *Speculum Vitae Humanae* (c. 1465), cited by Coulton, *Medieval Village,* 518; for the second citation, see Owst, *Literature and Pulpit,* 553.
Perhaps the most explicit peasant assertion of the authority of the *lex naturalis* (which
they identified with the *lex divina*) now available to us is that found in the documents
produced during the German Peasants' War of 1524–25. For a discussion, see Blickle,
Revolution of 1525, 168, and Heiko A. Oberman, "The Gospel of Social Unrest," in *The
German Peasant War of 1525—New Viewpoints,* ed. Bob Scribner and Gerhard Benecke
(London: Allen and Unwin, 1979), 39–51. Coulton is surely right when he says that the
Twelve Articles "rest upon [an] appeal from oppressive human law and custom to natu-
ral law" (*Medieval Village,* 546).

63. Honorius of Autun, *De imagine mundi:* "Huius tempore divisum est genus humanum in tria: in liberos, milites, servos. Liberi de Sem, milites de Japhet, servi de
Cham" (*PL* 172:166).

64. For Ham as a member of the race of Cain, see Oliver F. Emerson, "Legends of
Cain, Especially in Old and Middle English," *PMLA* 21 (1906), 925–26.

any argument that stigmatizes the vast majority of the population as damned beyond redemption—"curssed uppon þe grounde," as the York play put it—can hardly enter the mainstream of medieval political thought.[65] Yet there is evidence that, despite its exorbitance, this identification of the cursed Ham with rustics did achieve considerable currency. The popular *Cursor mundi*, first written in about 1300 and then rewritten into two other versions, appended to the usual geographical distribution of Noah's sons (Shem to Asia, Ham to Africa, and Japhet to Europe) Honorius's social analysis:

Kny3t & þral and fre man
of þese þre briþeren bigan;
Of Sem fre mon, of Iapheth kny3t,
Þral of Cam, waryed wi3te.[66]

More significant is the very popular *Liber de moribus hominum, et officiis nobilium ac popularium super ludo scachorum*, written in the early fourteenth century by Jacobus de Cessolis and in the course of the century translated at least twice into French and then later four times into German and once (by Caxton) into English. For de Cessolis not only enforces the identification of peasants as members of the race of Cain, but he uses the story of Ham's mockery to introduce a discussion of the four kinds of drunkenness (like a lion, a lamb, a swine, and an ape), a vice that is then associated with the laborer and seen as a spur to social disturbance: wines (in Caxton's translation) "make the poure [man] riche as longe as the wyn is in his hed and shortly dronkenshyp is the begynnynge of alle euylles."[67]

But the text that is most interesting in terms of the *Miller's Tale* is the *Liber armorum*, a brief treatise on heraldry included in the early fifteenth-century *Boke of Seynt Albans*.[68] For here the antipeasant myth

65. *Sacrificium Cayme and Abel*, in *The York Plays*, ed. Richard Beadle (London: Arnold, 1982), line 86.

66. Sarah M. Horrall, ed., *The Southern Version of Cursor Mundi* (Ottawa: University of Ottawa Press, 1978), 2133–36 (1:102–3).

67. William Caxton, trans., *The Game and Playe of the Chesse*, 2d ed. (Westminster: Caxton, 148[?]), reprinted in facsimile by William Figgins (London, 1855). For an edition of de Cessolis, see Ferdinand Vetter, ed., *Das Schachzelbuch Kunrats von Ammenhausen nebst den Schachbüchern des Jakob von Cessole und des Jakob Mennel* (Frauenfeld: Huber, 1892).

68. According to E. F. Jacob, "The Book of St. Albans," *BJRL* 28 (1944): 99–118, the *Liber armorum* is in part dependent upon both Nicholas of Upton's *De officio militari* (late 1420s–early 1430s) and a "Book of the Lineage of Cote Armour." The two other items in this compilation—treatises on hawking and hunting—are both based on early fourteenth-century sources.

of Ham is not only deployed in a way that makes its relevance to the *Miller's Tale* evident but that suggests that its late-medieval currency was a response to the debate about the nature of serfdom that was at the center of the class struggle taking place in fourteenth-century England. The *Liber armorum* begins by demonstrating "how gentilmen shall be knowyn from vngentill men and how bondeage began first" specifically in order to counter peasant claims of natural equality: "A bonde man or a churle wyll say, 'All we be cummyn of Adam.' So Lucifer with his cumpany may say, 'All we be cummyn of heuyn'. "[69] Lucifer and his rebel angels were the first group to be placed in bondage, followed by Cain, who was damned by God and by Adam for his fratricide: "By that did Cayn become a chorle and all his ofspryng after hym" (cciᵛ). Noah was descended from Abel's son Seth, and he in turn

> had .iii. sonnys begetyn by kynde; by the modre .ii. were named Cham and Sem and by the fadre the thirde was namyd Jafeth. Yit in theys .iii. sonnys gentilnes and vngentilnes was founde. In Cham vngentilnes was founde to his own fadre, dooun to discuver his preuytes and laugh his fadre to scorne. Jafeth was the yongist and repreued his brodre. Than like a gentilman, take mynde of Cham: for his vngentilnes he was become a chorle and had the cursyng of God and his fadre Noe. And whan Noe awoke he sayde to Cham his sonne, "Knowyst nott thow how hit become of Cayn, Adam['s] soon, and of his churlish blode? All the worlde is drownde saue we .viii. And now of the to begynne vngentilnes and a cause to destroye vs all—vppon the hit shall be and so I pray to God that it shall fall. Now to the I gyuve my curse, wycked kaytife for euer, and I gyuve to the the north parte of the worlde to draw thyn habitacion, for ther shall it be where [are] sorow and care, colde and myschef. As a churle thow shalt haue . . . the thirde parte of the worlde, wich shall be calde Europe, that is to say the contre of churlys." (ciᵛ–ciiʳ)

Nothing could more vividly illustrate the writer's sense of contemporary urgency than his or her willingness to override the traditional geographical endowments. Far from being exiled to distant Africa, the damned race of Ham is ubiquitously present in the here and now of late-medieval Europe, a presence that requires gentle readers to learn,

---

69. *The Boke of Seynt Albans* (St. Albans, 1486), fol. ciʳ; further page numbers will be included in the text. I have supplied the punctuation. The *Boke* has also been discussed by Coulton, *Medieval Village*, 232–33, and by Thrupp, *Merchant Class of Medieval London*, 288–319.

for their own self-protection, the way "to deseuer Gentilnes from vngentilnes" (ciʳ).⁷⁰ And so it is not surprising that aristocratic genealogies of the fifteenth century were careful to trace the descent of England's noble houses from Adam through Japhet.⁷¹ Finally, lest we doubt the currency of this identification of the serf with Canaan and the children of Ham, we actually find a somewhat inaccurate reference to it in that most orthodox of late-fourteenth-century texts, Chaucer's *Parson's Tale:* "This name of thraldom was nevere erst kowth til that Noe seyde that his sone Canaan sholde be thral to his bretheren for his synne" (X, 765).⁷²

What the *Miller's Tale* does, then, is to turn the myth of Ham against the clerical culture from which it originally arose. For here the searcher into hidden "pryvetee," far from being a peasant, is instead the astrologer-cleric Nicholas, who uses his illicit knowledge to mock and scorn John the Carpenter, the father Noah of the play he is staging.⁷³ Moreover, the characteristics that are ascribed to the biblical Ham by medieval clerical culture are here applied, with striking aptness, to Nicholas. Ham's name means, according to the commentators, *calidus,* and he represents a spirit that is *impatiens, inquietus,* and *commotior.*⁷⁴ He also represents, according to Augustine's authoritative exegesis,

> those who boast the name of Christian and yet live scandalous lives. For it is certain that such people proclaim Christ's passion, symbolized by Noah's nakedness, in their professions, while they dis-

70. The racist nature of the myth of Ham was made explicit in early nineteenth-century America, where it functioned as a justification for slavery; see Thomas Virgil Peterson, *Ham and Japheth: The Mythic World of Whites in the Antebellum South* (Metuchan: Scarecrow Press, 1978).

71. Alison Allan, "Yorkist Propaganda: Pedigree, Prophecy, and the 'British History' in the Reign of Edward IV," in *Patronage, Pedigree and Power in Later Medieval England,* ed. Charles Ross (Gloucester: Alan Sutton, 1979), 172.

72. This sentence is not found in the text that apparently served as Chaucer's source: Siegfried Wenzel, "The Source of Chaucer's Deadly Sins," *Traditio* 30 (1974), 368. For other contemporary examples of Ham as the progenitor of serfs, see Patricia Heath Barnum, ed., *Dives and Pauper,* EETS, OS (Oxford: Oxford University Press, 1976), 1:305; and John Wycliff, *Opera Minora,* ed. Johann Loserth (London: Paul, 1913), 146. Wycliff calls this opinion "foolish."

73. It is just possible that Chaucer derived the idea of having the role of Ham played by a cleric from Gower's identification of Ham in the *Confessio amantis* as the inventor of writing and the founder of *clergie* (G. C. Macaulay, ed., *The Complete Works of John Gower,* [London: Clarendon Press, 1900], 4, 2396–400 [1:366]); according to Macaulay's note to the passage, Gower derived his information from Godfrey of Viterbo's *Pantheon.*

74. See, for example, Ambrose, *Liber de Noe et arca* (PL 14:435); Isidore, *Quaestiones in Veterum Testamentum: In Genesin,* 8, 6 (PL 83:235–36).

honour it by their evil actions. It was of such people that we read in Scripture, "You will recognize them by their fruits."[75]

Most centrally, Ham is the heretic who reveals that which ought to remain a mystery, the *corporis mysterium* enacted in the passion and reenacted in the Eucharist: he "makes manifest that which was for the prophets a secret," and with this illicit knowledge he "deceives the simple"— the sort of "lewed man," like John, "That noght but oonly his bileve kan."[76] As John succinctly says, with (as we know from his prologue) the Miller's approval, "Men sholde nat knowe of Goddes pryvetee" (3454–56). The relevance of these characteristics to the Miller's Nicholas is self-evident. In his picture of Nicholas the Miller offers a biting exercise in cultural criticism, turning the materials of clerical culture against its proprieter and revealing by his very act of criticism how defamatory— and self-protective—are its misrepresentations.

V

Yet we must also recognize that the *Miller's Tale*, in its animosity toward John the Carpenter, contains as well an act of peasant self-criticism. In part, of course, we may have an expression here of the stresses and strains within the peasant community itself: John is a "riche gnof," and Robin represents himself in the tale as a servant boy who can be packed off to London and (so John at least thinks) to death by drowning without a second thought.[77] But again, I think we do best to understand the Miller's scorn for John as political in a deeper, more serious sense. Despite being a successful village craftsman, John not only allows himself

75. Augustine, *City of God*, 16, 2 (650–51). This interpretation is repeated throughout the Middle Ages, as by Isidore, *Quaestiones in Veterum Testamentum: In Genesin*, 8, 6 (*PL* 83:235–36), and by Rabanus Maurus, *Commentarius in Genesim*, 2, 9 (*PL* 107:525–26). So, too, the interpretation of Noah's drunken nakedness as representing Christ's passion is the standard exegesis.

76. Rabanus Maurus, *Commentarius in Genesim*, 2, 9 (*PL* 107:525), and Remigius, *Commentarius in Genesim*, 9 (*PL* 131:78). Cassian identified Ham as a worker in secret arts: see Williams, *Cain and Beowulf*, 30–31, and Gower, *Confessio amantis*, 4, 2396–400, ed. Macauley, *Complete Works*, 1:366.

77. For the relative wealth of carpenters, see Dyer, *Standards of Living*, 226–27. For their inclusion within the Statutes of Labourers, and for the accusation of overcharging, signs that they were profiting from postplague economic conditions, see Putnam, *Enforcement*, 75, 80–81, 163, and 214. For carpenters becoming country gentlemen in the fifteenth century, see Du Boulay, *Lordship of Canterbury*, 163. That Robin represents himself in so helpless a role in his *Tale* provides some evidence that although others saw millers as prosperous and powerful, millers thought of themselves otherwise.

to be intimidated by his lodger but has, by marrying the youthful Alisoun, violated a natural law that he, of all people, ought to understand; and when the Miller says that John married Alisoun because "he knewe nat Catoun, for his wit was rude" (3227), he is mockingly invoking an *auctoritas* to support a truth that ought to be self-evident to the truly natural man.[78] As Langland had put it, "kynde wit" is the companion of the commons and teaches "ech lif to knowe his owene."[79] Moreover, and more reprehensibly, John has also betrayed his class interests by handing himself over to a smooth-talking clerical con man.[80]

Thus it is John who is most severely punished at the end of the *Miller's Tale:* his wife is "swyved," his arm is broken, and his reputation as a man of probity is ruined. Yet even here, significantly enough, the Miller cannot finally withhold his sense that this punishment, however merited, is nonetheless enacted in the distasteful form of class victimization:

> The folk gan laughen at his fantasye;
> Into the roof they kiken and they cape,
> And turned *al his harm unto a jape.*
> For what so that this carpenter answerde,
> It was for noght; *no man his reson herde.*
> With othes grete he was so sworn adoun
> That *he was holde wood* in al the toun;
> *For every clerk anonright heeld with oother.*
> They seyde, *'The man is wood,* my leeve brother;'
> And every wight gan laughen at this stryf. (3840–49)

---

78. See Tillyard, *Poetry Direct and Oblique*, 88.

79. George Kane and E. Talbot Donaldson, eds., *Piers Plowman: The B-Text* (London: Athlone Press, 1975), Prol. 121–22. See also the poem written in 1392 by John Berwald of Cottingham, in which he insists that it would be "vnkind" (i.e., unnatural) for a villein to suffer "any villan hething," that is, the oppression or derision of any other villein; Rossell H. Robbins, ed. *Historical Poems of the 14th and 15th Centuries* (New York: Columbia University Press, 1959), 61; and see Dobson, *Peasants' Revolt*, 383–84.

80. An instance of clerical contempt for peasants with special relevance to the plot of the *Miller's Tale* is the widespread parodic prayer against rustics:

> Deus, qui multitudinem rusticorum congregasti et magnam discordiam inter eos et nos seminasti, da, quesumus, ut laboribus eorum fruamur et ab uxoribus eorum diligamur.

> O God, who brought forth a multitude of rustics and sowed great discord between them and us, grant, we beseech, that we may live off their labors and enjoy their wives.

Lehmann, *Parodie im Mittelalter* (Munich: Die Drei Masken, 1923), 178; see also 117, and Lehmann, *Parodistische Texte*, 22.

Before beginning to rehearse the *Miller's Tale* a nervous narrator had warned the "gentils" "nat [to] maken ernest of game" (3186); now at the end the Miller reverses the terms—and meaning—of the warning: when a group of clerks turn "al [a rustic's] harm unto a jape," more is at issue than simple comedy. The point is not only that the clerks band together against the rich artisan—an opposition that figures both the traditional medieval antagonism between clerks and peasants and also, in an oblique but nonetheless historically corroborated fashion, the larger conflict between the classes that was the central social phenomenon of Chaucer's England. Rather, it is that the terms the Miller uses here to represent the carpenter's oppression bear a powerfully political valence and force us to attend to the class consciousness to which the tale witnesses.

The clerks do not here merely silence John's arguments—"no man his reson herde"—but deny him rationality itself.[81] In twice insisting that the clerks considered John mad, the Miller is again invoking a terminology typical of medieval commentators (most of them, of course, clerics) on peasant behavior. And this madness is nowhere more visible than when the peasant seeks to promote his own interests. For the early fourteenth-century chronicler of the Abbey of Vale Royal, the "bestial men of Rutland" who had recourse to the courts and the king in a vain effort to prove that they were not the Abbot's serfs were *rabicanes*—mad dogs.[82] And as we should perhaps expect, the chroniclers of the Rising consistently use the language of insanity to describe the rebels. For Walsingham, the Rising as a whole is an expression of the *insania nativorum*—the madness of bondmen—and his account is both saturated with terms like *dementes, irrationibiles,* and *stulti* and invokes throughout the language of satanic possession: the rebels are *ganeones daemoniaci* (children of the devil), perhaps even

---

81. Not, of course, that this silencing is insignificant. In *Literature and Pulpit*, Owst provides a summary of a fourteenth-century sermon that attacks just this inability of the rich to hear the poor:

if a poor man . . . were to come asking help of some rich neighbours, "for the love of his father and mother and all those dear to him," they would deign neither to hear nor see him. If, redoubling his entreaties, he were to beg, "My Lord, for the love of Christ crucified and all the saints of God, help me, lest I be destroyed unjustly by my adversaries," still there would be "neither voice nor hearing." (315–16)

82. A long extract from the *Ledger Book of Vale Royal Abbey* (Lancashire and Cheshire Record Society, 1914), is translated by G. G. Coulton, *Medieval Village*, 132–35; for *rabicanes*, see 133.

pejores daemonibus (worse than devils).[83] Gower also describes the Rising as an expression of bestial madness: the rebels "were swine into which a cursed spirit had entered, just as Holy Writ tells of," and "just as the Devil was placed in command over the army of the lower world, so this scoundrel [Wat Tyler] was in charge of the wicked mob."[84] And even less vindictive observers invoke the language of madness and folly: a relatively disinterested macaronic poet calls the rebels "folus" and *stultes*, Knighton calls them *stultes* and refers to them as servants of the devil, Froissart compares them to devils from hell, and the monk of Westminster reinvokes *rabicanes*.[85]

"The man is *wood*," say the clerks about John when he tries to tell "his reson"—a designation important enough that the Miller first invokes it in his own voice and then has the clerks repeat it. The use of the language of folly and demonic possession to describe peasant resistance surfaces again in the *Canterbury Tales:* the lord in the *Summoner's Tale* begins by assuming that the churl John is a "fool" (2292) or—a term that is applied twice and implied once—a "demonyak" (2240, 2292; and cf. 2221). The point is that these are not simply terms of casual abuse but are derived from the language of moral censure with which the governing classes of medieval Europe, including fourteenth-century England, tried to stigmatize, and so to control, peasant protest. In having the unified mockery of the clerics pervert John's "resons" into the irrationality of madness, then, the *Miller's Tale* offers a bitter commentary upon not just the Rising of 1381 but upon the official language that sought to censor peasant resistance at the level of discourse as effectively as the instruments of government suppressed it politically.

VI

In searching for an ideological posture by means of which to distance himself from the cultic and increasingly caste-defined aristocratic culture of his time, Chaucer almost inevitably turned to the most vigorous oppositional force within his society—the rural world of peasant culture. In the *General Prologue* the Miller is represented in the conventional terms of peasant caricature: he is grossly ugly, with a flat nose, a huge mouth, and swinishly red hairs that protrude from a wart and match a beard also red "as any sowe or fox"—in sum, a threatening

83. Walsingham, *Historia anglicana*, 1:457–60, 472, 2:13, 16; see Dobson, *Peasants' Revolt*, 169–74, 272–75, 307–10.

84. Stockton, *Major Latin Works*, 58, 65.

85. For these terms, see Dobson, *Peasants' Revolt*, 144, 183, 189, 199, 278.

figure of peasant animality who uses his head not for rational thought (of which peasants are in any case incapable) but to enact invasive acts of violence: "Ther was no dore that he nolde . . . breke it at a rennyng with his heed" (I, 550–51).[86] And when he then invades the tale-telling game, he displays two of the most characteristic of peasant vices— drunkenness and a contempt for order.[87] In sum, the essential terms of the Miller's representation are not moral and psychological but social and political; and the consciousness articulated by his *Tale* is derived from the politics of late-medieval English society.

It is a consciousness, moreover, to which Chaucer grants remarkable scope and force, allowing it both to counter the hegemonic culture of the aristocracy and to subvert the language of class hatred promoted by certain forms of clerical discourse. Yet as we should expect, this authority is immediately, and severely, circumscribed. For as soon as the claims of peasant class consciousness are put forward they are countered. The *Reeve's Tale* accomplishes this subversion in two ways. One is to reveal the disunity within the peasant class itself, not simply by the antagonism between the Reeve and the Miller but by the Reeve's own betrayal of class interests. He is himself both an agent of seigneurial control and has social ambitions: he began life as a carpenter, he is now a reeve, and his dress and diction reveal clerical ambitions.[88] In short, he shows that the social identity asserted by the Miller is a fiction, that there is no class unity among the peasantry but only individuals.

86. For a discussion of the conventions governing the representation of peasants, see Alice M. Colby, *The Portrait in Twelfth-Century French Literature* (Geneva: Droz, 1965), 73–81; Beatrice White, "Poet and Peasant," in *The Reign of Richard II*, ed. F. R. H. Du Boulay and Caroline Barron (London: Athlone Press, 1971), 58–74.

87. Indeed, he is even given a name that is not only itself lower class—the male protagonist of the *pastrourelle*, for instance, is typically called Robin—but that seems to have carried implications of subversion and illegality: a number of fourteenth-century texts, including *Piers Plowman*, refer to criminals as Roberdesmen, and the term— perhaps like the Miller's own name—was probably derived from the stories of Robin Hood; see J. C. Holt, "The Origins and Audience of the Ballads of Robin Hood," *Past and Present* 18 (1960), reprinted in R. H. Hilton, ed., *Peasants, Knights and Heretics* (Cambridge: Cambridge University Press, 1976), 241. For Chaucer's familiarity with the Robin Hood rhymes, see *Troilus* 5, 1174, where Pandarus refers to "haselwode, there joly Robyn pleyde."

88. In theory the reeve was chosen by the tenants to represent them, and should therefore be distinguished from the bailiff, who was the lord's agent; but in practice the reeve often functioned as a bailiff: see H. S. Bennett, "The Reeve and the Manor in the Fourteenth Century," *EHR* 41 (1926): 358–65. In the later Middle Ages, according to Father Raftis, "the inability of the villagers to depend upon officials (reeves, for instance) as their 'men' left the peasant exposed to demands such as the poll tax" ("Social Change versus Revolution," 16).

The second way in which the Reeve subverts the politics of the *Miller's Tale* is by reinvoking the religious imperatives that the Miller, in his displacement of the Monk and his satire on clerical values, had sought to set aside. At the heart of the Reeve's attempt to "quite" (3916) the Miller is his all-out assault on one of the central principles that governs the Miller's world—that the natural and the supernatural, the sexual and the religious, animal nature and Christian imperatives, are in essential congruence. For the Reeve such a notion is a naive wish-fulfillment, a self-gratifying delusion. In his *Tale* Alisoun's innocent "Tehee" becomes the "Wehee" (4066) of the clerks' horse as he ramps among the "wilde mares" (4065) in the fen: the coltish gladness of the *Miller's Tale* is here shown to be the dangerous wildness of the stallion, and as Kolve has shown, the horse imagery that pervades the *Tale* invokes a traditional and uncompromising warning of the dangers of loosing the animal passions that inhabit man.[89]

The Reeve represents himself as painfully aware of those passions within himself (unlike Robin, who can see the mote in another's eye "but in his owene he kan nat seen a balke" [3920]); and in his *Prologue* he deploys a penitential language that speaks to man's sinful nature. The Reeve's screed on the four sins of old men and the dotage of age is a way to assert both his moral and his social superiority, and his aspirations to clerical status inform us as well why he was so oversensitive to the Miller's tale about a carpenter—the lowly craft he left behind on his way to becoming a reeve. But his "sermonyng" (3899) also establishes penitential values in the privileged position that the Monk would have given them had he been allowed to speak. Moreover, it articulates those values from the perspective of the end: the Reeve ostentatiously insists upon his age, and in his image of Death drawing the tap of life and letting the wine run out (including the wine of Southwark that has fueled Robin's revelry) he offers a challenge to the festivity that underwrites the tale-telling game as a whole.[90] The source of the Reeve's image here, as of his earlier one of the four coals that lurk in the old man's ashes, is Jean de Meun's *Testament,* and his words witness to a familiar medieval sense of terminality.

Osewald had described himself as a medlar pear, "an open-ers":

That ilke fruyt is ever lenger the wers,
Til it be roten in mullok or in stree.

89. Kolve, *Chaucer and the Imagery of Narrative,* 236–48.
90. Again, Kolve's discussion of this image demonstrates its centrality to the Reeve's consciousness (ibid., 222–33).

We olde men, I dred, so fare we:
Til we be roten, kan we nat be rype;
We hoppen alwey while the world wol pype. (3871–76)

It is under the sign of this condition, in which ripeness and rottenness
are indistinguishable, that the *Reeve's Tale* is told: his vision of life
haunted by an awareness of the end to which all things come, "myrthe
and revelrye" (4005) are for him always tainted by a retributive justice
that prefigures that of the ultimate Judge whom he is himself shortly to
confront. Hence he correlates the fabliau principle that "a gylour shal
hymself bigyled be" (4321) with the Old Testament principle of *oculum
pro oculo*, and he imposes upon both Robin the Miller and the narrative
agents of his *Tale* the harsh judgment he himself anticipates.[91] Nor is
this judgment in fact delayed: by revealing its teller's culpable ignorance of his own moral failures and his small-minded vindictiveness,
the *Reeve's Tale* comes ultimately to have most relevance to the Reeve
himself, to *quite* its own teller. Thus Chaucer's recasting of the fabliau
principle of *ars ut artem falleret* shows how this self-marginalized literary form can begin to accommodate the penitential imperatives of the
pilgrimage.

The Host, championing the holiday spirit as long as it remains
wholly without political force, will of course have none of it: not only is

91.   Paul Olson has shown that the text of Matthew 7:1–5 ("Judge not that ye be not
judged")—part of which the Reeve himself cites (3919–20)—governs the *Tale* ("The
Reeve's Tale: Chaucer's *Measure for Measure*," *SP* 59 [1962]: 1–17). The idea of correlating
this text with the fabliau principle of beguiling the guiler was perhaps suggested to Chaucer by the passage in the C-Text of *Piers Plowman* where Christ explains how by the
perfect symmetry of salvation history his sacrifice simultaneously fulfills and transcends
(i.e., *quites*) the Old Law:
        Þe old law techeth
    That gylours be bigiled and yn here gyle falle,
    And ho-so hit out a mannes eye or elles his fore-teth,
    Or eny manere membre maymeth oþer herteth,
    The same sore shal he have þat eny so smyteth.
    Dentem pro dente, et oculum pro oculo.
    So lyf shal lyf lete, ther lyf hath lyf anyented,
    So þat lyf quyte lyf, þe olde lawe hit asketh.
    Ergo, soule shal soule quyte and synne to synne wende,
    And al þat men mysdede, y man to amenden hit;
    And þat deth fordede my deth to releve,
    And both quykie and quyte that queynte was thorw synne,
    And gyle be bigyled thorw grace at þe laste.
    Ars ut artem falleret. (20, 381–92)
Langland's influence upon the *Reeve's Tale* is all the more likely since Chaucer probably
included a reeve in the *General Prologue* on Langland's model: see Jill Mann, *Chaucer and
Medieval Estates Satire* (Cambridge: Cambridge University Press, 1973), 163–67.

the Reeve's self-aggrandizing sermonizing itself a waste of the time of which he claims to have so little, but it is singularly out of place. Harry Bailly wishes to hurry the Reeve, but the language he uses bespeaks his own sense of festal temporality:

> What, shul we speke alday of hooly writ?
>
> . . . .
>
> Sey forth thy tale, and tarie nat the tyme.
> Lo Depeford! and it is half-wey pryme.
> Lo Grenewych, ther many a shrewe is inne!
> It were al tyme thy tale to bigynne. (3902–8)

Although the bourgeois mind defines here a quintessentially mercantile temporality, as it does again in the *Man of Law's Prologue* (16–32), it also wishes to protect the special time of holiday from the encroachments of an inappropriate spiritual earnestness. If it is already seven-thirty in the morning, it is *only* seven-thirty, and the Host wants to make sure that the pilgrims do not speak "*alday* of hooly writ." In the *Parson's Prologue* the shadows will lengthen and reveal it to be "foure of the clokke" (X, 5), which is the time for the language of penance; but that time has not yet arrived. The pilgrimage is both itself an act of satisfaction prescribed by the sacrament of penance and has at its goal another performance of the sacrament. But the Reeve's penitential *Prologue* and confessional *Tale* have introduced into the tale-telling game an earnestness it cannot sustain. Hence the penitential impulse that he articulates is simultaneously invoked and discredited: he is a fraudulent penitent, a social climber masquerading as a priest whose self-abasement is a warped self-gratification; and his inadvertently self-betraying *Tale* is a long way from a genuine confession.

Yet he has not only reintroduced into the tale telling the spiritual imperative the *Miller's Tale* was designed to neutralize, but he has also redirected the oppositional dynamics of the *Canterbury Tales* from the potential violence of political hostility to the less inflammatory debate between religious imperatives and literary interests. To be sure, this debate is central to the very premise of the *Canterbury Tales*: are the pilgrims heading from London to Canterbury under a spiritual guidance that comes to be embodied in the Parson, or is the Host returning them to the festal board at the Tabard? Is there a mode of literary discourse that can celebrate a wider range of human experience than a narrow piety will allow and yet not fall prey to a merely recreative revelry? That these literary topics become central questions as the *Canterbury Tales* unfold shows the extent to which the urgent social issues raised by the *Miller's Tale* have been disarmed.

The stigmatizing of the Miller's interruption is carried to its inevitable conclusion by means of the *Cook's Tale*. Although he means to recoup the disruptive energies of the *Miller's Tale*, the Cook reveals them to be not enlivening but destructive, not a necessary alternative to the hegemonic ideology of the *Knight's Tale* but a riotous excess that threatens the social order as a whole. This excess is embodied in the aptly named Perkyn Revelour. Initially described in terms that recall the innocent festivity of the *Miller's Tale* (4367–74), this rake's progress takes him from the socially approved processions or "ridyng[s]" (4377) of Cheapside first to the "disport" (4382) of gambling and theft, then to the public humiliation with which he is "lad with revel to Newegate" (4402), and finally to the "revel and disport" (4420) he shares with his "lowke" (4415), whose prostitute-wife "swyved for hir sustenaunce" (4422). The *Cook's Tale* is thus a story of degeneration and ejection—of "aquitance" (4411)—that itself *quites* the fabliaux that have preceded it. This operation is made explicit in the Cook's proverb, which refers to him and his *Tale* as well as to his protagonist: "Wel bet is roten appul out of hoord / Than that it rotie al the remenaunt" (4406–7). And his own performance is, appropriately, terminated before it can defile the *Tales* as a whole.

In making the Cook the voice of lower-class criminality, Chaucer links him with journeyman wage laborers and, beneath them, the marginals of urban society, the men whom the merchant patriciate was most concerned to keep under control for reasons that were made scandalously clear when they welcomed the rebellious peasants in 1381.[92] And in having him employed by the gildsmen, and serve as an expression of their social pretensions, Chaucer extends this culpability to the small, relatively powerless craft gilds.[93] The social meaning of the *Cook's Tale*, in other words, reveals Chaucer placing his poetry in the service of the dominant merchant patriciate from which he himself originally derived. So it is hardly surprising that the *Cook's Tale* is used to pass judgment upon the Miller's efforts to mount a political opposition to the hegemony of aristocratic values.

This judgment reappears one last time, in the penultimate moment of the *Canterbury Tales*. In the *Manciple's Prologue* the Cook's revelry has been reduced to inarticulate drunkenness. Unable to undergo the

92. For the marginals, see Bronislaw Geremek, *The Margins of Society in Late Medieval Paris*, trans. Jean Birrell (Cambridge: Cambridge University Press, 1987).

93. For the distinction between the powerful trade gilds or merchant companies, and the far weaker craft gilds, see Thrupp, *Merchant Class of Medieval London*, 27–41. For a different account of the *Cook's Tale*, which sees it as expressing the attitude of a conservative gildsman, see Kolve, *Chaucer and the Imagery of Narrative*, 257–96.

"penaunce" (IX, 12) of tale telling the Host there imposes on him, he is roused into ineffective rage by the Manciple's satire and launches a hapless attack that is mockingly described in the language of chivalry: "This was a fair chyvachee of a cook!" (50). Hogge of Ware here reveals his truly bestial nature: "Fy, stynkyng swyn!" (40), the Manciple says, and describes him—in the defamatory language that the *Game and Playe of the Chesse* applied to the lower orders as a whole—as "wyn ape" (44).[94] He is also described as devilish:

> Hoold cloos thy mouth, man, by thy fader kyn!
> The devel of helle sette his foot therin!
> Thy cursed breeth infecte wole us alle. (37–39)

In the *Vox clamantis* Gower identified the peasants as swinish, accused them of being inspired by the devil (their attack upon the Tower of London reminded him of the jaws of Hell), mentioned cooks as among the participants, and even designated one of the most vainglorious with the name of Hogg: "Hogg brandishes his pomp, for with his noble bearing he thinks he is greater than any king."[95] At the end of the *Tales*, then, Chaucer is also prepared to represent the rebellious Cook in Gower's abusive terms. The final word on this contretemps is the Host's citation of a prayer to St. Bacchus that parodies the Pater Noster, a festive gesture that definitively annuls the very revelry it seeks to reinvoke:

> O thou Bacus, yblessed be thy name,
> That so kanst turnen ernest into game!
> Worship and thank be to thy deitee! (99–101)[96]

And the Host concludes, "Of that mateere ye gete namoore of me" (102)—nor from anyone else. Thoroughly discredited by both this episode and the Manciple's mordant and insincere fable, festivity drains out of a game that is shortly to be brought to a definitive conclusion by the Parson. In this penultimate moment, then, the Cook's rebelliousness, and rebelliousness per se, stand for all that must be annulled if the *Canterbury Tales* is to be brought to its appointed and orthodox conclusion.

94. See above, note 67.
95. Stockton, *Major Latin Works*, 87, 59, 67.
96. For this prayer, see "Le Martyr de Saint Baccus," *Nouveau recueil de contes, dits, fabliaux, et autres pièces inédites des XIIIᵉ, XIVᵉ et XVᵉ siècles,* ed. Achille Jubinal (Paris: Pannier, 1839), 1:250–65, especially 251–52.

Chapter Six

The Wife of Bath and the Triumph of the Subject

"I think you've had it backwards all this time. You wanted to enter history. Wrong approach, Leon. What you really want is out. Get out. Jump out. Find your place and name on another level."

The tale-telling game restarts in Fragment II, as if the Miller had not interrupted, with a chronographia (II, 1–15) that repeats, and replaces, the one that originally introduced the *General Prologue* (I, 1–18).[1] "Lordynges," says the Host (II, 16), using a title that signals the highly placed male audience to whom he thinks it worthwhile to direct his attention,

> Wel kan Senec and many a philosophre
> Biwaillen tyme moore than gold in cofre;
> For "los of catel may recovered be,
> But los of tyme shendeth us," quod he. (25–28)

This language of bourgeois parsimony reinvokes the sober respectability that the churls of Fragment I had so scandalously flouted, a respectability then given legalistic force in the language with which the Host solicits the next tale from the Man of Law. "Ye been submytted, thurgh youre free assent, / To stonden in this cas at my juggement," he says, "*Acquiteth* you now of youre biheeste" (35–37)—a phrase that seeks to relocate fabliau *quiting* in an institutional and regulatory context. The Man of Law replies in kind: "Biheste is dette, and I wol holde fayn / Al my biheste" (41–42). Then he casts about for a "thrifty tale" (46)—one that is profitable or rewarding—that will now fulfill the prescription

---

1. For the *Man of Law's Introduction* as establishing a new beginning to the *Canterbury Tales,* see V. A. Kolve, *Chaucer and the Imagery of Narrative* (Stanford: Stanford University Press, 1984), 293–94.

that the Host tried vainly to invoke back when the Miller first inter-rupted ("Abyd," he had said to the Miller, "and lat us werken *thriftily*" [3131]). The pressures of social and legal constraint are thus poised to return the tale-telling game to the authoritarian orthodoxy that the Miller had originally challenged. And given the very substantial wealth of a sergeant of the law, the social ambitiousness of lawyers generally, and their role in enforcing the status quo, the Man of Law is an excel-lent choice to fulfill this role.[2]

Formally Fragments II and III replay the pattern of I: social authority is invoked by the Man of Law and countered by the Wife of Bath, a rebellion that is then dangerously exaggerated in the two *quiting* tales that follow, especially in the Summoner's scurrilous *fabliau* with which the four-tale movement concludes. But the terms of contention are in fact very different: we move from the political opposition generated by the class inequality of Fragment I to an ideological antithesis deter-mined by gender. Not that important class distinctions are not at work here as well. The highly placed Man of Law tells a story he learned from wealthy merchants about an empress of Rome—a story originally writ-ten by a cleric (Nicholas Trevet) for a royal nun (Mary of Woodstock, daughter of Edward I).[3] And the Wife of Bath is a rural commodity producer and tradeswoman whose economic independence chal-lenges the traditional order of feudal society and whose *Tale* concludes with a sermon on *gentillesse* that defines nobility in terms of virtue, not birth.[4] But these social determinants provide not the topic of the confrontation—which is gender—but its context.

2. For the very large income of a sergeant-at-law (£300 annually), see Christopher Dyer, *Standards of Living in the Later Middle Ages* (Cambridge: Cambridge University Press, 1989), 47; for the social advancement of lawyers, M. M. Postan, *The Medieval Economy and Society* (Harmondsworth: Penguin Books, 1975), 175; and for the interpenetration of the legal and mercantile classes, Sylvia Thrupp, *The Merchant Class of Medieval London* (Ann Arbor: University of Michigan Press, 1962 [1948]), 246. As the rage toward lawyers and legal records expressed by the rebels of 1381 shows, the legal system was widely per-ceived as serving the governing class.

3. On Trevet's *Chronicles* and their suitability for their patroness, see Ruth Dean, "Nicholas Trevet, Historian," in *Medieval Learning and Literature: Essays Presented to Rich-ard William Hunt*, ed. J. J. G. Alexander and M. T. Gibson (Oxford: Clarendon Press, 1976), 328–52.

4. See Mary Carruthers, "The Wife of Bath and the Painting of Lions," *PMLA* 94 (1979): 209–22, and D. W. Robertson, Jr., " 'And for my land thus hastow mordred me?': Land Tenure, the Cloth Industry, and the Wife of Bath," *ChR* 14 (1979–80): 403–20. For the importance of the workers in the cloth industry in the Rising of 1381, see Rodney H. Hilton, *Class Conflict and the Crisis of Feudalism* (London: Hambledon Press, 1985), 152. The independent commodity producer is postfeudal not because he or she produces

Moreover, gender itself is conceived largely, although not entirely, in metaphoric terms. What the Wife champions, as perhaps we should expect from a male author, is less the rights of her sex, much less those of her class, than the rights of selfhood. It is subjectivity per se that she promotes, a subjectivity that Chaucer, by no means uniquely, here associates with women. Throughout the Middle Ages women were denied social conceptualization, even existence as social—and historical—beings. Not only were they almost entirely excluded from public life, but their existence as part of the social totality was often ignored.[5] In the estates lists by which medieval society imagined itself, lay women are categorized not by economic, social, or political function but either by social status as determined by their male relatives or by marital status. Hence it is not surprising that when Marsilius of Padua defined the *populus,* he said that it included everybody but children, slaves, aliens—and women.[6] But perhaps this exclusion also carried with it (or so men thought) a sense of freedom, a liberation from the constraints of a highly regulatory social system. If women were denied social definition, did this not mean that the realm of the *asocial*—of the internal, the individual, the subjective—was peculiarly theirs? Men, as befitted historical beings, had social responsibilities; women, as befitted the socially invisible, had private lives. Men had careers; women had characters.

This familiar ideology of gender is deeply inscribed in Chaucer's representation of the feminine in the *Wife of Bath's Prologue and Tale.* What Chaucer's Wife wants is not political or social change; on the contrary, the traditional order is quite capable of providing the marital happiness she desires. To be sure, to acknowledge that the basic unit of social life is a socially undetermined selfhood entails important consequences that themselves carry the possibility (although by no means the necessity) of

---

commodities (which is true to some extent of virtually all agrarian production throughout the Middle Ages) but because the mode of production is *independent,* the defining characteristic of the feudal mode of production being its dependency (Postan, *Medieval Economy and Society,* 88).

5. For the "overwhelmingly private nature" ascribed to medieval womankind, which allowed them to be conceived "in iconic rather than narrative terms"—that is, without a history—see Diane Owen Hughes, "Invisible Madonnas? The Italian Historiographical Tradition and the Women of Medieval Italy," in *Women in Medieval History and Historiography,* ed. Susan Mosher Stuard (Philadelphia: University of Pennsylvania Press, 1987), 25–26.

6. Shulamith Shahar, *The Fourth Estate: A History of Women in the Middle Ages* (London: Methuen, 1983), 2–3; Marsilius of Padua, *The Defender of the Peace (Defensor pacis),* trans. Alan Gewirth (New York: Columbia University Press, 1956), 1, 12, 4 (45–46).

political change. And to see that the bearers of this message are women is also a political statement. But the implications of the politics of individualism are very different from the class-determined dissent articulated by the Miller: the selfhood privileged by individualism is by definition already common property. Thus the Wife avoids the kind of antagonistic political issues invoked by the Miller and offers in their place a less activist, more congenial message.

The revisionary process initiated by the Wife of Bath can be successfully completed, therefore, because her opposition is generated from a position that does *not* correspond to the most visible and politically specific oppositional forces at work in Chaucer's historical world. On the contrary, her invocation of the rights of the subject derives its force, as I shall argue in this chapter, from a dense and widespread web of precedents found in earlier medieval writing. Precisely the familiarity of her challenge, however brilliantly innovative the form in which it is articulated, makes it appealing and useful to Chaucer. Moreover, the final two movements of this staged, four-act drama of rebellion—the *Friar's* and the *Summoner's Tales*—are also constructed from highly traditional materials that while, again, brilliantly reaccented, nonetheless remain comfortably within the settled structures of medieval social ideology. Finally, Chaucer uses the opposition between the Man of Law and Wife of Bath to explore yet again the problematic of authorship that preoccupied him throughout his career. And here too the terms of representation are directed less toward the political specificities of writing within a class-bound context than with a highly generalized notion of cultural authority understood in terms of gender. It is with an examination of the staging of this problematic in the *Man of Law's Introduction* that we shall begin our analysis.

I

Not only does the Man of Law represent the attitudes and values of the governing classes, but he immediately identifies Chaucer with his own orthodoxy. He is, he claims, bereft of thrifty tales because Chaucer has exhausted the store—"And if he have nought seyed hem, leve brother, / In o book, he hath seyd hem in another" (51–52). In fact, the Man of Law's survey of what he calls Chaucer's "sermons" (87) is restricted to the poems of Ovidian pathos: the Ceyx and Alcyone episode in the *Book of the Duchess* and the tales of "noble wyves . . . and loveris" (59) included in the *Legend of Good Women*. But in aligning his *Tale* with this kind of writing, the Man of Law places it, as we have seen, in opposition to the developing *Canterbury Tales.*[7] And when Chaucer counters it with the *Wife of Bath's Prologue and Tale* he makes it clear that the specific term of opposition is the representation of women.

In the *Prologue* to the *Legend of Good Women* Queen Alceste reveals herself to be a victim who has internalized her own subjection. When the poet attempts to correct the god of Love's reductive reading of his poetry, Alceste denies him voice. "Lat be thyn arguynge," she says,

> For Love ne wol nat countrepleted be
> In ryght ne wrong; and lerne that at me! (F, 475–77)

—learn it, that is, from my imposition on you of the tyranny of which I am myself a victim. This economy of suffering is repeated throughout the Legends, as the dogged poet imposes upon his protagonists the tyranny under which he himself groans and so generates the virtuous female suffering he is condemned to celebrate. Each of the Legends thematizes the effacement of the subject that is the condition of its production. Just as the poet becomes an agent for Alceste's monolithic message, so does each of the good women bow before male tyranny in order to make manifest her virtue. And the condition of this self-defeating display of female superiority is that it always be seen from the outside, as object rather than subject. Consequently, the individual legends mute their protagonists: they continually gesture toward the Ovidian letters in which these women expressed, at least fictively, their own experience, but they never allow them, nor the female subjects they inscribe, presence in the poem. In this sense the most typical of the Legends is that of the definitively muted Philomela. But the female "tonge" that Tereus severed (2334) reappears in the vigorous "tonge" of that "verray jangleresse" (III, 638) the Wife of Bath—a reappearance that measures the distance between the *Legend* and the *Canterbury Tales* precisely in terms of the recuperation of the speaking subject.

The *Tale* told by the orthodox Man of Law is a Christianized version of the Ovidian tales of pathos told by Chaucer in the *Legend*—the dutiful author with whom the Man of Law identifies but whom the *Canterbury Tales* show to be in the process of supersession. As a foil to the *Wife of Bath's Prologue and Tale*, it offers a feminine virtue brought into existence by male authority. As Constance herself acknowledges, her redemptive mission is an effect of her father's tyranny—

---

7.   An excellent guide to these issues is provided by Alfred David, *The Strumpet Muse: Art and Morals in Chaucer's Poetry* (Bloomington: Indiana University Press, 1976), 118–34.

> I, wrecche woman, no fors though I spille!
> Wommen are born to thraldom and penance,
> And to been under mannes governance (285–87)

—and at the end of her career she pathetically begs her father to "sende me namoore unto noon hethenesse" (1112). This governance extends, moreover, to Alla's marital demands (708–14) and to Constance's pitiless exile by this "housbonde routhelees" (863). However edifying Constance's suffering may be, it is a function of the sexual authority of men, just as, at the level of narrative form, her exemplary role is a function of the generic authority of hagiography. Indeed, the disturbing instrumentality of her role in the *Tale* extends to the *Tale* itself: the Syrian merchants first pass on their "tidynges" of Constance's beauty to the Sultan along with their other wares, just as more recent merchants— "fadres of tidynges / And tales" (129–30)—later passed them on to the Man of Law, who finally transmits them to us. The tale is a mercantile "wynnynge" (127) with which the Man of Law will pay his "dette" (41) to the Host, a transaction that bears a striking similarity to the model of patronage described in the Prologue to the *Legend*, where the poet plays his "dette" (F 541) first with his balade, then with the Legends themselves. In sum, then, the *Legend* and the *Tale* both describe and exemplify the way men traffic in women.

With the completion of the *Man of Law's Tale* the Host calls upon the Parson—the counterpart to the Monk whom he had invited to follow the Knight in Fragment I. The Wife interrupts, setting aside the "lerned men of lore" (1168) whom the Host so much admires. Her tale, she tells us, "schal not ben of philosophie, / Ne phislyas, ne termes queinte of lawe" (1188–89): with these designations she is rejecting the kind of tales told by the Clerk, the Physician, and the Man of Law himself—all of them tales of good women (Griselda, Virginia, and Constance). But her brilliant manipulations of the authority of male learning are not accomplished, as we shall see, merely for purposes of parody. On the contrary, she seeks to find a means for the expression of the female subjectivity the *Legend* and the *Man of Law's Tale* effaced. Her program thus requires her to revise the model that prescribed her intervention in the first place, the *Miller's Tale*. The *Miller's Tale* is a narrative staging of the natural vitality and resourcefulness embodied in the "yonge wyf" Alison—values that reappear, with a sharply different valence, in the narrative told by Alison of Bath. The vernal innocence and beauty of the Miller's Alison served, as we saw, to elicit the male desire that motivated the tale. And in the last analysis, Alison evaded both the possessiveness of male desire and the severity of male judgment: the elegant plot spun its webs around her without actually entangling her, and she provided not only the model for the tale's climatic joke but also, and against all expectation, the norm by which we were invited to understand her world. Her inarticulate "Tehee!" (3740) fulfilled itself in the festivity first of the neighbors—"every wight gan laughen at this stryf" (3849)—and then of the pilgrims themselves, who "laughen at this nyce cas" (3855). Alison was not merely the heroine of the *Miller's Tale* but its presiding spirit.

And as such she partook of its limitations. She was, finally, no *more* articulate than her "Tehee," and her preeminence was never anything more than ludic: the political dynamic that motivated the *Tale* as a whole took place entirely apart from her. However ungraspable, she remained an object, "a prymerole, a piggesnye" (3268). Like the victimized maiden of the *Wife of Bath's Tale*, she elicited overmastering desire from the men of her world, but despite (or even because of) her resistance we cannot imagine her either leading them to enlightenment or herself purveying a saving wisdom. But of course this is not true of Alison of Bath, and when the feminine principle reinterrupts the tale-telling game it appears in a sharply expanded form. The Wife's *Prologue and Tale*, unlike the *Miller's Tale*, do not bespeak "Alison-ness" but are on the contrary spoken by it. No longer merely the protagonist of a fictive narration, the female both controls her own verbal world and the tale-telling game itself. And in this she becomes a model for the poet.

II

One of the more notorious of Alison of Bath's wanderings by the way is her digression into the realm of classical scholarship. In the midst of an Arthurian romance she interposes an Ovidian epyllion, a version of the tale of Midas and his ass's ears. Her stated purpose is to show that "we wommen konne no thyng hele" (950), but despite this apparently laudable attempt at self-criticism her telling is both inaccurate and incomplete. The male servant of the original becomes Midas's wife, and the crucial conclusion, in which the reeds whisper Midas's secret abroad, is suppressed. No wonder, then, that modern commentators have seen the Wife's Ovidianism as evidence of her irrepressible loquacity, her bad scholarship, even her moral turpitude.[8] But the very unanimity of

8. Judson Boyce Allen and Patrick Gallacher, "Alisoun through the Looking Glass: Or Every Man His Own Midas," *ChR* 4 (1970): 99–105; Richard Hoffman, *Ovid and the Canterbury Tales* (Philadelphia: University of Pennsylvania Press, 1966), 145–49; D. W. Robertson, Jr., "The Wife of Bath and Midas," *SAC* 6 (1984): 1–20.

these conclusions tempts a counterthought: does not the Wife here, as elsewhere, mean more than she says?

When Ovid's *famulus* revealed his lord's shameful secret he did so, paradoxically, by hiding it. He dug a hole and buried his *parva vox*, his whisper; his words were literally covered over (*obruta verba*).[9] In Alison's version the hiddenness of the wife's disclosure is imaged differently:

> And sith she dorste telle it to no man,
> Doun to a mareys faste by she ran—
> Til she cam there hir herte was a-fyre—
> And as a bitore bombleth in the myre,
> She leyde hir mouth unto the water doun. (969–73)[10]

Kneeling by the edge of the swamp and bumbling her message into the mire, Midas's wife provides an image of feminine speaking that suggests both obscurity and uncleanness. The metaphor governs, disturbingly, what we are also told, that the very ardor that impels her to speak is peculiarly feminine: the "conseil" swells within her as if she were with child, her heart is on fire as if she were in love. Her sense of relief is similarly physical: "Now is myn herte al hool, now is it oute" (977). Her speaking, in short, is coextensive with her nature as a woman and apparently as compulsive and untrustworthy as her sexuality. The obscurity of her speech is a function of the passion that urges her; its indecency a function of the carnality that characterizes her as a woman.

But the habits—or compulsions—of the Wife's almost entirely male audience may be equally suspect. As she is at pains to point out, the climax of Ovid's story is, in her version, not denied but strategically deferred: "The remenant of the tale if ye wol heere, / Redeth Ovyde, and ther ye may it leere" (981–82). This withholding ought to encour-

---

9. *Metamorphoses* 11, 187, 193.

10. The "bitore" or bittern was known as the "myredromylle" because, in the words of John Trevisa, it "is a bridde þat makeþ soun and voys in watir. . . . And he . . . is a bridde of greet glotonye and puttiþ þe bille down into þe watir and makeþ an horrible noyse and is enemye namliche to eles" (M. C. Seymour et al., eds., *On the Properties of Things: John Trevisa's Translation of Bartholomaeus Anglicus, De proprietatibus rerum* [Oxford: Clarendon Press, 1975], 1:635–36); see also Sidney J. H. Herrtage, ed., *Catholicon Anglicum*, EETS, OS 75 (London: Trübner, 1881), 50, 240. The Wife's use of the bittern image is appropriately antifeminist: reputed to have two stomachs or "wombes," as does a woman, its gluttony parallels the uncontrolled devouring which characterizes the feminine appetite. Chaucer probably got the image from Guillaume Deguileville's portrait of Gluttony, who has "com butor / deuz ventres" that are labeled "ivrece" and "Goufres, . . . Qui de mengier touz jours est prest" (*Le pèlerinage de la vie humaine*, ed. J. J. Stürzinger [London: Roxburghe Club, 1893], 325).

age her audience—or at least its learned members—to remember Ovid's version, and to recall that there the tattletale was not a woman at all but the trusted, male servant; that the secret of Midas's ears was no secret at all—the wind in the reeds wafted abroad the telltale sound *aures aselli;* and, most important, that the ears have a crucial significance. They are Midas's punishment for his foolish incapacity as a listener: called upon to judge between Pan's satyr songs and Apollo's divine hymns, he all too eagerly chose the carnal before the spiritual, the body before the mind. In discovering the full dimensions of Ovid's original, the reader comes to understand the Wife's strategy. The deferred conclusion explains both the misogynist surface with which she has covered over a tale of male deficiency and the need for the covering in the first place. For her telling argues that men, their listening obstructed by the carnality symbolized by their ass's ears, will naturally prefer the immediate self-gratifications of antifeminism to the severer pleasures of self-knowledge. The initial image of feminine speaking appears now to have been only an enticement, the deferral a test of the reader's patience: if men are really committed to a disinterested quest for truth they will avoid a surface misogyny in favor of the wisdom offered by the full story. Masculine listening can be as compelled as feminine speaking, a conclusion that rebounds with fine appropriateness upon the current critical responses to the Wife's digression. But can a man learn the lesson of his ass's ears when he has ass's ears? The Wife of Bath's text, here and elsewhere, solicits both body and mind, and it requires for its explication both an erotics and a hermeneutic. Who is equal to its demands? "Yblessed be God that I have wedded fyve! / Welcome the sixte, whan that evere he shal" (44–45).

The tale of Midas is a digression that exemplifies the characteristic method of the Wife's rhetoric. Most commentaries on the *Prologue and Tale* assume that the Wife has no rhetorical strategy at all: her garrulous ramblings are taken as a process of continual, unmotivated self-disclosure: she speaks, apparently, only that we may know her.[11] To demonstrate that this is not the case, I wish to analyze not only the *Prologue and Tale* themselves but a number of other texts, most available

11. The powerlessness of the Wife before her own language is an assumption shared by those who read her iconographically, as "a literary personification of rampant 'femininity' or carnality," in D. W. Robertson's well-known phrase (*A Preface to Chaucer* [Princeton: Princeton University Press, 1962], 321) or ethically, as a complex human character (see E. T. Donaldson, *Speaking of Chaucer* [London: Athlone Press, 1970], 174). The only real exception to this assumption is Theodore Silverstein, "The Wife of Bath and the Rhetoric of Enchantment," *MP* 58 (1961): 153–73, but see also Charles Koban, "Hearing Chaucer Out: The Art of Persuasion in the *Wife of Bath's Tale*," *ChR* 5 (1970–71): 225–39.

to Chaucer, in which the special status of feminine rhetoric had already
been explored. The larger purpose is to show that Chaucer, conceiving
of the Wife's performance as an act of deliberate self-fashioning,
sought to establish the construction of subjectivity—the representation of character—as itself a topic worthy of serious literary practice. It
is in this sense that the Wife's performance provided Chaucer with an
opportunity to represent and defend his own poetic activity.

The language of poetry, as enacted by the poet and received by the
reader, was often conceived in the Middle Ages in sexual, and specifically in feminine, terms. The voice of the poet is inescapably aligned
with that of women: his rhetoric is, to an important degree, always
feminine. Jean de Meun, for instance, draws a continuous parallel between the lover's "art d'amors" and the poet's art of writing about love:
"whoever writes about the thing—if he doesn't wish to turn aside from
the truth—ought to make the words resemble the deeds; for sounds,
neighbors to their things, ought to be cousins to the facts."[12] Cousins to
their deeds, Jean's words enact the reality they represent, a glossing
that is at once explanatory and obfuscating, pedagogic and seductive.
Similarly, when the Wife of Bath interrupts the Parson she substitutes
in no uncertain terms her carnal enticements for his moralistic preaching. "Nay, by my fader soule," she says,

> . . . schal he nat preche;
> He schal no gospel glosen here ne teche.
>
> . . . .
> My joly body schal a tale telle. (1178–85)

The Wife's analogy between her "joly body" and the *corpus* of her text
invokes a powerful medieval connection between sexuality and reading. The *locus classicus* for this connection is Augustine's misreading of
the *Aeneid*, when he was seduced into weeping for the death of Dido
while remaining unmoved by the dying of his own soul. This monitory
scene recurs throughout the later Middle Ages: Paolo and Francesca
(and Dante) relive it, Boccaccio anxiously argues against it, Chaucer—

---

12. . . . . quiconques la chose escrit,
     se du voir ne vous velt ambler,
   ' li diz doit le fet resambler;
     car les voiz aus chose voisines
     doivent estre a leur fez cousines. (15158–62)
All references to the *Roman de la Rose* are to the edition of Félix Lecoy, CFMA 92, 95, 98
(Paris: Champion, 1965–70), unless otherwise noted.

in the *House of Fame* and in the *Troilus*—reenacts it.[13] For each of these writers the relationship between the lovers *in* the text becomes a warning figure for the relationship that might develop between the male reader *and* the text. What Dido did to Aeneas the *Aeneid* did to Augustine: how can this reader protect himself against the "joly body" of the text?[14]

II

Antifeminist literature presents women as inveterate and interminable talkers, wagging their tongues like the clappers on bells. And for much of this literature a woman's voice is not merely part of her weaponry but the very mode of her existence, the substance from which she is constituted as well as the means by which she is made manifest. This poetry is a mimesis not of character but of language, a domestic counterpart to those texts, such as Rutebeuf's *Dit de l'herberie*, that record the patter of the street vendor.[15] A good example of a poem in which feminine speaking is virtually aligned with the poetic function is the *Liber lamentationum Matheoluli*.[16] Written at the end of the thirteenth century in Latin, this brilliant and vitriolic poem was translated into French in the 1370s by Jean Lefèvre, and it is doubtless this version that Chaucer

13. Augustine, *Confessions* 1, 13; Dante, *Inferno* 5; Boccaccio, *Genealogea deorum gentilium* 14, 18. In the *House of Fame* the Chaucerian reading of the *Aeneid* in the Temple of Venus is so compromised by the seductiveness of Dido that it reproduces not Virgil's epic of *pietas* but an Ovidian complaint; the narrator's seduction by Criseyde in the *Troilus* is well known.

14. The phrase "joly body" also occurs in the *Shipman's Tale*, which was almost certainly written originally for the Wife of Bath: "Ye shal my joly body have to wedde" (423), the wife says to her merchant husband. For the connection between sexuality and writing in the *Shipman's Tale*, see below, chapter 7. For the appearance of the phrase "au cuer joli, au cors inel" in the *Roman de la Rose*, and its punning on Jean de Meun's surname "Clopinel," see Daniel Poirion, ed., *Roman de la Rose* (Paris: Garnier-Flammarion, 1974), line 10566 and Poirion's note.

15. Edmond Faral and Julia Bastin, eds., *Oeuvres complètes de Rutebeuf* (Paris: Picard, 1960), 2:268–71; Faral and Bastin mention other instances on 267. For further discussion, see Mikhail Bakhtin, *Rabelais and His World*, trans. Hélène Iswolsky (Cambridge: MIT Press, 1968), 181ff. and bibliography cited there. A Chaucerian poem that draws on this tradition is the *Canon's Yeoman's Prologue* (misleadingly printed as *Pars prima* of his tale in the *Riverside Chaucer*).

16. *Les Lamentations de Matheolus et le Livre de leesce de Jehan Le Fèvre de Resson*, ed. A. G. Van Hamel (Paris: Bouillon, 1892–1905). Lefèvre also translated the pseudo-Ovidian *De vetula* as *La vielle* (see below, note 25) and several other works, including the unpublished *Epistre sur les misères de la vie* (MS B.N. fr. 19137), apparently a version of Innocent III's *De miseria humanae conditionis*, a treatise that Chaucer himself claimed to have translated.

knew.[17] While Matheolus includes explicit attacks on the potent feminine voice, his most telling strategy is to travesty the feminine idiom
directly, and his poem includes large chunks of wifely nagging. But it
shortly becomes ironically clear that the verbal energy that motivates
his poem derives from just this feminine copiousness. Once having
entered the poem, his wife's voice comes to possess it and even subverts the poet's attempts to regain control: in complaining about her
endless nagging Matheolus repeats himself verbatim and at length—
just like a woman.[18]

In one of his additions to Matheolus's text Jean Lefèvre furnishes a
suggestive image of the feminine idiom that makes explicit several of
the anxieties behind the misogynist tradition as a whole. He tells the
story of Carfania, a Roman matron who displayed her verbal mastery
by arguing cases before the courts. But at the moment of crisis Carfania
would reveal her true nature: "Carfania bent way over—she was a
greater jangler than a magpie, for she didn't plead wisely—she
showed her ass in court" (2:183–86).[19] Women try to hide behind masculine respectability but their carnality will out. A woman will say anything, the more embarrassing the better. Hence her wicked delight in
ferreting out masculine secrets that she may publish abroad—a theme
that is compulsively repeated throughout misogynist literature.[20] This

17. On Chaucer and Matheolus, see Zacharias P. Thundy, "Matheolus, Chaucer,
and the Wife of Bath," in *Chaucerian Problems and Perspectives: Essays Presented to Paul E.
Beichner*, ed. Edward Vasta and Zacharias P. Thundy (Notre Dame: University of Notre
Dame Press, 1979), 24–58.

18. In the Latin original Matheolus frames his long and chaotic complaint with a
repeated couplet: "Est horologium quod nulla cessat in hora / Uxor litigium dans, cujus
lingua sonora" (1, 331–32; cf. 1, 519–20, and also lines 322 and 545). Another brilliant
mimicry of the feminine idiom is Gautier Le Leu's *La Veuve*, a poem that captures femininity as it bespeaks the three crises of widowhood: first the lament for the dead husband,
then the chattering with a gossip that initiates the search for a new mate, and finally the
inevitable harangue of sexual disappointment that follows upon remarriage. This poem
has been discussed by Charles Muscatine, "The Wife of Bath and Gautier's *La veuve*," in
Romance Studies in Memory of Edward Billings Ham, ed. Urban T. Holmes (Hayward: California State College, 1967), 109–14.

19.   Cafurne en fu bien accroupie,
          Plus jangleresse qu'une pie,
          Car pas ne plaida sagement;
          Son cul moustra en jugement.

On Carfania or Afrania, see Claudine Herrmann, *Le role judicaire et politique des femmes sous
la Republique romaine* (Brussels: Latomus, 1964), 107–8.

20. Perhaps nowhere more fervently than in the *Roman de la Rose*, for example, lines
16317–676. The Wife of Bath brags that, if her husband had "pissed on a wal, / Or doon a
thyng that sholde han cost his lyf" (534–35) she would have tattled on him to her gossips,

fear of woman's shamelessness is at the domestic heart of medieval misogyny, a central source of the power that invests a speaker like the Wife of Bath. As she promises, "My joly body schal a tale telle." This is a verbal licentiousness that is at once frightening and exciting. When Carfania shows her *cul* in court she is mocking her male judges with both her carnality and theirs, simultaneously ridiculing their judicial solemnity and arousing their secret desires. For the male audience feminine speaking is never wholly divested of the titillating ambivalences of eroticism. Christine de Pisan, who doubtless knew better than most, speaks (apparently apocryphally) of the learned daughter of an Italian professor whose beauty forced her to lecture with a veil before her face.[21]

The double bind of antipathy and allure precipitated by feminine speech is wound more tightly when the woman happens to be old. The old woman has a double existence in medieval literature, as the randy widow searching for a new husband or as the practiced *entremetteuse* presiding over someone else's affair. The randy widow is virtually always a figure of mockery, but she is mocked less in fun than in outrage and even horror. The male fear of vidual sexuality appears throughout misogynist literature and is so profound a part of medieval life that it has left a mark even on the fugitive record of social history. The half-mocking, half-menacing village cavalcade known in France as the charivari and in England as the "skimmington" or "rough music" was one of the central ways by which the medieval community could bring its norms to bear upon the domestic life of the individual. Typical targets for these processions were child-beaters, adulterers, domineering wives, and widowers and—

---

but other texts detail far more intimate revelations. One wife recounts how when she returns from confession her husband wants to know "si j'ay pissé en ma chemise," but this scatological curiosity in fact hides a yet more shameful fascination with her adulterous acts with the priest. See "Sermon joyeux de la patience des femmes obstinées contre leurs maris," in *Recueil de poésies francaises de XVᵉ et XVIᵉ siècles*, ed. Anatole de Montaiglon (Paris: P. Jannet, 1856), 3:261–67.

21. The story is told about Novella d'Andrea at the University of Bologna in Christine's *Cité des dames*; see Pisan, *Book of the City of Ladies*, trans. Earl Jeffrey Richards (New York: Persea, 1982), 154. For a more recent instance of this way of understanding feminine writing, Nathaniel Hawthorne's comments on the pseudonymous and very popular Fanny Fern are exemplary: "The woman writes as if the Devil was in her; and that is the only condition under which a woman ever writes anything worth reading. Generally women write like emasculated men, and are only to be distinguished from male authors by greater feebleness and folly; but when they throw off the restraints of decency, and come before the public stark naked, as it were—then their books are sure to possess character and value" (cited by Beverly Voloshin, "A Historical Note on Women's Fiction," *Critical Inquiry* 2 [1975–76], 818).

especially—widows who remarried. Of all the offenders, domineering wives and widows who remarried a much younger man were by far the most common target of community disapproval.[22]

A taboo witnesses to a potency that is desired as well as feared, and the randy widow has her attractions. Matheolus suggests what these are in a passage that begins to move us from the widow to the *entremetteuse*. He offers us a commentary on Genesis 18, the account of Sarah's response to the news that she will bear Abraham a son:

> Sarah was old and toothless, and didn't seem lively enough for a coupling. But quickly enough she could make herself supple ("Mais asses tost se rendi souple"); when she knew that she was going to have a child the spear of pleasure pierced her. The old woman laughed when she thought that someone would make *la bonne chose* with her. It's an old woman's custom, when age overtakes her, she knows how to induct young folk and introduce them to the *jeu d'amour*. By her sayings and her words ("Par ses dis et par sa parole") she makes them dance to her tune.[23]

22. See Edward P. Thompson, " 'Rough Music': Le charivari anglais," *Annales* 27 (1972): 285–312; C. Gauvard and A. Gokalp, "Les conduites de bruit et leur signification à la fin du moyen âge: Le charivari," *Annales* 29 (1974): 693–704; Jacques Le Goff and Jean-Claude Schmitt, eds., *Le Charivari* (The Hague: Mouton, 1981); and Natalie Zemon Davis, *Society and Culture in Early Modern France* (Stanford: Stanford University Press, 1975), 97–151. The fear of widows is visible throughout the entire corpus of misogynist texts; one of the most extensive treatments of the theme is Boccaccio's *Il corbaccio,* translated by Anthony K. Cassell (Urbana: University of Illinois Press, 1975).

23. Sarre fu vieille et esdentee,
Ne sembloit pas entalentée
De recevoir charnele couple.
Mais asses tost se rendi souple;
Quand elle scot qu'enfant avroit,
Dart de leësce la navroit;
Vieille rit quant elle suppose
Qu'on li fera la bonne chose;
C'est coustume de vieille femme,
Que, puis que vieillesce l'entame,
Elle seult les jeunes induire
Et au jeu d'amours introduire.
Par ses dis et par sa parole
Les fait dancer a sa karole. (2, 1823–36)

This is by no means Matheolus's only expedition into biblical exegesis: among other interpretations, he also suggests that the risen Christ revealed himself to women because he knew that they would spread the word. Chaucer's Dame Prudence, in the *Tale of Melibee,* cites this example as well, although for her it is a sign of the high regard in which Christ held women (VII, 1075).

There are two kinds of teaching here, by the notorious feminine tongue
("Par ses dis et par sa parole") and by the old woman's well-practiced
body ("Mais asses tost se rendi souple"). She is truly a go-between: a
way of at once preparing for and getting to the young girl who is every
young man's fancy. As the passage to female sexuality she is endowed
with both its terrors and its delights. Too old to be a permanent mate,
she can be enjoyed with the abandon accorded the merely temporary
lover; but her age also renders her a monitory prefiguration of the fate
that awaits all lovers, a *memento temporis*. She is both beginning and end
and encloses the young man both temporally and psychologically. She
ushers her son/lover into manhood, but her very support demonstrates
his childish dependence.

　　These dark matters can also be illuminated by reference to the folk
rituals embodied in the wooing play. In its fullest form the wooing play
enacts the process of courtship for both youth and maiden, and the
crucial action for both is the rejection of an unseemly mate. But while
the maiden's rejected alternative is simply an old man, the youth is
challenged by an old woman who carries a baby. She is both mother
and sexual partner, and witnesses both to his past (as her son and perhaps lover) and to his future (as the young woman's husband and father to her family). While in the action of the play the maiden simply
rejects the old man, the youth is more violent: he beats and sometimes
even kills the old woman, suppressing the past that has made him
capable of grasping the future. These anthropological concerns are perhaps not as remote from the Wife of Bath's discourse as might at first
appear: in both *Prologue* and *Tale* age gives way to youth, and her rhetoric also invokes a festive and nuptial context.[24]

　　Alison of Bath also combines the roles of widow and go-between:
she is an *entremetteuse* who prepares the way to herself. The most important of Chaucer's literary precedents for this conflation of roles is the
pseudo-Ovidian *De vetula*, composed in the mid-thirteenth century,
probably by Richard of Fournival, and translated in the 1370s as *La
vieille* by Jean Lefèvre.[25] The story of *La vieille* can help us to understand
how the ambivalences embodied in the old woman can be explicated

　　24.　On the wooing play, see the two articles by Charles Read Baskerville, "Dramatic
Aspects of Medieval Folk Festivals in England," *SP* 17 (1920): 19–87, and "Mummers'
Wooing Plays in England," *MP* 21 (1924): 225–72.
　　25.　The *De vetula* has been edited by Paul Klopsch (Leiden: Brill, 1967), and by Doro-
thy M. Robathan (Amsterdam: Hakkert, 1968). Jean Lefèvre's adaptation, *La vieille, ou les
dernières amours d'Ovide*, has been edited by Hippolyte Cocheris (Paris: A. Aubry, 1861).
Its relevance to Chaucer is also discussed by William Matthews, "The Wife of Bath and
All Her Sect," *Viator* 5 (1974): 413–43.

into narrative, and it provides as well an important example of the eroticism of feminine discourse. The poem is a vast elaboration on the story of Dipsas in *Amores* 1, 8; it recounts "Ovid's" humiliation at the hands of an *anus* or *vetula* and his conversion from love to philosophy and finally to a saving adoration of none other than the Virgin Mary. Having fallen in love with a young girl, the middle-aged poet hires La Vieille as "une moienneresse" (2, 2831) to smooth his way, with disastrous results. Teased by her long-winded descriptions of the lady's beauty into a frenzy of anticipation, the lustful poet makes furious love to the woman awaiting him in the assigned bed, only to discover that he has lavished his attentions on the old woman herself. This sudden transformation of the virgin he was expecting into the "vielle chauve ridée" he has found is all too ironically apt, introducing into Ovid's own life the metamorphic principle he had previously recognized only in its effects on others: "Those mutations that I have told about—which are written in my large book—there is no mutation like to that which came to me, miraculously, when in so short a time it happened that she was old, ugly, and gray."[26] Here metamorphosis is nothing more nor less than aging, a process that applies to Ovid more immediately than he is at this point prepared to acknowledge. Consequently, he closes this episode with a vengeful description of La Vieille's withered body and with a truly horrible, excremental curse.

But the story is not over yet, and sixteen years later the lesson he had earlier evaded is now borne in on him. With the help of a chambermaid Ovid succeeds in seducing his long-sought-for beloved, and although she is now a wife and mother he discovers that her body is still all he could desire. But her character holds unsuspected and disquieting depths. For he learns that the trick played upon him sixteen years earlier had originated not with La Vieille but with the young girl herself: she had been trying to teach him, he now realizes, the bitter lesson that middle age should turn not back to its youthful past but forward to its inevitable if dismaying future. That this is a precept that she has herself now learned is shown by her own middle-aged choice of the elderly Ovid as a lover. The sixteen-year delay that his beloved has forced upon him has brought him not merely to age, then, but to the consciousness of age; and La Vieille, in having led him to herself, is now revealed

26.   Ces mutacions que j'ay dictes,
        Qui sont en mon grand livre escriptes,
        N'a point mutacion pareille
        Dont ce, me vint à grant merveille,
        Qu'en si pou de temps devenue
        Fut vielle, hideuse et chanue. (1, 3175–80)

to have been a "moienneresse" not to beauty but, inevitably if slowly, to wisdom. The human being he confronted when the sun rose on his bed of shame those many years ago was an image of his own future: an aged but unabated sexuality veiled by garrulity and nostalgia. That he did not recognize her wisdom until it was proffered to him by a desirable woman is of course a comment on Ovid's own, masculine limitations. For as the Wife of Bath's tale of Midas points out, men do not easily learn distasteful lessons about themselves, and as her *Tale* demonstrates, they often have to be taught twice.

Jean Lefèvre's *La vieille* thus provides suggestive precedents for the *Wife of Bath's Prologue and Tale*, if we think primarily in terms of narrative and theme: the dialectic of youth and age; the quest for beauty that discovers wisdom; sexuality as the bait with which women lure men toward self-knowledge; the old woman as a surrogate or veil for the maiden; the harsh lesson that is learned only when repeated in a milder form. But while part of my purpose is discussing the *Prologue and Tale* will be to show how Chaucer disposes these elements into his own configuration, my immediate interest remains the rhetoric of the Wife's discourse. From this narrower perspective the most relevant of *La vieille*'s strategies is its exploitation of the erotic possibilities of the old woman's garrulity. The ambivalent sexuality that invests the old woman is here expressed in *La Vieille*'s interlacing of delectable accounts of the young girl's body with self-pitying laments for her own age and poverty. Titillation and tedium alternate in her discourse, successfully arousing Ovid to a state of all too blind lust. Admittedly, however, this rhetorical strategy is elementary. The verbal sporting by which Chaucer creates the Wife of Bath is far more sophisticated, and we must look elsewhere, to the *Roman de la Rose*, for his precedent.

IV

Guillaume de Lorris abandoned the *Roman de la Rose* when it became apparent that the outcome of the lover's quest was dependent not upon his invention but upon the lady's generosity. Far from achieving the visionary authority to which he laid claim at the outset, Guillaume retreated to a graceful submission to the inevitability of history. Indeed, the literary embarrassment of an unfinished poem became in the context of extraliterary courtship a virtue: by not presuming to project the end of his story he demonstrates a *politesse* that marks him as worthy of his lady's favors. In part the impasse to which Guillaume brings the poem is a function of his reliance upon the formal strategy of personifi-

cation allegory, and fully to understand how La Vieille's discourse offers a solution requires us to explore this point in some detail. It is a
point important as well as our understanding of the Wife of Bath and of
her role in the *Canterbury Tales*. Both the *Canterbury Tales* and the *Roman
de la Rose* begin with incomplete fragments and both engage in progressively more intricate processes of self-reflection. That La Vieille plays a
crucial role in these processes is what I now hope to demonstrate and
so to suggest why the old woman should reappear when Chaucer's
poem reaches its own revisionary moment.

The personification allegory adopted by Guillaume inevitably promises the clarified understanding of vision. Within the enclosure of the
garden, so says the form of the discourse, the origin and essence of love
can be known and possessed: "l'art d'Amors est tote enclose" (38). The
poem's dream-time is the "tens enmoreus" (48) of an apparently perpetual youthfulness: Vieillesse is kept outside the walls, and the time of
which she is at once mistress and victim is exorcised with a curse (361–
92). The gate is opened by a Oiseuse who "mout avoit bon tens et bon
mai" (569), for the garden world has time to grow up but no time to
grow old, the special if temporary immortality of the young. That the
garden is also a *prison amoreuse* is the burden of the Narcissus episode.
The will to possession, whether by plucking the beloved or by codify-
ing love, derives from egoistic overreaching and issues in a bemused
admiration for one's own creation. The crystals in the fountain reproduce the garden with precisely the unmediated clarity and completeness to which the poem itself aspires:

> Just as a mirror shows the things which are set over against it and one
> sees there without covering both their color and their shape, in the
> same way I tell you truthfully that the crystal without deception re-
> veals the whole of the garden to him who gazes in the water. . . . There
> is no little thing, be it however hidden or shut, of which a demonstra-
> tion is not made there, just as if it were portrayed in crystal.[27]

27.   ausi con li mireors montre
        les choses qui sont a l'encontre
        et i voit l'en sanz coverture
        et lor color et lor figure,
        tot autresi vos di por voir
        que li cristaus sanz decevoir
        tot l'estre dou vergier encuse
        a celui qui en l'eve muse;

. . . .

        si n'i a si petite chose,

In the depths of the Fontaine d'Amour glimmers the lure of poetic inclusiveness, allegory's enticing promise to strip off the veil of the accidental to allow us to see the essence of things *facie ad faciem*. Many others have written of this fountain, says Guillaume, "But never will you hear the truth of the matter described better after I have set forth the mystery."[28] But the truth, as Narcissus has already discovered, is that the revealed essences are mere shadows (1484, 1492), that our vision remains always *per speculum in aenigmate*. In the autobiographical passage that shortly follows the description of the fountain, the whole of Guillaume's poem is revealed as a shadow, belatedly dependent upon a history that has not yet fully taken place. It is written as an offering to the very Rose that it represents, hoping by its representation or shadowing to earn a happy ending (3481–92). At the outset Guillaume told us that he believed "that a dream is significant of the good and the harm of people, that most people dream many things in a hidden way that they later see openly."[29] It now appears that this revelation will be accomplished not by allegory but by history, by the time that was so conclusively excluded from the garden in the frozen image of Vieillesse.

The entry of time into a poem posited upon its exclusion is a reversal radical enough to account for Guillaume's abrupt if apt withdrawal: his lover reaches an impasse that can be resolved only by the extrinsic decision of the lady. Jean de Meun, however, has higher ambitions, aspiring to bring both poem and amorous quest to simultaneous climax. He wants not to set his poem against or above history but to make temporality itself a key structural component. Love is not a timeless object, codified in a set of rules and enclosed within a *hortus conclusus*, but a process that must be enacted within the multivalent context of experience itself. But to introduce time into the poem—so sedulously excluded by Guillaume—is to introduce old age, with its penitential re-

---

     tant soit reposte ne enclose,
     dont demontrance ne soit feite
     con s'ele ert ou cristal portrete. (1553–68)

28. Mes ja mes n'oroiz mielz descrivre
     la verité de la matere,
     quant j'avré apost le mistere. (1598–1600)

29.   que songes est senefiance
     des biens as genz et des anuiz,
     que li plusor songent de nuiz
     maintes choses covertement
     que l'en voit puis apertement. (16–20)

trospections, and history, with its promised apocalyptic finale. It is, in short, to introduce into the poem larger perspectives that will inevitably call into question the amorous quest itself.

Jean's romance is built on the structural irony of a knight errant whose success depends upon not listening to the guides who direct him. These guides offer him commentaries on human experience that take a longer and larger view than his single-minded concentration on the rose—what Jean calls his "enterins corages" (10361)—will permit him to encompass. Each presents him with an image of his future that, were he to take it seriously, would dissuade him from his present course. Raison praises the wisdom of a Vieillesse who regards with scorn and remorse the follies of youth, and so offers the lover a prospect from which his sought-for end is revealed to be only a squalid means. Amis returns the poem to its narrower amorous concerns but provides two equally distasteful portraits of the future that awaits the experienced lover: either his own corrosive cynicism or the obsessions of the *mari jaloux*. The next pair of speakers repeats this pattern of expansion and contraction. Where Raison broadened the poem's perspective by invoking the Platonism of Boethius and Cicero, Faus Semblant turns to the chiliasm of William of St.-Amour. He introduces not merely the mendicant controversy, in other words, but the mendicant controversy as seen in an apocalyptic perspective. He opens the poem not merely to its historical context but to history as seen from the prospect of eternity, dwarfing the lover's petty concerns by comparison.

Then, like Amis, La Vieille returns the poem to the erotic life. But she does so in terms that are by no means as wholly negative as his. True to her lineage and function, she plays a role in the drama of the lover's quest that is genuinely ambivalent. She is an *entremetteuse* whose cynical teachings seem to make love impossible; a celebrant of carnality who witnesses to the devastations of a lifetime of love; a remorseful penitent reinvigorated by the memory of her sins; a guardian of the lady's virtue who betrays her charge. But her primary function, and the source of her ultimate affirmation, is to introduce the ambivalences of *temporality* into the poem in a fully human form. The temporality to which she witnesses is time as experienced and experience as time— the experience, in fact, of a lifetime. That she has a biography at all, rather than just a set of typifying habits, marks her off from the other interlocutors. But that she can dispose it before us as *autobiography* shows how fully self-possessed she is. The very existence of this selfhood requires and justifies the imperfections of temporality. As for the lover, her autobiography supports his passion and subjects it to ironies of which he is, quite appropriately, unaware. When young she loved as he loves, now old she has fallen into bitter regret. Youth and age, beauty and wisdom, means and end are enacted in the same personality. In sum, the antagonistic elements of the lover's world are at once joined and held apart by being disposed upon a temporal continuum and located within a capacious subjectivity.

La Vieille's autobiography is not, however, offered to us in linear sequence, with a beginning, middle, and end. Her discourse includes seven distinguishable themes, and these are presented as a series of interlocking subordinations. La Vieille's personal history begins and ends her discourse, providing a frame that contains and ameliorates her cynical Ovidian pedagogy. And this is true, in turn, of each of the succeeding six themes. The result is an overall structure of interlocking boxes, an *emboîtement*, as a diagram makes clear:[30]

---

30. My diagram follows the suggestion of Daniel Poirion, who identified this rhetorical structure in his *Le Roman de la Rose* (Paris: Hatier, 1973), 125. Poirion actually designs a similar diagram for Ami's discourse and suggests that one could also be constructed for Nature: see below, note 34. This kind of structure, known in studies of the epic as "ring composition," is a favorite Homeric ordering principle (Cedric H. Whitman, *Homer and the Heroic Tradition* [Cambridge: Harvard University Press, 1958], 249–84, 288–91, and 367–70) and is also visible in *Beowulf* (John D. Niles, "Ring Composition and the Structure of *Beowulf*," *PMLA* 94 [1979]: 924–35). Within the tradition in which Jean de Meun and Chaucer are working, however, the crucial precedent for chiastic structure is Ovid's *Metamorphoses* (Brooks Otis, *Ovid as an Epic Poet*, 2d ed. [Cambridge: Cambridge University Press, 1970], 45–90, and the diagrams passim). This is not to say that Ovid is the only Roman poet to avail himself of chiastic structure—see, for example, Gordon Williams, *Technique and Ideas in the* Aeneid (New Haven: Yale University Press, 1983), 75–78; Mario De Cesare, *The Altar and the City: A Reading of Virgil's* Aeneid (New York: Columbia University Press, 1974), 90; and David Vessey, *Statius and the* Thebaid (Cambridge: Cambridge University Press, 1973), 317–28—but he is the most persistent and, for the Middle Ages, the most influential. Within the twelfth-century romance, we find this structure enacted, for example, in Thomas's *Tristan* (Joan M. Ferrante, *The Conflict of Love and Honor* [The Hague: Mouton, 1973], 74–78) and in the two linked romances of Chrétien de Troyes, the *Chevalier de la charrette* (F. Douglas Kelly, *Sens and Conjointure in the* Chevalier de la charrette [The Hague: Mouton, 1966], 166–84) and, most explicitly and importantly, the *Chevalier au lion* (a preliminary account of the structure is offered in the diagram appended to Erich Köhler's *Ideal und Wirklichkeit in der höfischen Epik*, 2d ed. [Tübingen: Niemeyer, 1970]). Chrétien's use of *emboîtement* for thematic purposes both here and elsewhere provides an important precedent for its definition as a narrative *topos* specific to romance; indeed, narratives that have previously been identified as "interlaced" might be more properly described as chiastic. See, for example, Dale B. J. Randall, "A Note on Structure in *Sir Gawain and the Green Knight*," *MLN* 72 (1959): 161–63); Larry Benson, *Malory's* Morte Darthur (Cambridge: Harvard University Press, 1976), 34–35; James Nohrnberg, *The Analogy of the* Faerie Queene (Princeton: Princeton University Press, 1976).

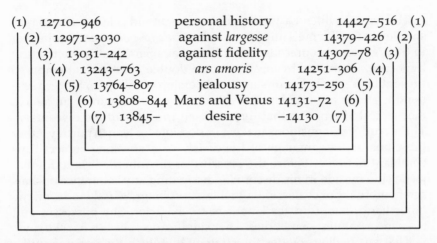

As well as its subordinating function, this *emboîtement* structure has a figurative intention. It imitates the poem's climactic action, the gradual exfoliation of the rose that the final lines of the poem so graphically and embarrassingly describe. La Vieille's verbal dilation upon her themes, in other words, is organized so as to match the rose's floral dilation. This means that her discourse is erotic in perhaps the most immediate way possible. In deferring the poem's longed-for conclusion, La Vieille's discourse stands as a barrier that tests the lover's patience and perseverance. And yet by being figured in the shape of the goal he seeks, her discourse lures him on; it reminds him of his rose at the very moment that it defers the rose. The structure of dilation translates the ambivalence of the old woman into the rhetoric of romance: it is the form of courtship. Jean's achievement, then, is not merely to exploit the meanings contained in the rhetorical term *dilatio*, a process that Chaucer will carry even further in the Wife of Bath's discourse. In a larger sense, he manages to translate the central Ovidian principle of amorous delay into stylistic terms and to show with impressive specificity how rhetorical structure can bear erotic value.[31]

31. Delay is of course, a *sine qua non* of courtship: "delay is a great bawd," says Ovid (*Ars amatoria* 3, 752: "maxima lena mora est"; see also 3, 473–74; "mora semper amantes / Incitat, exiguum si modo tempus habet"; and 2, 717–18: "Crede mihi, non est veneris properanda voluptas, / Sed sensim tarda prolicienda mora"). The same advice is repeated throughout Andreas Capellanus's *De Amore*, ed. and trans. P. G. Walsh (London: Duckworth, 1982), 94, 154, 176, 178, 194, and 196. Andreas does use the Ovidian term *mora* but prefers *dilatio* and its cognates, and may well be the source of the implied pun; for similar Andrean jesting, see Betsy Bowden, "The Art of Courtly Copulation," *M&H* 9 (1979): 67–85. The connection between dilation as delay and as opening is implicit throughout the *Roman*: Guillaume's failure in part 1 leads him to describe the gradually opening rose in

The way in which La Vieille's discourse provides Jean with a *formal* solution to Guillaume's impasse may best be grasped by comparing her to the figures who precede and follow. Faus Semblant is the truthful hypocrite, motivated by an "entencion double" that Jean attempts to present by a simple but unsuccessful version of interlace. Sincere self-denunciations are interleaved with outrageous braggings, an almost mechanical alternation that repeats itself throughout the discourse.[32] These crude juxtapositions make it impossible for Jean to portray either the ethos or the language of hypocrisy. As a speaking subject Faus Semblant dissolves before the pressure of the inherited rhetorics that jostle side by side in his discourse, dissipating any coherence of character before it can coalesce. La Vieille's autobiographical mode, on the other hand, subordinates language to character. She possesses and even incorporates—embodies—her significance: she is what she says.

That La Vieille provides the strategy by which the impasse of the poem's inheritance can be resolved is suggested, finally, by the way her discourse provides a model for the decisive statement now offered by Nature. Nature's message of universal generation and her explicitly feminine tone are first introduced into the poem by La Vieille. At times, indeed, Nature sounds like little more than La Vieille in a philosophical

---

terms that make it clear that more time must pass before possession (or penetration) can be accomplished—the whole time of the poem in fact (3339–60). A masculine version of this pun may be found in *Li consaus d'amours* by Richard of Fournival, in which courtship is called *prolongance* (Gian Battista Speroni, ed., *Medioevo romanzo* 1 [1974]: 217–78). I am indebted for my initial interest in dilation as the structural *topos* of romance to Patricia Parker, *Inescapable Romance: Studies in the Poetics of a Mode* (Princeton: Princeton University Press, 1979).

32.   As the following outline makes clear, in which the five separate movements of Faus Semblant's discourse, each marked by an interjection by Amors, are divided according to their alternating pattern of judgment and collusion. In each of the A speeches Faus Semblant expresses a sense of moral outrage at current ecclesiastical abuse, while in each of the B speeches he delights in his own complicity.

I:	10997–1006—A	V:	11499–568—B
	11007–52—B		11569–606—A
II:	11061–132—A		11607–756—B
	11133–92—B		11757–814—A
III:	11211–38—A		11815–66—B
	11239–376—B		11867–87—A
IV:	11383–478—A		11888–922—B
	11479–94—B		11923–38—A
			11939–46—B

Lines 11947–84 function as a conclusion and assert that the paradox of the truthful hypocrite allows of no solution.

mood, and she herself defines her discourse as a typically feminine indiscretion: "I am a woman, so I can't keep quiet but always want to reveal everything: a woman can hide nothing."[33] As we might expect, then, La Vieille's *emboîtement* also controls the structure of Nature's discourse—indeed, here the form proliferates into a plenitude of interlocking boxes.[34] Nature disposes the language of natural philosophy in the structures of erotic pursuit, providing a rhetorical synthesis of the poem's disparate materials that implies a larger, cultural reconciliation.

The total effect is to ground the poem's presiding personification in the specifics of human experience and to give that experience its fullest philosophical extension. Fulfilled by Nature, La Vieille's dilations are now seen as both a penetration into the self and an expansion outwards to encompass the whole of created nature. In temporal terms, La Vieille's erotic dialectic between delay and fulfillment becomes in Nature's discourse the greater dialectic between human action and providential vision. In both cases, deferral is a controlling concept. For man's participation in history to retain its significance, God's providential order must remain inscrutable, hidden until the end of time; for the meaning of erotic action to be fully explored, the plucking of the rose must be similarly delayed. The amorous quest and the pilgrimage of human life are at once insignificant and crucial: although their value

33. Fame sui, si ne me puis tere,
    ainz veill des ja tout reveler,
    car feme ne peut riens celer. (19188–90)

34. The basic structure is:

(1) 16801–954		18957–66 (1)
(2) 16955–18542*	planetary influence	18915–56 (2)
(3) 18543–606	comets	18897–914 (3)
(4) 18607	*nobilitas est virtus non sanguis*	18896 (4)

This relatively simple structure is amplified, however, by a series of further *emboîtements* that are embedded within the extended first half of the second movement (asterisked above):

(1) 16955–74	18535–42 (1)
(ai) 16975–7058	17860–74 (ai)
(aii) 17059	17859 (aii)

(bi) 17875–18027	18515–34 (bi)
(bii) 18028	18514 (bii)

depends entirely upon their conclusions they are themselves the only means by which conclusions can be reached.[35]

In sum, La Vieille's autobiographical mode introduces temporality into the poem in a form that aligns the lover's amorous obsessions with the poem's larger, more philosophical perspectives. Her mediation is accomplished, as we have seen, through the construction of subjectivity in language. The conflicting pressures that inevitably afflict the pilgrim's journey through the world are, if not resolved, at least contained within the capacious embrace of her selfhood, an embrace that is imaged in the *emboîtement* of her discourse. This is not to say, of course, that in disclosing her full dimensions La Vieille provides an unambiguous encouragement to Amanz's quest. On the contrary, she reveals that his goal is not a gradually dilating rose but a human being, and that the penetration he seeks to accomplish is not into a flower or even a body but into the labyrinths of personality. That this complicating knowledge would disable the intensity of Amanz's pursuit we may gather from his absence at her lecture. As I have said, each of his interlocutors offers advice he cannot afford to take, and the romance is built on the irony of a knight errant who can succeed only by ignoring his guides. But the threat posed by La Vieille is disarmed with special care: her words of feminine wisdom are mediated to the lover by a masculine Bel Acueil, who himself listens to her only after first deciding not to hear. As the Wife of Bath well knows, such are the vicissitudes of feminine speaking in a masculine world.

V

The last text we need to consider before returning our attention to the Wife of Bath is Roger de Collerye's *Sermon pour une nopce*.[36] Jean de Meun had labeled La Vieille's discourse a sermon, implicitly linking it with the genre of the *sermon joyeux*.[37] Conversely, de Collerye's sermon

35. The sharp disjunction between Genius's *sermon joyeux* on generation and his predication about the "parc du champ joli" presided over by "li filz de la Vierge" (19905–8) perhaps calls Nature's reconciliation into question; but it remains true that even Genius recognizes that the relationship between the two gardens is temporal as well as hierarchical and that entrance to the higher garden is accorded only after service in the lower: see lines 19877–909 and 20597–629.

36. Charles d'Héricault, ed., *Les Oeuvres de Roger de Collerye* (Paris: P. Jannet, 1855), 111–22. The sermon was written around 1500.

37. On this genre, see Emile Picot, "Le monologue dramatique dans l'ancien théâtre français," *Romania* 15 (1886): 358–422; 16 (1887): 438–542; 17 (1888): 207–75. Particularly relevant to this discussion are the sermons listed by Picot as numbers 14–28, 44–56, and especially 94: "Sermon joyeux des femmes" (c. 1420). Very similar to this text is the dia-

is delivered by a (presumably male) preacher "habillé en femme," and like the Wife of Bath he or she celebrates carnality in terms derived from Jean de Meun.[38] At the conclusion of the *sermon joyeux* the preacher rehearses his or her text or *thema:* "Listen, daughter, and hearken—which will be, without dilation, the conclusion to our sermon, and sleep well, just as I have taught you."[39] The reference to *dilation* in de Collerye's text recalls the opening of Jean de Meun's rose and invokes the rhetoric of preaching to which the term is primarily relevant. The *ars praedicandi* teaches that sermonizing is a process of revelation and illumination. Each scriptural text or *thema* contains the truth in all its fullness, a truth that the preacher is to explicate and spread abroad (*dilatare*). To this end he is endowed with certain keys (*claves*), techniques of dividing the text into elements that can be dilated upon to reveal the full significance hidden within the verbal form.[40] Faced with

---

logue *Gilote et Johane*, extant in MS Harley 2253 and dated 15 September 1293; see Achille Jubinal, ed., *Nouveau recueil de contes, dits, fabliaux, et autres pièces inédites des XIIIᵉ, XIVᵉ et XVᵉ siècles* (Paris: Pannier, 1842), 2:28–39, and Carter Revard, "Gilote et Johane: An Interlude in B. L. MS. Harley 2253," *SP* 79 (1982): 122–46. In *The Mediaeval Stage* (Oxford: Clarendon Press, 1903), E. K. Chambers briefly discusses the *sociétés joyeuses* that seem to have been the secular inheritors of the defunct feast of fools (1:383–84); see also Jean-Claude Aubailly, *Le théatre médiévale profane et comique* (Paris: Champion, 1975). For Latin and German material, see Sander L. Gilman, *The Parodic Sermon in European Perspective* (Wiesbaden: Steiner, 1974). Genius's first sermon on generation in the *Roman de la Rose* (19433–900) is a fine example of the genre, as are Gautier Le Leu's *Du con* and the sermon in praise of sexuality delivered by Bernart the Ass in the *Roman de Renart;* for the last of these, see Charles Muscatine, *Chaucer and the French Tradition* (Berkeley: University of California Press, 1956), 78. For Chaucer's use of the *sermon joyeux* in the *Manciple's Prologue*, see above, chapter 4, note 96.

38. Compare, for instance, the opening of the *Sermon pour une nopce* with Genius's discussion in lines 19763–66.

39. *Audi, filia, et vide,*
Qui sera, sans dilation,
De nostre predication
L'achevement, et bien couché
Ainsy que je vous ay touché. (261–65)

40. Of the many discussions of sermon theory, see especially Jean Leclercq, "Le magistère du prédicateur au XIIᵉ siècle," *AHDLMA* 15 (1946): 105–47, and Etienne Gilson, "M. Menot et la technique du sermon médiéval," in *Les idées et les lettres* (Paris: J. Vrin, 1932), 93–154. *Dilatio* (or *dilatatio*) is a term relevant primarily to preaching theory: rhetoricians prefer *amplificatio*, although the verbal form *dilato* and its cognates do appear. Heinrich Lausberg, *Handbuch der literarischen Rhetorik*, 2 vols. (Munich: Hueber, 1960), contains only a single reference to *dilatio*. On the other hand, a key text for the development of preaching theory is Richard of Thetford's *Ars dilatandi sermones:* for bibliography, see James J. Murphy, *Rhetoric in the Middle Ages* (Berkeley: University of California Press, 1974), 326–29. For *dilatio* and *divisio* in preaching theory, see also Simon Alcok's *De modo dividendi thema pro materia sermonis dilatanda*, ed. Mary F. Boynton in the *Harvard Theologi-*

an opened text, the listener is then moved to a corresponding open-
ness. "Delate my herte in thy love," says a fourteenth-century mystic,
and the metaphor harks back to Augustine's classic formulation: "My
heart is too narrow for you to enter: let it be dilated by you."[41]

De Collerye's explicit invocation of *dilatio* adds a special decorum to
his disposition of Jean's erotic motifs. The ambivalence that characteristically invests the discourse of the old woman is here enforced by the
sermon's occasion: as an entertainment for the wedding feast it is at
once preparation and deferral. Appropriately, then, this La Vieille provides titillation with an account of the delightful sufferings that await
the bride and dissuasion with a grim reminder that the pleasures of the
marriage bed will shortly become the harassments of family life. The
structure of the discourse similarly enacts the pattern of enticement
and delay, and it does so with a special attention to the rhetorical meaning of *dilatio*. The "old woman's" method of analysis is to broach a
series of discontinuous matters but then to develop each so that the
focus of attention returns always to herself. She opens by begging the
groom not to hurt his bride but soon pauses to demand a drink; restarts
with an account of the horrors of domestic life and adds an encomium
to the bride but then shifts to an extended defense of her own preaching; proffers more advice to the new husband but interrupts with self-
regarding pleas to the "seigneurs d'église" to have mercy on fallen
women; then justifies her own role as being to instruct "fillettes" in the
art of profitable love; and finally concludes with an extended autobiographical account of the experience that authorizes her words.

The total effect is a mix of frustration and enticement. As each element of the sermon is introduced only to be discarded we experience a
growing irritation; but in devaluing the words the preacher promotes
an all the more fascinating self. The dilations are a series of openings
into the same psychological space: the conclusion that is constantly
deferred is the self that is constantly proffered, the mystery that is at
once veiled and unveiled. The saving knowledge is thus contained not
in the *thema* ("Audi, filia, et vide") but in the subject to which the *thema*
points, and it is this subject that is opened by the keys of the *divisio* and

---

cal Review 34 (1941): 201–16; Margaret Jennings, ed., *The Ars componendi sermones of
Ranulph Higden* (Leiden: Brill, 1987), 112; and T. M. Charland, *Artes praedicandi* (Ottawa:
Presses de l'Université d'Ottawa, 1936), 194–211.

41.   William Atkynson, trans., *The Earliest English Translation of . . . the* De imitatione
Christi, ed. John K. Ingram, EETS, ES 63 (London: K. Paul, Trench and Trübner, 1893),
201; Augustine, *Confessions*, 1, 5: "Angusta est domus animae meae, quo venias ad eam:
dilatetur abs te."

spread abroad. In sum, this *sermon joyeux* brilliantly blends the random garrulity of La Vieille with the premediated manifestations of the preacher. In terms of literary history, it shows us how a later writer could adapt Jean de Meun's amorous rhetoric to the generic requirements of the *sermon joyeux;* and it does so in a way remarkably like the one that had earlier been devised by Chaucer in the Wife of Bath's *Prologue.* Indeed, the likeness of these two independent rewritings of Jean de Meun argues for a tradition of such rewritings, a tradition of which these texts are among the few surviving vestiges.[42]

VI

As everyone knows, the Wife of Bath's *Prologue* is divided into three parts, the first being the discussion of marriage versus virginity, the second the account of husbands one through three, and the last the account of husbands four and five.[43] I have no wish to quarrel with this self-evident disposition, but I do want to define more carefully then usual the kind of matter that is distributed among these three parts. Part one is a brief version of a *sermon joyeux.* The Wife's text is from 1 Corinthians 7:28: "If however you take a wife, you do not sin. And if a maiden marries, she does not sin: *but they will have trouble in the flesh because of this*" ("Si autem acceperis uxorem, non peccasti. Et si nupserit virgo, non peccavit: *tribulationem tamen carnis habebunt huiusmodi*").[44] She frames her sermon with two citations of this text, invoking it at the start as the "wo that is in mariage" and at the end in a direct quotation:

> An housbonde I wol have—I wol nat lette—
> Which shal be bothe my dettour and my thral,
> And have his tribulacion withal
> Upon his flessh, whil that I am his wyf. (154–57)

42. See, for instance, J. Morawski, "Parodie d'un passage du *Roman de la Rose* dans un *Sermon Joyeux,*" *Romania* 52 (1926): 159–60.

43. These natural divisions have been further authorized by Robert Pratt's analysis of Chaucer's use of different sources for these three parts, an analysis that nicely defines the disparate tones of the *Prologue* without requiring us to accept Pratt's complicated speculations about the order of composition: "The Development of the Wife of Bath," in *Studies in Medieval Literature in Honor of Professor Albert Croll Baugh,* ed. MacEdward Leach (Philadephia: University of Pennsylvania Press, 1961), 45–79.

44. The importance of this text to the Wife's *Prologue,* and its medieval interpretation, are well discussed by Britton J. Harwood, "The Wife of Bath and the Dream of Innocence," *MLQ* 33 (1972): 257–73. That the Wife delivers a sermon in the first 162 lines is of course well known, but that it is a *sermon joyeux* has not, to my knowledge, been suggested before.

By *tribulatio carnis* St. Paul meant the inevitable and unwelcome temptations that marriage imposes upon the flesh. For the Wife these temptations are to be embraced and celebrated, and her *sermon joyeux* explicates Paul's text to show that it means the opposite of what a more orthodox exegete would claim it says.[45] She does this by manipulating one of the most common of the *modi dilatandi* taught by the *ars praedicandi*, the citation of scriptural authorities.[46] She draws upon both Old and New Testaments but returns over and over again to the crucial seventh chapter of 1 Corinthians, citing it no fewer than eight separate times.[47] Her alternative reading of verse 28 can thus be supported even by the exegetical principle of intertextuality, taking one passage from a text to gloss another.[48] And as we would expect from a *sermon joyeux*, she unlocks the letter to discover an irreducible carnality. In other words, her exegetical method is not, as is usually argued, a sign of her moral limitations but a knowing strategy appropriate to her chosen genre.

With the Pardoner's interruption the Wife's discourse takes a new turn, although without abandoning the principles of sermon rhetoric. Responding to her as both professional colleague and sexual challenge, the Pardoner suggests a new dimension to her *explication de texte*:

> Ye been a noble prechour in this cas.
> I was aboute to wedde a wyf; allas!
> What sholde I bye it on my flesh so deere? (165–67)[49]

45. That the Wife's exegesis is heterodox is thoroughly demonstrated by Robertson, *Preface to Chaucer*, 317–31, and Harwood, "Wife of Bath," 258–63. Nonetheless, the specific advice that she offers in her sermon (insofar as she offers any) is less flagrantly illegitimate than some commentaries might lead us to think: see Donald R. Howard, *The Idea of the* Canterbury Tales (Berkeley: University of California Press, 1976), 250. The *sermon joyeux* as a genre, it should be pointed out, inverts the spirit of medieval orthodoxy but neither its structure nor its content: the Wife is not urging us to sin but to enjoy our inevitable limitations. Another reference to 1 Corinthians 7:28 and its exegetical meaning may be found in the "Envoy to Bukton," in which Chaucer also invokes the Wife as an authority on marriage:

Bet ys to wedde than brenne in worse wise.
But thow shal have sorwe on thy flessh, thy lyf,
And ben thy wives thral, as seyn these wise. (18–20)

46. See, for instance, Thomas Walys's treatment, in Charland, ed., *Ars praedicandi*, 390.

47. Lines 46–52, 64–65, 79–84, 87, 102–4, 129–30, 147–48, 154–60.

48. On intertextuality, see Augustine, *De doctrina Christiana* 3, 26–27; trans. D. W. Robertson (Indianapolis: Bobbs-Merrill, 1958), 101–2; and Woodburn O. Ross, ed., *Middle English Sermons*, EETS, OS 209 (London: Oxford University Press, 1940), xlvi–xlvii.

49. That there is a shift here in the subject of the Wife's discourse was first noted by Arthur K. Moore, "Alysoun's Other Tonne," *MLN* 59 (1944): 481–83; and Moore, "The Pardoner's Interruption of the *Wife of Bath's Prologue*," *MLQ* 10 (1949): 49–57.

Guided by the Pardoner's suggestion, the Wife now explicates Paul's *tribulatio carnis* not as sexual temptation but as domestic tyranny, and the festivity of the *sermon joyeux* takes a darker turn. There are, to be sure, appealing moments in her account of her mastery over the three old husbands: the very intimacy of her revelations assures her male audience that they are not old and foolish, that they might even qualify to be one of those with whom she has shared "many a myrthe" (399). Nonetheless, the total effect cannot help but be appalling: she presents herself as a nightmare of the misogynist imagination, a woman who not only exemplifies every fault of which women have been accused but preempts the very language of accusation.

The first two parts of the Wife's *Prologue,* then, offer a characteristically ambivalent self-image: the *sermon joyeux* is at once exciting and troubling in its vigorous sexuality and mastery of masculine modes of argument; the account of her first three marriages at once appalling and entertaining. And while the male listener might decide that this image of femininity is, on balance, more chilling than heating, these off-puttings are shortly to be revealed as preliminaries to a come-on. Like the Wife's tale of Midas, with its veiled revisions and deferred conclusion, the self-images of the first two parts are ways of testing the patience and persistence of her audience. The account of husband number four begins the process of opening up, in content and, more tellingly, form. "Now wol I speken of my fourthe housbonde" (452), she begins, and then allows an entrance into the poem of a twenty-seven-line passage of nostalgic self-definition, only to close it off with a repetition of virtually the same line: "Now wol I tellen of my fourthe housbonde" (480).

This passage provides a structural image of dilation, an opening into the subject that is framed by a delayed narrative movement, and it stands as a paradigm for the rest of the *Prologue,* which consists of small narrative movements intercalated and retarded with increasingly detailed self-revelations. These digressions are not, as Geoffrey de Vinsauf would say, leaps off to the side of the road, but motivations for the very narrative they retard.[50] Not only, in other words, does the interleaving of digressive meditations within the narrative provide an image of dilation, but the narrative itself is both an opening up and a standing still, a deepening explication of that which is already known.[51] The three parts of the *Prologue,* as the principles of sermon

50. Geoffrey of Vinsauf, *Poetria nova,* trans. Margaret F. Nims (Toronto: Pontifical Institute of Mediaeval Studies, 1967), 35.

51. On this as a principle of medieval poetics, see, for example, Ernest Gallo's com-

rhetoric prescribe, deal with the same text at three different levels of analysis: in part one *tribulatio carnis* is sexual temptation; in part two it is domestic tyranny; and now in part three it is the suffering of the un-loved spouse. As the Wife says about herself, commenting upon Jankin's antifeminist mockings, "Who wolde wene, or who wolde sup-pose, / The wo that in myn herte was, and pyne?" (786–87).

The sequence of the *Prologue* is thus both temporal, its three parts matching the stages of a woman's sexual life, and analytic. As an analy-sis the *Prologue* is a progressive series of glosses on a text, the gradual moralization of the letter *tribulatio*. The account of the first three hus-bands presents the Wife as object rather than subject: whatever inter-nal reality she may possess is hidden behind the carapace of anti-feminist rhetoric, and whatever human cost her mercenary marriages may have exacted remains uncomputed, at best a speculation in the mind of the sympathetic reader. The story of Jankin, however, renders these implications explicit, manifesting them in the expositions of nar-rative: the Wife becomes the victim of the antifeminism she previously manipulated, and the money she earlier extorted for her own sexual favors she now pays out for another's attentions. Beyond these ironic reversals, however, is a deeper revelation. For in telling us about Jankin she discloses a range of previously unacknowledged human feelings that include both a genuinely marital affection and a sense of disap-pointment, even discouragement. For in revealing the "wo . . . and pyne" of the early days of her marriage to Jankin she shows that she is capable of love as well as desire, that she covets his affection at least as much as his well-turned legs. Hence she is willing to abandon *maistrye* once she learns that he cares enough to grant it:

> God help me so, I was to hym as kynde
> As any wyf from Denmark unto Ynde,
> And also trewe, and so was he to me. (823–25)

At the heart of the Wife's dilated discourse, then, rests the subjectiv-ity that it both masks and discloses. The ambivalences of her old woman's identity are carefully anatomized and disposed on the narra-

---

ment on the teachings of the rhetoricians: "*Everything is already known from the beginning: that which follows is an unfolding, a manifestatio, of a nature, a type, an essence*" ("Mat-thew of Vendôme: Introductory Treatise on the Art of Poetry," *American Philosophical Soci-ety Proceedings* 118 [1974], 60). Also relevant here is the important definition in the *Rheto-rica ad Herennium* of *expolitio* as "standing in the same place:" "Expolitio est cum in eodem loco manemus et aliud atque aliud dicere videmur" (Harry Caplan, ed. and trans. [Cam-bridge: Harvard University Press, 1954], 364).

tive line of her rhetoric. The *sermon joyeux* presents a theatrical exaggeration of female sexuality, the account of the first three husbands an equally exaggerated feminine combativeness. The story of Jankin returns her to the human level on which her audience can meet and accept her. The complexities of this strategy, and its erotic value, are neatly ideogrammed in the episode that concludes her narrative, the tearing of the book. Initially, this episode eagerly offers itself to a misogynist reading, for the Wife behaves in what appears to be a typically feminine way, responding to Jankin's learned authority with irrational aggression and then using affection, even sexuality ("yet wol I kisse thee" [802]) to lure the unsuspecting husband within striking distance. But like so many of the other antifeminist readings elicited throughout both *Prologue* and *Tale*, this one proves to be merely preliminary. A more patient analysis reveals this episode to be a symbolic reenactment of both the Wife's life and her rhetoric. A violent assault precipitates an equally violent rejection; but then a more subtle approach disarms the opposition and allows for the beginnings of accommodation. The male listener is assaulted by the license and violence of the first two parts of the *Prologue* and inevitably responds by turning away; but the immediacy of autobiographical disclosure lures him back, and he is finally, perhaps to his surprise, prepared to admit that the Wife deserves her happiness. For both Jankin and for him, conditioned by the "booke of wikked wives" that is their common cultural inheritance, this recognition of the Wife's moral superiority is indeed a blow upon the cheek. But in both cases, once having achieved *maistrye*, the Wife abandons it in the interests of a larger purpose, whether it be marital harmony or the pleasure of the reader. As a wife she withdraws into gentle submission; as a speaker she replaces the complex self-promotions of her *Prologue* with a *Tale* that offers itself as pure entertainment.

To show that the canons of the *ars praedicandi* remain in force throughout the *Prologue* it is the Friar who gives formal notice of its conclusion. As well as his sexual interest, he shares with the Pardoner a professional concern with the Wife's preaching, as he snidely implies by criticizing the disposition of her discourse—"'Now dame,' quod he, 'so have I joye or blis, / This is a long preamble of a tale!'" (830–31)—just as later he will criticize its invention ("scole-matere" [1272]). The Wife's response to this critique demonstrates her uncontrite ingenuity. She allows the Friar a place in her tale by devising yet another preamble in which the Friar's malevolence is disarmed by the fairy-tale norms of her Arthurian fable. The "lymytours and othere hooly freres" are invited into the tale, in other words, only to be held in abeyance, suspended "as thikke as motes in the sonne-beem" (868) while the magic of her story fulfills itself. Far from violating her story, they too succumb to its charms, just as her sly allusion to the Friar's sexual conquests is both an insult and a compliment, a counterattack that is in the event a good-humored caress.

This sense of raising the mean and squalid into a higher, cleansing action, of transforming a petty desire by absorbing it into a larger, more generous motion, is characteristic of the *Tale* as a whole. The *Tale* presents a series of quests that are displaced into progressively more inclusive movements. The initial quest after a "maydenheed" succeeds only to reveal a new quest after the knight's own "heed," a movement that is in turn displaced into the primary action of the tale, a quest after the "thyng . . . that wommen moost desiren." An assault on beauty has thus been absorbed into a hard-earned approach to wisdom, a displacement that is then repeated in the narrative itself: the questing knight rushes toward a group of dancing maidens only to see them vanish, leaving behind the old "wyf." That they vanish in order to reveal the saving figure of the hag is a function of his motives in approaching them. "He drow ful yerne, / In hope that som wysdom sholde he lerne" (993–94), a sharp contrast to his earlier approach to women; and not surprisingly, the hag delivers her advice in a manner strikingly reminiscent of Midas's wife: "Tho rowned she a pistel in his ere" (1021). The wisdom the old wife purveys (that women desire mastery above all else) apparently concludes his efforts, but of course he then discovers that this quest was only preliminary to a further journey, the internalized quest of his marriage. Now the barrier becomes the moral severity of the bedtime sermon and the temptation the magical offer to have a wife who is either beautiful or faithful, a choice that ungenerously assumes that fidelity is possible only for the woman who has no alternative.[52] In rejecting this offer altogether and in allowing his wife to choose for herself, the knight is submitting to the *maistrye* of her wisdom. Now he can cast aside the veil of his own misogyny and achieve the ultimate goal of clarified vision: "Cast up the curtyn, looke how that it is" (1249). The deferrals of both *Prologue* and *Tale* have thus prepared for and authorized a final opening up that is truly a revelation. This is a climactic, all-inclusive movement that joins wisdom to beauty to allow

---

52. This is an assumption that is central to the misogynist attitude and so provides the knight with an opportunity to transcend his earlier consciousness. See Ovid, *Amores* 1, 8, 43: "she is chaste because no one asked" ("casta est, quam nemo rogavit"). In closing the Wife's discourse with a sermon Chaucer neatly imitates Jean's *emboîtement* structure. He also provides a revision of Genius's two sermons, with the temporality that is compressed in Genius's version here given its full extension.

for the proper matching of male and female: "And thus they lyve unto hir lyves ende / In parfit joye" (1257–58).

Yet the perfection at which the *Tale* arrives is marked with unreality, as the Wife well knows. Both *Prologue* and *Tale* playfully demonstrate the truth of the kind of proposition that a logician like the Clerk would call an *impossible*—a proposition whose contrary is self-evident. The Wife's particular proposition, moreover, has as its subject matter clerks themselves, as she herself points out: "For trusteth wel it is an impossible / That any clerk wol speke good of wyves" (688–89). Both *Prologue* and *Tale* are of course just such a speaking: in the *Prologue* clerical misogyny is appropriated by a woman's voice in order to articulate feminist truths, while in the *Tale* the presumably feminine genre of Arthurian romance gives way to a fully authentic clerical *topos*—*nobilitas est virtus non sanguis*—that is not only spoken by a woman but challenges the patriarchal ideology of property and inheritance.[53] Nonetheless, this success marks the limits of the Wife's achievement. Her accommodations and resolutions are more verbal than actual—she is herself, after all, on the lookout for husband number six—and her very verbalizations remain unavoidably dependent, feminine respeakings of a resolutely masculine idiom. Try as she (and Chaucer) might, she remains confined within the prison house of masculine language; she brilliantly rearranges and deforms her authorities to enable them to disclose new areas of experience, but she remains dependent on them for her voice. Her performance is a kind of transvestism, and she speaks "habillé en homme."

This dependence is at the very heart of the Wife's *Tale* and of the feminine desire that it at once defines and exemplifies. The *Tale*'s project is to answer the question Freud made notorious—"What thyng is it that wommen moost desiren?" (905)—and the *Tale* is itself motivated by what the Wife calls a "queynte fantasye" (516). Feminine wishfulness is initially defined, in a deliberately superficial way, as the simple desire for "maistrye" (1040). But as in the *Prologue*, mastery is sought

53. The source of the discussion of *gentillesse* in the sermon is John of Wales' preaching handbook, the *Communiloquium;* see Robert A. Pratt, "Chaucer and the Hand that Fed Him," *Speculum* 41 (1966), 624–27. It would be quite wrong to think that the topos that nobility derives from virtue not lineage was by definition antiaristocratic. On the contrary, it is cited by chivalric writers in order to argue not only that inherited nobility demands the exercise of virtue but that high lineage predisposes one to virtuous deeds. See, for example, Ghillebert de Lannoy's *Enseignements Paternels*, in Charles Potvin, ed., *Oeuvres de Ghillebert de Lannoy*, Académie Impériales et Royale des Sciences et Belles-Lettres (Louvain: Lefever, 1878), 460–61; and Malcolm Vale, *War and Chivalry: Warfare and Aristocratic Culture in England, France and Burgundy* (London: Duckworth, 1981), 22–28.

only that it may be surrendered, an abnegation that allows both spouses to escape from the economy of domination that blights marriage. The hag's answer to the knight's question is thus of a piece with the other, more explicitly but no less thoroughly misogynist answers he has been given in the course of his quest (925–51), and it serves as a misleading half-truth to cover over a larger understanding of the feminine personality. Yet while this dynamic neatly enacts for the *Tale* the *Prologue's* pattern of misogynist preliminary followed by a more authentic revelation, the truth that is in fact finally revealed is itself disturbingly irresolute in its sexual valence. For the point is not simply that the hag's transformation into a wife "bothe fair and good" (1241) expresses the Wife of Bath's secret hankering to trade her hard-won wisdom for more orthodox pleasures, but that the feminine wishes that are here fulfilled are themselves a function of *masculine* desire. The *Tale* tells us, first, that the husband who abandons *maistrye* will receive in return a wife who will fulfill his every wish ("And she obeyed hym in every thyng / That myghte doon hym plesance or likyng" [1255–56]), and second, that what women most desire is to be just this sort of obedient wife. The feminine desire that is anatomized throughout the *Tale* is here revealed to be, in its authentic form, determined by a desire that is not only masculine but is beyond scrutiny. The Wife's "queynte fantasye," in short, is a masculine wish fulfillment, and one in which she appears to be fully complicit.

That the Wife of Bath's *Tale* serves finally to articulate a fundamental orthodoxy is, to be sure, a not unexpected Chaucerian conclusion. But what *is* surprising is that this is not in fact the Wife's conclusion. When the hag had finished her account of *gentillesse* she closed with a high-minded invocation of divine grace:

> Yet may the hye God, and so hope I,
> Grante me grace to lyven vertuously.
> Thanne am I gentil, whan that I bigynne
> To lyven vertuously and weyve synne. (1173–76)

But when the Wife comes to conclude the whole of her performance she not only respeaks the hag's prayer in very different tones but actually allows it to modulate into its opposite, a curse:

> . . . and Jhesu Crist us sende
> Housbondes meeke, yonge, and fressh abedde,
> And grace t'overbyde hem that we wedde;
> And eek I praye Jhesu shorte hir lyves

That noght wol be governed by hir wyves;
And olde and angry nygardes of dispence,
God sende hem soone verray pestilence! (1258–64)

Coming hard upon the description of the "blisse" (1253) and "parfit joye" (1258) of the knight and his "new" wife, these discordant lines are deeply dismaying, and they constitute a final gesture as challenging and contradictory as, for instance, the Pardoner's offer of his relics. In part, certainly, the Wife is here reenacting the ambivalence that motivates her entire performance, luring the listener on with a seductive vision of feminine docility and then abruptly reminding him that the goal is not won without a struggle, that lasting peace emerges only from testing marital wars.[54] But beyond this, we are I think right to hear in the Wife's impenitent abrasiveness a subversion of her *Tale*'s wish-fulfilling promises, a jesting but nonetheless severe (*"verray* pestilence") judgment upon the masculine enterprise that has been constituted as her *Prologue* and *Tale*. For not only does her conclusion remind us that masculine consciousness is, in some of its forms, irredeemable—"olde and angry nygardes" will never be converted into "housbondes meeke, yonge, and fressh abedde"—it more tellingly suggests that the economy of domination will inevitably continue if the only alternative is a supervening, hegemonic masculinity. The Wife's conclusion, in short, undoes the very resolution at which she has herself arrived by suggesting that it may be merely the latest, most insidious move in an endless battle of the sexes.

When the Wife first appears she challenges her audience by first displacing the Parson's severe, Lollard-like moralism with her own ostentatiously unorthodox carnal rhetoric: "My joly body schal a tale telle." As we have seen, the Wife's analogy between her "joly body" and the *corpus* of her text is elaborately staged in both the form and the content of her performance, and with it she solicits a reading that is itself unorthodox in the terms of medieval hermeneutics. It is, nonetheless, a kind of reading that is prerequisite for the understanding of Chaucer's kind of poetry. For the orthodox reader, the "joly body" of the Wife's text can be disarmed by interpretation. Every text, according to Augustine, can and must be read so that it teaches the single lesson of the law of charity.[55] What is important about this hermeneutic is that

54. From this perspective, the conclusion to the *Tale* is analogous to the tearing of the book that serves to bring to a climax the struggle with Jankin, and specifically to the blow upon the cheek with which Alison greets Jankin's response to her apparent vulnerability.

55. *De doctrina Christiana* 3, 15, trans. Robertson: "What is read should be subjected to diligent scrutiny until an interpretation contributing to the reign of charity is produced" (93). See also 1, 36 and 3, 7 (30, 86).

it is preemptive: the reader knows before he approaches the text—and this is a deeply masculinist (although not exclusively male) mode of reading—what will be the result of his reading. His interpretive task is not to discover *what* the text means but its way of signifying the meaning it must have. Armed with the strength of the spirit, he is immune to the solicitations of the letter, for he knows that the letter is a mere covering, a veil to be torn aside and discarded in pursuit of the truth. Interpretation, in other words, is a way of mastering the text.

Maistrye and *acorde*, *auctoritee* and *experience*, the *joly body* and the *curtyn* that darkens it—these terms define the polarized values of the Wife of Bath's marital world. They are also terms that define alternative ways of reading her text. We can either master the text with the *auctoritee* of preemptive interpretation, or we can *acorden* with it through the negotiations of experience; we can display its carnality by hastily ripping off the *curtyn* of its rhetorical strategies, or we can patiently allow it to reveal itself to us. By offering a redefinition of reading—a way to make meaning that avoids the preemptions of Augustinian hermeneutics—the Wife of Bath is engaged in a project that is central to the poetic of the *Canterbury Tales* as a whole. For she offers a mode of reading that is at once literal and moral; and she insists that interpretation must be deferred, that meaning (whether literary or personal) is available only at the end (whether of a narrative or a life).

When the Wife of Bath preempts the Parson she displaces a voice that will provide a conclusion to the tale-telling so authoritative that it comes to include the tones of the author himself. The *Parson's Tale*, when it is finally allowed audience, is a treatise on confession that in turn preempts all discourse that is not conducted in the authorized language of penance. In rejecting "fables and swich wrecchednesse" the Parson rejects the whole of the *Canterbury Tales*, a rejection that Chaucer authorizes in the Retractions he appends to the *Parson's Tale*. For the *Canterbury Tales* to exist at all, then, the *Parson's Tale* must be deferred; and who could be a more appropriate agent of deferral than the Wife of Bath? The "joly body" of the Wife's text is thus a paradigm for the *Canterbury Tales* as a whole; just as her speaking is a dilation that defers her conclusion, so too are the *Tales* a "game" or "pleye" that postpones the penance of Canterbury. But as we have seen, this is a postponement and not a dismissal, and a digression that leads inevitably if eventually to the goal. Her rhetoric has as its goal not mere delectation but the higher pleasures of ethical understanding, an understanding that may properly be seen as preparatory to the Parson's absolutism. By introducing a rhetoric that is at once carnal and moral, in other words, the Wife of Bath ameliorates the harsh polarizations of Augustinian theory and opens up a space in which what we have come to call literature can find its home. And when we do finally arrive at the *Parson's Tale* we discover to our surprise that both penitential pilgrimage and playful tale telling have reached a simultaneous conclusion, that the Parson will now both "knitte up al this feste and make an ende." The longest way round has proved to be the shortest way home.

This is a conclusiveness that is profoundly satisfying and thoroughly medieval; but I am reluctant to deny to Chaucer's Wife either the nobility of her innovations or the last word. "Welcome the sixte, whan that evere he schal," she says; and we must admire her stamina. But if we really imagine an endless series, the pleasure of the text will quickly diminish. If we truly understand the Wife of Bath as a traditional figure, we will remember that the tradition she articulates depends for its own vitality on the threat of temporality. More, by making us wait so patiently for the right ending—or the right interpretation—it comes to seem, when it comes, so much the more right. She makes us ourselves desire an ending, and she herself insists that there is an ending to be desired:

> "Now wol I dye, I may no lenger speke."
> But atte laste, with muchel care and wo,
> We fille acorded by us selven two. (810–12)

VII

Chaucer is prepared to identify himself with the Wife's subversion of the authoritarian orthodoxy of the Man of Law because, as I have said, it does not correspond to an explicitly political position. The same strategy of disarming the political force of oppositional discourse is also visible in the final member of the four-tale movement of Fragments II–III, the *Summoner's Tale*. This *Tale* plays here the role that fell to the disgraced and excluded *Cook's Tale* in the first movement. Far from being chastened by the apparent failure of Fragment I, Chaucer seems defiantly to return here to the churlish world of mockery and retaliation that was forced into the pilgrimage by the Miller's interruption, the world of *quiting* that then came to such a bad end. In fact, the *Summoner's Tale* enacts *quiting* to an almost quintessential degree: not only does the *Tale* retaliate against the pompous Friar by deploying all of the traditional antifraternal arguments, but it mocks even fraternal propaganda by subjecting it to merciless ridicule.[56] *Quiting* is definitively recuperated, and in order to enforce

---

56. For full discussions, see Penn R. Szittya, *The Antifraternal Tradition in Medieval Literature* (Princeton: Princeton University Press, 1986), 231–46, and references cited there.

the parallelism with Fragment I Chaucer chooses as his spokesman for this recuperation the one other diseased pilgrim among the group, the scabrous Summoner whose inflamed face seems an appropriate counterpart to the disgusting "mormel" that adorns the Cook's leg.

Now our question becomes truly pressing: why does Chaucer complete this process with the Summoner while he apparently felt himself unwilling to go forward with the Cook? If the argument prosecuted thus far is correct, the answer lies in the realm of politics. And in terms of the conditions of fourteenth-century life, the Cook and the Summoner do indeed represent two very different worlds. The Cook derives from the threatening urban proletariat that stands as the economic and ideological counterpart to the emergent rural producers—a degraded urban version, in other words, of the Miller—while the Summoner, for all his gross immorality, is part of the apparatus of social control imposed upon medieval society by the church.[57] The Summoner, like the Reeve, is a bailiff, although in this case for the archidiaconal court that punished various spiritual and moral offenses, especially sexual ones. So that as his agent of successful subversion Chaucer has chosen not a genuinely rebellious figure but instead a representative of one of the most repressive forces in medieval society.

This conservatism is also thematized in the *Tale* itself. To be sure, the *Summoner's Tale* does recuperate the Miller's churlish irreverence by subjecting a pompous representative of clerical learning to the churlish wisdom of his intended victim. Yet the highly traditional nature of the Summoner's attack—its deployment of the well-worn topoi of antifraternal satire—functions to remove the *Tale* from the specific context of late-fourteenth-century English history. As Penn Szittya says about antifraternalism, "The poets, like the polemicists before them, are writing less about the friars than about an idea about the friars, less about men they have seen begging on the streets in London than about numberless and placeless figures who are the sons of Cain and allies of Antichrist, men whose final significance lies not in history but at its End."[58] Moreover, Thomas's churlish triumph is displaced from the peasant locale in which it is initially enacted to a seigneurial context: after receiving his insult from Thomas, the friar retreats to the manor house, where the insult is completed by the squire. In effect, then, the lines of social opposition are here drawn not along class lines (as in the *Miller's Tale*) but instead according to the traditional division of lay ver-

57. Thomas Hahn and Richard W. Kaeuper, "Text and Context: Chaucer's *Friar's Tale*," *SAC* 5 (1983): 67–101.
58. Szittya, *Antifraternal Tradition*, 230.

sus clerical. And, Thomas's churlish wit is revealed to be in need of a supplementary interpretation that can be provided only within the context of aristocratic play.

It is quite true, of course, that the *Tale* leads us to think that his gift always contained within it the wonderfully deflating meaning that the squire makes explicit, that—to put it crudely—the seigneurial class lives off the humor of its agricultural workers as well as off their labor. This is part of the recuperation of churlishness that the second four tales seek to accomplish. Yet live off it the lord and his *familia* do, and nothing in the *Tale* suggests that this is an arrangement that can or should be called into question. Far from there being any question of peasant independence or class antagonism, the *Summoner's Tale* presents us with a rural world united in its opposition to the fraternal orders—orders that had originally, of course, preached a dangerously radical social message but that are now represented as hopelessly, laughably corrupt.[59] The true forces of social change abroad in Chaucer's historical world are thus definitively disarmed, and we retreat into a world of aesthetic appreciation, in which peasant energy, however potentially threatening, is reduced to a playful manipulation of the images of the official culture that leaves the realities firmly in place.

Yet even here Chaucer does not wholly suppress the political. On the contrary, it returns at the end of the *Summoner's Tale* in a passage that both recalls the end of the *Miller's Tale* and invokes, in an oblique but unmistakable fashion, the radical political program that informed late-medieval peasant belligerence. Presented with the churl's problem

59.   Again, one of the means by which the fraternal orders are divested of social force, both here and elsewhere in fourteenth-century satire, is the relentlessly dehistoricized apocalypticism of the traditional criticisms. It was not always the case that antifraternalism relied upon these traditional topoi; see Carolly Erickson, "The Fourteenth-Century Franciscans and Their Critics," *Franciscan Studies* 35 (1975): 107–35; 36 (1976), 108–47. That the fourteenth-century fraternal orders still had the capacity to participate in movements for social justice is suggested by objections early in the century to their participation in peasant protests against monastic landlords at Bury St. Edmunds, at Christ Church, Canterbury, and at Sandwich (see A. G. Little, *Studies in English Franciscan History* [Manchester: University of Manchester Press, 1917], 98–99); similarly, complaints that they supported the rebels of 1381 (by Walsingham, for instance [*Historia anglicana*, 2:13], and by the author of the *Fasciculus Zizaniorum*, ed. W. W. Shirley [London: Longmans, 1858], 292–95) are probably antifraternal slanders, but they may just point to a shred of historical truth. Certainly, as Charles Oman long ago suggested, the social gospel preached by the friars—although in no sense only by them—must have contributed to the sense of the intolerability of social injustice that was a sine qua non of the revolt; see Charles A. Oman, *The Great Revolt of 1381* (Oxford: Clarendon Press, 1906), 20; see also Little, *Studies in English Franciscan History*, 155–57, and G. R. Owst, *Literature and Pulpit in Medieval England*, 2d ed. (Oxford: Blackwell, 1961), 548–93.

of how to divide a fart equally among a convent of thirteen friars, the
seigneurial household is itself divided. The lady is instantly dismissive:
"I seye a cherl hath doon a cherles deed" (2206). But the lord is intrigued, and when the terms of his puzzlement are located within the
political context of rural discontent they take on a startling relevance:

> The lord sat stille as he were in a traunce,
> And in his herte he rolled up and doun,
> "How hadde this cherl ymaginacioun
> To shewe swich a probleme to the frere?
> Nevere erst er now herde I of swich mateere.
> *I trowe the devel putte it in his mynde.*
> In ars-metrike shal ther no man fynde,
> Biforn this day, of swich a question.
> Who sholde make a demonstracioun
> That *every man sholde have yliche his part*
> As of the soun or savour of a fart?
> *O nyce, proude cherle, I shrewe his face!*
> Lo, sires," quod the lord, "with harde grace!
> *Who evere herde of swich a thyng er now?*
> *To every man ylike? Tel me how.*
> *It is an inpossible, it may nat be.*
> Ey, *nyce cherl,* God lete him nevere thee!
> The rumblynge of a fart, and every soun,
> Nis but of eir reverberacioun,
> And evere it wasteth litel and litel awey.
> Ther is no man kan deemen, by my fey,
> *If that it were departed equally.*
> What, lo, *my* cherl, lo, yet how shrewedly,
> Unto *my* confessour to-day he spak!
> I holde hym certeyn a *demonyak!*
> Now ete youre mete, and lat the cherl go pleye;
> *Lat hym go honge hymself a devel weye!*" (2216–42)

Taken aback by signs of mental power in a creature thought to lack the
capacity, the lord is intrigued but finally retreats into typical defama-
tions: the churl is either foolish ("nyce") or crazy ("a demonyak"—and
see the squire's words when he solves the puzzle: "He nys no fool, ne
no demonyak" [2292]). At issue, of course, is the burning peasant demand for equality: "To every man ylike? Tel me how. / It is an
inpossible, it may nat be." Not only a fart cannot be "departed equally,"
but neither can the goods of this world; and the lord closes with a curse

on any who would think otherwise—"Lat hym go honge hymself a devel weye!"—and returns to his meat, itself one of those goods with which he is so abundantly supplied and that peasants like Thomas so conspicuously lack. In short, Chaucer presents a brief allegory of the seigneurial reaction to peasant demands, and then shows, in the squire's translation of Thomas's challenge back into the dehistoricizing language of antifraternal discourse, how those demands are displaced and finally appropriated to the traditional structure of medieval society. And finally, of course, this is an allegory of Chaucer's own practice of articulating but finally containing the voice of political protest.

Chapter Seven

Chaucerian Commerce: Bourgeois Ideology and Poetic Exchange in the Merchant's and Shipman's Tales

"That's what they all want, isn't it, these people who live in corners inside themselves, in blinds and hidey-holes? A second and safer identity. Teach us how to live, they say, as someone else."

The *Tales* of Fragments I–III reveal an attitude toward history and the subject that is at once deeply ambivalent and characteristically Chaucerian. On the one hand is a persistent and penetrating interest in the specific historical conditions of life and a willingness not merely to represent but to accommodate dissonant voices and oppositional political forces. But on the other is a studied retreat from the sphere of history into a socially undetermined subjectivity, a realm of private value defined by its apartness from the public world of event. This is an ambivalence that we have come to recognize as a central characteristic of bourgeois liberalism. The very definition of life in terms of an opposition between society and the individual, history and the subject, is now understood to be typical of bourgeois ways of thinking, a model of life that seeks to preserve an arena free from social contamination. That Chaucer developed such a model is surely one of the reasons that he has become the only medieval poet whom modern readers recognize as a kindred spirit.

Does this also mean that Chaucer is a bourgeois writer in the sense that such a designation would have been understood in his own society? He was, after all, a product of the merchant patriciate, and his work in the customs immersed him in the world and ethos of commerce. There is also considerable evidence that Chaucer himself might

322

have thought of the *Canterbury Tales* as a bourgeois production. Critics have long noted that the account of English society that he offers in both the *General Prologue* and throughout the *Tales* gives unusually ample space to that middle range of society that could not easily be accommodated to either of the prevailing social models, neither the implicit binary division of society into "gentils" and "churls" nor the traditional ternary model prescribed by estates theory. And more recent criticism has further argued that the *Tales* are organized according to principles that seem to derive from a bourgeois locale. Paul Strohm has pointed out that "the social ethic of the pilgrimage" is that of the silent gildsmen: "fraternity, expressed through vital and egalitarian social interchange, is the order of the day."[1] Carl Lindahl has argued that the festive form of the *Tales* imitates "the mixed class revels" that were at the center of the ceremonial practices by which the urban governing classes sought to reaffirm the wholeness of the community.[2] The *quiting* principle by which the succession of *Tales* is articulated invokes, in R. A. Shoaf's words, "the sphere of economics, the marketplace, [as] the space where community, mutual and just exchange, is most visibly and strenuously tested."[3] Patricia Eberle has shown that the *Canterbury Tales* is saturated with commercial language, which not only carries implications about its audience but serves to locate the text within the world of *negotium*—the world of business, exchange, and commerce—rather than in the courtly world of *otium*.[4] Finally, while Chaucer's immediate circle was comprised of men who were, like himself, *gentil*, and whose professional and social lives centered on the court, many of his fifteenth-century readers, to judge from manuscript provenance, were "among the business and administrative classes, especially in London."[5]

1. Paul Strohm, "The Social and Literary Scene in England," in *The Cambridge Chaucer Companion*, ed. Piero Boitani and Jill Mann (Cambridge: Cambridge University Press, 1986), 14. See also Strohm's "Form and Social Statement in *Confessio Amantis* and *The Canterbury Tales*," *SAC* 1 (1979): 17–40, and *Social Chaucer* (Cambridge: Harvard University Press, 1989).

2. "The Festive Form of the *Canterbury Tales*," *ELH* 52 (1985): 531–74. See also Charles Phythian-Adams, "Ceremony and the Citizen: The Communal Year at Coventry 1450–1550," in *Crisis and Order in English Towns 1500–1700*, ed. Peter Clark and Paul Slack (London: Routledge and Kegan Paul, 1972), 57–85.

3. R. A. Shoaf, *Dante, Chaucer, and the Currency of the Word* (Norman: Pilgrim Books, 1983), 167–68.

4. Patricia Eberle, "Commercial Language and the Commercial Outlook in the *General Prologue*," *ChR* 18 (1983–84): 161–74.

5. Derek Pearsall, *The Canterbury Tales* (London: Unwin, 1985), 298. For Chaucer's circle, see Paul Strohm, "Chaucer's Audience," *L&H* 5 (1977): 26–41.

Most important, the *Tales* often promote values that, whatever their pedigree, are carefully detached from any specific social location. This is most tellingly the case with Chaucerian *gentillesse*, whose two primary spokespersons in the *Tales* are the Wife of Bath and the Franklin. Non*gentils* themselves, they tell tales derived from aristocratic models (an Arthurian romance, a Breton lai) but revised in order to counter the class-specific definition of *gentillesse* given by their immediate predecessors, the socially thrusting Man of Law and the snobbish Squire. What makes the Wife and the Franklin bourgeois is not that they promote specifically bourgeois values, whatever these might be, but that they place their tales in the service of an aristocratic value whose full force can be made available only when it is detached from its social origin. It is the effacement of social location that is the quintessentially bourgeois strategy. The Wife and the Franklin set aside their own social identities not in order to adopt other, better ones (both are quite candid about their non*gentil* status) but instead to promote values that, as formulated, transcend social determination. They assume that true values, and their true selves, are not socially determined at all—a claim that we have come to recognize as central to bourgeois ideology.

But was it so for Chaucer? Did the urban bourgeoisie of late-medieval England, and specifically the merchant patriciate from which Chaucer himself emerged, in fact maintain this conception of identity formation? It is to Chaucer's two tales of bourgeois commercialism, the *Merchant's* and the *Shipman's Tales*, that we must turn in order to frame an answer to this question. Criticism has generally assumed that these *Tales* represent Chaucer's rejection of the aggressive commercialism of the merchant class and a defense of the traditional organicism of medieval society. Thus the Merchant has been understood to be a secret usurer whose *Tale* overflows with acidic misogyny and a blasphemous disrespect for sacred images, while the *Shipman's Tale* is read as indicting a profit-and-loss mentality that turns all human values into commodities. But these readings seem to me both to simplify the textual evidence and to depend upon a set of assumptions about the economic and political shape of Chaucer's world that can no longer be maintained.

I

Literary medievalists have generally assumed that the commercial activity of the Middle Ages, and the urban culture it spawned, were oppositional forces within feudal society, that they contained the seeds of the capitalist future.[6] On the one hand, runs this familiar account, was the natural economy of the feudal countryside, a world bound together by ties of mutual obligation and stabilized by traditional standards of status; on the other was the monetized market economy of the city, pervaded with a dehumanizing cash nexus that commodified natural value, freed the individual from feudal collectivity, and gave free rein to an ambitious social mobility. But the idea that the merchant class was the prime mover in the economy and society of preindustrial England, that it functioned as a nonfeudal formation from which emanated the forces that finally transformed feudalism into capitalism, is much less a historical fact than one of capitalism's own, most cherished myths. It derives from the "commercialization" model of economic history that assumes that capitalism is the natural condition of economic man, that the history of economic life records the gradual liberation of the forces of innovation and production from the fetters of religious and social inhibition.[7] On this account, the crucial distinction within medieval culture is that between the country and the city, and the agent of economic and social progress is the merchant. According to Carlo Cipolla, "In medieval Europe the town came to represent an abnormal growth, a peculiar body totally foreign to the surrounding environment"; in M. M. Postan's phrase, cities were "non-feudal islands in a feudal sea."[8] The countryside, bound by ties of obligation enforced by the unchallenged dominance of the landowning nobility, represented the social backwardness of feudalism's subsistence economy, while the cities— where *Stadtluft machts frei*—provided (to cite Cipolla again) "a new and dynamic world . . . where sclerotic traditional institutions and discriminations no longer counted, and where there would be ample reward for initiative, daring, and industriousness."[9] Similarly, it was the

---

6. This discussion recapitulates some of the material offered at fuller length in chapters 3 and 5.

7. For an analysis of the "commercialization" model, see Robert Brenner, "Agrarian Class Structure and Economic Development in Pre-industrial Europe" and "The Agrarian Roots of European Capitalism," in *The Brenner Debate*, ed. T. H. Aston and C. H. E. Philpin (Cambridge: Cambridge University Press, 1985), 38–40, and 241–42. Also relevant is John Merrington, "Town and Country in the Transition to Capitalism," in *The Transition from Feudalism to Capitalism*, ed. Rodney Hilton (London: Verso, 1978), 170–95.

8. Carlo Cipolla, "The Origins," in *The Fontana Economic History of Europe: The Middle Ages*, ed. Carlo Cipolla (London: Fontana Books, 1972), 18; M. M. Postan, *The Medieval Economy and Society* (Harmondsworth: Penguin Books, 1975), 239.

9. Carlo Cipolla, *Before the Industrial Revolution: European Economy and Society, 1000–1700* (New York: Norton, 1980), 146; see also Robert S. Lopez, *The Commercial Revolution of the Middle Ages, 950–1350* (Englewood Cliffs: Prentice-Hall, 1971).

merchant who provided Europe with not simply the commercial activity that made possible a better life but with a culture that legitimized a range of attitudes upon which the future could be built: acquisitiveness and accumulation, to be sure, and calculative and calibratory attitudes toward space and time—but also a republican sense of "cooperation among equals" given expression in the horizontally organized guilds and confraternities that replaced the vertical repressiveness of feudal social relations.[10]

Another account is possible. To begin with, as we have seen, virtually all modern historians of medieval Europe agree that the notion that the medieval agricultural economy was a natural economy, innocent of either money or markets, is a figment of the Romantic imagination. On the contrary, from at least the eleventh century the medieval rural world was saturated not only with money but with sophisticated instruments of money management, including credit. The agrarian economy always directed a significant portion of its production to the market, and there existed since at least the twelfth century both a vigorous, monetized, and at times credit-based peasant land market, a market for agricultural wage labor, and small-scale but essential rural industry and commodity production. Conversely, the city, far from functioning as a productive and progressive element in the late-medieval English economy, served primarily as a site for the circulation of capital generated in the country, extracted by the landowning class, and spent by them in large part on luxury goods—including their most expensive luxury, warfare. The economically *dynamic* sector of the economy was not the city but the country, and the prime mover in the transition from feudalism to capitalism was not merchant capital but a rurally based independent commodity production financed by peasant producers able to retain more of their surplus value. Hence recent historians have concluded that, in Rodney Hilton's words, "the so-called commercial revolution in no way altered the feudal mode of production"; the city was not an anomalous formation but instead "an essential institution of medieval society, closely integrated with all strata of the rural population and constituting an essential element in the political structure of the feudal states."[11] Rather than themselves initiating a change in economic structure, cities were in fact the *result* of a growing seigneurial demand for luxury goods: seigneurial incomes in cash preceded rather

10. Cipolla, *Before the Industrial Revolution*, 148.
11. The first citation is from *Transition*, 23, the second from "Warriors and Peasants," *New Left Review* 83 (1974), 89. See also J. L. Bolton, *The Medieval English Economy, 1150–1500*, 2d ed. (London: Dent, 1980), 246–86.

than followed from the luxury trade and the growth of urbanization served to bring it into existence.

Second, the mental habits associated with capitalism—calculative and calibratory attitudes toward space, time, and labor, a concern with profit maximization, familiarity with financial transactions, and a general rationalization of economic life—were in no sense confined to the merchant class of the medieval city but were widespread throughout the late-medieval world.[12] Both the feudal nobility and the Church were at every level concerned with the acquisition and use of money. As an international institution the Church received virtually all of its revenues in the form of money and it routinely deployed vast amounts of cash—facts that were not lost upon its critics. And in the administration of their estates, monastic landowners took the lead in applying techniques of quantification and measurement, and strategies of management, that maximized profits and increased capital worth.[13] Similarly, the landholding nobility was more than a little familiar with commerce, the world of money, and the cash nexus. Landowners throughout the medieval period imposed a daunting array of money payments upon their tenants and showed, in the management of their estates, a shrewd alertness to the economic requirements of their changed circumstances.[14] Indeed, feudalism itself "was becoming," in the words of K. B. McFarlane, "for all practical purposes a complex network of marketable privileges and duties."[15]

12. In explaining the emergence of capitalism as the dominant form of economic organization in the West, Max Weber stressed above all its rational organization of free labor, a task that entailed the creation of both a pool of wage laborers (accomplished in England through the destruction of the peasant economy in the sixteenth century) and of a bourgeois class capable of such rational organization. This capacity to apply "exact calculation, which is the foundation of everything else," to the production of profit was initiated and sustained by merchants, who in this sense functioned as history's prime movers. For representative discussions, see Max Weber, *Selections in Translation*, ed. W. G Runciman, trans. Eric Matthews (Cambridge: Cambridge University Press, 1978), 138–73, 290–314, 331–40.

13. For the role of monasticism in the development of the calculative pursuit of profit-maximization, see H. E. Hallam, "The Medieval Social Picture," in *Feudalism, Capitalism and Beyond*, ed. Eugene Kamenka and J. S. Neale (Canberra: Australian National University Press, 1975), 29–49.

14. See Sylvia Thrupp, *The Merchant Class of Medieval London* (Ann Arbor: University of Michigan Press, 1962 [1948]), 243–44, 256–63; Harry A. Miskimin, *The Economy of Early Renaissance Europe, 1300–1460* (Cambridge: Cambridge University Press, 1975 [1969]), 32–47; and K. B. McFarlane, *The Nobility of Later Medieval England* (Oxford: Clarendon Press, 1973), 53.

15. K. B. McFarlane, *England in the Fifteenth Century* (London: Hambledon Press, 1981), 24.

Nor was the quintessentially noble activity of warfare in any sense free from the cash nexus. Since at least the twelfth century the feudal requirement of military service had been commuted into a cash payment, and soldiers of all ranks who participated in the Hundred Years War contracted for salary. Indeed, the best form of booty to be wished for was a noble prisoner who could then be ransomed for cash—about as pure an instance of the commodification of natural value as one can imagine. At the head of their ledgers merchants habitually wrote the motto, "In the name of God and of profit," a contradiction that commentators have seen as typifying the mercantile ethic.[16] And yet in his treatise on chivalry the preeminent French knight Geoffroi de Charny— who died at the battle of Poitiers defending his king's standard—said that the knight fought "de proffiter avecques l'onneur."[17] The nobleman was all too capable of operating in the commercial world, as many merchants discovered to their cost when the king and his barons used their political power to drain off merchant profit to finance their own chivalric adventures, especially the Hundred Years War.[18] Far from being undone by the unfamiliar *idea* of money, as elegant but fanciful literary accounts have suggested, it was the *fact* of money, or rather its absence, that distressed medieval aristocrats.[19] Most of their wealth was in land, whose value was severely undermined by the agricultural depression of the later Middle Ages; they developed extravagant tastes for luxury goods that they could not afford; and they insisted upon trying to recoup their losses by persistent recourse to the highly unreliable lottery of warfare.[20] Conversely, the peasantry, far from being sunk into rural idiocy by the unending round of toil, was in fact a highly stratified and politically self-aware class that took advantage of the many opportunities for self-improvement available in the changing

16. For a specific example of this motto, see Iris Origo, *The Merchant of Prato* (Harmondsworth: Penguin Books, 1963 [1957]), 9.

17. *Le Livre de chevalerie*, in *Oeuvres de Froissart*, ed. Kervyn de Lettenhove (Brussels: De Vaux, 1873), vol. 1, pt. 3, 468. For the profits of war, see above, chapter 3, 172 *n15*.

18. See R. E. Kaeuper, *War, Justice and Public Order: England and France in the Later Middle Ages* (Oxford: Clarendon Press, 1988), 32–116.

19. For a powerful version of such an account, see R. Howard Bloch, *Etymologies and Genealogies: A Literary Anthropology of the French Middle Ages* (Chicago: University of Chicago Press, 1983), 164–74.

20. For a general account, see Miskimin, *Economy of Early Renaissance Europe*, 14–72; Léopold Genicot in *The Cambridge Economic History*, ed. M. M. Postan (Cambridge: Cambridge University Press, 1966), 1:703–24; Christopher Dyer, *Standards of Living in the Later Middle Ages* (Cambridge: Cambridge University Press, 1989), 27–108.

world of late-medieval agriculture to develop into the most dynamic players in the economic game.[21]

Third, medieval cities, far from being "non-feudal islands in a feudal sea," replicated and even intensified the traditional feudal patterns of dominance and subordination that were actually breaking down in the rural world. Except for a brief, enigmatic period in the late 1370s and early 1380s, London, like other English cities, was run by a self-perpetuating oligarchy of leading merchants, while retailers and artisans—not to speak of journeyman wage laborers—were effectively excluded from political influence. In fact, probably less than a quarter of the adult males in London were enfranchised freemen, the rest being known as "foreigns."[22] Not surprisingly, then, the primary social value in late-medieval London was not freedom but public order. As Sylvia Thrupp has said,

> The central psychological prop of the economic and political inequalities that developed was in the individual's inescapable respect for authority. . . . The bourgeois context did nothing to free the individual from this kind of pressure but seems rather to have intensified it. . . . Among responsible citizens, . . . the necessity of public order was probably the dominating political idea.[23]

In order to submerge all signs of political or economic conflict beneath a sense of social wholeness, the ruling class of the medieval city both fostered rituals of corporate identity—such as the Corpus Christi processions—and maintained a highly visible and minutely graduated social hierarchy.[24] There were ranks both among and within the various fellowships, gilds, and councils that brought citizens together, distinctions that were carefully maintained by sumptuary legislation that translated otherwise indiscernible degrees of status into a manifest system of social hierarchy.[25] The effect was both to remind men of their place in the world and to distribute the signs of honor widely enough

21. See above, chapter 5, 247–53.

22. A. R. Myers, *London in the Age of Chaucer* (Norman: University of Oklahoma Press, 1973), 144–45.

23. Thrupp, *Merchant Class*, 16, 75.

24. See Phythian-Adams, "Ceremony and the Citizen," 69.

25. On the stratification within and among the various communal organizations of the city, see Charles Phythian-Adams, *Desolation of a City: Coventry and the Urban Crisis of the Late Middle Ages* (Cambridge: Cambridge University Press, 1979), 125. Claire B. Sponsler, "Society's Image: Estates Literature in Fifteenth-Century England," *Semiotica* 63 (1987): 229–38, shows that sumptuary legislation was sponsored by merchants themselves.

throughout urban society so that no one would feel wholly excluded.[26] And the goal was to fix the social system in place by emphasizing the subordination of the individual to the social whole. In sum, the socially dislocated countryside of postplague England almost certainly offered more scope for personal as well as economic freedom than did the tightly regulated and economically squeezed city. And to judge from the events of 1381, it was not in the city but in the country and its market towns that radical political change was conceivable.[27]

Finally, far from possessing a clear sense of social identity, the merchant class of medieval London gives every evidence of having been a class in search of a legitimizing ideology. London merchants seem to have constructed their social identity largely from the materials of other, noncommercial cultural formations. On the one hand, they aped the accoutrements and practices of *aristocratic* life: they adopted aristocratic modes of address for themselves, their wives, and their servants; designed for themselves heraldic devices, sometimes based on their commercial trademarks; joined with members of the gentry for both business and recreational purposes; and worked to win for their children—and in some cases, for themselves—entrance into the ranks of the rural landowning class.[28] They bought country residences and attached gardens—the classic space of aristocratic leisure—to their communal halls and to their city residences for, as one source says, "consolation and pleasure"; the secular books they read, such as the romances of the Auchinleck manuscript, were derived from aristocratic models and often expressed unabashedly aristocratic values; and to judge from the structure of the *pui*, the same went for their festive occasions.[29] As Nigel Saul has said, "The merchant class contributed little

26. Myers, *London*, 116–17. These various organizations also provided new city dwellers—of whom there were always a great many—with the sense of community they had enjoyed in the country; see Susan Reynolds, *Kingdoms and Communities in Western Europe, 900–1300* (Oxford: Clarendon Press, 1984), 73.

27. As Brenner says, "In truth, the historical record of urban support for the aspirations to freedom of the medieval European peasantry is not impressive" (*Brenner Debate*, 39). On the lack of enthusiasm for the rebellion in London, Thrupp comments: "The cult of secular equality implicit in the slogans of the peasants' revolt may have had its sympathizers in the city, but it found no prophets there" (*Merchant Class*, 26). For details, see Rodney Hilton, *Bond Men Made Free* (London: Methuen, 1973), 186–98.

28. For these statements, see Thrupp, *Merchant Class*, 16–18, 152, 144, 249–56, 120, 136, 247–63, 229–32.

29. On the *pui*, see John Hurt Fisher, *John Gower: Moral Philosopher and Friend of Chaucer* (New York: New York University Press, 1964), 78–86. On the bourgeois origins of the Auchinleck manuscript, A. I. Doyle, "English Books In and Out of Court from Edward III to Henry VII," in V. J. Scattergood and J. W. Sherborne, eds., *English Court Culture in the Later Middle Ages* (London: Duckworth, 1983), 164–65.

that was uniquely their own; rather, they preferred to assume the manners and values of the rural nobility."[30]

Merchants also fashioned their social identity from the materials of *clerical* culture. Sylvia Thrupp estimates that by the mid-fifteenth century, a remarkable 40 percent of male Londoners could read Latin and at least 50 percent English. "Parents were," she says, "genuinely anxious for their sons to be initiated into that world of Latin learning over which the church presided"; in the early fourteenth century one alderman mandated in his will that his sons should stay at school "until they could compose reasonably good verses."[31] Nor was it only the commercially useless learning of the clergy that attracted merchants, whose orthodox piety is clearly reflected in their large holdings of books of religious instruction. In the mid-fifteenth century Bishop Reginald Pecock tells of how men and women would frequently consult him about the views of current preachers.[32] And there must have been many such preachers: not only were there the pulpits of the Cathedral and St. Paul's Cross from which religious views were regularly disseminated, but the city supported both a large number of religious houses and an astonishing 120 parish churches, "probably more . . . than any other town in Christendom."[33]

There is, of course, a great deal of late-medieval writing that literary historians have understood as either emanating from or being directed toward the "middle class"—by which is generally meant everybody between the dignitary, whether lay or ecclesiastical, and the peasant. Certainly this literature articulates values and interests that are not aristocratic: it attacks the war with France, the depredations of an undisciplined nobility, the wastefulness and self-interest of the king's advisors, and clerical and fraternal corruption, and it promotes a pragmatic piety that interests itself in sometimes quite specific theological questions.[34] But what it declines to promote is a legitimizing self-definition of either the middle class in general or of merchants in particular. For one thing, it refuses to align itself with a socially specific perspective. Instead, as Anne Middleton has shown, it speaks in a "common voice":

30. Nigel Saul, *Scenes from Provincial Life: Knightly Families in Sussex 1280–1400* (Oxford: Clarendon Press, 1986), 187; and see Michael J. Bennett, *Community, Class and Careerism: Cheshire and Lancashire Society in the Age of* Sir Gawain and the Green Knight (Cambridge: Cambridge University Press, 1983), 132.

31. Thrupp, *Merchant Class*, 160.

32. Ibid., 181.

33. Myers, *London*, 75.

34. For a description of this writing, see Janet Coleman, *Medieval Readers and Writers, 1350–1400* (New York: Columbia University Press, 1981).

The voice of public poetry is neither courtly, nor spiritual, nor popular. . . . [It exemplifies] an ideal of communal responsibility founded
not primarily in an estates conception of one's duties, but in an altruis-
tic and outward-turning form of love that might be called "common
love" to emphasize the symmetry and contrast with that singular
passion which expresses itself in literature in the inward self-
cultivation sometimes called "courtly love."[35]

This voice—and Gower and Langland are two of its primary speakers—
defines itself against courtliness not because it represents another estate, but rather because it stands apart from and above *all* estates. It is a
vox populi; and if it is, in fact, generated by the bourgeoisie, it seeks to
efface the specificity of its social origins in the generality of its prescriptions and the universality of its tone. Second, what self-images merchants do sponsor are distinctly unflattering. In the later fifteenth century, Hugh Brice, a goldsmith, commissioned Caxton's translation of
The Mirror of the World for presentation to Lord Hastings—a work that
contained a vicious attack upon merchants.[36] Similarly, the books of cour-
tesy that were produced in the fifteenth century for what is usually taken
to be a mercantile audience sought to teach merchants how to shed the
social identity endowed them by their vocation and adopt the manners,
and with it the status, of the nobility.[37] Even in Elizabethan England, and
even in books directed to a middle-class audience, merchants and craftsmen were represented according to a set of values derived not from their
own class but rather from the aristocracy.[38]

The literature of middle-class England, in other words, may indeed
express the interests of the middle class but it nonetheless declines to
define much less to promote a specifically middle-class identity. If Boccaccio's *Decameron* is "a mercantile epic," and if Giovanni Sercambi's
Novelliero is the "chronicle of merchants," there is nothing comparable
in England—unless it is, a dubious proposition, the *Canterbury Tales.*[39]
What is missing in England, and is found in abundance in Italy, is both

35.   Anne Middleton, "The Idea of Public Poetry in the Reign of Richard II," *Speculum*
53 (1978), 95–96.

36.   Thrupp, *Merchant Class*, 163; for Hugh Brice, see Sponsler, "Society's Image,"
233.

37.   Sponsler, "Society's Image," 233.

38.   Laura Stephenson, *Praise and Paradox: Merchants and Craftsmen in Elizabethan Popular Literature* (Cambridge: Cambridge University Press, 1984).

39.   For Boccaccio, see Vittore Branca, *Boccaccio: The Man and His Works*, trans. Richard Monges (New York: New York University Press, 1976), 276–307; for Sercambi, Christian Bec, *Les marchands écrivains à Florence, 1375–1434* (Paris: Mouton, 1967), 175–98.

the aggressive economic individualism that characterizes Italian commercialism and the antiaristocratic politics of republican Italy. There are
good historical reasons for both of these gaps. For one thing, the accommodation of commercial to religious values had not developed as far in
England as on the continent, as is attested by both a nervous mercantile
piety and the scorn with which merchants were regarded by pious writers such as Langland.[40] And for another, English political structure neither allowed for urban independence nor permitted the merchant class
nearly as much responsibility for the governance of the realm as occurred in parts of *trecento* Italy, specifically Florence.

It appears to be the case, then, that English mercantile culture was
largely confected out of the materials of other cultural formations—
primarily aristocratic but also clerical—and lacked a center of its own. It
was a culture grounded in the historical realities of commercial life and
driven by interests that were historically constituted, but it was unable
to articulate much less justify this historical specificity. This produced, I
suggest, an early instance of what would become the most ineradicable
of bourgeois illusions: that the bourgeoisie is not a class driven by its
own interests and constituted by historical and economic conditions
but rather a group of free individuals with unlimited options—the idealized version of upward mobility. But in this, its earliest form, this
illusion derives not (as in the nineteenth century) from the impenetra-
ble strength of a bourgeois ideology that refuses to recognize itself.
Instead it is a function of weakness, of the very absence of ideology.

II

The *Merchant's Tale*, as its critical history has shown, is a remarkably
unstable, even volatile text. Part of its challenge derives from its
syncretism, its dizzying conjunction of widely disparate literary materials;[41] part derives from its refusal to provide a coherent perspective

40. Lester K. Little, *Religious Poverty and the Profit Economy in Medieval Europe* (Ithaca:
Cornell University Press, 1978); see also John H. McGovern, "The Rise of New Economic
Attitudes—Economic Humanism, Economic Nationalism—During the Later Middle
Ages and the Renaissance, A.D. 1200–1550," *Traditio* 26 (1970): 217–53. Langland expresses his contempt for commercialism in virtually all its forms throughout *Piers Plowman:* in his account of the pardon, for example, merchants are placed "in þe margyne" but
are pardoned *a poena et a culpa* only if they modify their business practices and spend all of
their profits on charitable works (B, 7, 18–39). For the highly prejudicial representation of
merchants in contemporary preaching, see G. R. Owst, *Literature and Pulpit in Medieval
England,* 2d ed. (Oxford: Blackwell, 1961), 352–61.
41. Robert Kaske has called it "perhaps the most skillful and richly allusive" of the

on this *bricolage*.[42] All conventions—indeed, all forms of medieval discourse—seem to be subject to its critique. The *Tale*'s denouement apparently reveals its central concern: although he has witnessed a scene of appetite and betrayal, January is deluded by May's words into believing that she has actually performed an act of physical restoration and marital loyalty. It is this capacity of language to deceive and befuddle—"he that mysconceyveth, he mysdemeth" (2410) is May's final apothegm—that is the target of attack. Alfred David has commented on "the narrator's obsession throughout the tale with what he considers to be sham language," and the performance as a whole can be read as an assault upon the delusive rhetoric that allows men to avoid reality in order to indulge their "heigh fantasye and curious bisyness" (1577).[43]

This conclusion may, however, be both too general and too absolute. The various elements that the *Tale* deploys are not simply items derived at random from the discursive world of late-medieval England. On the contrary, they are class-specific discourses: the Merchant's primary targets are the two great cultural formations that dominated his world, the Church and the aristocracy. For one thing, mercantile admiration for Latin learning is clearly visible in the *Tale*. Not just Cato and Seneca, those ubiquitous sources of medieval proverbs, but also Ovid, Claudian, and Martianus Capella are explicitly introduced into the narrative, Statius is present in allusions to characters from the *Thebaid* (1716, 1720–21), and familiar mythological figures (Orpheus, Hymen, Venus, Bacchus, Paris and Helen, Priapus, and Argus) make unascribed appearances. Clerical learning is equally well represented by the *Tale*'s mastery of the homiletics and liturgy of marriage, the fine points of canon law, the traditional discourse of clerical misogyny, and sophisticated techniques of exegesis. When, for instance, January says that he knows "the cause why / Men sholde wedde" (1441–42), the Merchant

---

Canterbury Tales ("Chaucer's Marriage Group," in *Chaucer the Love Poet*, ed. Jerome Mitchell and William Provost [Athens: University of Georgia Press, 1973], 55), while for G. G. Sedgewick it is "a dense mosaic of references, allusions, quotations" ("The Structure of the *Merchant's Tale*," *UTQ* 17 [1947–48], 344).

42. E. T. Donaldson speaks for most readers when he complains that "our moral judgment . . . finds no safe place to settle" in the *Tale* (*Speaking of Chaucer* [London: Athlone Press, 1970], 35); according to Derek Pearsall, "there is no centre to the poem, no literary convention within which it has its place in relation to reality, no body of moral value to which it refers" (*Canterbury Tales*, 207).

43. Alfred David, *The Strumpet Muse: Art and Morals in Chaucer's Poetry* (Bloomington: Indiana University Press, 1976), 173. See also Mary C[arruthers] Schroeder, "Fantasy in the 'Merchant's Tale,' " *Criticism* 12 (1970): 167–79.

produces a succinct and accurate survey of the relevant canon law.[44] The *Tale* opens with a 135-line account of marriage (1258–1392) largely derived from contemporary sermons—the sort of sermon the priest then delivers (1704–5) when he performs the marriage service according to current liturgical practice ("as is usage" [1706]);[45] and it closes with a final scene of such biblical resonance, including January's recital of the "olde lewed wordes" (2149) of the *Song of Songs* and the densely symbolic "struggle" in the pear tree within the *hortus conclusus* of his garden, that it has been for many years an exegetical gold mine for scholars.[46]

The *Tale* is equally saturated with the materials and tropes of courtly writing. The protagonist of the *Tale* is, after all, not a merchant but "a worthy knight," and the Merchant never allows us to forget that the action takes place within a courtly context and that much of the behavior it represents—both marital and extramarital—is governed by courtly norms of value. The marriage is celebrated with a flourish of the kind of classical allusion (1715–41) typically used by courtly writing to confer large significance upon local affairs; May withdraws to her bedchamber for four days after her marriage as was a "custume" of "thise nobles alle" [1889]); and the betrayal is endowed with tragic import by a "heigh style" of epic apostrophe (1783–94, 1866–74) and Boethian metaphysics (1967, 2057) and then enacted in a garden that combines the timeless significance of Pluto and Prosperpina with the current aristocratic practices described in the *Romance of the Rose* (2032).

But if the Merchant has been endowed with a *Tale* fashioned from materials appropriate to the synthetic culture of his class, his own atti-

44. The accuracy of January's account has been ratified by Henry Ansgar Kelly, *Love and Marriage in the Age of Chaucer* (Ithaca: Cornell University Press, 1975), 265. These lines derive from the same source as Chaucer used for the comparable passage in the *Parson's Tale*; see Lee Patterson, "The *Parson's Tale* and the Quitting of *The Canterbury Tales*," *Traditio* 34 (1978), 363–66.

45. See C. E. Shain, "Pulpit Rhetoric in Three *Canterbury Tales*," *MLN* 70 (1955): 235–45; J. D. Burnley, "The Morality of the *Merchant's Tale*," *YES* 6 (1976): 16–25; and Robert P. Miller, ed., *Chaucer: Sources and Backgrounds* (New York: Oxford University Press, 1977), 373–90.

46. For a representative sample, see James Wimsatt, "Chaucer and the Canticle of Canticles," in Mitchell and Provost, *Chaucer the Love Poet*, 66–90; Alfred L. Kellogg, "Susannah and the *Merchant's Tale*," *Speculum* 35 (1960): 275–79; Douglas Wurtele, "Ironical Resonances in the *Merchant's Tale*," *ChR* 13 (1978–79): 66–79; Emerson Brown, "Biblical Women in the Merchant's Tale: Feminism, Antifeminism, and Beyond," *Viator* 5 (1974): 387–412; and Kenneth A. Bleeth, "The Image of Paradise in the *Merchant's Tale*," in *The Lerned and the Lewed*, Harvard English Studies, 5, ed. Larry D. Benson (Cambridge: Harvard University Press, 1974), 45–60.

tude remains puzzling. Criticism of the *Tale* has consistently registered most readers' sense of the Merchant as a bitter cynic, desecrating the ideals of church and court. The opening encomium to marriage derisively rehearses the paradisal theory promoted by clerics but known in practice by laymen to be quite different. The institutional role of the church is represented as being simply to make "al siker ynogh with hoolynesse" (1708), even though the relationship being solemnized is a grossly commercial transaction that mocks the church's own teaching about the consensual basis of marriage.[47] The *Song of Songs* is slanderously described as "swiche olde lewed wordes"(2149) while the Marian images embodied in the garden are presented in what one offended critic has termed a "repulsive parody" that shows the Merchant taking "perverse delight in desecrating what others deem holy."[48] Courtly values apparently fare no better. The exchange between Justinus and the "court-man" (1492) Placebo witnesses to the corruption of court politics; the marriage presided over by the laughing Venus—amused indeed that January should "bicome hir knyght" (1724)—is a caustic commentary on the aristocratic habit of using self-glorifying classical allusions to elevate shameful marital practices; and the affair between "gentil May, fulfilled of pitee" (1995) and the "gentil squier" (1907) Damyan is a degrading representation of the noble cult of *fine amor*.

Yet such a reading of the *Tale* as entirely negative, as a demolition of every form of cultural value, not only overlooks certain elements of the text but posits for the teller an impossible condition of total cultural alienation. In fact, the Merchant's attitude toward the disparate discourses from which his *Tale* is constituted harbors affirmation as well as negation. Clearly he is proud of his capacity to deploy his learned materials, as his careful annotation of many of his allusions suggests ("thou poete Marcian" [1732], "O noble Ovyde" [2125], "In Claudyan ye may the stories rede" [2232]). When January sneers at Justinus's "scoleterms" (1569), or misrepresents the elementary canonical teaching that marital sexuality can be sinful ("A man may do no synne with his wyf, / Ne hurte hymselven with his owene knyf" [1839–40]), the Merchant wants to show us the ignorance of a man who would choose a wife "of his owene auctoritee" (1597). To "deffie Theofraste and herke me" (1310) is a perilous course: however much he mocks his authorities, the Merchant also accords them respect. So too, his deployment of sacred images may be blasphemous, but the very exegetical critics who have

47. On this point, see David Aers, *Chaucer, Langland and the Creative Imagination* (London: Routledge, 1980), 154–55.

48. Wurtele, "Ironical Resonances," 75.

been most offended have simultaneously demonstrated that these images harbor genuine moral opprobrium. The Merchant is, in fact, an exegetical critic of no little skill, motivated by what some have seen as "moral ferocity."[49] And the same ambivalence is present in the deployment of courtly discourse. When May is allowed to say, just before entering the garden, "I am a gentil womman and no wenche" (2202), the force of the irony derives from the Merchant's commitment to an idea of gentility that passes judgment on her depravity. The wedding of January and May may be a travesty, but John Burrow, among others, has rightly noted its "generous lyrical note, [its] festal dignity."[50]

For many years the criticism of the *Merchant's Tale* has been largely conducted over the question of the *Tale*'s valence: whether "everything in the tale is either mean, foolish, or ugly," or whether it tells the hopeful, essentially comic story of the conquest of age by youth.[51] Today the answer seems to be both. The *Tale* simultaneously subverts and puts faith in the class-specific discourses it deploys. The point is not that the Merchant nihilistically believes nothing but rather than he simultaneously does and does not believe everything. Teller of an almost perfectly self-canceling *Tale*, the Merchant is revealed as searching for but unable to find a system of values, beliefs, and meanings—an ideology—by which to endow his world with meaning. If the medieval social model of the three estates effaced the commercial classes, if moralists and social theorists provided relentlessly negative critiques of merchants, and if the merchant class itself failed to develop a coherent and assertive self-definition, then in the *Merchant's Tale* Chaucer explores this condition from the inside.

Moreover, and most brilliantly, he shows us that what this instability of social identity precipitates is an ideology of the subject. Lacking a

49. C. David Benson, *Chaucer's Drama of Style: Poetic Variety and Contrast in the* Canterbury Tales (Chapel Hill: University of North Carolina Press, 1986), 124.

50. J. A. Burrow, "Irony in the Merchant's Tale," *Anglia* 75 (1957), 202. J. S. P. Tatlock, "Chaucer's *Merchant's Tale*," *MP* 33 (1935–36): 367–81, reprinted in Richard Schoeck and Jerome Taylor, *Chaucer Criticism I: The* Canterbury Tales (Notre Dame: University of Notre Dame Press, 1960), described the mythological figures as "gusts of fresh air from the open heavens" (184), and more recent critics have spoken admiringly, in Derek Pearsall's words, of "the lovely opening to the final garden scene" and the "deflation and domestic comedy" of the argument between Pluto and Proserpina (*Canterbury Tales*, 206).

51. The first position is represented here by Norman Harrington, "Chaucer's *Merchant Tale*: Another Swing of the Pendulum," *PMLA* 86 (1971), 30; the second by Martin Stevens, "'And Venus Laugheth': An Interpretation of the *Merchant's Tale*," *ChR* 7 (1972–73): 118–31. The debate has been surveyed by Emerson Brown, Jr., "Chaucer, the Merchant, and Their Tale: Getting Beyond Old Controversies: Part I," *ChR* 13 (1978–79): 141–56.

secure social identity, the Merchant is overwhelmed by an inner self-hood, what he calls at the outset the "soory herte" (1244) that his *Tale* seeks to silence but everywhere expresses. Many critics have complained that to read the *Merchant's Tale* in terms of its teller is to overvalue a pilgrim to whom Chaucer grants only the most attenuated of representations.[52] Yet this is exactly the point: it is the *absence* of representability—of, that is, a social identity derived from a confidently articulated class ideology—that renders the Merchant vulnerable to merely personal feelings. Denied a secure prospect upon the world, the Merchant's gaze instead focuses with obsessive attention upon the inner landscape of unsatisfied desire that is staged in his own failed marriage. Lacking an ideology that would legitimize his commercial life and secure his participation in the political world of events, the bourgeois turns instead to the inner world of the self as the space of self-definition.

That the *Tale* is driven by a psychological dynamic deriving not from his social identity as a merchant but from his failed marriage is shown by the contradictions it harbors. January is both a repulsive old fool who deserves what he gets and a noble victim—"this good man" (1897), the Merchant calls him—betrayed by an uncaring wife whom he has endowed with his wealth and by a serpentlike retainer to whom he has shown nothing but "bountee and . . . gentillesse" (1917). January's thoughtful, even touching offer to May before they enter the garden, and her grossly duplicitous and irreverent reply, are there to solicit our sympathy for the old, blind husband. The *Tale* is pervaded with the contradictions of the Merchant's own feelings about himself: his shame and self-hatred for humiliating himself, his self-pity and anger at having been victimized. The same doubleness affects the role he means his *Tale* to play in the drama of the tale-telling game. He presents himself as a man overcome with grief—"of myn owene soore, / For soory herte, I telle may namoore" (1243–44)—whose *Tale* represents a tactfully reticent bid for sympathy: "I sey nat alle. / God shilde that it sholde so bifalle!" (1231–32). Yet he cannot resist offending the fellow

---

52. David Benson notes the disproportion between the injury the Merchant has presumably suffered and the emotion expressed by his *Tale:*

> The most serious problem with reading the *Merchant's Tale* primarily in terms of the pilgrim Merchant is that it is reductive in the extreme to attribute all the corrosive skill and dark power of what many see as one of Chaucer's most challenging tales to the unspecified disappointments of a new husband.

Chaucer's Drama of Style, 15. Similarly, Derek Pearsall objects that "the interpretation of the generally 'mercantile' values of the tale as generally appropriate to a Merchant is rather trite" (*Canterbury Tales,* 209).

pilgrims whose understanding he covets. He "quites" the Clerk, for example, by representing him as hopelessly credulous and perhaps a sodomite, and brutally transfers the Knight's creed of gentility—"Lo, pitee renneth soone in gentil herte!" (1986)—to the appetitive transactions between "fresshe May" and "gentil" Damyan.[53] The Merchant may desire sympathy but he tells a *Tale* designed to alienate precisely those pilgrims who might be prepared to give it to him.

Not surprisingly, then, the *Merchant's Tale* is on several levels *about* "fantasye" and self-enclosure, a theme expressed in the various acts of ironic literalization that mark the narrative. January wants a wife as malleable as "warm wex" (1430), wax that then materializes when May imprints the key to the garden; January's description of himself as being "as grene / As laurer" (1465–66) becomes the "laurer alwey grene" (2037) in the garden; the notion that a wife is the "fruyt of [man's] tresor" (1270) reappears in the "fruyt" (2336) in the pear tree that May desires; gazing on May "semed fayerye" (1743) to January, a fairydom that literalizes in the figures of Pluto and Proserpina; indeed, May herself is a literalized metaphor—she is both "lyk the brighte morwe of May" (1748) and is summoned up through an act of "heigh fantasye" (1577). The very governing metaphor of the *Tale*—that marriage is "paradys" (1265), a wife "paradys terrestre" (1332)—reappears as the literal garden where the denouement occurs. And most important, the *Tale* is itself just such a literalization: the Merchant's fleeting sneer about his wife in the *Prologue*—"thogh the feend to hire ycoupled were, / She wolde hym overmacche" (1219–20)—is nastily visualized in the final scene of the *Tale*, with May coupling in the tree with the satanic Damian, a scene in which even the underwriting metaphor of the seducing snake finds a material analogue in the penis with which Damyan "throng[s]" in: "Ye," says January, "algate in *it* wente!" (2376). It is the self-fulfilling dynamic of the jealous imagination that motivates the *Merchant's Tale* and that endows it with its sense of claustrophobic enclosure.

53. Specifically, the Merchant implies the Clerk does not realize what kind of woman an Italian nobleman really wants when he marries, how sovereigns actually respond when they receive advice they dislike, or what in fact happens to those who follow the Clerk's naive injunction to bow the "nekke under the blisful yok / Of soveraynetee, nought of servyse, / Whiche that men clepe spousaille or wedlock" (IV, 113–115). There is perhaps an even more pointed sneer at the Clerk when the Merchant describes January as one who "folwed ay his bodily delyt / On *wommen*, ther as was his appetyt, / As doon thise fooles that been seculeer" (1249–51)—the implication being that those in orders use not women but men for their pleasure. What lies behind this sneer is the attitude expressed in the medieval proverb "pedagogus ergo sodomiticus."

But if the *Tale* witnesses to self-absorption, it also aspires to self-understanding. It is the *ahistorical* nature of this effort that is crucial and that reveals the *Tale* as an externalization of the inner condition of an ideologically bereft merchant class. Far from representing in his *Tale* the forces within fourteenth-century England that were in fact at the heart of his situation, he seeks instead to efface from it every sign of historical specificity. Not only is the *Tale* set in an Italy stigmatized by his contemporaries as a locus of commercial and moral misbehavior, but his characters are endowed with names and characteristics that lift them out of history altogether and into a world of allegorical signifi-cance. Moreover, and most tellingly, the story he tells is not about the loss occasioned by specific historical conditions; it is, rather, about loss per se, the primal loss of innocence common to the Western cultural imagination. Indeed, in an act of significant overdetermination, the Merchant models his narrative upon both scriptural and classical para-digms, upon both Adam's exclusion from the garden of Eden and Proserpina's abduction from the eternal springtime of Sicily. What he endures is common to all men: "Assaye whoso wole, and he shal fynde / That I seye sooth" (1229–30).

History is thus understood by the Merchant not as a site of specific social and economic forces but as a generalized metaphysical condi-tion: fallenness rather than innocence, loss rather than possession. Yet the historically specific can never be definitively excluded: the very claim of ahistoricity is itself a function of historical determination, an expression of the social identity the Merchant finds such difficulty in defining. This paradox, and its dialectic of escape and engagement that defines escape *as* engagement, governs the crucial, emblematic ex-change between Pluto and Proserpina. This exchange is on its face ex-plicitly and unashamedly escapist: not only are the protagonists unreal—no longer even pagan deities, they are here reduced to fairies—but the topic of their debate is the quintessentially private mat-ter of marriage, the inner workings of an intimate relationship. Yet in the final analysis this moment represents less an evasion, a turn away from an intractable public history into the presumably more malleable world of the emotions, than a displacement. For it stages the central dilemma of the Merchant's historical condition—his sense of being ideologically adrift and denied a secure cultural formation—within the context of marriage. And it suggests that if this dilemma is insoluble it is also bearable.

The Merchant's *Tale* has revealed him to be at once disillusioned and credulous, bereft of ideals and yet still clinging to the possibility of belief. His narrative as a whole stages his sense of loss as the destruction of paradisal innocence and the entrance into the unforgiving world of history. Pluto and Proserpina both represent this process and enact it in their debate. Proserpina has been "ravysshed" by Pluto "in his grisely carte" (2230–33), and their dissension reveals the bitter effects of male violence. But it does more, for the target of Proserpina's attack is authority per se—"What rekketh me of youre auctoritees?" (2276), she angrily retorts to Pluto—as it is embodied here in the figure of Solomon. For Pluto Solomon is "wys and richest of richesse, / Fulfild of sapience and of worldly glorie" (2242–43); for Proserpina he is "a lecchour and an ydolastre" (2298) whose sayings do not, in any case, support the misogynist construction Pluto tries to put upon them. What Proserpina sets against authority is, like the Wife of Bath, the force of her experience and the intensity of her feeling: "I am a womman, nedes moot I speke, / Or elles swelle til myn herte breke" (2305–6). But it is the strategy of dismantling authority by revealing its historicity, by uncovering the specific, contingent individual from whom it issues, that represents the truly radical force of Proserpina's intervention. In rehearsing Solomon's delinquency, she undoes the transcendental claims of *auctoritee*, its pretense that it stands above and outside history. Indeed, this entire episode witnesses to the inescapability of history, both that of the arguing couple and of the wise man who would issue absolutist judgments. By insisting that Solomon is a man like any other, and not a particularly admirable one at that, Proserpina is attacking not just patriarchy but the strategy by which all ideological forms efface the contingency of their origins, their own existence as historically constructed. It is in this sense, then, that the argument between these two mythological figures rehearses the central dilemma of the Merchant's situation: Pluto represents a desire to remain ideologically secure, sheltered by a belief in male superiority despite the fact that his own violence reveals it to be without legitimacy; but Proserpina, relying upon experience and emotion to provide her with a sense of *self*-legitimization, steps outside ideology altogether. And if to us this seems impossible, we should remember that for the Middle Ages the disruptive desire of the female subject was seen as a threat precisely because it sought to locate itself outside and against all forms of cultural order.

In fact, the *Tale* as a whole is underwritten by a well-disguised but nonetheless profound belief in the liberating power of the feminine. For all its bitter misogyny, the narrative not only invokes various biblical types of the redemptive woman but tells a story of the humiliation and then recuperation of the male: January may (or may not) be deluded at the end, but he has achieved not only the status of long-

suffering victim but a genuine affection for his wife.[54] More specifically,
the Wife of Bath is a constant presence not only in this episode, where
her voice unmistakably subtends Proserpina's, but in the *Tale* as a
whole. To be sure, the *Tale* recycles the Wife of Bath's themes in a way
that puts her under attack as well as paying her homage. On the one
hand, January not only does not want one of "thise olde wydwes"
(1423) for a wife but, as a *senex amans* who buys his youthful spouse, he
stands as a grotesque, albeit male, version of the Wife herself; and Justinus cites her as an authority on the way in which a wife can serve as
"Goddes whippe" (1671) to urge her husband up to heaven, a grim
commentary on the demise of her five husbands. But it also acknowledges, at the deepest structural level, the power of feminine discourse.

The *Merchant's Tale* is structured according to two models: one is
Claudian's authoritative narrative of loss and lament, the other the
Wife's experience-based *Prologue and Tale* that teach us that happiness
can be won in this world. The *De raptu Prosperpinae* provides the narrative elements from which the *Tale* is constructed: January's unlikely
desire to marry and his celebration of the joys of wedded life and paternity; the presence and example of his brothers; the central role of Venus, her torch, the festal wedding celebrated by Orpheus, and the bless-
ing of the bed; the garden, its tree and fatal fruit; and above all the
disparity between bride and groom—all of these elements of his *Tale*
are derived by the Merchant directly from Claudian's poem.[55] Indeed,
when Claudian tells us he is impelled to song by his *mens congesta* (1, 5)
he provides a precedent for the "soory herte" (1244) that simultaneously inspires and censors the Merchant. But if the *De raptu
Proserpinae* provides the *Tale*'s narrative elements, they are disposed
according to a pattern established by the *Wife of Bath's Prologue and Tale*.
As with the Wife's *Prologue*, which begins with a *sermon joyeux*, the
Merchant's Tale opens with a mocking sermonlike discourse (1267–392).
Also like the Wife's *Prologue*, the Merchant then explores the topic of
marriage through a two-part narrative vastly expanded by the inclusion of the materials of the antimatrimonial and misogynist traditions
(the Wife's narrative is divided between the first three and the last two
husbands, the Merchant's between January's initial decision to marry

---

54. See Brown, "Biblical Women," 411–12.
55. Oddly enough, the extent to which the elements of the *Tale* derive from the *De
raptu Proserpinae* has not been fully described in Chaucer criticism. But see Mortimer J.
Donovan, "The Image of Pluto and Proserpina in the *Merchant's Tale*," *PQ* 36 (1957): 49–
60; Karl P. Wentersdorf, "Theme and Structure in the Merchant's Tale: The Function of
the Pluto Episode," *PMLA* 80 (1965): 522–27; and Charlotte Otten, "Proserpine: *Liberatrix
Suae Gentis*," *ChR* 5 (1970–71): 277–87.

[1245–66, 1393–576] and his choice of May [1577–688]). Finally, after the account of the marriage ceremonies (1689–749), the *Merchant's Tale* turns to a straightforward if expansively dilated narrative—the pear-tree fabliau—that is analogous to the Wife's similarly augmented Arthurian romance. Not surprisingly, then, when Pluto and Proserpina arrive at an accommodation of male and female it is one achieved under the sign of the Wife of Bath. When Proserpina contradicts Pluto she both speaks in the Wife's unmistakable voice and is also impelled, as we have seen, by an irresistible inner force: "I am a womman, nedes moot I speke, / Or elles swelle til myn herte breke" (2305–6).[56] And the accord at which Pluto and Proserpina finally arrive reenacts the mutual repudiation of *maistrye* by which Jankin and the Wife achieved marital happiness. The *Tale* as a whole is thus an attack on the female voice that becomes an act of deference, an initial rejection and then celebration of a socially undetermined subjectivity that is most fully embodied in the Wife.

Finally, the Pluto and Proserpina episode promises that history provides compensation as well as loss. The *Merchant's Tale* is posited on disenchantment, on the disillusion generated by the collapse of an impossible idealism brought in contact with reality: since all value has been invested in that which has been lost, what remains can only be worthless. If the dream of perfect mutuality is an empty fantasy, then it can only be replaced with a coercive patriarchy capable of governing the treacherous creatures women have revealed themselves to be. If husbands nod, wives will frolic. And if the ideological security guaranteed by authority is undone, then what remains is an unmoored world of pure contingency, a realm of historical difference in which no value reigns supreme. But this is not in fact what happens. When Pluto withdraws before Proserpina's wrath—"be no lenger wrooth; / I yeve it up!" (2311–12)—he is rewarded with a corresponding gesture of conciliation: "For sothe," she says, "I wol no lenger yow contrarie" (2319). This is no impossible dream of a utopianist mutuality: husband and wife remain independent and even in conflict, as is shown by the fact that their opposing gifts to January and May remain in force. But what has been uncovered is a resilient forbearance based on unspoken compromises. Agreeing to disagree, they acknowledge that difference is no longer insupportable. If history signifies loss, it also offers consolation; if the idealist is disinherited, the realist finds reparation. The unifor-

---

56. The Merchant is here referring to the Wife's self-representation in the figure of Midas's wife, who thought that the secret of Midas's ears "swal so soore aboute hir herte / That nedely som word hire moste asterte" (III, 965–68).

mity of monolithic ideologies yields to a differential reality, in which negotiation and exchange are the governing practices. We have entered, almost without noticing, the realm in which a merchant will be most at home.

It is in this way, then, that the debate between Pluto and Proserpina opens the narrative as a whole to the situational, individualistic, market-based ethic that accords with the Merchant's historical condition. That this ethic is defined in terms of marriage, and a marriage focused entirely upon relations between the conjugal couple, is itself an effect of the historical specificity of the Merchant's situation. For there is much evidence to suggest that it was within the bourgeois context that the companionate marriage developed most fully in the Middle Ages, a development that in turn placed spousal relations in question. Thus the late fourteenth century saw the growth of a literature that conceptualized marriage as a problem and that tried to confront the profound contradictions that inhabited late-medieval thinking about the marital relation. On the one hand was the traditional patriarchal ideology that preached male supremacy and wifely obedience, on the other the deeply felt and widely expressed need for a mutual, even intense love between the spouses. In order to follow out this line of investigation, however, we must return to social history; and a search for its most mature Chaucerian treatment will then direct us to the *Shipman's Tale*.

III

Historians of the family have recently challenged the familiar but misleading assumption that the companionate marriage, with its privileging of the conjugal unit at the expense of the kin group and the wider community, did not develop until the seventeenth century.[57] This does not mean, however, that the modern family was either fully developed in medieval England or that there were not important class differences

---

57. The leading exponents of the outdated view were Lawrence Stone, *The Family, Sex and Marriage in England 1500–1800* (London: Weidenfeld and Nicolson, 1977); J.-L. Flandrin, *Families in Former Times: Kinship, Household and Sexuality* (Cambridge: Cambridge University Press, 1979); and Edward Shorter, *The Making of the Modern Family* (London: Collins, 1976). For alternative views, see Alan Macfarlane, *Love and Marriage in England, 1300–1800* (Oxford: Blackwell, 1986); Macfarlane's review of Stone in *History and Theory* 18 (1979): 103–26; and R. A. Houlbrooke, *The English Family 1450–1700* (London: Longman, 1984). An excellent but now somewhat dated overview of this fast-developing field is provided by Michael Anderson, *Approaches to the History of the Western Family, 1500–1914* (London: Macmillan, 1980).

in both family structure and marital practice. Although the evidence is far from plentiful, what there is suggests that the practices and values that typify modern marriage found their nearest late-medieval analogues within the gentry and the wealthy urban classes. For the nobility, the need to preserve and extend the patrimony meant that marriage largely served the needs not of the individual but of the kin, as the parental control of marriage partners most vividly demonstrates. And the aristocratic life-style, which defined the household in terms of political community rather than domestic privacy, made the development of conjugal intimacy difficult.[58] Similarly, the family based economy within which both peasant and artisanal marriages were established naturally emphasized economic requirements at the expense of affectional needs: since the unit of production was equivalent to the unit of reproduction, the marital relation was inevitably absorbed into the social and economic system as a whole.

But the marital practices of the English merchant patriciate seem not to have been as fully governed by these economic and social imperatives. For one thing, merchant prosperity meant that economic pressures had sufficiently abated to allow for a sharp division between the male sphere of commerce and the female sphere of domesticity. Certainly there were merchant wives who engaged in trade or manufacture as, in the words of Sylvia Thrupp, "an outlet for surplus energy or a means of earning additional money to spend"; Thrupp cites several examples of merchant wives who became successful businesswomen.[59] But prescriptions for the behavior of merchant wives—such as the *Ménagier de Paris*, "The Good Wife Taught Her Daughter," "The Good Wyfe Wold a Pylgremage," and so on—make it clear that the bourgeois wife's primary sphere of interest was the home, that her task in life was to manage the domestic establishment with the same prudence and attentiveness as her husband applied to trade. And this is, as we shall see, precisely the attitude expressed by the merchant husband in the *Shipman's Tale*.

Moreover, London merchant families lacked the patrimonial sense of clan that characterized both the English nobility and the merchant class of Italy.[60] Thrupp points out that among London merchants "it had

58. See Kate Mertes, *The English Noble Household, 1250–1600* (Oxford: Blackwell, 1988).

59. Thrupp, *Merchant Class*, 170–72.

60. For the very different situation in Italy, where—in the words of Christian Bec, "Les *mercatores* de la cité du florin conçoivent les afaires dans le cadre de la *gente*" (*Les marchands écrivains*, 279)—see Martha C. Howell, *Women, Production, and Patriarchy in Late Medieval Cities* (Chicago: University of Chicago Press, 1986), 16–17; and Diane Owen

never been a universal custom for the son to follow his father's occupation" (204), which is probably one reason why very few sons had their
marriages arranged by their fathers. By and large, merchants seem to
have left the choice of a marriage partner up to their children (204–5),
marriage was quite late, and newly married couples, rather than moving
into the family household, established new domestic establishments on
their own—the "neolocal" arrangement that social anthropologists consider one of the prime requisites for conjugal marriage.[61] Merchants also
seem to have made a sharp distinction between the public world of trade
and the private world of domesticity, and they emphasized the family as
a haven in a heartless world. Certainly we see these values expressed
very explicitly in the *Shipman's Tale*, and the design of merchant houses,
with their enclosed gardens and small, private rooms, witnesses to the
same impulse.[62]

Of course merchant marriages served economic and social as well as
personal needs. Young men used marriage in order to acquire the capital
to set themselves up in business, and ambitious fathers used their financially well-endowed daughters to insert the family into the ranks of the
nobility. But the economic and social conditions in force among the merchant patriciate meant that the bonds that united husband and wife
could be stronger than those to kindred or community, and that the focus
of marital attention could consequently be upon the conjugal couple.
While the evidence is not extensive, what there is does indeed suggest
that for the literate urban middle class the affectional relations between
the spouses had become by the late Middle Ages an important topic of
discussion. While few domestic manuals have survived from the four-

---

Hughes, "Urban Growth and Family Structure in Medieval Genoa," *Past and Present* 66
(1975): 3–28.

61. See Macfarlane, *Love and Marriage*, 213–17; according to Thrupp, the age of marriage for men in late-medieval London was 24–26, for women, about 17 (*Merchant Class*,
192); for the late age of marriage in Coventry, see Phythian-Adams, *Desolation of a City*,
89–93.

62. On gardens, see Thrupp, *Merchant Class*, 136. According to Philippe Braunstein,
in the late-medieval town "people insisted on privacy, as is evident from the way in
which the rooms were divided among family members; the primary beneficiary was the
master of the house, who now enjoyed a private study to which he could retire" ("Toward Intimacy: The Fourteenth and Fifteenth Centuries," in *A History of Private Life*, vol.
2: *Revelations of the Medieval World*, trans. Arthur Goldhammer, ed. Philippe Ariès and
Georges Duby [Cambridge: Harvard University Press, 1988], 538). Philippe Contamine
points out that "it was 'bourgeois' to have a *comptoir*, a counting room, rather than an
ouvroir, a workroom, and even more bourgeois to have a study instead of (in addition to) a
counting room" ("Peasant Hearth to Papal Palace: The Fourteenth and Fifteenth Centuries," in Ariès and Duby, *History of Private Life*, 466).

teenth century, there are a good many in the later fifteenth and early sixteenth centuries that are directed specifically to the urban bourgeoisie. And a comparison of these texts to the few earlier instances that remain shows that the bourgeois reader would not have found "a great deal that was new or unusual in these texts," which "were disseminating . . . a rather unchanging style of successful bourgeois family life."[63] There are also other kinds of fourteenth-century texts that discuss marriage, and they witness to the same class interests. For instance, the French chivalric romances that were rewritten into English, which have plausibly been ascribed to the interests of a gentry and bourgeois audience, place the language of *fine amor* in the service of marriage—as does, of course, the *Franklin's Tale*.[64] John Gower's treatise on *Amantz Marietz* and his *Cinkante Ballades* seek to define a very similar ideology of married love, and so does—although it is hardly a marriage treatise—Thomas Usk's *Testament of Love*.[65] On the other side, literary historians have long maintained that misogynist and antimatrimonial writing has not merely a clerical but also a bourgeois provenance; indeed, Jean-Charles Payen recently argued that antimatrimonial literature is generated by a desire to attack the "embourgeoisement" of love and sexuality within marriage—an attack that witnesses to the extent to which bourgeois marriage was perceived as having a monopoly on the theory of the relations between the sexes.[66]

The effect of this bourgeois attention to marital relations was to make glaringly visible, as I have suggested, the contradiction between the traditional supremacy of patriarchy and the equally traditional desire for mutuality and love between the spouses. In many texts, these two components simply lie side by side, their opposition visible but unresolved. A thirteenth-century sermon, for instance, defines the spouses as "pares et socii" who are bound together by a "love founded on partnership" and who enjoy the "friendship of love"; yet it simultaneously deploys the degrading topoi of misogyny in order to justify the

63. Kathleen Davies, "Continuity and Change in Literary Advice on Marriage," in *Marriage and Society: Studies in the Social History of Marriage*, ed. R. B. Outhwaite (London: Europa Publications, 1981), 58–80.

64. Gervase Mathew, "Marriage and *Amour Courtois* in Late Fourteenth-Century England," in *Essays Presented to Charles Williams* (London: Oxford University Press, 1947), 128–35.

65. John Gower, *Works*, ed. G. C. Macauley (Oxford: Clarendon Press, 1899), 1:335–92; for Usk, see Kelly, *Love and Marriage*, 67.

66. Francis Lee Utley, *The Crooked Rib* (Columbus: Ohio State University Press, 1944), 15–20; Jean-Charles Payen, "La Crise du mariage à la fin du XIIIe siècle d'aprés la littérature française du temps," in *Famille et parenté dans l'occident médiévale*, ed. Georges Duby and Jacques Le Goff (Rome: Ecole Française, 1977), 413–20.

husband's superiority.[67] So too, the Ménagier de Paris counsels his young wife that "in all matters, in all terms, in all places and in all seasons, you shall do and accomplish without argument all [your husband's] commandments whatsoever"; yet he nonetheless posits as the goal of marriage a *mutual* obedience based on a shared love.[68] And in many texts either one or the other half of the contradiction is silently suppressed. While canonical and confessional texts allow for and occasionally even prescribe mutual love between the spouses, their overwhelming emphasis is on male supremacy and female submission; but in lay discussions, and in marriage sermons preached to the laity, male supremacy is quietly assumed while the emphasis is upon the way in which husband and wife are joined "in bodye, in fflesche, and in blode, and . . . in sawle by verre stedffaste luff," on how they enjoy an "amisté de mariage" in which "each holds the other to be better than himself."[69] What is significant about this application of the language of *amicitia* to marriage, both here and elsewhere (it underwrites, for example, Gower's treatise on *Amantz Marietz*), is that friendship had always been seen not only as the highest form of human bond but one that could exist only between equals: hence Cicero had maintained that it was impossible for men and women to be friends. For husband and wife to be urged to partake of the "amisté de mariage," then, the assumption of male superiority had to be silently set aside.

Not surprisingly, three of Chaucer's four tales of marriage in the *Canterbury Tales* are told by pilgrims whom we would now designate as "bourgeois": the Wife of Bath, the Merchant, and the Franklin. What is more important, however, is that those three pilgrims lack both an agreed-upon location within the fluid social world of fourteenth-century England and a stable public identity derived from an explicit

67. See the account of a sermon by Guibert de Tournai (d. 1288) by David d'Avray and M. Tausche, "Marriage Sermons in *Ad Status* Collections of the Central Middle Ages," *AHDLMA* 47 (1980): 71–119.

68. Eileen Power, trans., *The Goodman of Paris* (London: Routledge, 1928), 143, 147–48.

69. For the canonical writers, see John T. Noonan, "Marital Affection in the Canonists," *Studia gratiana* 12 (1967): 479–509, corrected by Michael M. Sheehan, "*Maritalis Affectio* Revisited," in Robert R. Edwards and Stephen Spector, eds., *The Olde Daunce: Love, Friendship, Sex and Marriage in the Medieval World* (Albany: State University of New York, 1991), 32–43, 254–60. For sermons and lay writers, the first citation is from *In nuptiis sollacio*, described by G. R. Owst, *Literature and Pulpit in Medieval England*, 2d ed. (Oxford: Blackwell, 1961), as a "typical marriage sermon of the day" (385) and found in CUL MS Gg.6.16, fols. 28b–30b; the citation is from fol. 29a. See also, in the same manuscript, *In Solemnizacione matrimonium*, fols. 32a–33b. The second citation is from Nicholas Oresme's gloss to his translation of the pseudo-Aristotelian *Oeconomica: Le Livre de Yconomique d'Aristote*, ed. and trans. Albert Douglas Menut, *Transactions of the American Philosophical Society*, n.s. 47, pt. 5 (1957), 813, 841.

class ideology.[70] They are thus the spokespersons for the private world of marriage in a way that the Clerk, whose allegorically inflected *Tale* invokes a far more spiritually and politically explicit set of values, is not. Moreover, the issue with which the marriage tales deal is in every case (including the Clerk's) the relation of patriarchy to mutuality. But they deal with it largely through gestures of avoidance. The Clerk insists, for example, that his *Tale* is not about marriage at all but about patience; and in both the *Wife of Bath's* and the *Franklin's Tales* the conflict between patriarchy and mutuality is reconciled through transformations that are explicitly marked as magical. The Wife tells an Arthurian romance presided over by an elf-queen and resolved through an act of enchanted metamorphosis, while the *Franklin's Tale* is a Breton lay, a kind of narrative that explicitly asserts its difference from real life. In the *Merchant's Tale* we have, in the conversation of Pluto and Proserpina in the garden prior to the denouement, a similar moment of resolution, and one also marked as outside the bounds of reality, unavailable to human beings embedded within history. Yet as I have argued, what is striking about the *Merchant's Tale* is that its climactic moment does not represent simply an evasion, a turn away from an intractable public history into the presumably more malleable world of the emotions. It is, rather, a displacement that proposes even if it does not fully explore a correspondence between the public world of commerce and the private world of marital negotiation. It is this correspondence that provides the argument of the *Shipman's Tale*. If marital relations are a specifically bourgeois issue, claims the *Tale*, then they can be represented in typically bourgeois terms and their problems will yield to the practices that prevail within the bourgeois world.

IV

The *Shipman's Tale* describes the process by which the circulation of a hundred franks among three people generates, as if by magic, a profit for all of them. The wife repays her creditors, the monk enjoys the wife, and the merchant gets in the place of a previously reluctant sexual partner one eager to do his bidding. Somehow, by a process we can only with difficulty specify, the very fact of exchange has produced a surplus value: something has come of nothing. Because we know, or think we

---

70. As Paul Strohm points out, the Franklin is "situated as close as he can be to the *gentils* without actually being *gentil* himself. . . . [He is] something of a 'new man' in his society, a person thriving (like Chaucer himself) in a social category largely ignored in traditional descriptions of society" (*Social Chaucer,* 107).

know, that this is impossible, we assume that there is something duplicitous in this process. And it is true that for the monk the hundred franks serve a double purpose, simultaneously paying for the wife's body and repaying the husband's loan; while the wife's body also does double duty, first in exchange for the hundred franks from the monk, then in place of their repayment to her husband. Yet to note that these two symmetrical acts of duplication provide the means by which something is made out of nothing is only to specify the mechanics of the process, not to understand it nor to judge it. Indeed, the very symmetry itself suggests that such double-dealing, however distasteful, may be inherent in the system of exchange itself. That the profit these transactions generate is unfounded continues to pose the central question. What is the founding premise of a system of exchange that enables it to produce, by its very workings, a surplus value? How can something come of nothing? Or to pose the question in less disinterested terms, what does the exchange system consume in order to generate profit?

That it is exchange per se that is the focus of Chaucer's interest in this narrative is shown by its ubiquity in the world of the *Tale*. The monk exchanges "diligence / To doon pleasaunce and also greet costage" (44–45) for a warm welcome: he gives the "eterne alliaunce" (40) of "cosynage" to his host, and money and food to the household staff, in return for their goodwill. Indeed, when the merchant remonstrates with his wife for not telling him that the monk had repaid the loan, she replies that she had thought the money was a gift offered as recompense for the hospitality he had received (406–10), a statement that reveals how habitual the act of exchange is in this world. Similarly, reciprocity between husband and wife is established both by their mutual marriage "dette" and, more important, by the division of duties the *Tale* defines. As the merchant husband makes provision for the household through his diligent pursuit of business, so is his wife enjoined to run "a thrifty houshold" (246): worldly comfort is exchanged for domestic order, an arrangement given symbolic expression in the *Tale*'s equivalence between the wife's "arraye" (12, 14, 179, 247, 418) and her husband's "worshipe" (13) and "honour" (179, 421).

Yet the central assumption upon which the order of the merchant's existence is based is precisely that there can be a *difference* between the domestic world of garden, feast hall, and marriage bed and the mercantile world of countinghouse and market fairs. Required by his "curious bisyness" to participate in the "queynte world . . . Of hap and fortune" (236–38), the merchant has established his "worthy hous" (20) as an alternative place of recreative festivity: accompanied by "a wyf . . . of excellent beautee" (3) and "gestes, grete and smale" (24) like his friend

the monk, the merchant "ete[s] and drynke[s] an
order both to celebrate his success and to prepare f
into the uncertain world of trade. What the actior
strates, however, is that this domestic retreat is undermin.. .
very reciprocity upon which it is based. For the bourgeois economy of
husbandly provision in return for wifely solicitude introduces into the
domestic world a principle of equivalence that appropriates it to the
exchange economy of mercantilism to which it is meant to serve as an
alternative: the domestic becomes an extension of the commercial. It is
this appropriation that the circulation of the hundred franks among the
protagonists definitively accomplishes, and the hegemony of the mercantile issues in that correspondence between the worlds of countinghouse and garden, and between marketplace and marital bed, that
has so disturbed modern readers. "While the merchant is doing his
accounts to determine 'how that it with hym stood' " (1269), as John
Scattergood has noted, "his wife is revealing to Daun John 'how that it
stant' (1310) as regards her personal happiness; while the merchant
works 'bisily' (1492) at Bruges, his wife and Daun John are leading 'a
bisy lyf' (1508) in bed together; and so on."[71] The same appropriation
motivates the puns that are so memorable a part of the *Tale*'s verbal
texture: the *cosynage* of kinship is undone by financial trickery, the
taillynge of marital sexuality becomes equivalent to the tallying of monetary debts.[72] The effect of these equivalences is to establish commerce
as the sole category of value: everything has its price.

The issue the *Tale* investigates, then, is nothing less than the primary
condition of economic man: when the worth of goods is determined
solely by their exchange value, then value is radically contingent. And
the more dimensions of life that fall within the sphere of economics, the
further the blight of contingency spreads. What is striking and impor-

71. V. J. Scattergood, "The Originality of the *Shipman's Tale*," *ChR* 11 (1976–77), 212.

72. Chaucer's pun on *cosynage* appears to be the first instance in English, but there is
a precedent (as yet unnoted) in French, in a text that Chaucer almost certainly knew. In
the *Roman de Renart* the fox attempts to persuade his intended victim Chantecler that they
are kinsmen, and after being disillusioned by Renart's attack upon him Chantecler says:
      Cousins Renart, dist Chantecler,
      nus ne se doit en vos fiër:
      dahez ait vostre cousinage!
      torner me dut a grant domage. (4443–46)
Ed. Mario Roques, CFMA (Paris: Champion, 1982), 2:37. For post-Chaucerian versions of
the pun in French, see Ruth M. Fisher, " 'Cosyn' and 'Cosynage': Complicated Punning
in Chaucer's *Shipman's Tale*," *N&Q* 12 (1965): 168–70; and Roy J. Pearcy, "Punning on
'Cosyn' and 'Cosynage' in Chaucer's *Shipman's Tale*," *AN&Q* 17 (1979): 70–71. For the
triple pun on "taillynge," see below, note 86.

tant about the *Tale*, however, is that Chaucer presents this condition in terms neither of specific historical forces, such as the development of a fully monetized market economy, nor of specific historical agents, such as merchants. On the contrary, he follows that tradition of medieval thinking that conceptualized the problem of commodification in transhistorical terms, as a condition endemic not to a specific historical moment but to historical life per se. Put bluntly, the *Shipman's Tale* argues that the correspondence between business and marriage, however dismaying, is an inevitable effect of being human. In addition, he recognizes that this condition is in no sense irremediable, that (as in the *Merchant's Tale*) there is reparation after loss, compensation for disinheritance. And most important and striking, he sees the agents of this recovery as being merchants themselves, those very beings who are most at the center of the exchange system itself: if the bourgeois life provides the site where marriage and business merge, it also provides the means to make both forms of life not merely legitimate but desirable. In effect, the *Shipman's Tale* provides what medieval English merchants so conspicuously lacked, a justification for the commercial life. And what is perhaps most telling of all, it defines this justification in terms that draw a powerful analogy between commerce and poetry, and specifically the kind of poetry that is unmistakably Chaucerian.

The central ideological problem that the market posed for the Middle Ages, as for more recent times, was that it derived value not from a transcendental and immutable standard that stood outside the exchange system but solely from the circulation of goods within the system itself. The market transforms all goods (including money itself) into commodities, which are by definition objects whose value is determined solely through exchange. That this process was a source of deep concern in the Middle Ages is shown not only by the instinctive medieval attacks upon merchants and financiers but also by the sophisticated attempts to think through the problem of the relation of value to price.[73] For canonists and Romanists, concerned with practical legislation to deal with economic evils such as fraud and monopoly, the problem was, to be sure, easily solved: the just price was simply the usual market price, a principle articulated in the ubiquitous if question-

73. For discussions of this issue, see Odd Langholm, *Price and Value in the Aristotelian Tradition* (Bergen: Universitetsforlaget, 1979); John T. Noonan, *The Scholastic Analysis of Usury* (Cambridge: Harvard University Press, 1957), 82–99; and especially John W. Baldwin, "The Medieval Theories of the Just Price," *Transactions of the American Philosophical Society*, n.s. 49 (1959): 3–92.

begging apothegm, "A thing is worth as much as it
But for theologians, for whom economic dealings f
gory of commutative justice, the theoretical issue r
found analysis. Since the justice of an exchange depends up͏o̵n̶ ͏ ,
ity, by what standard of value can one determine whether two goods
are of equal worth? By what norm, extrinsic to the exchange system
itself, can goods be measured? One tradition of thought answered this
question in terms of cost of production, an answer that necessarily remained within the sphere of the economic order by in effect com-
modifying labor.[75] But the more radical answer, and the one that offers
us the deepest insight into the medieval understanding of the economic order, was that proffered by the Aristotelian tradition presided
over by thinkers such as Albertus Magnus, Thomas Aquinas, and
Duns Scotus.

Following Aristotle's discussion in Book 5 of the *Ethics*, these theologians recognized that an object's intrinsic or natural properties were
irrelevant to its economic value. On the contrary, for them the common
standard of economic value was need: as John Baldwin says, "Human
want was the one measure which was necessary to make all economic
goods commensurable, comparable, and exchangeable."[76] This insufficiency had been called *chreia* by Aristotle and was termed *indigentia* by
the scholastics.[77] It was understood in far-reaching theological terms.
In the course of their analyses the scholastics invoked a key Augustinian text that defined the difference between natural and economic

74. "Res tantum valet quantum vendi potest." Baldwin provides a number of references and adds that "no Canonist of the later period has been found to disagree with this
basic conception of the just price" ("Medieval Theories," 54 nn. 101 and 102).

75. For discussions of this so-called objective standard of value, and its putative
proto-Marxism, see Langholm, *Price and Value*, 61–84.

76. Baldwin, "Medieval Theories," 74.

77. Aristotle, *Nicomachean Ethics* 5, 11. Albertus Magnus, *Ethica* 5, 2, 9, says that the
value of goods is not absolute but comparative "secundum usum *indigentiae*," a word
Albert uses throughout his discussion of the *contrapassum* of economic exchange (*Opera*,
ed. Auguste Borgnet [Paris: Vivès, 1891], 7:357); see also Thomas Aquinas, *In decem libros
Ethicorum Aristotelis ad Nicomachum Expositio* 5, 9, 981: "Et dicit, quod ideo possunt omnia
adaequari, quia omnia possunt commensurari per aliquid unum, ut dictum est; hoc
autem unum, quod omnia mensurat secundum rei veritatem est *indigentia*, quae continet
omnia commutabilia, inquantum omnia referuntur ad humanam indigentiam; non enim
apprentiantur secundum dignitatem naturae ipsorum: alioquin unus mus, quod est animal sensibile, maioris pretii esset quam margarita, quae est res inanimata: sed rebus
pretia imponuntur, secundum quod homines indigent eis ad suum usum (ed. Raymund
M. Spiazzi [Rome: Marietti, 1949], 270); for Scotus, see Langholm, *Price and Value*, 86–87,
who refers to Scotus's Commentary on the *Sentences* 4, 15, 2 (*Opera* [Lyon: L. Durand,
1639], 9:166).

orders in terms of original sin. In Book 11 of the *City of God*, Augustine had argued that *indigentia* is not a "natural" or rational emotion. "There is," he says, "a very wide difference between a rational consideration, in its free judgment, and the constraint of need. . . . Rational consideration decides on the position of each thing in the scale of importance on its own merits," because it recognizes that the order of nature locates immortal beings higher than mortal, and living beings above inanimate objects. But, he goes on,

> need only thinks of its own interests. . . . On this other scale we would put some inanimate things above some creatures of sense—so much so that if we had the power, we should be ready to remove these creatures from the world of nature, whether in ignorance of the place they occupy in it, or, though knowing that, still subordinating them to our own convenience. . . . A higher price is often paid for a horse than for a slave, for a jewel than for a maidservant. (11, 16)[78]

Under the pressure of *indigentia* the divinely ordained order of nature is displaced by man's fallen economic order, and the intrinsic value with which a being or object is endowed by its creator is replaced by a value derived from need. Moreover, this need is an insufficiency that is an effect of original sin. When through his original disobedience man defected from God, he fell away from his own perfection and became, in a biblical phrase often cited by Augustine, "like nothingness." "By aiming at more a man is diminished, when he elects to be self-sufficient and defects from the one who is really sufficient for him" (14, 13, 15).[79] The very existence of an economic order derives from this nothingness: it is a system of exchange driven by an *indigentia* caused by man's fall away from the original perfection of the order of nature.

In defining the worth of an object according to the severity of the need it fulfills, this tradition of thought invokes a standard of value extrinsic to the system of circulating goods. It can therefore explain why (to use the Aristotelian example commonly invoked by medieval commentators) a house is worth more than a pair of shoes. But the standard of value remains purely economic: nothing can *justify* the fact that a jewel is worth more than a maidservant. Thus this line of thought lays bare the problem

78. Augustine, *City of God*, trans. Henry Bettenson (Harmondsworth: Penguin Books, 1972), 448. For the original, see B. Dombart, ed., *De civitate Dei* (Leipzig: Teubner, 1909), 1:483–84.

79. Bettenson, *City of God*, 572, 575; Dombart, *De civitate*, 2:32. For the biblical citation, see Dombart, *De civitate*, 2:36.

of commodification that lies at the heart of the economic system. As soon as an object enters into the exchange system of the economic order, it loses its natural value and becomes a commodity, an object whose value is determined by the workings of an exchange system that is itself founded on nothingness, on the *indigentia* or lack entailed by man's alienation from the order of natural perfection.

The sense of the economic order as fallen, so clearly articulated in theoretical terms by the scholastics, is expressed elsewhere in medieval culture, as I have suggested, in a variety of less sophisticated ways. Perhaps the most common is the widespread sense that commerce is not only an effect of sin but is itself sinful, an animus that lies behind the many prohibitions directed against all sorts of commercial activities (and not just usury) throughout the Middle Ages.[80] Similarly widespread was a concern about the status of money. For the scholastics money was nothing other than a numerical statement of need, and some thinkers even realized that once money entered into the processes of economic exchange it became itself simply one commodity among others. But a more common attitude was a monetary realism that hoped that money could function as a universal standard of value by which an otherwise unfounded system of economic exchange could be stabilized.[81] Hence the anxiety—derived from concerns that were more than merely economic—about the stability of currency itself. Having disguised from themselves the mediatory role of money within an exchange economy, monetary realists endowed currency with a founding power; and they were therefore deeply concerned about abuses such as counterfeiting and devaluation that served to undermine it. For if money could not provide a standard of value, then the economic system was perforce revealed to be a process of ceaseless circulation in which the value of goods is determined not by their natural or intrinsic value but by an exchange value derived from the economic condition of need.

Now this understanding of the economic system is dramatized in the *Shipman's Tale* in its representation of profit as the creation of something from nothing. The profit that issues from the circulation of the hundred franks derives from loss—specifically, the loss of the values inherent in the ideal or original forms of the relationships obtaining

80. For a useful survey of medieval anticommercialism, see Raymond de Roover, *Business, Banking and Economic Thought in Late Medieval and Early Modern Europe*, ed. Julius Kirshner (Chicago: University of Chicago Press, 1974).

81. On monetary realism, see the discussion by Bloch, *Etymologies and Genealogies*, 164–74.

among the three protagonists. The marriage between merchant and wife, the kinship between monk and merchant, and the friendship between wife and monk are natural relations that are degraded—commodified—when they enter into the exchange system. Profit is what accrues from the reduction of the matrimonial bond, and of the ties of kinship and friendship, to business relationships. The argument of the *Tale*, in short, is that profit derives from the commodification of the natural order. This is a commodification, moreover, that is a function not of specific historical circumstances but of historicity per se. The *Tale* represents the economic order in the most highly conceptualized terms in which the Middle Ages understood it—as a function of a fallen and alienating history in which *all* men and women, including the poet and his readers, are necessarily implicated.

Despite assertions to the contrary, the *Tale* refuses to ascribe responsibility for the process it dramatizes to any particular historical class or social condition. Specifically, it refuses to explain the economic order in terms of a culpable mercantilism whose motives and morals can then serve as the efficient cause of deplorable social effects. Thus while the merchant husband may be the locus of mercantile values in the *Tale*, he displays throughout a personal probity and moral integrity in his dealings with his wife, with his friend the monk, and with his business associates that is wholly admirable.[82] He conducts himself not accord-

---

82. Scattergood is again correct in pointing out that "Chaucer is clearly familiar with the usual criticisms of the merchant class—indeed, there are allusions to these criticisms in this tale—but . . . refuses to exploit them. Contrary to the dictates of tradition he makes the merchant rather admirable" ("Originality," 221). For other defenses of the merchant, see John C. McGaillard, "Characterization in Chaucer's *Shipman's Tale*," *PQ* 54 (1975): 1–18; and Peter Nicholson, "The 'Shipman's Tale' and the Fabliaux," *ELH* 45 (1978): 583–96. Commentators have too quickly assumed that because the merchant relies upon credit in his business dealings (see lines 289, 303, 328–30, 365–68) he is a usurer: see, for example, Bernard S. Levy, "The Quaint World of the *Shipman's Tale*," *SSF* (1966–67): 112–18; and Thomas Hahn, "Money, Sexuality, Wordplay, and Context in the *Shipman's Tale*," in *Chaucer in the Eighties*, ed. Julian N. Wasserman and Robert J. Blanch (Syracuse: Syracuse University Press, 1986), 235–49. But in all these transactions the merchant appears to be the debtor not the creditor, and a debtor who is peculiarly at risk. The *chevyssaunce* (329) that he goes to Paris to make in order to redeem his bond from Lombard moneylenders is not, as is sometimes assumed, a particularly immoral form of borrowing but a particularly dangerous one. The term seems most commonly to have referred to a loan against future profits; and while it could designate a kind of bill of exchange used to evade the prohibitions against usury, it is by no means certain that this is the case either here or in the majority of other instances. See the citations in the *MED*, s.v., and especially the account offered by Gower in the *Mirour de l'Omme*, 7235–48 (*Works*, ed. Macauley, 1:84). The legitimacy of the transactions engaged in by both the merchant of the *Shipman's Tale* and the pilgrim Merchant have been ably defended by

ing to the manipulative double-dealing of which merchants were regularly accused by contemporary moralists but rather with a sobriety and reliability that they themselves took as the hallmark of the mercantile character. He represents, in effect, mercantile values at their most beneficent, an ideal image of what merchants no doubt most wanted themselves to be.[83] Indeed, his desire to establish a local enclave of domestic affection apart from the "curious bisynesse" (225) of merchandising witnesses to an awareness of the moral strains incumbent upon a man who must "make chiere and good visage, / And dryve forth the world as it may be" (230–31).

Moreover, not only is the merchant himself ethically superior to his faithless wife and hypocritical friend, but the mercantile ethos with which he is invested is shown to have a pragmatic force that renders him oddly invulnerable to their manipulations. As the elaborate plot spins its webs about him, he remains unaware of his own hoodwinking, with the effect that the commodification of the domestic world occurs almost literally behind the back (and certainly against the wishes) of the one individual who might be thought responsible for it. It may be, of course, that he is simply a victim protected by the same narrowness of vision that made possible his victimization in the first place. But there is another explanation. A master of exchange—he conducts his business with the financial instrument known literally as the bill of exchange—he recognizes that since the commercial system lacks an intrinsic standard of value it must rely upon *credit*—upon the faith in honest intentions that underwrites, for instance, the loan that he has himself "creaunced" (366), or pledged his faith to repay. And so too must the domestic system run on credit, which is why he chooses to accept his wife's account of the hundred franks. In effect, he preserves his own innocence by believing in that of his wife. And his example both provides an interpretive norm for the *Tale* as a whole—encouraging the reader to be as generous to the merchant as he is to his wife—and suggests that even the very economic order to which fallen man is condemned preserves vestiges of the primal innocence he has lost.

We witness here, then, much the same dynamic as in the *Merchant's Tale*. Commercialism is understood not as the effect of social and economic forces, nor as generated by class interests, but as a universal

---

Kenneth S. Cahn, "Chaucer's Merchants and the Foreign Exchange: An Introduction to Medieval Finance," *SAC* 2 (1980): 81–119.

83. See the discussion of the mercantile self-image by Gardner Stillwell, "Chaucer's 'Sad' Merchant," *RES* 20 (1949): 1–18. Stillwell's evidence is largely derived from the fabliau.

condition. It is entailed by the inevitable albeit culpable alienation of history per se, its fall away from an original order. Moreover, not only does Chaucer avoid the disparagement of merchants so characteristic of conventional thinking, he actually implies that those who are most capable of preserving a redemptive innocence within this world are merchants themselves. The exchange system within which they operate requires of them not a cynical disbelief in all values but just the opposite: the very recognition of contingency, of the fallenness of the world within which they operate, elicits from them a countervailing trust, a reliance upon goodwill. In the *Merchant's Tale* the polarization of value—prelapsarian innocence versus depravity, authority versus experience, patriarchy versus feminism—finds a moment of resolution in the mutual forbearance of Pluto and Proserpina. In the *Shipman's Tale* the agent of this forbearance is the merchant himself. And the series of puns by which resolution is enacted—"taillynge," "dette," and "good" are the most prominent—derive precisely from the commercial world within which the merchant operates and that now extends, with benevolent results, into the domestic space of his marriage. So that if in the negotiations between monk and wife commercialism at first subverts the domestic enclave, it is the same commercialism that in the end reconstitutes it.

The symbiotic relationship between contingency and credit that typifies commercialism is almost inevitably extended in the *Tale* to include the largest of transactional systems, and the one that implicates both poet and reader: language.[84] Just as the economic order represented in the *Tale* lacks an extrinsic norm by which value may be assessed, so does the verbal order from which it is constructed witness to a persistent instability of meaning. Take the merchant's final injunction to his wife:

> "Now wyf," he seyde, "and I foryeve it thee;
> But, by thy lyf, ne be namoore so large.
> Keep bet thy good, this yeve I thee in charge." (430–32)

That the merchant says more than he means witnesses to the presence within a single signifying system—the language of the market—of two originally disparate but now equivalent systems of value. The key

84. For another discussion of the *Tale* from this perspective, but one that relies on the deconstructionist analogy between language and money rather than on the larger analogy between language and exchange, see Gerhard Joseph, "Chaucer's Coinage: Foreign Exchange and the Puns of the *Shipman's Tale*," *ChR* 17 (1982–83): 341–47.

word "good" has both an ethical and a commercial referent, and fully to understand the passage we must be able to recognize the reciprocity that obtains between these two realms of experience and to exchange one for the other.

The interpretive maneuvers this passage requires are typical of the *Shipman's Tale* as a whole, saturated as it is with puns and *doubles entendres*. At the outset the merchant invites the monk "to *pleye* / With hym and with his wyf a day or tweye" (59–60); when the monk bids farewell to the wife after their dealings in the garden, he says, "Gooth now, and beeth as trewe as I shal be" (207); in describing the "curious bisynesse" (225) and "queynte world" (236) of "chapmanhede," the merchant unwittingly refers as well to the negotiations that have just taken place in the garden between his friend and his wife; and in advising his wife to "be to every wight buxom and meke, / And for to kepe oure good be curious" (242–43), he proffers advice that, when salaciously understood, she is all to eager to accept. So too, the "certein beestes" that Don John "moste beye, / To stoore with a place that is oures" (272–73), refer of course to his friend's wife, and when he tells the merchant that "God helpe me so, I wolde it [which can refer either to the place or to the 'beest'] were youres!" (274), he is making a mordant private joke; in return, the merchant offers the monk "nat oonly my gold, but my chaffare" (285), urges him to "take what you list, God shilde that ye spare" (286), and tells him to repay the money "whan it lith in youre ese" (291). After the monk has "repaid" the money, he tells the merchant he gave it to "oure dame / Youre wyf" (356–57) "upon youre bench" (358) and that he can prove it "by certeyn tokenes" (359) that he can rehearse to (or is it *about?*) her. The husband in turn accuses his wife of having "maad a manere straungenesse / Bitwixen me and my cosyn daun John" (386–87), which reminds us that when the monk had initially borrowed the money he had said, suggestively, that "Bitwix us two nedeth no strange fare" (263); and she defends herself by cursing the monk—"I kepe nat of his tokenes [whatever *they* are] never a deel" (403)—and claiming that she thought he had given her the money "For cosynage, and eek for bele cheere / That he hath had ful ofte tymes heere" (409–10). And she completes this defense by offering her tail as a tally upon which her husband can mark the marital and financial debt she owes him.

What must be included in this rehearsal of the *Tale*'s verbal complexity is its remarkably nuanced central scene, in which monk and wife reveal themselves to be master players of the game of sexual negotiation. The monk begins with an implicit sneer at the merchant as one of "thise wedded men, that lye and dare / As in a fourme sit a wery hare" (103–4) and then a provocative reference to the wife's sexuality ("I trowe, certes, that oure goode man / Hath yow laboured sith the nyght bigan" [107–8]) that he accompanies with a suggestive if no doubt inadvertent blush. The wife then replies with a theatricalized account of her marital sufferings that by its very exaggeration reveals itself as a gambit rather than a serious complaint. In response the monk, perhaps self-protectively, locates the conversation within the context of pastoral care by swearing an oath of confidentiality on his "portehors," but the wife quickly redirects this gesture toward a different kind of intimacy by also swearing an oath— an exchange that manages to remove the conversation from the sphere of spiritual advice and relocate it in that of sexual conspiracy. The wife then goes further by disavowing "cosynage [and] alliaunce" (139) as the basis of their relationship in favor of a more suggestive "love and affiance" (140), a gesture that the monk first matches and then extends by launching an attack on the merchant. By this point in the negotiations the two are securely bound together in opposition to the third member of the triangle; and when the wife embarks on a rather conventional version of the complaint of the *male mariée*, we are hardly surprised when it shortly turns to the crucial matter of the "plesance and service" (191) she will provide the monk if he will in turn provide her with a hundred franks. The conversation now reaches its inevitable climax with a violent act of possession—"And with that word he caughte hire by the flankes, / And hire embraceth harde, and kiste hire ofte" (202–3)—that fulfills the tentative gestures of collusion that have preceded it.

My purpose in rehearsing the intricacies of the *Tale*'s verbal texture is to enforce a sense of the interpretive demands it places upon its audience. Seeming always to mean more than it says, the *Tale* stimulates in its readers an unnatural alertness to the possibility of ambiguity; insecure in our grasp of such unstable linguistic material, and fearing an embarrassing revelation of our own naivete, we interrogate each element of the text in order to discover the playful or mocking meaning it conceals. The *Tale* serves, in short, as a textual version of the merchant's "queynte world" of commerce. Just as the "curious bisyness" of "chapmanhede" requires him to "stonde in drede / Of hap and fortune" (237–38), so the tricky verbal surface of the *Tale* solicits in the reader an analogous interpretive vigilance. Moreover, just as the *Tale* represents a world dominated by the ideology of exchange, so is it written in a language in which the natural or proper referent by which the value of a verbal sign should be determined can be exchanged for another, improper one. "Good," "beestes," and "chaffare" are words that properly refer to commodities, but when metaphorically applied to the marital order signify the merchant's wife. As medieval rhetorical discussions point out, this application is an impropriety: the *translatio* of metaphor is a transfer that exchanges the word's proper or natural referent for an improper one.[85] The dangers inherent in this exchange are most dramatically visible in the pun. Does the auditory image "cosynage" refer to "kinship" or to "trickery"? If to both, then we must acknowledge that the proper referent ("kinship") is interchangeable with the improper one ("trickery"), an equivalence that subverts the very distinction between proper and improper. The unstable verbal texture of the *Tale* represents, in short, a world in which words are no longer tied to an extralinguistic reality from which they receive their value. On the contrary, they have entered into a signifying system in which they can be promiscuously exchanged for other words: "good" means both "merchandise" and "wife." It is this promiscuity that is encapsulated in the term "taillynge," a triple pun that correlates the orders of sexuality, commerce, and tale telling into a mutually reciprocal system of interchangeable values.[86]

The unobtrusive mastery with which Chaucer destabilizes the verbal surface of his *Tale* shows how much at home he is within this "queynte world" of unfounded equivalence. Insofar as readers understand this verbal surface—and we all know what "queynte" *really* means—they too are natives of this territory. What is striking about the *Tale*, however, is that Chaucer leads us to acknowledge this habitation as a guilty complicity. For he aligns us with the culpable and all-too-knowing monk and wife against the ingenuous merchant. As monk and wife manipulate their victim and each other, we follow each move and note each ambiguity and *double entendre;* we understand them and their language in a way the merchant never can. And while he is protected by what amounts to a saving innocence, we are burdened with a guilty knowledge. Commonly described as cheerfully cynical, the *Tale* threatens to induce in its audience an analogous cynicism—it is the most Boccaccian of the *Canterbury Tales,* an anecdotal narrative that threatens to coopt its readers to its own sardonic world of self-interest by denying them access to a set of stable values.

Hence the typical response to the *Tale* is to read it as calling up its absent opposite—to invoke, that is, an orthodox set of values in terms of which judgment can be passed upon the narrative. Modern critics

85. On *translatio*, see above, chapter 2, 101–4.

86. The fact that "taillynge" refers to tale telling as well as sexual "tailing" and financial tallying is demonstrated by the scribal substitution of "talyng" for the *durior lectio* "taillynge"; see the rather misleading note to line 434 in Robinson's 2d ed. Gerhard Joseph has good comments on the fact that this third pun is not aural but visual ("Chaucer's Coinage," 354).

accomplish this by using the same exegetical strategies with which their medieval precursors disarmed the seductions of the letter. This process is familiar enough in Chaucer criticism generally, and it has been performed upon this particular *Tale* in a variety of instructive ways. The central scene between wife and monk in the garden has been read as a reenactment of both the fall and the meeting between the risen Christ and Mary Magdalen; the wife's greeting to her returning husband as an allusion to the apocryphal legend of Anna and Joachim; the language of pastoral care with which the monk initiates his negotiations with the wife as invoking a controlling penitential context; the oaths that dot the *Tale* as soliciting the orthodox teaching on oaths, which then reveals the protagonists' commitment to a base materialism; the wife's description as a parody of the wholly admirable *mulier fortis* of Proverbs 31:10–31; the merchant's moral philosophy as radically inadequate when judged by orthodox standards; and so on.[87]

These judgmental readings share a common refusal to accept the world of mercantile exchange at face value—hence their hostility to the merchant—and a desire to read the *Tale* in a way that will locate within it stable values capable of passing judgment upon the processes of commodification the *Tale* describes. Quite apart from their individual strengths and weaknesses, these interpretations are valuable because they make plain two qualities that characterize interpretation per se and that are themselves foregrounded in the elaborate medieval analysis of hermeneutics. One is that interpretation is an activity for a fallen world: not only does it seek to stabilize an otherwise unsteady text by invoking an extratextual norm of rectitude, but it is because both language and the reader have fallen away from a primal condition of integrity that truth must be encased within a form that requires decipherment.[88] The other point is that, for all its effort at returning the text to a

---

87. See, respectively, Lorraine Kochanske Stock, "The Reenacted Fall in Chaucer's *Shipman's Tale*," *SI* 7–8 (1981–82): 134–45; Gail McMurray Gibson, "Resurrection as Dramatic Icon in the *Shipman's Tale*," in *Signs and Symbols in Chaucer*, ed. J. P. Hermann and J. J. Burke (University: University of Alabama Press, 1981), 102–12; Theresa Coletti, "The Meeting at the Gate: Comic Hagiography and Symbol in the *Shipman's Tale*," *SI* 3 (1977): 47–56; Robert Adams, "The Concept of Debt in *The Shipman's Tale*," *SAC* 6 (1984): 85–102; George R. Keiser, "Language and Meaning in Chaucer's *Shipman's Tale*," *ChR* 12 (1977–78): 147–61; Theresa Coletti, "Biblical Wisdom: Chaucer's *Shipman's Tale* and the *Mulier Fortis*," *ChR* 15 (1980–81): 236–42; and Janette Richardson, *Blameth Nat Me: A Study of Imagery in Chaucer's Fabliaux* (The Hague: Mouton, 1970), 100–22.

88. The idea that interpretation is entailed by human sinfulness is most commonly expressed in the ubiquitous medieval notion that the divine truth is encased within symbols in order to conquer the reader's pride through hard work; see Henri de Lubac, *Exégèse médiévale: les quatres sens de l'Ecriture* (Paris: Aubier, 1959), 1:43–56. Hence too the

condition of rectitude, interpretation is itself necessarily implicated within the world of linguistic substitution it seeks to master. It is, after all, a strategy by which otherwise enigmatic narrative elements are exchanged for a set of known meanings, and as itself an economy—a system of exchange—it requires for its workings a hermeneutic just price, a configuration of meanings whose value is, somehow, beyond dispute. So that even if we disarm the *Tale* through exegetical interpretation, this very process forces upon us an awareness of our own location within the world of economic exchange. If for the poet this acknowledgement consists in the analogy between the ambiguous language from which his *Tale* is constructed and the unfounded system of commodity exchange it represents, for the reader it inhabits the very interpretive processes with which we seek to render the *Tale* morally efficacious.

Yet if we must acknowledge our location within the fallen world of history, the *Tale* simultaneously encourages us, as we have seen, to seek for a way to recover the kind of innocence that protects the merchant. This paradoxical demand is staged in the *Tale* in a detail of ostentatious irrelevance. When the wife goes walking in the garden early on Sunday morning she is accompanied by a companion:

A mayde child cam in hire campaignye,
Which as hir list she may governe and gye,
For yet under the yerde was the mayde. (95–97)

The few critics who have sought to understand this child have recognized that she serves as an innocent foil to the sordid transactions to which she is a witness.[89] Something of the same function is performed

---

medieval argument that were it not for the fall the divine truth would be immediately visible to man in God's book of nature; now, however, we have the Bible as a key with which to decipher it—although a key that must be itself deciphered (ibid., 1:122–25).

89.   See Charles A. Owen, Jr., "Morality as a Comic Motif in the *Canterbury Tales*," *CE* 16 (1955): 226–32; T. W. Craik, *The Comic Tales of Chaucer* (London: Methuen, 1964), 56; and Gibson, "Resurrection," 108–9. Analogous uses of a young girl as an innocent participant in an erotic transaction occur in the ninth story of Day 2 of the *Decameron* (a young man secretly gazes on the naked body of a woman who is sleeping with "una piccola fanciulla" and uses his knowledge of her body to persuade her husband that she is guilty of adultery), and in the fabliaux known as "De celui qui bota la pierre" (a boy not only witnesses the erotic dealings between his mother and the village priest but is unwittingly the agent of their undoing); see Boccaccio, *Opera*, ed. Cesare Segre (Milan: Mursia, 1963), 156, and Anatole de Montaiglon and Gaston Raynaud, eds., *Recueil général et complet des fabliaux* (Paris: Librairie des Bibliophiles, 1880), 4:147–49. I have discussed the child as an authorial emblem, especially in Fragment VII (begun by the *Shipman's Tale*), in "'What Man

in the *Merchant's Tale* by an odd simile the Merchant uses to describe January's reaction when he sees May and Damyan in the tree: "up he yaf a roryng and a cry, / *As dooth the mooder whan the child shal dye*" (2364–65), a line that expresses January's loss in terms of the loss of innocence, of the family, and of life itself.[90] The childish innocence these mercantile images express stands as a biographical equivalent to the historical golden age; and for the Shipman, both the maid's infant silence and her submission to the maternal figure of the wife bespeak an unfallen natural order against which the alienated order of commercial and verbal exchange is defined.

But she does more, for the form in which she is represented reexpresses with telling concision the dynamic of alienation that inhabits the *Tale* as a whole. Chaucer's lines contain an allusion to the natural signification that is the linguistic equivalent to the innocent world the child inhabits. According to medieval etymology, the word "yerde" is peculiarly appropriate to a maid child: *virgo*—virgin—is derived from *virga*—a branch or spring, what in Middle English is called a "yerde." Trevisa's fourteenth-century translation of Bartholomaeus Anglicus gives the rationale for this etymology: "And a maide hatte *virgo* and haþ þat name of grene age, as *virga* 'a ȝerde' is iseide as it were *viridios* 'grene'."[91] The word "yerde" thus invokes the innocent relation between word and thing that the fall has since ruptured. But it also contains the marks of that rupture, for in the process of translation the word has taken on other, less innocent meanings. One is the rod of discipline; empowered to "governe and gye" this maid child "as hir list," the wife is able to impose upon her the willful tyranny characteristic of fallen history. Another, more unsettling meaning is the sexual rod of the phallus: the maid child is not yet mature enough to receive the male sexuality for which the wife is now bargaining.[92] Given these

---

Artow?': Authorial Self-Representation in the *Tale of Sir Thopas* and the *Tale of Melibee*," *SAC* 11 (1989): 117–76. As I argue there, there is good reason to think that the late medieval idealization of childhood is a primarily bourgeois phenomenon.

90. For Tatlock, virtually the only critic to comment upon the line, this simile represents another example of the Merchant's capacity to sully even so sacred an emotion as maternal love: "this is hard to forgive him" ("Chaucer's *Merchant's Tale*," 183).

91. M. C. Seymour et al., ed., *On the Properties of Things: John Trevisa's Translation of Bartholomaeus Anglicus, De Proprietatibus Rerum* (Oxford: Clarendon Press, 1975), 1:320. For Trevisa's ultimate source, see Isidore of Seville, *Etymologiae* 12, 2, 21: "Virgo a viridiori aetate dicta est, sicut et virga, sicut et vitula"; see also 12, 1, 32 (ed. José Oroz Reta and Manuel Marcos Casquero [Madrid: Biblioteca de Autores Cristianos, 1982), 2:42, 62.

92. On this meaning, see *OED*, yard sb.[2], 11: "The virile member, penis." This is not a slang usage: see, for example, R. H. Helmholz, *Marriage Litigation in Medieval England* (Cambridge: Cambridge University Press, 1974), who cites a text that describes in sober

meanings, the word witnesses to its distance from an original natural order both in its specific significations and, more tellingly, in the ambiguity that characterizes the alienated language of history. The maid child thus invokes both an original innocence and the fact of its loss; and her fleeting appearance in this soon to be violated garden measures both distance from that origin and the force of nostalgia.

V

While the *Merchant's Tale* is tightly bound to its teller and is best read as an effort at self-definition and self-understanding, this is not true of the *Shipman's Tale*, whose roving textual history witnesses to its freedom from psychological specificity. Originally composed for the Wife of Bath, its subsequent assignment to the Shipman endows it with a teller who is appropriate but hardly inevitable. This lack of specificity is itself significant: the *Shipman's Tale* offers an account of bourgeois life from the outside, as a given historical condition, rather than, as in the *Merchant's Tale*, as a form of life subject to continual self-constitution and self-questioning. And the Shipman observes bourgeois life with shrewd accuracy: the division and equivalence of the spheres of commercial and domestic labor; the dominance of the conjugal relationship, and of marital sexuality, in the constitution of the family; and the practical equality of the partners despite the hierarchy prescribed by patriarchal ideology—these are characteristics that allow us to see in the *Tale* a reflection of contemporary social reality. But it is precisely the *givenness* of these characteristics, the unquestioning inevitability with which the *Tale* represents the bourgeois form of life, that serves as its deepest strategy of legitimization. And in its unspoken but all the more profound generalization of the commercial condition beyond the confines of the merchant class, as in its implication of both poet and reader in this process, it manages to redefine a historically specific form of life as life per se.

Taken together, then, the *Merchant's* and *Shipman's Tales* represent an effort both to know commercialism as an ideology and to mystify that knowledge. How are we to understand Chaucer's relation to this effort? There are, as Emerson Brown has well argued, suggestive links

---

legal prose the tests to which a husband's "yerde" or *virga* was subjected to demonstrate impotence (89 n. 53). See also Thomas W. Ross, *Chaucer's Bawdy* (New York: Dutton, 1972), 240–41, who denies an obscene sense here but does plausibly suggest that line 1387 in the *Knight's Tale*—"His slepy yerde in hond he bar uprighte"—contains a naughty double sense.

between the Merchant's social and geographical location and Chaucer's, and the language of his *Tale* finds an unmistakable echo in Chaucer's own "Envoy to Bukton."[93] Similarly, the *Shipman's Tale* draws a powerful analogy, as we have seen, between the worlds of merchant and poet, and here too the language of the *Tale* suggestively reappears in a Chaucerian lyric, "The Former Age."[94] To some extent, of course, the poet is present in every Canterbury pilgrim. But to what extent does the *Canterbury Tales* as a whole represent an effort to define a form of life that at once derives from mercantile canons of value and disguises that derivation, that projects, in classic bourgeois fashion, a class-specific version of reality as if it were reality per se? At the beginning of this chapter I summarized recent efforts to read the *Canterbury Tales* as a mercantile text, corresponding to Boccaccio's *Decameron* and Sercambi's *Novelliero*. That these efforts can be only partially successful not only does not impeach them but is, given Chaucer's strategy of legitimization, inevitable. In the *Merchant's* and *Shipman's Tales*—both of which, not coincidentally, find analogues and perhaps sources in Boccaccio's and Sercambi's texts—we can see that Chaucerian poetry does indeed, profoundly and even self-consciously, embrace the ideology of commerce. But it embraces it through an act of dehistoricization, representing it not as a specific historical form of social life but as life itself.

93.   Emerson Brown, Jr., "Chaucer, the Merchant, and Their Tale: Getting Beyond Old Controversies: Part II," *ChR* 13 (1978–79): 247–62.

94.   *The Former Age* is a lament for a lost golden age in which "no coyn ne knew man which was fals or trewe" (20), in which "no marchant yit ne fette outlandish ware" (22), and in which there was "no *taylage* by no tyrannye" (54). This poem about the loss of perfection lacks a line.

Chapter Eight
The Subject of Confession: The Pardoner and the Rhetoric of Penance

"The man is strange even to himself."

In the *Wife of Bath's Prologue and Tale* Chaucer used the rhetoric of misogyny to construct a feminine subjectivity. In the remarkably similar *Pardoner's Prologue and Tale*, he deploys the rhetoric of penance for an analogous act of self-constitution. That the Pardoner and the Wife of Bath form an odd couple among the Canterbury pilgrims at the level of theme has been well argued by a number of critics; there are also several formal analogies that link them together.[1] For one thing, both the Wife and the Pardoner find their immediate literary source in the *Roman de la Rose*, in the complementary figures of La Vieille and Faus Semblant. For another, the structure of their discourses are strikingly similar: a confessional prologue followed by a self-revealing tale, and the whole embedded in a carefully articulated dramatic context. But what is most important at the level of form is that in both cases their confessional narratives are preceded by tales that aspire to hagiographical authority: Man of Law-Wife of Bath, Physician-Pardoner.

The configuration of hagiography and confession, moreover, is one to which Chaucer will return once again in the course of the *Canterbury Tales*, and in circumstances that suggest its importance to him. In Fragment VIII, the *Second Nun's Tale* of St. Cecilia—the only fully fledged hagiography in the *Tales*, and almost certainly, in some form or other, an early work—is followed by the *Canon's Yeoman's Prologue and Tale*, a work that bespeaks belatedness in its relations both to the Chaucerian

---

1. See, for example, Anne Kernan, "The Arch-Wife and the Eunuch," *ELH* 41 (1974): 1–25.

career and to the drama of the *Tales*. The generic juxtaposition, in other words, is important enough to Chaucer that he not only reinvokes an early work but revises his original conception of the pilgrimage company in order to introduce a new character whose personal circumstances will be sufficiently dense to support a confessional narrative.[2] Moreover, the Canon's Yeoman's performance is articulated in a form precisely analogous to those of the Wife of Bath and Pardoner: a confessional prologue followed by an autobiographical tale, the whole embedded in a highly dramatic context.[3] And whereas the Wife and Pardoner depend on the specialized discourses of misogyny and penance for their self-construction, the Yeoman similarly relies upon alchemy, and an alchemy that is also given detailed representation in the *Roman de la Rose*.

Evidently, then, in trying to understand the *Pardoner's Tale* we should take seriously its pairing with the *Physician's Tale*. This is all the more the case because the Physician's narrative about the sacrifice of Virginia reinvokes the thematic context of the *Legend of Good Women* and the *Man of Law's Tale* and so suggests that the Physician-Pardoner pair will recall the topics at issue in the earlier confrontation of the Wife of Bath and the Man of Law.[4] We remember that the paradox at the center of the Man of Law's orthodoxy—that female virtue is actually generated by the male tyranny it seeks to chasten—was inverted in the *Wife of Bath's Prologue and Tale*, where female "maistrye" seeks to bring men to a world beyond hierarchy and domination, a golden age of innocent relations in which both men and women can receive their hearts' desires. Analogously, in the Wife's *Prologue and Tale* Chaucer contrasted the tyrannical violence of orthodox exegesis with a more patient form of reading, a dilatory postponement of meaning that yields a recuperative and inclusive understanding rather than the dismissive judgments rendered by a hermeneutic committed to the maintenance of hierarchy. These are parallel acts of utopianism, one social, the other textual, that the Pardoner will, in his own way, seek to achieve.

The *Physician's Tale* represents the Man of Law's masculine authori-

2.   The *Clerk's* and *Merchant's Tales* share a similar configuration, although the *Merchant's Tale* is less obviously confessional than the *Wife of Bath's*, *Pardoner's*, and *Canon's Yeoman's Prologues and Tales*.

3.   This structure is obscured by the inaccurate rubrics of the Ellesmere manuscript, which are unfortunately preserved in the *Riverside Chaucer*. See the edition by E. T. Donaldson, *Chaucer's Poetry*, 2d ed. (New York: Ronald Press, 1975).

4.   For the connection between the *Physician's Tale* and the *Legend*, see Anne Middleton, "The *Physician's Tale* and Love's Martyrs: 'Ensamples Mo Than Ten' as a Method in the *Canterbury Tales*," *ChR* 8 (1973–74): 9–32.

tarianism in an exaggerated form. "Of alle tresons sovereyn pestilence /
Is whan a wight betrayseth innocence" (91–92): as Virginia is betrayed
by Claudius, by Appius, and by Virginius, so does the *Physician's Tale*
betray the innocence of its quasi-hagiographical form. In a series of
parallel violations, Virginia becomes Claudius's thrall, the object of Appius's lust, and a token of Virginius's self-regarding commitment to
female chastity—a pattern of abduction that is extended to the Physician by the repeated appearance of the word "sentence." The "sentence" of Claudius's "cursed bille" (176–77, 190) is first enacted in the
"sentence of this justice Apius" (204, 172) and then preempted by the
harsher "sentence" that Virginius passes upon his helpless daughter:
"in pacience / Take thou thy deeth," he tells her, "for this is my sentence" (223–24). The final element of this series is the "sentence" (157)
of the *Tale* itself: "Forsaketh synne, er synne yow forsake" (286). The
Tale purports to celebrate Virginia's impeccable innocence but soon becomes preoccupied with the various forms of delinquency by which
innocence can be destroyed. Appius's lechery, Claudius's complicity,
and Virginius's self-regarding cruelty—displayed in a chilling speech
of mournful highmindedness—become the center of narrative interest.[5] And as if this were not enough, the Physician adds as well ostentatiously irrelevant discussions of the dangers of "feestes, revels,
and . . . daunces" (65) and of inattentive governesses (72–104). Just as
the "greet excellence" (10) that Nature has embodied in Virginia is destroyed by the fallen world she inhabits, so too is the transcendent
virtue she exemplifies eclipsed in the narrative. Far from dominating
the story in which she is so unhappily located—as do her hagiographical colleagues, Constance, Griselda, and Cecilia—Virginia is a
mere helpless victim. Her only act of conversion is to transform Appius
from a judge into a lecher—"Anon his herte chaunged and his mood, /

5. Virginius's culpability is clearly implied by the allusion to Jephthah (240–44),
whom medieval exegetes sharply criticized for his foolish oath; see Richard L. Hoffman,
"Jephthah's Daughter and Chaucer's Virginia," *ChR* (1967–68): 20–31. Equally damning
is his egregious speech to his daughter: "allas, that I was bore!" (215), he begins, then
refers to Virginia as the "endere of my lyf" (218), "my laste wo" (221), and "my laste joye
also" (222)—epithets that she could far better apply to him—and says that "my *pitous*
hand moot smyten of thyn heed" (226), an epithet that becomes deeply troubling when
he is then himself saved "for routhe and for pitee" (261) by his fellow citizens and in turn
intercedes for the wretched Claudius "of his pite" (272). When Virginia gives herself up
to him she cries, in scriptural tones, "Dooth with youre child youre wyl, a Goddes
name!" (250) and begs him that "he sholde smyte softe" (252); at the end of the *Tale* we are
told that "no man woot whom God wol smyte" (278). As with the *Clerk's Tale*, a merely
human figure takes on (or counterfeits) a divine authority; unlike the Clerk, the Physician
seems unaware of the presumption of this act.

So was he caught with beautee of this mayde" (126–27)—while she
fails to move her father: "wolde he from his purpos nat converte" (212).
Nor does her *Tale* have any conversionary force. "Hire beautee was hire
deth" (297), the Host says complacently; "This is a pitous tale for to
heere, / But natheless, passe over, is no fors" (302–3).

The *Physician's Tale*, in short, is a fraudulent or "counterfeit" hagiography. "Who kan me countrefete?" (13), Nature asks, and her interdictive
question is directed against both those who would attempt to work as
she works and, in a sense of which the Physician is unaware, against
those who would attempt to represent her.[6] The elaborate prosopopeia
of Nature with which the Physician ornaments his *Tale* is thus itself an
instance of the kind of counterfeiting against which she issues her prohibition. Virginia, on the other hand, had "no countrefeted termes . . . / To
seme wys" (51–52): she provides a norm of verbal innocence by which to
measure the narrator of her *Tale*. In the *General Prologue* we were told that
"in al this world ne was ther noon hym lik, / To *speke* of phisik and of
surgerye" (412–13). After the *Tale* Harry Bailey provides a litany of counterfeit medical terms: "urynals," "jurdones," "ypocras," "galiones,"
"boyste," "letuarie," "Saint Ronyon," "cardynacle."[7] "Seyde *I* nat wel?"
(311), he mockingly inquires. In its verbal fraudulence, the *Physician's
Tale*, like the pathetic figure it commemorates, is unable to transcend its
own fallen historicity: in ways it signally fails to understand, it is indeed
an "historial thyng notable" (156).

In foregrounding the question of authentic versus counterfeit language, the *Physician's Tale* establishes the terms of the Pardoner's performance. Moreover, the penitential nature of the Pardoner's speaking, a
characteristic underappreciated by criticism of the *Tale*, also raises the
question of paternal authority that is at the center of the *Physician's Tale:*
as Virginia bows to her father's idea of virtue, so does the Pardoner
engage in an action that seeks to reconcile him to the Divine Father. In
medieval thinking, sin results in insufficiency: the fall was a defection
that literally unmade (*de-ficere*) man, drawing him back to the nothingness from which he was originally fashioned. And its effect was to
alienate him from God, from nature, and from himself. The antidote to

6.   This is the primary sense of the passage from which Chaucer derived the account
of Nature, *Roman de la Rose*, 16219–228; that Chaucer himself agreed with this interdiction
is implied by his disclaimer in the *Parliament of Fowls* (316–18), where he declines to
describe Nature and refers us instead to the *De planctu Naturae*.

7.   A number of these terms are obviously comic neologisms: "urynals," "jurdones,"
"galiones," "Saint Ronyon," "cardynacle"; but while "ypocras," "boyste," and "letuarie"
are apparently authentic, they are homophones of words that cast a judgmental tone
upon the Physician's performance: hypocrisy, boasts, and lechery.

this alienation is an act of atonement accomplished through penance: by contrition, confession, and satisfaction the sinner can receive the divine grace that will recover for him the wholeness destroyed by sin. In this chapter I will argue that the subjectivity constructed in the *Pardoner's Prologue and Tale* is shaped according to the medieval understanding of the privation of sin and its antidote in the sacrament of penance, that the Pardoner's performance is best understood in terms of medieval confessional habits.

In the well-known words of Emile Benveniste, "It is in and through language that man constitutes himself as a *subject*, because language alone establishes the concept of 'ego' in reality, in *its* reality. . . . There is no other objective testimony to the identity of the subject except that which he himself thus gives about himself."[8] For Lacanian psychoanalysis, this act of linguistic identification is also one of self-alienation: "I identify myself in language," says Lacan, "but only by losing myself in it like an object."[9] Having entered into a symbolic order comprised above all by language,

> the subject is irremediably divided, because he is at once excluded from the signifying chain and "represented" in it. . . . By mediating himself in his discourse, the subject in effect destroys the immediate relation of self to self, and constructs himself in language . . . as he wishes to see himself, as he wishes to be seen, and thereby alienates himself in language.[10]

Moreover, this gap between self-presence and self-alienation is inscribed in the very dynamic of language itself. For the word effects the absence of that which it represents: as the subject is defined by its difference from the other of the unconscious, so does the signifier repress its signified.[11] Hence contemporary theory has insisted that language is characterized above all by privation, by the absence of a transcendental signified that might provide a legitimizing stability.

8. Emile Benveniste, "Subjectivity in Language," *Problems in General Linguistics,* trans. Mary Elizabeth Meek (Coral Gables: University of Florida Press, 1971), 224, 226.

9. Jacques Lacan, *Écrits,* trans. Alan Sheridan (London: Tavistock, 1977), 86.

10. Anike Lemaire, *Jacques Lacan,* trans. David Macey (London: Routledge and Kegan Paul, 1977), 68, 64.

11. On signification as repression, see Roland Barthes, *Elements of Semiology,* trans. Annette Lavers and Colin Smith (London: Jonathan Cape, 1967), 49; and Anthony Wilden, "Lacan and the Discourse of the Other," in Jacques Lacan, *Speech and Language in Psychoanalysis,* ed. and trans. Wilden (Baltimore: Johns Hopkins University Press, 1968), 272–76.

Described in the *General Prologue* as a "geldyng or a mare" (I, 691),
the Pardoner is presented as apparently lacking the male sexual organs
that would allow him to assume a straightforward gender identity.
That we are not certain that he is a castrate is, to be sure, part of the
mystery he at once discloses and withholds.[12] Yet his performance as a
whole—both *Prologue and Tale* and the dramatic context in which they
are located—enacts an Oedipal drama that has castration as its central
event and ultimate penalty.[13] That he is a professional orator alerts us
also to the relevance of the linguistic issue. And that his vocation locates him within the penitential system gives special point to the confessional nature of his discourse.[14] Put simply, my contention in the discussion that follows is that the Pardoner's discourse is offered as an effort
to satisfy paternal justice, that it is an act of penance that seeks to atone
for the transgression that has resulted in his "castration," whether it be
real or only presumed. Yet I want to argue as well that the Pardoner also
harbors a sense of victimization, and that his mockery of the penitential
system of which he is an agent is impelled by his sense that an injustice
has been worked upon him. Moreover, at the imaginative center of his
Tale is a scene that articulates the very desire that the paternal justice of
penance has proscribed. This is the moment when the Old Man describes his desire to divest himself of the burdens of his maturity by
returning to his maternal source:

12.   See Carolyn Dinshaw, *Chaucer's Sexual Poetics* (Madison: University of Wisconsin
Press, 1989), 156–57.
13.   That we are to understand the Pardoner as lacking testicles seems clear from the
General Prologue, both in the narrator's supposition—"I trow he were a geldyng or a
mare" (691)—and in the physical details of his description (on which see Walter Clyde
Curry, *Chaucer and the Medieval Sciences* [New York: Oxford University Press, 1926], 54–
70). Whether he is a *eunuchus ex nativitate*, as Curry unconvincingly claims, or a castrate,
is a distinction without a difference: if his testicles are absent, whether the deprivation
occurred before or after birth seems not to matter. It is perhaps also the case, as Monica
McAlpine has argued in "The Pardoner's Homosexuality and How It Matters," *PMLA* 95
(1980): 8–22, that Chaucer also presents him as a homosexual, which was in the Middle
Ages thought to be consistent with eunuchry. But none of the interpretive conclusions
that McAlpine draws from the Pardoner's presumed homosexuality could not also, and
in my view more appropriately, be understood in terms of castration.
14.   The purpose of pardoners as professional recipients of charity was to provide
parishioners with the opportunity to give alms and so be pardoned of the punishment
imposed upon them by their confessors as part of the satisfaction of penance. These are
pardons *a poena* (from the punishment of sin), although this Pardoner wrongly claims
that he has pardons *a culpa* (from the guilt of sin), the kind of pardons that only Christ
could provide. See Alfred L. Kellogg and Louis Haselmayer, "Chaucer's Satire of the
Pardoner," *PMLA* 66 (1951): 251–77.

Thus walke I, lyk a restelees kaityf,
And on the ground, which is my moodres gate,
I knokke with my staf bothe erly and late,
And seye "Leeve mooder, lete me in!" (728–31)

This scene—whose details will concern us at length at the end of the chapter—is related to the penitential action that the Pardoner seeks, in however oblique and displaced a fashion, to perform; but in its regressive and incestuous yearnings it speaks as well to the psychological dynamics of transgression and castration. The crucial point, I think, is that it imagines sufficiency not as atonement with the judgmental Father but as reengorgement by Mother Earth, a chthonic and unsanctified source of life. This is the moment of original unity that the entrance into the life of sin—and into the symbolic order of language—has ruptured; it represents a dream of childish innocence that the painful realities of age deny.

This is the Pardoner's version of the originality that in the *Physician's Tale* is embodied in the childish Virginia, and it makes explicit the incestuous emotions that hover about the parent-child relation represented in that *Tale*.[15] Rather than be violated by Appius's lust, Virginia must suffer the violence of paternal affection—Virginius strikes "for love and nat for hate" (225)—and her body can remain sexually intact only by enduring a fatal dismemberment at the hands of her father. That Virginius is here preempting Appius is made clear by his gesture of defiance: after severing the "heed" (255) of this "mayden" (132), he "presente[s]" (256) it to the judge in place of the maidenhead that Appius had originally sought, a substitution that surreptitiously witnesses to the illicit ambiguity of the emotions that move him. That the Old Man's expression of his desire is anything but surreptitious—although as criticism demonstrates, it is certainly capable of being either appropriated into another order of significance or ignored entirely—is itself part of its meaning. For it is here, I will argue, that the Pardoner articulates a mode of discourse that stands as an alternative to the inauthentic language of confession; and this privi-

15. Chaucer reduces Livy's *virgina adulta* to a "child" (250) of fourteen, which keeps her within the usual medieval age of innocence. According to Bartholomaeus Anglicus (following Isidore), because children before the age of fourteen are (presumably) incapable of sexual intercourse they are innocent: "And þerfore [for] purenes of kynde innocence suche children ben iclepid *pueri*" (M. C. Seymour et al., ed., *On the Properties of Things: John Trevisa's Translation of Bartholomaeus Anglicus, De Proprietatibus Rerum* [Oxford: Clarendon Press, 1975], 1:300). For Livy, see Edgar F. Shannon, "The Physician's Tale," in *Sources and Analogues of Chaucer's Canterbury Tales*, ed. W. F. Bryan and Germaine Dempster (London: Routledge and Kegan Paul, 1941), 402.

leging of an illicit language of the subject represents perhaps Chaucer's most radical imagining.

I

Of all the ways in which the Church affected the lives of medieval Christians, certainly the most ubiquitous and probably the most profound was through its administration of the sacrament of penance. At the Fourth Lateran Council in 1215 Pope Innocent III proclaimed the requirement of annual confession, and in succeeding centuries more and more of the religious life of medieval people came to be concentrated upon and articulated in terms of penance and the confessional.[16] For the Middle Ages, penance was an event that had both a subjective and an objective existence. Prescholastics such as Abelard and Lombard had stressed the justifying power of contrition alone, but the new and in some senses overwhelming responsibilities created by Innocent's decree encouraged the Scholastics to find a way to shift the focus away from the feelings of the penitent and toward the objective action of the sacrament itself. Hence, scholastic theology taught that justification is fully accomplished only by the sacrament itself, and while the penitent's disposition must be a sincere renunciation of sin, only by the sacrament (*ex opere operato*) can grace normally be received. In fact, even if the penitent's disposition is incomplete—if he feels not contrition but what the theologians called attrition—the sacrament itself could bring about the necessary psychological condition: *ex attrito fit contritus*, in the scholastic formula. With this doctrine scholasticism affirmed the importance of confession and satisfaction; it firmly located the power of binding and loosing with the Church in its administration of the sacraments (the *vis clavium*); and it went far toward removing contrition from the sphere of psychology altogether and raising it to the level of ontology.[17] For in this context the value of a penitential feeling now depended less on its motives or intensity than on whether it was informed (*formata*) with the grace made available through the sacrament. In substituting for the subjectivism of their predecessors the objectivity of sacramentalism, the Scholastics readjusted the focus of penitential

16.   See Thomas N. Tentler, *Sin and Confession on the Eve of the Reformation* (Princeton: Princeton University Press, 1977); Amédée Teetaert, O. C., *Les Confessions aux laïques dans l'église latine depuis le VIIIᵉ jusqu'au XIVᵉ siècles* (Paris: J. Gabalda, 1926); and the articles on Pénitence, Contrition, and Attrition in the *Dictionnaire de théologie catholique*, ed. Alfred Vacant and E. Mangenot, 16 vols. (Paris: Letouzay et Ané, 1903–72).

17.   P. de Letter, "Two Concepts of Attrition and Contrition," *Theological Studies* 11 (1950): 3–33.

attention and made the weighing of the remissive value of sorrow, whether by the priest or the penitent himself, both less delicate and less ultimate.[18]

But although sacramentalism sought to reassure the sinner by removing from him the emotionally intolerable and theologically unsound responsibility to earn the remission of his sins by the intensity of his own sorrow, it had in fact surprisingly little impact on vernacular religious writing. The desire of many serious-minded laymen for works of religious meditation was met by vernacular treatises whose ethical and hortatory purpose assumed, with the stubborn certainty of commonsense, that salvation could be won through striving and self-examination. Indeed, although scholastic sacramentalism quickly made its way into clerical confessional manuals it found almost no presence in the vernacular works of fourteenth-century England. For instance, the earnest analyses of contrition in works such as the *Parson's Tale* and *Jacob's Well*, both far more elaborate than the corresponding discussions in the *summae confessorum* written for priests, demonstrate how the growth of a lay audience encouraged a contritionist attitude.[19]

Moreover, there is the historical fact that most of the vernacular treatises were based ultimately on Raymond of Penyafort's *Summa de poenitentia*, a work that had a strong contritionist bias.[20] And there is the further fact that contemporary theological thinking was itself moving in the same contritionist direction. Franciscanism had always kept alive the Augustinian tradition of an extrasacramental means of remission

18. On the problem of sorrow in penitential theology, see Tentler, *Sin and Confession*, 233–301. One of the reasons urged for annual confession is that the sinner cannot be certain that his contrition is sufficient unless he partakes of the sacrament: John of Freiburg, *Summa confessorum* 3, 34, 28 (Lyon, 1518), fol. 186ᵛ; Antoninus of Florence, *Confessionale* (Chambéry [1485]), fol. 22ʳ.

19. *Parson's Tale*, X, 113–315, almost a fifth of the total; Arthur Brandeis, ed., *Jacob's Well*, EETS, OS 115 (London: K. Paul, Trench and Trübner, 1900), 168–78. By contrast, the *summae* are largely concerned with techniques for examining penitents and particularly the ecclesiastical legislation that governs specific cases: see Pierre Michaud-Quantin, *Sommes de casuistiques et manuels de confession au moyen âge, XIIᵉ–XVIᵉ siècles* (Louvain: Nauwelaerts, 1962), and L. E. Boyle, O.P., S.T.L., "The *Oculus Sacerdotis* and Some Other Works of William of Pagula," *TRHS*, 5th ser., 5 (1955): 81–110. It seems clear from Tentler's discussion that contritionist rigor is far more common in works written either in the late fifteenth or early sixteenth centuries and in the vernacular handbooks than in the fourteenth-century *summae*; see *Sin and Confession*, 233–63, and especially 244 n.18.

20. Amadeus Teetaert, O.C., "La Doctrine pénitentielle de Saint Raymond de Penyafort, O. P.," *Analecta Sacra Tarraconensia* 4 (1928), 156–58. The only vernacular work that I know that does show a clear awareness of sacramentalism is *The Clensyng of Mannes Sowle*, which distinguishes between attrition and contrition and describes contrition as "a sorwe of þe soule formed be grace" (MS Bodley 923, fols. 32ʳ–33ᵛ, 31ᵛ).

through contrition alone, and Duns Scotus finally shatttered the unity
of the way of justification not only by insisting on two ways but by
assigning to them sharply differing values.[21] According to Scotus, a
remedium generale is provided by the workings of the sacrament, an objective operation that exempts the penitent from virtually all responsibility. Certainly for the sacrament to be effective the penitent must remove any barriers to its working, but to the *parum attritus* this can mean
as little as not having the intention of sinning at the moment of confession. But in contrast to the minimalism of this penitential action, Scotus
defined as well an extrasacramental way of salvation that he designated the way of merit—*per modum meriti de congruo.* The more worthy
penitent is moved by an *attritio sufficiens* that is morally and psychologically identical to contrition and for the sake of which God grants the
grace that converts it ontologically into contrition. That this way is difficult and dangerous, fit only for the saint, makes it all the more strikingly genuine and casts a further shadow upon the *remedium generale* of
sacramentalism. The next step in the recuperation of contritionism was
for nominalist theology, with its commitment to the dignity and responsibility of the individual, to reject what it saw as Scotistic laxism and
insist instead that all remission must be to an important degree *de
congruo.* In terms of penance, this meant a return to the contritionism of
the prescholastics: Ockham quotes Lombard's distinction between an
inner and outer penance and agrees with him that it is the inner quality
alone that justifies.[22] While confession is defended by insisting that the
propositum confitendi is a part of contrition, the act itself is an effect of
contrition and remission rather than a cause of it.[23] It is contrition
alone, proceeding at least in part *ex puris naturalibus,* by which sins are
justified.[24]

21. On the double way of penance taught by Alexander of Hales and Bonaventure,
see Teetaert, *Les Confessions,* 262–66. For Scotus's teachings on penance, see Gordon J.
Spykman, *Attrition and Contrition at the Council of Trent* (Kampen: Kok, 1955), 70–84;
Heiko Augustinus Oberman, "Duns Scotus, Nominalism, and the Council of Trent," in
John Duns Scotus, 1265–1965, ed. John K. Ryan and Bernardine M. Bonansea (Washington: Catholic University of America Press, 1965), 311–44.
22. *Supra IV Libros Sententiarum* 4, 8–9, M: "per poenitentiam potest intellegi vel
actus exterior in parte sensitive vel interior. Loquendo de primo actu, sic dico, primo
quod nullus actus vel pena quecunque exterior necessario requiritur vel sufficit ad
deletorem peccati et infusione gratie" (*Opera plurima* 4 [Lyon, 1496]).
23. Ibid., P: "per sacramentum penitentis nunquam deleretur peccatum si esset
prius necessarium deleri per contritionem et attritionem."
24. Ibid., U: "possibile est aliquem actum detestandi sufficere ad deletionem culpe
et infusionem gratiae, quia ille actus quo aliquis detestatur peccatum propter deum quia
est dei offensium circumscripto omni alio sufficit." See also Gordon Leff, *Bradwardine and
the Pelagians* (Cambridge: Cambridge University Press, 1957), 203–6.

This contritionism becomes the standard teaching of nominalism, and even Bradwardine, with his fierce opposition to nominalist voluntarism, agrees that remission flows only from true contrition.[25] For him the sacrament is not the *causa efficiens* of grace but merely "a sign of a holy event."[26] But where he parts company with "Pelagians" like Ockham is in his insistence that the sinner cannot achieve contrition without a divinely infused *habitus*. Indeed, Bradwardine's concern raises the central problem of late-medieval contritionism and points us toward the relevance of this issue to the Pardoner. For he argues that by making Christians responsible for earning their own salvation the contritionists teach a lesson of despair: they not only limit God's power to save, they place upon sinners the responsibility to repay a debt that witnesses precisely to their unworthiness.[27]

The acuteness of Bradwardine's analysis is confirmed by the penitential writings that flourished in the later Middle Ages. On the one hand are those innumerable texts that focus upon the foulness of the sinner's condition. The sinner must set himself before himself, face to face with the defilement he has become. No longer the *imago Dei*, he is now the *imago terreni hominis* (1 Corinthians 15:49). "This image, if thou behold it wittily," says Walter Hilton, in a passage that could be paralleled virtually *ad infinitum* in medieval religious writing, "is all belapped with black stinking clothes of sin, as pride, envy, ire, accidie, covetise, gluttony and lechery. . . . This image and this black shadow though bearest about with thee where thou goest."[28] A true knowledge of himself humiliates the sinner, and he cries out to the Lord, "In thy truth thou hast humbled me."[29] Gratefully he abandons his corruption to the gnawings of the worm of conscience, receiving in his present pain a warrant against eternal agony.[30] Now is the moment for the crucifixion

25. For Bradwardine's rejection of attrition, see *De causa Dei* 1, 43 (London: John Billium, 1618): "Mandatum, inquit [Augustinus], si sit timore poenae, non amore iustitiae, serviliter sit non liberaliter, et ideo nec fit. Non enim frustuc bonus est, qui de charitatis radice non surgit" (380). See also Heiko A. Oberman, *Archbishop Thomas Bradwardine, A Fourteenth-Century Augustinian* (Utrecht: Kemink and Zoon, 1957), 163.

26. Ibid., 1, 43, 420; cited by Oberman, *Bradwardine*, 173.

27. Ibid., 1, 1, 27–29, 20–23.

28. Walter Hilton, *The Scale of Perfection*, 1, 52, ed. (and trans.) Evelyn Underhill (London: J. M. Watkins, 1948), 126; see also Julian of Norwich, *Revelations of Divine Love*, 40, ed. (and trans.) Grace Warrack (London: Methuen, 1949), 81–82.

29. For a particularly intense passage of self-hatred where this passage—Ps. 118(119):75—is cited, see Bernard of Clairvaux, PL 183:969–70.

30. The *vermis conscientiae* is a common figure in penitential writing; it receives an extended discussion in Deguileville's *Le Pèlerinage de l'âme*, ed. J. J. Stürzinger (London: Roxburghe Club, 1895), 45–51.

of the old Adam, the annihilation of the man of sin, the pulverizing force of contrition that destroys the dying to bring forth life.

But on the other hand, as we might expect, is a growing anxiety, and especially among ecclesiastics with responsibility for pastoral care, to balance the needs of discipline with those of consolation.[31] As Jane Douglass has pointed out, late-medieval religious writers show a "constantly recurring concern . . . about scrupulousness [that] must certainly grow out of nominalistic theology itself."[32] Hence, we find these writers (to cite one of them) urging priests not to "impose too rigidly and severely the halter of despair on the people."[33] For if the sinner is able to achieve forgiveness only through the intensity of his remorse, he will enter into a process of self-judgment in which he allows himself no quarter—with the almost predictable result that he will become so overwhelmed with self-loathing that he no longer believes himself worthy of the salvation he so desperately desires.

Moreover, the instinctive contritionism of late-medieval religious life, and the self-scrutiny it entailed, demanded of the sinner who would repent not merely emotional intensity but a punctilious—and, we may surmise, unattainable—emotional precision. For the contrition that provided the justification for sins was itself comprised of those very emotions that simultaneously constituted a damning despair. In his authoritative *Summa*, Penyafort listed six causes (really constitutive elements) of contrition, a list that was repeated *verbatim* by later writers:

> There are six causes inducing contrition: acknowledgement of sins committed; shame over these sins; hatred of the vileness of them; fear of judgment and of the pains of hell; sorrow for the loss of the heavenly home and for the many offenses against the Creator; and the threefold hope of pardon, grace and glory.[34]

Contrition is an uneasy balance of negation and assertion, a radical self-hatred and fear of God that is paradoxically joined to *spes triplex* and a

31. See Tentler, *Sin and Confession*, 249.

32. E. Jane Dempsey Douglass, *Justification in Late Medieval Preaching: A Study of John Geiler of Keisersberg* (Leiden: Brill, 1966), 154.

33. Godesalc Rosemondt, *Confessionale* (Antwerp, 1518); cited by Tentler, *Sin and Confession*, 261.

34. *Summa de poenitentia*, 3, 9 (Rome: Tallini, 1603): "Causae inductiuae contritionis sunt sex, cogitatio, et ex ea pudor de peccatis commissis: detestatio vilitatis ipsius peccati: timor iudicij, et poenae gehennae: dolor de amissione patriae caelestis, et multiplici offensa Creatoris: et spes triplex, veniae, gratiae, et gloriae" (443). Penyafort clarifies the nature of the first cause (*cogitatio*) with a reference to Isaiah 38:15: "I will acknowledge you all the days of my life in the bitterness of my spirit." See also the *Parson's Tale*, 135.

reliance on divine mercy. But at any moment these emotions are in danger of tipping over into a fatal exaggeration. "Therefore I say to you, that I shall teach you to hope and to fear," says Augustinus to Petrarch in the *Secretum*—but he must then immediately warn him against excesses of both hope (*praesumptio*) and, especially, fear (*desperatio*).[35] Presumption and despair are the Scylla and Charibdis of the spiritual life, the Devil's greyhounds, in the words of the *Ancrene Riwle*, "igedered to gederes . . . nexst þe ʒete of helle."[36] They are the prime elements of the medieval understanding of the impenitence that constituted the unforgiveable sin against the Holy Spirit—unforgiveable not because of its heinousness but because of the inner dynamic by which the presumptuous and/or despairing sinner refuses to ask for forgiveness.[37] And of these two, despair is both more central and more dangerous. Presumption removes the sinner from the penitential context entirely, reducing him to simply another instance of reckless procrastination. But despair actually arises from the self-confrontation that initiates penance and is disturbingly close to the genuine spiritual impulses that lead to salvation. It is not simply one of the *impedimenta* to contrition or even its obverse, for its terrors and self-negations are themselves an important part of the peni-

---

35. "Idcirco te alloquor, ut sperare doceam et timere." *Opera omnia* (Basle, 1554), 377.

36. Mabel Day, ed., *The English Text of the Ancrene Riwle*, EETS, OS 225 (London: Oxford University Press, 1952), 150–51. For an excellent discussion, see Susan Snyder, "The Left Hand of God: Despair in Medieval and Renaissance Tradition," *Studies in the Renaissance* 12 (1965): 18–59.

37. As developed throughout the Middle Ages, the concept of the *peccatum in Spiritum sanctum* came to include two not easily harmonized elements, personal impenitence (the "duritia cordis et cors impoenitens" of Romans 2:5) and an attack on Christian truth and the fellowship of the Church: see Augustine, *PL* 34:1266–67, *PL* 35:2097, 2103, *PL* 33:814, *PL* 38:445–67. The first element is usually defined by the terms *praesumptio, desperatio, obstinatio,* and *impoenitentia,* the second by *invidentia gratiae* and *oppugnatio fraternitatis.* While the relationship among these terms is never entirely settled, it is clear that *desperatio* plays a central role, being not merely an aspect of the sin but a primary cause, and in some cases the only element: for example, Bede, *PL* 92:63. In Lombard's authoritative discussion, which draws on accounts of both presumption and despair and, more tellingly, of the relationship of despair and impenitence, this emphasis on the centrality of despair is particularly marked: *Sententia* 2, 43, 1 (Quaracchi: Collegium S. Bonaventurae, 1916), 533–34; see also Aquinas, *ST* II, 2, 14, 2. Doubtless it is this history, as well as the peculiar mutuality of despair and impenitence—despair as usual cause and inevitable effect—that accounts for the definition in several fourteenth-century texts of the sin against the Holy Ghost as despair alone: *Parson's Tale,* 693–95; Robert Mannying, *Handlyng Synne,* ed. F. J. Furnivall, EETS, OS 119, 123 (London: K. Paul, Trench and Trübner, 1901–03), 386–87; T. F. Simmons and H. E. Nolloth, ed., *The Lay Folk's Catechism,* EETS, OS 118 (London: K. Paul, Trench and Trübner, 1901), 11; and Woodburn O. Ross, ed., *Middle English Sermons,* EETS, OS 209 (London: Oxford University Press, 1940), 56–57.

tential impulse. Five of the six *causae* listed by Penyafort are also char-acterisics of despair; indeed, in his influential discussion of penance William of Auvergne lists ten "virtuous emotions that shatter the old man," and they comprise a virtual litany of despair: *timor, pudor, dolor, ira, indignatio, abominatio, horror, odium, execratio,* and *detestatio.*[38] Possessed by these emotions, the penitent is well on the way to the abandonment of hope that constitutes despair. In trying to save his soul he risks losing it.

The dangerous instability of these negative feelings had long been recognized by writers on the spiritual life. According to St. Paul, there are two kinds of sorrow over sin, *tristitia secundum Deum,* which works repentance unto salvation, and *tristitia secundum saeculum,* which works death (2 Corinthians 7:10). For Augustine *tristitia* is so unstable an emotion that he admits, even in the midst of an attack on Stoic apathy, that "it is doubtful whether it can ever be beneficial."[39] And, says Cassian, whereas godly sorrow secures for the soul all the fruits of the Holy Spirit, its obverse is "impatient, hard, full of rancor and sterile habits, a culpable desperation [that is] . . . empty of the spiritual fruit-fulness by which renewal should take place."[40] Hence medieval coun-selors warn against the danger of contrition degenerating into despair, and autobiographical accounts in the literature of the fourteenth cen-tury show this to have been one of the hardest passages of the spiritual life.[41] Julian of Norwich warns that "the beholding of [our sinfulness] maketh us so sorry and so heavy, that scarcely we can find any comfort. And this dread we take sometimes for a meekness, but it is a foul blind-ness and a weakness."[42] Margery Kempe begins her autobiography and her spiritual life with the story of how her conscience and her con-fessor drove her from contrition to despair and then to madness.[43] And

---

38.	*De sacramento poenitentiae* 1, 6, *Opera omnia* (Paris: Hotot, 1674), 1:465. These *motus* are not themselves contrition but only preparatory to it (466–67). See P. Anciaux, "Le Sacrament de pénitence chez Guillaume d'Auvergne," *Ephemerides Theologicae Lovaniensis* 24 (1948): 98–118.

39.	"Scrupulosior quaestio est, utrum inveniri possit in bono" (*De civitate Dei* 14, 7, 2 [*PL* 41:411]).

40.	"Impatiens, dura, plena rancore et moerore infructuoso, ac desperatione poenali, . . . fructus spiritales evacuans, quos novit illa conferre" (*PL* 49:359); see Snyder, "Left-Hand of God," 58 and passim.

41.	Isidore, *PL* 83:617; Caesarius of Heisterbach, *Dialogus miraculorum* 2, 6, 2, 7; Aquinas, *4 Sent.* 17, 2, 4, 2.

42.	Julian, *Revelations,* 179.

43.	S. B. Meech and H. E. Allen, eds., *The Book of Margery Kempe,* EETS, OS 212 (London: Oxford University Press, 1940), 6–11. For a contemporary prayer against de-spair, see the poem listed in the *Index of Middle English Verse,* ed. Carleton Brown and R. H. Robbins (New York: Columbia University Press, 1943), number 1666.

in his *Livre de Seyntz Medicines,* Henry of Lancaster presents a homeo-
pathic explanation for the double effect of *tristitia:* it is a *triacle* drawn
from the venom of sin itself, and while in some it cures in those too
deeply infected it adds its force to the sin already present.[44] In sum, if
the ulcerous sinner is cleansed by the worm of conscience, he may also
(as Deguileville points out) be killed by it: "It's the worm of conscience,
who has teeth as hard as iron; he is so cruel and so lacerating, so penetrating and so piercing, that if he wounds him whom he would kill,
would strike and bludgeon, he will not cease burrowing until he will
have killed his host."[45]

In destroying its victim, despair operates in one of two ways. The
most dangerous is simply the working out of its own internal dynamic. A
sin not of commission but feeling—Donne's "sin of fear"—despair is
efficiently self-fulfilling: thinking himself lost, the man in despair refuses to ask for mercy; refusing to ask, he cannot receive; and not receiving, he becomes lost in deed as well as thought. In practical terms this
means that the man in despair avoids confession. "But he does not confess who despairs of the mercy of God," says Gregory flatly, and the
confessional manuals are virtually unanimous in warning against despair.[46] And yet, of course, the bitterest irony is that it is only by means of

44. Ed. E. J. Arnould (Oxford: Blackwell, 1940), 56–57. Walter Hilton uses the same
figure in his treatise *The Mixed Life,* printed by George G. Perry, ed., *English Prose Treatises
of Richard Rolle de Hampole,* EETS, OS 20 (London: Trübner, 1866), 38. J.-C. Payen, *Le Motif
de repentir dans la littérature française médiévale (des origines à 1230)* (Geneva: Droz, 1968),
mentions "le dit pieux *du triacle et du venim,* que nous avons lu dans le MS BN fr. 12471, f.
47: ce dit est une allegorie de la pénitence" (559 n. 8).

45.   Cest de conscience le ver
      Qui a les dens durs comme fer
      Si cruel est et si mordant
      Si poignant et si trespercant
      Que sil nauoit qui le tuast
      Qui le ferist ou assommast
      De tant runger ne fineroit
      Jusques son maistre oscist auroit.
Pelerinage de lhomme (Paris, 1511), fol. 16ʳ.

46. "Non confitetur autem qui desperat de misericordia Dei" (*PL* 79:649). For examples of the vernacular penitential manuals, see *Handlyng Synne,* 386–87; *Middle English
Sermons,* 275–76; *Parson's Tale,* 1070–75; Dan Michel, *Ayenbite of Inwyt,* ed. Richard Morris, EETS, OS 23 (London: Trübner, 1866), 179–80; W. Nelson Francis, ed., *Book of Vices
and Virtues,* EETS, OS 217 (London: Oxford University Press, 1942), 182–83. Relevant
here as well is the notion that despair is a function of the sinner's overdelicate fear of the
harshness of penance, which leads him to defer his confession; see, for example, Gregory, *PL* 75:1046–47. This theme is expressed in later discussions through the linking of
despair to sloth, a connection that develops historically from the merging of Cassian's
acedia, with its emphasis on physical torpor, with Gregory's *tristitia,* which includes the

confession that despair is finally conquered. To cite just one injunction among many, the *Speculum Christiani* reminds its readers that "Iudas offended more god in that he henge hym-selfe, than in that synne that he be-trayede Cryste. Therfor in verray confessyon knowleche ʒoure synnes and dooʒ penaunce, [and] the kyngdom of heuen schal come nere ʒou."[47]

The other way in which despair destroys its victim is through the excesses of desperation and final impenitence. According to Augustine, the despairing man is like a gladiator doomed to the sword: "Now I am a sinner, iniquitous, damned, and there is no hope of grace; then why should I not do whatever I wish, since nothing is forbidden? Why not enact all desires to the extent I can since after this there remains nothing but torment?"[48] And Gregory, in a passage particularly appropriate to the Pardoner, describes the hidden anxiety and inner torment of the despairing impenitent:

> For because he believes himself to be assailed by attacks from every side, despairing of salvation, he always grows in wickedness. Indeed, sometimes this perverse man anticipates divine judgment, and fears that it is to come upon him. . . . But he does not turn away from evil in order that it could itself be turned away from working his ruin. Accused by his conscience, he fears to be assailed; yet nonetheless he is always increasing that by which he is assailed. He scorns his return, despairs of grace, glories in sin; yet nonetheless, as a witness of his wickedness, he has fear within. And although it seems on the outside as if he commits evil deeds boldly, yet nonetheless within himself he trembles because of them.[49]

---

tristitia secundum saeculum of despair. This somewhat arbitrary arrangement is explained by later writers by the idea that sloth causes a neglect of spiritual duties, especially shrift, which leads in turn to the nightmare panic that the time for repentance is past, and thence to despair. Hence we find listed under sloth in the vernacular treatises the six steps to a bad end, the last being *wanhope*: for example, *Jacob's Well*, 112; *Ayenbite of Inwyt*, 33–34; and see Siegfried Wenzel, *The Sin of Sloth: Acedia in Medieval Thought and Literature* (Chapel Hill: University of North Carolina Press, 1967), 82.

47.   Gustaf Holmstedt, ed., *Speculum Christiani*, EETS, OS 182 (London: Oxford University Press, 1933), 72.

48.   "Jam peccator sum, jam iniquus, jam damnandus, nulla veniae spes est; cur jam non faciam quidquid libet, etsi nonlicet? Cur non impleam, quantum possum, quaecumque desideria, si post haec non restant nisi sola tormenta?" (*PL* 37:1301); see also *PL* 35:1651.

49.   Quia dum feriri se undique insidiis credit, salute desparat, semper ad nequitiam excrescit. Aliquando vero iste perversus etiam superna judicia attendit, et super se haec venire metuit. . . . Sed a malo non avertitur, ut etiam ipsa quoque

Licentiousness is a vain attempt at distraction, and beneath a reckless bravado works the anxiety of despair, tormenting the sinner with a foretaste of the eternal punishment that awaits him.

But spiritual writers insist that hope must never be abandoned for the man in despair. Even if contrition does collapse into despair the process can be reversed. In Deguileville's language, the worm of conscience can be broken by the hammer of contrition, while the lesson of the triumph of Mercy at the close of the *Castle of Perseverance* is not so much to cast out despair as to convert it to the work of penance.[50] The mystical writers tend to see despair as an early stage in the soul's progress toward God, the necessary *siccitas* of the dark night rather than the *accidia* of sin, and they accept its scourges and corrosion as both the punishment for sin and the pain by which the old Adam is destroyed that the Christ within may live.[51] Although the acts of desperation to which despair gives rise are perilous in the extreme, its negations are an important part of the penitential process, and any impulse that forces upon the sinner the reality of his condition can prove in the event to have been useful. The emotions that excite penance are, as we have seen, dangerously ambiguous: the four *impedimenta* to penance listed by Penyafort—*timor, pudor, spes,* and *desperatio*—are in other forms and contexts the causes of contrition.[52] But this ambiguity contains as well a spiritual opportunity: no matter how refractory or self-regarding the initial motives, they can be transformed by the penitential act itself into an offering acceptable to God. Putting aside the ontological changes effected *ex opere operato,* simply at the level of psychology the movement of the sinner toward contrition is, as medieval writers insisted, understood to be a gradual and even hesitent process.[53] Similarly, the

---

ab ejus interitu valeat averti. Accusante se autem conscientia feriri metuit, sed tamen semper auget quo feriatur. Contemnit reditum suum, desperat veniam, superbit in culpa; sed tamen testem suae nequitiae habet timorem. Et quamvis prava videatur foris audacter agere, de his tamen apud semetipsum cogitur trepidare.

PL 75:1007–8; see also PL 76:573.

50. Mark Eccles, ed., *The Macro Plays,* EETS, OS 262 (London: Oxford University Press, 1969), 91–111; see also, in the same volume, the conclusion to *Mankind,* 180–84.

51. Walter Hilton, "Bonum Est," in *Minor Works of Walter Hilton,* ed. Dorothy Jones (London: Burns, Oates, and Washbourne, 1929), 117; Julian, *Revelations,* 79; Paolo Molinari, S. J., *Julian of Norwich* (London: Longmans, 1958), 78–84; Wenzel, *Sin of Sloth,* 60–63.

52. *Summa de poenitentia,* 498–502.

53. While it remained true that only contrition could lead to justification, the psychological movement toward contrition was seen as gradual. In his *Liber poenitentialis,* for instance, Alanus de Insulis advises the priest to terrify the sinner into an initial change of

act of confession itself can excite in even the impenitent fruitful spiritual motions. "For many who arrive undevout," says Jacques de Vitry, "leave with tears and devotion," and according to Walter Hilton,

> Though the ground of forgiveness stand not principally in confession, but in contrition of the heart and in forthinking of sin, nevertheless I expect that there is many a soul that should never have felt very contrition, nor had full forsaking of sin, if confession had not been. For it falls oft times that in time of confession grace of compunction comes to a soul that never before felt grace, but aye was cold and dry, and far from feeling of grace.[54]

In sum, then, despite the efforts of scholastic theologians to render the question of the psychology of repentance moot by defining penance as a largely objective action, the pervasive contritionism of late-medieval religious thought reinstalled this psychology at the center of spiritual concern. And within this focus, discussions of contrition reveal an awareness—sometimes fugitive and even evasive, but sometimes clear-sighted and self-aware—of the immense and disturbing complexity that typified the intention to confess. Specifically, contritionism encouraged a self-scrutiny that often led to a scrupulousness and despair that preempted the confession that was the goal of the process in the first place. In proposing to locate the *Pardoner's Prologue and Tale* within this cultural context, I mean to endow his act of speaking itself with a spiritual value: he is, as we shall see, a man in despair whose discourse is best understood in confessional terms. That his language is complex and often self-conflicted is a function not of the presence of unassimilated and irrelevant literary conventions, nor even of a keenly observed psychological depth, but of a spiritual condition familiar to penitential theology.[55]

---

heart that could then be developed into a fully fledged contrition (*PL* 210:290). When joined to sacramentalism, as by William of Auvergne, this gradualism gave rise to the doctrine of attrition; see Spykman, *Attrition and Contrition*. In the fifteenth century, John Geiler organized the sinner's progress from faint stirrings of apprehension through to *timor filias* into ten distinct steps; see Douglass, *Justification*, 141 n. 1.

54. De Vitry, *In capite ieiunii*, quoted by Teetaert, *Les Confessions*, 288 n. 4: "Multi enim accedunt indevoti qui cum lachrymis et devotione recedunt." Hilton, *The Scale of Perfection*, 247.

55. The criticism of the Pardoner has traditionally fallen into one of these two schools. For examples of the now old-fashioned appeal to convention, see G. G. Sedgewick, "The Progress of Chaucer's Pardoner, 1880–1940," *MLQ* 1 (1940), reprinted in Edward Wagenknecht, ed., *Chaucer: Modern Essays in Criticism* (New York: Oxford University Press, 1959), 128–29; and P. M. Kean, *Chaucer and the Making of English Poetry*

As the confession of a man in despair, the *Pardoner's Prologue and Tale* is the enactment of a paradox: the impenitent man performs a penitential act. That the Pardoner's discourse is in no sense sacramentally legitimate is of course true, and its mimicry of the confessional mode reveals it to be, as we shall see, a familiar kind of medieval parody—a *confessio ficti* or *confessio renardi*. But the spiritual values with which his discourse is instinct will not allow us to dismiss it as an empty travesty. Indeed, in an important sense the Pardoner is less an exception than an exemplification of the workings of the penitential system: the paradox of the confession of despair is an extreme instance of the miracle of transformation that inhabits penance per se, a process that transforms its participants from sinners damned to eternal torment into newly cleansed Christians set on the road to salvation. Moreover, the fact that the Pardoner's confession is set outside a sacramental context translates the salvific claim made by confession into therapeutic terms. For the confession of despair tests the promise that underwrites all confession—that in giving himself up to the structures and language of penance the sinner will find relief from his inner torment. Confession promises a mode of self-representation that can minister to the privation caused by sin by restoring to the penitent an original wholeness. It is a language of replenishment that provides an antidote to the lack endemic to the human condition.

Nor is it a merely modern interest that formulates the confessional dynamic in these terms. For as I hope to show, the tradition of confessional writing in Middle English focuses precisely on the question of the relation of penitential language to the self, and this tradition pro-

---

(London: Routledge and Kegan Paul, 1972), 2:96–109. The argument of psychological realism, which depends upon treating a literary character as a real person, was first established by Kittredge's famous article in the *Atlantic Monthly* 72 (1893), reprinted in Wagenknecht, *Chaucer*, 117–25. The majority of contemporary critics, including those who draw upon recent psychoanalytic paradigms, adopt Kittredge's general position, with the exception of those who, like myself, seek to locate the Pardoner within traditional literary and theological contexts: in addition to Alfred L. Kellogg's fundamental essay, "An Augustinian Interpretation of Chaucer's Pardoner," *Speculum* 26 (1951): 465–81, see especially Robert P. Miller, "Chaucer's Pardoner, the Scriptural Eunuch, and the *Pardoner's Tale*," *Speculum* 30 (1955): 180–99, and Bernard F. Huppé, *A Reading of the* Canterbury Tales, rev. ed. (Albany: State University of New York Press, 1967), 209–20, who like myself reads the Pardoner as a man in despair. H. Marshall Leicester, " 'Synne Horrible': The Pardoner's Exegesis of His Tale, and Chaucer's," in *Acts of Interpretation: Essays in Medieval and Renaissance Literature in Honor of E. T. Donaldson*, ed. Mary J. Carruthers and Elizabeth D. Kirk (Norman: Pilgrim Books, 1982), 25–50, also argues that an exegetical reading can be accommodated to the norms of psychological realism. Leicester's discussion takes as one of its starting points an earlier version of this chapter, and my revision is much indebted to his subtle essay.

vides an important literary context for the *Pardoner's Prologue and Tale*. These are writings that stand apart from the theological and curatorial tradition that prescribes confessional procedures; they are texts, rather, that seek to represent the act of confession itself. Specifically at issue here are the Middle English penitential lyrics and the confession scene in *Piers Plowman;* and as we shall see, in both cases, and especially in Langland, the focus of these representations is upon the relation of confessional speaking to the suffering caused by sin. And the presence of these writings in the *Pardoner's Prologue and Tale* shows Chaucer systematically exploiting one of the central modes of self-representation available in late-medieval England.

II

If indeed the *Pardoner's Prologue and Tale* is to be considered a confession, what precedents are there in medieval literature, and specifically in Middle English, for this kind of writing? Is there a group of texts that can be seen as constituting a confessional genre? In fact, rather disappointingly, the Middle English works that can most accurately be called "confessions" are the texts known in the Middle Ages as *formae confitendi*—bare lists of topics on which the penitent is examined (the seven sins, the five wits, the deeds of mercy, and so on).[56] Occasionally, it is true, these *formae* are transposed from an interrogative into a declarative mood and, duly expanded, presented as the confession of an individual penitent. But because such *confessiones* are designed as aids to the reader's preconfessional reflection they necessarily avoid grounding themselves in an individuating subject: in order that each penitent can apply the *forma* to himself, while picking out only those sins that are in each instance relevant, they detail the sins in all their branches while carefully avoiding specificity.[57] But there are other texts that not only represent

56. A concise and unencumbered example of the *forma* can be found in Carl Horstmann, ed., *Yorkshire Writers: Richard Rolle of Hampole and His Followers* (London: Sonnenshein, 1896), 2:340–43. Versifications of the *forma* can be found in Andrew Clark, ed., *The English Register of Godestow Nunnery*, EETS, OS 129, 130, 142 (London: K. Paul, Trench and Trübner, 1911), 8–11; and James Kinsley, ed., *The Poems of William Dunbar* (Oxford: Clarendon Press, 1979), 13–21. See also Morton W. Bloomfield, *The Seven Deadly Sins* (East Lansing: Michigan State University Press, 1952), 387–88 n. 107.

57. See, for example, R. H. Bowers, "The Middle English *St. Brendan's Confession*," *Archiv für das Studium der neueren Sprachen* 175 (1939): 40–49; Jean Gerson, *La confession* (Paris [1490]); *La confession generale de frere Olivier Maillart* (Lyon [1485]). The function of the *confessio* is explained by the author of *The Clensyng of Mannes Sowle:* "In this forme of confessioun which I write I schal schewe ȝow diuers spices of ech of hem which in general ben cleped þe seuene dedely synnes. Scheweth tho in which ȝe ben gilty and leueth

the confession of an individual but focus precisely upon the relation of confessional speaking to the self who speaks. Works such as Middle English penitential lyrics and *Piers Plowman* attend above all, and with remarkable perspicuity, to the inner dynamic of the penitential action, and it is upon these texts that we should focus our attention.

While the lyric often does use the *forma* to make possible a complete rehearsal of sins, it is used as well in a more selective and exploratory way in order to structure a dramatized and personal act of penitential reflection.[58] Similarly, while many of these confessional poems are frankly instructive of doctrine or, more usually, emotion, seeking to provide the reader with a pattern of penitential feeling, others qualify this severe impersonality with an implicit psychological dialectic, seeking not simply to arouse or even express sorrow but to show it transformed and made fruitful by confession.[59] That this goal is rarely if ever achieved is itself a function of the way they define their project. For with impressive persistence they refuse to conceive of penitential speaking as less than problematic. Acutely aware of the complexity of contrition—of, that is, the dilemmas and self-contradictions that inhabit the intention that motivates the confessional act they record— these texts seek for a mode of discourse that will be both commensurate to that complexity and yet capable of accommodating the penitent to the institutional authority able to free him from his condition. Their results are, as we might expect, mixed; but what is of more central importance is the fact that they conceive of confessional discourse in problematic terms in the first place. For it is just this problematic that underwrites the complexities and self-contradictions that mark the surface of the *Pardoner's Prologue and Tale*.

An important instance, which shows how penitential anguish simultaneously motivates and forestalls speech, is the Harley lyric, "God, þat al þis myhtes may."[60] By his sin the speaker has alienated himself

---

the remenaunt" (fols. 73ᵛ–74ʳ). The vernacular treatises as a whole—including the *Parson's Tale*—are designed as aids to this kind of reflection.

58. For poems that use the complete *forma*, see the items listed in Brown and Robbins, *Index of Middle English Verse* as numbers 271, 965, 1602, 1959, 1969, 3231, 3233, and 3483; and for its more selective and exploratory use, numbers 253, 374, 1511, 1732, 1839, 2390. (To avoid the proliferation of bibliographical information, all Middle English lyrics will be identified by means of the Brown and Robbins *Index*.)

59. For poems that remain within the confines of demonstration, see *Index*, 1732, 2073, 2390, and 2483.

60. *Index*, 968; printed in Carleton Brown, ed., *English Lyrics of the XIIIth Century* (Oxford: Clarendon Press, 1939), 156–58. Theo Stemmler, "Interpretation des Mittelenglischen Gedichts *God Þat Al Þis Myhtes May*," *Anglia* 82 (1964): 58–75, has demonstrated the poem's careful construction.

from God—"ichabbe be losed mony a day, / er ant late y-be þy foo" (3–4)—and he is now overcome with self-disgust: "when y my-self haue þourh soht, / y knowe me for þe wrst of alle" (15–16); "Ich holde me vilore þen a gyw" (29). Anticipating the finality of judgment, the poet seeks to petition God before all efforts at speech have been foreclosed:

> when we bueþ dempned after vr dede
>   a domesday, when ryhtes bueþ tolde,
> when we shule suen þy wounde blede,
>   to speke þenne we bueþ vnbolde. (37–40)

But not only does the speaker disavow his previous discourse—"fals y wes in crop ant rote, / when y seyde þy lore wes lees" (45–46)—he now finds himself bereft of a language in which to articulate his conversion. Perilously close to despair, he stands speechless before his angry God: "Vnbold icham to bidde þe bote" (41); "louerd crist, whet shal y say?" (50). The poem skirts a spiritual abyss. While its very existence seeks to demonstrate that the penitent has avoided a self-destructive silence, he remains as alienated at the conclusion of the poem as he did at the outset, and his last stanza acknowledges a baffled sense of failure:

> Of myne deden fynde y non fro,
>   ne noþyng þat y þenke may.
> unwrþ icham to come þe to,
>   y serue þe nouþer nyht ne day. (51–54)

Hence the poem's conclusion returns the poet to his beginning, and his last line repeats his first: "In þy merci y me do, / god, þat al þis myhtes may" (55–56). What this speaker lacks is an authorized penitential language, a discourse that will allow him to articulate his insufficiency in terms that promise (even if they cannot in and of themselves provide) repletion. The poem's final line does seek to gesture toward such a language by representing the petitioner in a posture of prayer: it seeks, in an admittedly fragmentary and belated way, to fulfill *confessio peccati* in *confessio laudis*.[61]

A more familiar strategy of resolution and transcendence is to in-

---

61. For *confessio peccati* as *confessio laudis*, see Augustine, *Confessions* 1, 1, 1; 10, 3, 4; Alanus de Insulis, *PL* 210:273; Bernard of Clairvaux, *PL* 182:258. Peter von Moos has defined the genre of the Carolingian lyric *confessio* in "Gottschalks Gedicht *O mi custos— eine confessio*," *Frühmittelalterliche Studien* 4 (1970): 201–30; 5 (1971); 317–58. For other Middle English lyrics that use this theme, as in the refrain "Ay merci, God, and graunte mercy," see *Index*, 374, 2390, 2483, 2687.

voke a moral generalization that can absorb and in effect annul the painful emotion from which the poem takes its beginning. By understanding his life as an instance of a moral law, the penitent not only grants it a certain significance, however dismaying, but can also claim his new self-definition as evidence of his conversion from the past. The *sententia* by which he generalizes his personal experience completes both his poem and his life of sin: possessed of his bitter wisdom, he is self-evidently no longer the man he once was, and in the very course of the poem he is transformed from penitent into sage, directing his words to an audience that has not yet learned the lesson he knows so well. He becomes, in effect, an agent of the institutional authority from which he was originally alienated, and his assumption of these familiar tones marks his reassimilation into the body of the saved.

Hence a poem that begins "In my ʒowþe fulle wilde I was," and includes a carefully individualized confession, can end in a tone of severe impersonality:

> Man take hede what þu art!
> But wormys mete þu wote wel þis!
> Whanne þe erthe hath take his parte,
> Heven or helle wolle haue his.
> Yf þu doest welle þu goest to blis;
> Yf þu do eville vnto þy foo;
> Love þy lorde, and thynke on þis,
> Or wite þy self þyn owne woo![62]

Since he is himself no longer his "owne woo," as he was at the outset, the poet can cede his penitential feelings to others. But this transference is bought at the price of what seems to be a self-alienation, as the ritualistic moralism of this final stanza suggests. Indeed, the same poem appears in another manuscript with an additional sixty-four lines of deadeningly banal moralization tacked on: once the poet has entered into this order of discourse, there is no reason he could not go on forever.[63] Penitential feelings that can find no resolution in the language of the self are thus simply set aside in favor of a consoling self-righteousness.

This failure to find resolution, expressed as the bafflement of contri-

---

62. *Index*, 1511; printed in F. A. Patterson, ed., *The Middle English Penitential Lyric* (New York: Columbia University Press, 1911), 57–59.

63. F. J. Furnivall, ed., *Hymns to the Virgin and Christ*, EETS, OS 24 (London: Trübner, 1864), 35–39.

tion and its turn to despair, is enacted in a form most relevant to the *Pardoner's Tale* in the numerous poems in which the penitent is an old man. The speaker characteristically fears that he has repented too late, that his profession in old age of the values he abused in youth is belated and unwelcome.[64] As the speaker of the so-called *Poema Morale* says,

> Ich myhte habbe bet i-do heuede ich eny selhþe,
> Nv ich wolde and i ne may for elde ne for vnhelhþe;
> Elde is me bi-stolen on er þan ich hit wiste. . . .
> Þe wel nule do hwile he may ne schal he hwenne he wolde.[65]

Age is at once a symbol of sinfulness, the sin itself and, final irony, the punishment, a cheerless decay that stands as nature's mocking parody of the spiritual change that will now never be achieved. Here the old man turns from his anguish to a familiar exhortation to others to do penance; but in another poem, and one especially closely related to the figure of the Old Man in the *Pardoner's Tale*, the aging sinner remains lost in his own spiritual anguish. This poem is "Le Regret de Maximian" and is based on the first elegy of Maximianus, a text that also lies behind the Pardoner's representation of the Old Man.[66] In the Middle English poem Maximian's complaint is uncompromising in its despair. The speaker hates not only the old man he has become but the youth that brought him to it; the poem is an act of utter self-annulment, a betrayal of the past to the bitterness of the present. Even if he had his youthful strength back, he can think of no other use for it than to silence his badgering wife. As we might expect, the poem fails to arrive at a prospect from which the speaker's experience, however sad, can become significant. The act of speaking is thus useless: "Wat helpeþ al itold?" (80), he asks; he lacks even a *sententia* with which to redeem the past: "Deþ ich wolde fawe, / For I ne may tellen no sawe" (199–200). Hence the lament lacks both structure and direction and sinks sullenly to a closing obsession with the present: the self-possession of true recollection is impossible for the self-absorbed mind.

"Le Regret de Maximian" has a special interest for a discussion of the

---

64. Middle English lyrics on old age that focus on penitential themes can be found in *Index*, 349, 718, 880, 1115, 1216, 1454, 1511, 2272.

65. *Index*, 1272; printed in Richard Morris, ed., *An Old English Miscellany*, EETS, OS 49 (London: Trübner, 1872), 58–59 (lines 16–18, 36).

66. *Index*, 1115; I quote from Brown, *English Lyrics*, 92–100. For the relevance of Maximianus's elegy to the Pardoner's old man, see Frederick Tupper, "The Pardoner's Tale," in *Sources and Analogues*, 437; and George R. Coffman, "Old Age from Horace to Chaucer: Some Literary Affinities and Adventures of an Idea," *Speculum* 9 (1934): 249–77.

vicissitudes of contrition, for it has as virtually a companion piece another poem, entitled by its editor "An Old Man's Prayer," that seeks to show how bitter remorse can be transformed into a healing contrition by being articulated in the language of penance.[67] While "An Old Man's Prayer" also opens with bitterness, it revises the feelings and materials of lament in a penitential direction. God has created man both as a lover of "murþes" and a victim of time, and the paradox grieves and baffles the poet. He used to be a man of "semly sawes" (10) but this form of discourse has failed him: he does not now know "what bote is beste" (26). His remedy, however, is not to seek a new saw but a redefinition of the "murþes" that have been lost. Hence he changes his poem from lament to confession by describing his youth in terms of the seven deadly sins:

> whil mi lif wes luþer & lees,
> glotonie mi glemon wes,
>   wiþ me he wonede a while;
> prude wes my plow-fere,
> lecherie my lauendere—
>   wiþ hem is gabbe & gyle—
> Coueytise myn keyes bere,
> Niþe ant onde were mi fere,
>   þat bueþ folkes fyle,
> Lyare wes mi latymer,
> sleuþe & slep mi bedyuer,
>   þat weneþ me unbe while. (52–63)

This penitential perspective redefines both youth and age. The "murþes" of sin are now well left behind and age is not a betrayal but a respite for the penitent to bewail his sin: "Monne mest y am to mene, / lord, þat hast me lyf to lene" (66–67). Now the poet knows both that "murþes helpeþ me no more" (92) and "whet is þe beste bote": to "heryen him þat hath us boht, / vre lord þat al þis world haþ wroht, / fallen him to fote" (100–102). The "dredful deþ" that will not take him—

---

67. *Index*, 1216; I quote from the edition by Carleton Brown, ed., *Religious Lyrics of the XIVth Century*, 2d ed. (Oxford: Clarendon Press, 1952), 3–7. Brown suggests that the similarities between the poems can be fully accounted for by their common dependence on Maximianus's first elegy; but they extend beyond parallels in form and diction to a thematic counterpointing that suggests an intended relationship. Also relevant is the fact that both poems appear in MS Harley 2253, although Brown prints "Le Regret de Maximian" from the much better copy in MS Digby 86.

> why wolt þou dare
> bryng þis body þat is so bare
> ant yn bale ybounde (86–88)

—is now invoked both to release the speaker from a suffering he can no longer endure ("how mai hit lengore laste?" [51]) and to grant him the entrance to eternal bliss:

> Nou icham to deþe ydyht,
>   y-done is al my dede,
> god vs lene of ys lyht,
> þat we of sontes habben syht
>   ant heuene to mede! (103–7)

The old man's anguish is resolved not merely by the hope of salvation but by the prior and larger step of being understood within the penitential process in the first place: the sorrow of old age becomes the sorrow of contrition, and with the closing prayer the poem itself becomes an act of penance.[68]

In "An Old Man's Prayer" the spiritual negations of remorse and regret are articulated in the language of penance and so transformed into a saving contrition. The poem shows how the language of confession can prevent the sorrowful mind from sinking in on itself, as in "Le Regret de Maximian," directing it instead toward patterns of action and feeling in which sorrow becomes fruitful. But while this consoling conclusion accords well with medieval orthodoxy, the counterinstances urge us to recognize that the problem of penance will not yield to any final resolution. For at its heart resides one of the central paradoxes of the Christian *salus animarum:* man is responsible for his own salvation but cannot himself earn it. The force of this issue, and the literary energies that it released, are well demonstrated by the confession scene in *Piers Plowman.* Along with the *Pardoner's Prologue and Tale,* which it may well have served to influence, this is the most accomplished piece of penitential literature in Middle English. It expresses with brilliant economy both the literary manipulations that lie behind both Langland's and Chaucer's creations and the theological concerns that motivate them.[69]

---

68. For other poems that explicitly present themselves as acts of penance, see *Index,* 773, 775, 893, 1066, 3533, and 3774.

69. That Langland's inclusion of pardoners in the estates satire of his Prologue (B, Pro. 68–82) suggested to Chaucer that he too include a Pardoner in the *General Prologue* is

In his representation of the sins Langland draws upon a tradition of homiletic writing in which sinfulness is presented not as an inward condition of the soul but as a deed or at most a habit: the sinner recognizes himself not by what he is but by what he has done.[70] Even when personified and allowed to describe themselves, as in Deguileville's three *Pèlerinages* or in the Morality plays, the Sins remain exteriors, dutifully rehearsing the things that have been said about them: their speeches are hardly more than *tituli* to stand beside crude visualizations.[71] Although often they speak for no reason or in defiance of reason—Deguileville's Avarice carefully unfolds her devices to the pilgrim she is about to attack—their self-revelations are not removed from human range simply by being unmotivated.[72] Belial's "Ho, ho, beholde me!" in one of the Digby plays, for example, springs from a manic self-delight that in its consistent display stands as a sufficient motive; and Faus Semblant's self-exposure in the *Roman de la Rose* is compelled by the God of Love.[73] But even where motivation exists it does not proceed from the sinfulness that is at once embodied and expressed. Jean de Meun, for instance, accords to the paradox of the sincere hypocrite only a passing acknowledgement rather than allowing it to complicate Faus Semblant's self-revelations. The autobiography of medieval allegory, in other words, habitually severs the link between subjectivity and language that helps us to recognize the intention and ultimately the significance of human speech. In Langland's confession scene, on the other hand, the challenge of the allegorical

---

proposed by Jill Mann, *Chaucer and Medieval Estates Satire* (Cambridge: Cambridge University Press, 1973), 149–50, 208–12. This influence would then help to explain the analogy between Langland's confession of the sins and the Pardoner's confession in terms more specific than simply a shared cultural context.

70. For example, the passage on that most inward of sins, envy, in the *forma* of *The Clensyng of Mannes Sowle* details not the envious condition but situations that are the occasion for envious thoughts: "Also in my hert preuely I haue ben sory and lightly ben stered to envie when eny body hath ben better loued than I, more preised, better apparauled, more wurschipped or had more beaute, kunnynge, more of richesse þan I had; such steringes of preuey envie I haue had pasyngly" (fol. 95ʳ–ᵛ). The closest the vernacular treatises on the sins come to showing what envy or the other sins feel like is when they discuss sins of thought as part of the formula *in corde, in ore et in opere*.

71. An example of such a *titulus* is the couplet on pride printed by F. J. Furnivall, ed., *Political, Religious, and Love Poems*, EETS, OS 15 (London: Trübner, 1866), 234: "in alle maner þrifte, y passe alle þingge; / ʒif oni þing be lic me, to det i ssal him bringe."

72. Deguileville, *Pelerinage de lhomme* (Paris, 1511), fols. 67ʳ–72ᵛ.

73. "The Conversion of St. Paul," in *The Late Medieval Religious Plays of Bodleian MSS Digby 133 and E Museo 160*, ed. Donald C. Baker, John L. Murphy and Louis B. Hall, Jr., EETS, OS 283 (Oxford: Oxford University Press, 1982), 15. Daniel Poirion, ed., *Roman de la Rose* (Paris: Garnier-Flammarion, 1974), 10987–11002.

form is accepted, and the link between self-revelation and the self re-vealed is restored. And in forcing upon the Sins the confessional occa-sion they are designed to serve in others, Langland allows them to speak to and from their sinfulness.

At the center of this scene, then, is the central issue that we have been interrogating in this account of penitential writing: the relation of the act of speaking to the sin that is spoken about. This issue becomes central for Langland because he is prepared to take the short step from confession in terms of the sins to confession *by* the sins; but this is a step that requires him to combine the didactic and hortatory substance of one tradition with the investigative purposes of another, to fuse con-tent (the nature of Avarice) with form ("have I committed avarice?"). In Langland's scene Avarice confesses to itself, and the well-worn literary details become now the symptoms of an inward condition. The ques-tion is, can this condition be ameliorated through the act of linguistic self-representation that constitutes confession? By confessing to being itself the Sin enacts the paradox at the heart of penance. "Ich, Pruyde, pacientliche penaunce ich aske" (C, 7, 14), but once patient he is no longer prideful; "'I haue ben coueitous', quod þis caytif, 'I biknowe it here'" (B, 5, 198), but if he was Couetyse (or coueytouse), who is he now?[74] The scene turns not just on a quirk of the allegorical confession but, as we have seen, on the mystery of spiritual rebirth that is at the heart of penance. As the Sin confesses he is caught in the middle of a transformation from the old self that is extinguished in the words it speaks to the new self he hopes to become.

Now what is striking about Langland's scene is that this transforma-tion is habitually thwarted. In part this preemption is an effect of a bland obtuseness that bespeaks a deeper spiritual ignorance. Couetyse of the B text, when asked if he has made *restitution,* proudly describes robbing merchants while they were at *rest* and when corrected complains that he doesn't know any French. But at heart the failure of confession bespeaks a more profound dynamic than this, and Langland shows us how the suffering that is sin itself preempts and absorbs the contritional impulse. Throughout the scene Langland stresses the anguish of sin as much as its hardened impenitence: the self-consumption of Enuye, the endless rage of Wrathe, and the despair of Sloth are traditional attributes that here become an overwhelming spiritual wretchedness. As the author of one

74. Quotations from the A and B texts of *Piers Plowman* are from the editions by George Kane (London: Athlone Press, 1960) and George Kane and E. Talbot Donaldson (London: Athlone Press, 1975); quotations from the C text are from the edition by Derek Pearsall (London: Arnold, 1978).

of the vernacular treatises says, "What likyng haþ þe enuious of his enuye or þe irous of his wraþþe or hate or elles þe coueitous; certes, now[t] but payne."[75] Acutely alert to this suffering, Langland shows us not Sins that are moved by contrition but, in an achievement of far greater complexity, the vicissitudes to which contrition itself is subject within the sinful soul.[76] "Enuye with heuy herte asked after shrifte, / And criede '*mea culpa*' corsynge alle hus enemys" (C, 7, 63–64): the sorrow for sin and desire for amendment that constitute contrition are overwhelmed in the last half-line by the anguish and obsessions of envy. Again, Repentance asks him if he is sorry: " 'I am sory,' quod enuye, 'I am bote selde ooþer; / And þat makeþ me so mat, for I ne may me venge' " (B, 5, 128–29). Enviousness suborns and appropriates the contrition that is its only cure; the pain caused by the sin overwhelms the pain by which sin is cleansed.[77] The same question is asked of several of the other Sins. Can contrition survive Wrathe's fury? Is Glotone contrite or hung over? Can Couetyse worry about his soul when he has to worry about his money? Langland's scene demonstrates how sin destroys its own cure and so condemns itself to itself: he displays the mechanics of despair. By subverting the contrition that would destroy them, the Sins succeed in prolonging their lives of anguish. They condemn themselves to a dying without death and an ending without an end.[78]

Langland's interest in the dynamics of contrition and its relation to

75. *Ignorancia sacerdotum*, Bodley MS Eng. th. c. 57, fol. 8ʳ.

76. Greta Hort's Piers Plowman *and Contemporary Religious Thought* (London: SPCK, [1938]) convincingly demonstrates Langland's contritionism, although her suggestion that his opinions were self-consciously on the verge of heresy seems wide of the mark (130–55). As she says of the confession scene, "The key words of these confessions are not payment, money, but sorrow, shame, and purpose of amendment" (144). For a more recent discussion, see Robert Adams, "Piers's Pardon and Langland's Semi-Pelagianism," *Traditio* 39 (1983): 367–418.

77. In his *Pupilla oculi*, a revision of William of Pagula's *Oculus sacerdotis* written in 1384, John Burgo is careful to distinguish between the pain of contrition and the pain of sin:

Ita cor hominis conteri dicitur, quando affectus peccati secundum omnem sui partem in eo confringitur et totaliter a peccato resilit. Et dicitur huiusmodi contritio dolor voluntarie assumptus: ad differentiam doloris naturalis qui nec est meritorius nec demeritorius pro peccatis ponitus ad differentiam inuidie que est dolor voluntarius de bono alieno. ([Rouen, 1510], 5, 2, B)

78. Descriptions of damnation as an endless dying are ubiquitous in medieval writing; for Middle English examples, see Georgiana Lea Morrill, ed., *Speculum Gy de Warewyke*, EETS, ES 75 (London: K. Paul, Trench and Trübner, 1895), 14, and *The Book of Vices and Virtues*: "And þerfore wiþ good riȝt is þat penaunce cleped deep wiþ-outen ende, for euere-more a man or a womman lyueþ [þere] dyenge, and dyeþ euermore lyuynge" (71).

despair is confirmed by the processes of his revision. In the B text the comically stupid Couetyse falls into *wanhope* and needs the comfort of Repentance's words about the breadth of God's mercy (B, 5, 279–95). In the revision this humor gives place to Couetyse's own careful explanation (from Haukyn's confession in B, 13) of how the anxiety of the miser overcomes care for his soul—an account that once again establishes the power of sin to nullify its antidote. But Langland does not stop here; he strengthens the claims of Repentance by introducing at this point ʒeven ʒeld-aʒeyn and Robert the Ryfeler: they are not univocal allegorical figures but individuals with specific and detailed histories who by their repentance provide proof that despair can be overcome.[79] The effect of this revision is to move beyond the ontological paradox of the penitential action: having demonstrated his contrition by accepting the demands of satisfaction (*Reddite quod debes*), Couetyse is freed from himself and allowed to become a man who can be saved, whether ʒeven or Robert. For these two individuals are arguments against despair because their psychological complexity—their subjectivity—allows them to participate in the *salus animarum* of the Christian dispensation, a dispensation in which the being who was once Couetyse (or coueytouse) can now take his place.

To summarize, then, in the confession scene in *Piers Plowman* Langland revises earlier forms in order to focus upon the nature of contrition and its relation to sin, penitential concerns characteristic of medieval and especially fourteenth-century religious thought. At the center of his account of confession is the problematics of the penitential motive and the ambiguity of its expression. He offers two disparate models of penitential action. One is the confession of the Sins, in which the act of self-representation serves largely to enforce the sense of the intractability of sin: the contritional motive is undermined by the suffering of sin itself, and the act of confession elicits a self-display that preempts the possibility of self-understanding. The other is embodied in the repentances of ʒeven-ʒeld-aʒeyn and Robert the Ryfeler, who provide models of penitential action in which sin is disarmed by being subject to a larger structure of understanding. However we finally adjudicate between these two models of penitential theology, what remains most worthy of note is that they provide Langland's subject in the first place. For it is the inward dynamic of confession, and specifically the

79. There is, however, a loss of force in this revision, for when Robert is removed from his position in the B text following the final confession of Gloton he is no longer able to counter the despair aroused by the whole penitential sequence; see Elizabeth Kirk, *The Dream Thought of* Piers Plowman (New Haven: Yale University Press, 1972), 62–63.

uneasy relation of contrition to despair, that is Langland's central concern—a concern also in evidence, as we have seen, in the Middle English religious lyric. We find in these texts important and perhaps even influential precedents for Chaucer's exploration of the same issues in the *Pardoner's Prologue and Tale*. They offer us, moreover, not only confirming instances of the way in which the theological issues that vexed penitential thinking were enacted in literary texts but also examples of how the problem of verbal self-representation, which is so central to the modern understanding of privation and alienation, was itself part of the dynamic of medieval confessional writing. It is from this matrix that Chaucer's poem emerges.

III

In the *Pardoner's Prologue and Tale* Chaucer's revision of his inherited materials is in the same inward and problematic direction as in these other texts. The one-dimensional monologue of allegory is deepened here not by functioning as the Pardoner's confession but by becoming one element in a larger sequence of involuntary self-exposure that is fulfilled only in the *Tale;* and the *Tale* is in turn transformed by the context of its telling from an exemplum about avarice into a psychological allegory that reveals the Pardoner's despair. The confession of despair, like that of Pruyde or Couetyse, is a theoretical impossibility, and it is this paradox that requires these transformations of genre: the direct self-revelation of autobiography is distorted by strategies of manipulation and concealment, and the negatives of his condition are visible only in the displacements of fiction. It may be that sacramental healing is in fact brought no closer by the Pardoner's confession, but his act of speaking carries a spiritual significance and must be understood within a penitential context. Simply to write him off as an impenitent sinner, and to confine criticism to the task of categorizing and measuring his sinfulness, is to preempt understanding. Not that the desire for critical superiority over the Pardoner is not itself indicative of his significance. For in both his mutilation and in his willingness to imagine sufficiency in Oedipal terms, the Pardoner at once enacts masculinism's deepest fears and challenges a theological orthodoxy that is itself sustained by profoundly masculinist assumptions. However we seek to understand him, the Pardoner places upon our critical faculties, or at least those of the male reader, a sometimes intolerable strain.[80]

80. Criticism has generally stressed the Pardoner's spiritual hard-heartedness, and Kittredge's too memorable description of him as "the one lost soul among the Canterbury

The ironic smile with which the God of Love accepts Faus Semblant's pledge of loyalty is Jean de Meun's perfunctory gesture toward the discontinuity between character and speech implicit in the paradox of the truthful hypocrite. But whereas Jean de Meun evaded the force of the paradox by simply alternating passages of hypocritical piety with those of candid self-revelation, Chaucer defines his character as a professional speaker and so places this discontinuity at the center of his discourse. Language is the means by which the Pardoner creates himself for others and for himself, whether it be the cocksure prattle with which he simultaneously disguises and reveals his eunuchry, or the witty and learned sermon, embellished with telling exempla, with which he establishes his authority before the "lewed people." The *Prologue*, for all its apparent candor, participates in this image making. For there he presents a theatricalized self-representation of evil so extravagant that it necessarily calls itself into question.

The ostensible purpose of the *Prologue* is to demonstrate that the Pardoner knows himself to be "a ful vicious man" (459) motivated by an entirely "yvel entencioun" (408). Tyrannizing the priest and his parishioners, and willfully undermining the penitential system of which he is an agent, the Pardoner appropriates and debases even the scriptural image of the dove by which medieval preaching was typically legitimized:

> Thanne peyne I me to strecche forth the nekke,
> And est and west upon the peple I bekke,
> As dooth a dowve sittynge on a berne. (395–97)

And throughout he insists upon the almost allegorical simplicity of his own motives—"I preche of no thyng but for coveityse" (424)—and glories in his own hypocrisy: "Thus kan I preche agayn that same vice / Which that I use, and that is avarice" (427–28). Delightedly wringing the last penny from a widow with starving children, he consigns the

---

pilgrims" has found support in the enormous number of critical accounts that seek to pass theological and other sorts of judgment upon him. For a recent and powerfully argued instance of this forensic criticism, see R. A. Shoaf, *Dante, Chaucer, and the Currency of the Word* (Norman: Pilgrim Books, 1983), 211–27. As Felicity Currie points out in "Chaucer's Pardoner Again," *Leeds SE* 4 (1970), "What remains intriguing about the Pardoner is that he has elicited identical reactions from his fellow-pilgrims and from decades of critics. To all he is wicked and vile" (11). In "Chaucer's Idea of the Pardoner," *ChR* 14 (1979–80), Beryl Rowland says that "current sympathy with the sexually maladjusted has not yet contributed a convincing defence of the Pardoner" (142). My argument is not that the Pardoner's unusual circumstances solicit our sympathy but that they are themselves metaphorically representative, serving as the means by which he is able to typify both fourteenth-century penitential concerns and larger issues.

souls of his audience to an infernal black-berrying. "Ho, ho, be-holde me!" said Belial, "þe myȝte prynce of þe partys infernall," and the Pardoner's *Prologue* presents itself as an analogous display of self-delighting and unrepentant wickedness. Always the rhetorician, he at once offends the censorious *gentils* and titillates the raucous lower elements (represented by Harry Bailly) by playing to the full the role of the deliberate sinner, the man who has chosen with open eyes the path to his own damnation. Hence he speaks in the uncompromising, and subject-less, tone of allegory and sounds much like Deguileville's Avarice, who tells *her* pilgrim-victim that "I often go through the countryside showing false relics and objects to the simple people in order to hoodwink them out of their money."[81] But rather than being created by the conventions of medieval allegory, the Pardoner himself exploits them. Simultaneously entertaining and horrifying his audience, he adopts allegorical excess as a strategy by which he can at once reveal and conceal himself. The allegorical figure speaks in order to be fully known, while the very extravagance of the Pardoner's revelations hides him from us.[82]

But of course his hyperbole betrays the more complicated self it seeks to conceal. Insisting early and often that his motives are brazenly

---

81. Souvanteffois par le pais
     Faulx sainctuaires et fainctiz
     Va moustrant a la simple gent
     Pour faussement tirer argent.

Le Pelerinage de lhomme, fol. 70ᵛ; cf. *Canterbury Tales*, VI, 953, and I, 694–706. Lydgate's rewriting of these lines shows that he too was struck by the resemblance between Avarice and the Pardoner:

     som tyme by borows and by towns
     I walke about[en] with pardons,
     with reliks, and dedë bones,
     closyd vndar glase and stons:
     I shew them vndar sell and bull,
     and thus the pore people I pull,
     of ther sylvar I make them quite,
     in falsnes I ha so grete delyght.

The Pilgrimage of the Life of Man, ed. F. J. Furnivall (London: Roxburghe Club, 1905), 484 (lines 18103–10).

82. For this sense of the Pardoner's *Prologue* as a deliberate put-on, see James L. Calderwood, "Parody in *The Pardoner's Tale*," *ES* 45 (1964): 302–9; and John Halverson's excellent, "Chaucer's Pardoner and the Progress of Criticism," *ChR* 4 (1969–70): 184–202. This interpretation is close to the more familiar one that sees the Pardoner as an entirely self-conscious entertainer: for example, Paul E. Beichner, C.S.C., "Chaucer's Pardoner as Entertainer," *MS* 25 (1963): 160–72; Ralph W. V. Elliott, "Our Host's 'Triacle': Some Observations on Chaucer's 'Pardoner's Tale'," *REL* 7 (1966), 67–68; and Joyce E. Peterson, "With Feigned Flattery: The Pardoner as Vice," *ChR* 10 (1975–76): 326–36.

simple (403–4, 423–24, 432–33, 461), he also claims—and repeats the claim—that he is doing good works:

> But though myself by gilty in that synne,
> Yet kan I maken oother folk to twynne
> From avarice, and soore to repente. (429–31)
> . . . .
> For though myself be a ful vicious man,
> A moral tale yet I yow telle kan. (459–60)

What makes these hints persuasive is his own response to them, for in both cases he hastily withdraws from these disturbing complications to the comforting simplicity of an unqualified avariciousness. "But that is nat my principal entente," he insists, "I preche nothyng but for coveitise" (432–33), and he continues to claim that his moral tale serves only as a device "for to wynne" (461). And in both these cases, when his own complexity might become visible to himself and to his audience, he cuts off his line of thought with a misdirected and defensive conclusion: "Of this mateere it oghte ynogh suffice" (434); "Now hoold youre pees!"—although only he has been speaking—"my tale I wol bigynne" (462). These fugitive and embarrassed self-defenses show the Pardoner acknowledging in his spirit values he subverts in his working, a complication that occurs again in the notorious benediction with which he closes his *Tale*. In sum, he is by no means as unambiguously impenitent as he claims, and his attempt to reduce himself to the simplicity of allegorical evil itself witnesses to the painfully divided consciousness from which he seeks to escape. By turns derisory and hesitant, vaunting and awkwardly candid, the *Prologue* reveals in its very lack of clarity a spirit in conflict.

Chaucer's representation of this self-division is derived from medieval traditions of penitential theology and confessional writing. Quite apart from the spiritual condition of despair that, as we shall see, motivates the Pardoner's performance as a whole, the vaunting confession of the *Prologue* is itself a conventional penitential form. The *Prologue* is an instance of what in the *summae confessorum* is called a *confessio ficti*—the confession, that is, of an imposter—and of which a number of examples appear in vernacular literature.[83] Middle English instances include Lady Meed's confession to the friar in *Piers Plowman* and the Devil's confession with which Robert Mannyng closes *Handlyng Synne*.[84] The most

---

83. For the *confessio ficti* in the *summae*, see Tentler, *Sin and Confession*, 274–75, 279.
84. *Piers Plowman*, B, 3, 35–63; *Handlyng Synne*, 392–96.

common appearance of the *confessio ficti*, however, is in the Renart story, where Renart confesses no less than five times in all; indeed, his habit of misusing the sacrament led at least one cleric to label the perfunctory or uncontrite confession a *confessio renardi*.[85] The instance closest to Chaucer's poem, and one which he almost certainly knew, is Renart's confession to "frere Huberz" the kite.[86] Desperately hungry, Renart lures the kite within striking distance by confessing, apparently truthfully, that he has in his gluttony devoured even Hubert's children. He begs the horrified kite to forgive him, and when the charitable Hubert leans forward to bestow a kiss of peace Renart gobbles him up. The parallels between this scene and the situation of Chaucer's Pardoner are intriguing: the confession as a trap, the extravagant sinfulness, the crucial role of the kiss of peace, and the ambiguity of both confessions—in neither case can we easily separate truth from fiction—argue for a relationship of influence. But whether this episode is a specific source for Chaucer or not, the analogies suggest that in revising the allegorical monologue Chaucer moved in the direction of the *confessio renardi*. "ʒa, whanne þe fox prechyþ, kepe wel ʒore gees!" is a cautionary Middle English proverb that applies in the first instance to the "lewed people"; but by giving his Pardoner a confessional prologue Chaucer brings it to bear as well upon the pilgrims—and upon the reader.[87]

There is a further difference as well. For the *confessio renardi* remains irrepressibly and unredeemably cynical: the narrator's only comment on Renart's betrayal of Frere Huberz is a laconic "certes ci a mal pecheor / qui a mangé son confessor."[88] But in his reaccenting of these narrative elements, Chaucer uses the penitential situation to create a character who is anxious and dependent. For not only does the trap in this instance close on the Pardoner himself, but the whole relationship between his real and his created selves is less controlled and deliberate. We have already seen how the *Prologue* is a theatricalized self-representation that reveals as it conceals a motivational complexity that

85.   T. F. Crane, ed., *The Exempla . . . of Jacques de Vitry* (London: Folk-lore Society, 1890), 125: "Hec est confessio vulpis, que solet in Francia appellari confessio renardi." See John Block Friedman, "Henryson, the Friars, and the *Confessio Reynardi*," *JEGP* 66 (1967): 550–61; and J.-C. Payen, *Motif*, 547–48 n. 65.

86.   Mario Roques, ed., *Le Roman de Renart*, CFMA 88 (Paris: Champion, 1960), Branche XIV, 37–55. As Charles Muscatine has shown, the name of Chaucer's Friar Huberd is almost certainly taken from the *Roman de Renart* and most likely from this episode (*MLN* 70 [1955]: 169–72). See also John C. Jacobs, trans., *The Fables of Odo of Cheriton* (Syracuse: University of Syracuse Press, 1985), 95–96, for a very similar episode.

87.   For the proverb, see Eccles, ed., *Macro Plays*, 27; see also Friedman, "Henryson," 553 n. 9, and Sedgewick, "Progress," 130.

88.   "He is indeed a wicked sinner who eats his own confessor."

402 The Subject of Confession

yearns for a redemption it simultaneously disdains. This same ambiguity controls the *Tale*. Taken literally, as he recommends, it is an exemplum that means *radix malorum est cupiditas;* but read spiritually it is a moral allegory about the Pardoner himself, and it figures not avarice but despair. On the one hand, the rioters enact the Pardoner's life of self-damnation. Brazenly impenitent—"And ech of hem at otheres synne lough" (476)—they are perverse *imitatores Dei* in action as well as symbol. "Deeth shal be deed, if that they may hem hente!" (710) is their Christological claim; and as R. A. Shoaf points out, "The cry of the prophet [Hosea], 'O death, I will be thy death,' exegesis consistently understands as the triumphant claim of Christ the Redeemer."[89] They engage in the imitation of God symbolically as well: together a parodic Trinity—"we thre been al ones" (696)—they enact as well a dark Eucharistic ritual as "the yongeste of hem alle" (804) serves bread and poisoned wine.[90] And when, like the Pardoner, they issue from their tavern to misperform their divine mission, they receive their just desserts with terrifying efficiency.[91] In the guise of a story of three rioters, the *Tale* presents us with the facts of the Pardoner's case and the future that (he fears) awaits him. Thinking himself an Augustinian *venditor verborum*, the Pardoner is in fact a far more modern being, a Wordsworthian "traveller whose tale is always of himself."[92]

The penitential meaning of the Pardoner's history, with its tortuous inner complexities, is most powerfully expressed in the uncanny figure of the Old Man. Rather than the saintly wise man of the analogues, a

89. Shoaf, *Dante, Chaucer, and the Currency of the Word*, 220, and 274 n. 18.

90. In the A text of *Piers Plowman* Langland says laymen argue about theology and "telleth . . . of the trinite hou two slowen the thridde" (A, 11, 38–40). On Christians as imitators of God, see Ephesians 5:1–4. In the later Middle Ages the injunction to be an *imitator Dei* was directed specifically to those who were, like the Pardoner, preachers. As one medieval writer said, "Would that each preacher were to become such a diligent imitator of Jesus Christ, that he should preach not with the word alone but also with works" (Harry Caplan, "A Medieval Tractate on Preaching," in *Studies in Rhetoric and Public Speaking in Honor of James A. Winans* [New York: Century, 1925], 72). In fact, as Kellogg and Haselmeyer point out, pardoners were forbidden by papal injunction from preaching ("Chaucer's Satire of the Pardoner," 255–57). On the Eucharistic parody, see Robert E. Nichols, Jr., "The Pardoner's Ale and Cake," *PMLA* 82 (1967): 498–504; and Clarence H. Miller and Roberta B. Bosse, "Chaucer's Pardoner and the Mass," *ChR* 6 (1971–72): 171–84.

91. As Stephen Barney has well observed, the *Tale* shows how "the world properly behaves *sub specie aeternitatis*, turning intangibles into tangibles and rendering justice at the end of time" ("An Evaluation of the *Pardoner's Tale*," in Dewey Faulkner, ed., *Twentieth-Century Interpretations of the* Pardoner's Tale [Englewood Cliffs: Prentice Hall, 1973], 90).

92. *Prelude* 3, 198–99.

philosopher or hermit or even Christ, the Pardoner presents a figure who accurately reflects his own irreducible contradictions. Like the Pardoner, the Old Man proffers advice both needful—"Agayns an oold man, hoor upon his heed, / Ye sholde arise" (743–44)—and perilous: "turne up this croked wey" (761). Also like the Pardoner, he knows the truth but is unable to use it. In the terms of the story, he knows where Death is to be found but cannot find it himself, while tropologically he has won through to a gentle wisdom that has done little to relieve his own suffering.[93] Hence he too offers a closing benediction—"God save yow, that boghte agayn mankynde, / And yow amende!" (766–67)— that is in the event self-excluding. For the Old Man's fate is to remain ever unregenerate, whether this be expressed in the allegorical terms of exchanging age for youth or in the theological terms of exchanging the "cheste" of his worldly goods for the "heyre clowt" of penance.[94] As we should remember, he speaks with a voice traditional to the penitential lyric, that of the sinner whose repentance has come too late and whose wisdom is bought at the price of endless anguish. "Deþ ich wilni mest, / Whi nis he me I-core?"[95] These are Maximian's words in his "Regret," and it is precisely Maximianus's first elegy that Chaucer drew upon for this portrait and that directs us to the context of failed penance that helps to explain the Old Man. "Mors est iam requies, vivere mea poena," says the speaker of Maximianus's original poem, and it is this rest that is now denied the Old Man, this punishment that he must now suffer.[96] Like the *quaestor*—the Latin term for a pardoner—whom he faithfully expresses, the Old Man is condemned to a life-in-death of Cain-like wandering, and in his fruitless penitential yearnings he has descended into the hell of despair. Living death, wandering, and steril-

93. That the Old Man proffers the wisdom of age to the rioters is demonstrated by John M. Steadman, "Old Age and *Contemptus Mundi* in *The Pardoner's Tale*," *MAE* 33 (1964): 121–30.

94. Miller, "Chaucer's Pandoner, the Scriptural Eunuch," identifies the Old Man as the *vetus homo* of sin, the antithesis of the *novus homo* who has been reborn, and he points out the Old Man's thwarted penance: "He desires 'an heyre clowt to wrappe' himself in—i.e. the hair shirt of penance, and he wishes to be buried: for the Old Man must be crucified and buried that the New Man may live" (197). Subsequent criticism has rightly argued that to restrict the Old Man to this exegetical significance is unnecessarily reductive; see, for example, the qualifications of Miller's reading offered by Christopher Dean, "Salvation, Damnation, and the Role of the Old Man in the *Pardoner's Tale*," *ChR* 3 (1968– 69): 48 n. 28; and Alfred David, "Criticism and the Old Man in Chaucer's *Pardoner's Tale*," *CE* 27 (1965): 39–44.

95. Brown, *English Lyrics*, 99.

96. A. Baehrens, ed., *Poetae Latini Minores* (Leipzig: Teubner, 1883), 5:316.

ity: these are the characteristics of despair, and they are characteristics shared by the Old Man and by his creator and *alter ego*, the Pardoner.[97]

The Pardoner's own body invites a similar exegesis. Robert Miller, in a widely influential reading, has suggested that we interpret the Pardoner's evident sterility as revealing him to be a *eunuchus non dei*. But this is a by no means common exegetical figure, and if indeed it is to be invoked here then this is, at least to my knowledge, its only vernacular appearance. What also militates against its relevance here is that there is in fact another, homiletically common image of sterility that is both linked to penance, and specifically to despair, and that finds a striking presence in the *Tale* itself. This is the *arbor infructuosa*. The *radix malorum* of the sermon appears in the *Tale* as the "precious hoord" (775) the rioters find at the foot of an "ook" (765), a tree that the exegetes interpret as a symbol of despair.[98] The Pardoner himself is like the fig tree of Matthew 21:18–21 that offers to the hungry Lord not fruit but foliage and is withered with his curse: according to the exegetes, the foliage shows that the tree glories in vain words while lacking the fruit of good works.[99] The Pardoner is one of those "qui verba habent, et facta non habent," and his need is precisely for the "fruit worthy of penance" (Matthew 3:8) that can alone save him from the fire of judgment.[100] "For now the ax is placed to the root of the tree [*ad radicem arborem*]; therefore every tree that does not produce good fruit will be dug up and cast into the fire" (Matthew 3:10). Yet for all its judicial gravity, this sequence of biblical imagery includes a controlling message of mercy in the parable

97.   For texts that make these connections, see the following: Gregory, *PL* 75:821–22, 829; Isidore, *PL* 83:617; Rabanus Maurus, *PL* 107:506–7, *PL* 113:99; Aquinas, *ST* II, 2, 20, 1; Bernard, *PL* 183:989; and especially Bonaventure, in A. C. Peltier, ed., *Opera omnia* (Paris: Vivès, 1868), 13:455–56; see Snyder, "The Left Hand of God," 56–58. For instances in the vernacular, see Richard Morris, ed., *The Pricke of Conscience* (London: Asher, 1865), 7282–89, and Preface, xi; Robert Henryson, *Orpheus and Eurydice*, 310–16, 607–9, in Denton Fox, ed., *The Poems of Robert Henryson* (Oxford: Clarendon Press, 1981). Chaucer's own use of the language of despair is usually in a romantic context, a very common transference in medieval literature: *The Book of the Duchess*, 581–90; *Troilus and Criseyde* 4, 279–80; 1, 603–9; 2, 526–32; and see the "Complaint Against Hope," Kenneth G. Wilson, ed., *University of Michigan Contributions in Modern Philology* 21 (Ann Arbor: University of Michigan Press, 1957).

98.   For the oak as "duritia desperationis," see Bernard F. Huppé and D. W. Robertson, Jr., *Fruyt and Chaf: Studies in Chaucer's Allegories* (Princeton: Princeton University Press, 1963), 55; and Carolyn P. Collette, " 'Ubi Peccaverant, Ibi Punirentur': The Oak Tree and the *Pardoner's Tale*," *ChR* 19 (1984–85): 39–45.

99.   Hilary of Poitiers, *PL* 9:1037; Drumarthus, *PL* 106:1434; Rabanus Maurus, *PL* 107:1044; Radbertus, *PL* 120:714.

100.   Augustine, *PL* 37:1688; and see also *PL* 36:264 and, especially, 334: "Vide in verbis numerositatem, et in factis sterilitatem."

of the sterile fig tree in Luke 13:7–9. The *paterfamilias* commands that the tree be uprooted and destroyed, but the *cultor* advises that it be ditched and dunged and given one last chance; according to the exegetes the ditch is "humilitas poenitentis" and the dung "memoria peccatorum" and "cordis luctus et lacrymarum."[101] That "an evil tree cannot bring forth good fruit" (Matthew 7:18) remains an inviolable principle, but as Augustine (among others) insists, each righteous Christian has been *made* a fruitful tree: "Whoever therefore is today a good man, that is, a good tree, was found evil and has been made good."[102] The *radix arboris*, the human will, can be changed by penance from *cupiditas* to *caritas:* "so turn your eyes into yourself, descend into yourself, challenge yourself, appraise yourself, question yourself, and discover yourself: and what displeases you, destroy it; what pleases you, choose it and cultivate it."[103]

The *Pardoner's Tale* contains an accurate account of the Pardoner's own spiritual condition, but it is one that he is himself apparently incapable of reading. His understanding of the spiritual life is as obstinately literal as that of the rioters, who set out on a journey to kill "this false traytour Deeth" (699).[104] His sermon on the tavern vices conceives of sin in terms that are almost compulsively corporeal—the fall is ascribed not to disobedience but to gluttony—and his rhetoric throughout is pervaded with hyperbole pushed to the edge of personification: "O wombe! O bely! O stynkyng cod, / Fulfilled of dong and of corrupcioun!" (534–35). Indeed, we are encouraged to understand his spiritual impasse as an effect of his own literalistic misreading of himself. As we have seen, contrition includes powerful, at times overwhelming negations, its separate aspects traditionally termed *pudor, detestatio, dolor,* and *timor.* In self-evident ways each of these emotions is known to the Pardoner, but they derive not from spiritual self-inspection but from corporeal self-regard. Ashamed of a literal eunuchry, he hides behind a far more shameful spiritual sterility; fearing exposure to his companions, he mocks the

101. Augustine, *PL* 36:569, *PL* 36:1027, *PL* 38:467–70, *PL* 38:467–70, and *PL* 38:638–39; Gregory, *PL* 76:1229–30 and *PL* 79:51; Bruno of Segni, *PL* 165:402; Haymo, *PL* 118:698–99.

102. "Quisquis igitur homo hodie bonus est, id est, arbor bona, mala inventa est et bona facta est" (*PL* 38:467); see also *PL* 34:1305–6.

103. "Ut in semetipsum oculos convertat, in se descendat, se discutiat, se inspiciat, se quaerat, et se inveniat: et quod displicet, necet; quod placet, optet et plantet" (Augustine, *PL* 38:468).

104. The Pardoner's culpable literalism is a persistent theme in the criticism of the *Tale:* see, for example, A. Leigh DeNeef, "Chaucer's *Pardoner's Tale* and the Irony of Misinterpretation," *JNT* 3 (1974): 85–96; Warren Ginsberg, "Preaching and Avarice in *The Pardoner's Tale,*" *Mediaevalia* 2 (1976): 77–99.

judgment of God; his sorrow is not for "the loss of heaven and his many offenses against the Creator" but simply *de ipso;* and his hatred is not for "the vileness of sin" but for the vileness of his own body. In the *Parson's Tale* Chaucer quotes St. Paul's famous lament, "Allas, I caytyf man! who shal delivere me fro the prisoun of my caytyf body?"[105] In a sense that exceeds his comprehension, this is the meaning of the Pardoner's words. But only in the symbolic form of the "resteless kaityf" is he able to acknowledge his condition. Deprived by what the exegetes would call his "ariditas litterae" from understanding the spiritual meaning of his own discourse, the Pardoner enacts his confessional needs through a series of oblique displacements. The *Prologue* presents inflated self-advertisements and fugitive glimpses of a more genuine self; the *Tale* displaces into fiction the Pardoner's deepest self-understanding while hiding its meaning from the man who speaks. Finally the offer of the relics comes as the fitting conclusion to this sequence, an elliptical and compact gesture that is as self-contradictory as the Pardoner's previous utterances. On the one hand, it asks for inclusion, either in the fellow feeling of a jest or the earnest respect due a "suffisant pardoneer" (932); on the other hand, and especially in its taunting of the Host ("he is moost envoluped in synne" [942]), it solicits exclusion and punishment. The punishment that is then inflicted is painfully apt, for it brings into the open the physical source of the spiritual fruitlessness that only true confession can finally cure. In its full dimensions, then, as an invitation to be hurt and to be forgiven, this epilogue exactly fulfills the postconfessional part of penance: in its shaming of the Pardoner it provides—as the confessional handbooks advise—an appropriate punishment, and it serves to elicit a gesture of absolution: "Anon they kiste and ryden forth hir weye" (968).[106]

IV

This interpretation of the *Pardoner's Prologue and Tale* is satisfyingly efficient: it accommodates a dauntingly complicated verbal performance

---

105. Line 344, quoting Romans 7:24.

106. In the Mass, the Pax or kiss of peace is exchanged after the Fraction—the breaking of the bread that signifies both the act of sacrifice and the violation of community—and prior to communion: it is a way of restoring community before the act of communal eating (see John Bossy, "The Mass as a Social Institution, 1200–1700," *Past and Present* 100 [1983], 52). Discussions of penance almost always include the shame of exposure as part of the satisfaction for the sin; see Teetaert, *Les Confessions*, 277, 297, and passim. Also relevant here is the fact that the spiritual value of shame stems in part from its role in bringing the sinner to genuine contrition.

to a stable structure of imagery and thought derived from the penitential system of which the Pardoner is an agent, and it explains the Pardoner's own mutilation as a symbolic representation of his spiritual
condition. But like all interpretations, it is in no sense simply a disinterested explication of meanings with which the text is endowed, an innocent reading out of that which the author has written in. On the contrary, it responds to certain interests and needs—needs that the text
itself both solicits and, with characteristic self-awareness, dramatizes.
The agency of dramatization is the contretemps between the Host and
the Pardoner. We should remember that at the center of the Pardoner's
performance is the gap between intention and language: not only a
vicious man who can tell a moral tale, he is as well a speaker whose
language serves simultaneously to conceal and expose him, at once to
shroud his deepest spiritual needs and yet to enact them. Moreover,
this is a gap that is, as we have seen, meaningful in terms familiar to
both medieval and modern thought. On the one hand, it articulates the
medieval understanding of sin as privation, a lack that the language of
confession promises (perhaps overambitiously) to ameliorate. And on
the other hand, it expresses the modern analysis of the difference between self-representation and self-presence as a rift or split endemic to
a symbolic order that is itself the effect of a primal repression—a repression, moreover, that is both a disabling castration and the means by
which the male subject is constituted.

Now the point for our purposes is that these two orders of understanding are brought together in the final, enigmatic exchange between Host and Pardoner, an exchange that reveals as well the interpreter's own implication within this linguistic economy. For one thing,
it shows how the exegetical reading that the Pardoner's discourse elicits itself bespeaks the very need that motivates the Pardoner himself.
When the Host is offered the relics, he responds with a comment that
raises the issue not merely of the Pardoner's castration but of the linguistic instability that makes possible his verbal pyrotechnics:

> I wold I hadde thy coillons in myn hond
> In stide of relikes or of seintuarie.
> Lat kutte hem of, I wol thee helpe hem carie;
> They shul be shryned in an hogges toord! (952–55)

These lines are derived from a crucial passage in the *Roman de la Rose*, in
which Raison justifies to the prudish lover her use of the word *coilles* to
refer to the testicles that Jupiter cut off his father Saturn and threw into

the sea.[107] Raison argues that whether she used the word *reliques* or *coilles* is a matter entirely of convention, and she demonstrates her point by saying that if we used the word *coilles* to refer to what we now call relics then we would adore *coilles* in church, and we would kiss them and enshrine them in gold and silver—a passage that so offended the scribes that it is excised from several of the manuscripts.[108] This scribal squeamishness is indicative of just how much is invested in the fiction of a natural or innocent signification, in the belief, for instance, that the phonetic image *coilles* bears a relationship to testicles that is more than merely arbitrary. For we habitually assume that the relation of words to things is not conventional but natural, that words like *reliques* are necessarily tied to certain things and cannot wander promiscuously from, for instance, sacred and venerated objects to genitals.[109] It is just this instinctive belief in a natural and innocent signification that Raison subverts in her equation of *coilles* and *reliques*. Moreover, by deriving her example from the scene of Saturn's castration she invokes the initial act of severance by which the golden age of natural innocence was separated from the fallen world of history. Because of the absence or lack of verbal sufficiency, meaning is now a function of a convention that can (presumably) be changed at will. Hence the success of the Pardoner's verbal pyrotechnics: a castrate himself, he deploys words that are by definition empty to mean whatever he wants.[110]

Now it is the exegetical reading of the Pardoner that promises an antidote to this castrated language. When read exegetically, his *Pro-*

107. *Roman de la Rose*, ed. Poirion, lines 7064–152 (212–14). The relevance of this passage to the Pardoner's performance was first made clear to me by Carolyn Dinshaw in a paper delivered at the MLA in December 1984; and my reading of this passage is much indebted to her account and to that by R. Howard Bloch, *Etymologies and Genealogies: A Literary Anthropology of the French Middle Ages* (Chicago: University of Chicago Press, 1983), 137–41.

108. See the textual notes to lines 7120–21 in Ernest Langlois, ed., *Le Roman de la Rose*, SATF (Paris: Champion, 1921), 3:279.

109. Indeed, even Raison asserts the natural fitness of words and things—a fitness that her discourse as a whole serves to undermine—when she says that she was empowered by God to name things, and that she therefore named them "proprement" (7093): everything has, apparently, a proper name—precisely the assumption that her discussion of *reliques* and *coilles* shows to be unwarranted.

110. As Stewart Justman ("Literal and Symbolic in the *Canterbury Tales*," *ChR* 14 [1979–80]: 199–214) points out, "Words are of a symbolic order, a quantum apart from lived experience. There is nothing objectionable in an immoral man's telling a moral tale, but that act clearly implies that words are disconnected from reality. . . . The Pardoner may ironically remind us of the purely symbolic, un-real character of words. As a professional talker, the Pardoner finds it easy enough to exploit the falsity inherent in language" (207).

logue and Tale are an instance of what Roland Barthes in *S/Z*, itself a book about a book about castration, calls Replete Literature. Rather than "the *nothingness* of castration, [in which] the envelope of things cannot be authenticated [and] the dilatory movement of the signifier cannot be stopped," we have in an exegetically read *Pardoner's Tale* a classic or readerly text, one that is "like a cupboard where meanings are shelved, stacked, safeguarded (in this text, nothing is ever lost: meaning recuperates everything)."[111] The endless deferral that characterizes writing is in the readerly text cut short by a single, authoritative hermeneutic code.[112] To the reader armed with the repertory of exegetical meanings, the deceptive veiling with which the Pardoner seeks to conceal his despairing condition serves only to proclaim it. Despite his efforts to speak the merely literal language of exemplum, both he and his *Tale* are controlled by the spiritual subtext of an allegory that signifies despair. In other words, exegetical reading is a way of rendering the Pardoner harmless.

That he needs to be disarmed is demonstrated both by the apparently endless production of forensic readings of the Pardoner and by the reaction of the Host.[113] The Host fears that the Pardoner will force him to submit to a humiliating ritual of scatological adoration:

> Thou woldest make me kisse thyn olde breech,
> And swere it were a relyk of a seint,
> Though it were with thy fundement depeint! (948–49)

Alluding to the famous relic of St. Thomas's breeches that were awaiting the pilgrims at Canterbury, the Host in effect accuses the Pardoner of trying to preempt the pilgrimage by substituting his counterfeits for the true relics that urge them on their pilgrim way.[114] Yet the language of his accusation, with its fascination with the corporality that is itself so much a part of the Pardoner's own discourse, shows how profoundly the Host's imagination has been infiltrated by that which he here seeks to exorcise. In summoning up a parodic representation of the true relic, saturated now not with the healing power of sanctity but with bodily waste, he effaces, in a gesture of infantile regressiveness, the goal of his own spiritual efforts. Barthes is thus evidently right

111. Trans. Richard Howard (New York: Hill and Wang, 1974), 122–23, 200–201.
112. Ibid., 75.
113. See above, note 80.
114. For the allusion to St. Thomas's breeches, see Daniel Knapp, "The Relic of a Seint: A Gloss on Chaucer's Pilgrimage," *ELH* 39 (1972): 1–26.

when he says that to the masculinist mind, "Castration is contagious, it touches everything it approaches": the compulsions of the Pardoner become those of his audience.[115] The Host's parody unwittingly reveals how easy it is to imagine St. Thomas's holy breeches as fouled garments. Once the underwriting spiritual presence has been called into question, is it relics we kiss or feces?

The exegetical reading seeks to restore that presence. It stabilizes the letter with a spiritual truth that is anchored in institutional orthodoxy and reasserts a norm of linguistic rectitude that chastens the promiscuity of the letter. Yet in an important sense exegetics also partakes of the very condition it seeks to amend. It is a hermeneutics for a fallen world, and if it spiritually replenishes the letter it must also dispense with distracting and even illicit meanings. Allegorical reading is able to do its healing work only by first instituting a deep cleavage between the letter and the spirit. In order to be redeemed by spiritual significance, the letter must first be drained of historical value: youth in the *Pardoner's Tale* is a condition not of chronological earliness but spiritual rebirth; the Old Man is not an old man but spiritual despair; the rioters' oak tree is not a tree but an *arbor infructuosa*. And the Pardoner is not an individual member of the human community but Chaucer's "one lost soul." Exegetics is a hermeneutics of suspicion whose first step is an act of exclusion, of cutting off, that necessarily renders the text it finally does recuperate less than complete. And these are acts of repudiation that proclaim precisely the fear of insufficiency exegetics is designed to overcome.

What the exegetically augmented *Pardoner's Tale* must exclude is expressed in the Old Man's famous self-description, a passage that however well known will bear repeating:

> Ne Deeth, allas, ne wol nat han my lyf,
> Thus walke I, lyk a restelees kaityf,
> And on the ground, which is my moodres gate,
> I knokke with my staf, bothe erly and late,
> And seye 'Leeve mooder, leet me in!
> Lo how I vanysshe, flessh, and blood, and skyn!
> Allas, when shul my bones been at reste?
> Mooder, with yow wolde I chaunge my cheste

---

115. Barthes, 198. As John Halverson, "The Progress of Chaucer's Pardoner," rightly says about the confrontation with the Host, "It is not that the Pardoner is evil, but that he is somehow deadly" (200). For a reading in terms of this deadliness, see Derek Pearsall, "Chaucer's Pardoner: The Death of a Salesman," *ChR* 17 (1983–84): 358–65.

That in my chambre longe tyme hath be,
Ye, for an heyre clowt to wrappe me!'
But yet to me she wol nat do that grace,
For which ful pale and welked is my face. (727–38)

These lines articulate the desire for penitential conversion in terms that
are unavoidably Oedipal, and they pose for the reader a central interpretive problem: what is the relationship between these two orders of
understanding? On the one hand, the Old Man is expressing a desire
that is fully comprehensible within the terms of penitential action: he
wishes to exchange the chest of his worldly goods for the hair cloth of
contrition.[116] And yet on the other hand, the act imagined here is a
transaction conducted not with the Divine Father who sits in judgment
but with the Mother Earth who is the chthonic, and unsanctified,
source of life.[117] And when placed in this maternal context, these lines
solicit another reading: the chest can be construed as the coffin that
awaits the Old Man, and the hair clout as the swaddling clothes of
infancy—one of the primary meanings of the Middle English *clowt*—
and also perhaps as the even more primal genital hair within which can
be found the physical origin from which he took his beginning.[118]

116. See Miller, "Scriptural Eunuch," 197–98.
117. For a fourteenth-century account of Mother Earth, see the gloss by Nicole
Oresme to his translation of the pseudo-Aristotelian *Oeconomica*: "Et selon ce, les poetes
appellent la terre la grand mere, si comme Virgille, qui dit: Salve magna parens frugum
saturnia tellus [*Georgics* II, 73]. Et Ovide dit que les os de la grant mere laquelle est la terre:
Magna parens terra est; lapides in corpore terre ossa reor dici [*Metam.* I, 393]. Et en la
Saincte Escripture est dit: Usque in diem sepulture in matrem omnium [*Ecclicus.* 40:1]. Et
donques, aussi comme l'enfant est nourri du lait de sa mere, nature humaine est nourri
des fruis de la terre et est chose naturele" (Nicole Oresme, *La Livre de Yconomique
d'Aristote*, ed. and trans. Albert Douglas Menut, *Transactions of the American Philosophical
Society*, NS 47, part 5 [1957], 810). For pictorial representations, see Ilene H. Forsyth,
"Children in Early Medieval Art: Ninth through Twelfth Centuries," *Journal of Psychohistory* 4 (1976–77), 48 and n. 38; see also 32, where Forsyth describes how the illustrator of
the Utrecht Psalter illustrates Psalm 84:12 ("Truth shall spring out of the earth") with an
image of a newborn babe held aloft by its mother.
118. For "cheste" as coffin and "clowt" as swaddling clothes, see *MED*, s.v. In *Le
Regret de Maximian*, the speaker says, "Ich wolde ich were on rest, / Wel lowe leid in a
chest" (Brown, *English Lyrics of the XIIIth Century* (Oxford: Clarendon Press, 1939), 98
[lines 202–3]). For "clowt," see "Song of the Husbandman": "And at the londes ende lay
a litell crom-balle, / And there on lay a littel childe lapped in *cloutes*, / And tweyne of tweie
yeres olde opon another syde" (cited, Barbara A. Hanawalt, "Conception Through Infancy in Medieval English Historical and Folklore Sources," *Folklore Forum* 13 [1980]: 141);
and "Lullay, lullay litel child," a lullaby to the Christ Child, in Brown, *Religious Lyrics of the
XIVth Century*: "Child, it is a weping dale þat þu art comen inne, / þi pore *clutes* it prouen
wel, þi bed mad in þe binne" (83 [lines 13–14]).

The moment of fulfillment is thus imagined not as atonement with the Father but as reunion with the Mother, a return to primal oneness that the entrance into the fallen world of history has ruptured. And the confrontation with which the performance as a whole concludes provides the aetiology of this severance: presenting himself to the Host as "a *suffisant* pardoneer" (832), the Pardoner is threatened with castration: "Lat kutte hem of" (954). The claim of sufficiency—of self-sufficiency— transgresses a primal, paternal taboo, and the punishment consists in a maiming that undermines every effort at authenticity. Yet the dream persists, the phantasmic desire for a return to the Mother who will reengorge the child and make him whole and will cancel the death that awaits him by reuniting him with the maternal source of all life. Thus the Oedipal reading of these lines stands in contrast, even in opposition, to their penitential meaning. On the one hand is the desire to atone with the Father through self-abasement and suffering (the chest of worldly goods, the clout of penance); on the other is the desire to escape from the world of fallen history into an imagined sufficiency that is provided (however illicitly) by the mother and denied (with brutal consequences) by the father.

My purpose here is not to adjudicate between these readings but rather to use their difference to reapproach the Chaucerian fascination with origins, and especially with origins imagined in terms of the Theban legend. We can, I believe, trace the literary path by which a penitential motif was translated into Oedipal terms; and such an itinerary can make visible (although not explain) something of the mystery at the center of the Chaucerian imagination. For in the Middle Ages the classical figure of Oedipus became linked with the theological condition of despair, the agency of this linkage being the biblical figure of Judas. According to medieval exegetes, while Cain was the Old Testament type of *desperatio*, it was his New Testament fulfillment Judas who expressed in the most painful and uncompromising form the fatal economy of despair.[119] As religious writers endlessly repeat, Judas sinned more in hanging himself—that is, in preferring self-destruction to penance—than he did in selling Christ.[120] In order both to explain such impenitence and yet to reaffirm the power of divine mercy, the Middle

119. For Cain and Judas as types of despair, see Snyder, "The Left Hand of God," 31–34.

120. For one instance of the doubtless hundreds that could be cited, see Augustine: "Cum enim dixisset Judas, *Peccavi, quod tradiderim sanguinem justum;* facilius tamen desperatione cucurrit ad laqueum quam humilitate veniam deprecatus est" (PL 34:1266). For vernacular instances, see *Handlyng Synne,* 171; *Speculum Christiani,* 72.

Ages constructed for Judas a legendary pre-scriptural history that re-wrote the Oedipal narrative in penitential terms.[121]

Exposed as an infant by his parents in an effect to evade a prophecy that he would bring ruin to them and to his race, Judas became the adoptive son of a foreign king and queen. But in an envious rage he killed their natural son, a Cain-like act of fratricide for which he was driven out. Becoming then the trusted servant of Pontius Pilate (or, in some versions, Herod), he was ordered by his master to steal apples from an enclosed orchard; and it was in the course of this Adamic viola-tion that he killed the orchard's owner, who was (unbeknownst to him) his father. Then, as one version puts it, "lest, because of a single crime, he pass on to some greater risk,"[122] his master had him marry the man's widow, thus completing the fatal act of recursion—an act that one text significantly describes in the language of Thebanness: "In suos ortus monstrum revolvitur."[123] When Judas and his mother learned of their relationship, they sought relief from their horror by turning to the new teacher they had been told about, Jesus Christ. As the following pas-sage from the fullest, most sophisticated version of the legend makes clear, this climactic event was used to demonstrate God's capacity for forgiveness and renewal:

> Judas with his mother and wife went to him, and prostrate at his feet revealed to him the whole history of his crimes; indeed, he displayed the condition, grief, and tears of true penitence. Now the Lord Jesus, having seen the man, and since from the beginning he had renewed those who believed, knowing how far he had been from the kingdom of God, lest for all that he should be driven by despair further into peril, said: "At this point you can be saved if you will worthily repent, but while you live you must no longer give yourselves either to this or to other sins; and so that all occasion for sin will from now on be taken away from you, follow me and reject all impediments and worldly doings; and by imitating me you will in truth be able to receive eternal life."[124]

121. For these legends, see Paull Franklin Baum, "The Mediaeval Legend of Judas Iscariot," *PMLA* 24 (1916): 481–632. For the medieval Oedipus, see Lowell Edmunds, "Oedipus in the Middle Ages," *Antike und Abendland* 22 (1976): 140–55; and Edmunds, *Oedipus: The Ancient Legend and Its Later Analogues* (Baltimore: Johns Hopkins University Press, 1985), 61–88.

122. For this phrase, see Edmunds, *Oedipus*, 62. In other versions the marriage is undertaken either as an act of wickedness or to try to placate the outraged neighbors.

123. Baum, "Mediaeval Legend," 507.

124. Illum Iudas cum matre uxiorque adiit affususque pedibus eius criminis sui

But the lure of his evil origin was evidently too great for Judas, and with his betrayal of Christ and final despairing suicide a story that meant to argue for the power of penitential conversion comes finally to illustrate a darker lesson about the compulsions of wickedness.[125]

In a sense, of course, Judas's legendary assumption of the Oedipal crimes of parricide and incest serves simply to define him as an embodiment of wickedness; they are the classical counterparts, as it were, of his scriptural crimes of fratricide and the theft of fruit from the paternal garden. But in a deeper sense, these crimes bespeak not simply an irredeemable evil but a desire that is unspeakable but nonetheless unavoidable, a need that insists upon fulfillment, even at the cost of an ultimate exclusion. The father must be killed so that the mother may be possessed, and the final handing over of Christ to death is an inevitable reenactment of this act of initial return. As the son is called back to the mother, so is Judas called back to his original nature; and the paternal injunction of penance—"you can be saved if you will worthily repent"—must be rejected both now and forever. Despair is, after all, the inability to repent—the inability, that is, to change: the man in despair cannot get rid of the self of illicit desires in order to assume the reborn self of innocence.[126] It is in this sense, then, that despair is the

---

omnem historiam ei detexit, veri etiam penitentis habitum, luctum et lacrimas pretendit. Dominus autem Iesus intuitus hominem et quod noverat ab initio qui essent credentes, sciens quam longe esset a regno Dei, tamen ne desperatione salutis cogeretur amplius periclitari, 'Potes,' inquit, 'adhuc salvus fieri si digne penitueris, sed et hec et cetera peccata deinceps vitaveris nec etiam ad maiora te inclinaveris, et ut omnis occasio peccandi ulterius tibi tollatur, reiectis omnibus impedimentis et secularibus negoiciis sequere me meque imitando in veritate vitam eternam habere poteris.

Baum, "Mediaeval Legend," 508. See also 490–91 and 494.

125.   A rewriting of the Oedipus narrative in wholly positive penitential terms is found in the Legends of Pope Gregory; see Edmunds, "Oedipus in the Middle Ages" and *Oedipus,* 79–88.

126.   In *The Sickness Unto Death,* Søren Kierkegaard provided a powerful analysis of despair in which he focuses on just this quality of immobility, the despairing man's imprisonment within a hated self:

The fact that despair does not consume him is so far from being comfort to the despairing man that it is precisely this that keeps the gnawing pain alive and keeps life in the pain. This precisely is the reason why he despairs—not to say despaired—because he cannot consume himself, cannot get rid of himself, cannot become nothing. This is the potentiated formula for despair, the rising of the fever in the sickness of the self. . . . Hence it is a superficial view (which presumably has never seen a person in despair, not even one's own self) when it is said of a man in despair, "He is consuming himself." For precisely this it is that he despairs

appropriate condition of the Oedipus, which is itself perhaps the ulti-mate form of immobility. Unwilling to accept that the original union with the mother has been definitively ruptured, the Oedipus refuses to enter into the world of time and change. Instead he overrides the pater-nal prohibition in order to reclaim, over and over again, a maternal love that can alone render him "suffisant."

It is as a figure of despair driven by incestuous yearnings that the Old Man of the *Pardoner's Tale* invokes the figure of Judas. Perhaps he also invokes him, and his Old Testament prefiguration, Cain, in a spe-cific detail. Despite their crudeness, the following lines from the fourteenth-century *Cursor Mundi* express both the shared fate of Cain and Judas and part of its relevance to the Old Man:

> O judas and o caim als-sua,
> And o sli sinful manian maa,
> Þat wines for þair mikel sin
> Neuer to merci for to win,
> And suaget for þair wanhopping,
> Þai fall wit-vten vp-couering.
> For es namen mai merci haue
> Þat wil noght ask and efter craue.[127]

"Þai fall wit-vten vp-couering": here *Cursor Mundi* is referring to the legendary inability of Cain and Judas to reenter the earth from which they came. Cain is condemned to eternal wandering because the earth, having been polluted with his brother's blood, now refuses to receive him.[128] Driven by despair, Cain seeks for death but cannot find it: as Augustine says, in a suggestive passage, "he indeed sought for death, but no one would give to him what he had himself given to his

---

of, and to his torment it is precisely this he cannot do, since by despair fire has entered into something that cannot burn, or cannot burn up, that is, into the self. Trans. Walter Lowrie (Garden City: Doubleday Anchor Books, n.d.), 151–52. This ac-count can usefully be compared with the Augustinian analysis of sin, summarized in similar terms by Kellogg: "The pain [the sinner] would be rid of he can never escape, for the good nature, the work of God within him which experiences pain, can never be destroyed no matter how deeply he sins" ("Augustinian Interpretation," 467).

127. Richard Morris, ed., EETS, OS 68 (London: K. Paul, Trench and Trübner, 1878), 5:1476 (lines 25816–23).

128. See Oliver Emerson, "Legends of Cain, Especially in Old and Middle English," *PMLA* 21 (1906): 837–939; David Williams, *Cain and Beowulf: A Study in Secular Allegory* (Toronto: University of Toronto Press, 1982), 19–39.

brother."[129] Through Cain death entered the world, but he himself cannot now find the death he so desperately seeks—a condition succinctly
enacted by the Old Man, who can direct the rioters to death but cannot
find it himself. And as for Judas, in hanging himself he reinvokes
Cain's exclusion: according to the exegetes, he died suspended between earth and heaven because neither men nor angels would acknowledge him as a member of their respective orders.[130]

Hence, apparently, the Old Man's hopeless knocking on the earth
with his phallic staff—

> And on the ground, which is my moodres gate,
> I knokke with my staf, bothe erly and late,
> And seye "Leeve mooder, leet me in!'

—a gesture that is at once violent and pathetic, both sexually illicit
and, in its invocation of maternal care, oddly touching. Yet this is a
gesture that also invokes, with persuasive specificity, a central Theban
act; and it reveals to us that while the idea of the Old Man may have
been suggested to Chaucer by the scriptural figures of Judas and, to a
lesser extent, Cain, the terms in which he is actually imagined are
those of the original Theban model. The *Thebaid* opens with Oedipus
locked within his subterranean cavern, "beating with blood-stained
hands upon the hollow earth."[131] This is a gesture that replicates an
event that occurred at the beginning of Theban history: according to
Ovid's *Metamorphoses*, as the dragon-warriors were dying in their
fractricidal fury, they "beat their mother upon her breast warm with
blood."[132] It is this beating that the Old Man now reenacts, and when
we locate his action within this Theban context other Oedipal analogies become visible. The staff with which he knocks "bothe *erly* and
late," for instance, invokes both Oedipus's own crippled life—
hamstrung as a boy, blinded as an old man—and the Sphinx's rid-

---

129.   Augustine, *Contra Julianum:*
Cain vero fratricidae apparet omnibus immane peccatum, et scelus esse constat
horrendum. . . . Et cum ille audiens terram non sibi daturam fructum secundum
laborem suum, et super eam cum gemitu et tremore miserum se futurum, magis
mortis formidine quateretur, ne quis ei faceret, quod ipse fecerat fratri.
PL 45:1555; cited by Williams, *Cain and Beowulf*, 104 n. 28.

130.   As one of the legendary narratives about Judas states, "In aere etiam interiit, ut
qui angelos in coelo et homines in terra offenderat, ab angelorum et hominum regione
separaretur et in aere cum daemonibus sociaretur" (Baum, "Mediaeval Legend," 518 n.
29; and see 517–18).

131.   "Manibus cruentis / pulsat inane solum" (1, 54–55).

132.   "Sanguineam tepido plangebat pectore matrem" (3, 125).

dle.[133] So too, both the classical and medieval Oedipus are described in terms that unmistakably recall the theological condition of despair, and in a number of details the Old Man incorporates this understanding. In the *Thebaid* Oedipus outlives the sons whom he has cursed, and his lingering and grief-stricken old age is described by Statius as a "mortem imperfectam" (11, 582) and a "funera longa" (11, 696). And as Fulgentius said in his commentary on the *Thebaid*, Oedipus's self-blinding is a sign of how "the licentious mind, afflicted with horror at its sin, tortures itself."[134]

In the *Ovide moralisé*, the blinding and self-incarceration in an underground dungeon is a desperate effort to expiate this guilt: "He wishes to suffer penance, to offer his body to suffering; to expiate the sin of the father he has killed he encloses himself in a dungeon."[135] But according to the allegory, the darkness of both his blindness and his subterranean habitation mimics the infernal suffering he must forever endure. As Statius had said at the outset of the *Thebaid*, Oedipus "endured a long and living death"[136] and at the end of the poem, burdened with "a savage desire for a bitter death," he is exiled to a life of wandering and departs "scorning pardon."[137] This wandering then becomes part of the Theban fate: as Arcita says to Palemone in the *Teseida*, "it has been appointed to me to go about the world laden with sorrows," and as he departs from Athens he adds: "I leave my enamoured soul here as, beside myself, I go wandering and weeping."[138] Like the Oedipus of the Statian and medi-

---

133. In its medieval versions, the Sphinx's riddle was circular—four-three-two-three-four—and hence insisted upon the use of a staff by both the mutilated boy, pierced through his heels or shins, and the blind old man; see Edmunds, "Oedipus in the Middle Ages," 144 n. 15.

134. *Super Thebaiden*, in *Opera*, ed. R. Helm (Leipzig: Teubner, 1898): "Id est mens lasciua, horrore peccati afflicta, se ipsam excruciat" (183).

135. Bien veult penitance souffrir
    Et son cors a martire offrir,
    Pour espeneir le pechié
    Dou pere qu'il ot detrenchié
    Se mist en une croute enferme.

C. DeBoer, ed. *Ovide moralisé* (Amsterdam: Müller, 1930), lines 1525–29.

136. "Longaque animam sub morte tenebat" (1, 48). This line may in fact be a medieval variant on Statius's original; some of the MSS read "longaque animam sub nocte trahebat." If indeed the line I have quoted in the text is a medieval variant, it witnesses to the habit of understanding Oedipus as a man enduring the living death of despair.

137. "Saevae spes aspera mortis" (11, 715); "indignans veniam" (11, 741).

138. *Teseida* 3, 65: Non sai tu, Peritoo, come l'andare attorno per lo mondo pien d'affanni m'è conceduto?

eval traditions, then, the Old Man continues his life of living death; as one medieval Oedipus says, prefiguring the Old Man's progressive yet inconclusive decomposition ("Lo how I vanysshe, flessh and blood and skyn!"), "I deteriorate through sorrow; O, if only I could be made nothing!"[139] So too, just as Oedipus embodies a lesson about divine justice that his sons ignore, so does the Old Man in his relation to the rioters; and just as Oedipus curses his sons when they scorn his suffering, so does the Old Man condemn the rioters to a mutual betrayal and self-destruction that is characteristically Theban.

How are we to understand this late Chaucerian return to the recursive dynamic of Thebes? In order to frame an answer to this question we must first, I believe, acknowledge the ambivalence with which the Old Man is invested. Certainly the kind of exegetical reading that the text as a whole solicits encourages us to understand his Oedipal yearnings entirely in penitential terms, an understanding that passes upon them a harsh judgment. For within this interpretive category they represent an evasion of the severities of the penitential life, a reversionary movement that seeks to foreclose the possibility of spiritual conversion. Indeed, from the point of view of penitential (and, for that matter, psychoanalytic) orthodoxy, they mark his—and the Pardoner's—unregeneracy, the submission to a dark regressiveness that harks back to a dangerous, illicit origin. And it is precisely this transgression that is punished with the mutilation that makes the Old Man walk with a staff and that renders the Pardoner a gelding or a mare. But what makes me pause in assenting to this admittedly efficacious reading is its very power—its ability, that is, to appropriate the Pardoner to a scheme of understanding that the interpreter is able to deploy while remaining himself exempt. In other words the penitential reading dispenses with the embarrassment—the sense of interpretive transgression—that the Oedipal details themselves elicit. Is the staff really phallic? Are we right in thinking that the hair clout invokes the mother's pubic hair, at once identifying and concealing the orifice from which the child once issued and that the Old Man now seeks leave to reenter? There is no definitive answer to these questions, but the fact of embarrassment shows that we have moved into that area of human experience in which the Oedi-

---

3, 76: Io lascia l'alma qui innamorata e fuor di me vagabundo
          paigendo men vo. . . .
Bernadette Marie McCoy, trans., *The Book of Theseus* (New York: Medieval Text Association, 1974), 89, 91.
  139. *Planctus Oedipi*, in Edélestand du Méril, ed., *Poésies inédit du moyen âge* (Paris: Librarie Franck, 1854), 310–13: "Necesse me luctu deteri—/ O utinam nil possem fieri" (lines 51–52).

pal drama takes place, a drama in which all male readers, at least, are implicated.

One of the things we have to acknowledge, then, is the authenticity of the Old Man's yearning. Against the religious assertion that rebirth can be achieved only through submission to the paternal law and a consequent penitential suffering, he posits a dream of maternal renewal, an end to the sufferings of age through the free gift of the maternal love. That this is only a dream is shown by the Old Man's helpless wandering, which marks it as not merely unattainable but illegitimate. Yet his sad wisdom, and the sheer imaginative force with which he is endowed (so that every reader of Chaucer, no matter how casual, seems to remember him), invest him with an authority that is not easily dismissed. So too does his presence in a tale that has as its foil the *Physician's Tale*. For that is a tale, as we have seen, in which the salvific value of childhood is powerfully if finally ineffectively invoked. It is undone, moreover, by an incomprehending adulthood: Virginia is sacrificed to her father's idea of sexual purity, while the generic innocence of hagiography is demeaned at the hands of the all-too-experienced Physician. It is in the context of paternal violence, in other words, that the Old Man's desire for maternal love must be placed. And so too should we understand the Pardoner's desire for spiritual sufficiency as confronting both the Host's outraged masculinism and the divinely authorized injunctions of penance—injunctions that take as their enabling premise man's inevitable sinfulness, that is, his spiritual insufficiency. In short, if Virginia is a victim of paternal violance, so too are the Pardoner and his fictive alter ego, the Old Man. And so too, he implies, are all who groan under the burden of their inevitable and finally unavoidable sinfulness. Just as in the *Physician's Tale* paternal norms of righteousness can be satisfied only by the sacrifice of the innocent Virginia, so too for Christianity as a whole paternal indignation can be mollified only by the sacrifice of the only begotten son. This is the scandal to which the Pardoner constantly reverts in his discourse—*Prologue and Tale* are laced with allusions to the crucifixion and to its reenactment in the Mass, most explicitly in the denouement beneath the oak tree[140]—and which, in his mutilation, he has taken upon himself. And it is a scandal that he enacts but refuses to endorse.

In sum, the Pardoner's confession contains within it an anti-confession. It is a penitential act that challenges the legitimacy of the very penance it seeks to perform. In this sense the Pardoner's deliberate

---

140. On these allusions, see Rodney Delasanta, "Sacrament and Sacrifice in the *Pardoner's Tale*," *AnM* 14 (1973): 43–52.

mockery of the Church's penitential procedures should be seen as not merely a theatrically exaggerated representation of evil but as an oppositional political statement.[141] His _Prologue and Tale_ stage many of the issues central to the theological and ecclesiastical debates of late fourteenth-century England. The legitimacy of indulgences, relics, and pilgrimage; the definition of who can preach, where, and to whom; the question whether the justification of sins is best accomplished by a deeply felt contrition or by ritual participation in the sacrament of penance; the relation of spiritual office to individual virtue; and the validity of auricular confession: these controversies, each of which is relevant to the Pardoner's performance, are at the center of late-medieval religious debate.[142] In one sense, the Pardoner's abuses serve to justify the criticism of an ossified and empty formalism that the religious reformers of the time, whether orthodox or Lollard, leveled against the established Church. Yet insofar as the Pardoner presents himself as a deliberately extravagant instance of evil, he is himself mocking that formalism, is himself revealing the emptiness of the penitential procedures of which he is an agent.

Yet his criticism of religious formalism, unlike that of Langland or the Lollards, is not mounted in the name of a desire for a more intense spirituality, for a deeper, purer piety. On the contrary, the Pardoner speaks from the position of the victim, asking questions that are plaintive rather than accusatory. What kind of religious system is it that imposes upon its believers the spiritual torment he is forced to endure? Is the desire to be "suffisant" really anything more than a desire to be free of that endlessly painful sense of lack that characterizes the human condition per se? And should such aspirations be punished with social and religious exclusion, a cutting off from the corporate body of Christendom? Even more profoundly, the Pardoner's discourse poses an opposition between two kinds of language. On the one hand is the institutional language of penance, with its "exegetical edge" and its absolutist judgments; on the other is the language of mythography, with its ability to grant expression to illicit desires.[143] These are languages that yield two different Pardoners: on the one hand is Chaucer's one lost soul, the

141. See David Aers, _Chaucer, Langland and the Creative Imagination_ (London: Routledge and Kegan Paul, 1980), 89–106.

142. See R. N. Swanson, _Church and Society in Late Medieval England_ (Oxford: Blackwell, 1989); Anne Hudson, _The Premature Reformation: Wycliffite Texts and Lollard History_ (Oxford: Clarendon Press, 1988); and Margaret Aston, _Lollards and Reformers: Images and Literacy in Late Medieval Religion_ (London: Hambledon Press, 1984).

143. For the "exegetical edge" of the Pardoner's discourse, see Marshall Leicester in "Synne Horrible."

feminoid figure who has transgressed the paternal prohibition against sufficiency and been punished with castration; on the other is a man willing to dream of a sufficiency made possible by reunion with the original mother. In effect, the Pardoner's discourse is uneasily poised between a deforming institutional self-representation and a promise of authenticity, between Lacan's *parole vide* and *parole plein*—empty and full language. Perhaps a language of the self's deepest instincts, a discourse of self-presence, is only a dream—everything in contemporary thought conspires to make us think so. But perhaps also Chaucer had something to teach us when he not only imagined it but imagined it as written in the characters of myth.

In returning to the Theban matrix, Chaucer is recuperating and perhaps even redeeming an earlier obsession. The kind of earliness that Thebes represents to the Chaucerian imagination is invoked here in a form that marks it as both illicit and authentic, both fetal and genuine. Here Thebes represents a value that is not dissimilar to that embodied in the perfect earliness of Virginia. It is a phantasy of self-enclosure and self-presence, a perfect circularity. The world outside that circle is marked by time, change, and difference; and it is as well the world of language, in which words stand permanently at a distance from the things to which they refer. That this is a world which both the poet and the Pardoner manipulate to their benefit does not render it any less foreign, and together they gesture, in however oblique and even contradictory a fashion, to a moment not merely outside but before time, a moment of plenitude and fulfillment.

Afterword

"Everything is supposed to be something. But it never is. That's the nature of existence."

That the final object of this book's attention should be the *Pardoner's Prologue and Tale* is at once arbitrary and inevitable: arbitrary because Chaucer's analysis of the mutual construction of history and subjectivity continues throughout the *Canterbury Tales* (or at least until the *Parson's Tale*); inevitable because this profoundly Theban tale returns us to the point at which we began. In *Anelida and Arcite* Chaucer showed that modernity's presumption of an originary moment, a moment set outside and against history, is an impossible delusion; and by establishing Thebes as the site of both memory and modernity, the site where the father is killed yet always returns, he correlated the paradox of originality with his own self-construction as the father of English poetry. In *Troilus and Criseyde* and the *Knight's Tale* this dynamic was seen as constitutive of the self-understanding of the fourteenth-century aristocracy, a class that tried to ground itself upon moments of absolute value but remained trapped within a temporal recursion it only dimly understood. And after the false start of the highly politicized *Miller's Tale*, the way out of this dynamic became the socially undetermined (albeit socially generated) subjectivity of the Wife of Bath. Moreover, the Wife of Bath became the means to bring together two ideas that have subsequently been definitive for our literary tradition, the ideas of character and of literature. Put too explicitly, literature is here defined as a form of writing capable of representing, with specificity and understanding, the irreducible selfhood that constitutes the essence of human life. And this is a definition that shows that the ideas of literature and of selfhood as entities that transcend historical construction are mutually self-confirming. This is why for Dryden Chaucer presents God's plenty, since only God can make human character.

Yet it seems clear, and most of all from the *Pardoner's Prologue and Tale*, that this cannot be the whole story. On the contrary, here we see that the literary character named the Pardoner is both "real," in the sense that he possesses the inwardness and complexity that we ascribe to ourselves and to our fellow human beings, and fabricated from the materials of literary convention and contemporary religious culture. What this suggests, in other words, is that however much Chaucer may have been absorbed into the ideology of individualism that has come to dominate Anglo-American thinking, and however much his poetry may have solicited such cooption, he also thought, and imagined, socially. If Chaucer simultaneously courted and resisted the paternal role, as A. C. Spearing has well argued, so did he display a similar ambivalence toward the human nature that he portrays as at once universal and socially contingent.[1] And it is with the Pardoner, whose representation both asserts and subverts the idea of a unitary selfhood, that he also at once entreats and outrages paternal authority.

Although this book naturally witnesses to its author's political values, as well as to ideological presuppositions of which he is doubtless unaware, it has not been burdened with an explicit methodological or theoretical program. But as the Introduction makes clear, it is very much a book of the 1980s. This may ensure its obsolescence, but it also allows it to reflect something of what that decade has asked of literary scholars. "Think socially" is one of the mottos that has been in my mind as I tried to understand the shape of Chaucer's career and the claims of his writing. This motto derives its force from its opposition to what Catherine MacKinnon has described as "the five cardinal dimensions of liberalism: individualism, naturalism, voluntarism, idealism, and moralism." What this means, she explains, is that

> members of groups who have no choice but to live life *as* members of groups are taken as if they are unique individuals; their social characteristics are then reduced to natural characteristics; preclusion of choices becomes free will; material reality is turned into "ideas about" reality; and concrete positions of power and powerlessness are trans-

1. Spearing points out that Chaucer's

withdrawal of authority both from the tales and from their interpretations amounts to what might be called a de-authorization of the whole work, or, in the terms used by some more recent theorists, to the conscious transformation of the *Tales* from a "work" to a "text." . . . He is the first English poet to exist as an "author," the first to be known by name as the father of a body of work; and yet throughout his career he seems to be striving towards the culmination achieved in *The Canterbury Tales*, the relinquishment of his own fatherhood, the transformation of his work into a text.

(*Medieval to Renaissance in English Poetry* (Cambridge: Cambridge University Press, 1985), 105–6.

formed into relative value judgments, as to which reasonable people can form different but equally valid preferences.[2]

While MacKinnon's specific target in defining this complex of conceptual practices is the ideological defense of pornography, her analysis can be extended to include most of the other forms of inequality and exploitation that shape and misshape our lives, including our relation to the natural world. It is our inability to think socially, to recognize the social meaning and social consequences of our practices, including our habits of thought, that above all prevents us from dealing with problems whose gravity is self-evident.[3]

In this book I have tried to think socially about Chaucer. In terms of scholarly practice, this has meant locating each of his texts in relation to a discourse—a specific set of texts and practices—that can make explicit the social meaning of his poetry. It is for this reason that so many pages have been spent describing a few of the ways in which some medieval people thought about and acted out questions of history, class, gender, family, and religion. Although I hope that these descriptions will contribute a sense of depth and persuasiveness to the readings of the Chaucerian texts, their purpose is not to guarantee correctness: historical description can never provide a norm of interpretive rectitude. But it can make visible social meanings and so show how Chaucer, both in his championing of a sovereign selfhood and in his critique of it, participated and continues to participate in the making of our world. And perhaps it can help us to think socially about other, more urgent matters as well.

Nonetheless, this program has been tempered, at times even countered, by a different concern. For surely it is a mistake to think that the only meaning worth explicating is social meaning, just as group identity is by no means the only identity that matters. However much they may have served to mystify the concrete relations of social power, neither liberalism nor individualism can be simply banished into the outer darkness of the politically incorrect. One of the lessons we can learn from late-medieval writing is that there are moments in history when individualism is a powerfully liberating force: in a society in which identity is restricted to social function, and in which functions are assigned

2. Catherine A. MacKinnon, *Feminism Unmodified* (Cambridge: Harvard University Press, 1987), 137.

3. To give a simple example, were the social cost entailed in the production and disposal of consumer items included in their price, rather than silently dispersed throughout the public world, there would soon be a consensus in support of meaningful environmental protection.

in radically unequal ways, to think individually is to think progressively. Nor can we be certain that today is not one of those moments. The culture industry that so profoundly and pervasively shapes contemporary life imposes upon us all homogenized identities that can be resisted only by an insistence on heterogeneity and specificity—on, in effect, individuality. Moreover, to foreclose the possibility of acting for other than group reasons is to make inescapable an identity politics that undermines the coalition-building that the progressive forces of our society desperately need.

It is for these reasons that I have sought to chasten my first, global motto with another, far less ambitious one. Primo Levi was a Holocaust survivor who suffered terribly and finally fatally for his group identity but who was able to transform his suffering into writing of a luminous specificity and heroic generosity. Near the end of his life he offered a dictum against dicta:

> It is better to renounce revealed truths, even if they exalt us by their splendor or if we find them convenient because we can acquire them gratis. It is better to content oneself with other more modest and less exciting truths, those one acquires painfully, little by little and without shortcuts, with study, discussion, and reasoning, those that can be verified and demonstrated.[4]

Although it establishes a standard few of us can hope to meet, this is advice contemporary literary critics would do well to heed. That criticism cannot go back to the future is of course true, and the often smug naivete of the pretheoretical past is well left behind. But Levi's words both proscribe recourse to absolutizing, totalizing schemes and redirect our attention to the specific, the particular, the local, and the contingent. And this is not only the level at which words like "verification," "demonstration," and even "truth" become once more sayable— words that have for perhaps long enough been banished from the critical lexicon—but also here that the *relationship* between the individual and the social, in all its irreducible complexity, becomes visible. It is, finally, this relationship, as it is worked out in both Chaucer's poetic career and in his writing, that I have tried to understand.

4. Primo Levi, *The Truce*, trans. Stuart Woolf (London: Sphere Books, 1987), 396.

Bibliography
Index

Bibliography

I: Texts

à Kempis, Thomas. *The Earliest English Translation of . . .* De imitatione Christi. Trans. William Atkynson. Ed. John K. Ingram. EETS, ES 63. London: K. Paul, Trench and Trübner, 1893.

Alanus de Insulis. *Liber poenitentialis.* PL 210:281–304.

Alberic of Monte Cassino. *Flores Rhetorici.* Ed. D. Mauro Inguanez and H. M. Willard. Monte Cassino: Miscellanea Cassinese, 1938.

Albert of Stade. *Troilus.* Ed. Theodor Merzdorf. Leipzig: Teubner, 1875.

Albertus Magnus. *Ethica.* Vol. 7 of *Opera omnia.* Ed. Auguste Borgnet. Paris: Vivès, 1890–99.

Alcok, Simon. *De modo dividendi thema pro materia sermonis dilatanda.* Ed. Mary F. Boynton. *Harvard Theological Review* 34 (1941): 201–16.

Alliterative Morte Arthure. Ed. Mary Hamel. New York: Garland Press, 1984.

Ambrose of Milan. *De Noe.* PL 14:381–438.

Andreas Capellanus. *De amore.* Ed. and trans. P. G. Walsh as *Andreas Capellanus on Love.* London: Duckworth, 1982.

[Anselm of Laon et al.] *Glossa ordinaria.* PL 113:67–1316; 114:9–752.

Antoninus of Florence. *Confessionale.* Chambéry (1485?).

Aquinas, Thomas. *Commentum in quatuor libros sententiarum M. Petri Lombardi.* Vols. 6–7 of *Opera omnia.* Parma: Fiaccadori, 1852–73.

Aquinas, Thomas. *In decem libros Ethicorum Aristotelis and Nicomachum Expositio.* Ed. Raymund M. Spiazzi. Rome: Marietti, 1949.

Aquinas, Thomas. *Summa theologica.* 3 vols. Ed. Piero Caramello. Rome: Marietti, 1952–53.

Aristotle. *Rhetoric.* Trans. W. Rhys Roberts. New York: Random House, 1954.

Augustine. *On Christian Doctrine.* Trans. D. W. Robertson. Indianapolis: Bobbs-Merrill, 1958.

Augustine. *The City of God.* Trans. Henry Bettenson. Harmondsworth: Penguin Books, 1972.

Augustine. *Confessiones.* 2 vols. Ed. W. H. D. Rouse. Trans. William Watts. London: Heinemann, 1912.

Augustine. *Confessions.* Trans. John K. Ryan. Garden City: Image Books, 1960.

429

Augustine. *De civitate Dei*. 2 vols. Ed. Bernhard Dombart. Leipzig: Teubner, 1909.

Augustine. *De sermone Domini in monte*. PL 34:1230–308.

Augustine. *De vera religione*. PL 34:122–72.

Augustine. *Enarrationes in Psalmos*. PL 36:67–1028, 37:1033–968.

Augustine. *Epistolae*. PL 33:61–1094.

Augustine. *Epistolae ad Romanos inchoata expositio*. PL 35:2087–106.

Augustine. *Sermo 71*. PL 38:445–70.

Augustine. *Sermo 90*. PL 38:638–41.

Augustine. *Tractatus in evangelium Ioannis*. PL 35:1379–976.

Baehrens, Emil, ed. *Poetae Latini Minores*. 5 vols. Leipzig: Teubner, 1879–83.

Bartholomeus Anglicus. *On the Properties of Things: John Trevisa's Translation of Bartholomaeus Anglicus, De proprietatibus rerum*. 3 vols. Ed. M. C. Seymour et al. Oxford: Clarendon Press, 1975–88.

Bede. *De schematibus et tropis*. Trans. Gussie Hecht Tannenbaum. *Quarterly Journal of Speech* 48 (1962): 237–53. Reprt. *Readings in Medieval Rhetoric*. Ed. Joseph M. Miller, Michael H. Prosser, and Thomas W. Benson. Bloomington: Indiana University Press, 1973. Pp. 96–122.

Bede. *In Matthaei evangelium expositio*. PL 92:9–132.

Bede. *Opera Didascalica*. Vol. 1. Ed. C. W. Jones. Turnhout: Brepols, 1975.

Benoît de Sainte-Maure. *Chroniques des Ducs de Normandie*. 4 vols. Ed. Carin Fahlin. Uppsala: Almqvist and Wiksells, 1951–79.

Benoît de Sainte-Maure. *Le Roman de Troie*. 6 vols. Ed. Leopold Constans. SATF. Paris: Firmin Didot, 1904–12.

Bernard of Clairvaux. *Epistolae*. PL 182:67–716.

Bernard of Clairvaux. *Sermones in Cantica Canticorum*. PL 183:785–1198.

The Black Book of the Admiralty. 4 vols. Ed. Sir Travers Twiss. Rolls Series. London: Longman, 1871–76.

Blake, William. *Poetry and Prose of William Blake*. Ed. Geoffrey Keynes. London: Nonesuch Press, 1943.

Boccaccio, Giovanni. *Boccaccio on Poetry*. Trans. Charles Osgood. Indianapolis: Bobbs Merrill, 1956.

Boccaccio, Giovanni. *The Book of Theseus*. Trans. Bernadette Marie McCoy. New York: Medieval Text Association, 1974.

Boccaccio, Giovanni. *The Corbaccio*. Trans. Anthony K. Cassell. Urbana: University of Illinois Press, 1975.

Boccaccio, Giovanni. *Filostrato*. Trans. Nathaniel Edward Griffin and Arthur Beckwith Myrick. New York: Biblo and Tannen, 1967 (1929).

Boccaccio, Giovanni. *Genealogie deorum gentilium*. 2 vols. Ed. Vincenzo Romano. Bari: Laterza, 1951.

Boccaccio, Giovanni. *Opere*. Ed. Cesare Segre. Milan: Mursia, 1963.

Boccaccio, Giovanni. *Opere Minori in Volgare*. 2 vols. Ed. Mario Marti. Milan: Rizzoli, 1970.

Bode, Georg, ed. *Scriptores rerum mythicarum latini tres Romae nuper reperti*. 2 vols. Celle: Schulze, 1834.

Boethius. *The Theological Tractates and the Consolation of Philosophy*. Trans. "I. T." and rev. H. F. Stewart. LCL. London: Heinemann, 1918.

Boke of Seynt Albans. St. Albans, 1486.

Bonaventure. *Breviloquium*. vol. 2 of *Works*. Trans. José de Vinck. Paterson: St. Anthony Guild Press, 1960.

Bonaventure. *Opera omnia*. 15 vols. Ed. A. C. Peltier. Paris: Vivès, 1864–71.

Bonet, Honoré. *The Tree of Battles*. Trans. G. W. Coopland. Liverpool: Liverpool University Press, 1949.

The Book of Vices and Virtues. Ed. W. Nelson Francis. EETS, OS 217. London: Oxford University Press, 1942.

Bowers, R. H., ed. "The Middle English *St. Brendan's Confession*." *Archiv für das Studium der neueren Sprachen* 175 (1939): 40–49.

Bradwardine, Thomas. *De causa Dei*. London: John Billium, 1618.

Bradwardine, Thomas. "The *Sermo Epicinus* Ascribed to Thomas Bradwardine (1346)." Ed. Heiko A. Oberman and James A. Weisheipl. *AHDLMA* 25 (1958): 295–329.

Brown, Carleton, ed. *English Lyrics of the XIIIth Century*. Oxford: Clarendon Press, 1939.

Brown, Carleton, ed. *Religious Lyrics of the XIVth Century*. 2d ed. Oxford: Clarendon Press, 1952 (1924).

Bruno of Segni. *Commentaria in Lucam*. PL 165:333–452.

Burgo, John. *Pupilla oculi*. Rouen, 1510.

Caesarius of Heisterbach. *Dialogus miraculorum*. 2 vols. Ed. Joseph Strange. Cologne: Heberle, 1851.

Calendar of the Close Rolls (1272–1485). 45 vols. London: HMSO, 1892–1954.

Calendar of the Patent Rolls (1232–1509). 52 vols. London: HMSO, 1891–1916.

Cassian, John. *De institutis coenobiorum*. PL 49:53–476.

Catholicon Anglicum. Ed. Sidney J. H. Herrtage. EETS, OS 75. London: Trübner, 1881.

Cessolis, Jacques de. *The Game and Playe of the Chesse*. 2d ed. Trans. William Caxton. Westminster: Caxton (1481?); reprt. in facsimile, William Figgins. London, 1855.

Cessolis, Jacques de. *Das Schachzelbuch Kunrats von Ammenhausen nebst den Schachbüchern des Jakob von Cessole und des Jakob Mennel*. Ed. Ferdinand Vetter. Frauenfeld: Huber, 1892.

Chandos Herald. *La Vie du Prince Noir by Chandos Herald*. Ed. Diana B. Tyson. Tübingen: Max Niemeyer, 1975.

Charland, T. M., ed. *Artes praedicandi: contribution à l'histoire de la rhétorique au moyen âge.* Ottawa: Presses de l'Université d'Ottawa, 1936.

Charny, Geoffroi de. *Livre de Chevalerie. Les Oeuvres de Froissart.* Vol. 1, part 3. Ed. Kervyn de Lettenhove. Brussels: Devaux, 1873. Pp. 463–533.

Chaucer, Geoffrey. *The Canterbury Tales: A Facsimile and Transcription of the Hengwrt Manuscript, with Variants from the Ellesmere Manuscript.* Ed. Paul Ruggiers. Norman: University of Oklahoma Press, 1979.

Chaucer, Geoffrey. *Chaucer's Poetry: An Anthology for the Modern Reader.* 2d ed. Ed. E. Talbot Donaldson. New York: The Ronald Press, 1975 (1958).

Chaucer, Geoffrey. *Complete Works of Geoffrey Chaucer.* 7 vols. Ed. Walter W. Skeat. Oxford: Oxford University Press, 1894–97.

Chaucer, Geoffrey. *Odd Texts of Chaucer's Minor Poems.* 2 vols. Ed. Frederick J. Furnivall. Chaucer Society, 1st series, no. 23, 60. London: Trübner, 1868–80.

Chaucer, Geoffrey. *The Riverside Chaucer.* Ed. Larry D. Benson. 3rd ed. Boston: Houghton Mifflin, 1987.

Chaucer, Geoffrey. *The Tales of Canterbury.* Ed. Robert A. Pratt. Boston: Houghton Mifflin, 1974.

Chaucer, Geoffrey. *The Text of the Canterbury Tales.* 8 vols. Ed. John M. Manly and Edith Rickert. Chicago: University of Chicago Press, 1940.

Chaucer, Geoffrey. *The Works of Geoffrey Chaucer.* 2d ed. Ed. F. N. Robinson. Boston: Houghton Mifflin, 1957 (1933).

Cicero. *De inventione, De optimo genere oratorum, Topica.* Trans. H. M. Hubbell. LCL. Cambridge: Harvard University Press, 1949.

Clanvowe, John. *The Works of Sir John Clanvowe.* Ed. V. J. Scattergood. Cambridge: Brewer, 1975.

Clari, Robert de. *La conquête de Constantinople.* Ed. Philippe Lauer. Paris: Champion, 1924.

Claudian. *Poems.* 2 vols. LCL. Trans. Maurice Platnauer. London: Heinemann, 1922.

The Clensyng of Mannes Sowle. MS Bodley 923. Fols. 1–152.

Collerye, Roger de. *Les oeuvres de Roger de Collerye.* Ed. Charles d'Héricault. Paris: P. Jannet, 1855.

Compendium historiae Troianae-Romanae. Ed. H. Simonsfeld. *Neues Archiv der Gesellschaft für ältere deutsche Geschichtskunde* 11 (1886): 241–51.

Complaint Against Hope. Ed. Kenneth G. Wilson. University of Michigan Contributions in Modern Philology 21. Ann Arbor: University of Michigan Press, 1957.

Condé, Baudouin de, and Jean de Condé. *Dits et contes.* 3 vols. Ed. Auguste Scheler. Brussels: Devaux, 1866–67.

Courtois, Jean, the Sicily Herald. *Parties inédites de l'oeuvre de Sicile.* Ed.

Ferdinand Roland. Société des Bibliophiles Belges de Mons, 22. Mons: DeQuesme-Masquillier, 1867.

Crow, Martin, and Clair C. Olson, eds. *Chaucer Life-Records*. Oxford: Oxford University Press, 1966.

Cursor Mundi. 7 vols. Ed. Richard Morris. EETS, OS 57, 59, 62, 66, 68, 99, 101. London: K. Paul, Trench and Trübner, 1874–93.

Cursor Mundi: The Southern Version. 3 vols. Ed. Sarah M. Horrall. Ottawa: University of Ottawa Press, 1978–86.

Cuvelier. *Chronique de Bertrand du Guesclin par Cuvelier*. 2 vols. Ed. Ernest Charrière. Paris: Didot, 1839.

Dan Michel. *Ayenbite of Inwyt*. Ed. Richard Morris. EETS, OS 23. London: Trübner, 1866.

Dante. *Commedia*. 3 vols. Ed. and trans. Charles Singleton. Princeton: Princeton University Press, 1970–77.

Dante. *Vita Nuova*. Trans. Mark Musa. Bloomington: Indiana University Press, 1973.

Deguileville, Guillaume. *Le pèlerinage de l'âme*. Ed. J. J. Stürzinger. London: Roxburghe Club, 1895.

Deguileville, Guillaume. *Pelerinage de lhomme*. Paris, 1511.

Deguileville, Guillaume. *Le pèlerinage de la vie humaine*. Ed. J. J. Stürzinger. London: Roxburghe Club, 1893.

Deschamps, Eustache. *Oeuvres complètes*. 11 vols. Ed. A. Queux de Saint-Hilaire and Gaston Raynaud. SATF. Paris: Firmin Didot, 1878–1903.

"Deux traités sur l'amour tirés du MS. 2200 de la Bibliothèque Sainte-Geneviève." Ed. A. Långfors. *Romania* 56 (1930): 361–88.

Digby Plays. The Late Medieval Religious Plays of Bodleian MSS Digby 133 and E Museo 160. Ed. Donald C. Baker, John L. Murphy, and Louis B. Hall, Jr. EETS, OS 283. Oxford: Oxford University Press, 1982.

Dives and Pauper. vol. 1. Ed. Patricia Heath Barnum. EETS, 05 275. Oxford: Oxford University Press, 1975.

Drumarthus. *Expositio in Matthaeum evangelistam*. PL 106:1261–504.

du Méril, Edélestand, ed. *Poésies inédites du moyen âge*. Paris: Franck, 1854.

Dunbar, William. *The Poems of William Dunbar*. Ed. James Kinsley. Oxford: Clarendon Press, 1979.

Duns Scotus. *Quaestiones in Libros IV Sententiarum*. Vol. 9 of *Opera omnia*. 12 vols. Ed. Lucas Wadding. Lyon: L. Durand, 1639.

Einhard. *Vita Caroli. Two Lives of Charlemagne*. Trans. Lewis Thorpe. Harmondsworth: Penguin Books, 1969. Pp. 49–91.

The English Register of Godestow Nunnery. Ed. Andrew Clark. EETS, OS 129, 130, 142. London: K. Paul, Trench and Trübner, 1911.

The English Text of the Ancrene Riwle. Ed. Mabel Day. EETS, OS 225. London: Oxford University Press, 1952.

Excidium Troiae. Ed. E. Bagby Atwood and Virgil K. Whitaker. Cambridge: Mediaeval Academy of America, 1944.

Faral, Edmond, ed. *Les arts poétiques du XIIᵉ et du XIIIᵉ siècle: Recherches et documents sur la technique littéraire du moyen âge*. Paris: Champion, 1924.

Fournival, Richard of. *Li consaus d'amours*. Ed. Gian Battista Speroni. *Medioevo romanzo* 1 (1974): 217–78.

[Fournival, Richard of?]. *De vetula*. Ed. Paul Klopsch. Leiden: Brill, 1967.

[Fournival, Richard of?]. *De vetula*. Ed. Dorothy M. Robathan. Amsterdam: Hakkert, 1969.

Froissart, Jean. *Chroniques*. 14 vols. Ed. Siméon Luce, Gaston Raynaud, and Albert Mirot. Paris: Reynouard, 1869–1967.

Froissart, Jean. *Le Joli buisson de jonece*. Ed. Anthime Fourrier. Geneva: Droz, 1975.

Froissart, Jean. *Oeuvres de Froissart*. 25 vols. Ed. Kervyn de Lettenhove. Brussels: Devaux, 1867–77.

Fulgentius. *Mythologicon. Auctores Mythographi Latini*. Ed. August van Staveren. Amsterdam: Wetstenium and Smith, 1742.

Fulgentius. *Opera*. Ed. Rudolf Helm. Leipzig: Teubner, 1898.

Fulgentius metaforalis. Ed. Hans Liebeschütz. Leipzig: Teubner, 1926.

Furnivall, F. J., ed. *Political, Religious, and Love Poems*. EETS, OS 15. London: Trübner, 1866.

Geoffrey of Vinsauf. *Documentum de modo et arte dictandi et versificandi*. Trans. Roger P. Parr. Milwaukee: Marquette University Press, 1968.

Geoffrey of Vinsauf. *Poetria nova*. Trans. Margaret F. Nims. Toronto: Pontifical Institute of Medieval Studies, 1967.

[Gerson, Jean?]. *La confession*. Paris (1490?).

Gower, John. *The Complete Works of John Gower*. 4 vols. Ed. G. C. Macauley. Oxford: Clarendon Press, 1899–1902.

Gower, John. *The Major Latin Works of John Gower*. Trans. Eric W. Stockton. Seattle: University of Washington Press, 1962.

Grandson, Oton. *Oton de Grandson, sa vie et ses poésies*. Ed. Arthur Piaget. Lausanne: Librairie Payot, 1941.

Gray, Thomas. *Scalacronica*. Ed. Joseph Stevenson. Edinburgh: Maitland Club, 1836.

Gregory the Great. *Commentariorum in Librum I Regum libri sex*. PL 79:17–468.

Gregory the Great. *Moralium*. PL 75:509–1162; 76:9–782.

Gregory the Great. *XL Homiliarum in evangelia libri duo*. PL 76:1075–312.

Gregory the Great. *In septem psalmos poenitentiales expositio*. PL 79:549–658.

Guido delle Colonne. *Historia destructionis Troiae*. Ed. Nathaniel Edward Griffin. Cambridge: Mediaeval Academy of America, 1936.

Guido delle Colonne. *The History of the Destruction of Troy*. Trans. Mary Elizabeth Meek. Bloomington: Indiana University Press, 1974.

Guillaume de Saint-André. *Le Livre de Bon Jehan, Duc de Bretagne*. Printed with Cuvelier's *Chronique de Bertrand du Guesclin par Cuvelier*. Ed. E. Charrière. Paris: Didot, 1839.

Halm, Karl Felix von, ed. *Rhetores latini minori*. Leipzig: Teubner, 1863.

Haymo. *Homiliae de tempore*. PL 118:11–746.

Henry of Lancaster. *Le Livre de Seyntz Medicines*. Ed. E. J. Arnould. Oxford: Blackwell, 1940.

Henryson, Robert. *The Poems of Robert Henryson*. Ed. Denton Fox. Oxford: Clarendon Press, 1981.

Higden, Ranulf. *The Ars componendi sermones of Ranulph Higden*. Ed. Margaret Jennings. Leiden: Brill, 1987.

Higden, Ranulf. *Polychronicon*. 9 vols. Ed. Churchill Babington and Joseph R. Lumby. Rolls Series. London: Longmans, 1865–86.

Hilary of Poitiers. *Commentarius in Evangelium Matthaei*. PL 9:917–1078.

Hilton, Walter. *Minor Works of Walter Hilton*. Ed. Dorothy Jones. London: Burns, Oates and Washbourne, 1929.

Hilton, Walter. *The Mixed Life. English Prose Treatises of Richard Rolle de Hampole*. Ed. George G. Perry. EETS, OS 20. London: Trübner, 1866.

Hilton, Walter. *The Scale of Perfection*. Ed. and trans. Evelyn Underhill. London: J. M. Watkins, 1948.

Historia vitae et regni Ricardi Secundi. Ed. George B. Stow. Philadelphia: University of Pennsylvania Press, 1977.

Holinshed, Raphael. *Chronicles*. 2 vols. London: Johnson, 1807–08.

Honorius of Autun. *De imagine mundi*. PL 172:115–88.

Horace. *Satires, Epistles, and Ars Poetica*. Trans. H. Rushton Fairclough. LCL. Cambridge: Harvard University Press, 1961.

Hyginus. *Fabulae*. Ed. H. I. Rose. Leiden: A. W. Sythoff, 1963.

Hymns to the Virgin and Christ. Ed. F. J. Furnivall. EETS, OS 24. London: Trübner, 1864.

Ignorancia sacerdotum. Bodley MS Eng. th. c. 57. Fols. 1–141.

In nuptiis sollacio. Cambridge University Library MS Gg.6.16. Fols. 28^b–30^b.

In solemnizacione matrimonium. Cambridge University Library MS Gg.6.16. Fols. 32^a–33^b.

Isidore of Seville. *Etymologiae*. 2 vols. Ed. José Oroz Reta and Manuel Marcos Casquero. Madrid: Biblioteca de Autores Cristianos, 1982.

Isidore of Seville. *Quaestiones in Vetus Testamentum: In Genesin*. PL 83:207–38.

Isidore of Seville. *Sententiarum libri tres*. PL 83:537–738.

Jacob's Well. Ed. Arthur Brandeis. EETS, OS 115. London: K. Paul, Trench and Trübner, 1900.

John of Freiburg. *Summa confessorum*. Lyon, 1518.

Jones, Evan John, ed. *Medieval Heraldry: Some Fourteenth-Century Heraldic Works*. Cardiff: William Lewis, 1943.

Joseph of Exeter. *The Iliad of Dares Phrygius*. Trans. Gildas Roberts. Capetown: A. A. Balkema, 1970.

Joseph of Exeter. *Werke und Briefe*. Ed. Ludwig Gompf. Leiden: E. J. Brill, 1970.

Jubinal, Achille, ed. *Nouveau recueil de contes, dits, fabliaux, et autres pièces inédites des XIIIe, XIVe et XVe siècles*. 2 vols. Paris: Pannier, 1839–42.

Julian of Norwich. *Revelations of Divine Love*. Ed. and trans. Grace Warrack. London: Methuen, 1949.

Kempe, Margery. *The Book of Margery Kempe*. Ed. S. B. Meech and H. E. Allen. EETS, OS 212 (London: Oxford University Press, 1940).

Kempe, Margery. *The Book of Margery Kempe*. Trans. Barry Windeatt. Harmondsworth: Penguin Books, 1985.

Knighton. *Chronicon*. 2 vols. Ed. Joseph Rawson Lumby. Rolls Series. London: HMSO, 1889–95.

Langland, William. *Piers Plowman: The A-Text*. Ed. George Kane. London: Athlone Press, 1960.

Langland, William. *Piers Plowman: The B-Text*. Ed. George Kane and E. Talbot Donaldson. London: Athlone Press, 1975.

Langland, William. *The C Text of Piers Plowman*. Ed. Derek Pearsall. London: Arnold, 1978.

Lannoy, Ghillebert de. *Oeuvres de Ghillebert de Lannoy*. Ed. Charles Potvin. Académie Impériales et Royale des Sciences et Belles-Lettres. Louvain: Lefever, 1878.

The Lay Folk's Catechism. Ed. T. F. Simmons and H. E. Nolloth. EETS, OS 118. London: K. Paul, Trench and Trübner, 1901.

Lefèvre, Jean. *La vielle, ou les dernières amours d'Ovide*. Ed. Hippolyte Cocheris. Paris: A. Aubry, 1861.

Legnano, John of. *Tractatus de bello, de represaliis et duello*. Ed. Thomas Erskine Holland. Trans. J. L. Brierly. Washington: Carnegie Institution, 1917.

Lehmann, Paul, ed. *Parodistische Texte*. Munich: Die Drei Masken, 1923.

Liber lamentationum Matheoluli. Les Lamentations de Matheolus et le Livre de leesce de Jehan Le Fèvre de Resson. 2 vols. Ed. A. G. Van Hamel. Paris: Bouillon, 1892–1905.

Le Livre des faicts du Mareschal de Boucicaut. Nouvelle Collection des Mémoires relatifs à l'histoire de France depuis le xiiie siècle. Ed. Joseph F. Michaud and J. J. F. Poujoulat. Paris: Féchoz et Letouzey, 1881. Pp. 000–00.

Lombard, Peter. *Libri IV sententiarum*. Quaracchi: Collegium S. Bonaventurae, 1916.

Lorris, Guillaume de, and Jean de Meun. *Le Roman de La Rose.* 5 vols. Ed. Ernest Langlois. SATF. Paris: Firmin Didot, 1914–24.

Lorris, Guillaume de, and Jean de Meun. *Le Roman de la Rose.* 3 vols. Ed. Félix Lecoy. CFMA. Paris: Champion, 1965–70.

Lorris, Guillaume de, and Jean de Meun. *Roman de la Rose.* Ed. Daniel Poirion. Paris: Garnier-Flammarion, 1974.

Lull, Ramon. *Libro del ordre de cavayleria.* Trans. as *Le Livre de l'ordre de chevalerie.* Ed. F. Minervini. Bari: Adriatica, 1972.

Lull, Ramon. *Libro del ordre de cavayleria.* Trans. as *The Book of the Ordre of Chyualry.* Trans. William Caxton. Ed. A. T. P. Byles. EETS, OS 168. London: Oxford University Press, 1926.

Lydgate, John. *The Fall of Princes.* 4 vols. Ed. Henry Bergen. Washington: Carnegie Institution, 1923–27.

Lydgate, John. *The Pilgrimage of the Life of Man.* Ed. F. J. Furnivall. London: Roxburghe Club, 1905.

Lydgate, John. *The Siege of Thebes.* Ed. Axel Erdmann. EETS, ES 108. London: Kegan Paul, 1911.

Machaut, Guillaume de. *Poésies Lyriques.* 2 vols. Ed. V. Chichmaref. Paris: Champion, 1909.

Machaut, Guillaume de. *La Prise d'Alexandrie.* Ed. M. L. de Mas Latrie. Geneva: Flick, 1877.

The Macro Plays. Ed. Mark Eccles. EETS, OS 262. London: Oxford University Press, 1969.

Maillart, Oliver. *La confession generale de frere Olivier Maillart.* Lyon (1485?).

Malkaraume, Jean. *La Bible de Jehan Malkaraume.* 2 vols. Ed. J. R. Smeets. Assen: Van Gorcum, 1977–78.

Malory, Thomas. *Works.* 2d ed. 3 vols. Ed. Eugene Vinaver. Oxford: Oxford University Press, 1967.

Mannyng, Robert. *Handlyng Synne.* Ed. F. J. Furnivall. EETS, OS 119, 123. London: K. Paul, Trench and Trübner, 1901–03.

Mannyng, Robert. *The Story of England.* 2 vols. Ed. F. J. Furnivall. Rolls Series. London: Longmans, 1887.

Marsilius of Padua. *The Defender of the Peace.* Trans. Alan Gewirth. New York: Columbia University Press, 1956.

Martin of Poland. *Cronique martiniane.* Trans. Sébastien Mamerot. Ed. Pierre Champion. Paris: Champion, 1907.

Matthew of Vendôme. *Ars versificatoria.* Trans. Ernest Gallo as "Matthew of Vendôme: Introductory Treatise on the Art of Poetry." *Proceedings of the American Philosophical Society* 118 (1974): 51–92.

Le Ménagier de Paris. Trans. Eileen Power as *The Goodman of Paris.* London: Routledge, 1928.

Middle English Sermons. Ed. Woodburn O. Ross. EETS, OS 209. London: Oxford University Press, 1940.

Migne, J.-P. *Patrologia Cursus Completus: Series Latina*. 221 vols. Paris: Migne, 1844–91.

Montaiglon, Anatole de, ed. *Recuieil des poésies francaises de XVe et XVIe siècles*. 13 vols. Paris: P. Jannet, 1855–78.

Montaiglon Antole de, and Gaston Raynaud, eds. *Recueil général et complet des fabliaux*. 6 vols. Paris: Librarie des Bibliophiles, 1872–90.

Morris, Richard, ed. *An Old English Miscellany*. EETS, OS 49. London: Trübner, 1872.

[Netter, Thomas?]. *Fasciculus Zizaniorum*. Ed. W. W. Shirley. Rolls Series. London: Longmans, 1858.

Newburgh, William of. *Historia rerum Anglicarum. Chronicles of the Reigns of Stephen, Henry II and Richard I*. 2 vols. Ed. Richard Howlett. Rolls Series. London: Longmans, 1884–85.

Nicolas, Nicholas Harris, ed. *The Controversy between Sir Richard Scrope and Sir Robert Grosvenor*. 2 vols. London: Samuel Bentley, 1832.

Novati, Francesco, ed. *Carmina medii aevi*. Florence: Libreria Dante, 1883.

Ockham, William of. *Opera plurima*. 4 vols. Lyon, 1494–96.

Odo of Cheriton. *The Fables of Odo of Cheriton*. Trans. John C. Jacobs. Syracuse: University of Syracuse Press, 1985.

Oresme, Nicholas. *Livre de divinacion*. Ed. and trans. G. W. Coopland as *Nicole Oresme and the Astrologers*. Liverpool: Liverpool University Press, 1952.

Oresme, Nicholas. *Oeconomica: Le Livre de Yconomique d'Aristote*. Ed. and trans. Albert Douglas Menut. *Transactions of the American Philosophical Society*, n.s. 47, pt. 5 (1957): 785–853.

Origen. *The Song of Songs: Commentary and Homilies*. Trans. R. P. Lawson. Westminster: The Newman Press, 1957.

Orosius. *Historiarum adversum paganos libri septem*. Ed. Karl Zangemeister. Leipzig: Teubner, 1889.

Orosius. *Seven Books of History against the Pagans*. Trans. Irving Woodworth Raymond. New York: Columbia University Press, 1936.

Ovid. *The Art of Love and Other Poems*. Trans. J. H. Mozley. Rev. ed. G. P. Goold. LCL. London: Heinemann, 1939 (1929).

Ovid. *Heroides and Amores*. Trans. Grant Showerman. LCL. London: Heinemann, 1914.

Ovid. *Metamorphoses*. 2 vols. Trans. Frank Justus Miller. LCL. London: Heinemann, 1916.

Ovide moralisé. Ed. Cornelis DeBoer. Verhandelingen der koninklijke Akademie van Wetenschappen Te Amsterdam. Afdeeling Letterkunde, nieuwe reeks, 15, 21, 30.3, 37, 43. Amsterdam: Müller, 1915–36.

Patterson, F. A., ed. *The Middle English Penitential Lyric.* New York: Columbia University Press, 1911.

Petrarch, Francis. *Opera omnia.* Basle, 1554.

Petrarch, Francis. *Petrarch's Lyric Poems: The "Rime Sparse" and Other Poems.* Ed. and trans. Robert M. Durling. Cambridge: Harvard University Press, 1976.

"Picatrix": Das Ziel des Weisen von Pseudo-Magriti. Trans. Hellmut Ritter and Martin Plessner. London: University of London Press, 1962.

Pisan, Christine de. *Book of the City of Ladies.* Trans. Earl Jeffrey Richards. New York: Persea, 1982.

Pisan, Christine de. *Cent ballades d'amant et de dame.* Ed. Jacqueline Cerquiglini. Paris: Union Générale d'Editions, 1982.

Pisan, Christine de. *The Epistle of Othea to Hector.* Trans. Stephen Scrope. Ed. George F. Warner. London: Roxburghe Club, 1904.

Pisan, Christine de. *Le Livre des fais d'armes et de chevalerie.* Trans. as *The Book of Fayttes of Armes and of Chyualrye* by William Caxton. Ed. A. T. P. Byles. EETS, OS 189. London: Oxford University Press, 1932.

The Pricke of Conscience. Ed. Richard Morris. London: Asher, 1865.

Puttenham, George. *The Arte of English Poesie.* London: Richard Field, 1589.

Quintilian. *Institutio oratoria.* 4 vols. Trans. H. E. Butler. LCL. Cambridge: Harvard University Press, 1920–22.

Rabanus Maurus. *Commentaria in Genesim.* PL 107:413–670.

Rabanus Maurus. *Commentariorum in Matthaeum libri octo.* PL 107:727–1156.

Radbertus, Paschasius. *Expositio in evangelium Matthaei.* PL 120:31–994.

Raymond of Penyafort. *Summa de poenitentia.* Rome: Tallini, 1603.

Remigius of Auxerre. *Commentarius in Genesim.* PL 131:53–134.

Rhetorica ad Herennium. Ed. and trans. Harry Caplan. LCL. Cambridge: Harvard University Press, 1954.

Richard of Bury. *Philobiblon.* Ed. and trans. E. C. Thomas. Oxford: Basil Blackwell, 1970.

Robbins, Rossell Hope, ed. *Historical Poems of the 14th and 15th Centuries.* New York: Columbia University Press, 1959.

Robbins, Rossell Hope. *Secular Lyrics of the XIVth and XVth Centuries.* 2d ed. Oxford: Clarendon Press, 1955.

Roman d'Edipus. Paris: Collection Silvestre, 1858.

Le Roman de Renart. 6 vols. Ed. Mario Roques. CFMA. Paris: Champion, 1948–63.

Le Roman de Thèbes. 2 vols. Ed. Leopold Constans. SATF. Paris: Didot, 1890.

Rotuli Parliamentorum. 6 vols. Ed. J. Strachey. London, 1783.

Rutebeuf. *Oeuvres complètes de Rutebeuf.* 2 vols. Ed. Edmond Faral and Julia Bastin. Paris: Picard, 1959–60.

[Seissel, C. de?]. *Le premier volume de Oroze.* 3 vols. Paris: A. Verard, 1509.

Seneca. *Tragedies.* 2 vols. Trans. Frank Justus Miller. Cambridge: Harvard University Press, 1917.

Servius. *Commentarii in Vergilii Carmina.* 3 vols. Ed. Georg Thilo and Hermann Hagen. Leipzig: Teubner, 1884–1923.

Servius. *Servianorum in Vergili Carmina Commentariorum.* Ed. E. K. Rand et al. Lancaster: American Philosophical Society, 1946.

Speculum Christiani. Ed. Gustaf Holmstedt. EETS, OS 182. London: Oxford University Press, 1933.

Speculum Gy de Warewyke. Ed. Georgiana Lea Morrill. EETS, ES 75. London: K. Paul, Trench and Trübner, 1895.

Statius. *Silvae, Thebaid, Achilleid.* 2 vols. Trans. J. H. Mozley. LCL. London: Heinemann, 1928.

Stevenson, Joseph. *The Church Historians of England.* 5 vols. Glasgow: Seeleys, 1853–58.

Stow, John. *A Survey of London by John Stow.* 2 vols. Ed. Charles Lethbridge Kingsford. Oxford: Clarendon Press, 1908.

Symon de Phares. *Recueil des plus celebres astrologues et quelques hommes doctes.* Ed. Ernest Wickersheimer. Paris: Champion, 1929.

[Vincent of Beauvais?]. *Speculum Historiale.* Douai: Bellerus, 1624.

Virgil. *Eclogues, Georgics, Aeneid.* Rev. ed. 2 vols. Trans. H. Rushton Fairclough. LCL. London: Heinemann, 1932.

Vitry, Jacques de. *The Exempla or illustrative stories from the Sermones vulgares of Jacques de Vitry.* Ed. T. F. Crane. London: Folk-lore Society, 1890.

Walsingham, Thomas. *De archana deorum.* Ed. Robert A. van Kluyve. Durham: Duke University Press, 1968.

Walsingham, Thomas. *Historia anglicana.* 2 vols. Ed. Henry Thomas Riley. Rolls Series. London: Longman, 1863–64.

Walther, Hans, and Paul Gerhard Schmidt, eds. *Proverbia sententiaeque Latinitatis Medii Aevi. Lateinische Sprichwörter und Sentenzen des Mittelalters.* 9 vols. Göttingen: Vandenhoeck und Ruprecht, 1963–86.

William of Auvergne. *Opera omnia.* 2 vols. Paris: Hotot, 1674.

Windeatt, Barry A., ed. and trans. *Chaucer's Dream Poetry: Sources and Analogues.* Cambridge: Brewer, 1982.

Wycliff, John. *Opera Minora.* Ed. Joseph Loserth. London: Paul, 1913.

The York Plays. Ed. Richard Beadle. London: Arnold, 1982.

Yorkshire Writers: Richard Rolle of Hampole and His Followers. 2 vols. Ed. Carl Horstmann. London: Sonnenshein, 1896.

Young, Charles George, ed. *An Account of the Controversy between Reginald Lord Grey of Ruthyn and Sir Edward Hastings.* London: Privately Printed, 1841.

II: Studies

Adams, Robert. "The Concept of Debt in *The Shipman's Tale*." *SAC* 6 (1984): 85–102.

Adams, Robert. "Piers's Pardon and Langland's Semi-Pelagianism." *Traditio* 39 (1983): 367–418.

Aers, David. *Chaucer, Langland and the Creative Imagination*. London: Routledge and Kegan Paul, 1980.

Aers, David. "Review" of Terry Jones, *Chaucer's Knight: Portrait of a Medieval Mercenary*. *SAC* 4 (1982): 169–75.

Alexander, J. J. G. "Painting and Manuscript Illumination for Royal Patrons in the Later Middle Ages." *English Court Culture*. Ed. V. J. Scattergood and J. W. Sherborne. Pp. 141–62.

Alexander, J. J. G., and Paul Binski, eds. *The Age of Chivalry: Art in Plantagenet England 1200–1400*. London: Royal Academy of Arts, 1987.

Allan, Alison. "Yorkist Propaganda: Pedigree, Prophecy, and the 'British History' in the Reign of Edward IV." *Patronage, Pedigree and Power in Later Medieval England*. Ed. Charles Ross. Gloucester: Alan Sutton, 1979. Pp. 171–92.

Allen, Judson Boyce. *The Ethical Poetic of the Later Middle Ages*. Toronto: University of Toronto Press, 1982.

Allen, Judson Boyce, and Patrick Gallacher. "Alisoun through the Looking Glass: Or Every Man His Own Midas." *ChR* 4 (1970–71): 99–105.

Allmand, Christopher. *The Hundred Years War: England and France at War c. 1300–c. 1450*. Cambridge: Cambridge University Press, 1988.

Anciaux, P. "Le Sacrament de pénitence chez Guillaume d'Auvergne." *Ephemerides Theologicae Lovaniensis* 24 (1948): 98–118.

Anderson, David. "Theban History in Chaucer's *Troilus*." *SAC* 4 (1982): 109–33.

Anderson, Michael. *Approaches to the History of the Western Family, 1500–1914*. London: Macmillan, 1980.

Anderson, Perry. "Modernity and Revolution." *Marxism and the Interpretation of Culture*. Ed. Cary Nelson and Lawrence Grossberg. Urbana: University of Illinois Press, 1988. Pp. 317–33.

Angeli, Giovanna. *L'"Eneas" e i primi romanzi volgari*. Milan: Ricciardi, 1971.

apRoberts, Robert P. "Love in the *Filostrato*." *ChR* 7 (1972–73): 1–26.

Ariès, Philippe, and Georges Duby, eds. *A History of Private Life*. Vol. 2: *Revelations of the Medieval World*. Trans. Arthur Goldhammer. Cambridge: Harvard University Press, 1988.

Aston, Margaret. *Lollards and Reformers: Images and Literacy in Late Medieval Religion*. London: Hambledon Press, 1984.

Aston, T. H., and C. H. E. Philpin, eds. *The Brenner Debate: Agrarian Class*

Structure and Economic Development in Pre-Industrial Europe. Cambridge: Cambridge University Press, 1985.

Atwood, E. Bagby. "The *Excidium Troiae* and Medieval Troy Literature." *MP* 35 (1937–38): 115–28.

Aubailly, Jean-Claude. *Le théatre médiévale profane et comique.* Paris: Champion, 1975.

Auerbach, Erich. *Dante: Poet of the Secular World.* Trans. Ralph Manheim. Chicago: University of Chicago Press, 1961 (1929).

Baker, Robert L. "The English Customs Service, 1307–1343: A Study of Medieval Administration." *Transactions of the American Philosophical Society,* n.s. 51, part 6 (1961): 1–76.

Bakhtin, Mikhail. *Rabelais and His World.* Trans. Hélène Iswolsky. Cambridge: MIT Press, 1968.

Baldwin, Anna P. *The Theme of Government in* Piers Plowman. Cambridge: D. S. Brewer, 1981.

Baldwin, John W. "The Medieval Theories of the Just Price." *Transactions of the American Philosophical Society,* n.s. 49 (1959): 3–92.

Barber, Richard. *The Knight and Chivalry.* 2d ed. Ipswich: Boydell, 1974.

Barker, Francis. *The Tremulous Private Body: Essays on Subjection.* London: Methuen, 1984.

Barker, Juliet R. V. *The Tournament in England, 1100–1400.* Woodbridge: Boydell, 1986.

Barney, Stephen. "An Evaluation of the *Pardoner's Tale.*" *Twentieth-Century Interpretations of the* Pardoner's Tale. Ed. Dewey Faulkner. Englewood Cliffs: Prentice Hall, 1973. Pp. 83–95.

Barney, Stephen. "Troilus Bound." *Speculum* 47 (1972): 445–58.

Barnie, John. *War in Medieval English Society: Social Values and the Hundred Years War.* London: Weidenfeld and Nicolson, 1974.

Barraclough, Geoffrey. *The Mediaeval Empire: Idea and Reality.* Historical Association Pamphlets, G17. London: Historical Association, 1950.

Barthes, Roland. *Elements of Semiology.* Trans. Annette Lavers and Colin Smith. London: Jonathan Cape, 1967.

Barthes, Roland. *S/Z.* Trans. Richard Howard. New York: Hill and Wang, 1974.

Baskerville, Charles Read. "Dramatic Aspects of Medieval Folk Festivals in England." *SP* 17 (1920): 19–87.

Baskerville, Charles Read. "Mummers' Wooing Plays in England." *MP* 21 (1924): 225–72.

Baswell, Christopher C., and Paul Beekman Taylor. "The *Faire Queene Eleyne* in Chaucer's *Troilus.*" *Speculum* 63 (1988): 293–311.

Baum, Paull Franklin. "The Mediaeval Legend of Judas Iscariot." *PMLA* 24 (1916): 481–632.

Bayot, Alphonse. "La légende de Troie à la cour de Bourgogne." *Société d'Emulation de Bruges, Mélanges* 1. Bruges: de Plancke, 1908.

Bec, Christian. *Les marchands écrivains à Florence, 1375–1434*. Paris: Mouton, 1967.

Beichner, Paul E., C.S.C. "Chaucer's Pardoner as Entertainer." *MS* 25 (1963): 160–72.

Bellah, Robert N., Richard Madsen, William M. Sullivan, Ann Swidler, and Stephen M. Tipton. *Habits of the Heart: Individualism and Commitment in American Life*. New York: Harper & Row, 1986.

Bellamy, J. G. *Bastard Feudalism and the Law*. London: Routledge, 1989.

Bennett, H. S. "The Reeve and the Manor in the Fourteenth Century." *EHR* 41 (1926): 358–65.

Bennett, Michael. *Community, Class and Careerism: Cheshire and Lancashire Society in the Age of* Sir Gawain and the Green Knight. Cambridge: Cambridge University Press, 1983.

Bennett, Richard, and John Elton. *The History of Corn Milling*. 4 vols. London: Simpkin Marshall, 1898–1904.

Benson, C. David. *Chaucer's Drama of Style: Poetic Variety and Contrast in the* Canterbury Tales. Chapel Hill: University of North Carolina Press, 1986.

Benson, C. David. *The History of Troy in Middle English Literature*. Woodbridge: Brewer, 1980.

Benson, C. David. "The *Knight's Tale* as History." *ChR* 3 (1968–69): 107–23.

Benson, C. David. "'O Nyce World': What Chaucer Really Found in Guido delle Colonne's History of Troy." *ChR* 13 (1978–79): 308–15.

Benson, Larry D. *Malory's* Morte Darthur. Cambridge: Harvard University Press, 1976.

Benson, Larry D. "The Occasion of the *Parliament of Fowls*." *The Wisdom of Poetry: Essays in Early English Literature in Honor of Morton W. Bloomfield*. Ed. Larry D. Benson and Siegfried Wenzel. Kalamazoo: Institute for Medieval Studies, 1982. Pp. 123–44.

Benson, Larry D. "The Order of *The Canterbury Tales*." *SAC* 3 (1981): 77–120.

Benveniste, Emile. *Problems in General Linguistics*. Trans. Mary Elizabeth Meek. Coral Gables: University of Florida Press, 1971.

Bezzola, Reto R. *Les Origines et la formation de la littérature courtoise en Occident, 500–1200*. 5 vols. Paris: Champion, 1958–67.

Blaess, Madelaine. "L'Abbaye de Bordesley et les livres de Guy de Beauchamp." *Romania* 78 (1957): 511–18.

Blake, Kathleen A. "Order and the Noble Life in Chaucer's *Knight's Tale*?" *MLQ* 34 (1973): 3–19.

Blake, N. F. *The Textual Tradition of the* Canterbury Tales. London: Edward Arnold, 1985.

Blamires, Alcuin. "Chaucer's Revaluation of Chivalric Honor." *Mediaevalia* 5 (1979): 245–69.

Bleeth, Kenneth A. "The Image of Paradise in the *Merchant's Tale.*" *The Lerned and the Lewed.* Ed. Larry D. Benson. Harvard English Studies, 5. Cambridge: Harvard University Press, 1974. Pp. 45–60.

Blickle, Peter. *The Revolution of 1525: The German Peasants' War from a New Perspective.* Trans. Thomas A. Brady and H. C. Erik Midelfort. Baltimore: Johns Hopkins University Press, 1981.

Bloch, Marc. *Land and Work in Medieval Europe.* Trans. J. E. Anderson. Berkeley: University of California Press, 1967.

Bloch, R. Howard. *Etymologies and Genealogies: A Literary Anthropology of the French Middle Ages.* Chicago: University of Chicago Press, 1983.

Bloomfield, Morton. "*The Miller's Tale*—an unBoethian Interpretation." *Medieval Literature and Folklore Studies: Essays in Honor of Francis Lee Utley.* Ed. Jerome Mandel and Bruce A. Rosenberg. New Brunswick: Rutgers University Press, 1970. Pp. 205–11.

Bloomfield, Morton. *The Seven Deadly Sins.* East Lansing: Michigan State University Press, 1952.

Bois, Guy. *The Crisis of Feudalism: Economy and Society in Eastern Normandy c. 1300–1550.* Cambridge: Cambridge University Press, 1984.

Boitani, Piero. *Chaucer and Boccaccio.* Medium Aevum Monographs. Oxford: Society for the Study of Mediaeval Languages and Literature, 1977.

Boitani, Piero. "What Dante Meant to Chaucer." *Chaucer and the Italian Trecento.* Cambridge: Cambridge University Press, 1983. Pp. 115–39.

Bolton, J. L. *The Medieval English Economy 1150–1500.* London: Dent, 1980.

Borst, Arno, ed. *Das Rittertum im Mittelalter.* Darmstadt: Wissenschaftliche Gesellschaft, 1982.

Bossuat, André. "Les origines troyennes: leur rôle dans la littérature historique au xvᵉ siècle." *Annales de Normandie* 8 (1958): 187–97.

Bossy, John. "The Mass as a Social Institution, 1200–1700." *Past and Present* 100 (1983): 29–61.

Bowden, Betsy. "The Art of Courtly Copulation." *M&H* 9 (1979): 67–85.

Boyle, L. E., O.P., S.T.L. "The *Oculus Sacerdotis* and Some Other Works of William of Pagula." *TRHS*, 5th ser., 5 (1955): 81–110.

Branca, Vittore. *Boccaccio: The Man and His Works.* Trans. Richard Monges. New York: New York University Press, 1976.

Brenner, Robert. "Agrarian Class Structure and Economic Development in Pre-industrial Europe." *The Brenner Debate.* Ed. Aston and Philpin. Pp. 10–63.

Brenner, Robert. "The Agrarian Roots of European Capitalism." *The Brenner Debate.* Ed. Aston and Philpin. Pp. 213–327.

Brenner, Robert. "The Origins of Capitalist Development: A Critique of Neo-Smithian Marxism." *New Left Review* 104 (1977): 25–82.

Brewer, Derek. "Honour in Chaucer." *Essays and Studies* 26 (1973): 1–19.

Brewer, Derek, ed. *Chaucer: The Critical Heritage.* 2 vols. London: Routledge and Kegan Paul, 1978.

Brooks, Douglas, and Alastair Fowler. "The Meaning of Chaucer's *Knight's Tale." MAE* 39 (1970): 123–46.

Brown, Carleton. "Another Contemporary Allusion in Chaucer's *Troilus." MLN* 26 (1911): 208–11.

Brown, Carleton, and R. H. Robbins, ed. *Index of Middle English Verse.* New York: Columbia University Press, 1943.

Brown, Emerson. "Biblical Women in the Merchant's Tale: Feminism, Antifeminism, and Beyond." *Viator* 5 (1974): 387–412.

Brown, Emerson. "Chaucer, the Merchant, and Their Tale: Getting Beyond Old Controversies: Parts I and II." *ChR* 13 (1978–79): 141–56; 247–62.

Brown, R. A., and H. M. Colvin. "The King's Works 1272–1485." *The History of the King's Works.* 2 vols. Ed. R. A. Brown, H. M. Colvin, and A. J. Taylor. London: HMSO, 1963.

Bryan, W. F., and Germaine Dempster, eds. *Sources and Analogues of Chaucer's Canterbury Tales.* London: Routledge and Kegan Paul, 1941.

Burckhardt, Jacob. *The Civilization of the Renaissance in Italy.* Trans. S. G. O. Middlemore. London: Phaidon Books, 1965 (1860).

Burnley, J. D. "The Morality of the *Merchant's Tale." YES* 6 (1976): 16–25.

Burrow, J. A. *Essays on Medieval Literature.* Oxford: Clarendon Press, 1984.

Burrow, J. A. "Irony in the Merchant's Tale." *Anglia* 75 (1957): 199–208.

Burrow, J. A., ed. *Geoffrey Chaucer: A Critical Anthology.* Harmondsworth: Penguin Books, 1969.

Bush, Douglas. "Chaucer's 'Corinne,' " *Speculum* 4 (1929): 106–8.

Butterfield, Herbert F. *The Whig Interpretation of History.* London: G. Bell, 1931.

Cahn, Kenneth S. "Chaucer's Merchants and the Foreign Exchange: An Introduction to Medieval Finance." *SAC* 2 (1980): 81–119.

Calderwood, James L. "Parody in *The Pardoner's Tale." ES* 45 (1964): 302–9.

Caplan, Harry. "A Medieval Tractate on Preaching." *Studies in Rhetoric and Public Speaking in Honor of James A. Winans.* Ed. A. M. Drummond. New York: Century, 1925. Pp. 61–90.

Carruthers, Mary. "The Wife of Bath and the Painting of Lions." *PMLA* 94 (1979): 209–22.

Carton, Evan. "Complicity and Responsibility in Pandarus' Bed and Chaucer's Art." *PMLA* 94 (1979): 47–61.

Cassirer, Ernst. *The Individual and the Cosmos in Renaissance Philosophy.* Trans. Mario Domandi. New York: Harper Torchbooks, 1964 [1927].

Chambers, E. K. *The Mediaeval Stage*. 2 vols. Oxford: Clarendon Press, 1903.

Champion, Pierre. *La Librairie de Charles d'Orléans*. Paris: Champion, 1910.

Chatillon, F. "Regio Dissimilitudinis." *Mélanges E. Podechard*. Lyon: Facultés Catholiques, 1903. Pp. 85–102.

Chenu, Marie-Dominique. *Nature, Man, and Society in the Twelfth Century*. Trans. Jerome Taylor and Lester Little. Chicago: University of Chicago Press, 1968.

Chrimes, S. B. "Richard II's Questions to the Judges, 1387." *Law Quarterly Review* 72 (1956): 365–90.

Cipolla, Carlo M. *Before the Industrial Revolution: European Society and Economy, 1000–1700*. 2d ed. New York: Norton, 1980 (1976).

Cipolla, Carlo M., ed. *The Fontana Economic History of Europe: The Middle Ages*. London: Fontana Books, 1972.

Clark, Elaine. "Debt Litigation in a Late Medieval English Vill." *Pathways to Medieval Peasants*. Ed. J. Ambrose Raftis. Toronto: Pontifical Institute of Mediaeval Studies, 1981. Pp. 247–79.

Clark, John. "Trinovantum—The Evolution of a Legend." *JMH* 7 (1981): 135–51.

Claxton, Ann. "The Sign of the Dog: An Examination of the Devonshire Hunting Tapestries." *JMH* 14 (1988): 127–79.

Cloetta, Wilhelm. *Beiträge zur Literaturgeschichte des Mittelalters und der Renaissance*. Vol. 1: *Komödie und Tragödie im Mittelalter*. Halle: Niemeyer, 1890.

Clogan, Paul M. "Chaucer and the *Thebaid* Scholia." *SP* 61 (1964): 599–615.

Clogan, Paul M. "Chaucer's Use of the *Thebaid*." *English Miscellany* 18 (1967): 9–31.

Clogan, Paul M. "Medieval Glossed Manuscripts of the *Thebaid*." *Manuscripta* 11 (1967): 102–11.

Clogan, Paul M. "The *Planctus* of Oedipus: Text and Comment." *M&H* 1 (1970): 233–39.

Coffman, George R. "Old Age from Horace to Chaucer: Some Literary Affinities and Adventures of an Idea." *Speculum* 9 (1934): 249–77.

Colby, Alice M. *The Portrait in Twelfth-Century French Literature*. Geneva: Droz, 1965.

Coleman, Janet. *Medieval Readers and Writers 1350–1400*. New York: Columbia University Press, 1981.

Coleman, Olive. "The Collectors of Customs in London under Richard II." *Studies in London History Presented to Philip Edmund Jones*. Ed. A. E. J. Hollaender and William Kellaway. London: Hodder and Stoughton, 1969. Pp. 181–94.

Coletti, Theresa. "Biblical Wisdom: Chaucer's *Shipman's Tale* and the *Mulier Fortis*." *ChR* 15 (1980–81): 236–42.

Coletti, Theresa. "The Meeting at the Gate: Comic Hagiography and Symbol in the *Shipman's Tale*." *SI* 3 (1977): 47–56.

Coletti, Theresa. *Naming the Rose: Eco, Medieval Signs, and Modern Theory.* Ithaca: Cornell University Press, 1988.

Collette, Carolyn P. "'Ubi Peccaverant, Ibi Punirentur': The Oak Tree and the *Pardoner's Tale*." *ChR* 19 (1984–85): 39–45.

Constans, Leopoid. *La Légende d'Oedipe étudiée dans l'antiquité, au moyen âge et dans les temps modernes.* Paris: Maisonneuve, 1881.

Contamine, Philippe. *War in the Middle Ages.* Trans. Michael Jones. Oxford: Blackwell, 1984.

Cooper, Helen. *The Structure of the Canterbury Tales.* Athens: University of Georgia Press, 1983.

Coulton, G. G. *The Medieval Village.* Cambridge: Cambridge University Press, 1925.

Courcelle, Pierre. *Les "Confessions" de Saint Augustine dans la tradition littéraire: Antécédents et postérité.* Paris: Etudes Augustiniennes, 1963.

Courcelle, Pierre. "Tradition néo-platonicienne et traditions chrétiennes de la 'region de dissemblance.' " *AHDLMA* 32 (1957–58): 5–33.

Cowgill, Bruce Kent. "The *Knight's Tale* and the Hundred Years' War." *PQ* 54 (1975): 670–79.

Craik, T. W. *The Comic Tales of Chaucer.* London: Methuen, 1964.

Crane, R. S. *The Languages of Criticism and the Structure of Poetry.* Toronto: University of Toronto Press, 1953.

Cripps-Day, F. H. *The History of the Tournament in England.* London: Quaritch, 1918.

Cropp, Glynnis M. "*Le Livre de Boece de Consolation:* From Translation to Glossed Text." *The Medieval Boethius: Studies in the Vernacular Translations of* De Consolatione Philosophiae. Ed. Alastair Minnis. Cambridge: Brewer, 1987. Pp. 63–88.

Currie, Felicity. "Chaucer's Pardoner Again." *LeedsSE* 4 (1970): 11–22.

Curry, Walter Clyde. *Chaucer and the Mediaeval Sciences.* 2d ed. New York: Barnes and Noble, 1960 (1926).

Curtius, E. R. *European Literature and the Latin Middle Ages.* Trans. Willard R. Trask. New York: Harper & Row, 1963.

Davenport, W. A. *Chaucer: Complaint and Narrative.* Cambridge: Brewer, 1988.

David, Alfred. "Criticism and the Old Man in Chaucer's *Pardoner's Tale*." *CE* 27 (1965): 39–44.

David, Alfred. *The Strumpet Muse: Art and Morals in Chaucer's Poetry.* Bloomington: Indiana University Press, 1976.

Davies, Kathleen. "Continuity and Change in Literary Advice on Marriage." *Marriage and Society: Studies in the Social History of Marriage.* Ed. R. B. Outhwaite. London: Europa Publications, 1981. Pp. 58–80.

Davis, Natalie Zemon. *Society and Culture in Early Modern France.* Stanford: Stanford University Press, 1975.

Davis, Ralph H. C. "William of Poitiers and His History of William the Conqueror." *The Writing of History in the Middle Ages: Essays Presented to Richard William Southern.* Ed. R. H. C. Davis and J. M. Wallace-Hadrill. Oxford: Clarendon Press, 1981. Pp. 71–100.

d'Avray, David, and M. Tausche. "Marriage Sermons in *Ad Status* Collections of the Central Middle Ages." *AHDLMA* 47 (1980): 71–119.

Dean, Christopher. "Salvation, Damnation, and the Role of the Old Man in the *Pardoner's Tale.*" *ChR* 3 (1968–69): 44–49.

Dean, James. "Time Past and Time Present in Chaucer's Clerk's Tale and Gower's *Confessio Amantis.*" *ELH* 44 (1977): 401–18.

Dean, James. "The World Grown Old and Genesis in Middle English Historical Writing." *Speculum* 57 (1982): 548–68.

Dean, Nancy. "Chaucer's *Complaint,* A Genre Descended from the *Heroides.*" *CL* 19 (1967): 1–27.

Dean, Ruth. "Nicholas Trevet, Historian." *Medieval Learning and Literature: Essays Presented to Richard William Hunt.* Ed. J. J. G. Alexander and M. T. Gibson. Oxford: Clarendon Press, 1976. Pp. 328–52.

Delasanta, Rodney. "Sacrament and Sacrifice in the *Pardoner's Tale.*" *AnM* 14 (1973): 43–52.

de Letter, P. "Two Concepts of Attrition and Contrition." *Theological Studies* 11 (1950): 3–33.

de Man, Paul. *Blindness and Insight.* 2d ed. Minneapolis: University of Minnesota Press, 1983 (1970).

Dembowski, Peter F. *Jean Froissart and his* Meliador: *Context, Craft, and Sense.* Lexington: French Forum, 1983.

DeNeef, A. Leigh. "Chaucer's *Pardoner's Tale* and the Irony of Misinterpretation." *JNT* 3 (1974): 85–96.

Denholm-Young, Noel. *The Country Gentry in the Fourteenth Century.* Oxford: Clarendon Press, 1969.

Dennys, Rodney. *The Heraldic Imagination.* London: Barrie and Jenkins, 1975.

Derrida, Jacques. *Writing and Difference.* Trans. Alan Bass. Chicago: University of Chicago Press, 1978.

Di Cesare, Mario. *The Altar and the City: A Reading of Virgil's* Aeneid. New York: Columbia University Press, 1974.

Dinshaw, Carolyn. *Chaucer's Sexual Poetics.* Madison: University of Wisconsin Press, 1989.

Dobb, Maurice. *Studies in the Development of Capitalism.* New York: International Publishers, 1947.

Dobson, R. B., ed. *The Peasants' Revolt of 1381.* London: Macmillan, 1970.

Dollimore, Jonathan. *Radical Tragedy: Religion, Ideology and Power in the Drama of Shakespeare and His Contemporaries.* Chicago: University of Chicago Press, 1984.

Donaldson, E. Talbot. "Arcite's Injury." *Middle English Studies Presented to Norman Davis in Honour of his Seventieth Birthday.* Ed. Douglas Gray and E. G. Stanley. Oxford: Clarendon Press, 1983. Pp. 65–67.

Donaldson, E. Talbot. "The Idiom of Popular Poetry in the *Miller's Tale.*" *English Institute Essays, 1950.* New York: Columbia University Press, 1951. Pp. 116–40.

Donaldson, E. Talbot. "The Ordering of the *Canterbury Tales.*" *Medieval Literature and Folklore Studies: Essays in Honor of Francis Lee Utley.* Ed. Jerome Mandel and Bruce A. Rosenberg. New Brunswick: Rutgers University Press, 1970. Pp. 193–204.

Donaldson, E. Talbot. *Speaking of Chaucer.* London: Athlone Press, 1970.

Donovan, Mortimer J. "The Image of Pluto and Proserpina in the *Merchant's Tale.*" *PQ* 36 (1957): 49–60.

Douglass, E. Jane Dempsey. *Justification in Late Medieval Preaching: A Study of John Geiler of Keisersberg.* Leiden: Brill, 1966.

Doyle, A. I. "English Books In and Out of Court from Edward III to Henry III." *English Court Culture.* Ed. V. J. Scattergood and J. W. Sherborne. Pp. 163–81.

Doyle, A. I., and M. B. Parkes. "The Production of Copies of the *Canterbury Tales* and the *Confessio Amantis* in the Early Fifteenth Century." *Medieval Scribes, Manuscripts and Libraries: Essays Presented to N. R. Ker.* Ed. M. B. Parkes and Andrew G. Watson. London: Scolar Press, 1978. Pp. 164–210.

Dragonetti, Roger. *La technique poétique des trouvères dans la chanson courtoise.* Bruges: De Tempel, 1960.

Dryden, John. *Of Dramatic Poesy and Other Critical Essays.* 2 vols. Ed. George Watson. London: J. M. Dent, 1962.

DuBoulay, F. R. H. "The Historical Chaucer." *Geoffrey Chaucer: Writers and Their Background.* Ed. Derek Brewer. London: G. Bell, 1974. Pp. 33–57.

DuBoulay, F. R. H. *The Lordship of Canterbury: An Essay on Mediaeval Society.* London: Nelson, 1966.

DuBoulay, F. R. H., and Caroline Barron, eds. *The Reign of Richard II: Essays in Honour of May McKisack.* London: Athlone Press, 1971.

Duby, Georges. *Rural Economy and Country Life in the Medieval West.* Trans. Cynthia Postan. Columbia: University of South Carolina Press, 1968.

Duby, Georges. *The Three Orders: Feudal Society Imagined.* Trans. Arthur Goldhammer. Chicago: University of Chicago Press, 1980.

Dunger, Hermann. *Die Sage vom trojanischen Kriege in den Bearbeitungen des Mittelalters und ihre antiken Quellen.* Leipzig: Vogel, 1869.

Dyer, Christopher. "The Social and Economic Background to the Rural Revolt of 1381." *The English Rising of 1381.* Ed. R. H. Hilton and T. H. Aston. Cambridge: Cambridge University Press, 1984. Pp. 9–42.

Dyer, Christopher. *Standards of Living in the Later Middle Ages.* Cambridge: Cambridge University Press, 1989.

Eagleton, Terry. *William Shakespeare.* Oxford: Blackwell, 1986.

Ebel, Julia. "Troilus and Oedipus: The Genealogy of an Image." *ES* 55 (1974): 15–21.

Eberle, Patricia J. "Commercial Language and the Commercial Outlook in the *General Prologue*." *ChR* 18 (1983–84): 161–74.

Eberle, Patricia J. "The Politics of Courtly Style in the Court of Richard II." *The Spirit of the Court: Selected Proceedings of the Fourth Congress of the International Courtly Literature Society.* Ed. Glyn S. Burgess and Robert A. Taylor. Cambridge: Brewer, 1985. Pp. 168–78.

Economou, George D. "Chaucer's Use of the Bird in the Cage Image in the *Canterbury Tales*." *PQ* 54 (1975): 679–84.

Edmunds, Lowell. *Oedipus: The Ancient Legend and Its Later Analogues.* Baltimore: The Johns Hopkins University Press, 1985.

Edmunds, Lowell. "Oedipus in the Middle Ages." *Antike und Abendland* 22 (1976): 140–55.

Edmunds, S. "The Library of Savoy: Documents." *Scriptorium* 24 (1970): 318–27; 25 (1971): 253–84; 26 (1972): 269–93.

Edwards, A. S. G. "The Unity and Authenticity of *Anelida and Arcite:* The Evidence of the Manuscripts." *SB* 41 (1988): 177–88.

Ehrhart, Margaret J. *The Judgment of the Trojan Prince Paris in Medieval Literature.* Philadelphia: University of Pennsylvania Press, 1987.

Ehrhart, Margaret J. "Machaut's *Dit de la fonteinne amoureuse,* the Choice of Paris, and the Duties of Rulers." *PQ* 59 (1980): 119–39.

Elbow, Peter. "How Chaucer Transcends Oppositions in the *Knight's Tale*." *ChR* 7 (1972–73): 97–112.

Elliott, Alison Goddard. "The *Facetus:* or, The Art of Courtly Living." *Allegorica* 2 (1977): 27–57.

Elliott, Ralph W. V. "Our Host's 'Triacle': Some Observations on Chaucer's 'Pardoner's Tale'." *REL* 7 (1966): 61–73.

Elster, Jon. *Making Sense of Marx.* Cambridge: Cambridge University Press, 1985.

Emerson, Oliver F. "Legends of Cain, Especially in Old and Middle English." *PMLA* 21 (1906): 837–939.

Erickson, Carolly. "The Fourteenth-Century Franciscans and Their Critics." *Franciscan Studies* 35 (1975): 107–35; 36 (1976): 108–47.

Evans, Joan. *Magical Jewels of the Middle Ages and the Renaissance, Particularly in England.* Oxford: Clarendon Press, 1922.

Faith, Rosamond. "The 'Great Rumour' of 1377 and Peasant Ideology." *The English Rising of 1381*. Ed. R. H. Hilton and T. H. Aston. Cambridge: Cambridge University Press, 1984. Pp. 43–73.

Farnham, Willard. *The Medieval Heritage of Elizabethan Tragedy*. Berkeley: University of California Press, 1936.

Ferguson, Arthur B. *The Indian Summer of English Chivalry: Studies in the Decline and Transformation of Chivalric Idealism*. Durham: Duke University Press, 1960.

Ferrante, Joan M. *The Conflict of Love and Honor*. The Hague: Mouton, 1973.

Ferry, Luc and Alain Renaut, *French Philosophy of the Sixties: An Essay on Antihumanism*. Trans. Mary H. S. Cattani. Amherst: University of Massachusetts Press, 1990.

Finberg, Herbert P. R. *Tavistock Abbey: A Study in the Social and Economic History of Devon*. Cambridge: Cambridge University Press, 1951.

Fineman, Joel. *Shakespeare's Perjured Eye: The Invention of Poetic Subjectivity in the Sonnets*. Berkeley: University of California Press, 1986.

Fisher, John Hurt. *John Gower: Moral Philosopher and Friend of Chaucer*. New York: New York University Press, 1964.

Flandrin, J.-L. *Families in Former Times: Kinship, Household and Sexuality*. Cambridge: Cambridge University Press, 1979.

Fleming, John V. "Deiphoebus Betrayed: Virgilian Decorum, Chaucerian Feminism." *ChR* 21 (1986–87): 182–99.

Forsyth, Ilene H. "Children in Early Medieval Art: Ninth through Twelfth Centuries." *Journal of Psychohistory* 4 (1976–77): 31–70.

Freccero, John. "Dante's Novel of the Self." *The Christian Century* (1965): 1216–18.

Freccero, John. *Dante: Poetics of Conversion*. Ed. Rachel Jacoff. Cambridge: Harvard University Press, 1986.

Friedman, John Block. "Henryson, The Friars, and the *Confessio Reynardi*." *JEGP* 66 91967): 550–61.

Funkenstein, Amos. "Periodization and Self-Understanding in the Middle Ages and Early Modern Times." *M&H* 5 (1974): 3–23.

Fyler, John M. "*Auctoritee* and Allusion in *Troilus and Criseyde*." *Res Publica Litterarum* 7 (1984): 73–92.

Fyler, John M. *Chaucer and Ovid*. New Haven: Yale University Press, 1979.

Galway Margaret. "Geoffrey Chaucer, J.P. and M.P." *MLR* 36 (1941): 1–36.

Gauvard, C., and A. Gokalp. "Les conduites de bruit et leur signification a la fin du moyen age: *Le charivari*." *Annales* 29 (1974): 693–704.

Gaylord, Alan. "Chaucer's Tender Trap: The *Troilus* and the 'Yonge, Fresshe Folkes'." *English Miscellany* 15 (1964): 25–45.

Gaylord, Alan. "Friendship in Chaucer's *Troilus*." *ChR* 3 (1968–69): 239–64.

Gaylord, Alan. "The Role of Saturn in the *Knight's Tale*." *ChR* 8 (1973–74): 172–90.

Gaylord, Alan. "Uncle Pandarus as Lady Philosophy." *Papers of the Michigan Academy of Science, Arts, and Letters* 46 (1961): 571–95.

Genet, Philippe, ed. *Four English Political Tracts*. Camden Society, 4th ser., 18 (1977).

Genicot, Léopold. "Crisis: From the Middle Ages to Modern Times." *The Cambridge Economic History of Europe*. Vol 1: *The Agrarian Life of the Middle Ages*. 2d ed. Ed. M. M. Postan. Cambridge: Cambridge University Press, 1966. Pp. 660–741.

Georgianna, Linda. *The Solitary Self: Individuality in the* Ancrene Wisse. Cambridge: Harvard University Press, 1981.

Geremek, Bronislaw. *The Margins of Society in Late Medieval Paris*. Trans. Jean Birrell. Cambridge: Cambridge University Press, 1987.

Gibson, Gail McMurray. "Resurrection as Dramatic Icon in the *Shipman's Tale*." *Signs and Symbols in Chaucer*. Ed. J. P. Hermann and J. J. Burke. University: University of Alabama Press, 1981. Pp. 102–12.

Giddens, Anthony. *Central Problems in Social Theory*. Berkeley: University of California Press, 1979.

Gilman, Sander L. *The Parodic Sermon in European Perspective*. Wiesbaden: Steiner, 1974.

Gilson, Etienne. *Les idées et les lettres*. Paris: J. Vrin, 1932.

Ginsberg, Warren. "Preaching and Avarice in *The Pardoner's Tale*." *Mediaevalia* 2 (1976): 77–99.

Given, James Buchanan. *Society and Homicide in Thirteenth-Century England*. Stanford: Stanford University Press, 1977.

Given-Wilson, Christopher. *The English Nobility in the Late Middle Ages*. London: Routledge and Kegan Paul, 1987.

Given-Wilson, Christopher. "The King and the Gentry in Fourteenth-Century England." *TRHS*, 5th ser. 37 (1987): 87–102.

Given-Wilson, Christopher. *The Royal Household and the King's Affinity: Service, Politics, and Finance in England 1360–1413*. New Haven: Yale University Press, 1986.

Goodman, Anthony. *The Loyal Conspiracy: The Lords Appellant Under Richard II*. London: Routledge and Kegan Paul, 1971.

Gorra, Egidio. *Testi inediti di Storia Trojana*. Turin: C. Triverio, 1887.

Gransden, Antonia. *Historical Writing in England*. 2 vols. London: Routledge and Kegan Paul, 1974–82.

Green, Richard Firth. *Poets and Princepleasers: Literature and the English Court in the Late Middle Ages*. Toronto: University of Toronto Press, 1980.

Greenblatt, Stephen. *Renaissance Self-Fashioning: From More to Shakespeare*. Chicago: University of Chicago Press, 1980.

Greene, Thomas M. *The Light in Troy: Imitation and Discovery in Renaissance Poetry.* New Haven: Yale University Press, 1982.

Greif, Wilhelm. *Die mittelalterlichen Bearbeitungen Trojanersage.* Marburg: Friedrich, 1885.

Gueneé, Bernard. "La Culture historique des nobles: le succès des *Faits des Romains* (XIIIᵉ–XVᵉ siècles)." *La Noblesse au Moyen Age.* Ed. Philippe Contamine. Paris: Presses universitaires de France, 1976. Pp. 261–88.

Gueneé, Bernard. "Histoires, annales, chroniques: essai sur les genres historiques au moyen âge." *Annales* 28 (1973): 997–1016.

Gueneé, Bernard. *Histoire et culture historique dans l'occident médiéval.* Paris: Aubier, 1980.

Gueneé, Bernard. *States and Rulers in Later Medieval Europe.* Trans. Juliet Vale. Oxford: Blackwell, 1985.

Guiette, Robert. "D'une poésie formelle en France en Moyen Age." *Romanica Gandensia* 8 (1960): 9–23.

Habermas, Jürgen, "Modernity—An Incomplete Project," *New German Critique* 22 (1981). Reprinted in *Interpretive Social Sciences: A Second Look.* Ed. Paul Rabinow and William M. Sullivan. Berkeley: University of California Press, 1987. Pp. 141–56.

Hahn, Thomas. "Money, Sexuality, Wordplay, and Context in the *Shipman's Tale.*" *Chaucer in the Eighties.* Ed. Julian N. Wasserman and Robert J. Blanch. Syracuse: Syracuse University Press, 1986. Pp. 235–49.

Hahn, Thomas, and Richard W. Kaeuper. "Text and Context: Chaucer's *Friar's Tale.*" *SAC* 5 (1983): 67–101.

Haller, Robert S. "The *Knight's Tale* and the Epic Tradition." *ChR* 1 (1966–67): 67–84.

Halverson, John. "Aspects of Order in the *Knight's Tale.*" *SP* 57 (1960): 606–21.

Halverson, John. "Chaucer's Pardoner and the Progress of Criticism." *ChR* 4 (1969–70): 184–202.

Ham, Edward B. "*Knight's Tale* 38." *ELH* 17 (1950): 252–61.

Hamilton, G. L. *The Indebtedness of Chaucer's* Troilus and Criseyde *to Guido delle Colonne's* Historia Trojana. New York: Columbia University Press, 1903.

Hammond, Eleanor Prescott. "A Burgundian Copy of Chaucer's *Troilus.*" *MLN* 26 (1911): 32.

Hammond, Eleanor Prescott. *Chaucer: A Bibliographical Manual.* New York: Macmillan, 1908.

Hanawalt, Barbara A. "Conception Through Infancy in Medieval English Historical and Folklore Sources." *Folklore Forum* 13 (1980): 127–57.

Hanawalt, Barbara A. *Crime and Conflict in English Communities, 1300–1348.* Cambridge: Harvard University Press, 1979.

Hanna, Ralph, III. "Problems of 'Best Text' Editing and the Hengwrt Manuscript of *The Canterbury Tales.*" *Manuscripts and Texts: Editorial Problems in Later Middle English Literature.* Ed. Derek Pearsall. Cambridge: Brewer, 1987. Pp. 87–94.

Hanning, Robert. "Review Essay." *History and Theory,* 12 (1973): 419–34.

Hanning, Robert. " 'The Struggle between Noble Designs and Chaos': The Literary Tradition of Chaucer's Knight's Tale." *The Literary Review* 23 (1980): 519–41.

Hanning, Robert. *The Vision of History in Early Britain.* New York: Columbia University Press, 1966.

Harrington, Norman. "Chaucer's *Merchant's Tale:* Another Swing of the Pendulum." *PMLA* 86 (1971): 25–31.

Harriss, G. L. *King, Parliament, and Public Finance in Medieval England to 1369.* Oxford: Clarendon Press, 1975.

Harvey, P. D. A., ed. *The Peasant Land Market in Medieval England.* Oxford: Clarendon Press, 1984.

Harwood, Britton J. "The Wife of Bath and the Dream of Innocence." *MLQ* 33 (1972): 257–73.

Hatton, Thomas J. "Chaucer's Crusading Knight: A Slanted Ideal." *ChR* 3 (1968–69): 77–87.

Helmholz, R. H. *Marriage Litigation in Medieval England.* Cambridge: Cambridge University Press, 1974.

Helterman, Jeffrey. "The Dehumanizing Metamorphoses of *The Knight's Tale.*" *ELH* 38 (1971): 493–511.

Herrmann, Claudine. *Le role judicaire et politique des femmes sous la Republique romaine.* Brussels: Latomus, 1964.

Hertz, Neil. *The End of the Line.* New York: Columbia University Press, 1985.

Herz, Judith Scherer. "Chaucer's Elegiac Knight." *Criticism* 6 (1964): 212–24.

Hewitt, H. J. *The Organization of War under Edward III, 1338–62.* Manchester: Manchester University Press, 1966.

Hilton, Rodney. *Bond Men Made Free.* London: Methuen, 1977 (1973).

Hilton, Rodney. *Class Conflict and the Crisis of Feudalism.* London: Hambledon Press, 1985.

Hilton, Rodney. *The English Peasantry in the Later Middle Ages.* Oxford: Clarendon Press, 1975.

Hilton, Rodney. "Medieval Market Towns and Simple Commodity Production." *Past and Present* 109 (1985): 3–23.

Hilton, Rodney. *A Medieval Society: The West Midlands at the End of the Thirteenth Century.* London: Weidenfeld and Nicolson, 1966.

Hilton, Rodney. "Towns in Societies—Medieval England." *Urban History Yearbook* (1982): 7–13.

Hilton, Rodney. "Warriors and Peasants." *New Left Review* 83 (1974): 83–94.

Hilton, Rodney., ed. *The Transition from Feudalism to Capitalism*. London: Verso, 1978.

Hoffman, Richard. "Jephthah's Daughter and Chaucer's Virginia." *ChR* 2 (1967–68): 20–31.

Hoffman, Richard. *Ovid and the Canterbury Tales*. Philadelphia: University of Pennsylvania Press, 1966.

Holt, J. C. "The Origins and Audience of the Ballads of Robin Hood." *Past and Present* 18 (1960); reprinted *Peasants, Knights and Heretics*. Ed. R. H. Hilton. Cambridge: Cambridge University Press, 1976. Pp. 236–57.

Holt, R. H. "Whose Were the Profits of Corn Milling?" *Past and Present* 116 (1987): 3–23.

Holton, R. J. *Cities, Capitalism and Civilization*. London: Allen and Unwin, 1986.

Holton, R. J. *The Transition from Feudalism to Capitalism*. New York: St. Martin's Press, 1985.

Homans, George C. *English Villagers of the Thirteenth Century*. Cambridge: Harvard University Press, 1941.

Hort, Greta. Piers Plowman *and Contemporary Religious Thought*. London: Society for Promoting Christian Knowledge, [1938].

Hoskins, William G. *The Midland Peasant: The Economic and Social History of a Leicestershire Village*. London: Macmillan, 1957.

Houlbrooke, Ralph A. *The English Family 1450–1700*. London: Longman, 1984.

Howard, Donald R. *Chaucer: His Life, His Works, His World*. New York: Dutton, 1987.

Howard, Donald R. "Experience, Language, and Consciousness: *Troilus and Criseyde*, II, 596–931." *Medieval Literature and Folklore Studies: Essays in Honor of Francis Lee Utley*. Ed. Jerome Mandel and Bruce A. Rosenberg. New Brunswick: Rutgers University Press, 1970. Pp. 173–92.

Howard, Donald R. *The Idea of the* Canterbury Tales. Berkeley: University of California Press, 1976.

Howell, Martha C. *Women, Production, and Patriarchy in Late Medieval Cities*. Chicago: University of Chicago Press, 1986.

Hudson, Anne. *The Premature Reformation: Wycliffite Texts and Lollard History*. Oxford: Clarendon Press, 1988.

Hughes, Diane Owen. "Invisible Madonnas? The Italian Historiographical Tradition and the Women of Medieval Italy." *Women in Medieval History and Historiography*. Ed. Susan Mosher Stuard. Philadelphia: University of Pennsylvania Press, 1987. Pp. 25–57.

Hughes, Diane Owen. "Urban Growth and Family Structure in Medieval Genoa." *Past and Present* 66 (1975): 3–28.

Hughes, Muriel J. "The Library of Philip the Bold and Margaret of Flanders, First Valois Duke and Duchess of Burgundy." _JMH_ 4 (1978): 145–88.

Huizinga, Johan. _Men and Ideas._ Trans. James S. Holmes and Hans van Marle. New York: Meridian Books, 1959.

Huizinga, Johan. _The Waning of the Middle Ages._ Trans. F. Hopman. London: Edward Arnold, 1924.

Hulbert, James Root. _Chaucer's Official Life._ Menasha: Collegiate Press, 1912.

Hulbert, James Root. "What Was Chaucer's Aim in the _Knight's Tale?_" _SP_ 26 (1929): 375–85.

Hult, David. _Self-Fulfilling Prophecies: Readership and Authority in the First_ Roman de la Rose. Cambridge: Cambridge University Press, 1986.

Hultin, Neil C. "Anti-Courtly Elements in Chaucer's _Complaint of Mars._" _AnM_ 9 (1968): 58–75.

Hunt, Tony. "The _Song of Songs_ and Courtly Literature." _Court and Poet._ Ed. Glyn S. Burgess. Liverpool: Francis Cairns, 1981. Pp. 189–96.

Huppé, Bernard F. _A Reading of the_ Canterbury Tales. Rev. ed. Albany: State University of New York Press, 1967.

Huppé, Bernard F., and D. W. Robertson, Jr. _Fruyt and Chaf: Studies in Chaucer's Allegories._ Princeton: Princeton University Press, 1963.

Jacob, E. F. "The Book of St. Albans." _BJRL_ 28 (1944): 99–118.

Jaeger, C. Stephen. _The Origins of Courtliness: Civilizing Trends and the Formation of Courtly Ideals 939–1210._ Philadelphia: University of Pennsylvania Press, 1985.

James, Mervyn. _English Politics and the Concept of Honour, 1485–1642. Past and Present,_ Supplement No. 3. Cambridge: Cambridge University Press, 1978.

James, Mervyn. _Society, Politics and Culture: Studies in Early Modern England._ Cambridge: Cambridge University Press, 1986.

Jauss, Hans Robert. "La transformation de la forme allégorique entre 1180 et 1240: D'Alain de Lille à Guillaume de Lorris." _L'Humanisme médiévale dans les littératures romanes du XIIᵉ au XIVᵉ siècle._ Ed. Anthime Fourrier. Paris: Klincksieck, 1964. Pp. 107–46.

Javelet, Robert. _Image et ressemblance au douzième siècle._ 2 vols. Paris: Letouzey et Ané, 1967.

Jay, Martin. _The Dialectical Imagination: A History of the Frankfurt School and the Institute of Social Research 1923–1950._ Boston: Little, Brown, 1973.

Jones, George Fenwick. "Chaucer and the Medieval Miller." _MLQ_ 16 (1955): 3–15.

Jones, Michael. "'Mon Pais et ma Nation': Breton Identity in the Fourteenth Century." _War, Literature and Politics in the Late Middle Ages._ Ed. C. T. Allmand. Liverpool: University of Liverpool Press, 1976. Pp. 144–68.

Jones, Richard H. *The Royal Policy of Richard II: Absolutism in the Later Middle Ages.* Oxford: Blackwell, 1968.

Jones, Terry. *Chaucer's Knight: The Portrait of a Medieval Mercenary.* Baton Rouge: Louisiana State University Press, 1980.

Joseph, Gerhard. "Chaucer's Coinage: Foreign Exchange and the Puns of the *Shipman's Tale.*" *ChR* 17 (1982–83): 341–47.

Justman, Stewart. "Literal and Symbolic in the *Canterbury Tales.*" *ChR* 14 (1979–80): 199–214.

Kaeuper, Richard W. *War, Justice and Public Order.* Oxford: Clarendon Press, 1988.

Kamenka, Eugene, and J. S. Neale, eds. *Feudalism, Capitalism and Beyond.* Canberra: Australian National University Press, 1975.

Kaske, Robert E. "The 'Canticum Canticorum' in the 'Miller's Tale'." *SP* 59 (1962): 479–500.

Kaske, Robert E. "Chaucer's Marriage Group." *Chaucer the Love Poet.* Ed. Jerome Mitchell and William Provost. Athens: University of Georgia Press, 1973. Pp. 45–65.

Kaske, Robert E. "The Knight's Interruption of the *Monk's Tale.*" *ELH* 24 (1957): 249–68.

Kaye, Harvey J. *The British Marxist Historians.* London: Polity Press, 1984.

Kean, Patricia M. *Chaucer and the Making of English Poetry.* 2 vols. London: Routledge and Kegan Paul, 1972.

Keen, Maurice. "Chaucer's Knight, the English Aristocracy and the Crusade." *English Court Culture in the Later Middle Ages.* Ed. V. J. Scattergood and J. W. Sherborne. Pp. 45–61.

Keen, Maurice. *Chivalry.* New Haven: Yale University Press, 1984.

Keen, Maurice. "Chivalry, Nobility and the Man-at-Arms." *War, Literature, and Politics in the Late Middle Ages.* Ed. C. T. Allmand. Liverpool: Liverpool University Press, 1976. Pp. 32–45.

Keen, Maurice. "Huizinga, Kilgour and the Decline of Chivalry." *M&H* 8 (1977): 1–20.

Keen, Maurice. "The Jurisdiction and Origins of the Court of Chivalry." *War and Government in the Middle Ages: Essays in Honour of J. O. Prestwich.* Ed. John Gillingham and J. C. Holt. Woodbridge: Boydell, 1984. Pp. 159–69.

Keiser, George R. "Language and Meaning in Chaucer's *Shipman's Tale.*" *ChR* 12 (1977–78): 147–61.

Kekewich, Margaret. "Edward IV, William Caxton, and Literary Patronage in Yorkist England." *MLR* 66 (1971): 481–87.

Kellogg, Alfred L. "An Augustinian Interpretation of Chaucer's Pardoner." *Speculum* 26 (1951): 465–81.

Kellogg, Alfred L. "Susannah and the *Merchant's Tale.*" *Speculum* 35 (1960): 275–79.

Kellogg, Alfred L., and Louis Haselmayer. "Chaucer's Satire of the Pardoner." *PMLA* 66 (1951): 251–77.

Kelly, Douglas. *Sens and Conjointure in the* Chevalier de la charrette. The Hague: Mouton, 1966.

Kelly, Douglas. "*Translatio Studii:* Translation, Adaptation, and Allegory in Medieval French Literature." *PQ* 57 (1978): 287–310.

Kelly, Henry Ansgar. *Love and Marriage in the Age of Chaucer.* Ithaca: Cornell University Press, 1975.

Kendrick, Laura. "Fame's Fabrication." *Studies in the Age of Chaucer Proceedings 1, 1984: Reconstructing Chaucer.* Ed. Paul Strohm and Thomas Heffernan. Knoxville: New Chaucer Society, 1985. Pp. 135–48.

Kendrick Laura. *The Game of Love: Troubadour Wordplay.* Berkeley: University of California Press, 1988.

Kernan, Anne. "The Arch-Wife and the Eunuch." *ELH* 41 (1974): 1–25.

Kibler, William W. "Poet and Patron: Froissart's *Prison amoureuse.*" *L'Esprit Créateur* 18 (1972): 32–46.

Kierkegaard, Søren. *The Sickness Unto Death.* Trans. Walter Lowrie. Garden City: Doubleday Anchor Books, n.d.

Kilgour, Raymond Lincoln. *The Decline of Chivalry as Shown in the French Literature of the Late Middle Ages.* Cambridge: Harvard University Press, 1937.

Kirk, Elizabeth. *The Dream Thought of* Piers Plowman. New Haven: Yale University Press, 1972.

Kittredge, George L. "Chaucer's Lollius." *Harvard Studies in Classical Philology* 28 (1917): 47–133.

Kittredge, George L. "Chaucer's Pardoner." *Atlantic Monthly* 72 (1893): 829–33.

Knapp, Daniel. "The Relic of a Seint: A Gloss on Chaucer's Pilgrimage." *ELH* 39 (1972): 1–26.

Knight, Stephen. *Geoffrey Chaucer.* Oxford: Basil Blackwell, 1985.

Koban, Charles. "Hearing Chaucer Out: The Art of Persuasion in the *Wife of Bath's Tale.*" *ChR* 5 (1970–71): 225–39.

Köhler, Erich. *Ideal und Wirklichkeit in der höfischen Epik.* 2d ed. Tübingen: Niemeyer, 1970.

Kolb, David. *The Critique of Pure Modernity: Hegel, Heidegger, and After.* Chicago: University of Chicago Press, 1986.

Kolve, V. A. *Chaucer and the Imagery of Narrative: The First Five Canterbury Tales.* Stanford: Stanford University Press, 1984.

Kolve, V. A. *The Play Called Corpus Christi.* Stanford: Stanford University Press, 1966.

Kosminsky, Evgeny A. *Studies in the Agrarian History of England in the Thir-*

teenth Century. Ed. Rodney H. Hilton. Trans. Ruth Kisch. Oxford: Blackwell, 1956.

Krüger, Karl Heinrich. *Die Universalchroniken.* Typologie des sources du Moyen Age, fasc. 16. Turnhout: Brepols, 1976.

Lacan, Jacques. *Écrits: A Selection.* Trans. Alan Sheridan. London: Tavistock, 1977.

Lacan, Jacques. *Speech and Language in Psychoanalysis.* Trans. Anthony Wilden. Baltimore: Johns Hopkins University Press, 1968.

Ladner, Gerhart B. *The Idea of Reform: Its Impact on Christian Thought and Action in the Age of the Fathers.* Cambridge: Harvard University Press, 1959.

Lambert, Malcolm D. *Medieval Heresy: Popular Movements from Bogomil to Hus.* London: Edward Arnold, 1977.

Lambert, Mark. "*Troilus,* Books I–III: A Criseydan Reading." *Essays on Troilus and Criseyde.* Ed. Mary Salu. Cambridge: D. S. Brewer, 1979. Pp. 105–25.

Langholm, Odd. *Price and Value in the Aristotelian Tradition.* Bergen: Universitetsforlaget. 1979.

Lausberg, Heinrich. *Handbuch der literarischen Rhetorik: Eine Grundlegung der Literaturwissenschaft.* 2 vols. Munich: Hueber, 1960.

Lawler, Traugott. *The One and the Many in* The Canterbury Tales. Hamden: Archon Books, 1980.

Lawton, David. *Chaucer's Narrators.* Cambridge: Brewer, 1985.

Leach, Edmund. "Caste, Class and Slavery: The Taxonomic Problem." *Caste and Race: Comparative Approaches.* Ed. Anthony de Reuck and Julie Knight. Boston: Little Brown, 1966. Pp. 5–16.

Leclercq, Jean. *The Love of Learning and the Desire for God.* Trans. Jean Misrahi. New York: New American Library, 1962.

Leclercq, Jean. "Le magistère du prédicateur au XIIe siècle." *AHDLMA* 15 (1946): 105–47.

Leff, Gordon. *Bradwardine and the Pelagians.* Cambridge: Cambridge University Press, 1957.

Legge, M. D. *Anglo-Norman Literature and Its Background.* Oxford: Clarendon Press, 1963.

Le Goff, Jacques, and Jean-Claude Schmitt, eds. *Le Charivari.* The Hague: Mouton, 1981.

Lehmann, Paul. *Parodie im Mittelalter.* Munich: Die Drei Masken, 1923.

Leicester, H. Marshall, Jr. "The Art of Impersonation: A General Prologue to the *Canterbury Tales.*" *PMLA* 95 (1980): 213–24.

Leicester, H. Marshall Jr. " 'Synne Horrible': The Pardoner's Exegesis of His Tale, and Chaucer's." *Acts of Interpretation: The Text in its Contexts,*

700–1600. *Essays in Medieval and Renaissance Literature in Honor of E. T. Donaldson.* Ed. Mary J. Carruthers and Elizabeth D. Kirk. Norman: Pilgrim Books, 1982. Pp. 25–50.

Lemaire, Anike. *Jacques Lacan.* Trans. David Macey. London: Routledge and Kegan Paul, 1977.

Lenaghan, R. T. "Chaucer's Circle of Gentlemen and Clerks." *ChR* 18 (1983–84): 155–60.

Lester, G. A. "Chaucer's Knight and the Earl of Warwick." *N&Q* 28 (1981): 200–202.

Lester, G. A. "Chaucer's Knight and the Medieval Tournament." *Neophilologus* 46 (1982): 460–68.

Levi, Primo. *The Truce.* Trans. Stuart Woolf. London: Sphere Books, 1987.

Levy, Bernard S. "The Quaint World of the *Shipman's Tale.*" *SSF* 4 (1966–67): 112–18.

Levy, F. J. *Tudor Historical Thought.* San Marino: Huntington Library, 1967.

Lewis, C. S. "What Chaucer Really Did to *Il Filostrato.*" *Essays and Studies* 17 (1932): 56–75.

Lindahl, Carl. "The Festive Form of the *Canterbury Tales.*" *ELH* 52 (1985): 531–74.

Lindenbaum, Sheila. "The Smithfield Tournament of 1390." *JMRS* 20 (1990): 1–20.

Little, A. G. *Studies in English Franciscan History.* Manchester: University of Manchester Press, 1917.

Little, Lester K. *Religious Poverty and the Profit Economy in Medieval Europe.* Ithaca: Cornell University Press, 1978.

Lloyd, T. H. *The English Wool Trade in the Middle Ages.* Cambridge: Cambridge University Press, 1977.

London, H. Stanford. *Royal Beasts.* East Knoyle: Heraldry Society, 1956.

Loomis, Roger Sherman. *A Mirror of Chaucer's World.* Princeton: Princeton University Press, 1965.

Lopez, Robert S. *The Commercial Revolution of the Middle Ages, 950–1350.* Englewood Cliffs: Prentice-Hall, 1971.

Lowes, John Livingston. *Convention and Revolt in Poetry.* Boston: Houghton Mifflin, 1919.

Lowes, John Livingston. *Geoffrey Chaucer and the Development of his Genius.* Boston: Houghton Mifflin, 1934.

Lowes, John Livingston. "The Prologue to the *Legend of Good Women* Considered in its Chronological Relations." *PMLA* 20 (1905): 749–864.

Lubac, Henri, de. *Exégèse médiévale: les quatres sens de l'Écriture.* 4 vols. Paris: Aubier, 1959–64.

McAlpine, Monica. *The Genre of* Troilus and Criseyde. Ithaca: Cornell University Press, 1978.

McAlpine, Monica. "The Pardoner's Homosexuality and How it Matters." *PMLA* 95 (1980): 8–22.

McCall, John P. *Chaucer Among the Gods: The Poetics of Classical Myth*. University Park: Pennsylvania State University Press, 1979.

McCall, John P. "Five-Book Structure in Chaucer's *Troilus*." *MLQ* 23 (1962): 297–308.

McCall, John P. "The Trojan Scene in Chaucer's *Troilus*." *ELH* 29 (1962): 263–75.

McCall, John P., and George Rudisill, Jr. "The Parliament of 1386 and Chaucer's Trojan Parliament." *JEGP* 58 (1959): 276–88.

Macfarlane, Alan. *Love and Marriage in England, 1300–1800*. Oxford: Blackwell, 1986.

Macfarlane, Alan. *The Origins of English Individualism: The Family, Property and Social Transition*. Oxford: Blackwell, 1978.

Macfarlane, Alan. "Review" of Lawrence Stone, *The Family, Sex, and Marriage in England, 1500–1800*. *History and Theory* 18 (1979): 103–26.

McFarlane, K. B. *England in the Fifteenth Century: Collected Essays*. London: Hambledon Press, 1981.

McFarlane, K. B. *Lancastrian Kings and Lollard Knights*. Oxford: Clarendon Press, 1973.

McFarlane, K. B. *The Nobility of Later Medieval England*. Oxford: Clarendon Press, 1973.

McGaillard, John C. "Characterization in Chaucer's *Shipman's Tale*." *PQ* 54 (1975): 1–18.

McGovern, John H. "The Rise of New Economic Attitudes—Economic Humanism, Economic Nationalism—During the Later Middle Ages and the Renaissance, A.D. 1200–1550." *Traditio* 26 (1970): 217–53.

MacIntyre, Alasdair. *After Virtue*. 2d ed. Notre Dame: University of Notre Dame Press, 1984 (1981).

McKeon, Richard. "Rhetoric in the Middle Ages." *Critics and Criticism: Ancient and Modern*. Ed. R. S. Crane. Chicago: University of Chicago Press, 1952. Pp. 260–96.

MacKinnon, Catherine A. *Feminism Unmodified*. Cambridge: Harvard University Press, 1987.

McKisack, May. *The Fourteenth Century*. Oxford: Clarendon Press, 1959.

Magoun, Francis P. "Chaucer's Summary of Statius' *Thebaid* II–XII." *Traditio* 11 (1955): 409–20.

Mann, Jill. *Chaucer and Medieval Estates Satire: The Literature of Social Classes and the* General Prologue *to the* Canterbury Tales. Cambridge: Cambridge University Press, 1973.

Markus, R. A. *Saeculum: History and Society in the Theology of St. Augustine*. Cambridge: Cambridge University Press, 1970.

Martin, John E. *Feudalism to Capitalism: Peasant and Landlord in English Agrarian Development*. Atlantic Highlands: Humanities Press, 1983.

Marx, Karl. *Capital*. 3 vols. Ed. Frederick Engels. New York: International Publishers, 1967.

Marx, Karl. *Grundrisse: Foundations of the Critique of Political Economy*. Trans. Martin Nicolaus. Harmondsworth: Penguin Books, 1973.

Mathew, Gervase. *The Court of Richard II*. London: John Murray, 1968.

Mathew, Gervase. "Marriage and *Amour Courtois* in Late Fourteenth-Century England." *Essays Presented to Charles Williams*. London: Oxford University Press, 1947. Pp. 128–35.

Matter, Hans. *Englische Gründungssagen von Geoffrey of Monmouth bis zur Renaissance*. Heidelberg: Winter, 1922.

Matthews, William. "The Wife of Bath and All Her Sect." *Viator* 5 (1974): 413–43.

Mazzotta, Giuseppe. *Dante, Poet of the Desert*. Princeton: Princeton University Press, 1979.

Meech, Sanford. *Design in Chaucer's "Troilus."* Syracuse: Syracuse University Press, 1959.

Merelman, Richard M. *Making Something of Ourselves: On Culture and Politics in the United States*. Berkeley: University of California Press, 1984.

Merrill, Rodney. "Chaucer's *Broche of Thebes*: The Unity of *The Complaint of Mars* and *The Complaint of Venus*." *Literary Monographs* 5 (1973): 3–61.

Merrington, John. "Town and Country in the Transition to Capitalism." *The Transition from Feudalism to Capitalism*. Ed. Rodney Hilton. London: Verso, 1978. Pp. 170–95.

Mertes, Kate. *The English Noble Household, 1250–1600*. Oxford: Blackwell, 1988.

Meyer, Paul. "Les premières compilations françaises d'histoire ancienne." *Romania* 14 (1885): 36–76.

Michaud-Quantin, Pierre. *Sommes de casuistiques et manuels de confession au moyen âge, XII^eXVI^e siècles*. Louvain: Nauwelaerts, 1962.

Middleton, Anne. "Chaucer's 'New Men' and the Good of Poetry." *Literature and Society*. Ed. Edward W. Said. Baltimore: Johns Hopkins University Press, 1980. Pp. 15–56.

Middleton, Anne. "The Idea of Public Poetry in the Reign of Richard II." *Speculum* 53 (1978): 94–114.

Middleton, Anne. "Narration and the Invention of Experience: Episodic Form in *Piers Plowman*." *The Wisdom of Poetry: Essays in Early English Literature in Honor of Morton W. Bloomfield*. Ed. Larry D. Benson and Siegfried Wenzel. Kalamazoo: Medieval Institute Publications, 1982. Pp. 81–122.

Middleton, Anne. "The *Physician's Tale* and Love's Martyrs: 'Ensamples Mo Than Ten' as a Method in the *Canterbury Tales.*" *ChR* 8 (1973–74): 9–32.

Mieszkowski, Gretchen. "'Pandras' in Deschamps' Ballade for Chaucer." *ChR* 9 (1974–75): 327–36.

Miller, Clarence H., and Roberta B. Bosse. "Chaucer's Pardoner and the Mass." *ChR* 6 (1971–72): 171–84.

Miller, Robert P. "Chaucer's Pardoner, the Scriptural Eunuch, and the *Pardoner's Tale.*" *Speculum* 30 (1955): 180–99.

Miller, Robert P. "The *Miller's Tale* as a Complaint." *ChR* 5 (1970–71): 147–60.

Miller, Robert P., ed. *Chaucer: Sources and Backgrounds.* New York: Oxford University Press, 1977.

Minnis, Alastair. *Chaucer and Pagan Antiquity.* Cambridge: Brewer, 1982.

Minnis, Alastair. *Medieval Theory of Authorship: Scholastic Literary Attitudes in the Later Middle Ages.* 2d ed. London: Scolar Press, 1988.

Miskimin, Harry. *The Economy of Early Renaissance Europe, 1300–1460.* Cambridge: Cambridge University Press, 1975.

Moffatt, Michael. *Coming of Age in New Jersey: College and American Culture.* New Brunswick, N.J.: Rutgers University Press, 1989.

Molinari, Paolo, S. J. *Julian of Norwich.* London: Longmans, 1958.

Mollat, Michel, and Philippe Wolff. *Ongles bleus, Jacques et Ciompi: les révolutions populaires en Europe aux XIVe et XVe siècles.* Paris: Calman-Lévy, 1970.

Momigliano, Arnaldo. *Essays in Ancient and Modern Historiography.* Middletown: Wesleyan University Press, 1975.

Mommsen, Theodor. *Medieval and Renaissance Studies.* Ed. Eugene Rice. Ithaca: Cornell University Press, 1959.

Monfrin, Jacques. "Les traducteurs et leur public en France au Moyen Age." *L'humanisme médiéval dans les littératures romanes du XIIe au XIVe siècles.* Ed. Anthime Fourrier. Paris: Klincksieck, 1964. Pp. 247–62.

Monfrin, Jacques. "La traduction française de Tite-Live." *Histoire littéraire de la France.* Vol. 39. Paris: Imprimerie Nationale, 1962. Pp. 358–414.

Moore, Arthur K. "Alysoun's Other Tonne." *MLN* 59 (1944): 481–83.

Moore, Arthur K. "The Pardoner's Interruption of the *Wife of Bath's Prologue.*" *MLQ* 10 (1949): 49–57.

Morawski, J. "Parodie d'un passage du *Roman de la Rose* dans un *Sermon Joyeux.*" *Romania* 52 (1926): 159–60.

Murphy, James J. *Rhetoric in the Middle Ages.* Berkeley: University of California Press, 1974.

Muscatine, Charles. *Chaucer and the French Tradition.* Berkeley: University of California Press, 1957.

Muscatine, Charles. "Form, Texture, and Meaning in Chaucer's *Knight's Tale.*" *PMLA* 65 (1950): 911–29.

Muscatine, Charles. "The Name of Chaucer's Friar." *MLN* 70 (1955): 169–72.

Muscatine, Charles. *Poetry and Crisis in the Age of Chaucer.* Notre Dame: University of Notre Dame Press, 1972.

Muscatine, Charles. "The Wife of Bath and Gautier's *La veuve.*" *Romance Studies in Memory of Edward Billings Ham.* Ed. Urban T. Holmes. Hayward: California State College, 1967. Pp. 109–14.

Myers, A. R. *London in the Age of Chaucer.* Norman: University of Oklahoma Press, 1973.

Neilson, George. *Trial by Combat.* Glasgow: William Hodge, 1890.

Neuse, Richard. "The Knight: The First Mover in Chaucer's Human Comedy." *UTQ* 31 (1962): 299–315.

Nichols, Robert E., Jr. "The Pardoner's Ale and Cake." *PMLA* 82 (1967): 498–504.

Nicholson, Peter. "The 'Shipman's Tale' and the Fabliaux." *ELH* 45 (1978): 583–96.

Niles, John D. "Ring Composition and the Structure of *Beowulf.*" *PMLA* 94 (1979): 924–35.

Nohrnberg, James. *The Analogy of the* Faerie Queene. Princeton: Princeton University Press, 1976.

Noonan, John T. "Marital Affection in the Canonists." *Studia gratiana* 12 (1967): 479–509.

Noonan, John T. *The Scholastic Analysis of Usury.* Cambridge: Harvard University Press, 1957.

North, J. D. "Kalenderes Enlumyned Ben They: Some Astronomical Themes in Chaucer," *RES* 20 (1969): 129–54; 257–83; 418–44.

Norton-Smith, John. "Chaucer's *Anelida and Arcite.*" *Medieval Studies for J. A. W. Bennett.* Ed. Peter Heyworth. Oxford: Clarendon Press, 1981. Pp. 81–99.

Oberman, Heiko A. *Archbishop Thomas Bradwardine, A Fourteenth-Century Augustinian.* Utrecht: Kemink and Zoon, 1957.

Oberman, Heiko A. "Duns Scotus, Nominalism, and the Council of Trent." *John Duns Scotus, 1265–1965.* Ed. John K. Ryan and Bernardine M. Bonansea. Washington: Catholic University of America Press, 1965. Pp. 311–44.

Oberman, Heiko A. "The Gospel of Social Unrest." *The German Peasant War of 1525—New Viewpoints.* Ed. Bob Scribner and Gerhard Benecke. London: Allen and Unwin, 1979. Pp. 39–51.

Olson, Glending. "Deschamps' *Art de dictier* and Chaucer's Literary Environment." *Speculum* 48 (1973): 714–23.

Olson, Glending. "Making and Poetry in the Age of Chaucer." *CL* 31 (1979): 272–90.

Olson, Glending. "Toward a Poetics of the Late Medieval Court Lyric." *Vernacular Poetics in the Middle Ages.* Ed. Lois Ebin. Kalamazoo: Medieval Institute Publications, 1984. Pp. 227–48.

Olson, Paul A. *The Canterbury Tales and the Good Society.* Princeton: Princeton University Press, 1985.

Olson, Paul A. "Chaucer's Epic Statement and the Political Milieu of the Late Fourteenth Century." *Mediaevalia* 5 (1979): 61–87.

Olson, Paul A. "The *Reeve's Tale:* Chaucer's *Measure for Measure.*" *SP* 59 (1962): 1–17.

Oman, Charles A. *The Great Revolt of 1381.* Oxford: Clarendon Press, 1906.

Origo, Iris. *The Merchant of Prato.* Harmondsworth: Penguin Books, 1963 (1957).

Otis, Brooks. *Ovid as an Epic Poet.* 2d ed. Cambridge: Cambridge University Press, 1970.

Otten, Charlotte. "Proserpine: *Liberatrix Suae Gentis.*" *ChR* 5 (1970–71): 277–87.

Owen, Charles A., Jr. "The Alternative Reading of *The Canterbury Tales:* Chaucer's Text and the Early Manuscripts." *PMLA* 97 (1982): 237–50.

Owen, Charles A., Jr. "Morality as a Comic Motif in the *Canterbury Tales.*" *CE* 16 (1955): 226–32.

Owen, Charles A., Jr. *Pilgrimage and Storytelling in the Canterbury Tales: The Dialectic of "Ernest" and "Game."* Norman: University of Oklahoma Press, 1977.

Owst, G. R. *Literature and Pulpit in Medieval England.* 2d ed. Oxford: Blackwell, 1961.

Palmer, J. J. N. *England, France and Christendom, 1377–99.* London: Routledge and Kegan Paul, 1972.

Palmer, J. J. N. "The Last Summons of the Feudal Army in England." *EHR* 83 (1968): 771–75.

Palmer, J. J. N. "The Parliament of 1385 and the Constitutional Crisis of 1386." *Speculum* 46 (1971): 477–90.

Palmer, Nigel F. "Latin and Vernacular in the Northern European Tradition of the *De Consolatione Philosophiae.*" *Boethius: His Life, Thought and Influence.* Ed. Margaret Gibson. Oxford: Blackwell, 1981. Pp. 362–409.

Panofsky, Erwin. *Renaissance and Renascences in Western Art.* Stockholm: Almqvist and Wiksell, 1960.

Parker, Patricia. *Inescapable Romance: Studies in the Poetics of a Mode.* Princeton: Princeton University Press, 1979.

Parkes, M. B. "The Influence of the Concepts of *Ordinatio* and *Compilatio* on the Development of the Book." *Medieval Learning and Literature: Essays Presented to Richard William Hunt.* Ed. J. J. G. Alexander and M. T. Gibson. Oxford: Clarendon Press, 1976. Pp. 115–41.

Parr, Johnstone. "The Date and Revision of Chaucer's *Knight's Tale.*" *PMLA* 60 (1945): 307–24.

Parr, Johnstone. "Reply." *PMLA* 63 (1948): 736–39.

Partner, Nancy F. *Serious Entertainments: The Writing of History in Twelfth-Century England.* Chicago: University of Chicago Press, 1977.

Pasquali, Giorgio. *Storia della tradizione e critica del testo.* 2d. ed. Florence: Le Monnier, 1962 (1934).

Pastoureau, Michel. *Les armoiries.* Typologie des sources du moyen âge occidental, 20. Turnhout: Brepols, 1976.

Patterson, Lee. *Negotiating the Past: The Historical Understanding of Medieval Literature.* Madison: University of Wisconsin Press, 1987.

Patterson, Lee. "The *Parson's Tale* and the Quitting of the *Canterbury Tales.*" *Traditio* 34 (1978): 331–80.

Patterson, Lee. " 'What Man Artow?': Authorial Self-Definition in the *Tale of Sir Thopas* and the *Tale of Melibee.*" *SAC* 11 (1989): 117–76.

Payen, Jean-Charles. "La Crise du mariage à la fin du XIIIe siècle d'aprés la littérature française du temps." *Famille et parenté dans l'occident médiévale.* Ed. Georges Duby and Jacques Le Goff. Rome: Ecole Française, 1977. Pp. 413–30.

Payen, Jean-Charles. *Le Motif de repentir dans la littérature française médiévale (des origines à 1230).* Geneva: Droz, 1968.

Pearsall, Derek. *The Canterbury Tales.* London: Unwin, 1985.

Pearsall, Derek. "Chaucer's Pardoner: The Death of a Salesman." *ChR* 17 (1983–84): 358–65.

Pearsall, Derek. *John Lydgate.* London: Routledge and Kegan Paul, 1970.

Pearsall, Derek. *Old English and Middle English Poetry.* London: Routledge and Kegan Paul, 1977.

Pearsall, Derek. "The *Troilus* Frontispiece and Chaucer's Audience." *YES* 7 (1977): 68–74.

Peck, Russell A. *Chaucer's Lyrics and* Anelida and Arcite: *An Annotated Bibliography (1900–1980).* Toronto: University of Toronto Press, 1983.

Peck, Russell A. "Social Conscience and the Poets." *Social Unrest in the Late Middle Ages.* Ed. Francis X. Newman. Binghamton: Medieval and Renaissance Texts and Studies, 1986. Pp. 113–48.

Peterson, Joyce E. "With Feigned Flattery: The Pardoner as Vice." *ChR* 10 (1975–76): 326–36.

Peterson, Thomas Virgil. *Ham and Japheth: The Mythic World of Whites in the Antebellum South.* Metuchan: Scarecrow Press, 1978.

Phythian-Adams, Charles. "Ceremony and the Citizen: The Communal

Year at Coventry 1450–1550." *Crisis and Order in English Towns 1500–1700: Essays in Urban History.* Ed. Peter Clark and Paul Slack. London: Routledge and Kegan Paul, 1972. Pp. 57–85.

Phythian-Adams, Charles. *Desolation of a City: Coventry and the Urban Crisis of the Late Middle Ages.* Cambridge: Cambridge University Press, 1979.

Pickering, F. P. *Literature and Art in the Middle Ages.* Coral Gables: University of Miami Press, 1970.

Pickford, C. E. "The Royal Boar and the Ellesmere Chaucer." *PQ* 5 (1926): 330–40.

Picot, Emile. "Le monologue dramatique dans l'ancien théatre francais." *Romania* 15 (1886): 358–422; 16 (1887): 438–542; 17 (1888): 207–75.

Pitt-Rivers, Julian. "Honour and Social Status." *Honour and Shame: The Values of Mediterranean Society.* Ed. J. G. Peristiany. London: Weidenfeld and Nicolson, 1965. Pp. 19–77.

Poirion, Daniel. *Le poéte et le prince: Evolution du lyrisme courtois de Guillaume de Machaut à Charles d'Orléans.* Paris: Presses universitaires de France, 1965.

Poirion, Daniel. *Le Roman de la Rose.* Paris: Hatier, 1973.

Postan, M. M. *Essays on Medieval Agriculture and General Problems of the Medieval Economy.* Cambridge: Cambridge University Press, 1973.

Postan, M. M. *The Medieval Economy and Society.* Harmondsworth: Penguin Books, 1975 (1972).

Postan, M. M. *Medieval Trade and Finance.* Cambridge: Cambridge University Press, 1973.

Powell, Edgar. *The Rising in East Anglia in 1381.* Cambridge: Cambridge University Press, 1896.

Pratt, R. A. "Chaucer and the Hand that Fed Him." *Speculum* 41 (1966): 619–42.

Pratt, R. A. "Chaucer's Use of the *Teseida*." *PMLA* 62 (1947): 598–621.

Pratt, R. A. "Chaucer and the Visconti Libraries." *ELH* 6 (1939): 191–99.

Pratt, R. A. "The Development of the Wife of Bath." *Studies in Medieval Literature in Honor of Professor Albert Croll Baugh.* Ed. MacEdward Leach. Philadelphia: University of Pennsylvania Press, 1961. Pp. 45–79.

Pratt, R. A. "Geoffrey Chaucer, Esq., and Sir John Hawkwood." *ELH* 16 (1949): 188–93.

Pratt, R. A. "Was Chaucer's *Knight's Tale* Extensively Revised After the Middle of 1390?" *PMLA* 63 (1948): 726–36.

Prior, Sandra Pierson. "Parodying Typology and the Mystery Plays in the Miller's Tale." *JMRS* 16 (1986): 57–73.

Putnam, Bertha Havens. *Enforcement of the Statute of Labourers.* New York: Columbia University Press, 1908.

Rabinow, Paul, and William M. Sullivan, eds. *Interpretive Social Sciences: A Second Look.* Berkeley: University of California Press, 1987.

Raftis, J. Ambrose. "Social Change versus Revolution: New Interpretations of the Peasants' Revolt of 1381." *Social Unrest in the Late Middle Ages.* Ed. Francis X. Newman. Binghamton: Medieval and Renaissance Texts and Studies, 1986. Pp. 3–22.

Ramsey, R. Vance. "The Hengwrt and Ellesmere Manuscripts of the *Canterbury Tales.*" *SB* 35 (1982): 133–55.

Ramsey, R. Vance. "Paleography and Scribes of Shared Training." *SAC* 8 (1986): 107–44.

Randall, Dale B. J. "A Note on Structure in *Sir Gawain and the Green Knight.*" *MLN* 72 (1959): 161–63.

Raynaud de Lage, Guy. "Les romans antiques dans l'*Histoire ancienne jusqu'à César.*" *Moyen Age* 63 (1957): 267–309.

Reeves, Marjorie. "History and Prophecy in Medieval Thought." *M&H* 5 (1974): 51–75.

Renoir, Alain. "Thebes, Troy, Criseyde, and Pandarus: An Instance of Chaucerian Irony." *SN* 32 (1960): 14–17.

Revard, Carter. "*Gilote et Johane:* An Interlude in B. L. MS. Harley 2253." *SP* 79 (1982): 122–46.

Réville, André, and Charles Petit-Dutaillis. *Le Soulèvement des Travailleurs d'Angleterre en 1381.* Paris: Picard, 1898.

Reynolds, L. D., and N. G. Wilson. *Scribes and Scholars.* Oxford: Clarendon Press, 1968.

Reynolds, Susan. *Kingdoms and Communities in Western Europe, 900–1300.* Oxford: Clarendon Press, 1984.

Rezak, Brigitte Bedos. "The Social Implications of the Art of Chivalry: The Sigillographic Evidence (France 1050–1250)." *The Medieval Court in Europe.* Ed. Edward E. Haymes. Munich: Wilhelm Fink, 1986. Pp. 142–75.

Richardson, Janette. *Blameth Nat Me: A Study of Imagery in Chaucer's Fabliaux.* The Hague: Mouton, 1970.

Robbins, Rossell Hope. "Chaucer and the Lyric Tradition." *Poetica* 15/16 (1983): 107–27.

Robbins, Rossell Hope. "Dissent in Middle English Literature: The Spirit of (Thirteen) Seventy-Six." *M&H* 9 (1979): 25–51.

Robbins, Rossell Hope. "Geoffroi Chaucier, Poète Français, Father of English Poetry." *ChR* 13 (1978–79): 93–115.

Robbins, Rossell Hope. "The Lyrics." *A Companion to Chaucer Studies.* Rev. ed. Ed. Beryl Rowland. New York: Oxford University Press, 1979. Pp. 380–402.

Robbins, Rossell Hope. "The Middle English Court Love Lyric." *The Interpretation of Medieval Lyric.* Ed. W. T. H. Jackson. New York: Columbia University Press, 1980. Pp. 205–32.

Robbins, Rossell Hope. "Poems Dealing with Contemporary Conditions." *A Manual of the Writings in Middle English 1050–1500.* Vol. 5. New Haven: Connecticut Academy of Arts and Sciences, 1975. Pp. 1385–536, 1631–725.

Robbins, Rossell Hope. "The Structure of Longer Middle English Court Poems." *Chaucerian Problems and Perspectives: Essays Presented to Paul E. Beichner.* Ed. Edward Vasta and Zacharias P. Thundy. Notre Dame: University of Notre Dame Press, 1979. Pp. 244–64.

Robbins, Rossell Hope. "The Vintner's Son: French Wine in English Bottles." *Eleanor of Aquitaine: Patron and Politician.* Ed. William W. Kibler. Austin: University of Texas Press, 1976. Pp. 147–72.

Robertson, D. W., Jr. "'And for my land thus hastow mordred me?': Land Tenure, the Cloth Industry, and the Wife of Bath." *ChR* 14 (1979–80): 403–20.

Robertson, D. W., Jr. "Chaucerian Tragedy." *ELH* 19 (1952): 1–37.

Robertson, D. W., Jr. "The Historical Setting of Chaucer's *Book of the Duchess.*" *Medieval Studies in Honor of Urban Tigner Holmes.* Ed. John Mahoney and John Esten Keller. Chapel Hill: University of North Carolina Press, 1965. Pp. 169–95.

Robertson, D. W., Jr. *A Preface to Chaucer.* Princeton: Princeton University Press, 1962.

Robertson, D. W., Jr. "The Probable Date and Purpose of Chaucer's *Knight's Tale.*" *SP* 84 (1987): 418–39.

Robertson, D. W., Jr. "The Probable Date and Purpose of Chaucer's *Troilus.*" *M&H* 13 (1985): 143–71.

Robertson, D. W., Jr. "The Wife of Bath and Midas." *SAC* 6 (1984): 1–20.

Robertson, Stuart. "Elements of Realism in the *Knight's Tale.*" *JEGP* 14 (1915): 226–55.

Rogers, J. E. Thorrold. *A History of Agriculture and Prices in England.* 7 vols. Oxford: Oxford University Press, 1866–1902.

Root, R. K. *The Textual Tradition of Chaucer's Troilus.* Chaucer Society, 1st ser., 99. London: K. Paul, Trench and Trübner, 1916.

Roover, Raymond de. *Business, Banking and Economic Thought in Late Medieval and Early Modern Europe.* Ed. Julius Kirshner. Chicago: University of Chicago Press, 1974.

Rosenthal, Joel. "Mediaeval Longevity and the Secular Peerage, 1350–1400." *Population Studies* 27 (1973): 287–93.

Roskell, J. S. *The Impeachment of Michael de la Pole, Earl of Suffolk in 1386.* Manchester: Manchester University Press, 1984.

Roskell, J. S. *Parliament and Politics in Late Medieval England.* London: Hambledon, 1983.

Ross, Thomas W. *Chaucer's Bawdy.* New York: Dutton, 1972.

Rowe, Donald W. *O Love O Charite! Contraries Harmonized in Chaucer's* Troilus. Carbondale: Southern Illinois State University Press, 1976.

Rowland, Beryl. "Chaucer's Idea of the Pardoner." *ChR* 14 (1979–80): 140–54.

Rubinstein, Nicolai. "The Beginnings of Political Thought in Florence: A Study in Medieval Historiography." *JWCI* 5 (1942): 198–227.

Salter, Elizabeth. *Chaucer: The Knight's Tale and the Clerk's Tale*. London: Edward Arnold, 1962.

Salter, Elizabeth. *Fourteenth-Century English Poetry: Contexts and Readings*. Oxford: Clarendon Press, 1983.

Saul, Nigel. "The Despensers and the Downfall of Edward II." *EHR* 99 (1984): 1–33.

Saul, Nigel. *Scenes from Provincial Life: Knightly Families in Sussex 1280–1400*. Oxford: Clarendon Press, 1986.

Scattergood, V. J. "Literary Culture at the Court of Richard II." *English Court Culture in the Later Middle Ages*. Ed. V. J. Scattergood and J. W. Sherborne. London: Duckworth, 1983. Pp. 29–43.

Scattergood, V. J. "The Originality of the *Shipman's Tale*." *ChR* 11 (1976–77): 210–31.

Scattergood, V. J., ed. *The Works of Sir John Clanvowe*. Cambridge: D. S. Brewer, 1975.

Scattergood, V. J., and J. W. Sherborne, eds. *English Court Culture in the Later Middle Ages*. London: Duckworth, 1983.

Schibanoff, Susan. "Argus and Argyve: Etymology and Characterization in Chaucer's *Troilus*." *Speculum* 51 (1976): 647–58.

Schirmer, Walter F., and Ulrich Broich. *Studien zum literarischen Patronat im England des 12. Jahrhunderts*. Cologne: Westdeutscher Verlag, 1962.

Schmidt, A. V. C. "The Tragedy of Arcite: A Reconsideration of the *Knight's Tale*." *EIC* 19 (1969): 107–17.

Schroeder, Mary C[arruthers]. "Fantasy in the 'Merchant's Tale'." *Criticism* 12 (1970): 167–79.

Schweitzer, Edward C. "Fate and Freedom in *The Knight's Tale*." *SAC* 3 (1981): 13–45.

Sedgewick, G. G. "The Progress of Chaucer's Pardoner, 1880–1940." *MLQ* 1 (1940): 431–58.

Sedgewick, G. G. "The Structure of the *Merchant's Tale*." *UTQ* 17 (1947–48): 337–45.

Sennett, Richard. *The Fall of Public Man: On the Social Psychology of Capitalism*. New York: Knopf, 1977.

Seymour, M. C. "Hypothesis, Hyperbole, and the Hengwrt Manuscript of the *Canterbury Tales*." *ES* 68 (1987): 214–19.

Seznec, Jean. *The Survival of the Pagan Gods: The Mythological Tradition and Its*

Place in Renaissance Humanism and Art. Trans. Barbara Sessions. Bollingen Series, 38. New York: Pantheon Books, 1953.

Shahar, Shulamith. *The Fourth Estate: A History of Women in the Middle Ages.* Trans. Chaya Galai. London: Methuen, 1983.

Shain, C. E. "Pulpit Rhetoric in Three *Canterbury Tales.*" *MLN* 70 (1955): 235–45.

Shannon, Edgar F. *Chaucer and the Roman Poets.* Cambridge: Harvard University Press, 1929.

Sheehan, Michael M. "*Maritalis Affectio* Revisited," in *The Olde Daunce: Love, Friendship, Sex and Marriage in the Medieval World.* Ed. Robert R. Edwards and Stephen Spector. Albany: State University of New York, 1991. Pp. 32–43, 254–60.

Shoaf, R. A. *Dante, Chaucer, and the Currency of the Word.* Norman: Pilgrim Books, 1983.

Shorter, Edward. *The Making of the Modern Family.* London: Collins, 1976.

Sidney, Sir Philip. *An Apology for Poetry.* Ed. Geoffrey Shepherd. London: Nelson, 1965.

Silverstein, Theodore. "The Wife of Bath and the Rhetoric of Enchantment." *MP* 58 (1961): 153–73.

Silvia, Daniel. "Some Fifteenth-Century Manuscripts of the *Canterbury Tales.*" *Chaucer and Middle English Studies in Honor of Rossell Hope Robbins.* Ed. Beryl Rowland. London: Allen and Unwin, 1974. Pp. 153–61.

Smalley, Beryl. *English Friars and Antiquity in the Early Fourteenth Century.* Oxford: Basil Blackwell, 1960.

Smith, Paul. *Discerning the Subject.* Minneapolis: University of Minnesota Press, 1988.

Snell, K. D. M. "English Historical Continuity and the Culture of Capitalism: The Work of Alan Macfarlane." *History Workshop* 27 (1989): 154–63.

Snyder, Susan. "The Left Hand of God: Despair in Medieval and Renaissance Tradition." *Studies in the Renaissance* 12 (1965): 18–59.

Southern, R. W. "Aspects of the European Tradition of Historical Writing: 1. The Classical Tradition from Einhard to Geoffrey of Monmouth." *TRHS,* 5th ser., 20 (1970): 173–96.

Spearing, A. C. *Medieval to Renaissance in English Poetry.* Cambridge: Cambridge University Press, 1985.

Specht, Henrik. *Poetry and the Iconography of the Peasant: The Attitude to the Peasant in Late Medieval English Literature and in Contemporary Calendar Illustration.* Copenhagen: Akademisk Forlag, 1983.

Spiegel, Gabrielle M. "Genealogy: Form and Function in Medieval Historical Narrative." *History and Theory* 22 (1983): 43–53.

Sponsler, Claire B. "Society's Image: Estates Literature in Fifteenth-Century England." *Semiotica* 63 (1987): 229–38.

Spurgeon, Caroline, ed. *Five Hundred Years of Chaucer Criticism and Allusion, 1357–1900.* 3 vols. Cambridge: Cambridge University Press, 1925.

Spykman, Gordon J. *Attrition and Contrition at the Council of Trent.* Kampen: Kok, 1955.

Squibb, G. D. *The High Court of Chivalry.* Oxford: Clarendon Press, 1959.

Steadman, John M. *Disembodied Laughter: Troilus and the Apotheosis Tradition.* Berkeley: University of California Press, 1972.

Steadman, John M. "Old Age and *Contemptus Mundi* in *The Pardoner's Tale.*" *MAE* 33 (1964): 121–30.

Steel, Anthony. "The Collectors of Customs in the Reign of Richard II." *British Government and Administration: Studies Presented to S. B. Chrimes.* Ed. H. Hearder and H. R. Loyn. Cardiff: University of Wales Press, 1974. Pp. 27–39.

Stemmler, Theo. "Interpretation des Mittelenglischen Gedichts *God Pat Al Pis Myhtes May.*" *Anglia* 82 (1964): 58–75.

Stephenson, Laura. *Praise and Paradox: Merchants and Craftsmen in Elizabethan Popular Literature.* Cambridge: Cambridge University Press, 1984.

Stevens, John. *Music and Poetry in the Early Tudor Court.* London: Methuen, 1961.

Stevens, Martin. "'And Venus Laugheth': An Interpretation of the *Merchant's Tale.*" *ChR* 7 (1972–73): 118–31.

Stevens, Martin. "The Ellesmere Miniatures as Illustrations of Chaucer's *Canterbury Tales.*" *SI* 7–8 (1981–82): 113–34.

Stewart-Brown, Ronald. "The Scrope and Grosvenor Controversy, 1385–1391." *Transactions of the Historic Society of Lancashire and Cheshire* 89 (1937): 1–22.

Stillwell, Gardner. "Chaucer's 'Sad' Merchant." *RES* 20 (1949): 1–18.

Stock, Lorraine Kochanske. "The Reenacted Fall in Chaucer's *Shipman's Tale.*" *SI* 7–8 (1981–82): 134–45.

Stone, Lawrence. *The Family, Sex and Marriage in England 1500–1800.* London: Weidenfeld and Nicolson, 1977.

Storey, R. L. "Gentlemen-bureaucrats." *Profession, Vocation, and Culture in Later Medieval England.* Ed. Cecil H. Clough. Liverpool: Liverpool University Press, 1982. Pp. 90–129.

Storey, R. L. "Liveries and Commissions of the Peace, 1388–90." *The Reign of Richard II.* Ed. DuBoulay and Barron. Pp. 131–52.

Stow, George B. "Chronicles versus Records: The Character of Richard II." *Documenting the Past: Essays in Medieval History Presented to George Peddy Cuttino.* Ed. J. S. Hamilton and Patricia J. Bradley. Woodbridge: Boydell, 1989. Pp. 155–76.

Strohm, Paul. "Chaucer's Audience." *L&H* 5 (1977): 26–41.

Strohm, Paul. "Chaucer's Fifteenth-Century Audience and the Narrowing of the 'Chaucer Tradition'." *SAC* 4 (1982): 3–32.

Strohm, Paul. "Form and Social Statement in *Confessio Amantis* and *The Canterbury Tales.*" *SAC* 1 (1979): 17–40.

Strohm, Paul. "The Origin and Meaning of Middle English *Romaunce.*" *Genre* 10 (1977): 1–28.

Strohm, Paul. *Social Chaucer.* Cambridge: Harvard University Press, 1989.

Strohm, Paul. "The Social and Literary Scene in England." *The Cambridge Chaucer Companion.* Ed. Piero Boitani and Jill Mann. Cambridge: Cambridge University Press, 1986. Pp. 1–18.

Strohm, Paul. "*Storie, Spelle, Geste, Romaunce, Tragedie:* Generic Distinctions in the Middle English Troy Narratives." *Speculum* 46 (1971): 348–59.

Stroud, Theodore A. "Boethius' Influence on Chaucer's *Troilus.*" *MP* 49 (1951–52): 1–9.

Sundwall, McKay. "Deiphobus and Helen: A Tantalizing Hint." *MP* 73 (1975): 151–56.

Szittya, Penn R. *The Antifraternal Tradition in Medieval Literature.* Princeton: Princeton University Press, 1986.

Tatlock, J. S. P. "Chaucer's *Merchant's Tale.*" *MP* 33 (1935–36): 367–81.

Tatlock, J. S. P. *The Development and Chronology of Chaucer's Works.* Chaucer Society, 2d ser., 37. London: Trübner, 1907.

Taylor, Karla. *Chaucer Reads* The Divine Comedy. Stanford: Stanford University Press, 1989.

Teetaert, Amédeé, O.C. *Les Confessions aux laïques dans l'église latine depuis le VIIIe jusqu'au XIVe siècles.* Paris: J. Gabalda, 1926.

Teetaert, Amédeé, O.C. "La Doctrine pénitentielle de Saint Raymond de Penyafort, O.P." *Analecta Sacra Tarraconensia* 4 (1928): 121–82.

Tentler, Thomas N. *Sin and Confession on the Eve of the Reformation.* Princeton: Princeton University Press, 1977.

Teskey, Gordon. "Milton and Modernity." *Diacritics* 18 (Spring, 1988): 42–53.

Theiner, Paul. "The Medieval Terence." *The Lerned and the Lewed.* Ed. Larry Benson. Cambridge: Harvard University Press, 1974. Pp. 231–48.

Thomas, Antoine. "Le *De claustro anime* et le *Roman de Troie.*" *Romania* 42 (1913): 83–85.

Thomas, Antoine, and Mario Roques. "Les traductions françaises de la *Consolatio Philosophiae* de Boèce." *Histoire littéraire de la France* 37 (1938): 419–88.

Thompson, Edward P. " 'Rough Music': Le charivari anglais." *Annales* 27 (1972): 285–312.

Thorndike, Lynn. *A History of Magic and Experimental Science.* 8 vols. New York: Columbia University Press, 1923–64.

Thrupp, Sylvia. *The Merchant Class of Medieval London, 1300–1500.* Ann Arbor: University of Michigan Press, 1962 (1948).

Thundy, Zacharias P. "Matheolus, Chaucer, and the Wife of Bath." *Chau-*

cerian Problems and Perspectives: Essays Presented to Paul E. Beichner. Ed. Edward Vasta and Zacharias P. Thundy. Notre Dame: University of Notre Dame Press, 1979. Pp. 24–58.

Tillyard, E. M. W. *Poetry Direct and Oblique*. London: Chatto and Windus, 1945.

Tobin, Patricia Drechsel. *Time and the Novel*. Princeton: Princeton University Press, 1978.

Tout, T. F. *Chapters in the Administrative History of Mediaeval England*. 6 vols. Manchester: Manchester University Press, 1920–33.

Tuck, Anthony J. *Crown and Nobility, 1272–1461: Political Conflict in Late Medieval England*. London: Fontana Press, 1985.

Tuck, Anthony J. *Richard II and the English Nobility*. New York: St. Martin's, 1974.

Tuck, Anthony J. "Richard II's System of Patronage." *The Reign of Richard II: Essays in Honour of May McKisack*. Ed. F. R. H. DuBoulay and Caroline Barron. London: Athlone Press, 1971. Pp. 1–20.

Twycross, Meg. *The Medieval Anadyomene: A Study in Chaucer's Mythography*. Medium Aevum Monographs 9, n.s. 1. Oxford: Blackwell, 1972.

Tyson, Diana B. "Patronage of French Vernacular History Writers in the Twelfth and Thirteenth Centuries." *Romania* 100 (1979): 180–222, 584.

Ullmann, Walter. "Dante's 'Monarchia' as an Illustration of a Political-Religious 'Renovatio.'" *Traditio-Krisis-Renovatio aus theologischer Sicht: Festschrift Winfried Zeller*. Ed. Berndt Jaspert and Rudolf Mohr. Marburg: Elwert, 1976. Pp. 101–13.

Ullmann, Walter. *Medieval Foundations of Renaissance Humanism*. London: Elek, 1977.

Ullmann, Walter. "Reflections on the Medieval Empire." *TRHS*, 5th ser., 14 (1964): 89–108.

Underwood, Dale. "The First of the *Canterbury Tales*." *ELH* 26 (1959): 455–69.

Utley, Francis Lee. *The Crooked Rib*. Columbus: Ohio State University Press, 1944.

Vacant, Alfred, and E. Mangenot, eds. *Dictionnaire de théologie catholique*. 16 vols. Paris: Letouzay et Ané, 1903–72.

Vale, Juliet. *Edward III and Chivalry: Chivalric Society and Its Context, 1270–1350*. Woodbridge: Boydell Press, 1982.

Vale, Malcolm. *War and Chivalry: Warfare and Aristocratic Culture in England, France and Burgundy at the End of the Middle Ages*. London: Duckworth, 1981.

Vance, Eugene. "Mervelous Signals: Poetics, Sign Theory, and Politics in Chaucer's *Troilus*." *NLH* 10 (1979): 293–337.

Vessey, David. *Statius and the* Thebaid. Cambridge: Cambridge University Press, 1973.

Voloshin, Beverly. "A Historical Note on Women's Fiction." *Critical Inquiry* 2 (1976): 817–20.

von Moos, Peter. "Gottschalks Gedicht *O mi custos*—eine *confessio*." *Frühmittelalterliche Studien* 4 (1970): 201–30; 5 (1971): 317–58.

Wagenknecht, Edward, ed. *Chaucer: Modern Essays in Criticism*. New York: Oxford University Press, 1959.

Wagner, Anthony Richard, ed. *A Catalogue of English Mediaeval Rolls of Arms*. Harleian Society Publications, 100. Oxford: Oxford University Press, 1950.

Wagner, Anthony Richard. *Heralds of England*. London: HMSO, 1967.

Wagner, Anthony Richard. *Heralds and Heraldry in the Middle Ages*. London: Oxford University Press, 1956.

Wallace, David. "Chaucer's Continental Inheritance: The Early Poems and *Troilus and Criseyde*." *The Cambridge Chaucer Companion*. Ed. Piero Boitani and Jill Mann. Cambridge: Cambridge University Press, 1986. Pp. 19–39.

Wallace, David. "'Whan She Translated Was': A Chaucerian Critique of the Petrarchan Academy." *Literary Practice and Social Change in Britain, 1380–1530*. Ed. Lee Patterson. Berkeley: University of California Press, 1990. Pp. 156–215.

Wallace-Hadrill, J. M. "History in the Mind of Archbishop Hincmar." *The Writing of History in the Middle Ages: Essays Presented to R. W. Southern*. Ed. R. H. C. Davis and J. M. Wallace-Hadrill. Oxford: Clarendon Press, 1981. Pp. 43–70.

Waswo, Richard. "The Narrator of *Troilus and Criseyde*." *ELH* 50 (1983): 1–25.

Webb, Henry J. "A Reinterpretation of Chaucer's Theseus." *RES* 23 (1947): 289–96.

Weber, Max. *Selections in Translation*. Ed. W. G. Runciman. Trans. Eric Matthews. Cambridge: Cambridge University Press, 1978.

Wedel, Theodore Otto. *The Medieval Attitude Towards Astrology*. New Haven: Yale University Press, 1920.

Wentersdorf, Karl P. "Theme and Structure in the *Merchant's Tale:* The Function of the Pluto Episode." *PMLA* 80 (1965): 522–27.

Wenzel, Siegfried. *The Sin of Sloth: Acedia in Medieval Thought and Literature*. Chapel Hill: University of North Carolina Press, 1967.

Wenzel, Siegfried. "The Source of Chaucer's Seven Deadly Sins." *Traditio* 30 (1974): 351–78.

Westlund, Joseph. "The *Knight's Tale* as an Impetus for Pilgrimage." *PQ* 43 (1964): 526–37.

Wetherbee, Winthrop. *Chaucer and the Poets: An Essay on* Troilus and Criseyde. Ithaca: Cornell University Press, 1984.

Whately, Gordon. "Heathens and Saints: *St. Erkenwald* in its Legendary Context." *Speculum* 61 (1986): 330–63.

White Beatrice. "Poet and Peasant." *The Reign of Richard II.* Ed. F. R. H. Du Boulay and Caroline Barron. London: Athlone Press, 1971. Pp. 58–74.

Whitman, Cedric H. *Homer and the Heroic Tradition.* Cambridge: Harvard University Press, 1958.

Wiener, Norbert. *The Human Use of Human Beings: Cybernetics and Society.* Garden City: Doubleday, 1954.

Wilcox, Donald J. *The Development of Florentine Humanist Historiography in the Fifteenth Century.* Cambridge: Harvard University Press, 1969.

Williams, Gordon. *Technique and Ideas in the* Aeneid. New Haven: Yale University Press, 1983.

Williams, Raymond. *Marxism and Literature.* Oxford: Oxford University Press, 1977.

Wimsatt, James I. "*Anelida and Arcite:* A Narrative of Complaint and Comfort." *ChR* 5 (1970–71): 1–8.

Wimsatt, James I. "Chaucer and the Canticle of Canticles." *Chaucer the Love Poet.* Ed. Jerome Mitchell and William Provost. Athens: University of Georgia Press, 1973. Pp. 66–90.

Wimsatt, James I. *Chaucer and the French Love Poets.* Chapel Hill: University of North Carolina Press, 1968.

Wimsatt, James I. "The *Dit dou Bleu Chevalier:* Froissart's Imitation of Chaucer." *MS* 34 (1972): 388–400.

Wimsatt, James I. "The Lyric Element in *Troilus and Criseyde.*" *YES* 15 (1985): 18–32.

Wimsatt, James I. "Guillaume de Machaut and Chaucer's Love Lyrics." *MAE* 47 (1978): 66–87.

Wise, Boyd Ashby. *The Influence of Statius upon Chaucer.* Baltimore: J. H. Furst, 1911.

Woledge, Brian. *Bibliographie des romans et nouvelles en prose française antérieurs à 1500.* Geneva: Droz, 1975.

Wood, Chauncey. *Chaucer and the Country of the Stars.* Princeton: Princeton University Press, 1970.

Wood, Chauncey. *The Elements of Chaucer's* Troilus. Durham: Duke University Press, 1984.

Wurtele, Douglas. "Ironical Resonances in the *Merchant's Tale.*" *ChR* 13 (1978–79): 66–79.

Zink, Michel. *La subjectivité littéraire autour de siècle de saint Louis.* Paris: Presses universitaires de France, 1985.

Zink, Michel. "Time and the Representation of the Self in Thirteenth-Century French Poetry." *Poetics Today* 5 (1984): 611–27.

Zumthor, Paul. *Essai de poétique médiévale.* Paris: Seuil, 1972.

Index

Abel, 262–63, 268
Abelard, Peter, 9, 374
Adams, Robert, 362n, 395n
Adorno, Theordor, 7n
Aers, David, 167n, 198n, 336n, 420n
Alain de Lille, 370n, 383–84n, 388
Alberic of Monte Cassino, 103
Albert of Stade, 111n
Albertus Magnus, 220, 353
Alcok, Simon, 305–6n
Alexander of Hales, 376n
Alexander, J. J. G., 187n
Allan, Alison, 269n
Allen, Judson Boyce, 102n, 286n
Alliterative Morte Arthure, 199n
Allmand, Christopher, 174n
Ambrose, 269n
Anciaux, P., 380n
Ancrene Riwle, 379
Andalò di Negro, 216, 217n
Anderson, David, 132n
Anderson, Perry, 24
Andreas Capellanus, 263n, 301n
Angeli, Giovanna, 98n
Anne of Bohemia, Queen of England, 162n, 187, 236–37n
Antoninus of Florence, 375n
apRoberts, Robert P., 141n
Aquinas, Thomas, 220, 353, 379n, 380n, 404n
Aristotle, 102n, 353
Arras, Gautier d', 10
Ars praedicandi, 305–6, 307–8, 311–12
Arundel, Thomas, archbishop of Canterbury, 44
Arundel, Richard Fitzalan, earl of, 157–59, 187
Ascham, Roger, 14n
Ashby, George, 14n, 16n, 17
Aston, Margaret, 44, 420n
Astrology, 216–22, 227

Atkynson, William, 306n
Aubailly, Jean-Claude, 305n
Aucassin et Nicolette, 264
Auchinleck manuscript, 330
Audelay, Sir James, 214
Auerbach, Erich, 10n
Augustine, 8, 18, 66–67, 84, 87n, 89–90, 96, 132–33, 152, 261n, 262–63, 269–70, 289, 306, 308n, 315–16, 353–54, 375–76, 379n, 380, 382, 388n, 402, 404n, 405, 412n
Ayenbite of Inwit, The, 381n, 382n

Baker, Robert L., 37n
Bakhtin, Mikhail, 290n
Baldwin, Anna, 192n
Baldwin, John W., 352n, 353, 353n
Ball, John, 257–58
Barber, Richard, 171n
Barker, Francis, 8
Barker, Juliet R. V., 93n, 170n, 187, 192n, 194n
Barney, Stephen, 67n, 112n, 137n, 402n
Barnie, John, 93n, 156n, 177, 189
Barraclough, Geoffrey, 90n
Barthes, Roland, 371n, 409–10
Bartholomaeus Anglicus, 364, 373n. See Trevisa, John
Baskerville, Charles Read, 294n
Baswell, Christopher, 110n
Baum, Paull Franklin, 413n, 414n, 416n
Bayot, Alphonse, 94n
Beauchamp, Richard, earl of Warwick, 57n
Beauchamp, William, 35
Bec, Christian, 332n, 345n
Bede, 88, 95, 102n, 379n
Bedford, John, duke of, 234n
Beichner, Paul E., 399n
Bellah, Robert N., 3–5
Bellamy, J. G., 192n